Social Work and Law

Judicial Policy and Forensic Practice

Sunny Harris Rome

George Mason University

PEARSON

Boston Columbus Indianapolis New York San Francisco Upper Saddle River
Amsterdam Cape Town Dubai London Madrid Milan Munich Paris Montréal Toronto
Delhi Mexico City São Paulo Sydney Hong Kong Seoul Singapore Taipei Tokyo

Editorial Director: Craig Campanella
Editor in Chief: Ashley Dodge
Editorial Product Manager: Carly Czech
Editorial Assistant: Nicole Suddeth
Vice President/Director of Marketing: Brandy Dawson
Executive Marketing Manager: Wendy Albert
Marketing Assistant: Frank Alarcon
Digital Media Editor: Paul Deluca

Production Manager: Fran Russello
Full Service Production: Suganya Karuppasamy/Element LLC
Cover Administrator: Jayne Conte
Cover Designer: Suzanne Behnke
Cover Image Credit: Fotolia: grungy room © Phase4Photography
Interior Design: Joyce Weston Design

Credits and acknowledgments borrowed from other sources and reproduced, with permission, in this textbook appear on the appropriate page within text.

Library of Congress Cataloging-in-Publication Data
Rome, Sunny Harris.
  Social work and law : judicial policy and forensic practice / Sunny Harris Rome.
     p. cm.
  Includes bibliographical references and index.
  ISBN-13: 978-0-205-77689-4
  ISBN-10: 0-205-77689-2
  1. Social workers—Legal status, laws, etc.—United States. 2. Public welfare—Law and legislation—United States. 3. Judicial power—United States. 4. Social legislation—United States.
  5. Judicial review—United States. 6. Evidence, Expert—United States. 7. Sociological jurisprudence.
  I. Title.
  KF390.S6.R66 2013
  344.7303—dc23

                                                           2012033082

10 9 8 7 6 5 4 3 2 1 - CRW - 16 15 14 13 12

ISBN-10:   0-205-77689-2
ISBN-13: 978-0-205-77689-4

Contents

iii

UNIT II: CHILDREN AND FAMILIES   118

6. Child Abuse and Neglect   118

UNIT III: HEALTH AND JUSTICE   239

11. Juvenile Justice   239

12. Criminal Justice   259

20. Legal Rights of Students   471

Preface

The convergence of social work and law is a fascinating one. Courts make decisions every day that impact individuals locked in disputes or fighting for their rights. These people are often our clients. It is the courts that decide whether parents retain custody of their children, whether older adults are mentally competent to manage their own affairs, and whether tenants in low-income neighborhoods are entitled to repairs from their landlords. Courts also make decisions that have broad policy implications affecting the entire nation. They decide who is entitled to protection under the Americans with Disabilities Act, what constitutes sexual harassment, and what rights prisoners retain while incarcerated. Finally, courts help define the scope of social work practice, both in terms of roles within the courtroom and legal standards for acceptable practice.

There are two primary ways to approach the topic of social work and law. First, we can look at the judiciary as an important instrument of social policy. We need only consider some of the Supreme Court's decisions, such as *Brown v. Board of Education* or *Roe v. Wade,* to see its enormous impact on civil rights, human rights, and social justice. Second, we can examine ways in which social workers themselves interact with the court system. It is this bundle of knowledge and skills that we mean when we refer to "forensic social work practice". This might include, for example, responding to subpoenas; conducting interviews with child abuse victims that will survive scrutiny in court; testifying as experts in domestic violence, guardianship, or disability cases; and conducting evaluations that will affect the outcomes of child custody, civil commitment, or criminal sentencing hearings.

This book addresses both of these aspects of social work and law. It is designed for students in BSW programs, MSW programs, dual-degree programs in social work and law, and certificate programs in forensic social work practice. Practicing social workers may also find it useful in enhancing their understanding of the legal context relevant to their everyday work.

The book is organized into four units. Unit I provides important background information on how the legal system operates and the role of social workers in the legal environment. It provides brief introductions to the topics of law and judicial policy and law and forensic practice. It also discusses how social workers should practice within the law, minimizing our risk of malpractice, and provides ideas on how to influence judicial decision making.

Units II, III, and IV address a wide range of specific topic areas, in each instance presenting an overview of the law and legal processes and their relevance to social work. Unit II examines various topics related to children and families, including child maltreatment, adoption, child custody, domestic violence, and aging. Unit III addresses issues related to health and justice, including health, mental health, juvenile justice, criminal justice, and the death penalty. Unit IV addresses a number of topics related to civil liberties and civil rights, including race discrimination, sex discrimination, discrimination based on sexual orientation, the legal rights of immigrants, and the legal rights of students.

In addition to basic content, each chapter features one or more special topics, some of which highlight forensic social work roles and skills, and some of which highlight intriguing issues or controversies. Most chapters end with an excerpt from an actual court case. These judicial opinions were carefully chosen and edited to provide the reader with an opportunity to become more comfortable with reading and analyzing this primary source material. Each sample case is followed by discussion questions.

My intent is to create a resource that will introduce students to fundamental legal concepts and procedures and illustrate how they are operationalized across a range of topics and fields of practice. Given the breadth of social work's interaction with the legal system, it is possible to provide only a starting point; no treatment of any topic purports to be exhaustive. The initial unit provides a necessary backdrop to understanding the content that follows, and the remainder of the book can be used selectively by focusing on those topics of greatest interest to particular student groups.

Social work curricula have come a long way in recognizing the relevance of legislation to social work interests and practice; major federal laws are routinely covered in policy classes, for example. The role of the courts has crept in more incrementally, often as one topic of many in courses addressing specific policy or practice issues. Meanwhile, more and more universities are offering dual-degree programs in social work and law. As of 2008, the Council on Social Work Education (CSWE) identified 42 such programs, making it the most common dual-degree combination available to social work students. This book supports this trend toward recognizing the unique and important relationship between social work and law. It fills a gap in social work education by addressing the role of the judicial branch in policy development. It also extends preparation for social work practice by exposing students to some of the socio-legal competencies expected of all practitioners, as well as those needed by forensic social work experts. In today's litigious society, in which the rights of client groups and our own professional practice are constantly subject to challenge, it is essential to understand the law. This book provides a first step on that journey.

Acknowledgments

Completion of this project would not have been possible without considerable assistance. For that, I owe a debt to gratitude, first and foremost, to a host of amazing students and former students who contributed, in ways large and small, to the book's conceptualization, research, and writing. They are Jenna Addington, Alicia Akakpo, Michael Beattie, Sarah Beddoe, Tenezeah Bishop, Nicole Cardarelli, Tracy Connor, Kristin Dart, Angela Dixon, Thomas Faulconer, Jenny Freeze, Katie Griffith, Ryan Hanlon, Brynn Harris, Teresa Hollandsworth, Hannah Kane, Lauren Kipfer, Christine Lee, Sheree Levitsky, Sue Ellen Mawhinney, Cass Mercer, Kristin Miller, Ruth Rocci, Mark Taylor, Sarah Weston, and Rachel Wiggins. I thank my dean and department chair for their support, and my colleagues in the Department of Social Work for their patience and camaraderie. Looking back, I cannot help but be grateful to my own professors in both social work and law for cultivating my ongoing interest in this area. And lastly, a heartfelt thanks and much love to my family for their steadfast encouragement: my husband, Chip; children, Anna and Robert; mother, Viola; and brother, Steve.

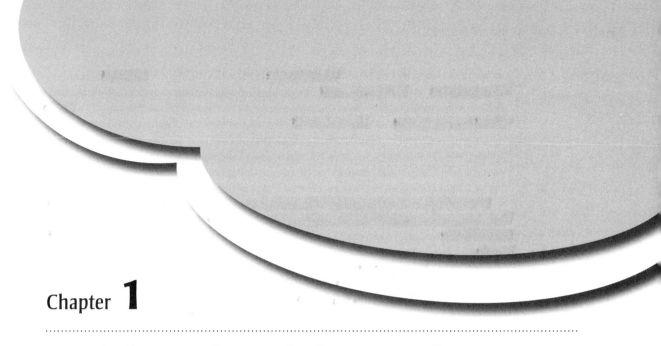

Chapter **1**

Social Work and the Legal System

The gist of the law is justice, and its purpose is the common good. The content of social work is the correction and prevention of injurious social relations, and its aim, in common with that of the law, is the public well-being. It is strange at first sight, therefore, that they should be looked upon as separate fields, only now converging toward a common method with a common goal (Kelso, 1929, p. 17).

History and Rationale

Although they differ in many ways, the fields of social work and law have long had a close association. As early as 1879, members of the National Conference of Charities and Corrections engaged in legal strategies to advance social justice for vulnerable groups, including people in poverty, those with disabilities or mental illness, and victims of exploitation (Rome, 2008). Less than a decade later, the Chicago Protective Agency for Women began assisting survivors of domestic violence by safeguarding their legal rights in cases of separation and divorce (Burgess, 2002). By the late 19th and early 20th centuries, the Charity Organization Societies had adopted a structural view of poverty which regarded community institutions as the key to alleviating social ills; this was epitomized by the work of Josephine Lowell who was instrumental in drawing attention to conditions in jails, hospitals, and orphanages and was a strong supporter of organized labor (Day, 2009). During the Progressive Era of the early 20th century, settlement houses brought together the wealthy and the poor and became important agents of social reform. Hull House, the settlement house in Chicago founded by Jane Addams, attracted numerous activists including Florence Kelley and Mary O'Sullivan, who sought political reforms on behalf of women, children, and immigrants. The accomplishments of these leaders, and others such as Lucy Flower, Grace Abbott, and Julia Lathrop, cleared the way for the first child labor laws, public assistance for women in poverty, maternal and child health programs, the mental hygiene movement, veterans' services, old age and disability assistance, unemployment insurance, and the first juvenile court (Day, 2009). Many of their successes were achieved through legal and political advocacy, with the support and assistance of attorneys.

One of these lawyers, Robert Weeks deForest, is credited with helping establish what is now the School of Social Work at Columbia University (Coleman, 1999; Hijiya, 1980). In the 1920s, social workers served as advocates within local police departments. In the 1930s, they used the New Deal as a catalyst to address the legal needs of people in poverty (Albert, 2000). In the 1940s, social workers became leaders in delinquency prevention and treatment. By the late 1950s, child guidance clinics employed social workers to act as court liaisons. In the 1960s and 1970s, social workers began to assume greater roles in probation (Roberts & Brownell, 1999). In the decades since, social workers have taken on new roles in victim assistance; offender reentry and community-based treatment; and specialized courts for cases involving mental health, domestic violence, homelessness, truancy, and drugs.

This link between social work and law is not at all surprising. Clients often manifest multiple needs and face multiple challenges that require the attention not only of social workers but also of lawyers, police officers, judges, or corrections professionals. Social workers may interact with the legal system in a wide variety of ways. For example, clients may need the support of social workers as they face unwanted legal actions such as eviction, psychiatric commitment, or criminal prosecution. Social workers may be called upon to work with clients who are mandated by the courts to receive anger management or drug treatment services. Social workers also provide mental health and other services to inmates reentering the community after serving their sentences. Social workers often become involved with the legal system in order to protect a client's interests or assure his or her safety. For example, a client may be seeking child custody or visitation, may need to arrange for guardianship on behalf of an older relative, or may require protection from the threat of domestic violence. Clients facing immigration issues, special education challenges, or workplace discrimination also rely on social workers to be knowledgeable about the legal rights, constraints, and processes that will play a role in defining their well-being and success. Whatever the focus of a social worker's professional practice, it is to his or her advantage to be conversant with, and comfortable in, the legal environment. Although social workers should never give legal advice, they can play an important role in helping clients navigate the legal arena.

Every topic in this text—from domestic violence to immigration—in some way involves a legal process. To illustrate, let's look briefly at two fields in which many social workers are employed: child welfare and mental health. Child welfare workers in child protective services (CPS), foster care, and adoption routinely appear in court to testify about risks to a child's well-being; the advisability of removal, reunification, or termination of parental rights; efforts made by both the agency and the parents to achieve safety and stability for those children; and the appropriateness of specific custody, visitation, or adoption arrangements. Yet, even though social workers play a key role in identifying risk, providing services, and evaluating options, the fate of vulnerable families ultimately is a legal decision. Social workers need to understand how the legal process works in order to maximize the effectiveness of their input. Similarly, mental health practice has significant legal aspects. Take, for example, the decision about whether or not a person with mental illness should be committed for psychiatric treatment without his or her consent—a decision with profound implications for the client, the family, and the community. Social workers and other behavioral health providers should be knowledgeable about what the legal requirements are for involuntary commitment in their state and should understand the process by which these decisions are made. Social workers are often involved in conducting mental health assessments and in making follow-up recommendations. In the interests of social justice, they should also be familiar with their clients' legal rights in these circumstances, in order to help ensure that those rights are consistently protected.

Social workers also become involved with the judicial system as advocates. They and the organizations they work with can help identify clients or situations that might serve as *test cases* to promote important policy interests. Groups that provide legal advocacy, particularly in the area of civil rights, are always on the lookout for sympathetic victims whose cases they can bring to court in order to force decisions on important issues. Social work organizations can also provide input into cases coming before the court by submitting *amicus curiae* ("friend of the court") briefs. The National Association of Social Workers (NASW), for example, is actively involved in promoting social justice and shaping social policy not only in the state and federal legislatures but in the courts as well. The policy interpretations handed down by the judiciary on issues such as reproductive rights, same-sex marriage, and immigration present us with both opportunities and constraints as we strive to serve our clients' best interests. We have an obligation to ensure that legal rules, procedures, and actions have a positive, rather than negative, impact on both our clients and the larger society. As Madden and Wayne (2003) suggest, social work should use its "collective wisdom, research, and practice experiences to influence changes that make the law more therapeutic" (p. 346).

Finally, the law also plays an important role in shaping social work practice. Social work licensing laws prescribe the basic requirements of eligibility for professional practice, including minimum educational attainment, supervision, and continuing education. State laws govern the qualifications for various social work and related positions in public agencies including who, and under what circumstances, the title "social worker" may be used. Judges define clients' rights to receive treatment, to refuse treatment, and to expect their communications with social workers and other providers to remain confidential. And although we do our best to adhere to the highest principles of the Code of Ethics and engage in competent, ethical practice, it is inevitable that some of us will face allegations of professional malpractice that bring us or our agencies into contact with the courts. Knowing what our legal obligations are, in addition to our ethical ones, is essential. Every practicing social worker needs to know how to avoid, as well as defend against, a malpractice suit.

We begin our exploration of the legal system by reviewing the different types of law, the nature of the legal environment, how our court system is structured, and some basic vocabulary. This is followed by a discussion of social work roles in the legal system, including how social workers interface with professionals from other disciplines. Special sections highlight two social workers and their experiences in legal settings.

Understanding the Judicial System

The Different Types of Law

Each branch of government plays a role in the development and implementation of the laws that govern our nation. *Statutory law* is another name for laws made by the legislature. *Administrative law* refers to laws made by the executive branch of government. *Case law,* the focus of this text, involves laws made by the judiciary. You probably are most familiar with statutory law: This includes the laws (statutes) that are passed by the U.S. Congress and various state legislatures, as well as by local units of government (at this level, they are referred to as *ordinances*). Administrative law includes regulations crafted by government agencies to elaborate on what the legislature has enacted and to provide guidelines for implementation. Case law refers to opinions by judges that establish accepted interpretations of statutes, regulations, and constitutions.

Each branch of government makes its own contribution to the policy process, and each presents different opportunities for social work practitioners. The legislature's basic contribution is to make the laws. As advocates, we often focus on the legislature because its members are elected by the public and are therefore the most open to influence; they need to be accountable to their constituents in order to stay in office. As a result, social workers engage in legislative advocacy, hoping to influence legislative outcomes on behalf of their clients. Power in the legislature is spread among many players. At the national level, in order to succeed, a policy proposal needs the support of at least 51 of the 100 senators and 218 of the 435 representatives; in some instances, when a two-thirds or three-fifths majority is required, even broader support is necessary. Although the numbers are different, the same principle holds true in state legislatures: A majority of lawmakers must be on board for change to occur. There are several important implications here: The decentralization of power means that compromise is inevitable; it also presents a challenge to social work advocates and reinforces the importance of widespread civic engagement. There is a growing body of social work research on legislative advocacy, including the civic engagement of both social workers and social work clients (Ritter, 2007; Rome & Hoechstetter, 2010; Rome, Hoechstetter, & Wolf-Branigin, 2010). In addition to working as professional lobbyists, social workers serve as staff to local, state, and federal legislators—and run for elective office. According to NASW (2011a), seven current members of Congress are social workers (two senators and five representatives), and approximately 175 social workers hold state or local elective office (NASW, 2011b). Social workers are also active in political campaigns, while those in academia, consulting firms, nonprofit and for-profit agencies, and think tanks provide research and policy analysis that inform the debate around social issues and influence legislative outcomes.

Unlike the members of the legislative branch of government, members of the executive branch (with the exception of the president and vice president) are either appointed or employed as civil servants, rather than being elected. As a result, the public has less leverage with them than with legislators. Yet the regulations that executive agencies generate are an important contribution to social policy and social work practice. In providing the details needed for implementation, they can make a law more or less effective. For example, a bill passed by the legislature and signed by the president may require "qualified mental health professionals" in a particular setting. It would then be left to the appropriate agency in the executive branch to determine how that term is defined and whether, for example, social workers are or are not included. The same holds true for social work practice. Virginia law, for example, requires a "clinical course of study" in order to be eligible to sit for the state's clinical licensing exam. It is the regulations that specify what coursework and fieldwork that actually entails. Many social workers hold positions within the executive branch's local, state, and federal government agencies; others seek to educate them on pending issues or submit comments on proposed regulations in order to shape policy implementation.

Finally, although the judiciary is widely regarded as being the most authoritative branch of government, producing decisions that are more durable than those of the other branches, its reach in some ways is the most restricted. In order for the courts to act, a law must already have been enacted, implemented, and challenged. Of the three branches, the judiciary is least open to influence; it is designed to be insulated from politics. Yet judges and courts can have a profound and far-reaching effect on social justice and client well-being. When we think of the roles of courts and judges, we generally envision them settling disputes between an individual *plaintiff* and an individual *defendant* or determining whether or not someone has broken the law. Although the court does indeed perform these functions, it sometimes casts a much wider net by conducting what is known as judicial review. *Judicial review* is a procedure by which courts evaluate the validity of a statute, regulation, or administrative decision. For example, courts have stepped in to overturn laws that deprive people of their constitutional right to due process. Courts also consider challenges brought by individuals and organizations to specific actions such as the denial of food stamps or the expulsion of a student. Judicial review also gives courts the authority to evaluate whether an agency followed the proper procedure in issuing a regulation. For example, agencies issuing regulations are typically required to hold public hearings, solicit public comments, conduct cost-benefit analyses, or write environmental impact statements. The court may invalidate a regulation that was passed in violation of these rules. Finally, many statutes describe the powers of government agencies, and courts can invalidate agency actions that go beyond the scope of their mandate. The roles that social workers can play in relation to the judicial branch are described throughout the chapters that follow.

The Different Types of Courts

The U.S. legal system features two parallel sets of courts: state courts and federal courts. Federal courts have jurisdiction over (1) issues concerning the U.S. Constitution and federal statutes, regulations, or treaties and (2) disputes involving citizens of different states (what is referred to as *diversity jurisdiction*). Most other claims are handled through the state court system. Figure 1.1 depicts the two court systems. Each is arrayed hierarchically; cases begin at the bottom rung (federal district court or state trial court) and can be appealed to the next level.

In addition, some courts have very specific purposes. These include, for example, bankruptcy courts, juvenile and domestic relations ("family") courts, traffic courts, probate courts, and immigration courts. These are referred to as courts of *limited jurisdiction*.

A court's decision in a case is binding only on the courts within its designated geographic area. For example, there are 94 federal district courts in the United States; a case

FIGURE 1.1 **Chain of Appeals in Federal and State Courts**

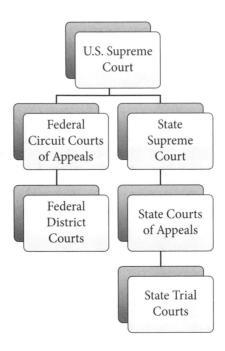

decided by a particular district court applies only within that district. Similarly, there are 13 circuit courts of appeals. A decision by a particular circuit court applies only to the states that comprise that circuit. To illustrate, a decision rendered by the Fourth Circuit Court of Appeals is binding in the states that make up the fourth circuit: Maryland, West Virginia, Virginia, North Carolina, and South Carolina. A decision by the Eighth Circuit Court of Appeals is binding on North and South Dakota, Minnesota, Nebraska, Iowa, Missouri, and Arkansas. Table 1.1 identifies the various circuits in the continental United States.

In the state court system, the same principle applies. A decision by a state's supreme court applies only within that state. So, for example, a decision by the California Supreme Court is binding throughout the state of California. A decision in one of California's state courts of appeals would be binding on the trial courts (in California, these are called superior courts) within its jurisdiction. Only decisions by the U.S. Supreme Court are binding nationwide. Looking at it slightly differently, lower courts are expected to make decisions that are consistent with those that have previously been made by the courts above them.

Any case *adjudicated* (tried) in a lower court can automatically be appealed to the next highest court. In the federal courts, decisions by district courts can be appealed to circuit courts. In the state courts, trial court decisions can be appealed to state courts of appeals (*appellate courts*) and decisions of those courts can in turn be appealed to the state supreme court. The exception to this is the U.S. Supreme Court, to which there is no automatic right of appeal. To ask the Supreme Court to hear a case, one of the parties petitions for a *writ of certiorari*. The Supreme Court receives thousands of such requests each term but accepts only about 100 to 150 cases per year.

TABLE 1.1 **States Comprising the Federal Circuits**

First Circuit	South Carolina	Eight Circuit	Nevada
Maine	Virginia	Arkansas	Oregon
Massachusetts	West Virginia	Iowa	Washington
New Hampshire	**Fifth Circuit**	Minnesota	**Tenth Circuit**
Puerto Rico	Louisiana	Missouri	Colorado
Second Circuit	Mississippi	Nebraska	Kansas
Connecticut	Texas	North Dakota	New Mexico
New York	**Sixth Circuit**	South Dakota	Oklahoma
Vermont	Kentucky	**Ninth Circuit**	Utah
Third Circuit	Michigan	Alaska	Wyoming
Delaware	Ohio	Arizona	**Eleventh Circuit**
New Jersey	Tennessee	California	Alabama
Pennsylvania	**Seventh Circuit**	Guam	Florida
Virgin Islands	Illinois	Hawaii	Georgia
Fourth Circuit	Indiana	Mariana Islands	**D.C. Circuit**
Maryland	Wisconsin	Montana	Washington, D.C.
North Carolina			

Regardless of the court, whenever a case is on appeal only the legal question at issue is debated and resolved. There are no witnesses testifying and there is no new presentation of facts or evidence. Each side to the dispute submits a written brief outlining the issues of law they are contesting, and the lawyers on each side have an opportunity to present their arguments orally. If the court agrees with the decision previously made by the lower court, it *affirms* that decision. If it disagrees, it can *reverse* the decision. In some cases, it will *remand* (return) the case to the lower court so the court can reconsider the case in light of the higher court's legal determinations.

Comparing Civil and Criminal Proceedings

We often speak of criminal and civil cases. *Criminal cases* are technically brought by the government, rather than by the alleged victim of a crime. You can usually identify a criminal case because its name will be *People v. Someone*, or *State v. Someone* or *U.S. v. Someone*. The stakes in criminal cases are considered particularly high because the punishment that ensues can include incarceration. As a result, the rights of the individual defendant (the accused) are more vigorously safeguarded than in civil cases. To this end, it is the government that must prove guilt (the government has the *burden of proof*), and it must do so *beyond a reasonable doubt*. This is the most stringent of the existing *standards of proof*. In other words, to successfully make its case, the government has to make an extremely persuasive showing that leaves little room for the possibility of error or uncertainty. In reality, of course, this stringent standard can be compromised by human factors, including how sympathetic the parties appear, the talents and abilities of their respective attorneys, and biases that enter into an otherwise rational system of justice.

Social workers might become involved in criminal proceedings in a number of ways. A social worker who provides services to either the alleged perpetrator or the victim might be called to testify as a fact witness and provide information to the court about his or her client. Alternatively, a social worker might be called as an expert witness to educate the court about some particularly complex aspect of a case: the dynamics of intimate partner violence, for example, or the behavioral symptoms of a particular mental illness. A forensic social worker might also conduct an assessment that is offered into evidence in a criminal child abuse case or might complete a life history of a defendant facing the death penalty in order to persuade the jury to reduce the defendant's sentence.

Cases that are not criminal are considered *civil*. In these cases, brought by one party against another, the stakes are typically lower. Punishments can include *damages* (fines) or *equitable relief* (the loser is required to do, or not do, something). The person bringing the suit (the *plaintiff*) has the burden of proof, and he or she must prove the case by a *preponderance of the evidence*. Under this, the lowest standard of proof, all that is required is that it be *more likely than not* that the accused is guilty. Although the vast majority of civil cases require only a preponderance of the evidence, in a limited number of instances, proof of guilt must be shown by *clear and convincing evidence*. This standard requires more than a preponderance of the evidence but less than proof beyond a reasonable doubt. Clear and convincing evidence has been applied to several types of proceedings in which, for a civil case, the stakes are unusually high; examples include involuntary mental health commitment and termination of parental rights.

Some observers have attempted to quantify the three standards of proof, suggesting, for example, that a preponderance of the evidence requires 51% certainty of guilt, clear and convincing evidence requires 75% certainty, and beyond a reasonable doubt requires 98% certainty. Although these designations are arbitrary, they aim to provide a clearer picture of otherwise ambiguous standards. Perhaps they can best be understood relative to one another, with beyond a reasonable doubt being a highly difficult threshold to meet, clear and convincing evidence falling in the middle, and preponderance of the evidence being the easiest threshold to meet.

Social workers may be involved in civil proceedings if they need to defend themselves or their agency against a malpractice claim. They might also be called upon to provide information that sheds light on a client's eligibility for disability (or other) benefits. A social worker might be called as a fact witness in a child abuse case, an elder abuse case, or a case in which his or her client is suing someone or being sued. Finally, a social worker might be called as a forensic expert to conduct a mental health assessment for a civil commitment or to make a recommendation in a child custody dispute.

Regardless of the nature of their involvement in a case, social workers need a basic understanding of the burden of proof and standard of proof required for particular types of cases. Although these distinctions may seem like technicalities, they can make a profound difference in who will prevail. For example, as discussed in Chapter 15, when President Reagan's attempted assassin, John Hinckley, was found not guilty by reason of insanity, the public was outraged by the lack of a conviction. This led many states to change their laws, rendering it more difficult to make out a successful insanity defense. They did this by shifting the burden of proof from the prosecutor to the defendant, and changing the standard of proof from a mere preponderance to clear and convincing evidence. In other words, a criminal defendant would now bear the burden of affirmatively proving that he or she met the legal definition of insanity, and a higher level of proof would be required to do so. In another example, as part of a 2011 plan to crack down on sexual assaults and harassment, the Obama administration notified colleges and universities that they must use a preponderance of the evidence standard in weighing allegations of sexual misconduct. Many of these institutions were requiring higher standards at the time—clear and convincing evidence or proof beyond a reasonable doubt—so this meant reducing the standard of proof, thus making it easier to find someone guilty. This was a win for victims, but it raised concerns that the low threshold for proof of guilt might result in more innocent people mistakenly being convicted (Khadaroo, 2011).

How a Court Case Proceeds

Social workers are most often involved in court cases as witnesses. Unless a social worker is one of the actual parties to a lawsuit (the target of a malpractice case, for example), his or her contact with the court system is likely to begin and end with the trial itself. It is helpful to bear in mind, however, that the legal maneuvering on a case begins well before the case comes to court and may result in a case settling or being dismissed before a trial is even held.

In a civil case, the process begins when the plaintiff files a *complaint* that specifies the legal basis for the lawsuit (the *cause of action*) and puts the parties on notice that redress is being sought in court. The defendant may file a *motion* to have the complaint dismissed or may submit an *answer* to the complaint by contesting some or all of the plaintiff's assertions. Meanwhile, both attorneys begin to compile information about the case through a process known as *discovery*. This typically entails the examination of relevant documents, responding to *interrogatories* (questions that must be answered in writing, under oath), and the *deposing* of witnesses. Social workers sometimes are called to appear for a *deposition*. This questioning resembles testifying in court, but it is usually conducted in a lawyer's office with only the witness, the attorneys, and a court reporter present. Finally, a *pretrial conference* between the judge and the attorneys is held to clarify the issues that will be dealt with at trial. All of this occurs before ever entering a courtroom. In fact, the vast majority of cases are settled out of court, avoiding a trial altogether.

In a criminal case, the initial complaint identifies which part of the criminal code the accused is charged with violating. The process then continues with an *arraignment* during which the accused is read the formal charges, is advised of his or her legal rights, and enters a plea. The plea can be *guilty, not guilty,* or *nolo contendere/no contest* (forgoing the right to a trial without an admission of guilt). *Bail* (a sum of money) may be set by the judge in an effort to ensure that the accused appears for trial; if the judge determines that no bail is necessary, the accused may be *released on his her own recognizance*. In felony cases, before a case can proceed to trial, the U.S. Constitution requires there be *probable cause* to believe the accused committed the crime. In federal courts and in many states, this determination is made by a *grand jury*. In others, it is made by a judge during a *preliminary hearing* (or *probable cause* hearing). If the judge finds probable cause or the grand jury issues an *indictment*, either the parties will enter into a *plea agreement* or the case will be scheduled for trial. As in civil cases, there may be a flurry of pretrial motions and pretrial conferences that help shape the issues that will come before the court. There also is a period of discovery. Unlike in civil cases, however, the prosecution is required to share with the defense any evidence that might exonerate the defendant—and, in many states, the defense must share with the prosecution any evidence that substantiates guilt.

In both civil and criminal cases, a trial may be a *bench trial* (presided over by a judge) or a *jury trial*. Defendants accused of serious crimes are guaranteed the right to a jury trial (although that right can be waived), and most states make jury trials available to defendants in most civil trials. Many of you have probably been solicited for jury duty in your hometown. Being called for jury duty, however, does not mean you will actually serve on a jury. The jury pool is whittled down through a process known as *voir dire*, in which potential witnesses are questioned and can be dismissed because of hardship or *for cause* (e.g., the juror is related to one of the parties). Each side is also permitted a limited number of *peremptory challenges*; that is, the lawyer can ask the court to dismiss specific members of the jury pool without providing any reason at all. The U.S. Supreme Court has set some limits on these peremptory challenges, for example, by prohibiting the dismissal of jurors based solely on race (*Batson v. Kentucky*, 1986) or sex (*J.E.B. v. Alabama*, 1994).

In high-stakes cases, people hire jury consultants at a cost of tens, sometimes hundreds, of thousands of dollars—rather than leave the composition of the jury to chance. As famed attorney Melvin Belli once said, "You can pick the facts if I can pick the jury" (Winegar, 2006). For many years, experience in the courtroom yielded rules of thumb about jury selection, suggesting, for example, that social workers, teachers, artists, musicians, students, unskilled laborers, and welfare recipients are likely to favor the plaintiff in a civil action and the defendant in a criminal case, whereas the inverse is true of accountants, bankers, police officers, small business owners, military officers, landlords, engineers, and scientists. Similarly, younger jurors and jurors from "oppressed" racial and ethnic groups were thought to favor plaintiffs in civil suits, and older jurors and those from "nonoppressed" groups were thought to favor the defendants (Winegar, 2006). These and other generalizations have been roundly criticized for their lack of an evidence base and their perpetuation of stereotypes. A body of literature has emerged, however, that relies on extensive polling data and analysis to predict juror behavior based on demographic characteristics, attitudes, personality types, and prior experience. Over the past several decades, mathematical models have been developed that purport to define the ideal jury in specific kinds of cases. Various computer applications have been marketed to serve a similar purpose to jury consultants, but at lower cost (Glover & Burke, 2007).

The O.J. Simpson murder trial provides a good example of the importance of jury selection. In that case, the jury consultant for the defense conducted repeated polls of the local population and determined, for example, that the overwhelming majority of people who regularly read the newspaper thought O.J. was guilty, whereas the overwhelming majority of those who watched T.V. talk shows believed he was innocent. She also collected information about prevailing attitudes toward spousal abuse and trust in police, two important issues in the case. Meanwhile, she asked each potential juror to complete a 78-page questionnaire from which 150,000 pieces of information about each individual were computerized. Combining the polling data with the data about each prospective juror, she was able to produce a rating of each juror's likelihood of voting to acquit. Using this information, the defense attorney shaped the jury to his advantage: for example, not a single member of the final jury regularly read the newspaper (Winegar, 2006).

Once a jury is impaneled, the trial itself can begin. The plaintiff's attorney (or in a criminal case, the prosecutor) provides an *opening statement,* laying out the theory of the case and providing a preview of the evidence to be presented. This is followed by the opening statement by the defendant's lawyer. Each side (beginning with the plaintiff) then proceeds to call witnesses and to offer evidence in support of its case. Whether or not particular evidence is admissible is determined by the *rules of evidence.* For example, the evidence presented must be relevant and not unduly likely to prejudice the jury. The rules of evidence also prohibit the admission of hearsay (although there are some exceptions). *Hearsay* refers to information that witnesses know only secondhand—someone else told them that it was true. Although social workers who testify in court are not expected to know all the rules of evidence (they can leave this to the attorneys), it is helpful to keep in mind that some of the information and evidence they have to offer may not be acceptable under court rules. This should not be taken personally; these technicalities are in place to help ensure that the court considers only legitimate, truthful, and accurate information.

Following the presentation of witnesses and physical evidence by both sides, each side (beginning with the plaintiff or prosecutor) delivers its *closing argument,* summarizing the evidence and hammering home its theory of the case. In a jury trial, the judge then issues *jury instructions,* explaining the basis on which the jury is to formulate its verdict. In criminal trials, all federal courts and the vast majority of states require that the jury verdict be unanimous. In civil trials, the trend has been away from unanimity with most states now permitting a two-thirds or five-sixths majority instead (Diamond, Rose & Murphy, 2006). If the jury is unable to muster the required number of votes, the judge will declare a *mistrial,* and the plaintiff or prosecutor must decide whether or not to start over with a new trial. Finally, if a guilty verdict ensues, the court will issue a *sentence* or other penalty. As described previously, the losing party retains the right to appeal.

Understanding the Legal Environment

Like any system, the legal system has a distinct culture complete with norms, roles, relationships, procedures, and expectations. In order to interact effectively with the legal system, social workers need to understand the legal environment, its players, and how it differs from the human services environment with which we are more familiar.

Roles of Legal Professionals

Most prominent among the cast of characters that inhabits the legal environment, of course, is the *judge.* All federal judges, as well as judges in state trial and appellate courts, are required to be lawyers. Judges may be selected in a variety of ways, depending on the jurisdiction. Judges preside in the courtroom and make a host of decisions outside the courtroom that shape what happens at trial. At pretrial hearings, judges determine whether or not there is sufficient evidence to warrant going to trial at all. In criminal proceedings, they set bail. They rule on the admissibility of evidence, decide motions brought by attorneys, accept or reject plea bargains, and ensure that all rules governing the proceedings are consistently followed. In the absence of a jury, judges determine guilt or innocence and what punishment or sentence will ensue. When a jury is present, the judge provides the jury with instructions on the law and on how to consider the evidence presented. On rare occasion, the judge may overrule a jury verdict *(judgment notwithstanding the verdict)* if he or she believes such a verdict could not possibly have been reached on the strength of the evidence presented. Judges have also been known to increase or decrease the amount of damages assessed by a jury.

A *magistrate* is similar to a judge but presides over some lower court proceedings, usually on specific kinds of matters. Magistrates' roles vary from state to state. In Virginia, for example, they can determine whether probable cause for an arrest exists, whether to issue search warrants, and whether defendants should be detained while awaiting trial. They also issue emergency protective orders in domestic violence cases and hear petitions for mental health commitments. Unlike judges, magistrates are often not required to have law degrees; some states, in fact, have only recently required a bachelor's degree for this position.

Lawyers, or *attorneys*, advise clients on legal matters and represent them in court. All states require that practicing attorneys be licensed members of the bar. Before sitting for the bar exam, lawyers complete a minimum of three years of full-time graduate study. Prosecutors are lawyers who represent the government in bringing criminal charges. Depending on the jurisdiction and the court where the case is heard, the prosecutor may more accurately be called the *district attorney, states' attorney, commonwealth's attorney,* or *county attorney.* Defense attorneys represent the accused. A defense attorney provided free of charge (if the defendant cannot afford one) is referred to as a *public defender.*

Proceedings involving children or other vulnerable groups may also require the involvement of a *guardian ad litem.* These are persons assigned by the court to represent the best interests of a child or incapacitated adult. Professional qualifications for the role vary by state. In Wisconsin, for example, *guardians ad litem* are required to be attorneys. In Florida, anyone can qualify. The law in Maine, on the other hand, specifically identifies lawyers, social workers, psychologists, and psychiatrists as qualified to assume the position.

PREPARING CHILDREN FOR COURT: MY ROLE AS A FAMILY ADVOCATE
Megan Steel, MSW

When I began my employment as the family advocate at a child advocacy center, my responsibility was to develop and manage programs related to legal advocacy for child victims of sexual abuse, as well as for victims of domestic violence. A child advocacy center is designed to serve as a "one-stop shop" for abuse victims, so children and their families can receive services and talk to allied professionals such as police officers, child protective service workers, and therapists at one child-friendly location. I worked with an interdisciplinary team composed of the aforementioned professionals to support families during the investigative and legal processes of child sexual abuse cases. I developed and managed three

programs: the Family Advocacy program, designed to support parents of victims by providing appropriate referrals and emotional support at various points in the case; the Domestic Violence program, which involved providing referrals, emotional support, and legal advocacy to parent victims attending the center; and CourtHelp, an educational program for child witnesses.

Of the three programs I managed, CourtHelp was the one that best demonstrates how social work professionals can practice in legal settings while still maintaining their professional identity. CourtHelp is designed as an educational program to teach children ages 5–17 how to serve as effective witnesses in civil and criminal court cases, while reducing the chance they experience secondary trauma as a result. Testifying before a judge, various legal professionals, and their abuser is an intimidating experience for many adult victims who understand the legal process. Imagine this experience through the eyes of the children: Adults are wearing clothes that they have never seen, using words that they have never heard, and asking them intimate details about arguably the most traumatizing experience in their life in front of the person who victimized them.

Before each child appeared before the court, I met with him or her in our child-friendly office and described what to expect while inside the courtroom. I used a miniature mock courtroom to illustrate where he or she would sit, where the support team would sit, and where the abuser would sit. We talked about the meanings of words that would be used, as well as everyone's role in the courtroom. For example, when I explained the role of the bailiff to children, I described him as their personal bodyguard who would prevent their abuser from hurting them—or that a judge would be like a referee from their soccer game who makes sure that everyone plays fair. It is important that the children connect what they see in the courtroom to experiences in their everyday lives because it reduces their anxiety about being in an unfamiliar place. I often went through this routine with non-victim siblings and parents as well. The most challenging part was figuring out how to describe complex legal phrases and issues in words that children of various ages, and from various socioeconomic and ethnic backgrounds, could understand.

Often I accompanied families to the hearings to answer questions on site or accompanied them to meetings with the commonwealth's attorney. It was helpful for the families to have a social worker as an intermediary. For example, 10-year-old Mary was referred by child protective services after having been repeatedly sexually assaulted by her biological father. Mary's father was the son of a leader of a cult based in Africa, and many of his followers had formed a small community in the area. Mary, her sister, her mother, her grandmother, and her two brothers met with me to discuss what would happen if she testified at her father's trial. The family was extremely distraught over the allegations of abuse, the effect the trial would have on the family's financial situation, and rumors that the cult's followers intended to protest at the trial. I provided emotional support, answered their questions, and accompanied the family to the weeklong trial. Despite the fact that members of the cult lined the courthouse hallway every day to glare at Mary and her family, Mary testified and her father was convicted of sexual assault. He is currently in prison.

Although my work required me to understand many specifics that were not taught to me in a social work classroom, the instruction I received in case management and the importance of empathy and cultural competence did enable me to play an important role on the interdisciplinary team. Despite the challenges, working as a family advocate for the child advocacy center and seeing children empowered in the courtroom were extremely rewarding experiences.

Comparing Social Work and Law

Many social workers report feeling uncomfortable when they interact with the legal system. This discomfort, in turn, can lead to poor performance. To ensure that we do our best for our clients, it is critical that we understand how the legal system works, know what to expect from the attorneys we are likely to encounter, and accept that we are operating in a cultural environment that works differently from our own. Consider the following:

- **The legal system is *triangular* in nature.** It is defined by three distinct points: the plaintiff, who initiates a lawsuit; the defendant against whom the suit is brought; and an impartial decision maker (judge or jury), often referred to as the *trier of fact*. Multiple advocates and decision makers, by comparison, populate the human service system.

- **The legal system is *adversarial*.** Two sides are, by definition, pitted against each other and only one can win. It is this adversarial climate that often poses a challenge to social workers whose orientation tends to be more cooperative and conciliatory, rather than competitive and confrontational (Barsky & Gould, 2002). Social workers are trained to value collaboration in problem solving and to seek win-win solutions; in law, the adversarial process is considered essential to the protection of individual client rights.

- **The legal system focuses on the individual.** Although social workers view the world from a systems perspective, recognizing biopsychosocial and spiritual influences on individual behavior, the legal system typically views the individual as singularly responsible for his or her own actions rather than in relation to the surrounding environment (Center for Social Services Research, 2002; Coleman, 2001).

- **The legal system tends to see issues as black or white** (Barsky & Gould, 2002). Social workers, on the other hand, are trained to appreciate subtleties and nuances; we operate in the gray areas of human emotion, motivation, and behavior. Social workers are trained to accept ambiguity and appreciate the role of professional discretion; the legal system requires conformity to formal rules and procedures (Weinstein, 1997). Although this serves the legal system well by introducing a measure of predictability and fairness, the lack of flexibility can be frustrating for social workers who tend to be less bound by structure and may be less accustomed to adhering to detailed rules.

- **The legal system puts less emphasis on individuals' strengths.** Although social work is premised on identifying and building on individuals' strengths, this perspective is not necessarily shared within the legal environment (Kelly, Smith, & Gibson, 2009). The "good guys" versus "bad guys" orientation of law enforcement and corrections often challenges social work's belief in the dignity of every individual and the potential for positive change. This difference in attitude can be especially salient when working with alleged perpetrators or providing court-ordered treatment.

- **The legal system accords greater status to lawyers than to social workers** (Barsky & Gould, 2002; Center for Social Services Research, 2002). As a "host" environment, its personnel often have had limited experience with social workers; they may lack a full appreciation for our training, competencies, roles, and ethical requirements. These attitudes may be extremely frustrating for social workers who want to be respected in a legal setting.

Among the legal professionals with whom social workers are likely to have contact, lawyers are undoubtedly the most prominent. Although social workers and lawyers often collaborate, differences in their roles, objectives, and ethical standards can make working together challenging (Barsky & Gould, 2002). Numerous studies, mostly centering on child welfare practice, have documented the presence of conflict between the two groups (Center for Social Service Research, 2002; Russel, 1988; Vandervort, 2008). Early studies of how social workers and lawyers view each other provided evidence of the kinds of stereotyping that can inhibit a productive working relationship. Social workers have described attorneys as analytical, inflexible, ruthless, partisan, arrogant, patronizing, and uncaring; lawyers have described social workers as emotional, ineffectual, nurturing, and unprofessional (Fogelson, 1970; Sloane, 1967). In keeping with these characterizations, the court system has been described as having a masculine organizational culture (Kearney & Sellers, 1997), and social work has been described as featuring a "feminine ethic of care" (Freedberg, 1993). Although studies such as those by Smith (1970) and Weil (1982) found social workers and lawyers sharing some positive perspectives on each other (lawyers empathized with social workers and lauded their concern for others; social workers respected the ability of lawyers to be assertive), the persistent presence of gender stereotypes is unmistakable. Despite the passage of time since many of these studies were conducted, it seems little has changed. A more recent qualitative study of the relationship between attorneys and social workers in child welfare found a pervasive belief that "legal professionals do not understand the mindset of social workers and that social work and the legal mindsets do not mix" (Center for Social Services Research, 2002, p. 15).

Conflicts between social workers and attorneys have been attributed to a variety of factors. One author suggests that lawyers are primarily left-brained, whereas social workers are primarily right-brained, so the two disciplines attract fundamentally different types of people (Lau, 1983). Others identify role confusion as a major source of conflict (Stein, 2004). Researchers have found, for example, that social workers and lawyers often disagree about who should assume primary responsibility for the various tasks associated with cases in family court (Brennan & Khinduka, 1971; Center for Social Services Research, 2002; Russel, 1988). Golick and Lessem (2004) acknowledge that defining "the roles of lawyers and social workers in an interdisciplinary practice is clearly a work in progress" (p. 206). Status issues often strain the working relationship, as well. Finally, differences in ethical obligations can create interprofessional conflict. The bottom line, however, is that despite their differences, social workers and lawyers share two important passions: a commitment to justice and loyalty to the client.

It is important to recognize that social workers and lawyers are shaped by significantly different educational experiences (Staller & Kirk, 1998; Taylor, 2005), play different roles in the legal process (Stein, 2004), and are guided by different ethical considerations (Vandervort, 2008). Lawyers, first and foremost, have a duty to zealously represent the interests of their clients. This is indeed admirable, but it can cause considerable confusion and consternation to social work practitioners. To begin with, social workers and lawyers employ different definitions of the term *client* (Stein, 2004). Whereas a social worker may work with more than one individual as a client (e.g., a couple or a family), a lawyer is ethically prohibited from doing so and may regard social workers' doing so as a conflict of interest. Whereas social workers seek to reconcile the needs of the various individuals in a client group by finding a win-win solution for all, the lawyer's duty is simply to win. This single-mindedness of purpose shows itself not just in relation to who is considered the client, but also in how lawyers go about pursuing what their clients want.

Social workers and lawyers see their roles as different in scope. As Senior U.S. District Court Judge Jack B. Weinstein (1999) writes, "the social worker tends to expand an inquiry when a social problem is presented to get to the root causes, to solve related difficulties of the whole person, and to stay with the case with continuing help. The lawyer tends to narrow the question, to address and solve the present issue, and then to close the case" (p. 391).

A correlate of social work's more holistic approach is that a social worker's duty to the client always must be balanced against a competing responsibility to the larger community (Vandervort, 2008). That is why, for example, all states require that social workers report suspected cases of child maltreatment and, in many states, the maltreatment of vulnerable adults. Although this requirement compromises our duty to maintain client confidentiality, it serves an important interest in protecting the public. This dual responsibility also explains our profession's expectation that we engage in political advocacy in the name of social justice. Lawyers, however, have only a single obligation: to fight for the individual client. As a result, the exceptions to confidentiality that hold true for social workers, for example, do not hold true for lawyers. The lawyer's duty to the client has different parameters; generally speaking, fewer exceptions are ethically permissible. Social workers may find a lawyer's failure to consider the broader implications of his or her actions irresponsible; in fact, however, a lawyer who demonstrates single-minded loyalty to the client is simply acting as his or her professional ethics require.

This dual responsibility on the part of the social worker to both the client and the larger society also leads social workers to pursue therapeutic goals (what is best for the client) while lawyers pursue legal goals (the outcome the client desires). Stein (2004) provides the following example:

> Cassie was 15 when she was arrested for possession of cocaine. The arresting officer found the cocaine after conducting what her lawyer would later conclude was an illegal search. It was clear to both her court-appointed social worker and the court-appointed attorney that Cassie had a drug problem, that it was likely, based on the information she provided, that she was prostituting herself to obtain money to buy drugs, and that a drug rehabilitation program would be in her best interest. Cassie had no interest in entering a rehabilitation program, and she was clear in telling this to her attorney. (p. 12)

In this example, the attorney's goal would be to get the search thrown out and the charges against Cassie dropped. The social worker's goal, on the other hand, would be to have the judge order Cassie into a drug rehabilitation program. This is an excellent example of how each profession's ethical guidelines require the pursuit of different objectives. Even though we may regard the lawyer's behavior as counterproductive, the lawyer would be professionally remiss if he or she failed to advocate for the client's wishes. It is important to keep in mind that social workers and lawyers are not always working toward the same goal; acting in the best interests of the client may have a different meaning for each. Both professions play important roles in the overall scheme of things, but one must not be confused with the other.

Finally, in zealously representing their clients, lawyers often use information and relationships strategically in order to advance their case. In the interests of the client, a lawyer may be cooperative and open at one point in the process, then withhold potentially helpful information and seem obstructionist at another (Vandervort, 2008). None of this is personal. It is simply the lawyer's way of doing what he or she is ethically bound to do: promote the legal interests of his or her client. If social workers are to be effective in the legal system, they must learn not to be offended by the lawyer's behavior, but rather to recognize that the legal process is an adversarial one and that the lawyer is doing his or her job.

Working Collaboratively

The differences between social work and law—and between social workers and attorneys—present challenges, but they are not irreconcilable. In fact, social workers increasingly partner with lawyers, are employed in legal settings, and participate alongside lawyers and other professionals on multidisciplinary teams. Through collaboration, social workers and attorneys can not only better meet the holistic needs of clients but also "ameliorate social conditions repugnant to both fields" (Albert, 2000, p. 332).

Whether as consultants, collaborators, or employees, social workers can be found in private law firms, courts, jails, forensic hospitals, detention centers, probation departments, advocacy organizations, prosecutors' offices, public defenders' offices, and legal aid programs. Social workers partner with law enforcement to provide crisis intervention, victim-offender mediation, and victim/witness assistance. Social workers also work as forensic evaluators who advise the courts on whether defendants are competent to stand trial and whether they satisfy the criteria for an insanity defense. They may be called upon to provide social histories; to offer sentencing recommendations; and to provide court-ordered anger management, parenting education, substance abuse treatment, or family therapy. Many social workers work with youth involved in the juvenile justice system; they are employed as probation officers, residential treatment counselors, gang prevention specialists, and family court staff (Ritter, Vakalahi, & Kiernan-Stern, 2009). Judges depend on evaluations and recommendations by social workers in making disposition determinations (Saltzman & Furman, 1999). In correctional settings, social workers may provide counseling to inmates with HIV, mental illness, or drug addiction. They can assist in monitoring medication, provide group therapy and substance abuse education, train correctional staff on how to handle inmates with mental illness, and serve as liaisons between the prisoner and the outside world. Social workers may also serve as advocates, helping to ensure that inmates—particularly those with mental health needs—have access to appropriate services. Once an inmate is released, social workers often provide follow-up treatment services in the community, including support for family members (Coleman, 1999). Solomon Draine (1995) described the successful use of interdisciplinary teams in providing intensive case management to people with mental illness who were leaving jail and facing homelessness. The Michigan Prisoner Reentry Initiative includes social work students among those providing housing assistance, job search skills, and counseling to men and women on parole (Young, 2009).

Social workers also work in public defenders' offices, many of which have begun to adopt a more holistic view of client representation. The social work role can include obtaining client social histories; conducting interviews and evaluations; and locating resources to address clients' employment, housing, mental health, physical health, and financial needs. Social workers can make referrals, provide crisis intervention and counseling, and assist attorneys in developing sentencing recommendations (Wiggins, 2009). Similarly, social workers also work alongside attorneys who represent immigrants facing detention or deportation. In this capacity, they perform psychosocial assessments, provide links to needed community services, and educate and support extended family members. Finally, social workers and lawyers may work jointly in cases of domestic violence. Attorneys prosecute batterers, obtain restraining orders, and argue for child custody and visitation rights; social workers, meanwhile, help survivors deal with the psychological impact of abuse, provide needed support, and facilitate safety planning. The complementary skills of social workers and lawyers permit a more holistic approach to addressing domestic violence (St. Joan, 2001).

WORKING IN THE OFFICE OF THE PUBLIC DEFENDER
Tonia Copeland, MSW

My field placement for the 2009–2010 academic year was at the Office of the Public Defender (OPD) in Rockville, Maryland. It was my first experience with the justice system. I have to admit that I initially struggled to make the connection between social work and the OPD; in light of my previous experiences, however, the field coordinator wanted to introduce me to something different. And a different experience it was! I know it will have a lasting effect on my understanding of social work and will be an experience I take with me throughout my professional career.

Social workers at the OPD were responsible for helping the lawyers with mitigation—that is, seeking reduced sentences for people who were convicted of crimes. In mitigation work, the relationship with the client and the written assessment are the most important aspects of the job. The lawyers send requests to the social workers for a particular case (i.e., murder, rape, malicious wounding, armed robbery). In an ideal situation, the social worker would have months to prepare; however, in some cases, the social worker has two weeks to build rapport and then complete an assessment to present to the judge. The interview with the client is the most crucial aspect of the assessment. Assessments also involve interviewing family members, school officials, and professionals from other agencies involved with the client.

The majority of the interviews took place at the Montgomery County Correctional Facility (MCCF), which houses OPD's juvenile and adult clients. "Nervous" does not begin to describe my feelings as I walked into MCCF for the first time! Going through the metal detector and being searched by the security officer were pretty routine; however, going through the multiple doors of the facility was a little unnerving. We walked through one door and then waited for that door to close behind us before the officials, sitting behind black glass, opened the next door. This process happened at every door we had to enter. I recall walking down the hallways to our cli-ents' living area and passing inmates who were not handcuffed or escorted by a security officer. Several thoughts ran through my mind including the concern that I might be attacked; I'd have nowhere to run because I was behind all those locked doors.

I used a biopsychosocial-spiritual model in conducting the client assessments. The assessment covered every imaginable aspect of the clients' lives, from birth to the present. The interview covered their living environment; whether or not their parents were married when they were born; their relationship with each parent; their relationship with each sibling; whether they have any children; their performance in school including their grades; any suspensions or expulsions in school; any medication and/or health problems; any mental illnesses experienced by the client or their family; any mental, sexual, and/or physical abuse; any substance abuse issues experienced by the client and/or family; whether they had any religious beliefs; and whether or not the client had thought of or attempted suicide. Every aspect of the clients' and their family's life was uncovered in order to identify trauma, victimization, or any themes or issues that could be expounded upon in order to present the client as a person in need of treatment instead of prolonged incarceration.

My first lesson in empathy occurred during this field placement. The lesson occurred in court. I attended the sentencing of my field instructor's client who was initially charged with first-degree murder but pled guilty to second-degree murder as part of a plea agreement. We sat on the defendant's side of the courtroom. The lesson began when the victim's family walked in. The amount of venom in the victim's mother's gaze was indescribable. I immediately thought that I was sitting on the wrong side of the courtroom. However, observing my field instructor consoling her client's mother, who repeatedly stated "I have lost my son," reminded me of the social worker's purpose in this particular environment. Who better to look past a person's actions in order to advocate for them than a social worker. My field instructor's client was first and foremost a person. Granted, he committed what is described as a heinous crime, but there is an explanation behind the action—an explanation deserving of treatment. My field instructor's ability to console the mother and attempt to alleviate her pain was a true demonstration of empathy; it convinced me that social workers have an important role to play in legal settings.

Most of my work at OPD involved conducting research and interviews in order to complete mitigation assessments, but I also assisted with waiver transfers, attended court hearings, attended team meetings to discuss cases, researched alternative placements for juvenile clients, and researched community resources. In fact, I had experience with nearly every aspect of social work practice in a legal setting. I now plan to obtain my clinical license and gain the vital skills needed to work with incarcerated persons and their families.

Low-income clients are often the focus of collaborative efforts between social workers and lawyers. Gollick and Lessem (2004) describe the creation of a university-based free legal clinic serving older adults and people with disabilities. Staffed largely by students who were supervised by professional attorneys and a professional social worker, the clinic addressed problems including housing evictions and denials or terminations of public benefits. Despite encountering numerous challenges in fostering effective teamwork between the law students and social work interns, there were clear rewards. The authors found the social work students to be particularly adept at understanding client concerns and problems. They also played a significant role in alleviating client anxiety around involvement in the legal process. They helped identify needed community resources. Finally, they were able to provide important follow-up services to clients, once the legal case was complete.

A number of additional models of collaboration have arisen around the rapidly increasing older adult population. "The legal needs of older persons and their families tend to be multifaceted and often require a multidisciplinary approach" (Arnason, Fish & Rosenzweig, 2001, p. 6). To this end, social workers may be employed as staff in "elder law" practices or may forge reciprocal working relationships in which each professional refers clients to the other. In this way, the social worker can focus on the psychosocial needs of the client while the attorney addresses important legal concerns. A client who needs help with probate, guardianship, or long-term care financing, for example, could also receive support in dealing with attendant feelings of loss, grief, or stress. The social worker's skills in outreach, engagement, interviewing, assessment, counseling, and accessing resources and benefits can complement the attorney's legal skills and provide the client with a more complete and satisfying experience (Pierce, Gleason-Wynn, & Miller, 2001).

Multidisciplinary teams that include both social workers and lawyers have also addressed both child and adult maltreatment. For example, the first Elder Abuse Forensic Center opened in 2003 in California, bringing together Adult Protective Services (APS) social workers, law enforcement officials, members of the district attorney's office, medical professionals, mental health services providers, victim advocates, and domestic violence experts. Under this model, these diverse professionals commit to a sustained, collaborative process that includes frequent consultation and a range of case management activities.

Research suggests that the forensic center model is successful in enhancing both the effectiveness and efficiency of addressing elder abuse (e.g., Wiglesworth, Mosqueda, Burnight, Younglove, & Jeske, 2006). A similar model addresses child maltreatment. Known as a child advocacy center, it uses multidisciplinary teams to conduct one-stop, child-friendly forensic interviews, examinations, and treatment in cases of suspected abuse or neglect. This approach minimizes trauma for the victim while facilitating the collection of evidence for both protecting the child and prosecuting the abuser.

In order for social workers and legal professionals to collaborate successfully, they must approach the working relationship with "respect, understanding, and a willingness to learn" (Wiggins, 2009, p. 1). Because their roles, objectives, training, and ethical obligations differ in important ways, communication is critical (Center for Social Services Research, 2002). Clear and realistic expectations of each professional should be delineated, including who will assume which tasks and what resources are necessary to do the job well. Lines of supervision should be clear and should respect the need for each professional to seek consultation from those in his or her own field. The potential for ethical conflicts should be discussed up front; when their resolution is unclear, a plan should be established for processing them (Galowitz, 1999). Finally, cross-disciplinary training should be initiated so that each professional has an opportunity to become familiar with the other. In venues where social workers and lawyers work together—whether in public defenders' offices, courthouses, or correctional facilities or on multidisciplinary teams—having some insight into each profession's roles and obligations can become the foundation for negotiating positive and productive collaborations. In sum, "regardless of the differences in approach, law as well as social work are helping professions. Both can cooperate in obtaining the speedy, efficacious and most cost-effective way of dealing with people who are hurting" (Weinstein, 1999, p. 399).

Alternatives to the Traditional Court System

So far, we have discussed various aspects of the traditional legal system with which social workers should be familiar. Beginning in the late 1980s, however, a movement began to reconceptualize the justice system and to establish a new brand of courts known as *problem-solving courts*. Beginning with the first drug court in Miami, this new approach now encompasses a wide variety of specialized courts that deal with cases involving domestic violence, homelessness, truancy, mental health, driving while intoxicated (DWI), sex offenses, and parole reentry, among others. What they all have in common is a commitment to addressing the underlying problem leading to the defendant's behavior, rather than simply perpetuating "revolving door justice" in which defendants serve their time but are soon rearrested and incarcerated again. The goal of problem-solving courts is to change "the life trajectories of victims, offenders, and community residents" by creating specialized courtrooms in which long-term goals replace short-term ones, judges stay involved in each case over the long haul, the impact of environmental factors on individual behavior is taken into account, multidisciplinary teams work together to achieve results, and attorneys on both sides work collaboratively to facilitate positive behavior change for the defendant (Berman & Feinblatt, 2005, p. 11). Although controversial, these courts present new opportunities for social work practitioners. In many ways, they reflect important social work values. They are dedicated to identifying and treating both the individual and the social problems that contribute to unlawful behavior (Mirchandani, 2008). They feature a model in which psychosocial assessment and treatment expertise—the domain of social work professionals—are integral to success.

Evaluation results, to date, are promising. Drug courts, which number upward of 1,000 in the United States, have been shown to have positive effects in reaching targeted populations, keeping offenders in treatment, providing effective monitoring and community supervision, and reducing jail costs. Overall, they appear to have a positive effect on reducing long-term recidivism rates (Berman, Rempel, & Wolf, 2007; Mitchell, Wilson, Eggers, & MacKenzie, 2012). Comparatively little research has been conducted on mental health courts, although new studies are currently underway. So far, findings suggest that these courts are effective in linking offenders to services, providing a higher level of service, and reducing subsequent arrests. Domestic violence courts, of which there are now at least 300, show small improvements in satisfaction with the court process and delivery of services to survivors and their families, reductions in the number of cases dismissed, increases in guilty pleas, and improved perpetrator compliance with treatment programs and other court-ordered sentences (Casey & Rottman, 2003). Despite these apparent advantages, some observers worry that circumventing the adversarial nature of the traditional legal system may undermine offenders' rights by coercing them into unwanted guilty pleas and treatment (Tyuse & Linhorst, 2005).

By redefining the relationship between social work and the justice system, problem-solving courts provide exciting opportunities for cross-disciplinary collaboration. According to Tyuse and Linhorst (2005), social workers can interact with problem-solving courts by helping develop new venues or by working in agencies that are part of the network courts rely on for service provision. In any event, social work practitioners should be familiar with the problem-solving court movement, as well as with the traditional justice system's processes and procedures.

Summary and Conclusion

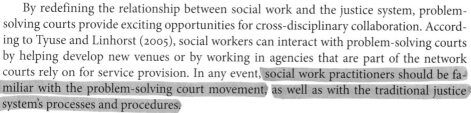

Social workers have a long history of using the law to meet client needs and to pursue social justice. Over time, social workers have increasingly partnered with legal professionals, become employed in legal settings, provided consultation to the courts, and participated with attorneys on multidisciplinary teams. Practicing in the legal environment can be challenging for social workers. In order to be effective, they need to understand how the legal system compares to the human service system in terms of its roles, processes, expectations, culture, and ethical mandates. This chapter introduced basic information about the legal system, including the different types of courts, different types of proceedings, how a court case unfolds, and alternatives to the traditional justice system. The legal profession provides numerous opportunities for engagement by social workers; doing so has enormous potential benefits.

CHAPTER 1 PRACTICE TEST

The following questions will test your application and analysis of the content found within this chapter. For additional assessment, including licensing-exam-type questions on applying chapter content to practice behaviors, visit **MySearchLab**.

1. Your state has been rocked by a scandal in which social workers fraudulently filed millions of dollars in Medicare claims. In response, the governor wants to make it easier to convict health professionals accused of these types of offenses. One way to accomplish this would be to

   a. change the standard of proof.

   b. rely on precedent.

   c. require judicial review.

   d. allow peremptory challenges.

2. You are a child welfare worker, appearing in court in connection with a case involving parental neglect. You approach the mother's lawyer, hoping that a frank discussion will generate a solution that is best for all involved. He rebuffs your efforts. Which of these observations would explain his response?

   a. He is behaving unethically.

   b. He lacks the necessary interpersonal skills to perform his job effectively.

   c. He is behaving consistently with the adversarial nature of the judicial process.

   d. He is behaving consistently with the ecological framework that grounds legal representation.

3. When a case is on appeal

   a. The court hears only the most important witnesses.

   b. Evidence can be introduced but no witness testimony is permitted.

   c. Only legal issues are considered, so no testimony or evidence is presented.

   d. The U.S Supreme Court will automatically hear the case if the lower court's holding is reversed.

4. In selecting a jury

   a. Only the judge has input regarding who may serve.

   b. Lawyers can strike selected jurors if they have good cause.

   c. Lawyers can eliminate jurors in order to ensure representation of a particular race or sex.

   d. No outside consultants are permitted to influence the process.

5. In what ways is the problem-solving court model a good fit with social work's orientation?

6. What strategies can be employed to facilitate positive collaborations between social workers and attorneys?

MYSEARCHLAB CONNECTIONS

Reinforce what you learned in this chapter by studying videos, cases, documents, and more available at **www.MySearchLab.com**

Watch these Videos

✶ Women's Rights Movement in Nineteenth Century America, The

- *How did women (including many social worker pioneers) of the nineteenth century go about seeking legal equality with men?*

Read these Cases/Documents

∆ Jane Addams, from Twenty Years at Hull House (1910)

- *What social work values seem to have motivated Jane Addams to pursue the social reforms that she did?*

∆ Frances Perkins and the Social Security Act (1935, 1960)

- *How does Frances Perkins exemplify the use of legal channels to effect social change?*

Explore these Assets

- NASW Code of Ethics

Research these Topics

- Restorative Justice
- Interdisciplinary Collaboration

Assess Your Knowledge

Go to **MySearchLab** to test your knowledge of key topics in this chapter with topic-specific quizzes. Conclude your assessment by completing the chapter exam.

✶ = CSWE Core Competency Asset
∆ = Case Study

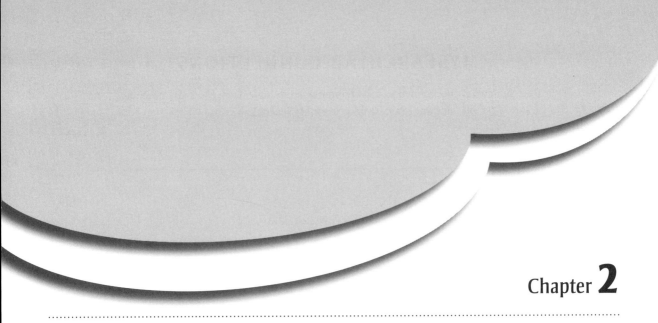

Chapter **2**

Law and Judicial Policy

When we hear the term *policy*, most of us think of laws that are passed by the legislature. Because legislative policy is more amenable to change and more open to public influence than policy made by the other branches of government, it has become the focus of many social work courses and field placements, as well as the centerpiece of the profession's lobbying efforts. With so much emphasis on legislative policy making, however, the profound role of the courts in shaping policy is often obscured. Yet their interpretations of laws and regulations can have far-reaching effects. Judicial decisions help define our clients' life chances and the realities of social and economic justice.

The Role of Case Law in Policy

As students, we are taught that the legislative branch of government makes laws, the executive branch enforces laws, and the judicial branch interprets laws. Our focus in this text is on the judiciary's interpretive role and its contribution to policy outcomes. When legislators pass laws, and when agencies write regulations, it is impossible to anticipate every situation to which the law might be applied. As new circumstances surface, it is the courts that interpret the law to fit each new set of facts. These interpretations, in turn, become part of our understanding of the underlying policy. For example, the Americans with Disabilities Act has been before the courts many times. Courts have considered whether an asymptomatic condition (such as HIV) falls within the policy's definition of disability. Similarly, the courts have considered whether someone whose disability can be remedied with the assistance of corrective devices (e.g., glasses or prostheses) is entitled to the law's protections. In these instances, the courts are interpreting the language of the statute and regulations, providing guidance on how the law should be applied as new situations present themselves.

All of us can name landmark Supreme Court cases that we think of as constituting important national policy. *Brown v. Board of Education*, for example, decided in 1954, addressed the issue of school desegregation, concluding that separate schools for White and Black students were inherently unequal and thus violated the U.S. Constitution. *Roe v. Wade*, decided in 1973, used a constitutional interpretation to lay out the parameters of a right to abortion. Circuit courts, state courts, and local district courts also issue opinions that impact nearly every sphere relevant to social work practice, including housing, education, child welfare, health, mental health, corrections, and disabilities.

Judicial opinions of interest to us as social workers are handed down by the dozens every year. During the 2009–2012 Supreme Court terms, the Court considered cases addressing affirmative action, strip searches in schools, the rights of English language learners and special education students, voting rights, campaign finance, age discrimination, gun rights, immigration, assisted reproductive technology, informed consent, health care reform, separation of church and state, domestic violence, Indian land rights, disability rights, labor unions, race discrimination, sex discrimination, fairness in sentencing, rights of linguistic minorities, prisoners' rights, the insanity defense, civil commitment of sex offenders, child abduction, the right to counsel, death penalty mitigation, and juvenile justice. Specific cases will be discussed later as various topic areas are explored.

Although technically mere interpretations of the law, these decisions help determine how public policy is operationalized. Because each case involves an actual, real-life application of an existing law, it is the court's interpretation that determines how a bill passed by Congress actually plays out on the ground. Let's consider an example. In 2009, the U.S. Supreme Court heard a case called *Forest Grove School District v. T.A.*, which concerned the rights of a student with a diagnosed learning disability. Under the Individuals with Disabilities Education Act (IDEA), all students are entitled to a free and appropriate public education. The question here was whether a student who transferred from a public school without ever having previously received special education services was entitled to receive them at his new private school. When T.A.'s parents requested special education services, the school district found him ineligible. A hearing resulted in the opposite conclusion, and the school district was ordered to reimburse T.A.'s parents for the cost of his private school tuition. The district court reversed that decision, concluding that IDEA bars reimbursement unless the student has previously received special education services. The court of appeals reversed again, concluding that the courts can grant reimbursement in appropriate circumstances. The U.S. Supreme Court was the final arbiter, interpreting IDEA to permit reimbursement of private special education services if the public school fails to provide them and the private school placement is appropriate, regardless of whether the student has previously received special education services through the public schools. This decision by the Supreme Court put to rest the conflicting interpretations by the lower courts and resulted in a concrete benefit to T.A. and countless other students who might find themselves in a similar situation.

Comparing Statutory Law and Case Law

Using statutory law (laws passed by the legislature) as a point of comparison to case law will help us understand the unique ways in which case law operates. Consider the following differences between case law and statutory law:

- **Unlike the legislature, a court cannot initiate decision making; it can act only after a case comes before it.** If a legislator wants to change a particular policy, he or she can introduce a bill. Let's say, for example, that a member of the Colorado General Assembly (the state legislature) wants to amend state law to allow felons to have their voting rights reinstated once they are on parole. If there is a sponsor in the other chamber as well, a bill would be drafted, debated, amended, and voted on first by one chamber and then by the other; any differences between the two chambers' versions would be resolved and put to a vote, and, if signed by the governor the bill would become law. A court, on the other hand, cannot simply decide that such a policy should be in force and proceed to create it. The court has to wait until an existing law adversely affects an actual person who comes to court to have the conflict resolved. In our example, a felon on probation would have to be stripped of his or her voting rights and bring an action in court contesting the law or the way in which it was applied. It is only then that the court could consider the law, rendering a new interpretation or striking it down, resulting in policy change. Colorado does have a law that deprives felons of their voting rights and then automatically reinstates them when the "term of imprisonment" is completed. The legislature has not made efforts to explicitly apply the reinstatement provision to those on parole, but if a state legislator were so inclined, he or she could simply introduce a bill to that effect. As it happens, such a case did come before the Colorado courts. In *Danielson v. Dennis* (2006), a parolee argued that his voting rights should have been reinstated when his confinement ended and his parole began. The Colorado Supreme Court disagreed, leaving the law unchanged and clarifying that being on parole is considered part of one's term of imprisonment. Even if the court had interpreted the law differently, it could not even have considered the case unless and until an actual person was affected by the law and brought his or her challenge to court.

  Marriage equality is another example. In Iowa, gay marriage became legal in 2009 as the result of *Varnum v. Brien*. In this case, six couples successfully brought suit challenging the state's ban on same-sex marriage after being refused marriage licenses because of their sexual orientation. Had they not come forward, the court would have been unable to weigh in on this controversial issue. In Maryland, on the other hand, a bill to the same effect was passed by the state legislature and signed by the governor in 2012; if approved by voters, it will become law. Any member of the legislature can introduce a policy change; courts, on the other hand, can only respond to the cases that come before them.

- **Unlike statutory law, case law is based on precedent.** As just discussed, any legislator can introduce a bill on any issue, without any preconditions. Once a bill is passed and a new law is in place, it typically can be revised or reversed by a simple majority vote. Legislators are influenced by myriad factors, but there is no particular expectation that they will be bound by prior legislative decisions. A prominent example was the effort of the new Republican-led House of Representatives to repeal the Obama health care reform plan in early 2011, a mere 10 months after its enactment. Courts, on the other hand, are bound by *precedent* (also known as the doctrine of *stare decisis*). The idea, at least in theory, is that the law should be settled and not be subject to the whims of the public or the changing composition of the court. It is this general imperviousness to change that lends the courts' determinations an aura of authority and stability. Courts use precedent by examining relevant prior decisions and applying them to the cases now before them.

In *People v. Cabral* (1993), a California court considered the case of a man who was convicted of sexually abusing his daughter. While in custody, the man was advised by two other prisoners that he might be able to get a shorter sentence if he voluntarily participated in a treatment program for sex offenders. Seeking admission to such a program, Cabral sent a letter to the psychologist in charge, acknowledging the abuse. At trial, the letter was admitted into evidence against him. Cabral argued that the letter contained confidential communication that should be accorded privilege (i.e., it should be legally protected from disclosure in court). In ruling against him, the court relied on a similar 1981 case, *Montebello Rose Co. v. Agricultural Labor Relations Board*, involving the attorney-client privilege. In that case, the court determined that in order for communication with an attorney to be privileged, its dominant purpose must be the furtherance of the attorney-client relationship, that is, the solicitation of legal advice. Cabral's argument that his letter should fall within the psychotherapist-client privilege was rejected because its dominant purpose was *not* deemed to be therapeutic but rather strategic: to evade imprisonment. The point here is that the court in *Cabral*, as it does in nearly every case, based its determination on decisions made in previous, similar cases.

Is *stare decisis* absolute? No. The court may diverge from previous holdings for several reasons: The new case may have facts that make it different in significant ways from previous cases, the changing composition of the court may in fact result in a different outcome, or changing social conditions can lead the court in a new direction. For example, in *Stanford v. Kentucky* (1989), the U.S. Supreme Court ruled that capital punishment was unconstitutional when applied to youth whose crimes were committed before they were age 16 but maintained that it was constitutional for those 16 and older. In 2005, the Court in *Roper v. Simmons* considered another death penalty case and, this time, ruled that capital punishment is unconstitutional when applied to youth who committed their crimes before they were 18. How do we explain the discrepancy? What about precedent? Between the time the *Stanford* case was decided and the time *Roper v. Simmons* was decided, public opinion had significantly shifted away from executing juveniles. In addition, new research on adolescent brain development played a significant role in informing the Court's more recent consideration of the juvenile death penalty.

Similarly, in *Lawrence v. Texas* (2003), the Supreme Court overturned a 1986 decision (*Bowers v. Hardwick*) in which it had upheld the constitutionality of antisodomy laws. Rather than relying on the earlier case as precedent, the Court declared that it had misconstrued the legal question; posing the question differently allowed the Court to reach a different conclusion. The composition of the Court also had changed, as had public opinion. The first case, *Hardwick*, was decided in the early days of the AIDS crisis when AIDS was widely regarded as a "gay" disease. Progress in our understanding of the AIDS epidemic and an increasing acceptance of homosexuality contributed to the Court's willingness to disregard—and even overturn—an important precedent.

- **In case law, every decision is specific to a set of facts.** Because courts consider actual disputes, rather than theoretical questions, their decisions apply to the specific facts before them. Judges do not make global determinations but rather base their analyses and opinions on the individual situation at hand. In considering a case, the judges must determine whether the scenario is similar enough to that of previous cases to call for the application of settled law or different enough to require a different approach and outcome. In *Vernonia School District v. Acton* (1995), the U.S. Supreme Court upheld the constitutionality of a school district policy requiring the random drug testing of all students in extracurricular athletic programs. A few years later, in 1998, the Colorado Supreme Court considered a slightly different policy in *Trinidad School District No. 1 v. Lopez*. Here, *all* students participating in extracurricular activities—not just athletes—were subject to random drug tests. A member of the marching band objected to the policy and the court agreed, finding it unconstitutional. In reaching its conclusion, the court emphasized the ways in which the facts in this case differed from those in *Vernonia*. First, the court recognized that participants in marching bands have a greater expectation of privacy than student athletes because the latter shower and dress in communal facilities. Second, the athletes in *Vernonia* were believed to be the primary instigators of the school's rampant drug use and disorder; no such evidence suggested the same was true of the band members in *Trinidad*. Finally, the concern that drug use created a safety hazard for athletes was found to be unsupported in relation to members of the marching band. The court considered these differences in the facts of the case to be significant enough to reach a different conclusion than the Supreme Court had reached in *Vernonia*. Interestingly, a similar case was later considered by the U.S. Supreme Court in *Board of Education v. Earls* (2002). In this case, by a vote of 5–4, the Court upheld an Oklahoma school district policy that required random drug testing of students who participated in any and all extracurricular activities. Essentially, they concluded that the facts were indistinguishable in any important way from those in *Vernonia*, so they reached the same result. This is how case law evolves; it is cumulative. As each slightly different set of facts is examined, the law is reinterpreted and our understanding of it is refined.

How Statutory Law and Case Law Interact

Although legislatures and courts impact policy in different ways, it is not unusual for an issue to bounce back and forth between the two as each body shapes the outcome. An example is late-term abortion (described by opponents as "partial birth abortion"). Nebraska passed a law criminalizing late-term abortions; challenges to it reached the U.S. Supreme Court in 2000. In a 5–4 decision (*Stenberg v. Carhart*), the Court struck down the law as unconstitutional, in part because the statute's definition left somewhat vague the question of which abortions would be covered. In 2003, Congress passed its own law, the Partial Birth Abortion Ban Law, being careful to "fix" the constitutional deficiencies that the Supreme Court had identified in Nebraska's law. The Partial Birth Abortion Ban Law then made its way to the Supreme Court based on a challenge that the law unconstitutionally provided no exception for the health of the mother. The law was upheld, nonetheless, by a 5–4 vote (*Gonzales v. Carhart*), in part because Justice Sandra Day O'Connor had retired and been replaced by a more conservative justice, Samuel Alito.

This jockeying back and forth between the legislature and the courts has also characterized the law on marriage equality. In a May 2008 decision, the California Supreme Court found that the state had violated its constitution by refusing to grant marriage licenses to same-sex couples. Gay marriage was essentially legalized and couples began to be married. In response, a constitutional amendment (Proposition 8) to prohibit same-sex marriage was put on the ballot in November 2008 and was approved by voters. Proposition 8 was subsequently challenged; the state supreme court found it to have been lawfully enacted but ruled that those same-sex marriages performed before November 2008 would remain valid. Meanwhile, in October 2009, the state legislature passed a bill allowing out-of-state same-sex marriages to be recognized in California. And in October 2010, a U.S. district court, in the case of *Perry v. Schwarzenegger*, declared Proposition 8 to be unconstitutional.

As these examples suggest, legislatures sometimes pass laws with which the courts subsequently find fault. In order to clarify the intent of a law—or cure problems identified by the courts—the legislature may then revise the law in the hope that it will withstand judicial scrutiny. This can happen any number of times; eventually, the legislature gives up, passes a version of the law that goes unchallenged, or fashions a law that the courts approve. One final example to illustrate this point: In 2008, the U.S. Supreme Court decided in a landmark case, *District of Columbia v. Heller*, that a D.C. policy restricting the possession of handguns and other firearms for private use at home was unconstitutional. The case is regarded as a referendum on the meaning of the Second Amendment, interpreting the Constitution to grant individuals the right to bear arms. In response to the Supreme Court's ruling, the D.C. Council (the legislative body) revised its gun laws to be as restrictive as possible while still meeting the letter of the law enunciated in the Court's decision. Those restrictions were subsequently challenged in a civil suit (taking it once again into the court's domain) and upheld by a district court judge in 2010.

Although many of these examples involve decisions by the U.S. Supreme Court, important policy issues are raised across the judicial spectrum. The reality is that the vast majority of cases are actually decided by lower federal courts and by state courts. It is these decisions that often shape our day-to-day lives and those of our clients. Most social workers, for example, are familiar with the case of *Tarasoff v. Board of Regents of the University of California* (1976). This is the case that established a duty for therapists to warn third parties who might be endangered by a client. In fact, this was a decision by the California Supreme Court. However, it laid the groundwork for similar laws and court decisions across the country. Although not a decision by the U.S. Supreme Court, it is considered a landmark case in relation to social work practice. Similarly, it is state court decisions that have catapulted marriage equality to the top of the national agenda, raising questions about how restricting marriage to heterosexuals is compatible with the guarantees of various state constitutions. Although the issue of gay marriage has yet to reach the U.S. Supreme Court, the actions of lower federal courts and of state courts have made an indelible mark on the national landscape when it comes to the rights of same-sex partners. Keeping this in mind, we turn our attention to the U.S. Supreme Court. Its makeup, role, and decision-making processes are discussed next.

The U.S. Supreme Court

The U.S. Supreme Court, known as "the highest court in the land," is generally considered to be the most respected and authoritative of our government institutions. Its members are appointed by the president and approved by the Senate, rather than elected. Its procedures and deliberations enjoy a level of secrecy not afforded other parts of the U.S. government. Appointments for life are meant to ensure insulation from the whims of public opinion and pressure groups, affording the Court a unique stability and neutrality on issues of great importance to the nation.

The Court convenes in the U.S. Supreme Court Building, which is located next to the U.S. Capitol in Washington, D.C. Despite changes in leadership and the passage of time, the Court remains grounded in a sense of history and tradition (O'Brien, 2005). Brass spittoons, goose-quill pens, and pewter inkwells still adorn the courtroom, and the justices are seated in order of seniority.

Nine justices serve on the U.S. Supreme Court. In 2012, they were Chief Justice John G. Roberts Jr., Atonin Scalia, Anthony M. Kennedy, Clarence Thomas, Ruth Bader Ginsburg, Stephen G. Breyer, Samuel A. Alito Jr., Sonia Sotomayor, and Elena Kagan. Historically, an overwhelming majority of Supreme Court justices have been Caucasian males with Ivy League educations. Most were appointed to the Court after serving in lower federal and state courts (O'Brien, 2005). As American society has increasingly recognized the rights of women and minorities, they have slowly become more visible on the Court as well. To date, there have been two African American justices, Thurgood Marshall (appointed by Lyndon B. Johnson in 1967) and Clarence Thomas (appointed by George H. W. Bush in 1991). The introduction of women to the Court came later and has included Sandra Day O'Connor (appointed by Ronald Reagan in 1981), Ruth Bader Ginsburg (appointed by Bill Clinton in 1993), Sonia Sotomayor (appointed by Barack Obama in 2009), and Elena Kagan (appointed by Barack Obama in 2010). Justice Sotomayor is the Court's first Hispanic justice. Of the current justices, one (Thomas) is African American, three (Ginsburg, Sotomayor, and Kagan) are female, and all but four (Ginsburg, Breyer, Sotomayor, and Kagan) were nominated by Republican presidents. Table 2.1 identifies these and the other Supreme Court justices appointed since 1950, their terms of service, and the president who appointed them.

While they are on the bench, justices earn a modest salary considering their qualifications and expertise. In 2009, associate justices of the Court received an annual salary of $208,100 and the chief justice received $217,400 (National Taxpayers Union, 2010). Compare this to celebrity Judge Judy's annual earnings of more than $25 million (ABC News, 2009)!

Because all appointments are for life, vacancies occur only when a member resigns, retires, or dies. If the integrity of a justice's behavior is in question, he or she may be impeached by the House of Representatives and face a trial in the Senate for high crimes

| | | TABLE 2.1 Supreme Court Justices Appointed Since 1950 |

TABLE 2.1   Supreme Court Justices Appointed Since 1950

Name	Dates of Service	Appointed By
Earl Warren	1953–1969	Dwight D. Eisenhower
John Marshall Harlan	1955–1971	Dwight D. Eisenhower
William J. Brennan Jr.	1956–1990	Dwight D. Eisenhower
Charles E. Whittaker	1957–1962	Dwight D. Eisenhower
Potter Stewart	1958–1981	Dwight D. Eisenhower
Byron R. White	1962–1993	John F. Kennedy
Arthur J. Goldberg	1962–1965	John F. Kennedy
Abe Fortas	1965–1969	Lyndon B. Johnson
Thurgood Marshall	1967–1991	Lyndon B. Johnson
Warren E. Burger	1969–1986	Richard Nixon
Harry E. Blackmun	1970–1994	Richard Nixon
Lewis F. Powell	1971–1987	Richard Nixon
William H. Rehnquist	1972–2005	Richard Nixon
John Paul Stevens	1975–2010	Gerald R. Ford
Sandra Day O'Connor	1981–2006	Ronald Reagan
Antonin Scalia	1986–Present	Ronald Reagan
Anthony M. Kennedy	1988–Present	Ronald Reagan
David S. Souter	1990–2009	George H.W. Bush
Clarence Thomas	1991–Present	George H.W. Bush
Ruth Bader Ginsburg	1993–Present	Bill Clinton
Stephen G. Breyer	1994–Present	Bill Clinton
John G. Roberts	2005–Present	George W. Bush
Samuel Anthony Alito Jr.	2006–Present	George W. Bush
Sonia Sotomayor	2009–Present	Barack Obama
Elena Kagan	2010–Present	Barack Obama

and misdemeanors. In reality, removal from office is a rarity (O'Brien, 2005). In the entire history of the Supreme Court, only seven justices have been convicted and removed. Vacancies through death and retirement are much more common. In 2005, for example, Justice Sandra Day O'Connor announced her intention to retire; President George W. Bush nominated John G. Roberts to fill her seat on the Court. However, Chief Justice Rehnquist passed away in the midst of that confirmation process, necessitating the immediate appointment of yet another justice. President Bush withdrew Roberts from consideration for Justice O'Connor's seat and instead nominated him to assume the role of chief justice (Baker, 2005; Lane, 2005). The Senate confirmed his nomination. Third Circuit Judge

Samuel Alito was then nominated to fill Justice O'Connor's seat and was confirmed by the Senate after prolonged debate (Grunwald, Becker, & Russakoff, 2005). The opportunity to appoint new justices to the Supreme Court comes rarely and is prized by presidential contenders. Voters often underestimate the importance of a president's being able to fill Court vacancies.

As social workers we need to be cognizant of the enormous difference the composition of the courts can make in the public policies that ensue and how well or poorly they reflect our professional values.

Judicial Selection

The Constitution (Article II, Section 2) defines the process of appointment for Supreme Court justices. Simply put, the president submits a nominee to the Senate, which must approve the nomination by a majority vote. In fact, it is the attorney general who identifies potential nominees. Before their names are shared with the Senate, the American Bar Association (ABA) provides the White House with a rating of each (well qualified, qualified, or not qualified) based on the criteria of integrity, professional competence, judicial temperament, and health. Ideally, Supreme Court justices are selected on the basis of objective qualifications (Baum, 2007). Because the Court has such enormous power to shape public policy, however, the confirmation process often becomes highly political. Presidents, members of Congress, political operatives, and interest groups all understand that they can benefit from choosing someone who shares their beliefs and perspectives. As a result, the nomination and confirmation of Supreme Court justices have become increasingly partisan and contentious processes.

A notable example of this more politicized process was President Reagan's nomination of Robert Bork to the Supreme Court in 1987; liberals vehemently opposed Bork's appointment on the basis of his right-wing views regarding abortion, affirmative action, and civil rights. After a highly acrimonious confirmation fight, Bork was rejected by the largest margin in history (Greenhouse, 1987). Clarence Thomas's nomination in 1991 drew headlines when he was accused by Anita Hill, a former employee, of sexual harassment. He was ultimately confirmed, despite the fact that many African American and civil rights groups took issue with his conservative views and the American Bar Association's recommendation panel split on whether or not he was qualified for the position. In 2005, President Bush's nomination of Harriet Miers was torpedoed by Republicans—members of his own party—who feared she was not sufficiently committed to a conservative agenda; she withdrew from consideration. With media scrutiny intensifying and the broader public weighing in through social media, blogs, and talk radio, the confirmation process has become both more open and more dominated by interest groups and media politics (Silverstein, 2007). The politically charged environment surrounding the appointment of Supreme Court justices has changed the nature of confirmation hearings as well; nominees are increasingly reticent to comment on matters of consequence or controversy. Like other advocacy groups and professional associations, NASW takes positions on Supreme Court nominees. Most recently, it opposed the confirmation of Justices Roberts and Alito and supported the nominations of Justices Sotomayor and Kagan (National Association of Social Workers, 2005, 2006).

The Leanings of the Court

With the additions of Chief Justice Roberts and Justice Alito, the Court has become noticeably more conservative. Researchers from the University of Chicago (Landes & Posner, 2009) analyzed the records of all the justices who have served on the Court since 1937 and then ranked the justices from most to least conservative. Four members of the current Court—Thomas, Scalia, Roberts, and Alito—ranked in the top five. That means that four of the five most conservative justices in the past 70 years are on the bench today. Only one of the current justices—Ginsburg—ranked among the 10 *least* conservative justices over the past 70 years. This conservatism has been apparent in cases involving criminal law, campaign finance, abortion rights, civil rights, and separation of church and state. For example, the Court reached further than ever before in permitting restrictions on the right to an abortion in the combined cases of *Gonzales v. Carhart* and *Gonzales v. Planned Parenthood* (2007). In these cases, it upheld a federal law criminalizing late-term abortions even when the mother's health is at stake. Until this point, restrictions on abortion had consistently required an exception for the health of the mother in order to be considered constitutional. This incursion into women's reproductive rights is regarded as a significant step on the road toward reversing *Roe v. Wade*. In another example, the Court removed existing restrictions on corporate-funded advertising that supports or opposes political candidates (*Citizens United v. Federal Election Commission*, 2010). President Obama famously decried this decision, which gives business more influence in deciding elections, during his 2010 State of the Union address. As a general rule, Justices Roberts, Alito, Scalia, and Thomas comprise a conservative bloc within the Court, with Justices Ginsburg, Breyer, Sotomayor, and Kagan taking more liberal positions. Justice Kennedy, like Justice O'Connor before him, most often acts as the swing vote in closely divided cases—although observers note that he more often votes with the conservative justices than with the liberals. A notable exception to the prevalence of conservative outcomes is *National Federation of Independent Business v. Sebelius* (2012), in which a five-member majority of the Court (the four liberal justices plus Chief Justice Roberts) upheld the major provisions of President Obama's health care reform plan, the Affordable Care Act.

In addition to assessing the Court's conservative or liberal leanings, observers often examine the degree to which justices can be characterized as strict constructionists or activists. A *strict constructionist* is one who is faithful to the actual language of the law being scrutinized or who applies its original meaning or seeks to enforce what was intended by its authors. For strict constructionists, there is little room for interpretation in light of the advances that have occurred with the passage of time. Judicial *activists*, on the other hand, are those who use the court as an instrument of policy making by basing their interpretations on contemporary realities; they see legal texts, including the Constitution, as living documents whose meaning evolves over time. Critics accuse judicial activists of "legislating from the bench" by ignoring the dictates of the law and substituting their own view of what is best for society. Although strict constructionists are most often conservatives, judicial activism occurs on both ends of the spectrum. For example, the 1970s was a time of significant judicial activism by liberals as the Court issued groundbreaking rulings in areas including reproductive freedom and civil rights. More recently, however, conservative jurists have shown their activist stripes as well. Examples include the 2000 *Bush v. Gore* decision, in which the Court entered uncharted territory when it effectively decided the outcome of a contested presidential election, and the 2007 case of *Ledbetter v.*

Goodyear Tire and Rubber Co., in which the Court severely limited the opportunity to seek redress for pay discrimination, contradicting precedent and the manifest intent of the law.

The Operations of the Court

The Court's yearly term begins on the first Monday in October and typically extends until late June. The time is divided between *sittings* (when the justices hear oral arguments and issue rulings) and *recesses* (when they discuss pending cases and draft opinions). Although the justices meet together to conduct Court business, they spend a majority of their time in separate, secluded chambers with their staff, examining cases and formulating individual opinions (O'Brien, 2005). Each justice typically employs three or four clerks who play an important role in the process by recommending which new cases the Court should accept and drafting the initial opinions of decided cases.

There is no right of appeal to the U.S. Supreme Court. Instead, those seeking a hearing by the Court petition for *certiorari* (*cert* for short). The Court receives approximately 7,000 such petitions each year. Only 100 to 150 are accepted. The Court employs what is known as the "Rule of Four": At least four justices must agree to hear a case in order for a *cert* petition to be granted. Once *cert* is granted, each side submits a written brief of up to 50 pages. The brief is each party's opportunity to lay out its legal arguments. Outside individuals and organizations that have an interest in the case may also submit "friend of the court" or *amicus* briefs. NASW submits about 15 *amicus* briefs per year, sometimes as the sole or primary author and other times as a signatory to a brief authored by another organization. In recent years, NASW has submitted briefs on issues including same-sex marriage, gay adoption, employment rights, mandatory drug testing, health care reform, and student rights.

Oral arguments are held before the justices, with each side having 30 minutes to present its case. High-profile cases may receive more time; for example, 5-1/2 hours were set aside for oral arguments on the Affordable Care Act (health care reform). Oral argument resembles a dialogue, with the justices frequently interrupting the attorneys to ask questions. No testimony is presented and no evidence is introduced. The only subject being debated is the law. It is often possible to gain some insight into the justices' positions on the case by paying close attention to the concerns they voice during oral arguments, along with their demeanor and the comments that they share. Oral arguments on recent cases can be heard online through the Oyez Project (www.oyez.com). Transcripts of oral arguments are also available online.

Twice a week, the justices meet in *conference,* which begins with the age-old ritual of each justice shaking hands with every other justice. They then discuss the pending petitions for *cert* and the cases heard since their last meeting. Six justices are required for a quorum. Both the discussion and the voting occur in order of seniority. In the event that not all justices are present and the vote is split, the judgment from the court below is affirmed. The most senior justice voting with the majority writes—or assigns the writing of—the Court's opinion. If there is a dissent, the most senior justice in the minority authors that opinion or determines who will. Most of the justices rely on their clerks to write the initial drafts of their opinions. Once a draft is written, it is circulated among the justices who provide comments and occasionally even change their votes. For example, they may agree with the holding but disagree with the arguments contained in the opinion as written. Rather than join the majority, they may choose to author a separate *concurring opinion*—or they may actually change sides. Most often, their concerns about the draft lead the author of the opinion to reconsider the arguments made and either broaden or narrow them in order to hold onto support by a majority of the justices. In this respect, each opinion is the result of compromise. Each justice must sign off on the final version of the Court's opinion before it is released. The vast majority of the Court's decisions are announced in the spring or early summer, at the end of the term.

Like the confirmation process, the drafting and announcing of Supreme Court opinions can be highly political. In *Roe v. Wade*, for example, Chief Justice Warren Burger believed the antiabortion law being challenged was constitutional, yet he reserved his vote until everyone else voted to see which way the vote would go. Seeing that the majority of the Court in fact opposed the law and believed it to be unconstitutional, he then voted with the majority (against his own conviction) so that he could assign the writing of the opinion. He assigned it to Justice Harry Blackmun, who he believed would take the most limited approach in ruling the law unconstitutional. Similarly, in the famous civil rights case of *Korematsu v. United States* (1944), the justices intentionally delayed announcing their opinion affirming the constitutionality of Japanese internment camps until after President Roosevelt was reelected and the last of the camps was shut down. This way they sidestepped what would certainly have been a politically divisive decision (Irons, 2006).

All Supreme Court justices are expected to participate in the collective decisions of the Court. In the event that involvement with a particular case would constitute a conflict of interest, however, federal law requires that the justice be *recused*, or excused from service. Justice Thomas, for example, recused himself in a case concerning the exclusion of women from the Virginia Military Institute (*United States v. Virginia,* 1996) because his son had previously been enrolled there as a student.

How Judges Make Decisions

One of the hallmarks of judicial decision making is that judges rely on precedent. That is, they examine decisions that have been made previously and act in concert with those decisions. Courts may depart from precedent in two ways: by distinguishing a case on the basis of the facts and by overturning a prior case. In the former instance, the court concludes that precedent does not apply because the facts in the current case differ in some significant way from the facts that guided a prior decision. In the latter instance, on rare occasion, a court explicitly overrules a previous holding, nullifying its effects. For example, in *Gideon v. Wainwright* (1963), the Supreme Court overruled an earlier decision (*Betts v. Brady,* 1942) in order to permit indigent defendants to have appointed counsel in all state criminal trials. When the Court overrules a prior decision, it typically concludes that its original decision was in error, or it acknowledges that changes have occurred that necessitate a different interpretation of the law. On a more contemporary note, with the Supreme Court becoming more conservative, many observers are anticipating the possible overturning of the *Roe v. Wade* abortion decision.

In addition to relying on precedent, the courts have a long history of relying on research findings to inform their deliberations. The use of social science research dates back to *Muller v. Oregon* (1907) in which the Supreme Court upheld a state law that limited the number of hours women could be required to work. Justice Louis Brandeis based his opinion on more than 90 reports that had been gathered by investigators, supporting the notion that long working hours were dangerous for women. Social science research is now routinely introduced in court proceedings for a wide variety of purposes, including determining the facts of a case, providing context, and planning litigation (Monahan & Walker, 1998). It can also be used to evaluate procedural innovations. In *Brown v. Board of Education* (1954), the Court relied on extensive research findings documenting the deleterious effects of segregation on the personality development of children. In the sensational 1993 case in which the Menendez brothers were tried for murdering their parents, the defense attorney introduced research evidence on the dynamics of battered child syndrome, arguing (unsuccessfully) that her clients had been driven to commit the murders as a result of childhood abuse. Social science research has also been used in the development of mathematical models used strategically by attorneys in the jury selection process to identify the characteristics of an ideal jury. Finally, judges have used research on the reliability of videotaped testimony by child witnesses to determine its admissibility in court.

As professionals who are both consumers and conductors of social science research, it is important to recognize the role that social workers can play in shaping judicial outcomes. If anything, the courts have become increasingly open to considering the research findings of various disciplines as part of their legal deliberations. In *Roper v. Simmons* (2005), the Supreme Court outlawed the use of the death penalty for minors after relying heavily on brain research showing that the capacity to appreciate consequences and regulate our behavior is not fully developed until adulthood. Similarly, in a more recent death penalty case (*Kennedy v. Louisiana,* 2008), the Supreme Court cited research presented in NASW's *amicus* brief supporting the argument that making child rape a capital offense would increase the emotional trauma experienced by victims because it would necessitate prolonged participation in the trial process.

The public often assumes that court decisions revolve around the substantive issue at hand. However, decisions can be premised on factors other than an actual policy question. A case can be won or lost because the person bringing the case does not have *standing*; that is, he or she is not in fact eligible to bring such a case. An example is *Elk Grove Unified School District v. Newdow* (2004), which challenged the constitutionality of including the words "under God" in the Pledge of Allegiance. Mr. Newdow (an atheist) brought the suit on behalf of his daughter, an elementary school student, claiming that having to recite these words violated her First Amendment right to freedom of religion. The district court disagreed and dismissed the suit. The court of appeals reversed, finding in favor of Newdow. The U.S. Supreme Court never reached the First Amendment question at all. It found that Newdow did not have standing to bring the case on behalf of his daughter because her mother had previously been awarded sole custody. Other reasons that a court reaches a particular conclusion can be equally technical. If the case is brought under a certain law or theory, the court must consider it in light of that particular law or theory. In *DeShaney v. Winnebago County DSS* (1989), the Supreme Court held that the Department of Social Services has no duty under the 14th Amendment to protect a child from ongoing, obvious abuse. This does not mean that the department was not at fault—only that a case could not successfully be made under the 14th Amendment. In another example (*Johnson v. State*, 1992), a woman reported to her obstetrician that she had smoked pot and crack cocaine three to four times every other day throughout her pregnancy. The Florida Supreme Court found that she was *not* guilty of violating the state law in question, which prohibited "delivery of a controlled substance." This does not mean that the court condones the behavior, nor does it tell us how the court would come down on the policy issue of criminalizing drug use during pregnancy. It simply tells us that the mother was not guilty under the court's interpretation of this particular state statute. These are just two examples of the many reasons that a court might render a particular decision in a particular instance. Readers should be careful not to simply look at the court's holding and assume it to be a policy decision on the merits of the case. It is important to examine the court's rationale—its reasoning—to understand what is really at stake.

Reading and Analyzing a Case

As discussed previously, case law involves an iterative process in which courts examine one specific set of facts at a time and interpret existing law in relation to those facts. These cumulative interpretations help us understand what the law really means when applied in the real world. Reading and analyzing judicial opinions allow us as social workers to have a more accurate, thorough, and nuanced understanding of how legal controversies are resolved, how the law is interpreted, on what bases these far-reaching decisions are made, their potential implications for key social work constituencies, and the likely direction of future judicial responses. Like any primary source material, case law provides us with an understanding that surpasses that of secondary sources and media accounts. Although it may involve unfamiliar terminology and new ideas, analyzing court opinons is a transdisciplinary skill that improves with practice and can provide us with unparalleled insight into the court's role in shaping social policy.

Every case involves a story. In lower court cases (state trial courts and federal district courts), we typically are presented with a more detailed account of the facts, the testimony, and the evidence. Once on appeal, however, the legal issues take center stage and become the focus of the court's argument. As an aid to capturing the essential features of a court opinion, law students often learn to "brief" a case. A *case brief* (not to be confused with the lengthy briefs attorneys submit that lay out their arguments for the court) is a specific method of note taking or outlining. It is presented here because it is a useful way for social workers to summarize the important elements as they read and analyze a case. Generally speaking, a case brief includes the following parts: (1) case name and citation, (2) facts, (3) issue, (4) holding, (5) rationale, and (6) summary of concurring/dissenting opinions.

The *case name* identifies the opposing parties in the litigation. In *Roe v. Wade*, for example, Roe was a pseudonym for the woman who challenged the Texas antiabortion statute. Wade was the attorney general. *Bush v. Gore* bears the names of the two presidential contenders whose close election in 2000 was decided through Supreme Court intervention. The party bringing the case (the plaintiff or petitioner) is typically listed first. In criminal cases, the government—represented by the term *People* or *U.S.* or *State*—is always the plaintiff. In cases involving juveniles, initials are often used to protect the identity of the child—for example, *In re D.L.* or *In the Matter of S.H.*

Following the case name is the *citation*. It tells us how to locate the court's written opinion. The citation 410 U.S. 113 (1973), for example, is the citation for *Roe v. Wade*. The initial number refers to the volume in the series of books (U.S.) in which the case appears, and the number following is the starting page. If you went to the library to look for a hard copy of the case, you would first find the United States Reports (abbreviated "U.S."), pull volume 410 off the shelf, and turn to page 113. The date indicates the year in which the case was decided. Given the current accessibility of court opinions online, the citation

TABLE 2.2   **Case Law Collections**

Reporter Abbreviation(s)	Name of Reporter	Court(s) Covered
Federal Reporters		
L. Ed., L. Ed. 2d	*U.S. Supreme Court Reports, Lawyers' Edition*	U.S. Supreme Court
S. Ct.	*Supreme Court Reporter*	U.S. Supreme Court
U.S.	*United States Reports*	U.S. Supreme Court
F., F.2d, F.3d	*Federal Reporter*	U.S. Courts of Appeals
F. Supp., F. Supp. 2d	*Federal Supplement*	U.S. District Courts
Regional Reporters		
A., A.2d	*Atlantic Reporter*	CT, DC, DE, MD, NJ, NH, ME, PA, RI, VT
N.E., N.E.2d	*North Eastern Reporter*	IL, IN, MA, NY, OH
N.W., N.W.2d	*North Western Reporter*	IA, MN, MI, ND, NK, SD, WI
P., P.2d, P.3d	*Pacific Reporter*	AZ, AK, CA, CO, HI, ID, KS, MT, NM, NV, OK, OR, UT, WA, WY
S.E., S.E.2d	*South Eastern Reporter*	GA, NC, SC, VA, WV
So., So. 2d	*Southern Reporter*	AL, FL, LA, MS
S.W., S.W.2d, S.W.3d	*South Western Reporter*	AR, KY, MO, TN, TX

Source: From *Guide to Legal Abbreviations and Citations* from the University of Southern California Law Library Research Guide, available at http://lawlibguides.usc.edu/content.php?pid=269818&sid=2225794. Copyright © USC Gould School of Law. Reprinted with permission.

may be less necessary—although having the information handy can be helpful in locating a case more expeditiously. Popular websites for locating U.S. Supreme Court cases include www.FindLaw.com, www.StreetLaw.org, www.law.cornell.edu/supct/, supreme.justia.com, and www.supremecourt.gov/. A good online source for lower court opinions is LexisNexis Academic, available through most university libraries.

The citation is important for another reason; it identifies which court rendered the opinion. Just as a case citation that directs you to "U.S." indicates a U.S. Supreme Court decision, an "F.Supp" citation indicates a decision by a federal district court; "N.W.2d" indicates a decision by a state court. Table 2.2 identifies the various abbreviations used to denote the major compilations of court opinions and the court that each represents. Why do we want to be aware of which court rendered the opinion? As discussed in Chapter 1, it tells us how large a geographic area is bound by the court's decision. A decision by the U.S. Supreme Court is binding nationwide; decisions by a circuit court of appeals are binding only on that circuit; and decisions by a federal district court are binding only within that district. State court decisions are binding only within that state. This helps us understand the role of precedent by sorting out which prior decisions a particular court is governed by, and whom its current opinion will govern in turn.

If you are briefing a case, you would next turn to the *facts*. Here we are looking for a brief recitation of the relevant parts of the story. The facts are a crucial part of each case, because the court is making a decision about how the law applies only to the specific situation before it. Try to provide enough information to jog your memory and to establish a context for the court's deliberations, but avoid including extraneous details that likely have little or no bearing on the issue the court is deciding. The facts of a case can usually be summarized in three to four sentences.

Next is the *issue* in the case. This is a concise statement that identifies the legal question under consideration. In *District of Columbia v. Heller*, the 2008 gun control case decided by the U.S. Supreme Court, a statement of the issue might be "Whether the D.C. law prohibiting possession of usable handguns by individuals in their homes violates the Second Amendment to the Constitution." In the 2005 Supreme Court case of *Roper v. Simmons*, a statement of the issue might be "Whether applying the death penalty to youth younger than age 18 when their crimes were committed constitutes cruel and unusual punishment."

The next two items comprise the centerpiece of the brief. First is the *holding*. This is the outcome of the case. Which party won? What is the court saying? In the example of *Roper v. Simmons*, the holding might be "Judgment for Simmons. The Eighth Amendment prohibits the death penalty for youth who were younger than age 18 when their crimes were committed." This is followed by the *rationale*, a summary of the court's reasoning. How did it reach its conclusion? The court can decide the cases before it in several ways. Sometimes it examines the actual wording of the statute at issue using accepted rules of *statutory construction*. Sometimes it examines the legislative history to ascertain the policy makers' intent. Often the court draws on precedent—previous rulings that have applicability to the case at hand. You will see these cases cited in the text of the court's opinion. For example, in the case of *Graham v. Florida* (2010), the Supreme Court considered whether it is constitutional to sentence a juvenile to life without the possibility of parole for a non-homicide offense. The Court approached the case in much the same way it had previously approached the question of capital punishment for juveniles in *Roper v. Simmons*. That decision, in turn, was based on the Court's reasoning in *Atkins v. Virginia* (2002), where it found the application of the death penalty to offenders with intellectual disabilities unconstitutional.

Over time, the Supreme Court has developed specific tests or principles to guide its consideration of particular types of cases. To be constitutional, for example, a confession must be "knowing, intelligent, and voluntary"; the courts determine this by examining "the totality of the circumstances." To determine whether a law constitutes cruel and unusual punishment, the court considers "the evolving standards of decency" as reflected in whether the punishment is proportionate to the offense and whether there is evidence of consensus among the states. These considerations guide the court's rationale—its reasoning in reaching its conclusion. The rationale is important because it provides a window into the factors the court takes into consideration and how it might decide other cases that raise similar issues in the future.

Finally, certain members of the court sometimes author or join a minority opinion that either concurs with, or dissents from, that of the majority. It can be useful to briefly summarize these *concurring* or *dissenting opinions*. They give us a broader understanding of the issue by exposing us to both sides of the argument. In close cases, it is especially important because with a slight change in facts—or a change in the court's composition—the minority opinion today may become the majority opinion at a later date.

Presented next is a short case followed by a sample brief. As you read the case, try to use the briefing format discussed earlier. Who the parties are to the dispute, which facts are most important, what legal issue the court is deciding, what conclusion it reaches, and why. Try comparing your brief to the sample brief provided. As you progress through the text, you will find other cases that pertain to particular topics. Try briefing them as a way of capturing and analyzing the important information.

Sample Case

DORNHECKER v. MALIBU GRAND PRIX CORP.
828 F.2d 307 (1987)

Edith H. Jones, Circuit Judge.

The behavior of a co-worker at the Malibu Grand Prix Corporation proved too racy for Marvelle Dornhecker. She worked there in a corporate staff position for four days in December 1984 before resigning because of sexual harassment to which, she felt, the company was insensitive. This Title VII lawsuit followed, and the district court awarded her $25,000 compensatory damages. Malibu appeals.

We shall assume, without deciding, that Mrs. Dornhecker was the victim of unwelcome sexual harassment that was sufficiently pervasive to alter the conditions of her employment and create an abusive working environment. The perpetrator was one Robert Rockefeller, a contract consultant to the corporation in marketing, who was slated to attend a series of out-of-town presentations with Mrs. Dornhecker and other Malibu representatives during December 1984. Rockefeller's conduct in the presence of Mrs. Dornhecker was public, clownish and boorish. During two days of her business trip with the company to Cincinnati and Miami, Rockefeller put his hands on her hips in an airport ticket line and dropped his pants in front of the passengers while waiting to board the airplane. He touched her breasts. Finally, when a number of Malibu employees attended a business dinner at the Downunder Restaurant in Fort Lauderdale, he put his stocking feet on the cocktail table directly in front of her and "playfully" choked her when she complained. The co-workers were appalled.

The events most pertinent to this appeal commenced when Mrs. Dornhecker, overcome by Rockefeller's disgusting lack of professionalism, rushed to the ladies' room immediately after this last incident and dissolved, in her words, into hysterical tears. Her immediate supervisor, Krysia Swift, followed and tried to console her. Although Swift had not seen the choking incident, she agreed to talk to the company president about it. The next morning, December, 6, Mrs. Dornhecker herself addressed Peabody, the president, and the court found that he "told plaintiff that she would not have to work with Rockefeller after the Florida trip." The Florida presentations were then scheduled to last one-and-a half more days. It is undisputed that Rockefeller did not attend the remaining presentations in Fort Lauderdale, and his contract with Malibu went un-renewed at the end of December. Mrs. Dornhecker was not present to savor these events: she believed management was unresponsive, and shortly after talking to Peabody on December, 6, she left Fort Lauderdale, explaining her departure only with a brief note in her supervisor's hotel mail slot.

The critical issue in this case for purposes of Title VII liability is whether Malibu, knowing about Mrs. Dornhecker's claims of sexual harassment, failed to take prompt remedial action. The district court found that Malibu did not. This is clearly erroneous. Since the demise of the institution of dueling, society has seldom provided instantaneous redress for dishonorable conduct. In this case, the district court found that Malibu's president personally reassured Mrs. Dornhecker that Rockefeller would not be working with her after the Florida trip. This assurance occurred approximately 12 hours after Mrs. Dornhecker had tearfully confronted Krysia Swift in the ladies' room and first acquainted her with Rockefeller's behavior. Considered in terms of the speed with which the company addressed Mrs. Dornhecker's complaint or the length of time it proposed to resolve that complaint, Malibu's remedial action was unusually prompt.

Malibu's handling of the problem was also decisive. Ordinarily, an organization requires time to respond to embarrassing, emotional and often litigation-spawning claims of sexual harassment. Careers and corporate image rest on the company's handling of such charges. Here, Krysia Swift witnessed an hysterical outpouring from Mrs. Dornhecker, whom she had known and worked with for only two days, and whose reaction to offensive conduct Swift could hardly have been expected to assess in a moment. Whether Swift brushed off the charges or was just trying to defuse Mrs. Dornhecker's condition in the ladies' room is unclear but irrelevant. The next morning Peabody informed Mrs. Dornhecker that Rockefeller would only work with her one-and-a-half more days. Had Malibu believed it needed more time to consider Mrs. Dornhecker's complaints or what to do about them, it would have been reasonable. Rockefeller, despite his faults, had helped to purchase Malibu for its owners and held an employment contract. In this case, one cannot reasonably demand the employer to ignore its experience with the alleged offender or to examine a charge of sexual harassment based on one side of the story, in a vacuum. Malibu speedily evaluated Mrs. Dornhecker's complaints.

The judgment of the district court is reversed.

Sample Case Brief

1. **Case Name & Citation:** *Dornhecker v. Malibu Grand Prix Corp.*, 828 F.2d 307 (1987).

   The parties are an employee and employer. The lower (district) court found in favor of Ms. Dornhecker (the employee).

2. **Facts:** A contract consultant sexually harassed an employee during a business trip. When the harassing behavior came to the attention of the employee's supervisor, the supervisor notified the company's president who assured the employee that she would not have to work with the offender once the business trip (scheduled to last an additional 1-1/2 days) concluded. The employee was dissatisfied with the response and resigned.

3. **Issue:** Whether the company, knowing about Ms. Dornhecker's claims of sexual harassment, failed to take prompt remedial action.

4. **Holding:** Judgment reversed. Judgment for Malibu Grand Prix (employer).

   Malibu responded to Ms. Dornhecker's complaints within a reasonable period of time.

5. **Rationale:** The company's response was both prompt and decisive. The company president provided assurances to the employee only 12 hours after the behavior was

made known. Claims of harassment must be handled carefully and only after weighing both sides of the story.

6. **Concurrence/Dissent:** None

Summary and Conclusion

Judges contribute to public policy by interpreting laws and regulations. These interpretations shed light on how a policy would apply to various situations in real life. Courts make decisions every day that are relevant to social work interests. These include decisions about health, mental health, employment, civil rights, disabilities, family violence, child custody, criminal and juvenile justice, and education. Lower federal and state courts hear witnesses and examine evidence, whereas appeals courts consider only issues of law. The U.S. Supreme Court is the most secretive yet authoritative of our government institutions. Its justices have skewed more conservative in recent years. The Supreme Court decides which cases it will consider, hears oral arguments, reads briefs, and issues opinions. Appointments to the Court are highly political. Cases are often decided based on precedent and may be driven by legal considerations other than the merits of the case. Briefing a case is a method of summarizing its main points. Briefs are designed to capture the title and citation of a case, the important facts, the issue, the holding, and the rationale.

CHAPTER 2 PRACTICE TEST

The following questions will test your application and analysis of the content found within this chapter. For additional assessment, including licensing-exam type questions on applying chapter content to practice behaviors, visit **MySearchLab**.

1. You work in a local high school. One of the student athletes is threatened with suspension after being caught on camera swearing during an away game against a rival school. You decide to find out whether or not the school is within its rights to suspend her for this behavior. You discover that in another case the court upheld the suspension of a student who was caught swearing in class. Which of the following is the best explanation for the court reaching a different conclusion in this case?

   a. The previous case was decided more than 10 years ago.
   b. Precedent doesn't apply in cases involving free speech.
   c. The facts of the case are different.
   d. Interpreting the law is the province of the legislative branch.

2. The current U.S. Supreme Court
   a. is composed of all conservatives.
   b. is composed of all liberals.
   c. leans conservative.
   d. leans liberal.

3. Decisions by a federal circuit court are binding on
   a. all federal courts.
   b. all appeals courts.
   c. all courts within that state.
   d. all courts within that circuit.

4. You feel strongly that the law in your state should permit same-sex partners to be covered by protective orders. Your best course of action would be to seek a remedy through
   a. the legislature, because it can initiate new policies.
   b. the judiciary, because it can initiate new policies.
   c. the executive branch, because its role is to interpret the Constitution.
   d. a magistrate.

5. Think of a Supreme Court case with which you are familiar. How do you think the Court's holding has shaped our understanding of policy in that area?

6. Discuss the advantages and disadvantages of a strict constructionist approach to the Constitution. Do you favor such an approach, or do you prefer an activist orientation? Which do you think is more consistent with social work values? Why?

MYSEARCHLAB CONNECTIONS

Reinforce what you learned in this chapter by studying videos, cases, documents, and more available at **www.MySearchLab.com**.

Watch these Videos

* Proposition 8
    * *Which branch of government do you think should resolve the issue of same-sex marriage: the courts or the legislature? What would be the advantages of each?*

Explore these Assets

* Interactive Case Study: You Are the President and Need to Nominate a Supreme Court Justice

Research these Topics

* Recent Supreme Court decisions
* Biographies of the U.S. Supreme Court justices

Assess Your Knowledge

Go to **MySearchLab** to test your knowledge of key topics in this chapter with topic-specific quizzes. Conclude your assessment by completing the chapter exam.

---

* = CSWE Core Competency Asset   Δ =Case Study

Chapter **3**

Law and Forensic Practice

As described in the previous chapter, courts play a vital role in shaping important social policies. They also, of course, have a role in regulating our day-to-day experience by settling disputes between individuals and defining legal rights and obligations. For example, the courts may determine the outcome of a child custody dispute, whether an older adult is competent to handle his or her own affairs, whether a person with mental illness can be hospitalized against his or her will, or whether a school system has provided the required educational opportunities to a student with a disability. Social workers can use their knowledge and skills to contribute to these legal processes by engaging in activities that include forensic interviewing, testifying, and conducting forensic evaluations. Although *forensic social work* can be defined in a variety of ways, the material in this text focuses on practice that brings social workers into contact with the courts.

Overview of Forensic Practice

It is not unusual for social workers, regardless of their area of practice, to find themselves interacting with the legal system. Many social workers may be unprepared for these experiences and thus find them to be nerve wracking and intimidating. Possessing certain basic knowledge and skills will help them feel more comfortable and perform more competently in their contacts with the legal system. These include knowing how to respond to a subpoena and testify as a fact witness (discussed later) and how to maintain proper documentation and protect against malpractice claims (discussed in Chapter 5).

In addition to becoming familiar with these basics, some social workers choose to develop a repertoire of skills in order to become forensic specialists. Forensic specialists are expected to have advanced clinical skills and to complete specialized training in working with the courts or the justice system. Even though social workers have a long tradition of applying their expertise in legal settings, forensic social work was slow to emerge as a recognized area of specialization. Physicians have the distinction of being the first professional group whose expertise (related to both physical and mental health) was accepted in court. This dominance of the medical profession in the legal realm remained clearly visible until the 1980s (Ashford, 2009). Even when social workers became an accepted part of the treatment team, state laws often permitted their involvement in legal affairs only if supervised by psychiatrists. Beginning in the 1970s, however, psychologists and other nonphysicians began to challenge this reliance on psychiatrists in the court system (Dix & Poythress, 1981). In the years since, psychologists have been recognized by an increasing number of states as competent in many areas of forensic practice, and social workers continue to make steady progress toward that goal.

The use of the term *forensic social work* is fairly new. Some define it narrowly to refer to social work practice in criminal justice settings. According to others, it encompasses anything and everything concerning the law. The *Social Work Dictionary* defines forensic social work as "the practice specialty in social work that focuses on the law, legal issues, and litigation, both criminal and civil" (Barker, 2003, p. 166). An informal survey in 1982 suggested that many more social workers were engaged in forensic practice than expected (Hughes & O'Neal, 1983). Based on those findings, the National Organization of Forensic Social Work (NOFSW) was founded in 1983; it continues to serve the growing community of forensic social work practitioners. The National Association of Social Workers (NASW), similarly, has organized a Specialty Practice Section on Social Work and the Courts.

Today, social workers routinely testify as expert witnesses; provide consultation and training to judges, attorneys, law enforcement officers, and corrections staff; perform court-ordered assessments and evaluations; conduct mediation; and provide treatment and case management services to victims, offenders, and families impacted by crime (Ashford, 2009). They are involved in cases involving domestic violence, divorce and child custody, disability, mental health, child abuse and neglect, adoption, immigration, criminal justice, juvenile justice, probation and parole, education, and elder abuse. Forensic social workers can be found in psychiatric hospitals, prisons and jails, public defenders' offices, law firms, child advocacy centers, law enforcement agencies, family courts, child protective service agencies, alternative treatment programs, and detention centers (Rome, 2008). Many have careers as clinical social workers and engage in forensic work as a part-time, ancillary activity (Barker & Branson, 2000). This chapter provides an overview of some of the more common forensic social work roles; others are discussed in various chapters throughout the book.

Forensic Interviewing

One role that a forensic social work specialist might play is to conduct forensic interviews. A forensic interview is an interview method in which a neutral, trained professional gathers factual information in order to assist the court in reaching the best possible decision.

Forensic interviews are most often conducted in the context of criminal cases—with both victims and perpetrators—in order to help determine whether or not a crime occurred, and if so, what the details surrounding its occurrence are. These interviews can be conducted by a variety of professionals including law enforcement officers, physicians, nurses, psychologists, psychiatrists, social workers, defense attorneys, and prosecutors. Increasingly, particularly in cases of child or elder abuse, these professionals work on multidisciplinary teams and conduct the interview as a group in order to spare victims the trauma of having to tell their story over and over again. Forensic interviews may take place in a wide range of settings including hospitals, mental health agencies, social service departments, schools, police departments, and courts. They may also take place in child advocacy centers or elder abuse forensic centers, which are highlighted elsewhere in this chapter.

Forensic interviews typically comprise one component of the evidence offered in a criminal case. These cases often involve the physical or sexual abuse of children, the abuse or exploitation of people with disabilities or older adults, or cases of sexual assault. In some instances, the outcome of a case may depend heavily on the results of a forensic interview; in cases of child sexual abuse, for example, there often are no witnesses and little or no physical evidence to corroborate an allegation. In order for the interview to withstand legal scrutiny, the interviewer must possess special knowledge and skill and follow specific procedures. Social workers and others who conduct forensic interviews must be exceedingly careful not to lead, coach, or coerce the person being interviewed lest the credibility of the information they elicit be compromised. In order to be successful, social workers should know how to conduct a proper forensic interview and should understand the differences between forensic interviewing and clinical interviewing.

Comparing Forensic and Clinical Interviews

Most social workers are accustomed to conducting clinical interviews as part of their work with clients. The purpose of clinical interviewing is to lay the foundation for some type of therapeutic intervention. The clinical interview allows social workers to assess the strengths and needs of an individual or family in order to develop a plan for treatment. Clinical interviewing can occur in any setting and often occurs on a regular, ongoing basis throughout the duration of the therapeutic relationship. Forensic interviews, on the other hand, are time limited and highly structured and serve the limited purpose of collecting evidence for a court proceeding. In forensic interviewing, the goal is to obtain a truthful and accurate account of what occurred; only the facts—not feelings or subjective experiences—are important. The interviewer should avoid approaching the interview with the intent of eliciting a disclosure or confession (because not every case will turn out to actually involve a crime), but rather should focus on gathering truthful information that can guide the court in reaching a sound conclusion. Neutrality is the key in forensic interviewing; this includes using neutral statements, questioning, and body language that in no way suggests or reinforces a particular response. It is not the interviewer's role to advocate for the client, nor is it the interviewer's role to provide emotional support.

Much controversy has surrounded the question of whether it is advisable for the same social worker to serve the same client in both therapeutic and forensic capacities. This dilemma is not unique to social workers but is shared by other mental health practitioners as well. On one hand, having the same professional serve in both capacities could spare the client the stress of having to adjust to another professional at a time of profound vulnerability.

If in the course of therapy, for example, a client discloses an adverse event, the treating social worker could move seamlessly into a forensic role in order to pursue the details for subsequent prosecution. Alternatively, if the relationship begins through a forensic interview and a disclosure results, the interviewer could continue to see the interview subject thereafter as a therapy client. Many observers caution, however, that the disadvantages outweigh the possible benefits. From a legal perspective, keeping the clinical and forensic roles entirely separate minimizes the possibility of bias and keeps the interview "clean" for court. There is less opportunity for the interviewer to become sidetracked into acting as an advocate for the client (Kuehnle, 1998). Conflicts of interest can also be avoided because forensic questioning has the potential to undermine the therapeutic relationship. The interviewer is required to provide a full accounting to the court, even if the information paints the client in an unflattering light; if a negative legal outcome ensues, the client may be too resentful to continue a constructive relationship with the social worker. Recognizing this, the American Academy of Psychiatry and the Law (2005) has specified that "treating psychiatrists should . . . generally avoid acting as an expert witness for their patients or performing evaluations of their patients for legal purposes." Finally, most clinical social workers are not trained in forensic interviewing; practicing outside the scope of one's expertise is a serious violation of both law and ethics and can result in harm to the client.

Using an Interview Protocol

Compared to clinical interviews, forensic interviews are highly structured. The interviewer typically uses a specific protocol to guide the questioning process. Various protocols are available for this purpose; they vary in terms of complexity and may target different populations. The important considerations are that the protocol be appropriate to the situation and that the interviewer be trained in the use of that particular tool. The advantages of using a protocol for forensic interviewing are many. First, it increases uniformity from one interview to another. Imagine testifying in court regarding an interview you conducted. It comes to light that you usually ask your interview subjects one set of questions, but in this case you asked different questions. Clearly, the responses you elicited will be suspect. By sticking to a routine, structured protocol, there is less opportunity for (and appearance of) bias. Protocols also keep the interviewer on track and help ensure that nothing is inadvertently omitted. And because these protocols have been tested for reliability and validity, and many are evidence-based or endorsed by professional associations, the interview results are more likely to hold up in court if challenged.

Although specific interview protocols vary, they all allow for an initial period of rapport building, they encourage free narrative on the part of the interviewee, they allow for more focused questions if needed to spur conversation or elicit detail, and they conclude with an opportunity for the interview subject to ask questions. To get an idea of how an interviewing protocol might work, we use the Step-Wise Interview (Yuille, Hunter, Joffe, & Zaparniuk, 1993) as an example. Imagine that the interview is with an alleged victim. The interviewer's role is to question the subject in a way that will allow a disclosure of maltreatment, if it in fact occurred, while ensuring its admissibility as evidence in court.

Phase 1: Introduction   During this phase, the interviewer introduces him or herself and describes the purpose of the interview. If the interview is being recorded, the interviewer explains this to the subject and seeks consent.

Phase 2: Rapport Building   This phase sets the tone for rest of the interview and can end up being the deciding factor in whether or not a disclosure is made (Collins, Lincoln, & Frank, 2002). It provides an opportunity to get to know the interview subject and to make him or her feel at ease. Approaching the interview using cultural competence is an important ingredient for success. Typically, the interviewer begins with a broad, open-ended question such as *Tell me about your family* or *How did you spend the holiday weekend?* The questions should be neutral and nonthreatening and designed simply to break the ice. With children or people with intellectual disabilities, this phase can also be used to get a sense of the subject's developmental competencies, including their ability to observe, remember, and communicate (Faller, 2007). This is also a time when the interviewer might share some ground rules, including the following: *If you don't know the answer to a question, it's O.K. to say "I don't know"* or *If you don't understand something I ask, just tell me and I'll try to ask it differently.* If the interviewer has any concerns about whether the interview subject can distinguish between truth and falsehood or is willing to tell the truth, this phase can also include efforts to test the subject's truth-telling ability and to reinforce the importance of talking only about events that really happened.

Phase 3: Raising the Topic of Concern   After the ice has been broken, the interviewer gently guides the conversation in the direction of the event that triggered the investigation (child abuse, sexual assault, etc.). It is important to avoid assumptions and not to put words into the subject's mouth. Examples might include the following: *Do you know why you're here today? Why do you think you're here? Has anything been worrying you? Tell me about what's worrying you.* The interviewer should be careful not to introduce information known from other sources, because the goal is to have any possible disclosure come entirely and voluntarily from the interview subject alone.

Phase 4: Disclosure   The best possible outcome of a forensic interview would be for a disclosure of victimization and all attendant details to come directly from the interview subject, with no involvement whatsoever on the part of the interviewer. Although this rarely occurs, free narrative by the interview subject should be encouraged as much as possible. If the subject starts talking, do not interrupt. As information is shared, encourage additional information with prompts such as *Tell me more* or *Then what?* Open-ended questions can be used to facilitate a response. Keep in mind, however, that disclosure is a process, not an event. It typically involves several stages: an initial denial, a tentative disclosure, a full disclosure, a recantation (the subject changes his or her mind and "takes it back"), followed by a reaffirmation. If you have reason to believe that a crime was committed but a disclosure is not forthcoming, it can be helpful to return to rapport building until the subject feels more comfortable or to conduct multiple interviews.

Phase 5: Clarification   Before the interview comes to an end, it is important to restate what the subject has said and ask for any corrections.

Phase 6: Closing the Interview   In this final phase, the interviewer explains what will happen next, addresses any lingering questions or concerns, and thanks the interview subject for his or her help.

Types of Questioning

As was discussed earlier, open-ended questions should be used as much as possible in order to reduce the risk that the interviewer is influencing responses. Remember that the results of the interview will be presented to the court; the less directive the interviewer, the more credibility the interview results will be considered to have. Because open-ended questions are often not sufficient—especially when the participant is reluctant to share very sensitive and painful information—an *hourglass* approach is recommended. Here, the interviewer relies on open-ended questions as much as possible, but when the conversation stalls or detailed information is not forthcoming, more focused questions are introduced, followed if necessary by closed-ended questions. As soon as the interview is moving along productively again, however, the interviewer returns to using open-ended questions.

What do we mean by *focused* questions? These are questions that direct attention to a particular person, place, or topic but steer clear of the alleged act of victimization itself. For example, the interviewer might ask *Where do you usually go after work?* or *Tell me about the time you stayed overnight at Grandpa's house.* What are *closed-ended* questions? These would include multiple-choice and yes-no questions. If you ask a multiple-choice question, include an "other" option so that the interview subject does not feel boxed into giving an incorrect response. Here is an example: *Were you in the bedroom, the bathroom, or some other room?* Yes-no questions should be used very sparingly, because they tend to be more restrictive and give subjects less opportunity to generate their own information. Once a disclosure is made, specific details can be elicited using *who, what, where, when,* and *how* questions.

Finally, some kinds of questions are never acceptable. These are questions that are leading or coercive. A *leading* question tells the interview subject exactly what response you want to hear. It puts words in the subject's mouth: *Your boss was harassing you, wasn't he?* or *Isn't it true that your boss was harassing you?* Needless to say, there is no way of knowing whether the answer given is genuinely coming from the subject or whether the subject is just going along with what he or she perceives as the interviewer's agenda.

Documentation

Because information gained in forensic interviewing can be used in a criminal proceeding, the results of the interview should be carefully documented so they can withstand judicial scrutiny. Typically, forensic interviews are videotaped. The tape should start rolling before the interviewer and subject enter the room. The interviewer should identify who is present and state the date, the time, and the location. Once the camera starts, it should never be stopped or interrupted until the interview is completed and everyone has left the room. By taping continuously, no one can claim that the footage was altered. Videotaping has several advantages. Perhaps most important, it produces a verbatim record of what the victim said and provides a record of his or her nonverbal communication. At the same time, it captures the interviewer's questions and behavior. If any doubt is raised about the interviewer's skill or impartiality, the videotape can be presented as evidence that the interviewer remained neutral and followed accepted protocol (Wakefield, 2006). When more than one jurisdiction is involved in a case—for example, the victim lives in one county but the crime occurred in another—the alleged victim can be interviewed near her home and the tape can then be sent to investigators in the other jurisdiction for follow-up. The videotape can also be used if the interview subject recants or to refresh the subject's memory before going to court (Faller, 2007). One cautionary note, however: Once available, the videotape can also be used by the other side to impeach the victim or to challenge the competence or neutrality of the interviewer.

In addition to videotaping, many forensic interviewers take notes. Every effort should be made to write down exactly what is said without paraphrasing; the less interpreting the interviewer engages in, the better. Nothing should be kept secret from the interview subject; even children should be informed that you will be taking notes and advised that they are welcome to see what you are writing. Instead of the interviewer taking notes, sometimes one person will ask the questions and a second will write down what is said. Regardless of which approach is used, the original notes should be kept on file even after the report is submitted to the court.

Drafting the Report

The result of a forensic interview is a written report that is filed with the court and about which the interviewer may be called to testify. As is generally true with forensic reports, it should identify who was interviewed, where, when, and for how long; it should share the information received from the subject; it should state the interviewer's opinion; and it should explain the basis for that opinion, referencing the data that led to the interviewer's conclusion. Remember that no matter how good a job the interviewer does, there can never be 100% certainty about what actually transpired. The interview subject may falsely allege that a crime occurred (a *false positive*), or, more commonly, he or she may deny having been victimized when a crime indeed took place (a *false negative*). For this reason, the interviewer must keep an open mind, explore all possible explanations, and avoid jumping to conclusions. In reaching a determination, it is crucial to consider the possibility that the interview subject lied, exaggerated, minimized, fantasized, miscommunicated, was coached, or is seeking attention. It is the forensic interviewer's job to responsibly consider the results of the interview and apply his or her best professional judgment in rendering an opinion for the court.

Testifying in Court

Another common role for social workers is to testify as a witness in court. Although practitioners in child welfare are especially likely to fill this role, any social worker may need to testify at some point in his or her career. The testimony will often be offered in connection with a current client, although it is possible to be called to testify regarding a former client as well. The circumstances under which a social worker might be called as a witness are many—for example, the client might be seeking to qualify for disability on the basis of a mental illness, asserting his or her competence against efforts by a family member to assume guardianship, bringing assault charges in a domestic violence case, defending against a criminal allegation, or seeking custody in a divorce settlement. In the child welfare context, agency social workers routinely testify as to the facts surrounding abuse or neglect and the client's compliance with services required as a condition for reuniting the family. Being able to provide effective testimony is critically important in all of these instances because it can sway the outcome of a court case and have a profound impact on those involved. It should be considered part and parcel of the ethical duty of "competence" that is central to our professional identity.

There are two types of witnesses, *fact witnesses* and *expert witnesses.* Social workers may be called in either capacity. This section discusses testifying as a fact witness (expert witnesses are discussed in Chapter 4). A fact witness is a direct observer of events that are relevant to the case being presented in court; the witness's role is to accurately convey the facts in order to assist the judge or jury in making the best possible decision. Fact witnesses can appear in court willingly (e.g., to address a parent's progress in a child neglect case in which reunification is the goal), or they may be mandated to appear through a subpoena. Although important, testimony provided by a fact witness is not conclusive in its own right; it is one factor among many that may influence the outcome of the case (Barker & Branson, 2000).

RESPONDING TO A SUBPOENA

A subpoena is a legally enforceable method of requiring someone to appear in court or to produce evidence. The former is called a *subpoena ad testificandum,* and the latter is called a *subpoena duces tecum.* In most jurisdictions, the court clerk issues a signed form to the attorney, who fills in the specifics regarding the name of the case; which party is issuing the subpoena; and the date, time, and place where the person being summoned must appear (or, in the case of a *subpoena duces tecum,* which documents must be made available, when, and where). A subpoena must be served either in person or by registered mail. In every jurisdiction, the recipient is required to respond within a strict time limit (usually 14 days).

If you receive a subpoena (which most practicing social workers do at some point in their careers), be sure you clearly understand who is issuing it and what is requested. Complying with a subpoena invariably results in the court having access to confidential client information; therefore, inform your client immediately and seek his or her written consent. To ensure that any consent is valid, you might want to suggest that the client consult with an attorney. Be sure to notify your supervisor, as well.

If the client declines consent, consult with your attorney to be sure you proceed in a manner that is consistent with all applicable state laws and ethical guidelines. Although a subpoena is legally enforceable in that the recipient is required to respond, the subpoena itself does not require the disclosure of information. Resisting disclosure of information is therefore an acceptable response. You may do this by filing an objection with the attorney who issued the subpoena, challenging the request and explaining your reasons for objecting. You almost certainly will want to file a *motion to quash* or a *motion to modify* the subpoena. These are documents drawn up by your attorney and filed with the court. Granting a motion to quash essentially nullifies the subpoena; granting a motion to modify typically reduces the amount of documentary evidence required. Reasons for a motion to quash or modify include that the subpoena's terms are oppressive or unreasonable (providing inadequate time to comply, requesting too much information, requiring the recipient to travel an unreasonable distance), the subpoena is defective (fails to include all necessary information), or the subpoena requires the sharing of privileged information that the client has not consented to disclose. A motion to quash or modify is particularly appropriate when the information can be obtained through another source or by other means that would not require the social worker to breach confidentiality.

Note that even if you, as the recipient, choose to challenge the subpoena by having your attorney file a motion to quash or to modify, you must respond within the allotted time period. Ignoring the subpoena is not an option.

Upon receiving a motion to quash or modify, the court will balance the client's right to privacy against the importance of the information in ensuring a fair trial. Before reaching a conclusion, the judge may choose to review the disputed records *in camera* (privately) to determine their relevance to the case. If the judge concludes that the subpoena is appropriate, the court will issue a *motion to compel*. Unlike the original subpoena, a motion to compel is considered to be a court order that must be obeyed; failure to comply with a motion to compel by appearing as a witness or submitting the requested documents places the recipient at risk of being found in contempt, which is punishable by a fine or imprisonment. Even when ultimately complying, social workers should be careful to disclose only the information specifically required by law and should make it known that they are doing so reluctantly (Sarnoff, 2004).

The NASW Code of Ethics (2008a) provides guidance to social work practitioners on responding to subpoenas. According to Sec. 1.07(j),

> Social workers should protect the confidentiality of clients during legal proceedings to the extent permitted by law. When a court of law or other legally authorized body orders social workers to disclose confidential or privileged information without a client's consent and such disclosure could cause harm to the client, social workers should request that the court withdraw the order or limit the order as narrowly as possible or maintain the records under seal, unavailable for public inspection.

In other words, in the absence of client consent, social workers are expected to respond to a subpoena by declining to provide confidential information and waiting instead for the court to mandate disclosure.

Preparing to Testify

Effective testimony requires thorough preparation and practice prior to taking the stand. Social workers should approach their role as witnesses with the same thoughtfulness and savvy that they bring to other aspects of their practice. As we discussed in Chapter 1, the legal system is unique; it has its own culture, players, expectations, rules, and procedures. Before you appear as a witness, think through what you know about how that system operates and strategize about how you can maximize your effectiveness—not just in general, but specifically in the legal environment. How will the courtroom's formality and the adversarial posture of the attorneys shape what is expected of you as a witness? How would you anticipate this experience being different from the experiences you have had in other professional settings?

A social worker can take several steps before arriving in court. All witnesses, no matter how many times they have testified, can be nervous about taking the stand; feeling prepared will help. First and foremost, thoroughly review the client's file and course of treatment. Refresh your memory of the client's background, presenting issues, and any progress made. You might want to prepare a note card with important dates and key words that can assist your recall while on the stand. Having the basic information at your fingertips will earn you credibility and allow you to feel more confident as you testify. In addition to reviewing the case file, meet with the attorney who is calling you as a witness to avoid any surprises. The attorney can clarify when you need to appear, where you should wait, how long you are likely to be needed, whether or not you are free to discuss the case or your testimony with others, and what to do when your testimony is finished. He or she can help you feel at ease by identifying possible questions that could be asked and by critiquing your responses. You should also consider practicing or role-playing with a colleague or supervisor to prepare for your actual court appearance. Remember to focus on both your verbal and nonverbal communication, including clarity, volume, word choice, body language, and posture, because all of these may impact the effectiveness of your testimony.

If you have not testified before, it is a good idea to seek out colleagues with experience in the courtroom and listen to what they have to say. Be sure you are familiar with courthouse protocol. Find out how much time you will need to allow for travel, parking, and going through security. Many courthouses limit the items that you are permitted to bring; our local courthouse, for example, confiscates cell phones with cameras. Find out the name of the judge who will be presiding and the names of both attorneys. If at all possible, arrange to visit the courthouse in advance of your testimony so you have a sense of where you will wait; where the attorneys, judge, court reporter, and bailiff will be located; and where you sit when you take the stand. Ideally, you should observe the same kind of case in which you will be testifying. Make note of how the lawyers, judge, and witnesses behave, and how the case proceeds. If your observation raises any new questions, contact the attorney for whom you will be testifying and share your questions or concerns.

Phases of Questioning at Trial

The questioning of witnesses typically is divided into three phases: direct examination, cross-examination, and re-direct. *Direct examination* refers to "the initial questioning of a witness by the party who called the witness" (Gifis, 2008, p. 124). In other words, during direct examination, the attorney for whom you are testifying (sometimes referred to as the "friendly" attorney) will ask questions designed to elicit from you all information he or she believes is important to the case. Your role as a witness is not to serve as an advocate for the client but rather to recount the facts as accurately as possible. Although rules restrict the types of questions the attorney may ask (e.g., leading questions are prohibited), the lawyer may encourage you to elaborate in order to get all of the relevant facts out on the table. Remember that the attorney is on your side; just follow his or her lead and tell your story.

On *cross-examination*, which is conducted by the opposing attorney, questions are designed to "check or discredit the witness's testimony, knowledge, or credibility" (Merriam-Webster, 1996, p. 116). In this phase, witnesses are often put on the defensive; attorneys can ask leading questions in an effort to uncover inconsistencies in your testimony or to cast you in a negative light. Because opposing counsel is using the cross-examination to find ways of undercutting your testimony, it is best to answer each question honestly but succinctly, without volunteering additional information. Minimizing the information you share will also help protect your client from the disclosure of potentially damaging and extraneous private information.

Finally, the friendly attorney has an opportunity to engage in *re-direct*, during which he or she will try to restore the witness's credibility and reinforce those points most important to his or her side of the case. Throughout the testimony, regardless of who is asking the questions or which phase of the questioning is taking place, the best rule of thumb is to simply tell the truth. You, as a fact witness, have a better grasp of what happened than anyone else in the courtroom. Your job is to convey the information as you know it.

Guidelines for Testifying

Once you have prepared for your testimony by becoming familiar with the environment, the players, and the protocol—and by reviewing the facts related to the client and the case—it is time to think about how you can be most effective on the stand. Following are some guidelines for testifying in the capacity of a fact witness:

• Behave Professionally

Remember that the court is a formal setting. The expectation is that witnesses, including social workers, will dress in business attire; because much can be gained from impressing the judge or jury (and much can be lost by attracting attention for being inappropriately dressed), be sure your attire is professional. Professionalism should also extend to your behavior. Be alert and pay attention when you are on the stand; do not chew gum, mumble, slouch, or speak to the judge or attorneys too casually. Refer to the judge as "your honor" and to the attorneys as "Mr." or "Ms." You want to do everything you can to be taken seriously so that the information you share will be valued.

• Be Clear About Your Role

One of the most difficult challenges social workers face when they testify as witnesses is to remember that they are there to provide the court with facts, not to act as advocates for their clients. As social workers, it is natural for us to want to make a good impression and to make our clients look good; we often have strong feelings about the preferred outcome of the case. Even so, when you are asked a question, provide a truthful response. Be careful not to cherry-pick information to please the lawyer or to protect your client; making your client look like a saint or demonizing the opposing party will likely undermine your credibility, render your testimony useless, and interfere with the court's being able to make the best possible decision. Your value as a witness is that you can relay the facts. Just as you would in your written documentation, your testimony should describe specific, concrete, observable phenomena; you should resist the temptation to introduce bias or judgmental statements or conclusions. For example, rather than saying that someone was "drunk," you might indicate that there were empty liquor bottles on the floor, that the person's speech was slurred, or that his or her footing was unsteady. Rather than describing an apartment as "filthy," you might indicate that the sink was full of dirty dishes, that there was a strong smell of urine, or that you observed a thick layer of dust on the floor and the countertops (North Carolina Division of Social Services, 2000). It is the judge's job to interpret the facts; it is your job to present them. The more straightforward and unbiased your testimony, the more valuable it will be.

• Concentrate on Your Delivery

Although your first and most important obligation is to report the facts accurately, you also should make an effort to communicate those facts as effectively as possible. As with any presentation, it is important to make eye contact with your audience; this conveys confidence and certainty. It also minimizes the likelihood that your testimony will be dismissed as boring. Some disagreement exists about whom the witness should look at when testifying. One school of thought is that the witness should maintain eye contact with the trier of fact (judge or jury) throughout the course of the testimony. Another school of thought suggests that testimony should be regarded as a dialogue—and that the natural thing is to look at whoever asked the question (whether one of the attorneys or, occasionally, the judge).

Once you are on the stand, one approach may feel much more natural to you than the other; do what feels right. Just be sure to avoid looking down at your hands, staring into space, or rifling through any notes you may have brought with you. In addition to maintaining eye contact, be sure to speak slowly, loudly, and clearly. Remember that everyone in the courtroom (including the court reporter, when present) should be able to hear and understand you. Similarly, try to avoid using gestures; words are what count. Avoid using slang. Use acronyms or abbreviations sparingly—and only if you are sure that your meaning will be fully understood. Take your time. Consider pausing briefly after each question so you can gather your thoughts and so the attorneys have an opportunity to voice any objections before you begin to answer. If an attorney objects, stop and await the judge's ruling on the objection. If the objection is *overruled*, proceed to respond to the question. If the objection is *sustained*, remain silent and wait for the next question to be offered. Remember that objecting is the province of the attorneys; they are the ones who are responsible for conforming to the rules of evidence. Leave it to the judge and the attorneys to determine what is and is not admissible; all you have to do is answer the questions as directed.

Cross-examination can bring its own perils. It is during cross-examination that social workers often feel attacked or devalued by the other side. Keep in mind that it is opposing counsel's job to zealously represent the interests of his or her client; being aggressive toward a witness is part of that strategy—it is not about you personally. You can do a number of things, as a witness, to avoid setting yourself up for a fall during cross-examination, including the following:

• Be Concise

Although you have an obligation to respond to opposing counsel's questions, you should avoid volunteering any more information than what was asked for. Try to resist the temptation to elaborate. If counsel asks if you have had regular contact with the client, say "yes"—without offering details not requested (why, where, when, how often, under what circumstances, etc.). If the lawyer wants those additional details, he or she will ask for them. If the attorney asks a question you do not know the answer to, simply say "I don't know." If you don't remember something, just say "I don't remember." If the lawyer correctly points out an error or inconsistency on your part, politely concede the point and move on. The more you dwell on things, the worse it may get. Occasionally, the lawyer will ask an open-ended question. In that case, respond as concisely as possible and try not to volunteer information beyond what was requested. Rambling is a big mistake; it will confuse the judge and jury and will provide opposing counsel with additional ammunition. Your goal is to be responsive without volunteering information needlessly. If you are chatty on the stand, the lawyer will see that all he has to do is let you talk—and, odds are, you will box yourself into a corner and his work will be done for him.

• Be Confident

Remember that you are the one who knows the facts. Just answer the questions asked. If you preface your responses with phrases such as "I guess" or "I believe," you will project an air of uncertainty. The more straightforward your responses are, the better your testimony will be. Similarly, there is no need to say "to the best of my knowledge" or "to the best of my recollection." You have taken an oath to tell the truth, so the court assumes that whatever you say is to the best of your knowledge and recollection. Hedging your comments detracts from the confidence you want to display; the more confident you seem, the more credibility your testimony will have. In addition to the words you use, your body language can also convey confidence. Keep an eye on your posture; sit up straight and stay alert. Even when you are asked to step down at the conclusion of your testimony, leave the stand with confidence (regardless of how you think it went). Smile, keep your head up, stand straight, and walk with purpose.

• Stand Up for Yourself

Lawyers are notorious for trying to catch witnesses off guard by using rapid fire, leading, or confusing questions. Do not let them get away with it! Never answer a question that you do not really understand or feel bullied into providing a misleading response. It is not unusual, for example, for a lawyer to ask a compound question; this is a question that is really two questions in one. Suppose the lawyer says, "Isn't it true that Mrs. Smith was at work all night and left her child alone?" One part of the statement may be true (she was at work all night), but the other may be false (she left her child alone). Rather than simply answering "yes" or "no," it is best to ask for the question to be rephrased—or indicate that these are really two questions and you're happy to answer each one separately. There are also times when the lawyer will ask for a "yes" or "no" response, but you know that there is more to the story and are concerned that a simple "yes" or "no" would be misleading. In these circumstances, it is appropriate to say "yes, but" and attempt to continue. If the lawyer cuts you off, politely tell the judge that you cannot answer the question accurately with a "yes" or "no" response. Most likely, the judge will allow you to continue. Sometimes, despite your best efforts, you will misspeak or make a mistake. If this happens, correct the error at the first opportunity or signal your lawyer, who can give you an opportunity to correct it during re-direct. If the opposing attorney ever mischaracterizes something you have said (e.g., summarizes your testimony inaccurately), do not hesitate to set the record straight. Never let the lawyer put words in your mouth.

• Keep Your Cool

During cross-examination, opposing counsel will attempt to rattle you. Remember that this is a strategy and not a personal attack. Stay calm. Do not let the attorney trick you into getting angry, defensive, or sarcastic. The last thing you want to do is get into a power struggle. If something does not go your way, move on. Do not be stubborn. Getting into a power struggle will distract from your testimony and cast you in a negative light. Remember that your body language is just as important as your words. Clenching your fists or rolling your eyes will make you seem less likeable, less confident, and therefore less trustworthy. You can minimize the opportunities for an attack by sticking to the facts. Be sure not to exaggerate any of your claims. If you say that the client was "always" on time for treatment or "never" left her child unsupervised, your entire testimony can be discredited if the lawyer introduces even a single exception. Similarly, if instead of relating the facts, you hazard a guess, speculate, or make an assumption, you leave yourself open to being proven uncertain at best, and wrong at the worst.

Conducting Forensic Evaluations

Another role social workers may have in a court proceeding is to conduct a forensic evaluation of a person involved in a case. A forensic evaluation is the legal equivalent of a clinical intake assessment. It involves the collection and interpretation of biopsychosocial data, but in a specific legal context. Unlike with clinical assessments, the aim of the forensic evaluation is not to provide a basis for treatment; rather, the goal is to provide objective information and conclusions that can help the court render a legal decision. As with other forensic activities, it is important to follow accepted guidelines in order to ensure the admissibility of the evaluation in court. Forensic evaluations may be used by the court to help inform a wide range of legal determinations including, for example, whether a person is competent to manage his or her own affairs, make his or her own medical decisions, or stand trial; whether a person with mental illness can be committed for psychiatric treatment without his or her consent; whether a person exhibits an injury or disability for purposes of receiving benefits; whether a defendant in a criminal case should receive a harsher or lighter sentence; and who should have custody of a child subsequent to a divorce or dependency proceeding.

Before accepting a role as a forensic evaluator, it is important to consider whether you have the requisite qualifications, are able to remain unbiased, and have ruled out any conflict of interest relating to the case or parties involved (American Academy of Child and Adolescent Psychiatry, 1997). Consistent with what we have discussed in relation to other forensic activities, when a social worker assumes the role of forensic evaluator, the expectation is that he or she will use professional skills to provide factual, objective, and accurate information to the court, rather than act as an advocate for the client. Regardless of the type of evaluation performed, the most important consideration is that it be able to withstand legal scrutiny and be admitted into evidence in court.

Types of Forensic Evaluations

The discussion that follows is not meant to be exhaustive but rather to provide a brief introduction to several types of forensic evaluations that social work practitioners might be called upon to conduct. These include child custody, mental health, guardianship, disability, alternative sentencing, and mitigation evaluations. Several of these are discussed further in subsequent chapters.

In *child custody evaluations*, the social worker (or other professional conducting the assessment) interviews each parent, the child or children, and others who are familiar with the family. Each parent is also observed interacting with each of the children. The evaluator's goal is to assess the fit between each child's developmental and socioemotional needs and the ability of each parent to meet those needs. The evaluation identifies each party's parenting strengths and weaknesses, as well as any presenting issues that might affect their ability to raise a child. Psychological testing of both the children and the adults is often used as part of the evaluation process. These tests provide objective data that can be used to reinforce other findings. The evaluator's recommendation is derived from interviews, observations, home visits, review of documents, testing, and contacts with collaterals (others who know the child and family); it is relayed to the court through the submission of a written report and oral testimony, both of which are designed to help the court determine an appropriate custody plan for the child (Rich, 2010). The "best interests of the child" is the prevailing legal standard for custody decisions. Although state laws operationalize this concept in various ways, the goal is to determine the custody arrangement that will best meet the developmental and emotional needs of the child. Additional information on conducting child custody evaluations can be found in Chapter 8.

Forensic social work practitioners might conduct several types of *mental health evaluations*. Mental health evaluations are used to inform legal determinations regarding competence to stand trial, the validity of an insanity defense, and the appropriateness of involuntary mental health commitment. In all of these, the evaluator looks at presenting issues related to a person's mental health status. An evaluation concerning *competency to stand trial* begins with a thorough mental status examination to determine a defendant's current level of functioning. With the help of specific protocols, the evaluator then ascertains whether mental illness has rendered the defendant incapable of understanding the proceedings against him or her or of assisting in his or her defense. If the court finds the defendant incompetent to stand trial, the defendant is committed for treatment until competency is restored (Swenson, 1997; Voskanian, 2011). Forensic evaluation may also be used to determine the validity of an *insanity defense*. The evaluator collects evidence to support an opinion regarding whether the client was mentally ill at the time the offense was committed, and if so, whether he or she lacked the ability to appreciate the criminality of his or her conduct (Knoll & Resnick, 2007). Finally, mental health evaluations are also used in *commitment* cases to determine the appropriateness of involuntary hospitalization. Here, the evaluator must determine whether the person is a danger to self or others and whether it is necessary to resort to hospitalizing the person against his or her will. All three of these mental health evaluations—competence to stand trial, the insanity defense, and civil commitment—are discussed in greater detail in Chapter 15.

Forensic assessment is also commonly used with older adults and people with intellectual disabilities. The purpose of evaluation with these special populations is to determine their ability to handle their own affairs and to assess the need for guardianship. *Guardianship* is a legal means of protecting people who cannot take care of themselves, make decisions that are in their own best interest, or handle their assets. The fact that a person has reached an advanced age or has an intellectual disability does not automatically dictate the need for guardianship. The test for determining the need for guardianship focuses on the person's ability to make decisions and to function independently, which is determined through psychological and developmental testing. Guardianship evaluations include a description of the presenting disability; an evaluation of mental, physical, and behavioral functioning; and a recommendation for or against guardianship based on this information (TSA, 2010).

SPECIALIZED FORENSIC CENTERS

Cases of elder abuse and child maltreatment are complex and often involve numerous agencies working simultaneously to explore different aspects of a case. The initial abuse is typically reported to the local protective service agency, an investigation is initiated by law enforcement, doctors or nurses conduct a medical examination, prosecutors ready the case for court, and mental health professionals conduct assessments and provide treatment to the victims and their families. This division of the case into multiple responsibilities assumed by multiple people often results in ineffectiveness and inefficiency. Agencies with differing values and conflicting goals may complicate the process of assisting victims and prosecuting perpetrators. More important, as a result of these agencies' independent efforts, victims of abuse are required to interact with a seemingly endless array of people asking probing questions about sensitive and traumatic events. Child advocacy centers (CACs) and elder abuse forensic centers (EAFCs) reflect a model that has been developed to address these concerns. Both use a victim-friendly, multidisciplinary approach to gather the necessary information for prosecution while shielding the victims from unnecessary stress.

The first elder abuse forensic center was established in the United States in 2003. An EAFC is typically composed of professionals from law enforcement, social services, medicine, law, psychology, geriatrics, financial management, and real estate. This collaboration is intended not only to "build on the strengths and expertise of each agency to effectuate positive solutions for complex abuse cases, strengthen communication between partner agencies, and assist in the prosecution and prevention of elder abuse" (San Francisco Elder Abuse Forensic Center, 2011), but also to reduce the burden of repeated interviews on victims (Schneider, Mosqueda, Falk, & Huba, 2010).

Professionals involved with elder abuse forensic centers often work in a shared location and regularly conduct joint case meetings. A shared location ensures that the multidisciplinary team interacts regularly and "has easy access to each other for relationship building and case consultation purposes" (McNamee & Mulford, 2007, p. 6). Medical and psychological experts conduct in-home assessments to help determine the occurrence and nature of the abuse, the victim's competence, and a course of action (McNamee & Mulford, 2007). Education and training by EAFCs allow comprehensive information and multiple perspectives to be communicated to other agencies, students, and the general public. Through consultation, established EAFCs provide expert case input and technical assistance to other jurisdictions that are pursuing cases of older adult mistreatment.

Child advocacy centers developed in the United States in the 1980s. A child advocacy center is a child-focused, community-oriented, multidisciplinary approach to coordinating investigation, prosecution, and treatment in child maltreatment cases. Originally, CACs focused primarily on protecting child victims of sexual abuse, but many have now incorporated physical abuse and domestic violence into their services (Hornor, 2008). CACs were designed to "reduce the stress on child abuse victims and families created by traditional child abuse investigation and prosecution procedures and to improve the effectiveness of the response" (Cross et al., 2008, p. 1). Like EAFCs, child advocacy centers are facilities in which representatives from different disciplines are located; this creates a sense of safety, comfort, and privacy for children and families and ensures better team communication and cooperation.

No two CACs look exactly alike because they are designed to address the distinctive needs of the community in which they are situated. A CAC typically includes individuals from law enforcement, child protective services, the prosecutor's office, the medical and mental health professions, and victim advocacy services. They work collaboratively to conduct forensic interviews, medical examinations, and mental health assessments; create action plans for investigation and treatment; and prosecute perpetrators (Simone, Cross, Jones, & Walsh, 2005). All of this is done in a child-friendly setting without the need for the victim to repeat the details of a traumatic event to multiple agencies, multiple times.

The joint intervention and investigation processes featured in EAFCs and CACs have numerous benefits. Participating agencies share a common goal and philosophy and learn to better communicate and cooperate with one another (Simone et al., 2005). They also learn about other agencies involved in elder abuse and child abuse cases and learn to consider their cases from the perspectives of different disciplines. Clients, meanwhile, benefit from multidisciplinary coordination; their safety can be protected and the offenders prosecuted, all with maximum sensitivity and efficiency.

In injury or *disability evaluations*, a social worker may be asked by the court to assess the emotional and psychological damage suffered as a result of an injury or disability. Psychological testing is used to determine the presence or degree of disability and to support the legitimacy of a claim. Brain damage as a result of an injury can also be assessed through the use of neuropsychological testing. The results of the evaluation assist the court in assigning liability for the injury (Rich, 2010). Disability evaluations can also be used to support claims for benefits.

Finally, forensic social workers may also be involved in alternative sentencing and mitigation. *Alternative sentencing* refers to identifying offenders who can be better served in the community than in the correctional system. It involves working with prosecutors to divert low-level offenders from incarceration and substituting court supervision and treatment. Social workers may conduct screenings to determine eligibility for alternative sentencing, work with families to ascertain their level of support and commitment, link the offender to appropriate community resources, and report to the court on an offender's participation and treatment progress. Social workers also work with defense attorneys to prepare *mitigation* evaluations in order to secure lighter sentences for criminal defendants. This involves compiling life histories for presentation to the court. A life history is a distillation of extensive information about a person's past and current life circumstances and how they bear on the commission of the offense. It may include information about a past trauma, abuse, addiction, or other struggles the defendant has confronted, along with strengths, contributions, and accomplishments that cast the defendant in a positive light. The life history is a holistic assessment that seeks to "humanize" the defendant; the idea is that a deeper understanding of the whole person and his or her circumstances will lead the court to see the defendant as less blameworthy for his or her actions and therefore deserving of a lighter sentence. Mitigation evaluation is discussed in greater detail in Chapter 13.

Drafting a Forensic Report

The results of a forensic evaluation are typically provided by way of a written report that becomes part of the evidence at trial; sometimes the evaluator will also be required to testify. The most helpful reports are impartial, well documented, thorough, and solid enough to withstand cross-examination. Even though individual states specify the details of how various types of reports should be prepared, reports for court tend to follow a similar format. Table 3.1 identifies the key elements that are typically included in a forensic report (Barsky & Gould, 2002; Guidelines for Forensic Evaluations, 2004; Massachusetts Department of Mental Health, 2008).

When preparing a forensic report for the court, specificity is very important. For example, in an analysis of 52 child custody reports filed by psychologists with various family courts, a number of shortcomings were identified. These included neglecting to specify what procedures were used, which specific tests were administered, which collaterals were contacted, and which specific documents had been reviewed; neglecting to explain how informed consent was obtained; neglecting to provide a child history, a clinical description of the parties, and details of the parent-child observations conducted; neglecting to respond directly to the relevant legal questions and criteria; and neglecting to adequately explain how the data presented were relevant to the evaluator's opinion. This last item is particularly important. As the authors acknowledge, "It is important for the reader of the report to understand the evaluator's data source and how the information contributed to the evaluator's opinions and conclusions" (Bow & Quinnell, 2002, p. 173). Although these particular findings are specific to child custody evaluation, lack of specificity is a hazard

TABLE 3.1   **Key Components of Forensic Reports**

Identifying Data

Subject's name, date of birth, sex, race/ethnicity, marital status, referring court, docket number, charge (if relevant), names and phone numbers of both attorneys, names and phone numbers of other collateral informants

Assessment Procedures

Documentation of informed consent, interviews conducted (dates, length, location, names of those present), observations conducted (dates, length, location, names of those present), documents reviewed, physical evaluations and psychological tests, collateral sources contacted, pertinent contacts with counsel

Background Information

Subject's developmental history, education history, employment history, military history, medical history, psychiatric history, substance abuse history, criminal justice involvement, relationship history, current living situation

Current Status

Current behavioral observations; description of current mental status; results of recent medical examinations, psychological tests, and lab work; treatment received (including medication), responses to treatment, intervention results

Opinion & Recommendation

Restatement of legal criteria, opinion on each question posed by the court, illustration of abilities and deficits relative to each legal question, specific behavioral observations and data that support each opinion or recommendation

Signatures

that could apply to any forensic report; social workers preparing submissions for the court are advised to make sure that their documentation is detailed and thorough.

Ethical Considerations in Forensic Practice

Fulfilling the duties related to forensic social work can sometimes create ethical tensions. After all, we are duty bound as professionals to put our clients' interests first. The forensic role, however, is substantially different from the clinical one. As has been discussed previously, forensic practice is premised on the interviewer, evaluator, or witness providing neutral, unbiased information; in a forensic context, the social worker serves the court rather than the client. Although an integral part of the social work role, behaving as an advocate is inappropriate here; it will devalue the social worker's contribution and may interfere with the court's ability to make a sound decision, undermining the fairness of the proceeding. In many instances, the information provided by the social worker will be helpful to the client. Sometimes, however, the reverse may be true. A social worker who is subpoenaed to testify, for example, may be legally required to divulge confidential client information, including information that casts the client in a negative light. For this reason, it is vitally important that social workers discuss with their clients the limits of confidentiality and advise them immediately of any role that the social worker will play in the legal arena. Clients need to understand that you will have no control over how information will be used, once it is disclosed to the court. Be aware that if you assume a forensic role, the therapeutic relationship with your client may not survive; the client may not feel comfortable continuing to work with you. Even when no therapeutic relationship exists and your role is limited to conducting a court-ordered interview or evaluation, the information you provide may result in an unwelcome outcome. The NASW Code of Ethics recognizes the potential tensions here. It states, "Social workers' primary responsibility is to promote the well-being of clients. In general, clients' interests are primary. However, social workers' responsibility to the larger society or specific legal obligations may on limited occasions supersede the loyalty owed clients, and clients should be so advised" (NASW, 2008). In other words, although our primary duty is to promote the client's well-being, we also have a duty to uphold the law. As a result of our dual responsibilities to both the client and to the larger society, we may well find ourselves facing ethical uncertainties. As with any ethical dilemma, it is advisable to be familiar with these various professional and legal expectations, consult with colleagues and supervisors, and follow best practice standards.

Summary and Conclusion

As evidenced in this chapter, social workers are often required to wear many hats. Practitioners should be aware of the various roles they may play, including forensic ones. Social workers undertake some forensic activities as part of their day-to-day practice, including testifying in court as fact witnesses. Social workers might choose to undertake other roles as forensic specialists. Included in this category are forensic interviewing and conducting various forensic evaluations related to mental health, child custody, guardianship, criminal sentencing, and disability. Social workers need to appreciate the differences between therapeutic and forensic practice. Therapeutic practice focuses on the client's subjective emotional experience. In forensic practice, the goal is to use our knowledge and skills to provide the court with objective, factual information to inform the judge's or jury's decision. Social workers should be familiar with the various forensic roles open to them; these roles present unique professional opportunities to shape legal outcomes that can profoundly impact the clients we serve.

CHAPTER 3 PRACTICE TEST

The following questions will test your application and analysis of the content found within this chapter. For additional assessment, including licensing-exam type questions on applying chapter content to practice behaviors, visit **MySearchLab**.

1. You are a social worker conducting a forensic interview with an alleged victim of a sexual assault. Your goal is to
   a. provide a sympathetic view of the victim.
   b. ensure that the victim is afforded his or her legal rights.
   c. elicit a factual account of what transpired to help the court reach its conclusion.
   d. help the victim overcome the trauma resulting from the assault.

2. Using a protocol during a forensic interview is advantageous because
   a. it protects against bias.
   b. it allows the interviewer to ask leading questions.
   c. anyone can administer it without needing any special training.
   d. it is based entirely on observations, so the victim need not respond to questions.

3. One of your colleagues is about to testify in court for the first time. She is especially worried about how to handle the cross-examination. Based on your vast experience on the stand, you wisely advise her to
   a. avoid getting defensive.
   b. elaborate on her answers to be sure she has included all relevant details.
   c. object if an objection is called for.
   d. refrain from correcting the attorney if he mischaracterizes her responses

4. When submitting a written forensic report,
   a. use the opportunity to advocate for your client.
   b. be sure the information you provide is specific.
   c. do not waste time documenting the sources of your information.
   d. remember that there are uniform specifications that have been adopted by every state.

5. If you were asked to testify in court, describe what you would do to prepare.

6. Discuss some of the ethical issues a social worker might confront in the course of forensic practice.

MYSEARCHLAB CONNECTIONS

Reinforce what you learned in this chapter by studying videos, cases, documents, and more available at **www.MySearchLab.com**.

Read these Cases/Documents

Δ Child Sexual Abuse Case: Melindar

- *What challenges are involved when conducting forensic interviews with family members of a child sexual abuse survivor? How can they be overcome?*

Research these Topics

- careers in forensic social work

Assess Your Knowledge

Go to **MySearchLab** to test your knowledge of key topics in this chapter with topic-specific quizzes. Conclude your assessment by completing the chapter exam.

$\star$ = CSWE Core Competency Asset   Δ = Case Study

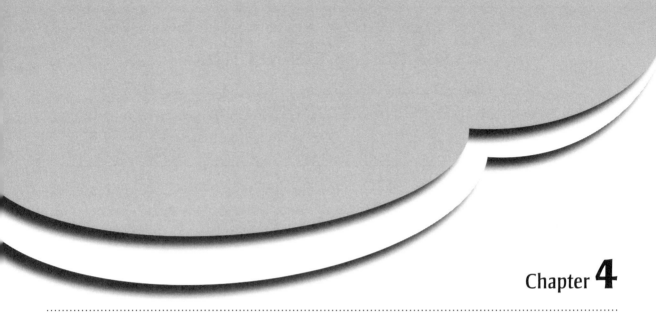

Chapter **4**

Influencing the Judicial System

Decisions by the courts can profoundly affect individual clients and families, as well as set policy for the entire nation. As social workers, we have an interest in ensuring that judicial decisions reflect social work values and priorities, regardless of whether they are made by a local judge in a child welfare case or by the U.S. Supreme Court in a high-profile civil rights action. Unfortunately, strategies for influencing the judicial system are too often neglected. Social work advocacy tends, instead, to focus on legislative change. It makes sense that the U.S. Congress and various state and local legislatures would be our primary targets because the legislative branch of government is designed to be open to influence. As citizens, we can use the ballot box to hold our elected policy makers accountable for their actions. Influencing the judicial branch is trickier. This is not to say it is impossible, however. This chapter discusses three strategies for affecting judicial outcomes: participating in the selection of judges, submitting *amicus* ("friend of the court") briefs, and presenting expert testimony. Participating in judicial selection allows us to help shape the composition of the court; submitting *amicus* briefs and providing expert testimony are tools designed to influence the rulings in specific cases. Social work has a unique perspective to offer, as well as important knowledge and skills. Influencing the legal system is yet another way of satisfying our ethical mandate to challenge social injustice through social and political action.

Participating in Judicial Selection

Most social workers recognize that when it comes to promoting legislation consistent with social work interests, having the right people in office is a tremendous advantage. The same is true in the judicial context. Who wears the robe can make the difference between punitive and compassionate outcomes when disputes between individuals are settled or when policies are advanced. The judicial selection process provides social workers with an opportunity to put judges on the bench who share our professional values. The discussion that follows describes what the selection process entails and identifies potential avenues for influence.

Selecting State Court Judges

The process for selecting judges varies by state and by type of court. As discussed in Chapter 1, the United States has two court systems: state courts and federal courts. More than 25,000 judges preside over the nation's state courts (American Bar Association, 2001), which hear approximately 100 million cases each year (American Judicature Society, 2008). States use two primary methods to put these judges in office: appointment and election. The United States is one of only three countries (the others being Japan and Switzerland) where most judges are elected (Jost, 2009). In fact, more than half the states choose at least some of their judges through elections (AJS, 2008). In the remaining states, the governor or the legislature, with the help of impartial nominating commissions, appoints judges to the bench. Identifying which states use which methods can be exceedingly complicated. In reality, many states use a combination of approaches, depending on the type of judicial vacancy being filled. In addition, states often employ one method to determine the initial selection of judges and another to determine the retention of judges whose initial terms have expired.

In those states that select judges through popular election, candidates wage campaigns and compete against one another just as candidates for other elective offices do. In most of these states, the elections are nonpartisan; in other words, candidates appear on the ballot without any political party affiliation. This is designed to minimize the influence of politics in the selection of judges. A minority of states, however, elect some or all of their judges through partisan elections in which candidates run as members of specific political parties. As with elections to legislative office, the election of judges has become increasingly competitive. Issues that are often debated in the courtroom have become debate topics in the election process as well. Examples include the death penalty, reproductive rights, environmental regulation, and education (Committee for Economic Development, 2002). Although candidates are not permitted to express their positions on issues currently before (or likely to come before) the court, their past decisions and conduct may be scrutinized by the voters. Not surprisingly, the increase in competition for voter support has prompted an increase in campaign spending. Between 2000 and 2009, money raised by state supreme court candidates totaled $206.4 million, more than double the $83.3 million raised in the previous decade (Justice at Stake, 2011). Organized groups including the National Education Association, National Association of Realtors, and AT&T have entered the fray as well, becoming significant sources of both financial support and influence (AJS, 2008). Organizations spend millions of dollars in contributions, direct mail campaigns, advertising, and voter turnout programs in an effort to elect like-minded candidates who can advance their interests on the bench. Some fear that the involvement of organized groups has encouraged judges who depend on voter support for reelection to inappropriately consider public opinion in making their rulings. Several recent high-profile cases reinforce these concerns. One, for example, involved a judge in West Virginia who heard a case against a coal company whose chief executive officer had contributed $3 million to the judge's campaign. Conflicts of interest such as this have prompted a number of states to revise their judicial selection procedures. Four states now publicly finance their judicial elections; others have switched to appointing their judges rather than electing them (Schouten, 2010).

There is no question that this politicizing of the courtroom invites the possibility that a judge's impartiality will be compromised; however, arguments can be made on the other side as well. Some believe that when citizens have a voice in judicial selection, judges can be held more accountable for their decisions. Furthermore, the data suggest that partisan elections are more effective than gubernatorial appointments in putting racial minorities on the bench. As Table 4.1 illustrates, minority judges are poorly represented in many states. States courts in Maine, Montana, New Hampshire, North Dakota, Rhode Island, Vermont, and Wyoming lack even a single African American, Asian/Pacific Islander, Hispanic, or Native American judge. Whatever side one takes in the debate over judicial elections, social workers can exert influence by campaigning and voting for those candidates who most respect our professional priorities and values. We can also play a role in educating the public about judicial candidates and about the opportunity to become involved in shaping judicial outcomes by voting in judicial elections.

TABLE 4.1   Minority Judges by State

State	African American	Asian/Pacific Islander	Hispanic American	Native American	Other	Total
Alabama	10	0	0	0	0	6% (163)
Alaska	0	1	0	0	0	2% (48)
Arizona	4	5	9	0	0	9% (201)
Arkansas	14	0	0	0	0	10% (139)
California	87	85	121	4	73	23% (1631)
Colorado	6	0	15	0	0	11% (186)
Connecticut	17	2	3	0	0	12% (184)
Delaware	3	0	0	0	0	10% (31)
District of Columbia	47	1	5	0	0	56% (95)
Florida	35	2	51	1	1	13% (668)
Georgia	24	0	0	0	0	11% (221)
Hawaii	0	23	0	0	6	67% (43)

State	African American	Asian/Pacific Islander	Hispanic American	Native American	Other	Total
Idaho	0	0	1	0	0	2% (51)
Illinois	102	7	26	0	0	14% (967)
Indiana	17	1	4	0	0	7% (320)
Iowa	5	1	0	0	0	3% (199)
Kansas	5	0	3	0	0	4% (188)
Kentucky	2	0	0	0	0	1% (160)
Louisiana	51	0	0	0	0	18% (291)
Maine	0	0	0	0	0	0% (24)
Maryland	32	0	1	0	0	19% (173)
Massachusetts	9	3	0	0	0	11% (112)
Michigan	21	0	4	0	0	10% (256)
Minnesota	13	3	1	3	1	7% (315)
Mississippi	11	0	0	0	0	16% (70)
Missouri	13	0	3	0	1	5% (373)
Montana	0	0	0	0	0	0% (68)
Nebraska	1	0	0	0	0	1% (143)
Nevada	2	1	2	0	1	8% (71)
New Hampshire	0	0	0	0	0	0% (31)
New Jersey	41	1	24	0	0	14% (483)
New Mexico	4	1	25	0	1	30% (103)
New York	48	5	23	0	0	16% (461)
North Carolina	9	0	0	1	0	8% (131)
North Dakota	0	0	0	0	0	0% (49)
Ohio	19	1	1	0	0	4% (470)
Oklahoma	7	0	0	1	0	3% (277)
Oregon	0	0	1	0	0	1% (191)
Pennsylvania	29	1	2	0	0	7% (470)
Rhode Island	0	0	0	0	0	0% (27)
South Carolina	6	0	0	0	0	9% (67)
South Dakota	0	0	0	1	0	2% (43)
Tennessee	14	0	0	0	0	8% (184)
Texas	23	3	77	1	4	19% (569)
Utah	1	4	1	1	0	8% (83)

(continued)

TABLE 4.1   **Minority Judges by State (continued)**

State	African American	Asian/Pacific Islander	Hispanic American	Native American	Other	Total
Vermont	0	0	0	0	0	0% (34)
Virginia	18	0	0	0	0	11% (168)
Washington	11	5	1	0	1	8% (217)
West Virginia	1	0	0	0	0	3% (37)
Wisconsin	7	1	4	0	0	4% (269)
Wyoming	0	0	0	0	0	0% (29)
Total	**769**	**157**	**408**	**13**	**89**	**1436**

Srouce: From *National Database on Judicial Diversity in State Courts* by the ABA Standing Committee on Judicial Independence. Copyright (c) 2011 by the American Bar Association. Reprinted with permission. This information or any or portion thereof may not be copied or disseminated in any form or by any means or stored in an electronic database or retrieval system without the express written consent of the American Bar Association.

In the states where judges are appointed, a nominating commission generally identifies, recruits, and screens prospective candidates for office and forwards a list of qualified candidates to the governor, who makes the final decision. Nominees are evaluated based on their experience, integrity, professional competence, commitment to judicial impartiality, and service to the law (ABA, 2001). More than half of the states and the District of Columbia use nominating commissions in making all or some of their judicial appointments; only five states appoint judges without any aid from a nominating commission. In three of them, the governor makes the appointments, and in the remaining two, the state legislature does (Berkson, Caufield, & Reddick, 2010). Typically, nominating commissions are composed of between five and nine individuals, both attorneys and non-attorneys, who serve terms of 3 to 6 years. The chair is a nonvoting member who is a former or current judge (ABA, 2001; CED, 2002). Commission members are chosen by state authorities which, depending on the state, might be the governor, the legislature, state supreme court judges, or officers in the state bar association. These commissions are expected to be nonpartisan and to evaluate judicial candidates based entirely on merit. Although the vast majority of states that appoint their judges believe that nominating commissions are important in ensuring impartiality, critics have raised questions about allowing this important responsibility to rest in the hands of a small and elite group that does not necessarily represent the views of the public at large.

Most judges are appointed for a limited term and must then be reappointed. States vary in how this reappointment process works, and different processes may be employed within a single state depending on the court in question. As a result, countless variations exist. Rhode Island, for example, appoints its state supreme court judges for life. Massachusetts allows judges to serve until they reach the age of 70 (CED, 2002). Arizona holds a "retention" election (during which the judge runs unopposed) after the initial 2-year appointment by the governor; a majority vote in favor of retention is required to keep the judge in office. In Hawaii, the judicial selection commission is responsible for both initial appointments and subsequent reappointments, and in Maine, judges are reappointed by the governor pending confirmation by the legislature (AJS, 2010).

Supporters of the appointment method of selection argue that, unlike other methods, appointment encourages the consideration of more qualified candidates because nominees are not subject to election by the public and thus need not double as politicians. Although influencing the selection of judges is more difficult in the case of appointment than in the case of election, social workers can nonetheless become involved by lobbying the appointing official (whether it is the governor or the state legislators) for or against particular candidates. They can also serve on state nominating commissions.

Selecting Federal Judges

Federal judges include those who preside in district courts, federal circuit courts of appeals, and the U.S. Supreme Court. Article III of the Constitution mandates that all federal judges, who are appointed for life, be nominated by the president and confirmed, or approved, by the U.S. Senate. Party affiliation and policy preferences are significant considerations when a president makes these judicial appointments. As one might expect, federal judges appointed by Democratic presidents tend to be more liberal, and those appointed by Republican presidents tend to be more conservative. Because of the Senate's role in the confirmation process, senators belonging to the same party as the president often influence the selection of judges in their home states; this is known as *senatorial courtesy*. If the Senate is controlled by the opposite party, the president may take into consideration potential difficulties in the confirmation process but usually tries, nonetheless, to appoint judges whose policy preferences resemble his own (Giles, Hettinger, & Peppers, 2001).

Nominating commissions have a role in the selection of federal judges just as they do for state judges, although the process works somewhat differently. As discussed earlier, state court nominating commissions make candidacy suggestions directly to the appointing official (governor or legislature). In contrast, nominating commissions for federal judges (also called *screening panels* or *advisory committees*) typically submit the names of potential candidates to U.S. senators, who in turn decide which nominees to forward to the president for consideration. The precise role and makeup of these nominating bodies varies by state (AJS, 2011). In addition to seeking advice from the Senate, presidents often rely on staff within the White House and the U.S. Department of Justice to assist in the judicial selection process. Although the roles of the individuals involved may vary with each president, the office of the U.S. Attorney General and the Justice Department's Office of Legal Policy usually play a key role in the identification of prospective candidates (Brand, 2010).

Countless commentators have noted the increasing role of ideology in the judicial selection process. Critics contend that decisions should be made solely on merit, without reference to the candidate's views. Others believe that ideology is a natural and appropriate consideration because "an individual's beliefs dictate how he or she will decide cases once on the bench" (Chemerinsky, 2003, p. 620). Presidents and senators from both political parties have delayed or blocked the appointment of candidates with whom they disagree. From our perspective as advocates, merit and viewpoint are equally important. Social work is a profession with an explicit set of values and priorities, and advancing the rights of marginalized client groups is an integral part of our role. We have an obligation to help put on the bench competent decision makers most likely to support us in that effort.

Because federal judges are appointed and not elected, the public must use creative strategies to influence the selection process. Considering the important role these judges play, however—and the fact that they are appointed for life—every opportunity to have input into the process should be embraced. Remember that the appointment and confirmation of federal judges is political. This means that social workers and others can advocate for or against specific candidates by lobbying the White House and seeking to influence the Senate's confirmation vote. As discussed in Chapter 2, this has become increasingly common in the case of U.S. Supreme Court nominees. The National Association of Social Workers (NASW), for example, spoke out against the appointment to Chief Justice Roberts and Justice Alito while supporting the appointment and confirmation of Justices Sotomayor and Kagan. This same activism can be applied to the selection of district and appellate court judges as well. Important social work interests are at stake, not only in terms of policy but also in terms of diversity. Despite recent gains by minorities and women, approximately 85% of the judges on the federal bench are White and approximately 80% are male (Wheeler, 2009). We and our clients have everything to gain by getting involved, and nothing to lose.

Submitting *Amicus* Briefs

In addition to influencing who the decision makers are by participating in judicial selection, social workers can influence the outcome of individual cases by filing *amicus* briefs. *Amici curiae* ("friends of the court") are people who provide input for the court to consider even though they are not directly involved as parties in the case. *Amici curiae* may be individuals, for-profit or not-for-profit organizations, professional associations, government agencies, interest groups, or other entities. With the assistance of an attorney, *amici curiae* submit legal briefs that supplement those of the parties in the case. Because judges may not be well versed in all the details underlying various perspectives, *amicus* briefs provide an opportunity for outside experts to share with the court relevant research, background information, alternative legal arguments, technical or statistical data, and other contextual elaboration that might help inform the court's decision (Flango, Bross, & Corbally, 2006). *Amicus* briefs can also bring attention to issues of public concern such as civil rights, human rights, gender equality, capital punishment, environmental protection, and so on.

In addition to the useful information they contain, *amicus* briefs provide judges with a window into how their decisions might be received by other judges, other branches of government, and the public at large. Taking this into consideration helps minimize the possibility that judges' decisions will be overridden, altered, or not enforced by their peers because they are not aligned with public opinion (Epstein & Knight, 1998). In addition, when the court demonstrates an awareness of public opinion, it may generate important support for the legal system as a whole (Kearney & Merrill, 2000). Recognizing public opinion in decision making assures the public that the court is a responsive institution, acting in society's best interests.

The number of *amicus* briefs submitted annually has increased considerably since the 1960s. As the role of *amici curiae* has expanded, submitting friend of the court briefs has become less of a strategy for providing information to the court and more of an advocacy strategy. In fact, *amicus* briefs have become the most popular method of influencing the judicial process, particularly on appeal. *Amicus* briefs play an important role in the democratic process, allowing citizens to voice their positions and influence judicial decision making. Some say that *amicus* briefs are to judges what lobbying is to legislators (Collins, 2007).

Rules for Submitting *Amicus* Briefs

Rules for submitting an *amicus* brief vary by state, but most follow the U.S. Supreme Court rule that requires *amici curiae* to obtain permission from both parties in the case or from the court before filing a brief. On occasion, courts specifically invite experts or organizations to submit *amicus* briefs. More often, the filing of an *amicus* brief is initiated without an explicit invitation. In this instance, as one would expect, parties to the case are more likely to permit the filing of a brief if it supports their particular position (Corbally, Bross, & Flango, 2004). When *amici curiae* file briefs in support of one of the parties, the goal is not only to advocate for the party involved but also to influence the policy that will result from the court's decision (Collins, 2007). After all, case outcomes have potentially far-reaching implications for other individuals not directly involved in the case. Of course, the mere act of submitting an *amicus* brief does not guarantee that the judge will rule in one's favor; it may, however, cause the judge to consider arguments not otherwise before the court (Simpson & Vasaly, 2004).

Although *amicus* briefs have a presence in lower federal courts and state courts, they are most often filed in the U.S. Supreme Court, the *court of last resort* (Corbally et al., 2004). By submitting *amicus* briefs in U.S. Supreme Court cases, *amici curiae* attempt to influence the judicial process from the top down, engaging the most influential court first and expecting the resulting decisions to trickle down to the lower courts (Collins, 2007). The filing of *amicus* briefs shows the justices that the issue under consideration is important to the public and extends beyond the parties in the case, thus suggesting broader political and policy implications. In addition, receiving an *amicus* brief with a large number of cosigners reminds the Court that many groups and individuals will be impacted by the Court's decision.

Although the participation of *amici curiae* is not limited in the U.S. Supreme Court, it is limited in state courts where *amicus* briefs have a narrower presence. Some state courts allow briefs only in certain cases, such as those expected to have a profound impact on the public interest; others accept only those briefs submitted by an impartial source, rather than by supporters of one of the parties (Corbally et al., 2004). Interestingly, even if the court permits the submission of an *amicus* brief, judges are not obligated to read it or to consider the arguments and information it contains. However, research shows that persuasive arguments do in fact influence judicial decision making when they are presented by organized interests, and that participation by *amici curiae* increases the likelihood the supported party will succeed (e.g., Kearney & Merrill, 2000).

To ensure that briefs are effective, they should be well written, concise, and clearly organized, and they should fully explain the relevance of their arguments to the case and emphasize their sociopolitical value (Foggan & Dancey, 2004). Briefs that are poorly organized and irrelevant to the case do not advance the brief's position and burden the court. Submitting briefs that repeat arguments and information presented by other briefs is discouraged; instead, organizations should consolidate their arguments into a single brief submitted collaboratively. This allows organizations to share knowledge, resources, and the financial burden of preparing a brief while demonstrating to the court the breadth of interests that will be affected by its decision. Such collaborations also build relationships with like-minded organizations while showing organizational members that important issues are actively being addressed on their behalf (Collins, 2004). Similarly, early coordination between *amici curiae* and the party they support has come to be expected (Foggan & Dancey, 2004).

Every state has its own guidelines for writing and filing *amicus* briefs; therefore, *amici curiae* should be sure to follow specific state instructions regarding the content of briefs and comply with deadlines for submission. *Amicus* briefs for the U.S. Supreme Court are limited to 30 pages; those submitted in lower courts are often limited to half the length of the briefs submitted by the actual parties. An *amicus* brief typically describes the individuals or organizations that are submitting the brief, summarizes their interest in the case, provides an overview of its arguments, and details each argument citing relevant legal authorities. Because the purpose is to supplement the information already being submitted by the parties rather than repeating it, the brief should clarify why it is important both to the specific case and to the greater development of the law (Foggan & Dancy, 2004). Although only required by some courts, it is also recommended that a complete list of authors, cosigners, and financial supporters be included in all briefs (Corbally & Bross, 2001). *Amici curiae* should be sure to confirm the rules of the jurisdiction where the brief is being filed to ensure that all regulations are followed.

Social Workers and *Amicus* Briefs

Social workers file *amicus* briefs both on their own behalf and in collaboration with other professional groups and organizations. Social workers have a distinctive viewpoint that can be valuable to the court, derived from knowledge of human development and behavior, social policy expertise, and evidence-based research. NASW and its chapters, for example, participate as *amici curiae* in cases that they deem significant in light of the association's Code of Ethics, which mandates advocacy for improved social conditions and social justice. NASW has filed approximately 200 briefs in the past three decades, on its own or in collaboration with other organizations including the American Civil Liberties Union (ACLU), National Women's Law Center, Children's Defense Fund, American Psychological Association, National Education Association, and National Alliance on Mental Illness. The issues addressed include capital punishment, civil rights, child welfare, disabilities, discrimination, due process, education, equal protection, health care, human rights, juvenile justice, sexual orientation, social work practice, and women's issues (NASW, 2011).

Among the *amicus* briefs submitted by NASW during the first half of 2011 are two supporting the rights of lesbian parents in guardianship and child custody proceedings, four supporting the Affordable Care Act (federal health care reform) against various challenges, two supporting plaintiffs in sex discrimination actions (one concerning girls' sports and the other concerning employment discrimination), and one seeking to protect the privacy of patients' mental health treatment records.

Of particular note is the fact that NASW's *amicus* briefs have been cited as part of several U.S. Supreme Court opinions. In reaching its decision in *Jaffee v. Redmond* (1996), the case that established privileged communications for clinical social workers, for example, the Court relied on information in NASW's *amicus* brief identifying clinical social workers as the predominant providers of psychotherapy in the United States. In the more recent (and very controversial) case of *Kennedy v. Louisiana* (2008)—a case in which the Supreme Court decided that the death penalty cannot constitutionally be applied in cases of child rape—the Court cited NASW's arguments that (1) extensive court proceedings, such as those involved in death penalty cases, would exacerbate the trauma experienced by child victims, and (2) permitting the death penalty for child rape would increase the underreporting of sexual abuse. Given these and other examples, it is safe to say that filing an *amicus* brief can indeed have an impact on the outcome of a case.

As social workers, we can play an important role by encouraging the organizations with which we work and affiliate to submit or sign onto *amicus* briefs. It is an important mechanism for providing the court with our knowledge and expertise in pursuit of positive judicial outcomes.

Testifying as an Expert Witness

A third way in which social workers can influence the judicial system is by serving as expert witnesses at trial. As discussed in Chapter 3, social workers can be called upon to testify in two capacities: as fact witnesses and as expert witnesses. Whereas fact witnesses provide the court with firsthand information about what transpired relative to a particular dispute, expert witnesses help educate the court about technical issues requiring specialized knowledge. They are individuals who, by virtue of their education, training, or experience, have the ability to interpret or explain complex information (Polowy & Gilbertson, 2004). Depending on their credibility, expert witnesses and the evidence they present may have a profound effect on the outcome of a case. As with any forensic role, the objective is not to advocate for a particular person or position but rather to assist the court in making a sound decision by increasing its understanding of topics that are outside the ordinary experience of the judge or jury. Note that testifying as an expert is closely linked to conducting forensic evaluations (discussed in Chapter 3), because evaluators are often called upon to testify regarding the results of the evaluations conducted.

Becoming an Expert Witness

Unlike fact witnesses who may be subpoenaed to testify, expert witnesses always become involved in a case voluntarily. They may be hired by either party or may be appointed by the judge. Experts are typically identified through referral by other attorneys, university faculty, researchers, other expert witnesses involved in a case, professional associations, or online directories and databases (Schultz, 1989). Experts may also be identified through their recent presentations, speeches, or publications.

Social workers and others who are interested in being hired as expert witnesses should take action to ensure that they are properly qualified. This includes making sure they have the requisite educational background, experience, and licensure or certification; making professional presentations in their area of expertise; publishing on the topic; working or training alongside recognized experts; and staying current through continuing education and reading the scholarly literature.

If asked to serve as an expert witness, one should consider a number of factors. First, remember that expert witnesses are expected to maintain their objectivity. Given the nature of the case, will you be comfortable with this—or will you be tempted to act as an advocate? Also, will the attorney who is hiring you accept your being unbiased or will he or she pressure you to compromise your objectivity in order to win the case? Second, expert witnesses may testify only within their area of expertise. This is both a legal issue and an ethical one reflected in the NASW Code of Ethics. What is the nature of the case?

On what topic will you be expected to speak—and is it clearly within the scope of your expert education, experience, and training? Finally, you have an ethical obligation to practice competently. Will you have access to all of the materials you will need in order to perform responsibly? Will the time and payment afforded you allow you to do your best?

It is common practice to sign a contract or letter of agreement before beginning work on a case. Unlike fact witnesses, expert witnesses are paid for their time; even those appointed by the court are entitled to "reasonable" compensation. Most expert witnesses charge the same or somewhat more than the hourly rate they charge as practitioners; note that charging substantially more can cast doubt on your objectivity. As it is, cross-examination often includes an insinuation that the expert witness is being paid to render a particular opinion. If opposing counsel asks about the payment you are receiving while you are on the stand, simply indicate that you are being paid for your time, not to reach any specific conclusion. Never allow counsel to tarnish your professionalism. Remember that whatever hourly rate you set should include not only your time in court (both waiting around and actually testifying) but also the time you spend in preparation: conducting research, reviewing files, interviewing, drafting reports, and preparing or practicing your testimony (Barker & Branson, 2000) You might also expect to incur travel costs or need to engage consultants or administrative help. In addition to clarifying how much you will be paid, be sure to negotiate when and how you will be paid. What will happen, for example, if the case settles before you testify? Or the court finds you unacceptable as an expert witness?

If you do decide to testify, you will need to prepare. Effective expert witness testimony is a complex task that requires practice; even an experienced expert witness must prepare for each case because every case is different, involving different parties, facts, evidence, and issues. Here are some suggestions that will help you feel more comfortable and testify more effectively:

- **Meet with the attorney who is hiring you.** Meeting with the attorney provides an invaluable opportunity to ask questions and to clarify your role. The attorney will explain what you can expect in court and how he or she envisions your testimony contributing to the case. Together you can review the important facts and evidence. Be sure to arrange for access to any materials you might need. Rehearsing your testimony will allow both you and the attorney to identify any weaknesses in the content of your testimony or in your delivery. The lawyer can also help prepare you for cross-examination (Barker & Branson, 2000).
- **Carefully review your resume.** Be sure that it is current, complete, and accurate. Barksy and Gould (2002, p. 156) recommend including your professional title and contact information, training and education, degrees and professional licenses, employment history and years of experience, supervisory experience, awards or other recognition, trainings conducted, prior court experience, work under recognized experts, membership in professional associations, publications, presentations, continuing education, consultation provided, methods of practice, and recognized specializations. Pay special attention to those items most directly related to the area in which you will testify. Be ready to summarize what you learned from each of your various employment and educational experiences. Be sure to include every experience that can help explain the basis for your knowledge, skills, and expertise (North Carolina Division of Social Services, 2000). Go over the resume with the friendly attorney and find out what questions he or she

will be asking in court about your professional background, so you can prepare to respond intelligently.

- **Be sure you are familiar with the latest research on the topic as well as any controversies.** You should also review cases similar to the one in which you are testifying in order to examine recent judicial trends in your topic area. Think about how best to communicate your information to the court. Even though you have a responsibility to be familiar with the literature, it is always possible that opposing counsel, on cross-examination, will ask about a study you have not read; be prepared to cite those studies on which your opinions are based and to explain the rationale behind various therapeutic techniques and interventions. Depending on the complexity of the topic, you might also want to prepare notes, slides, or charts to better explain the topic and its relevance.

- **Brush up on courtroom procedures.** If acting as an expert witness is a new role for you, find an opportunity to observe the testimony of other expert witnesses in order to increase your comfort with the courtroom environment and procedures. Many witnesses who are new to testifying, for example, do not realize that expert witnesses can end up spending considerable time just waiting, usually in seclusion from other witnesses to ensure the objectivity of their testimony. There is no way to know how long things will take, so witnesses need to be available to spring into action at a moment's notice. Testifying may also require spending time away from work, necessitating special arrangements to cover job responsibilities. Because your goal is to be both knowledgeable and effective, it is important to have experience with the judicial process as well as expertise on the topic under consideration by the court (Barker & Branson, 2000).

Remember that when you testify as an expert witness, a lot is on the line. Inadequate preparation may result in inaccurate testimony or in compromised objectivity. Lapses in your credibility could adversely affect the outcome of the case and tarnish your professional reputation.

Testifying Effectively

Prior to the trial, expert witnesses may be required to participate in a deposition. As described in Chapter 1, a deposition involves testifying under oath in response to oral or written questions, in the presence of both sides' attorneys and a court reporter. The deposition serves as an opportunity for both parties to hear the content of the expert's testimony and to assess his or her demeanor and credibility (Pollack, 2004). Following a deposition, the expert witness has the right to receive a transcript of the testimony and to verify its accuracy. The expert should take advantage of this opportunity to carefully review the transcript and take steps to correct the written record if necessary (Schultz, 1989).

Once the case goes to trial, before the expert's testimony can begin, the judge must certify that the witness is indeed qualified to testify as an expert in the case. This entails a process known as *voir dire*. Based on the information in your resume, each attorney will question you regarding your credentials and their relevance to the type of expertise sought. This process allows the judge to evaluate your specialized knowledge, education, professional experience, affiliations, publications, and reputation in the field. Keep in mind that someone who is qualified as an expert in one subject area may not be considered qualified in another (Barker & Branson, 2000). The friendly attorney will usually ask you to elaborate on your background in order to impress upon the court how very qualified you are, whereas the opposing attorney will challenge your qualifications and attempt to disparage your expertise. This is why taking the time to review your resume is so essential. You do not want to give opposing counsel any opportunity to find fault; especially hazardous are inconsistencies and inaccuracies that might make you appear to be exaggerating your experience or credentials. Occasionally, when a witness has extensive and highly impressive credentials, opposing counsel will short-cut the process by stipulating that the witness is qualified; this is a strategy to avoid exposing the jury to a lengthy recitation of the witness's stunning accomplishments.

Once the court accepts the witness as an expert, the testimony begins. First, the friendly attorney questions the expert witness; then, the opposing attorney cross-examines the expert witness. Finally, the friendly attorney is permitted to question the expert witness again on re-direct. Once the testimony is finished, the expert's involvement in the case is complete; the judge will indicate whether or not the witness is permitted to remain in the courtroom for the remainder of the hearing. As is true with fact witnesses (discussed in Chapter 3), the expert witness can expect direct examination to provide an opportunity to share information fairly liberally; because this is the side that hired you, the questions will be gentle and encouraging. By contrast, the purpose of cross-examination will be to discredit your testimony. Re-direct provides your attorney with an opportunity to re-establish your credibility if necessary and reinforce the key elements necessary to the case.

Perhaps the greatest difference between expert witnesses and fact witnesses is that expert witnesses are permitted to offer opinions. These opinions can be based on direct observation or on evidence provided during the hearing; they must reflect knowledge derived from professional experience, education, training, and a thorough knowledge of the scholarly literature. Sometimes the expert will have had direct experience with one of the parties in the case—for example, a mental health expert might have evaluated the competency of a criminal defendant. Other times, the expert testifies about a condition or phenomenon in the abstract—for example, stress experienced by first responders in disaster situations. Sometimes, the court will ask about the specific parties or facts in the case; other times, the expert may be asked to respond to a hypothetical situation. In any case, it is essential that you clearly explain the factual basis for your opinion, interpretation, or conclusions. Any opinion you offer must be stated with a *reasonable degree of certainty*—the same degree of certainty you would require of yourself in reaching conclusions as a competent, practicing professional. Your purpose is to educate the court, so steer clear of jargon; you will be most effective if you think of yourself as a teacher and are able to explain things in simple language that nonexperts will understand. It is also important for the jury to like and trust you; if you, as a witness, do not come across as credible, your testimony may not be taken seriously. Be careful not to alienate the jury by seeming arrogant, patronizing, impatient, or defensive. All of the guidelines discussed in Chapter 3 related to testifying as a fact witness are equally applicable to expert witnesses: behave professionally, be clear about your role, and concentrate on your delivery.

Social Workers as Expert Witnesses

Social workers are valued as expert witnesses on the basis of their knowledge, skill, experience, training, and education (Barker & Branson, 2000). Initially, social workers were called upon to testify almost exclusively in family and child welfare cases because of their involvement in identifying and reporting child maltreatment (Gothard, 1989; Polowy & Gilbertson, 2004). For example, in *Bostic v. State* (1989), a social worker was called as an expert witness in a case involving the alleged sexual abuse of a girl by her father. The social worker, Elizabeth Scollan, testified regarding how children typically behave after being sexually abused, noting that children are often reluctant to report incidents of abuse and are likely to minimize the experience when reporting. On appeal, Bostic (the father) argued that Scollan's testimony should be excluded because she had previously counseled him, and any information shared would therefore be privileged. The court disagreed, noting that Scollan's testimony was not based on firsthand knowledge of Bostic and his family but rather on her expert knowledge and experience regarding the characteristics of sexually abused children in general. This is the hallmark of an expert witness. The judge subsequently affirmed Bostic's conviction on two counts of sexually abusing a minor. This case is one of many in which social workers have used their experience with child maltreatment to provide valuable information to the court and to influence the outcome of a case.

Since the 1980s, the use of social workers as expert witnesses has proliferated. This was reinforced, in part, by the U.S. Supreme Court's decision in *Jaffee v. Remond* (1996) which extended the psychotherapist-client privilege to clinical social workers, placing them on an equal footing with other mental health professionals in terms of their qualifications, knowledge, and expertise. Today, social workers testify as expert witnesses in a wide array of cases, including those involving parental rights, trauma, civil commitment, guardianship, criminal justice, competency, domestic violence, disability, substance abuse, sexual harassment, addictions, and education (Sarnoff, 2004; Schultz, 1989). Social workers have also drawn on their expertise with cultural competence to testify about the history of discrimination against African Americans in the United States (*Mallory v. Ohio,* 1997) and Native Alaskan culture (*L.G. v. State of Alaska,* 2000). Even as the use of social workers as expert witnesses has expanded, some state laws continue to restrict who is permitted to testify in certain types of cases. As discussed in Chapter 15, for example, some states continue to permit only psychiatrists and psychologists to testify regarding competency to stand trial. Thus, as always, it is important to be aware of specific rules governing expert testimony within your state.

When social workers testify as expert witnesses, they are bound by the NASW Code of Ethics, just as they are when engaging in any other aspect of professional practice. This includes providing testimony that is honest, unbiased, and based on fact. Social workers should never base their conclusions on their personal ideology, nor agree to alter their testimony in order to meet the needs of the party paying their fee. Social workers are encouraged to refuse requests for expert testimony in which skewed or misleading testimony is expected. Similarly, it is advisable to decline to testify if you disagree with the position of the requesting party and may have difficulty maintaining your objectivity and professionalism (Barker & Branson, 2000).

Remember, too, that an expert witness may testify only within the scope of his or her expertise. Social workers must be scrupulous about making clear the range and limitations of their knowledge, and resisting the temptation to comment on matters outside their area of specialization. For example, it would be unethical to testify about adolescent depression if your specific area of expertise is depression in older adults—or for an expert completing a child custody evaluation to testify as to the relative merits of the educational approaches used by schools in the parents' respective neighborhoods. If you hold yourself out as an expert, you also have an ethical obligation to keep up with the current practice research through reading the literature and attending appropriate professional trainings, workshops, and continuing education events. Social workers should not only be familiar with the research in their field but also should be able to assess its validity. Being able to identify promising practices and evidence-based approaches is an important aspect of competent practice as an expert witness.

Finally, Chapter 3 discussed some of the confusion that can result from having the same social worker acting in both therapeutic and forensic roles. The same holds true when social workers are asked to serve as both fact witnesses and expert witnesses in the same case. Although there is some disagreement on the issue, most observers see this as a "dual relationship" of the type prohibited by the Code of Ethics. In the *Bostic* case described earlier, for example, Scallon was called as an expert witness in a case regarding her own clients. A conflict of interest was averted only because she testified exclusively about the dynamics of child maltreatment and was not required to provide information regarding her therapeutic relationship with the parties in the case (Sarnoff, 2004). Social workers should err on the side of caution and decline to serve in more than one capacity in relation to the same client.

In addition to serving as expert witnesses, social workers may also work with attorneys as consultants. Experts who are hired as consultants will not necessarily testify during a trial, but they may contribute to a case by suggesting relevant books and literature to read; recommending qualified expert witnesses to hire; identifying additional research to be conducted; and advising on trial strategy, questions for direct examination or cross-examination, and jury selection (Schultz, 1989). An expert consultant, like an expert witness, can play an important role in influencing the outcome of a case.

Summary and Conclusion

Influencing the judicial system can be more difficult than influencing the legislature because it is designed to be insulated from public opinion. Social workers can, however, influence judicial outcomes in several ways; it is important to try to do so because these decisions often have important effects not only on the dispute before the court but also on public policies. Social workers can participate in the election of judges by engaging in ballot-based activities including working on electoral campaigns and voting in judicial contests. When judges are appointed rather than elected, social workers can seek to sit on state nominating commissions and can participate in lobbying activities targeting those charged with appointing and confirming judicial candidates. To influence the outcomes of specific cases, social workers can work with like-minded individuals and organizations to submit *amicus* briefs. These are written documents, submitted by outsiders, that supplement the arguments presented by the parties in court. They often address issues with broad policy implications. NASW is among those organizations that use *amicus* briefs as a tool for social reform. Another method of influencing specific cases is to serve as an expert witness. Expert witnesses must be qualified by the judge on the basis of specialized knowledge. Their role is to help the court understand technical or complex material that is relevant to the case. As with any professional activity, social workers have a duty to properly prepare and perform competently. The opportunities for social workers to serve as expert witnesses are expanding; by assuming this role, we can make a direct contribution to the outcome of judicial proceedings while demonstrating to the public the depth of our professional knowledge and skills.

CHAPTER 4 PRACTICE TEST

The following questions will test your application and analysis of the content found within this chapter. For additional assessment, including licensing-exam type questions on applying chapter content to practice behaviors, visit **MySearchLab**.

1. The selection of U.S. Supreme Court justices has increasingly involved consideration of the candidates'
   a. experience.
   b. ideology.
   c. integrity.
   d. objectivity.

2. The role of an expert witness is to
   a. advocate for one of the parties.
   b. provide factual information about the case at hand.
   c. educate the court about a complex issue that most people don't understand.
   d. sway the jury.

3. You are asked to appear as an expert witness by the attorney representing a woman accused of embezzlement. He plans to present a defense based on the woman's addiction to shopping. Although you have no experience with compulsive shopping, you do specialize in treating compulsive gambling. Should you accept the job?
   a. Yes, because your clinical license is sufficient to qualify you to testify as an expert.
   b. Yes, because all compulsive behavior shares certain similarities.
   c. No, because you lack professional competence in the area of specialization required.
   d. No, because you have never testified as an expert witness before.

4. The purpose of an *amicus* brief is to
   a. detail the state rules governing the judicial proceedings.
   b. provide an impartial legal analysis without offering an opinion.
   c. reiterate the arguments made by the parties in the case.
   d. supplement the arguments made by the parties in the case.

5. State judges can be appointed or elected, depending on the state. What are the advantages and disadvantages of each of these methods of selection?

6. As a social worker, which avenue of influencing judicial decision making do you think has the most potential? Explain why.

MYSEARCHLAB CONNECTIONS

Reinforce what you learned in this chapter by studying videos, cases, documents, and more available at **www.MySearchLab.com**.

Research these Topics

- bias in judicial selection: Tracy Thorne-Begland
- NASW amicus briefs

Assess Your Knowledge

Go to **MySearchLab** to test your knowledge of key topics in this chapter with topic-specific quizzes. Conclude your assessment by completing the chapter exam.

⋆ = CSWE Core Competency Asset   Δ = Case Study

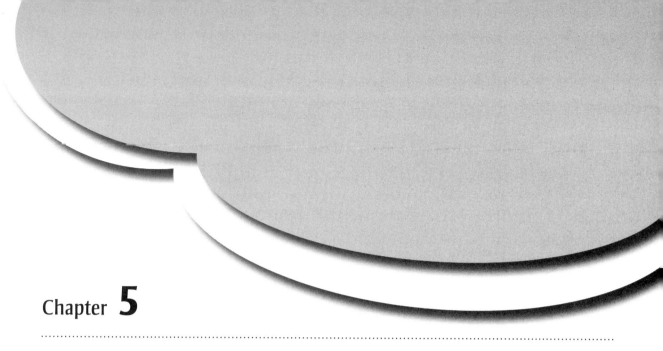

Chapter **5**

....

Practicing Within the Law

One of the most obvious areas in which social work and law intersect is in the legal regulation of professional practice. Whereas state laws and regulations dictate who may practice as a social worker, a rich history of case law defines the boundaries of acceptable practice. As with any other socio-legal issue, our understanding of professional malpractice continues to evolve as courts address specific cases that raise new questions of interpretation. Although we as social workers strive to ensure that we practice competently and within the law, the possibility always exists that we will be sued by a client for malpractice.

Malpractice suits against social workers were relatively rare until the early 1970s, but the number of suits has increased dramatically since—as have lawsuits against other professional practitioners. Among the most common complaints against social workers are incorrect treatment, sexual misconduct, client suicide or attempted suicide, and dual relationships, including maintaining a social or business relationship with a client in addition to a professional one (Dolgoff, Lowenberg, & Harrington, 2009). This chapter addresses the legal definition of malpractice, how malpractice cases proceed in court, common types of malpractice actions, and steps that social workers should take to minimize their risk of liability. A special section highlights the topic of e-therapy.

Overview of Malpractice Law

....

Suing for malpractice is one of several remedies available to victims of inappropriate care or treatment. Malpractice is a form of negligence. It is a civil action that involves failure to perform in a reasonably professional manner. Victims may also lodge complaints against practitioners with state licensing boards (Dolgoff et al., 2009). Generally speaking, there are two broad categories of malpractice. First, malpractice can involve acts of commission, meaning the social worker or other professional does something he or she should not have done. This can include doing the right thing in the wrong way—such as failing to obtain the client's informed consent before releasing treatment records—or doing something that is in and of itself wrongful or unlawful—for example, extorting money from a client. Alternatively, malpractice can involve an act of omission whereby the provider fails to carry out a duty owed to the client. Failing to properly monitor a suicidal patient would be considered such an act (Cournoyer, 2008; Reamer, 2003; Roberts, Monferrari, & Yeager, 2008).

Defining Malpractice

The law does not expect social workers, or other professional practitioners, to be perfect. It does, however, demand that we conform to our profession's *standard of care*. This involves "practicing with the skill and care expected of a prudent practitioner engaged in the same kind of professional practice, with the same degree of training, in a similar community, and under similar circumstances" (Israel, 2011, p. 35). A malpractice action is made up of four required elements. To be successful, the person bringing the suit (the plaintiff) must establish that each of these conditions is met:

1. A legal duty existed between the professional and the client at that time.
2. The professional was derelict in his or her duty.
3. The client suffered harm or injury.
4. The harm or injury was directly and proximately caused by the dereliction of duty.

Let's take a look at these, one by one, to see what they actually entail. First, *the social worker must owe a legal duty to the client*. When a client contacts a social worker and the social worker agrees to see the client, a professional relationship has been established and the social worker has incurred a duty to the client (Dickson, 1995). Thus, a client who has been in therapy with a social worker—whether for six years, six months, six days, or six hours—would be owed a professional duty. Getting more technical, the triggering of the duty depends on the professional actually beginning to provide an agreed-upon service. In that case, if the client has scheduled an appointment but not yet met with the provider for treatment, no duty would be considered to exist. Perhaps the most ambiguous case would be a social worker who has conducted only an initial intake interview. Whether or not the duty was triggered would likely depend on the interview's purpose: If it were to collect preliminary information so that the client and provider could decide whether or not to pursue a therapeutic relationship, no duty would be incurred. If, on the other hand, the client and provider already share an expectation of working together and the information collected will be used to inform a course of treatment, a duty likely does exist. Ordinarily in malpractice cases, whether or not a duty exists is clear; if there is any doubt, social workers should play it safe by erring on the side of caution and assuming that a professional duty is incurred as soon as any substantive interaction with a client has begun.

The second element requires that *the professional somehow failed to carry out his or her duty*. How do we know what that duty entails? We know that the duty involves acting consistently with the standard of care in the relevant profession. At one time, the expected standard of care depended in part on what was commonplace in the community where the professional was practicing. For example, a social worker in a rural community would be held to the standard of care expected of an ordinary, reasonable, prudent professional in the same community or in other rural communities where social workers have comparable access to training, technology, and treatment techniques (Swenson, 1997). However, advances in technology, including the Internet, have minimized disparities across communities. As a result, social workers are now invariably held to a broader national standard that encompasses the profession at large. To determine what that standard requires, courts examine relevant state laws as well as the profession's ethical guidelines—in our case, the NASW Code of Ethics. Standards for specific areas of practice may also be relevant. NASW has promulgated standards related to child welfare, palliative and end-of-life care, practice in long-term care facilities, adolescents, genetics, cultural competence, school social work, case management, family caregiving with older adults, clients with substance use disorders, technology, and practice in health care settings. Other organizations may also have relevant standards; examples include the Association for the Advancement of Social Work with Groups and the Child Welfare League of America. In addition to the standard of care derived from these professional ethical codes and standards, social workers are also held to any specific standard of care that is relevant to the school of thought or treatment modalities that characterize their practice. For example, a practitioner who provides play therapy or cognitive behavioral therapy can be held to the standard of care expected of professionals utilizing those specific treatment approaches (Shapiro & Smith, 2011).

If the standard of care is not entirely clear, the court will look at the process the professional engaged in before the action in question occurred: Did the social worker consult with colleagues? Obtain appropriate supervision? Review the relevant ethical standards, laws and policies, and scholarly literature? Properly document the decision-making process? Obtain legal advice? If the social worker took all reasonable, responsible steps before acting—even if the action taken turns out to have been a mistake—the court is unlikely to find a legal dereliction of duty.

Under the third element, ***the client has to have suffered harm or injury***. What qualifies as harm or injury? Physical injury is the most obvious, but the harm could also be emotional or financial. Emotional injury is, of course, the most difficult to prove. It is up to the client to demonstrate the existence of both the injury and its severity (Dickson, 1995; Reamer, 2003; Shapiro & Smith, 2011; Swenson, 1997).

The fourth element is that **the professional's negligence is the cause of the injury**. The client has to be able to show a direct link between what the provider did (or failed to do) and the harm or injury suffered by the client. This connection can be difficult to prove, in part because most social work clients are already experiencing emotional problems. If, for example, a social worker was treating a client with an eating disorder, and the client claimed that wrongful termination of her therapy caused her to stop eating, she would have to show that her condition was more acute after the termination than before; simply demonstrating that she had an eating disorder would be insufficient. In addition, as with all human behavior, any client experience can have multiple possible causes. Consider a client whose depression worsens following an unconventional treatment but whose spouse was struggling with a terminal illness during that same time. It might be difficult to make a case that it was the treatment—and not the spouse's condition—that caused the client's worsening depression. Finally, some other event may intervene between the time of the act in question and the onset of the harm. If a client saw other therapists after working with you but before the onset of the injury, for example, it would be difficult to show that it was your behavior, and not the behavior of another therapist, that directly and proximately caused the harm.

Remember that to prove malpractice all four of these elements must be substantiated. Malpractice is an excellent example of where ethics and law diverge: If the social worker acted in a way that failed to meet the standard of care, what he or she did would be unethical—but it does not constitute malpractice (a legal wrong) unless the behavior also caused demonstrable harm or injury to the client.

Going to Court

It is critical for social workers to be prepared to properly handle malpractice suits because legal liability is a risk routinely associated with social work practice. As professionals entrusted with people's well-being, no matter how scrupulous we are, there is always a possibility of being sued. Familiarity with the legal process is a must. In the event that you are sued for malpractice, the first step is to contact your insurance company, which will assign an attorney to your case. Even if your agency is insured, and even if it has legal counsel, it is better to have your own insurance coverage and to employ your own attorney. Never discuss the case with anyone other than your attorney, especially not your client, lest you admit guilt or make any incriminating statements that can be used against you (Houston-Vega, Nuehring, & Daguio, 1997). Always be candid with your lawyer; this will allow him or her to provide the strongest possible defense.

Most malpractice claims are filed in state courts (Shapiro & Smith, 2011). The client (plaintiff) who is claiming to have suffered a wrong at the hands of the social worker or other professional initiates the case. Every state has a *statute of limitations* that defines how long the client can wait before filing a lawsuit for malpractice. In Virginia, for example, the statute of limitations is 2 years from the date of injury; if the injury occurred while the client was a minor, the case must be filed within 2 years of reaching the age of majority. Although most states have statutes of limitations of 2 to 3 years, they range from 1 year in Tennessee to 10 years in Oregon.

In malpractice suits, as with other civil lawsuits, guilt must be proven by a *preponderance of the evidence*. As discussed in Chapter 1, this is the easiest threshold to meet; the client need only show that it is more likely than not that the social worker's negligence caused his or her injury (Shapiro & Smith, 2011; Swenson, 1997). The plaintiff ordinarily has the burden of proof. If, however, the provider's negligence appears obvious (e.g., the social worker had sex with a teenage client), the burden of proof shifts to the defendant, who must prove that he or she is innocent of the allegation.

If the client prevails in court, he or she is awarded *compensatory damages*. This refers to a monetary award equal to what it would take to make the client "whole" again, as if the wrongdoing had not occurred. For example, if a client is persuaded by the social worker to invest in a business the social worker owns and the client loses money, compensatory damages might reflect the amount of money invested plus lost interest. In rare and extreme cases, if the social worker's behavior rises to the level of being *reckless, malicious, or willful*, the client may be eligible for *punitive damages* as well. Punitive damages go beyond what is needed to compensate the victim for the provider's wrongdoing; instead, they are designed to express strong disapproval on the part of the court. For example, a California court of appeals awarded $6,000 in punitive damages (in addition to nearly $5 million in compensatory damages and $1 million in attorneys' fees) after the Orange

County Social Service Agency and two of its social workers used fabricated evidence to remove two children from their mother. The social workers lied in court and filed false reports, resulting in the children remaining separated from their mother for 6-1/2 years, despite the absence of any serious physical injury or imminent danger to the child (Court of Appeal, 2010).

Professional Review of Ethics Complaints

Although not acting in a legal capacity, NASW provides a forum for reviewing griev-ances alleging ethical transgressions by professional social workers. This process may be pursued instead of, or in addition to, the initiation of a malpractice suit. Its goal is to "promote the quality and effectiveness of social work practice and to protect the public from unprofessional, unfair, or unscrupulous conduct" (NASW, 2005a, p. x). This pro-fessional review process conducted by NASW can take the form of either *mediation* (in which a neutral third party assists in resolving the conflict) or *adjudication* (in which a panel determines whether a violation occurred and recommends corrective action or sanctions). In the event of adjudication, each side can make a statement, respond to questions from the panel, and question witnesses. If a violation is confirmed, conse-quences can include requiring additional training or supervision, ordering restitution, publishing the finding in the *NASW News*, suspending or expelling the violator from NASW membership, suspending or revoking an NASW-issued credential, notifying state regulatory or credentialing bodies, notifying the violator's malpractice insurer, or issuing of a letter of censure. In her review of 894 grievances filed with NASW over a 10-year period, Strom-Gottfried (2000) reported that 47.8% resulted in adjudication; of those, violations of the Code of Ethics were found in 62.3%. The most common complaints con-cerned boundary issues, primarily sexual contact with clients and dual social relation-ships. These were followed by complaints alleging a variety of types of inferior practice. Although the professional review process does not result in legal consequences, being brought up on ethics charges can have serious adverse implications for a social worker's reputation and practice.

Informed Consent

Practicing within the law requires that social workers consistently seek clients' informed consent before initiating treatment. Although it began in medicine, requiring informed consent is now accepted practice throughout the health, mental health, and substance abuse fields. Social workers must seek informed consent before a client undergoes volun-tary hospitalization or receives treatment including, for example, medication, restraints, electroconvulsive therapy (ECT), substance abuse treatment, or family planning services. You may also be familiar with informed consent requirements in relation to conducting research. Requiring informed consent is consistent with the social work value of client self-determination. The idea is that people should have the right to control what happens to them, including the type and extent of intervention they believe will advance their own best interests.

Legal Requirements of Consent

Informed consent is both an ethical and a legal obligation. In order to be valid, the following three conditions must be met:

1. The client must be competent to consent.
2. The consent must be voluntary.
3. The information provided must be adequate.

Let's consider each of these in turn. First, ***the client must be competent to consent***. Competence here has a specific legal meaning. Basically, the client must be capable of understanding the information provided, weighing its implications, and communicating his or her decision. All adults are presumed to be legally competent to consent unless a court has made a formal determination of incompetence because of age, intellectual disability, mental illness, and so on. Never assume that a client is incompetent; even a client moving in and out of lucidity may be competent to provide consent. Keep in mind, too, that a person can be legally competent for some purposes but not others; the same person, for example, could be competent to provide informed consent for treatment but not competent to stand trial in a criminal proceeding.

An important illustration of the issue of competency to consent is the U.S. Supreme Court case of *Zinermon v. Burch* (1990). Burch was found walking along the highway, injured and disoriented. He was taken to a mental health center where staff reported that he was bruised and bloodied, confused, psychotic, hallucinating, and believed he was in heaven. He was diagnosed with paranoid schizophrenia and given medication. Three days later, he was referred to a public hospital where he signed a voluntary admission form. After five months with no lawyer or hearing, he was released. He subsequently brought suit claiming that he'd been admitted and treated without ever having been competent to consent and that he should, under the circumstances, have been afforded the legal rights that attach to being hospitalized involuntarily. The Supreme Court agreed, concluding that hospitals must have a process in place for confirming competence to consent before a patient can be voluntarily admitted.

The second condition that must be met for consent to be valid is that ***the client's consent must be given voluntarily***. This is not always as simple as it sounds. Because of the power differential between the social worker and the client, there is always a risk of coercion. Our clients typically come to us when they are needy or in crisis; this makes them particularly vulnerable to influence. Low-income clients, for example, may be inclined to consent if treatment is predicated on receipt of a much-needed benefit. A 1974 class action suit against the U.S. Department of Health, Education and Welfare (now the Department of Health and Human Services) provides a shocking example. In that case (*Relf v. Weinberger*), low-income women were threatened with having their welfare benefits discontinued unless they submitted to tubal ligation (sterilization). The most popular targets were women giving birth who were receiving Medicaid. Pressure to consent can occur in more subtle ways. In one of my own research studies, youth who had recently aged out of foster care were provided with gift cards each time they completed an interview. I had to be very careful about how much the gift cards were worth (enough to compensate them fairly for their time, but not enough to "bribe" them to participate)—lest their consent not be entirely voluntary. Clients sometimes will provide consent because they think that is what the social worker wants—or that the social worker will somehow benefit from their participation in a particular treatment or intervention. Finally, a client may agree simply because he or she assumes that the social worker knows best. Because coercion can be subtle, if the social worker has any question about whether the client's consent is in fact totally voluntary, it is best to encourage the client to take his or her time reviewing the information provided before making a decision (Shapiro & Smith, 2011). It is also important for clients to understand that they are free to change their minds at any time, for any reason—or for no reason at all. Should this occur, be sure to document both the client's agreement and his or her revocation of consent.

Many social workers work with involuntary clients who are mandated to receive services, usually as the result of a court order. This occurs most often in the context of child abuse proceedings, criminal prosecutions, divorce proceedings, and domestic violence cases (Israel, 2011). Given that they are mandated to receive services, how can their participation ever be considered voluntary? If they consent to participate in treatment in order to avoid imprisonment or end litigation, isn't that coercive? In fact, because the court has the ultimate authority to make decisions regarding services for the client in cases of court-ordered treatment, the court is empowered to provide informed consent on the client's behalf.

The third condition that must be met for informed consent to be valid is that ***the information provided to the client must be adequate***. This goes to the "informed" part of "informed consent." Clearly, it is not necessary that the social worker provide every client with every possible shred of information about every possible treatment; there are limits to what must legally be shared. Where do we draw the line? The seminal case on this topic is *Sard v. Hardy* (1977). This was a medical case involving a woman who was pregnant for the third time. Her first child had died from complications and, although her second was born healthy, she was concerned about the possible risks and felt she could not afford to continue having children after this pregnancy. Her doctor agreed and recommended sterilization. On his advice, Sard underwent a tubal ligation in conjunction with her third Caesarian section. Despite the procedure, she subsequently became pregnant for a fourth time. She sued her doctor for failing to discuss any alternatives with her, for failing to advise her that the procedure might not be successful, and for failing to tell her of the increased risk of ineffectiveness when tubal ligations are performed at the time of C-section delivery.

In determining Dr. Hardy's legal obligation in regard to providing information, the Maryland Court of Appeals applied a legal test known as *materiality*. Under this test, one is required to share any and all information that is *material* to the client's decision—that is, anything that would be likely to influence whether or not the client chooses to consent. Most agree that this would include the nature and purpose of the treatment, probable risks, probable benefits, costs, potential effects on other people and on other life activities, and reasonable alternatives. Keep in mind that different facts may also be material to different clients. For example, the fact that a particular medication has been found to produce confusion in older adults would be material to an older adult but not to a younger person. Similarly, whereas a remote likelihood that a medication could cause significant weight gain might be material to a teenage girl on the cheerleading squad, the same likelihood might not be considered material to others.

Typically, we obtain informed consent by asking clients to sign a form. If social workers are taking their legal and ethical responsibilities seriously, they should never use a general, all-purpose form when seeking informed consent. Instead, the form should be as specific as possible and should use simple language that the client can understand. An example is shown in Figure 5.1. In addition to having the client read and sign a form,

FIGURE 5.1	Sample Informed Consent Form

UTSA

The Department of Counseling – Community Family Life Center

Informed Consent for Counseling

Instructions: Please enter your information into the appropriate fields, check boxes, or item lists. Once you have entered your information, you may save the data so it will appear the next time you open the form. Create a new name for your copy and save it on your computer.

STUDENT INFORMATION

Student Name:

Practicum / Internship Site:

Academic Degree:	Study Program:	Course:

SITE SUPERVISOR INFORMATION

Site Supervisor Name:	Title:
Phone:	Email:

UNIVERSITY SUPERVISOR INFORMATION

University Supervisor Name:	Title:
Phone:	Email:

INFORMED CONSENT

- **Introduction** – Please take time to read and understand this form. This informed consent document is intended to give you general information about my counseling services. If you have any questions about signing this document and/or would like a copy of this document, please ask me and I will provide you with this information. The Counseling Department at the University of Texas at San Antonio requires that I obtain your signature, acknowledging that I have provided you with this information, before I provide you with any professional services. Please understand that you may end this Agreement at any time.
- **Nature of Counseling** – There may be both benefits and risks while participating in counseling. Counseling may improve your ability to relate with others, provide a clearer understanding of yourself, your values, and your goals. Since counseling may also involve discussing unpleasant parts of your life, you may also experience uncomfortable feelings. Counseling often leads to better relationships, solutions to specific problems, and significant improvement in feelings of distress. Please understand that there are no guarantees of what you will experience.

  In your first session, I will provide you with some sense of what counseling will involve and how I will work with you to address your concerns. Whenever they arise, please discuss any questions you may have with me. You have the right to ask about or to decline any part of your counseling. You also have the right to request another counselor. You have the right to an explanation of any tests/questionnaires and you may decline participation at any time. You also have the right to a summary (which may be either verbal or written) of any test results.
- **Emergency** – In some instances, you might need immediate help at a time when I am unavailable or cannot return your call. These emergencies may involve thoughts of harming yourself or others, or thoughts

of committing dangerous acts. If you find yourself in any emergency situation, please contact the site or university information listed on this form. If, for whatever reason, that option is not available to you, please visit the nearest hospital emergency room.

- **Supervision** – You have the right to know the name of my supervisor(s) and how to contact her or him. Because of my training, my supervisor may ask about our counseling for confidential supervisory and train ing purposes. Occasionally, I may find it helpful to consult with other professional staff about a case. If you don't object, I will not tell you about these consultations unless I feel that it is important for our work together. I will note all consultations in my clinical notes.
- **Confidentiality** – The law protects the privacy of all communications between a client and a counselor. In most situations, I can only release information about our professional relationship if you sign a written authorization form.
- **Limits of Confidentiality** – There are some situations in which I am legally obligated to take actions that I believe may be necessary to protect you or others from harm. If such a situation arises, I will make every effort to fully discuss it with you before taking any action and will limit disclosure to what is necessary.
  - If I have reason to believe that a child or vulnerable adult is being neglected or abused, the law requires that the situation be reported to the appropriate state agency.
  - If I believe you present a clear and substantial danger of harm to yourself or another/others, I am ethi- cally obligated to take protective actions.

These actions may include contacting family members, seeking hospitalization for you, notifying any po- tential victim(s), and notifying the police. While this summary is designed to provide an overview of confi- dentiality and its limits, please let me know of any questions or concerns you may have.

- **Statement of Acknowledgement** – I have read and understand the statement and have had the opportu- nity to discuss it before revealing personal information about myself.

SIGNATURES		
Client's Signature	Printed	Date
Signature of Parent/Guardian (if client is under 18)	Printed	Date
Student Counselor's Signature	Printed	Date
Site Supervisor's Signature	Printed	Date

Source: Informed Consent for Counseling form. Reprinted with permission of the UTSA Community Family Life Center.

social workers should discuss the content with the client. Informed consent is a process—a dialogue—that includes information sharing, conversation, questions, and answers. Although courts have upheld signed forms as evidence of informed consent when a competent client was afforded the opportunity to ask questions, courts have rejected them when it is clear that no real understanding occurred. In *Sard v. Hardy*, for example, Mr. Sard signed the consent form despite being functionally illiterate and Mrs. Sard signed the form without reading it, while being rushed into surgery. Remember that clients' understanding and ex- pectations may vary depending on their cultural background and linguistic competence; it is the practitioner's responsibility to provide whatever assistance is necessary to ensure that the client indeed understands the information given. Most of us know, from our own experience, the value of discussing proposed medications, treatments, or interventions with health or mental health care providers. It is not unusual for people to sign a consent form without actually reading it all the way through—or to feel pressured to just sign it and move on. Most of us would probably find ourselves attending more closely to a conversation with the practitioner than to a written form. The bottom line here is to facilitate self-determination on the part of the client, whatever that entails. The social worker should always be able to document what information was provided, why it was adequate, and why a decision was made to withhold any information not shared with the client. Likewise, if the client refuses or withdraws consent, it is important to discuss any possible adverse consequences and ask him or her to sign a release in which the client assumes responsibility for his or her decision.

Substituted Judgment

As discussed previously, informed consent cannot be legally valid unless the client is competent to provide consent. There are, however, those who lack the ability to participate in the decision-making process as a result of their physical or mental condition. When this is the case, a court-ordered guardian (often a spouse or relative who holds the client's *health care proxy*) assumes responsibility for providing informed consent on their behalf. This is known as *substituted judgment* or *consent by proxy*. The trick here is that whoever has legal decision-making authority must make the decision he or she believes the client would make, if able—rather than what he or she believes is best. For example, if a client was known to have stated when she was competent that she was opposed to taking psychotropic medications, then substituted judgment would require her proxy to refuse psychotropic medications on her behalf—even if the psychiatrist and family members insist that they are necessary for the client's benefit. Social workers have a professional obligation to ensure that the guardian acts in a manner consistent with the client's wishes (NASW, 2008). In an excruciating case called *In re A.C.* (1990), a pregnant woman was dying of cancer. According to her doctors, delivering the fetus would precipitate the mother's death, whereas letting the pregnancy continue would jeopardize the survival of the fetus. The mother was too ill to be capable of making an informed decision. The hospital sought guidance from the court. Without ever making a determination of the mother's competency or seeking to determine what cause of action she would likely have preferred, the court ordered a caesarian section. Sadly, the fetus died 2-1/2 hours after the procedure was performed and the mother died 2 days later. The D.C. Court of Appeals later ruled that the trial court had erred in not using substituted judgment.

How exactly should one go about determining what decision an incompetent client would have made? If a client moves in and out of lucidity—and therefore is sometimes competent and sometimes not—substituted judgment should be suspended in favor of decisions made by the client while competent. For those who are consistently incompetent, determining their wishes is easiest if they have committed them to writing in the form of a living will, advance directive (see discussion in Chapter 10), or mental health advance directive (see Chapter 15). Absent that, one should look at the client's previous treatment decisions, any previous statements made by the client about his or her wishes, and evidence of the client's personal values. Although this is unquestionably the ethical course to take, it is less clear that these indicators amount to legally sufficient evidence. In 1990, the U.S. Supreme Court considered the case of Nancy Cruzan (*Cruzan v. Missouri Department of Health*), an accident victim in a persistent vegetative state. Her parents sought to remove her feeding tube; the court intervened and denied the request. The Supreme Court, in reviewing the lower court's decision, concluded that there was insufficient evidence that Nancy would have consented to the removal of the feeding tube. It reached this conclusion despite that fact that Nancy had told her roommate the previous year that she would never want to live as a "vegetable." In addition, her family and friends believed that she would want the feeding tube removed, and the *guardian ad litem* representing her interests concurred. An outraged, four-justice minority of the Court asserted that the decision should rest with the family and that the state's role should be limited to ensuring that whoever makes the decision on the patient's behalf is someone with proper motives whom the patient would have selected.

What about when it truly is impossible to determine whether or not the client would have consented, if competent? Suppose there simply is no clear indication on which to rely? In those cases, the courts suggest going with the decision that most people would make in a similar situation. Even if a client is incompetent and unable to consent, social workers are advised to discuss the treatment with the client so he or she has the best possible understanding of what to expect (Dolgoff et al., 2009; NASW, 2008). Because informed consent is an ongoing process, any changes to the treatment must be approved by the client (if competent) or by the proxy before being implemented (Davis et al., 2003).

Exceptions to Informed Consent

The requirement that informed consent be obtained before treatment or services are initiated has several accepted exceptions. The first is a *waiver*. Because the right to informed consent belongs to the client, the client can choose to waive informed consent. This might occur when the client prefers not to know all the facts—or simply trusts the provider to do what is best. Should this happen, the social worker needs to encourage the client to discuss the situation and make an informed decision; if the client continues to decline, the social worker should explain the possible consequences of waiving informed consent, document the conversation, and have the client sign a written disclaimer.

Second, the requirement for informed consent can be suspended in the case of an *emergency*. This is only applicable when the client is unable to make an informed decision and limited treatment is urgently necessary to save the client's life or health or to protect others from harm.

The third exception is *incapacity*, when the client is incapable of providing informed consent because of mental disability or age. Minors generally are not considered capable of giving informed consent, in which case the consent of a parent or legal guardian is required. However, state laws vary on this issue. Some states allow exceptions for specific types of treatment. Oregon and Minnesota, for example, allow minors to access medical or mental health services related to pregnancy, sexually transmitted infections, and substance abuse (Minnesota Coalition against Sexual Assault, 2010; Oregon Health Authority, 2011). Virginia also allows minors to consent to services involving the prevention, diagnosis, and treatment of mental illness or emotional disturbance (Code of Virginia, § 54.1-2969 [E]). In Rhode Island, minors may only consent to substance abuse services if a physician determines that requiring parental consent would be deleterious to treatment; in Maine, only minors who are emancipated, married, or in the Armed Forces may consent to mental health treatment (NASW, 2007).

A final exception to the requirement for informed consent is *therapeutic privilege*, which means that it is permissible to dispense with informed consent if disclosure of all the facts would have a substantially negative impact on the physical or psychological well-being of the client, or render the client unable to make a rational decision. The exception was developed as a way to reconcile the doctrine of informed consent with the physician's duty to "do no harm." Not surprisingly, this exception is highly controversial; many observers regard it with skepticism, maintaining that any practice that compromises the client's right to self-determination is inadvisable.

Confidentiality and Privilege

Understanding confidentiality is essential to practicing within the law and is especially important because breach of this client right is one of the most common types of malpractice by social workers. The concepts of privacy, confidentiality, and privilege are related but distinct. *Privacy* refers to the right to be left alone or to refrain from sharing information. *Confidentiality* is the right not to have private information shared with a third party (someone other than the social worker). *Privilege*, a subcategory of confidentiality, is the client's right not to have confidential information shared in legal proceedings (NASW, 2004).

    Confidentiality is the cornerstone of an effective therapeutic relationship between social worker and client, as well as one of the key ethical precepts of the social work profession (Houston-Vega et al., 1997; NASW, 2004). Social workers have both an ethical and a legal duty to protect client confidentiality. In order for a client to truly benefit from social work services, it is often necessary for him or her to share intimate life details. Clients need to be able to trust that the information they share with their social worker will not be shared with others. Therefore, confidentiality can be considered a "prerequisite for effective practice" (Macarov, 1990, p. 70). The NASW Code of Ethics first specifically addressed confidentiality in 1979. The revised Code, adopted in 1996 and revised in 2008, more than tripled the number of provisions relating to confidentiality. The bottom line is that "social workers should protect confidentiality of all information obtained in the course of professional service, except for compelling professional reasons" (NASW, 2008, Sec. 1.07 [c]).

    What exactly is within the scope of the right to confidentiality? According to NASW (2004), a social worker cannot disclose "any information related to the fact that an individual has sought mental health services" (p. 4), including the fact that the person is, or has been, in treatment; any communications made by the client during treatment; observations by the therapist; the results of psychological or laboratory tests; diagnostic information; and prognosis. Confidentiality covers both oral communication and documents containing client-related information, regardless of whether they are in hard copy or electronic format (Dickson, 1995). The right to confidentiality even survives the client's death (Reamer, 2003). In addition to the guidelines provided in the NASW Code of Ethics, each state's law contains a definition of client confidentiality in that state. Social workers should be familiar with both the laws in their state and the Code of Ethics.

Intentional Disclosure of Confidential Information

Despite its critical role in the social worker–client relationship, confidentiality is not absolute; there are exceptional situations in which social workers may be required or permitted to divulge confidential information. All states define some circumstances under which client confidentiality can legally be breached in order to protect the client or members of the public. The scope of these exceptions is one factor that distinguishes social work ethics from legal ethics (as discussed in Chapter 1). When client information is disclosed without the client's consent, it is advisable to document the facts and circumstances surrounding the disclosure and the ethical and legal grounds that led to the decision to breach client confidentiality (NASW, 2004). Even when the law requires disclosure of confidential information, social workers must make every effort to protect the client by releasing the least amount of information necessary (Houston-Vega et al., 1997).

Although the legal exceptions to confidentiality vary by state, the following discussion addresses those that are most common. Again, not all of these are recognized by all states. Be sure to find out what state law allows or requires in the state where you are practicing.

Duty to warn

All states permit client confidentiality to be breached in order to save a third party from harm. These laws derive from *Tarasoff v. Board of Regents of the University of California* (1976). That case concerned a young man from India, Prosenjit Poddar, who was studying naval architecture at the University of California, Berkeley. He became interested in a young woman named Tatiana Tarasoff. She, however, rejected him. He subsequently became depressed and sought counseling, confiding to the treating psychologist that he intended to kill Tatiana. After consulting with two psychiatrists, the psychologist notified campus police with the intention of having Poddar committed for observation. After briefly detaining him and searching his apartment, however, the police released him. Two months later, after discontinuing therapy, Poddar killed Tatiana. Her parents filed suit against the psychologist and others at the university. The lower courts concluded that although therapists owe a duty of care to their clients, no such duty is owed to third parties. The California Supreme Court disagreed, articulating for the first time a duty on the part of mental health providers to protect someone other than the client—even though that may mean divulging the client's confidential communication. Although the *Tarasoff* case technically applies only in California, all states have carved out some sort of duty to warn. The specifics of these laws vary somewhat, but a duty to warn is typically triggered when the following four elements are present:

1. The client poses a threat of violence to a third party.
2. The violent act is foreseeable.
3. The violent act is imminent.
4. It is possible to identify the probable victim.

Remember that for there to be a duty to warn, all four elements must be met (depending on the state's law). For an element to be met, the social worker must have some actual evidence to support the determination. The whole idea is to limit disclosure to only those situations in which it is truly warranted so that client confidentiality can be protected unless absolutely necessary.

The first element, *a threat of violence*, is self-explanatory. The client communicates intent to harm someone else. The second element, *foreseeability*, refers to there being a significant likelihood that the violent act will in fact occur. Evidence of foreseeability typically includes having access to a weapon or having a clear plan of action. The idea here is to be reasonably sure that this was more than an idle threat or a client venting or letting off steam. Imagine if therapists rushed out to breach confidentiality every time a client expressed frustration or anger by saying, in passing, "I'm going to kill her." The third element, *imminence*, refers to the likelihood that the act will occur relatively soon. Again, the point is to help the therapist distinguish between real and hypothetical danger to a third party. A threat to kill one's father "someday" is not the same as a threat to kill him "on my way home from work tomorrow night." Finally, the fourth element is ***identifying the probable victim***. This can be done through explicit reference (the client names the intended target) or by inference (the therapist can figure out the intended target even though he or she was not explicitly named). In the *Tarasoff* case, for example, Poddar didn't actually name Tatiana—but her identity was clear to the treating psychologist. Some states have rejected or reinterpreted this final element. The sample case at the end of this chapter, *Hamman v. County of Maricopa*, provides an example.

As mentioned previously, the parameters of the duty to warn vary by state. Twenty-two states (including Delaware, Kentucky, Michigan, New Hampshire, and Utah) have an actual, affirmative duty to warn. Another 17 (including Florida, Missouri, Oregon, and Texas) permit, but do not require, therapists to warn third parties. The remaining states (including Nevada, North Carolina, and Wisconsin) do not address the duty to warn by statute, but in some of them a duty to warn has been established by the courts (NASW, 2008b).

Although the duty to warn is by now well established across the country, it continues to engender uncertainty and controversy. Despite a plethora of statutes, judicial opinions, and ethical guidelines, ambiguous situations arise that require social workers and other professionals to make a judgment call. For example, what constitutes a threat of violence? The same communication by a client might be regarded as a threat by one therapist but not another (Reamer, 1991). And if the comment made by a client is in fact perceived to be a threat, how far must a therapist go to adequately protect the intended target? In *Tarasoff*, the psychologist notified campus police but the court found that insufficient. The language of the opinion merely says that "when a therapist determines, or should determine, that his patient presents a serious danger of violence to another, he incurs an obligation to use reasonable care to protect the intended victim against such danger." What constitutes "reasonable care"? Was the psychologist obligated to warn Tatiana? Or notify her parents? Should he have involved the local police rather than the campus police? Or taken additional steps to have Poddar committed? The lack of clear guidelines leaves considerable room for interpretation, often making it unclear whether or not confidentiality should be breached. As in every instance of ethical uncertainty, social workers should seek advice from supervisors and colleagues; it would also be prudent to consult with an attorney. Be sure to document the process undertaken in making a determination, including the reasons for doing what you did.

Duty to protect a client from self-harm

Much like the duty to warn, the therapist's duty to protect clients from self-harm also requires balancing the importance of preserving confidentiality against keeping someone safe. The most common situation involving a duty to protect is suicide. The conditions that justify warning a third party of the threat of violence (the *Tarasoff* criteria) are generally used to determine whether there is a duty to protect a client who is threatening harm to him or herself. Although the presence of an imminent threat is necessary, foreseeability of the suicide is often the key variable in determining whether the situation warrants breaching confidentiality. If a client expresses suicidal intent and appears to have a concrete plan, including access to a weapon, a breach of confidentiality may be necessary to prevent harm to the client. The situation may require contact with other professionals or the client's family, or involuntary commitment (NASW, 2004). As always, it is important to become familiar with the laws in your specific state and to document your decision-making process.

Duty to report suspected abuse

As discussed further in Chapters 6 and 10, respectively, social workers are mandated reporters of suspected child maltreatment and in many states of suspected elder abuse. Confidentiality can be breached in these circumstances because protecting those who are vulnerable and unable to protect themselves is considered more important than protecting a client's privacy. Clients should be advised of these exceptions to their right to confidentiality at the onset of any therapeutic relationship.

Duty to report a client's HIV status

Controversy and ambiguity surround a therapist's duty to report a client's HIV or AIDS status to sexual partners. Many states do not have legislation that directly addresses whether such reporting is required or permissible. Those states that do address the issue do so in a variety of ways. In California and Utah, notifying a client's sexual and needle-sharing partners is required; in Georgia, only the client's spouse must be notified. Massachusetts and New Mexico have no specific provisions regarding the notification of sexual partners, whereas laws in Pennsylvania and Rhode Island explicitly indicate that no notification is required (National HIV/AIDS Clinicians' Consultation Center, 2011). Some argue that the same principles that justify the duty to warn apply equally to the necessity of reporting a client's HIV status; others argue that reporting will only encourage discrimination against people with HIV and AIDS (Reamer, 1991). This issue is discussed further in Chapter 14.

When no clear guidelines exist, social workers must make difficult choices about whether or not to breach client confidentiality. However, social workers can take steps to minimize the risk of liability. According to Houston-Vega et al., "The decision to intentionally breach confidentiality must be based on an accurate assessment of all the facts surrounding a particular situation and the ability to articulate a statutory or ethical basis for the breach" (1997, p. 23). Consulting an attorney who is familiar with state confidentiality law is a good starting point for making an informed decision. Sometimes a potentially difficult situation can be avoided by involving the client in the process, as long as doing so poses no additional risk. For example, a social worker might ask the client for permission to warn a potential victim—or have the client voluntarily notify a sexual partner of his or her HIV status. Social workers can protect themselves by consulting with colleagues, seeking supervision, referencing relevant laws and ethical guidelines, and documenting their decision-making process and rationale (Reamer, 2003).

Unintentional Disclosure of Confidential Information

In addition to situations in which confidential information is deliberately breached, there are instances in which it is breached inadvertently due to carelessness. To preserve confidentiality of client information and minimize malpractice risk, it is important to be cognizant of how we are handling confidential material. Client information that is generated, transmitted, or stored electronically should be secured with passwords or special software. It is good practice to log off or lock the computer when leaving the room and to avoid leaving client files in plain sight. Any client-related files that are saved onto portable media such as disks, external hard drives, or flash drives should be secured in a location with restricted access. Hard copies of documents should be stored in a locked, fireproof file cabinet in or near your office. When faxing confidential information, call the recipient before sending the documents to ensure that they can be retrieved immediately. Be careful not to leave confidential documents in Xerox machines or wastebaskets; shred any materials you intend to discard. Confidential conversations should take place in a setting where privacy is reasonably expected (NASW, 2004). For example, if a client happens to run into you in the restroom or elevator and starts to discuss his or her treatment plan, encourage the client to delay the conversation until you are in the privacy of a room or office. When you are with the client in the presence of others, the client's name should not be used. Never discuss a client or client issue where you can be overheard. If you need to review a client's file before a session, do so in your office rather than in a public space where people may be walking by. Use the telephone to discuss confidential information only in emergency situations. Avoid leaving messages on answering machines, voice mail, or cell phones. Retrieve and erase your own messages promptly.

Inadvertent breaches of confidentiality can be easily avoided if you pay attention to your surroundings and take your client's right to privacy seriously. It is also important to be clear about who is entitled to client information, both within and outside the agency. To be safe, never share information outside the agency without the client's consent. Inside the agency, information should be shared only on a genuine need-to-know basis. Your clients should have a full understanding of what your policies are regarding the sharing of information.

Confidentiality with Minors

As do adults, minors have a right to confidentiality. Because their legal status differs from that of adults, however, the scope of that right varies from state to state depending on the specific context. In states where minors are entitled to receive health or mental health services without parental consent, they are typically afforded the right to control access to their client information. On the other hand, in states where parental consent is required for a minor to engage in treatment, the child's information can be shared with the parent. Although this holds as a general rule, individual states have their differences. In certain situations, social workers will invariably have to use their best judgment in deciding whether to share a minor's private communications. If the state statute does not specify whether a minor has the right to confidentiality, it is usually advisable to share information with the parent or guardian unless doing so would be harmful to the client. As with any other controversial decision, it is important to document your rationale.

Privileged Communications

If confidential communication is *privileged*, it is protected from disclosure in legal proceedings. Privilege is actually an exception to the general rule that all testimony should be allowed, because it is through testimony that the truth emerges and justice is served. Because withholding information in court potentially undermines justice, privilege is accorded only to those special relationships in which the ability to share private information without the risk of disclosure is considered essential. You are probably familiar with some forms of privilege already, including the attorney-client privilege, spousal privilege, and clergy (or "priest-penitent") privilege. Licensed social workers in federal court were accorded privilege through the 1996 U.S. Supreme Court decision in *Jaffee v. Redmond.*

The right to privilege belongs to the client and is designed to allow the social worker to uphold the client's best therapeutic interests. State laws, however, determine whether communication between social workers and their clients is or is not considered privileged in state court proceedings. Twenty-one states, including Arkansas, Idaho, and Maine, expressly extend privilege to social workers. Other states, such as Arizona, Florida, and Louisiana, extend privilege to mental health professionals broadly, a category that includes social workers. Three states (Alaska, North Dakota, and Oklahoma) specifically exclude social workers in client privilege laws, and four states (Alabama, Hawaii, Pennsylvania, and Wyoming) have no general statutory provision on privilege or have not had the opportunity to adjudicate the issue (NASW, 2004). As with confidentiality, there are legal exceptions to privilege. Some common examples include the following: The client waives privilege; the client is suing his or her therapist; the client threatens a criminal act; the client threatens to commit suicide; or the therapist suspects child maltreatment (Albert, 2000). Social workers should be familiar with state laws regarding privilege that apply to them and should consult with an attorney if they have questions about a specific situation.

As mentioned previously, the most important legal decision regarding social workers and privileged communication is *Jaffee v. Redmond* (1996). In that 6–2 decision, the U.S. Supreme Court concluded that communications with licensed social workers in the context of psychotherapy are privileged under the Federal Rules of Evidence. The case involved a police officer, Mary Lu Redmond, who shot and killed a man named Ricky Allen when she responded to a "fight in progress" call. Redmond was subsequently sued by Allen's family, which alleged that she had used excessive force. After discovering that Redmond had received counseling after the shooting, Allen's attorney sought access to the statements Redmond had made to her therapist, a licensed clinical social worker. The social worker refused to relinquish her notes, claiming that they were privileged. The district court rejected the social worker's argument but the court of appeals reversed, recognizing a psychotherapist privilege applicable to licensed social workers. The U.S. Supreme Court affirmed. In reaching its decision, the Court emphasized the importance of a trusting relationship for psychotherapy to be effective. It also found that a psychotherapist privilege serves the public interest by making it more likely that those who need mental health treatment receive it. The Court noted that all 50 states and the District of Columbia already had adopted some form of psychotherapist privilege and that social workers provide a significant portion of the country's mental health treatment. Finally, the Court concluded that little benefit would accrue from *not* recognizing the privilege. In the absence of privilege, the Court reasoned, people would be less likely to share information in the first place—thus limiting the very existence of the kinds of information being sought.

In a biting dissent, Justice Scalia took issue with the notion of a psychotherapist privilege, suggesting that the majority of the Court overstated its importance: "Ask the average citizen: Would your mental health be more significantly impaired by preventing you from seeing a psychotherapist, or by preventing you from getting advice from your mom? . . . Yet there is no mother-child privilege" (p. 22). As for extending the privilege to social workers, he suggested that their training lacks rigor when compared to that of other professional groups including attorneys, psychiatrists, and psychologists: "Does a social worker bring to bear at least a significantly heightened degree of skill—more than a minister or rabbi, for example? I have no idea, and neither does the Court" (p. 28). Even so, the *Jaffee* decision unquestionably represents a major success for the social work profession. It places social workers on a par with other mental health professionals and recognizes, at the highest level, the importance of the confidential services that social workers provide.

The Treatment Process

Social work practice is fraught with risks. Although we do our best, we sometimes make mistakes. In addition to violating confidentiality (discussed earlier), many of these errors involve faulty assessment, treatment, or termination. Being aware of the risks we face, and embracing strategies to address them, is an important part of competent practice. Even simple mistakes can have profound consequences for vulnerable clients.

Proper Assessment and Diagnosis

Assessments can be faulty for several reasons. The social worker might fail to identify a presenting problem and consequently neglect to provide diagnosis or treatment. Alternatively, an assessment that is not sufficiently thorough could result in an inaccurate diagnosis. Finally, a proper assessment could result in an improper diagnosis because the social worker has misinterpreted the data or relied on faulty assumptions. Improper assessments and inaccurate diagnoses can be extremely harmful to clients because it is these procedures that determine the course of treatment. Failing to recognize a problem, or improperly diagnosing the problem, can result in the wrong intervention being applied. This, in turn, can result in ineffective treatment or treatment that is actually detrimental to the client's well-being. As always, the law does not require perfection; it requires, however, that our assessment, diagnosis, and treatment procedures conform to professional standards of care.

Perhaps the most challenging issues around proper assessment and diagnosis arise with clients at risk of suicide. Although the law does not expect social workers to be able to accurately predict every suicide, social workers are expected to adequately assess suicide risk and to take reasonable precautions to protect the client from self-harm (Reamer, 2003). Social workers should determine whether the client's situation poses an emergency risk (client is likely to commit suicide within the next 24 hours) or a long-term risk (client is likely to commit suicide within the next 2 years) and respond accordingly (Houston-Vega et al., 1997).

A comprehensive assessment for suicide risk would include the following steps (Jacobs, 2003):

- Conduct a thorough biopsychosocial assessment.
- Identify risk factors and protective factors.
- Ask directly about suicidal intent.
- Determine the level of suicide risk.
- Document the results of the assessment.

The ***biopsychosocial assessment*** should involve: (1) identifying the presence of mental illness (e.g., depression, schizophrenia, personality disorder, or substance abuse), (2) identifying any personal or family history of physical and/or mental illness (including prior instances of self-harm, suicide attempts, or history of mental illness), (3) identifying the client's personal strengths (including coping skills) and vulnerabilities, (4) understanding the client's psychosocial situation (including both stressors and supports), and (5) identifying specific symptoms of suicidality (including plans, behaviors, or intent on the one hand, and reasons for living on the other).

In addition to understanding the client's history and circumstances by performing a biopsychosocial assessment, examining risk and protective factors can aid social workers in determining the likelihood of suicide. **Risk factors** (those associated with an increased likelihood of suicide) include being male, unmarried, an older adult, or Caucasian; being unemployed, socially isolated, or having low socioeconomic status; having a mental illness, physical illness, or substance abuse issue; feeling hopeless or anxious, having low self-esteem; being impulsive or aggressive; having previously attempted suicide; engaging in black-and-white thinking; having survived childhood abuse, neglect, or loss; and having a family history of suicide, abuse, or mental illness. After identifying the presence of risk factors, the social worker should separate out those that are amenable to change from those that are not. For example, it would be impossible to modify a client's family history of abuse; it might, however, be possible to address the client's feelings of hopelessness or lessen the client's anxiety. Separating out those factors that can potentially be modified can help inform a treatment plan for reducing suicide risk.

Protective factors (those factors that have been found to reduce the risk of suicide) include being pregnant or having children at home, having strong religious beliefs, possessing positive coping skills, having access to an array of social supports, and enjoying a positive therapeutic relationship with the social worker. As always, identifying strengths allows the social worker to consider a treatment plan that will build on both the personal assets of the client and those that reside in the client's environment.

It is commonplace for the social worker to engage in **direct suicide inquiry** with the client. During this phase of the assessment, the social worker asks the client about his or her intent, taking note of any ambivalence; suicidal ideation, including its intensity, frequency, and lethality; and whether the client has rehearsed the suicide in any way. It is also important to ask about the existence of a concrete suicide plan, including identification of a time, place, and method; access to a weapon or other means; and the presence or absence of a suicide note. Some observers have cast doubt on the effectiveness of direct inquiry in accurately assessing suicide risk. Most agree, however, that it can be useful as one element in a more comprehensive assessment process (Jacobs & Brewer, 2004).

In **determining the level of risk**, the social worker should consider the results of the direct inquiry together with the clinical assessment and any risk or protective factors identified. Before reaching a conclusion, it is advisable to seek consultation or supervision if any questions remain. Because the risk of suicide can wax and wane over time, it is important to reevaluate the client's suicide risk at regular intervals. In terms of malpractice risk, **documentation** is critical because it can help substantiate that the social worker practiced according to the standard of care. Documentation should address the level of risk, the evidence on which this conclusion is based, and the treatment plan the social worker recommends for reducing the level of risk. It is especially important to document whether the client has access to a firearm and any instructions provided as a result. Documentation should occur at the time of initial intake and after every subsequent reevaluation.

A number of instruments have been developed for the purpose of assessing suicide risk. These include the Beck Hopelessness Scale, Beck Depression Inventory, Scale for

Suicide Ideation-Worst Point, Lifetime Parasuicidal Count, Linehan Reasons for Living Scale, Suicide Potential Lethality Scale, and SAD PERSONS Scale (Roberts et al., 2008). To look at one example, SAD PERSONS is an acronym for 10 major risk factors that predict the possibility of suicide: *S*ex, *A*ge, *D*epression, *P*revious attempt, *E*thanol (alcohol) abuse, *R*ational thinking loss, *S*ocial supports lacking, *O*rganized plan, *N*o spouse, and *S*ickness. For each risk factor that is present, a point is scored, and the risk for suicide is assessed on a scale from 1 to 10. Recommendations for action are also available based on the score. The scale is intended to be used in conjunction with a direct suicide inquiry, a psychosocial evaluation, and an identification of factors in the client's life that might help prevent suicide (Patterson, Dohn, Bird, & Patterson, 1983).

Much has been written about the details of assessing suicide risk among clients. The previous discussion is meant only to provide an introductory overview. Before practicing with potentially suicidal clients, it is important to read the current literature, participate in relevant continuing education and training, obtain proper supervision, and consult with experienced colleagues. A social worker cannot be held responsible for a client's suicide if proper assessment and diagnostic steps were taken. It is only if the suicide was reasonably foreseeable—in other words, the social worker ignored or missed obvious clinical signs of suicidality—that liability for malpractice may attach.

Proper Treatment

The basic legal question in terms of proper treatment is whether the social worker's intervention was consistent with the standard of care in the profession. Negligent treatment can arise from mistreating a client, using a technique for which one is inadequately trained, engaging in a nontraditional intervention that lacks an evidence base, or practicing outside the bounds of the profession.

As mentioned previously, a status differential exists between a social worker and a client. The social worker is the well-educated professional whom vulnerable clients depend upon for their safety and well-being. This imbalance can sometimes lead to social workers taking advantage of clients. The exploitation can be as blatant as beating a client, having sex with a client, or persuading a client to leave the social worker money in his or her will. It can also happen in more subtle ways. Seemingly harmless acts such as getting together with a client socially or providing a comforting touch can open the door to exploitation. This is why avoiding dual relationships is so important. Entering into a business deal with a client, hiring a client's family member, or dating a client's friend can confuse the therapeutic relationship, interfere with the social worker's judgment, and jeopardize the success of treatment efforts. Social workers need to be vigilant about avoiding any behavior that could result in taking advantage of a client or in undermining the therapeutic process.

Social workers might be tempted to use new techniques without the proper training. This is both ethically and legally risky, as well as potentially damaging to the client. One of the approaches being used in cases of post-traumatic stress disorder is eye movement desensitization and reprocessing (EMDR). Simply put, EMDR involves recalling traumatic memories while tracking an object from side to side with your eyes. Of course, it is much more complicated than that; the actual protocol involves a detailed eight-phase process (EMDR Institute, 2011). Conducting EMDR requires specialized skill and training.

Because of the intense nature of the subject matter involved, conducting EMDR without the necessary training can result in harm to clients with specific vulnerabilities including pregnancy, heart problems, eye problems, and certain other mental or physical conditions. A social worker who treats a client using EMDR but who failed to receive proper training could be subject to a charge of malpractice.

Nontraditional interventions should also be avoided. In an extreme example (*Cool v. Olson,* 1997), a longtime patient sued a Wisconsin psychiatrist for convincing her that she had multiple personalities (including angels and a duck), implanting false memories of childhood abuse (including eating babies and having sex with animals), and performing an exorcism to rid her of her demons. His insurance company also sued the doctor after he submitted claims totaling $300,000 for group therapy, claiming he was counseling Ms. Cool's 126 personalities. In the end, the case settled for $2.4 million. Although the use of nontraditional practices such as exorcism is relatively rare, it is important to be knowledgeable about the proven effectiveness of various treatment modalities. The developing emphasis on evidence-based practice provides social workers with an important tool in identifying interventions that can be used with maximum efficacy and minimum risk. Keeping up with the literature is important; using techniques that are known to be safe and effective is the best route to take.

Practicing or giving advice outside the bounds of one's profession can also constitute improper treatment. Social workers, for example, should never give legal advice. Nor should they prescribe medication. We are legally and ethically bound to limit our practice to those areas within the recognized sphere of our professional expertise. Failing to do so can have serious adverse consequences for our clients. Even within a social work practice, if a client exhibits problems that exceed our expertise, it is important to refer them to others who can offer them the required degree of competence (Saltzman & Furman, 1999).

Earlier in the chapter, we discussed the difficulties inherent in assessing clients for suicide risk. It should not go unmentioned that proper treatment includes the proper supervision and monitoring of those deemed suicidal. Legally, a social worker can be liable for a client's suicide only if the suicide could reasonably have been prevented. Once a proper assessment and diagnosis have been made and a client is found to be at risk of suicide, a range of options may be employed to protect the client, including the following:

- Increasing the frequency of therapy sessions
- Contacting the client by telephone between appointments
- Having the client sign a safety contract
- Referring the client for a medication evaluation
- Notifying the client's family or friends
- Taking steps to detain or hospitalize the client

Expectations in inpatient settings are generally more stringent than those in outpatient settings because mental health professionals are thought to be in a position to exercise greater control over those confined to inpatient facilities. In any case, when professionals know or should have known of a suicide risk, they have a legal duty to take reasonable steps to ensure the client's safety. It is critical to document your actions along with your decision-making process and rationale. It is also important to be familiar with your agency's policies on working with suicidal clients as well as state laws regarding duty to warn, duty to protect, and civil commitment.

E-THERAPY

The confluence of mental health and electronic communication is becoming more common and more complex as the technological age continues to advance. In 2004, 23% of Internet users searched for information online regarding stress, anxiety, depression, and other mental health issues (Fox, 2005). Websites offering e-therapy have also proliferated. E-therapy can involve both self-guided online sites and online counseling with a qualified mental health professional. In the latter case, therapy is conducted via email, video conferencing, or chat; the use of Skype, in particular, has become increasingly popular (Strong, 2010). "Over the past ten years, the use of the Internet for the provision of mental health (and health) education, advice, and treatment, has skyrocketed" (Deardorff, 2010). Given that, it is important for practitioners and clients to be aware of both the benefits and the risks of participating in Internet-based mental health treatment. Although there is little high-quality, evidence-based research on the effectiveness of e-therapy (Postel, deHaan, & DeJong, 2008), it has numerous supporters who tout its benefits. Anecdotal accounts suggest that some clients find e-therapy less stressful and more convenient than face-to-face sessions. Clients who might otherwise be intimidated by the prospect of therapy are more inclined to seek help. Many people report feeling freer to express themselves honestly. Interruptions in the therapy process can also be minimized; instead of having to cancel sessions while out of town, clients and practitioners can continue contact. From a therapeutic standpoint, e-therapy may also reduce the occurrence of transference, projection, and countertransference (Recupero & Rainey, 2005).

Although it may indeed have numerous advantages and be the method of choice for some therapists and some clients, e-therapy poses some noteworthy risks that social workers should take under advisement. First, the sense of anonymity that often accompanies Internet communication may lead some clients to disclose information they might otherwise choose to withhold. If a client is in crisis, the practitioner may be unable to effectively intervene to protect the client from self-harm or to warn third

parties who might be in harm's way. A social worker should never be left in this position, unable to satisfy his or her professional obligations. However, this risk can be alleviated by limiting clients to the surrounding geographic area and insisting on adequate background information, contact information, and verification of identity.

Second, e-therapy may also carry an increased risk of misdiagnosis or misunderstanding (Recupero & Rainey, 2005). Absent the availability of nonverbal cues, it may be difficult for the social worker to correctly interpret the client's communication or assess his or her affect. Videoconferencing or Skype could lessen this risk, as could requiring that an initial intake assessment be conducted face-to-face.

Third, there are risks to confidentiality. Hackers can intercept messages, resulting in the unauthorized disclosure of sensitive information. Unlike with face-to-face therapy sessions, e-therapy can generate a verbatim record of everything said—and this material can be retrieved even after it has been deleted. Studies show that social workers who perform e-therapy demonstrate low levels of compliance with ethical standards concerning confidentiality (Santhiveeran, 2009). Although some websites warn clients that breach of confidentiality by hackers is a potential risk, others fail to address confidentiality issues at all. Some websites guarantee confidentiality; others state that disclosure will occur only if required by law. Clients should always be advised of the inherent risks to confidentiality, including strategies they can employ to minimize these risks (firewalls, encryption, password protection, etc.).

It is essential that clients be advised up front of the benefits and material risks of participating in e-therapy generally. Informed consent is more important than ever in this new and uncertain context; all relevant considerations, including the current state of evidence-based research, should be fully discussed and questions answered via synchronous communication. The social worker should be especially careful to disclose any limitations to the e-therapy relationship, including his or her lack of specific training or experience with this particular form of mental health treatment. Uncertainties regarding the status of professional licensure should also be shared. Licensure is typically restricted to the state in which one practices; therefore, providing e-therapy to clients across state or national lines may raise important concerns. Similarly, clients should be aware of the legal recourse that exists in the event of malpractice. Finally, social workers should be sure to discuss with each client various alternatives to e-therapy so clients can make an informed decision about whether this is the best modality for their treatment (Recupero & Rainey, 2005).

Proper Termination

The legal concept underlying termination of service is *abandonment.* Once a client and social worker begin a therapeutic relationship, the social worker incurs a legal duty to either sustain the relationship as long as necessary or refer the client to another provider (Reamer, 2003; Swenson, 1997). This does not mean that you have to accept every client in the first place—but once you do, you have established a legal duty of care and must either continue the relationship or terminate properly. Although most cases of abandonment involve improper termination, it also refers more generally to a social worker being unavailable to the client when needed. As always, social workers must be aware of the scope of their duty to their clients as articulated in the NASW Code of Ethics.

The timing of termination is critical. Ideally, treatment should continue until both the provider and the client are in agreement that the identified goals have been reached. Sometimes, however, either the client or the provider will terminate prematurely. In the former case, if the client is not considered to be a danger to self or others, the social worker should encourage the client to process his or her decision and should explain why additional treatment is advisable. If the client is in crisis, or the social worker suspects that the client may be a danger to self or others, steps should be taken to keep the client or others safe by notifying family or law enforcement or taking steps to have the client committed. Whenever a client initiates termination against the advice of the provider, the client should be asked to sign a statement indicating that the risks of premature termination were discussed and that he or she nonetheless chose to terminate services (Houston-Vega et al., 1997).

Sometimes it is the social worker who prematurely terminates with a client. This can occur because the client is uncooperative or does not seem to be progressing or because the client's insurance is exhausted and the client cannot pay. It can also occur because of the social worker's personal circumstances, for example, if he or she is relocating or retiring from practice. Finally, it can result from the social worker's poor clinical judgment. Social workers should never simply discontinue services; instead, they should provide clients with other available options for continuing treatment (Swenson, 1997). Before terminating with a client unilaterally, it is also advisable to discuss the case with one's supervisor. For a difficult client, for example, it may be possible to continue treatment with additional consultation or support; in fact, doing so could present an opportunity for professional growth. When clients' insurance companies refuse to authorize coverage of services, social workers should notify clients of their right to appeal the decision and assist them with the appeals process. Social workers are permitted to terminate services to clients who have overdue bills as long as the client has been informed of his or her financial obligations and the potential consequences of nonpayment, and the client does not pose an imminent danger to self or others (NASW, 2008).

To ensure proper termination, social workers should make every effort to give the client as much advance notice as possible, should provide the client with several referrals and check back to see if the client has followed through, and should carefully document any situation in which either the social worker or the client initiates termination prematurely.

In addition to discontinuing services, abandonment can occur through failing to be responsive to client needs. Most often, this involves being unavailable to the client in the case of an emergency. It is the social worker's responsibility to be reachable outside of scheduled hours, to arrange for coverage in the case of illness or vacation, and to provide clients with emergency instructions.

Terminating prematurely can constitute malpractice, as can sustaining treatment beyond the point where it continues to benefit the client. The timing of termination should be mutually agreed upon by the client and the provider and should be based on the client's progress in meeting the agreed-upon treatment goals.

Social Work Records

Proper record keeping is both a legal and an ethical obligation for social workers. Service quality can be enhanced through the documentation of critical information, including clinical assessments, diagnoses, treatment plans, and client progress. Such documentation assists social workers in remembering the details of their interactions with clients, thereby minimizing the possibility that important information will be forgotten or confused. It allows for continuity from session to session and keeps social workers accountable for their actions by requiring that they commit to writing the rationale for their treatment decisions. It also facilitates coordination among staff members within an agency, should someone need to fill in for, or take over from, the client's primary provider. In these instances, which may already be disconcerting to the client, it is important to be able to rely on proper documentation to ensure continuity and maximize the likelihood that relevant information will be readily available.

Proper Documentation

We know that careful and accurate documentation is necessary to facilitate competent and effective service delivery. Failure to adhere to the standard of care regarding record keeping can also subject a practitioner to liability for malpractice. Although what a social worker decides to record may depend on the agency or the client, a *client record* (also called a *case file* or *client file*) typically includes intake forms, fee information, confidentiality agreements, informed consent forms, social histories and assessments, diagnoses, symptoms underlying the diagnoses, treatment goals, treatment plans, dates of contact, progress notes, and termination summaries, as well as supplementary materials including contacts made with third parties, appointment books, photographs, medical and psychological tests, drawings, videotapes, and correspondence.

How information is recorded is just as important as being sure that a client record is complete. According to the NASW Code of Ethics (2008), social workers have a duty to protect client privacy to the greatest extent possible by limiting documentation to information that is directly relevant to the delivery of services. Compliance with this guideline requires us to distinguish between essential and nonessential information, and objective and subjective observations. Information that is not clinically relevant—including uncalled for remarks about the client or third parties—should never be included in client records; it can be damaging to the client and reflects poorly on the social worker's competence.

Notes of client sessions should be taken contemporaneously, if at all possible, because they are more likely to be accurate than those recorded after the fact. Many social workers prefer not to take notes during the session, however, because it can be a distraction or can lead clients to feel that the social worker is being less attentive. If this is the case, documentation should occur as soon after the session as possible. Each entry should be typed or completed in ink, dated, and signed.

Failure to keep adequate records can have serious consequences. In the case of *Abille v. United States* (1980), it led to a patient's death. The patient, who was experiencing depression and suicidal thoughts, was originally assigned a status level of S-1—meaning that he was not allowed to leave his unit in the psychiatric hospital without a staff escort. A few days later, thinking that his status had been changed to S-2 (which allows for fewer restrictions), the duty nurses permitted him to attend mass in the building, unescorted. The next day, they permitted him to shave with a razor and to go to breakfast, again unescorted. Shortly after leaving the ward, he jumped to his death from a seventh-floor window. The nurses were unable to recall who had authorized the change in Abille's status from S-1 to S-2 but indicated that it had been posted as S-2 on the patients' sign-in board. The physician in charge testified that he had authorized the change; however, there was no written record to that effect. The only documentation of a change in patient status was added by a nurse, after Abille's suicide. The court concluded that the nurses were negligent for permitting Abille to move about without supervision in the absence of a proper medical order changing his status. The court also found the physician guilty of malpractice for failing to enter progress notes (there were none in the file), medical orders, or other records identifying his actions and explaining the basis for his judgments. According to the court, his actions "fell below the applicable standard of care" (p. 708). As this case indicates, failing to provide proper documentation or being sloppy with documentation can have serious consequences for both clients and providers. Although few social workers relish the task, conscientious record keeping is a necessary part of competent professional practice.

Responsible record keeping also involves retaining records in accordance with accepted privacy standards. How long records must be retained typically becomes an issue of concern when a social worker retires, closes a practice, relocates, or dies without leaving instructions on how to handle existing records. The minimum period required for record retention varies from state to state. In Virginia, for example, client records must be kept for 10 years after the last treatment contact; for juveniles, they must be kept for 5 years past the age of majority or 10 years after the last treatment contact, whichever is later. So, if you were seeing a client from the time she was 13 until she turned 15, you would have to wait until she was 25 (10 years after the last treatment contact) before disposing of her records. Alternatively, if your last treatment with a juvenile was at age 8, you could dispose of her records at age 23—that would be 5 years after she reached the age of majority. In Louisiana, social workers are required to maintain client records for at least 6 years after the last contact, and records of minor clients must be kept for 6 years after the client reaches the age of majority. State laws also specify how long records must be retained in the event of a client's death.

A few states have laws that specifically mention social workers in regard to the retention of records; it is more common, however, for laws to generally address medical or hospital records rather than referencing social work records directly (NASW, 2005b). If you practice in a state without specific record retention requirements for social workers, it is a good idea to research the record retention laws for related professions. It might also make sense to check your state's statute of limitations for malpractice suits. As discussed earlier, a statute of limitations specifies the time within which a person may file a lawsuit. Many social workers choose to retain records according to the statute of limitations, especially if it is longer than the record retention requirement, to be sure that they are not caught unprepared should legal action be taken against them. When it is time to dispose of records, hard copies should be shredded and information held electronically should be permanently deleted.

Protecting Records from Disclosure

Even though the primary purpose of documentation is to facilitate effective service delivery, it is also important to recognize that the information contained in client records can make its way into court. It is never safe to assume that only you will have access to client files; documentation should always be approached with the assumption that, at some time, others will closely examine it. This is especially true if you are working with clients whose profiles make legal action more likely: couples in a violent relationship, families facing termination of parental rights, clients with paranoid ideation, or clients who have been litigious in the past (Barsky & Gould, 2002). Client records can be subpoenaed any time a client is involved in a lawsuit, including when the client sues the social worker for malpractice. In the latter case, proper recording can be a way of protecting the social worker by providing evidence of his or her adherence to the standard of care. In any event, it is always important to think about how client information is gathered, entered, preserved, and discarded.

The prospect of client records being subpoenaed is frightening to many practitioners. In an effort to safeguard client information, social workers and others have devised strategies for protecting client records from disclosure. Unfortunately, none is without its drawbacks. For example, some recommend recording only minimum information about a client; however, doing so could result in harm to both the client and the practitioner. By minimizing documentation, the social worker runs the risk of omitting information that could be therapeutically necessary, thus resulting in poor practice. It might also do an injustice to the social worker, should he or she face malpractice charges and be left without adequate information to support a defense. Alternatively, some social workers elect to keep two sets of records. The problem here is that all records can still be subpoenaed; meanwhile, the behavior casts doubt on the social worker's ethics and credibility. Another strategy is to code information in the record so outsiders cannot understand it. Of course, the court can require the social worker to decode the information; again, doing this leaves the impression that the social worker is trying to hide something and can impeach his or her credibility (Barsky & Gould, 2002).

The practice of separating subjective notes from objective information has been the subject of considerable debate. The term *clinical notes* or *psychotherapy notes* is meant to encompass a mental health provider's personal notes documenting or analyzing what transpires during a counseling session. Clinical notes are afforded a different level of privacy under the Health Insurance Portability and Accountability Act (HIPAA) than is afforded the rest of the client record, but only if they are separately maintained. Even though both clinical notes and objective client information can be subpoenaed, keeping them separate allows the court to more easily distinguish fact from opinion; it might also allow the court to permit submission of a summary of the notes rather than the notes themselves. On the other hand, social workers who keep separate personal notes are often tempted to record information outside the scope of what is therapeutically relevant, potentially harming the client and creating an enhanced risk of malpractice. Although social workers may think that maintaining personal notes on their clients enhances their practice by allowing them to better process their thoughts and decisions, it can be argued that the same goal can be achieved with less risk by conscientiously adhering to professional and legal standards.

It should go without saying that client information should never be shared without explicit consent from the client. If an attorney contacts you for information—or you receive a subpoena (see Responding to a Subpoena, in Chapter 3), discuss the request with your client. When the client is the one bringing the lawsuit (e.g., to support a claim of disability), he or she may well agree to release the records. In that case, be sure you have obtained informed consent and that the client signs a release clearly identifying what information may be released, by whom, to whom, for what purpose, and over what period of time. If clinical notes are stored separately from the rest of the client record, separate consent is required. Even if you think disclosure is ill advised, once the client consents to share the information, you must honor his or her decision. If, on the other hand, the client refuses consent, you are ethically bound to make every reasonable and legally defensible effort to maintain the client's privacy by resisting disclosure of client records.

Falsifying Information

Social workers and others may be tempted to falsify client or treatment information. This can amount to fraud, which is both unlawful and unethical. For example, social workers may feel pressured to alter documentation in client records for the sake of the agency's reputation, to avoid a potential lawsuit, or to appear to comply with accreditation or other practice standards. *Abille v. United States* (discussed earlier) provides an example of this. One of the nurses entered a change in the patient's status not only after the fact but after the patient had died. Doing so not only failed to absolve her of malpractice liability in the case, it undoubtedly made things worse.

Many agencies direct their staff to correct mistakes in the files in anticipation of external audits. Although correcting errors to create an accurate record is important, care should be taken to never delete or erase the mistaken information; instead, it should be crossed out with a single line so the original is still visible to the reader. The person making the correction should place his or her initials and the date of the change in the margin. If an explanation is warranted, it can be appended to the record. The point is for any and all changes to be transparent; that way, the reader knows that a correction was made and that the social worker has nothing to hide.

Sometimes information is falsified in order to promote the practitioner's financial interests. Social workers may bill insurance companies for sessions that did not occur or may falsify diagnostic codes for reimbursement (Reamer, 2003). In the previously discussed

Cool v. Olson case, the psychiatrist filed a false insurance claim hoping to reap extra profit. As a result, he was sued for fraud. More commonly, social workers are tempted to falsify claims in order to benefit not themselves but their clients. For example, a social worker may intentionally misdiagnose a client to avoid labeling the client or to make the client's treatment eligible for continued coverage. Although the motives here are altruistic, the practice is nonetheless legally unacceptable. Similarly, social workers should never alter or dispose of client records in order to keep private, unflattering, or potentially incriminating information from being shared in court.

Summary and Conclusion

Social workers have both a legal and an ethical duty to practice in conformity with the law. Although the law does not require perfection, it does require that our actions comport with those of a reasonable, prudent professional in the same or similar circumstances. Despite one's best efforts, however, it is always possible to be sued for malpractice. Malpractice is a type of civil action in which a social worker or other practitioner is alleged to have acted negligently. In addition to bringing suit, clients alleging malpractice can file grievances with NASW; a finding of fault can result in a range of sanctions for the social work practitioner.

In order to practice within the law, social workers should routinely seek informed consent, maintain client confidentiality, engage in proper assessment and diagnosis, ensure ethical and competent treatment, and keep complete and accurate records. Even though malpractice suits cannot always be avoided, social workers can reduce the risk of liability by staying current with the relevant scholarly literature, participating in continuing professional education, becoming familiar with relevant state laws, brushing up on the Code of Ethics and other practice guidelines, discussing challenging situations with colleagues, conscientiously documenting the rationale for every course of action, and seeking legal consultation when necessary.

Sample Case

The following case is one of the many cases that followed in the wake of the *Tarasoff* decision. It raises new and important questions about the duty to warn. Try briefing the case, using the method described in Chapter 2. Then consider the questions that follow.

HAMMAN V. COUNTY OF MARICOPA
775 P.2d 1122 (1989)
Supreme Court of Arizona

Holohan, Justice (Retired)

We granted the plaintiffs' petition for review to determine the nature and extent of a psychiatrist's duty to third parties injured by the psychiatrist's patient. The plaintiffs filed a tort action against the defendants for injuries inflicted on Robert Hamman by John Carter, a patient of the defendant, Dr. Manuel Suguitan. The superior court granted the defendants' motion for summary judgment, and the Court of Appeals affirmed the judgment of the lower court in part and reversed in part.

Facts

*** John Carter is the son of plaintiff Alice Hamman, and stepson of plaintiff Robert Hamman. On January 5, 1982, the Hammans brought Carter to the Maricopa County Hospital emergency psychiatric center because Carter had been exhibiting strange behavior. Dr. Suguitan, a psychiatrist who had previously admitted Carter to the hospital in August 1981, interviewed Carter for about five minutes and noted the following symptoms: (1) anxious but cooperative, (2) fear and apprehension about a place to live, (3) loose associations and blocking, (4) inappropriate affect, (5) tries to conceal depression by grimacing, and (6) employs denial and projection. Dr. Suguitan did not review the medical records of Carter's 1981 hospitalization. After interviewing Carter, Dr. Suguitan had a discussion with Mrs. Hamman, the specifics of which are disputed by the parties. Mrs. Hamman stated in her deposition that she told Dr. Suguitan the details of Carter's abnormal behavior since his hospitalization in August 1981. She described various incidents of strange behavior, a few instances of violent conduct, and a recent incident in which Carter was discovered to be carrying photos of animals with their heads cut off. Mrs. Hamman also testified in her deposition that she told Dr. Suguitan that she and Mr. Hamman feared that Carter would either be killed or kill somebody. . . . Mrs. Hamman further testified that Dr. Suguitan told her that Carter was schizophrenic and psychotic, but that he was "harmless." Dr. Suguitan denied in his deposition that Mrs. Hamman told him about the specific details of the patient's conduct, and he denied that he ever told her that Carter was "harmless."

Dr. Suguitan did not refer to Carter's medical records from his previous hospitalization at Maricopa County. Those records would have shown among other things that Carter expressed jealousy of his stepfather and that the treatment plan had been to "seclude and restrain" the patient from agitation, assaultive, or dangerous behavior. Carter had also been examined and treated in the past at Desert Samaritan Hospital. Dr. Suguitan did not review the patient's medical records from that hospital. Those records would have revealed that Carter had a history of drug abuse and violent behavior, and he had made statements that he wanted to punish someone.

On January 5, 1982, as Mrs. Hamman discussed Carter's behavior and the Hammans' fear of him, she repeatedly begged Dr. Suguitan to admit Carter to the hospital. Dr. Suguitan refused to admit Carter. Instead, he wrote a prescription for Navane, gave it to Mrs. Hamman, and instructed her to give Carter 10 milligrams of Navane each morning and night. Dr. Suguitan admits he ordered this treatment knowing that Carter had not been taking the Navane which had been previously prescribed for him in August, 1981. Mrs. Hamman stated that Dr. Suguitan then told her to call him again in one week. Dr. Suguitan states that he advised Mrs. Hamman to take Carter to Tri-City Medical Center for follow-up care.

Upon being denied admission, Carter fled down the street brushing his teeth. The Hammans eventually persuaded him to get in their truck and go home. They gave him the medication as prescribed that night and again the following morning and night on January 6.

Although Mrs. Hamman tried to give Carter his medication on the morning of January 7, Carter refused to take it. At approximately 11:00 a.m. that day, Mr. Hamman while working on a home project with an electric drill, was attacked without warning by Carter. He repeatedly beat Hamman over the head with wooden dowels. Mr. Hamman suffered a heart attack during the beating as well as severe brain damage from the blows to his head. Carter later stated he believed Mr. Hamman was going to physically attack Mrs. Hamman with the drill, and that he (Carter) reacted as he did to protect his mother. Carter was later criminally charged for the beating, but found not guilty by reason of insanity.

The Hammans subsequently filed this civil action. The complaint contained three counts charging medical malpractice by Dr. Suguitan while employed by Maricopa County, general negligence, and a claim against Maricopa County for negligent training and supervision of psychiatric personnel.

The defendants filed a motion for summary judgment, essentially contending Dr. Suguitan owed no duty to the Hammans because Carter had never communicated to Suguitan any specific threat against the Hammans. The trial court granted the defendants' motion, and entered judgment against the plaintiffs dismissing all their claims for relief. . . . The majority of the Court of Appeals followed the "specific threats to specific victims" approach. *See Brady v. Hopper,* 570 F. Supp. 1333 (1983). Under this view, a psychiatrist incurs no duty to any third party unless his patient communicates to the psychiatrist a specific threat against a specific person. ***

The issue taken for review is whether Dr. Suguitan and Maricopa County owed a duty to the Hammans, absent a specific threat by the patient against them, properly to diagnose, treat or control the patient.

Analysis

A negligence action may be maintained only if there is a duty or obligation, recognized by law, which requires the defendant to conform to a particular standard of conduct in order to protect others from unreasonable risks of harm. ***

The landmark case regarding the duty of a psychiatrist to protect others against the conduct of a patient is Tarasoff v. Regents of Univ. of Cal., 551 P.2d 334 (1976). In Tarasoff, the plaintiff alleged that the defendant therapists had a duty to warn their daughter of the danger posed to her by one of the therapists' patients. The Tarasoff plaintiffs were the parents of Tatiana Tarasoff, a young woman killed by the patient. Two months prior to the killing, the patient informed his therapist that he intended to kill a young woman. Although the patient did not specifically name Tatiana as his intended victim, the plaintiffs alleged, and the trial court agreed, that the defendant therapist could have readily identified the endangered person as Tatiana. . . .

The Tarasoff court held that the psychiatrist-patient relationship was sufficient ... to support the imposition of an affirmative duty on the defendant for the benefit of third persons. The court ruled that when a psychiatrist determines or, pursuant to the standards of the profession, should determine that a patient presents a serious danger of violence to another, the psychiatrist incurs an obligation to use reasonable care to protect the intended victim against such danger. According to the Tarasoff court, discharge of that duty may require the psychiatrist to warn the intended victim or others reasonably likely to notify the victim, to notify the police, "or to take whatever other steps are reasonably necessary under the circumstances."

Although the Tarasoff decision did not state that a psychiatrist's duty to third parties arises only when his patient communicates a specific threat concerning a specific individual, numerous subsequent decisions interpret Tarasoff. For example, in Brady, John

W. Hinckley, Jr. injured the plaintiffs in his attempt to assassinate President Reagan. The suit alleged, in part, that Hinckley's psychiatrist had negligently diagnosed and treated him. The Brady court held that the psychiatrist owed no duty to the plaintiffs because Hinckley had not made specific threats against a readily identifiable victim.

Similarly, in Thompson v. County of Alameda, 614 P.2d 728 (1980), the parents of a young child sued the county for the wrongful death of their son. The juvenile offender, James F., killed the child within 24 hours of his release from confinement into the temporary custody of his mother. James stated he would kill a child in the community at random, and the county knew it. Nonetheless, county officials released him without warning local police, parents, or James's mother. Distinguishing Thompson from Tarasoff, the majority of the California Supreme Court refused to impose "blanket liability." The court stated that liability may be imposed only in those instances in which the released offender posed a predictable threat of harm to a named or readily identifiable victim. James made a generalized threat to a segment of the population. Consequently, the majority refused to impose upon the psychiatrist a duty to protect such a large group in the community.

Other courts, however, have not required a specific threat as a prerequisite for liability. Instead, they require that the psychiatrist reasonably foresee that the risk engendered by the patient's condition would endanger others. For example, in Petersen v. State, 671 P.2d 230 (1983), a patient was hospitalized for several weeks and treated with Navane after his psychiatrist diagnosed him as having schizophrenic and hallucinogenic symptoms. The hospital allowed the patient to go home for Mother's Day, but required him to return that night. Upon his return, hospital personnel observed the patient driving recklessly and spinning his car in circles on hospital grounds. The psychiatrist nevertheless released the patient the following morning and continued to prescribe Navane even though he knew of the patient's reluctance to take such medication. Five days later, the patient drove through a red light at 50–60 miles per hour, striking plaintiff's car and injuring her. The Petersen court emphasized the importance of foreseeability in defining the scope of a person's duty to exercise due care. In affirming plaintiff's claim based on negligent treatment of the patient, the court ruled that the psychiatrist had a duty to protect any person foreseeably endangered by the patient.

A somewhat narrower interpretation of this "foreseeably endangered" approach is illustrated in Jablonski by Pahls v. United States, 712 F.2d 391 (1983). In Jablonski, a psychiatric patient, Phillip Jablonski, had an extensive record of psychiatric and criminal problems and had on numerous occasions tried to kill his ex-wife. Jablonski threatened to use violence against the mother of his girlfriend, Melinda Kimball. Rather than imprison Jablonski, he was allowed to undergo a psychiatric examination at the Loma Linda Veteran's Administration Hospital. The police informed Dr. Berman, the Hospital's head of psychiatric services, of Jablonski's prior criminal record and recent violence. Dr. Berman, however, failed to relay this information to the treating psychiatrist. As a result, the treating psychiatrist diagnosed Jablonski as "potentially dangerous" but did not admit him. He concluded that there was no emergency and no basis for involuntary hospitalization. The psychiatrist did not attempt to obtain Jablonski's prior medical records, which documented his numerous attempts to kill his ex-wife and indicated "future violent behavior was a distinct probability." A second evaluation four days later again indicated Jablonski was dangerous, but the psychiatrist found no basis for involuntary hospitalization. Two days thereafter, Jablonski attacked and killed his girlfriend, Melinda Kimball. . . .

Applying Tarasoff, the district court found three separate instances of the psychiatrists' malpractice: failure to (1) transmit the information from the police, (2) obtain Jablonski's past medical records, and (3) warn Jablonski's girlfriend. In affirming the findings of the district court, the Court of Appeals noted that the case fell somewhere between the extremes of the specific threats cases and the broad "foreseeably endangered" cases. The appellate court held that, although no specific threats were made, Jablonski's record of violence toward his ex-wife indicated that his girlfriend was a more "sufficiently targeted" victim than were random members of the community. The court reasoned that review of the medical records and police report provided the necessary information that Jablonski's girlfriend was a foreseeable victim. Hence, the failure to obtain the records was vital to the conclusion that the psychiatrists breached their duty to protect third parties.

In the present case, the Court of Appeals would limit a psychiatrist's duty and liability to cases in which there are specific threats against third parties, i.e., the Brady approach. The plaintiffs concede that Carter never made any specific threats against Mr. Hamman.

Standard

We believe the Brady approach is too narrow. Tarasoff envisioned a broader scope of a psychiatrist's duty when the court stated: "[O]nce a therapist does in fact determine, or under applicable professional standards reasonably should have determined, that a patient poses a serious danger of violence to others, he bears a duty to exercise reasonable care to protect the foreseeable victim of that danger." Additionally, we agree with those cases interpreting Tarasoff which state that a psychiatrist should not be relieved of this duty merely because his patient never verbalized any specific threat. We recognize the concern about adopting a rule which would be too inclusive, subjecting psychiatrists to an unreasonably wide range of potential liability. However, we believe that the approach used by the Ninth Circuit in Jablonski allays such fears and represents a sound analytical foundation for the facts before us. In holding that Jablonski's girlfriend (Kimball) was a foreseeable victim, the court stated:

> Unlike the killer in Tarasoff, Jablonski made no specific threats concerning any specific individuals. Nevertheless, Jablonski's previous history indicated that he would likely direct his violence against Kimball. He had raped and committed other acts of violence against his wife. His psychological profile indicated that his violence was likely to be directed against women very close to him.

Dr. Suguitan was aware that schizophrenic-psychotic patients such as Carter are prone to unexpected episodes of violence. He knew that Carter was living with and being cared for by the Hammans. Dr. Suguitan, in denying Carter's admission to the hospital, released the patient into the care of the Hammans. If indeed Dr. Suguitan negligently diagnosed Carter as harmless, the most likely affected victims would be the Hammans. Their constant physical proximity to Carter placed them in an obvious zone of danger. The Hammans were readily identifiable persons who might suffer harm if the psychiatrist was negligent in the diagnosis or treatment of the patient.... We reject the notion that the psychiatrist's duty to third persons is limited to those against whom a specific threat has been made. We hold that the standard originally suggested in Tarasoff is properly applicable to psychiatrists. When a psychiatrist determines, or under applicable professional standards reasonably should have determined, that a patient poses a serious danger of violence to others, the psychiatrist has a duty to exercise reasonable care to protect the foreseeable victim of that danger. The foreseeable victim is one who is said to be within the zone of danger, that is, subject to probable risk of the patient's violent conduct. *** The psychiatrist to fulfill his duty to those within the zone of risk must take the action reasonable under the circumstances.

Conclusion

The rule which we adopt does not impose upon psychiatrists a duty to protect the public from all harm caused by their patients. We do not, however, limit the duty of the psychiatrist to third parties only in those instances in which a specific threat is made against them. We hold that the duty extends to third persons whose circumstances place them within the reasonably foreseeable area of danger where the violent conduct of the patient is a threat.

That part of the Court of Appeals' opinion which is inconsistent with views expressed herein is vacated. The judgment of the trial court is reversed, and the case is remanded for further proceedings consistent with this opinion.

Questions

1. The psychiatrist in this case made a number of errors that could constitute negligence. What are they? For each one you can identify, describe what should have been done instead.

2. The *Tarasoff* case established that a mental health professional owes a duty of care not only to the client but to third parties who there is reason to believe might be harmed by the client. *Hamman* focuses on what is often considered to be the fourth prong of a "duty to warn" analsysis: an identifiable victim. How does the *Hamman* opinion alter this requirement? What is the court's basis for concluding that the psychiatrist had a duty to warn the Hammans? Do you agree? Why or why not?

3. Given what we know about Carter's violent tendencies, how would you define the "foreseeable zone of risk"? Does it reach beyond his parents? If so, where does it end?

4. Consider this case from the perspective of a social work practitioner. How do you think your legal responsibility for warning potential third-party victims should be defined? Do you prefer the *Tarasoff* definition, the *Hamman* definition, or some other definition? Explain.

CHAPTER 5 PRACTICE TEST

The following questions will test your application and analysis of the content found within this chapter. For additional assessment, including licensing-exam type questions on applying chapter content to practice behaviors, visit **MySearchLab**.

1. If you are sued by a client for malpractice, the first thing you should do is
   a. contact your insurance company.
   b. discuss the issue with your client in the hope of reaching an amicable agreement.
   c. line up colleagues who might be able to serve as character witnesses for you.
   d. suspend your practice.

2. Compensatory damages
   a. are designed to make an example of the offender's bad behavior.
   b. are designed to make the victim whole again.
   c. are awarded in malpractice cases only if punitive damages are unwarranted.
   d. require community service instead of a monetary settlement.

3. A person with Alzheimer's disease
   a. may be competent to consent during periods of lucidity.

   b. should be deemed to have given valid consent if he or she signs a consent form.
   c. should be deemed to consent if the provider thinks it is in her best interests.
   d. should never be considered competent to give informed consent.

4. You are treating a 22-year-old client with a history of having been abused as a child. Although she and her parents have been estranged since she entered foster care at age 15, she continues to harbor considerable anger and resentment toward her father. In one of your sessions, she says, "If I ever see him again and he lays a hand on me, I'll kill him." Under the law, do you have a duty to breach confidentiality to warn her father of possible harm?
   a. Yes, the harm is foreseeable.
   b. Yes, you can identify the possible victim.
   c. No, the harm is not imminent.
   d. No, your client is an adult.

5. Describe what is involved in properly terminating a therapeutic relationship.

6. Discuss the various strategies a social worker might employ to monitor a client considered to be at risk for suicide.

MYSEARCHLAB CONNECTIONS

Reinforce what you learned in this chapter by studying videos, cases, documents, and more available at **www.MySearchLab.com**.

Read these Cases/Documents

Δ Ethical Practice*

- *How would you describe the relationship between social workers' ethical responsibilities and their responsibilities under the law? Can you give an example of where law and ethics coincide? Of where they're different?*

Δ Computerized Record Keeping

- *Given the rapid advance in electronic record-keeping and communication, what steps should social workers take to protect client interests? To protect themselves from malpractice?*

Explore these Assets

- Techniques for Generalist Practice: Planning for Absence or Departure

Research these Topics

- NASW Committee on Inquiry
- How HIPAA applies to social work practice
- Confidentiality and minors (in school and non-school settings)

Assess Your Knowledge

Go to **MySearchLab** to test your knowledge of key topics in this chapter with topic-specific quizzes. Conclude your assessment by completing the chapter exam.

---

* = CSWE Core Competency Asset   Δ = Case Study

Child Abuse and Neglect

In the United States, parents generally have a right to bring up their children free from state intervention. Supreme Court cases from the early 1900s to the present time have reinforced the right of parents to control most aspects of their children's lives, including education (*Meyer v. Nebraska*, 1923; *Pierce v. Society of Sisters*, 1925), health care (*Parham v. J.R.*, 1979), and associations with other adults (*Troxel v. Granville*, 2000). An exception arises when state intervention is needed to shield children from serious harm. The government's involvement with child abuse and neglect, or *child maltreatment*, stems from the legal concept of *parens patriae*. This doctrine asserts that when parents fail to provide proper care for their children, the government has a role in intervening to protect children's interests (Crosson-Tower, 2009; Ramsey & Abrams, 2003; U.S. Department of Health and Human Services, 2009). In order to intervene, the state must demonstrate that the need to protect the child from harm outweighs the constitutional rights of the parents (Ramsey & Abrams, 2003).

The U.S. government's role in child protection began in the late 19th century. Prior to this time, private religious and community-based organizations handled issues of child maltreatment (U.S. Department of Health and Human Services, 2009). In the past century or so, the field of child welfare has undergone significant development with the enactment of numerous federal and state laws. Key among these federal laws are the following:

- **Child Abuse Prevention and Treatment Act of 1974 (CAPTA, P.L. 93-247):** Provides assistance to states in identifying and preventing child abuse and neglect, establishes grants to train personnel and promote innovative prevention programs, and creates a system for the collection and dissemination of research on child maltreatment.

- **Indian Child Welfare Act of 1978 (ICWA, P.L. 95-608):** Establishes rules specifically to govern child welfare cases involving Native American children. Prior to this Act, Indian children were removed from their families and placed in boarding schools run by government or church organizations. ICWA established procedures to transfer jurisdiction to tribes and allow tribal intervention in state court proceedings.
- **Adoption Assistance and Child Welfare Act of 1980 (P.L. 96-272):** Provides guidelines aimed at ensuring child safety, decreasing the length of time spent in temporary foster care, and promoting permanent placements.
- **Family Preservation and Support Services Program Act of 1993 (P.L. 103-66):** Promotes the provision of services designed to strengthen families and prevent the need for removal of children from the home.
- **Multiethnic Placement Act of 1994 (P.L. 103-82):** Prohibits agencies from delaying or refusing prospective adoption or foster care placements in order to attain a match based on race, color, or national origin.
- **Adoption and Safe Families Act of 1997 (P.L. 105-89):** Shortens the timeline for attempting reunification before requiring termination of parental rights.
- **Fostering Connections to Success and Increasing Adoptions Act of 2008 (P.L. 110-351):** Promotes care by extended family members for children who are removed from home. The Act permits payments to relative caregivers who assume legal guardianship of children in foster care, extends Medicaid eligibility to children in kinship guardianship arrangements, and authorizes states to adopt procedures aimed at helping children reconnect with family members.

This chapter begins by providing background information on child abuse and neglect as a context for examining legal aspects of the field that are particularly relevant to social work. These legal aspects include child abuse reporting, civil and criminal processes, out-of-home care, reunification, termination of parental rights, and children as witnesses in court. Special sections highlight recovered memory syndrome and forensic interviewing of children. A sample case is provided that raises important considerations for policy and practice.

Background

The American approach to child welfare is distinctive within the larger, global context. Some countries have more comprehensive approaches than we do and others have yet to recognize the need for action. Katz and Hetherington (2006) describe two basic child welfare models: *dualistic* (focusing on the child) and *holistic* (focusing on the family). In a dualistic system, the government exercises two potentially contradictory functions: (1) preventing child maltreatment by strengthening families and (2) rescuing child victims, often by removing them from the home. The looming possibility of court intervention into family life plays an important role in defining the dynamics of this type of child welfare system. Our approach to child maltreatment in the United States would be considered dualistic. In contrast, holistic models promote early intervention and are focused on the full range of factors that can harm a child's social and emotional development, including child abuse. These models often rely upon local resources, including voluntary and faith-based organizations, to provide services that support families. The state's role is mainly to ensure funding for these resources. Holistic systems predominate throughout continental Europe as well as in Nordic countries (Katz & Hetherington, 2006). In the French system, for example, family ties are severed only as a last resort; the priority is on improving the child–parent relationship because most children, even if removed, are eventually returned to their birth families (Dumaret & Rosset, 2005).

Some nations do not have any type of coordinated response to child abuse and neglect. In many of those that do, the emphasis is on punishment through the criminal justice system, rather than on comprehensive strategies that recognize the rights of children and incorporate evidence-based practice (Bennett, 2005). In China, the government does not recognize child maltreatment as a social problem in any official way, despite the fact that many adults admit to having experienced abuse as children. This lack of response is driven by cultural attitudes, including respect for family privacy and the acceptability of corporal punishment to demonstrate both discipline and love (Qiao & Chane, 2005). In Syria, where violence against children remains pronounced at home, at school, and on the streets, there are no guidelines for identifying and reporting maltreatment, and there is no systematic approach to addressing it. Child mental health services do not exist, and there are no treatment programs for offenders. The concept of children's rights is unfamiliar to most families and child labor is often still the norm (Essali, 2005). In Belarus, 85,500 children remain in orphanages, including children who were abandoned, whose parents' parental rights were terminated, whose parents are imprisoned, or whose parents were convinced to relinquish their "disabled" children to the state. It is only in the past decade that these children have been integrated into the community, beginning with visits to host families (Bonner, 2005).

Definitions of Child Maltreatment

Definitions of child abuse and neglect appear in federal legislation and are more specifically defined by state statute. The Child Abuse Prevention and Treatment Act (CAPTA) defines child abuse and neglect as "any recent act or failure to act on the part of a parent or caretaker which results in death, serious physical or emotional harm, sexual abuse or exploitation, or an act or failure to act which presents an imminent risk of serious harm" (42 U.S.C.A. §5106g). This definition establishes a set of baseline behaviors that is further delineated on a state-by-state basis. State definitions vary considerably, with some being very broad and others very detailed. As social workers, it is important to be familiar with the definitions in the state where we practice.

As part of its definition, each state identifies specific categories of child maltreatment that trigger government intervention. These categories typically include physical abuse, neglect, sexual abuse/exploitation, emotional abuse, parental substance abuse, and abandonment. Brief descriptions of these types of maltreatment and examples of state statutes are found in Table 6.1. Although statutes differ from state to state, many states adopt the same or similar language.

TABLE 6.1 Types of Child Maltreatment

Type	Description	Sample State Statute
Physical abuse	Non-accidental physical injury to a child	Georgia (Ann. Code § 19-7-5[b]) *Child abuse* means physical injury or death inflicted upon a child by a parent or caretaker by other than accidental means
Neglect	Deprivation of adequate food, shelter, clothing, medical care or supervision	Massachusetts (Ann. Laws Ch. 119, § 51A) Injured, abused, or neglected child means a child under age 18 who is suffering from neglect, including malnutrition, or who is determined to be physically dependent upon an addictive drug at birth
Sexual abuse	Use of a child for the sexual gratification of an adult	Idaho (Idaho Code § 16-1602) Abused means any case in which a child has been the victim of sexual conduct including rape, molestation, incest, prostitution, obscene or pornographic photographing, filming, or depiction for commercial purposes, or other similar forms of sexual exploitation harming or threatening the child's health, welfare, or mental injury to the child
Emotional abuse	Injury to the psychological or emotional stability of the child	Arizona (Rev. Stat. § 8-201) Abuse means the infliction of or allowing another person to cause serious emotional damage to the child, as evidenced by severe anxiety, depression, withdrawal, or untoward aggressive behavior, and such emotional damage is diagnosed by a medical doctor or psychologist, and the damage has been caused by the acts or omissions of an individual having care, custody, and control of a child.

Source: Child Welfare Information Gateway (2007a).

Physical Abuse

Generally defined as "any non-accidental physical injury to the child," physical abuse can include kicking, burning, striking, or biting the child or any action that results in a physical impairment. Physical symptoms may also include suspicious injuries that the parents cannot explain (Downs, Moore, & McFadden, 2009). Some states also include "acts or circumstances that threaten the child with harm or create a substantial risk of harm to the child's health or welfare" (Child Welfare Information Gateway, 2007a). Generally speaking, medical evidence must be presented to prove that a child's injury was not accidental (Ramsey & Abrams, 2003).

Neglect

Neglect is generally defined as deprivation of adequate food, shelter, clothing, medical care, or supervision (Child Welfare Information Gateway, 2007a; Downs et al., 2009). Approximately 20 state statutes also include failure to provide education. Many include medical neglect, although the specific definition varies. Seven states (Mississippi, Ohio, North Dakota, Oklahoma, Tennessee, Texas, and West Virginia) include the failure to secure needed mental health treatment in their definitions of medical neglect (Child Welfare Information Gateway, 2007a). Some also include provisions for children whose condition is characterized as "failure to thrive," which means that the child is suffering from a growth deficiency without an identifiable physical cause. Untreated, failure to thrive children may experience permanent physical, cognitive, and emotional damage (Ramsey & Abrams, 2003).

Sexual Abuse/Exploitation

Sexual abuse involves the use of a child for the sexual gratification of an adult (Crosson-Tower, 2008). CAPTA defines sexual abuse as

> (1) The employment, use, persuasion, inducement, enticement, or coercion of any child to engage in, or assist any other person to engage in, any sexually explicit conduct or simulation of such conduct for the purpose of producing a visual depiction of such conduct; or (2) The rape, and in cases of caretaker or interfamilial relationships, statutory rape, molestation, prostitution, or other form of sexual exploitation of children, or incest with children. (42 U.S.C.A. § 5106g[4])

Sexual abuse is often difficult to prove because of a lack of physical evidence. Because it generally occurs in private, there may also be no witnesses to provide testimony (Ramsey & Abrams, 2003).

Emotional Abuse

Emotional abuse, or psychological maltreatment, is not an isolated event but a pattern of psychologically harmful behavior that may include rejecting the child, isolating the child from normal experiences, terrorizing the child, creating a climate of fear, ignoring the child, or engaging the child in psychologically destructive behavior (Crosson-Tower, 2008). The courts have also considered but rejected maltreatment charges against parents who permit their children to witness violence in the home. In *New Jersey Department of Youth and Family Services v. S.S.* (2004), a woman was holding her 21-month-old infant in her arms while her husband punched her, tried to choke her, and threatened to kill her. The court concluded that there was no evidence of harm to this particular child arising from the domestic violence and thus overturned her conviction for child abuse.

Parental Substance Abuse

Several states include parental substance abuse as evidence of child maltreatment. Parental substance abuse is defined in some jurisdictions (including Arkansas, Colorado, Illinois, Iowa, Louisiana, Massachusetts, Michigan, North Dakota, South Dakota, Wisconsin and the District of Columbia) as prenatal exposure to harm resulting from the mother's use of illegal drugs or other substances. It is important to note that some states do *not* recognize parental substance abuse as child abuse or neglect. Prosecutions of substance abusing parents under endangerment and abuse statutes have often failed; in fact, the majority of courts have refused to bring criminal charges under these circumstances. The U.S. Supreme Court went one step further, ruling that even administering drug tests to pregnant women without their knowledge violates their constitutional rights (*City of Charleston v. Ferguson*, 2001).

Abandonment

Eighteen states and the District of Columbia include abandonment in their definitions of child abuse and neglect when a "parent's identity or whereabouts are unknown, the child has been left by the parent in circumstances in which the child suffers serious harm, or the parent has failed to maintain contact with the child or to provide reasonable support for a specified period of time" (Child Welfare Information Gateway, 2007a). In order to decrease the number of abandoned infants put at risk, all states have enacted "safe haven" or "baby Moses" laws. These laws allow parents in crisis to safely relinquish their babies at designated locations (such as hospitals, police stations, fire stations, and churches) without threat of prosecution. Once the child is relinquished, most states require the safe haven provider (if not a hospital) to transfer the infant to a hospital and to notify child protective services.

Incidence and Trends

The Children's Bureau of the U.S. Department of Health and Human Services publishes an annual *Child Maltreatment Report* based on data provided by the National Child Abuse and Neglect Data System. According to the most recent report (U.S. DHHS, 2011a), in 2010, child protective services workers received approximately 3.3 million reports involving nearly 6 million children. A total of 695,000 children were found to be maltreated (down from a high of more than 1 million in the early 1990s) and approximately 1,560 of those children died (U.S. Department of Health and Human Services, 2011). Figure 6.1 shows the percentage of victims by maltreatment type. Neglect represents the highest

| FIGURE 6.1 | Reported Maltreatment Types of Victims, 2010 |

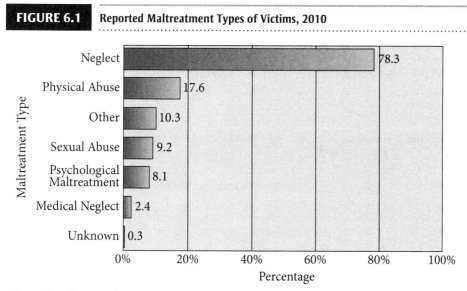

Source: http://www.acf.hhs.gov/programs/cb/pubs/cm10/cm10.pdf#page=31

percentage of cases at 78.3%, which is not surprising. Courts often find neglect when a child has been injured but there is insufficient evidence to prove intentional child abuse (Goldstein, 1999). In addition, poverty often contributes to neglect when families experiencing financial need cannot access appropriate supports (Ramsey & Abrams, 2003). Physical abuse cases comprise the next largest percentage at 17.6%, followed by sexual abuse at 9.2% and psychological abuse at 8.1%.

Research suggests that teenage parents and parents who were themselves abused as children are at increased risk for engaging in child maltreatment (Child Welfare Information Gateway, 2006a; Schuyler Center for Analysis and Advocacy, 2008). Additional risk factors include parental or family substance abuse; depression, stress, or other mental health problems; family violence such as intimate partner violence; unemployment; poverty; community violence; family isolation; lack of parental knowledge of child development and children's needs; and lack of support for dealing with children with disabilities or developmental delays (Council on Virginia's Future, 2010).

Consequences of Child Maltreatment

Childhood is a time of enormous physical, social, and emotional growth. Child maltreatment can have a significant impact on a child's physical, behavioral, and psychological development (Downs et al., 2009; Hagele, 2005). In some cases, child maltreatment can cause impaired development of the brain (DeBellis & Thomas, 2003). These impairments have long-term consequences for cognitive, language, and academic abilities (Watts-English, Fortson, Gibler, Hooper, & DeBellis, 2006). According to the National Survey of Child and Adolescent Well-Being (U.S. DHHS, 2003), children placed in out-of-home care as a result of maltreatment had lower scores than the general population on measures of cognitive capacity and language development. In addition, maltreated children may experience delays in fine and gross motor skills. Child abuse and neglect have well-documented effects on child development that, for many victims, persist into adulthood (National Clearinghouse on Child Abuse & Neglect Information, 2001).

Although not all child maltreatment victims suffer behavioral consequences, child abuse and neglect may make some maladaptive behaviors more likely. Studies indicate that abused and neglected children are 25% more likely than other children to experience delinquency, drug use, teen pregnancy, and low academic achievement (Kelley, Thornberry, & Smith, 1997). They are also more likely to continue unhealthy behaviors into adulthood, including smoking cigarettes, abusing alcohol, and using illegal drugs (Dube et al., 2001). Approximately one-third of maltreated children will go on to victimize their own children (Prevent Child Abuse New York, 2003). Finally, research suggests that children subject to abuse and neglect may experience poor mental and emotional health, including anxiety, depression, eating disorders, and suicide (Silverman, Reinherz, & Giaconia, 1996). Emotional conditions including posttraumatic stress disorder, dissociative disorders, panic disorders, and reactive attachment disorder may also be associated with child maltreatment.

The consequences of child abuse and neglect differ for each child. Contributing factors include the child's age and developmental status when the abuse occurred; the frequency, type, and severity of abuse; and the relationship between the victim and the abuser (Chalk, Gibbons, & Scarupa, 2002; English, Widom, & Brandford, 2004). Overall, however, studies show that adults who were maltreated as children have twice the number of serious health problems as non-maltreated adults, including an increased incidence of alcohol and substance abuse disorders (Hagele, 2005).

The Life Cycle of a Child Maltreatment Case

An elaborate set of processes is brought into play when child abuse or neglect is suspected. This process begins with a report that is followed by an investigation, development of a case plan, court proceedings, and the possible placement of the child in substitute out-of-home care. Social workers play various roles throughout the life cycle of a maltreatment case, many of which are highlighted in the following discussion. Although many child protective services (CPS) workers are not degreed social workers, the two terms will be used here interchangeably.

Reporting Suspected Maltreatment

All 50 states, the District of Columbia, and the U.S. territories have mandatory reporting laws for child abuse and neglect. Social workers as well as other professionals including teachers, law enforcement officials, mental health professionals, and child care workers are required by law to report child abuse or neglect if they have actual knowledge of abuse or neglect, if they suspect or have reason to believe a child has been abused or neglected, or if they have observed that the child is subjected to conditions that would reasonably result in harm (Child Welfare Information Gateway, 2008; Crosson-Tower, 2009). This is known as the *reasonable suspicion* or *reasonable cause to suspect or believe* standard. Eighteen states have enacted universal reporting laws under which any person suspecting child abuse or neglect is required by law to report it (Persky, 2012).

Mandated reporters may face criminal and civil penalties for *failure to report* (Goldstein, 1999; Ramsey & Abrams, 2003), but only if it is done willfully or maliciously. The consequences vary considerably by state and may involve fines of between $100 and $5,000 and jail time of between 10 days and 5 years. Thirty-eight states treat failure to report as a misdemeanor and in several states (Arizona, Florida, and Minnesota), the violation may be upgraded to a felony in more serious cases of maltreatment (Child Welfare Information Gateway, 2007b). At the other end of the spectrum from failing to report is *false reporting*, which is generally defined as willfully or intentionally making a report of child abuse or neglect that the reporter knows to be false. Approximately 30 states recognize false reporting in state statutes and define penalties that may include misdemeanor or felony charges. In six states (California, Colorado, Idaho, Indiana, Minnesota, and North Dakota), a person may also be civilly liable for damages. Some states have adopted enhanced penalties for false reports made with malicious intent (Child Welfare Information Gateway, 2007b). For example, Idaho law specifies that when a "defendant acted with malice or oppression, the court may award treble [triple] actual damages or treble statutory damages, whichever is greater" (Idaho Code § 16-1607). Similarly, in Kentucky, "any person who knowingly makes a false report and does so with malice shall be guilty of a Class A misdemeanor" (Rev. Stat. § 620.050[1]). Malicious false reporting most often occurs in hotly contested child custody cases as a way of gaining the upper hand over a competing parent.

Despite the proliferation of mandatory reporting laws, problems remain with both the underreporting and overreporting of child maltreatment. Many incidents of child abuse and neglect are never reported. People are often unsure about whether abuse or neglect actually took place; they may not realize that only reasonable suspicion, not certainty, is required. Others are unaware of whom to contact if abuse or neglect does occur—or may believe that the involvement of government authorities will result in removal of the child, thus doing more harm than good. Some are concerned about the repercussions of being identified as the reporter and may be reluctant to risk angering the family (American Humane, 2008). Professionals may fear that reporting will affect their trust relationship with the client (Downs et al., 2009; Goldstein, 1999). Finally, some are unwilling to get involved or may believe that someone else will take care of the situation (American Humane, 2008).

In contrast, overreporting can also occur. In 2006, 60% of all reports made to child protective services agencies were unfounded (Downs et al., 2009). Even among those reports that receive significant attention, less than one-third actually make their way to court (Ramsey & Abrams, 2003). The number of false reports proliferates following the appearance of a high-profile child maltreatment case in the media or following an increase in community awareness. For example, in the five months following the widely publicized discovery of four dead children in the home of D.C. resident Banita Jacks, reports to the city's CPS hotline increased by 400% (Myers, 2008). Unfortunately, this can have negative consequences by overwhelming the agency with unnecessary investigations, thereby diverting scarce resources from those cases with greatest need (Child Welfare Information Gateway, 2008).

The Investigation Phase

Once a report of suspected child abuse or neglect is received, CPS determines whether or not the case fits within the state's definition of child maltreatment and the criteria for investigation. Approximately 70% of reports pass this hurdle and are subsequently investigated (McCarthy et al., 2003;). CPS then initiates an agency investigation, usually within 24 hours, to determine whether or not the allegation is true and to assess the safety level of the child. Agencies often rely on specially trained social workers to make contact with those involved and to complete the investigation. This typically involves a visit to the child's residence or to the site of the alleged maltreatment and interviews with the alleged perpetrators, victims, siblings, and other non-offending adults in the home. Other sources of information during the investigation may include police, teachers, coaches, mental health professionals, and other community service providers involved with the family (U.S. Department of Health and Human Services, 2003).

During an investigation, CPS workers must respect the parent's constitutional rights under the Fourth Amendment to be free from unreasonable search and seizure (Goldstein, 1999; Ramsey & Abrams, 2003). Searches without a warrant may be conducted only in an emergency or in circumstances otherwise permitted by state law (Ramsey & Abrams, 2003). Most states allow CPS workers to interview children without a parent present. Child interviews without parental consent have traditionally been permissible when a child is at school or in the temporary custody of another adult. In order to interview a child privately in the home over the parent's objection, a court order is required.

INTERVIEWING CHILD VICTIMS

The purpose of conducting a forensic interview with a child witness or victim is to collect evidentiary information that will stand up in court. All of the rules discussed in Chapter 3, in relation to forensic interviewing generally, apply equally when interviewing children. However, conducting forensic interviews with children presents special challenges. Depending on their age and level of maturity, children may have limited recall and communication skills (Tang, 2006). They also may be highly reluctant to disclose abuse or may provide inaccurate information. For this reason, it is imperative that skilled forensic interviewers—including trained forensic social work professionals—be involved in the interview process: "Although children are capable of providing accurate, reliable, and forensically useful information, they are vulnerable to suggestion. Leading, suggestive, or coercive questioning can not only result in a child making inaccurate statements, it can cause the child to develop a subjectively real memory for an event that never happened" (Wakefield, 2006, p. 57). Given the sensitive nature of interviewing children, researchers and practitioners have developed a number of helpful guidelines (Faller, 2007):

- Whenever possible, before meeting with the child, interview the child's caregiver to discuss the child's history and any observed behaviors.
- Interview the child alone if he or she is old enough to be separated from the parent.
- Remember that gradual disclosure is common. Young children may do better with an extended interview over two to six sessions that are brief in duration.
- Be aware of the child's stage of development, cultural needs, and the possible impact of trauma on both memory and communication.
- When videotaping the interview, explain to the child what you are doing and show the child the equipment. Introduce anyone who will be observing. Explain to the child that you will be writing down what he or she tells you. Build trust by demonstrating that there will not be any secrets.
- Avoid using play, fantasy, or imagination. Draw a clear distinction between play time and truth time.
- Use the rapport-building phase to assess the child's ability to observe, remember, and communicate.
- Keep your language simple and appropriate to the developmental age of the child. Avoid compound questions and double negatives.
- With young children, include a truth-telling step in your protocol. Use this to ascertain the ability and willingness of the child to tell the truth.
- Stress that it is acceptable for the child to say "I don't know" in response to a question.
- Reinforce that because you were not there when the event occurred, the child needs to explain to you what happened.
- Use the child's own language. Double-check what he or she means when using slang or "family names" for body parts. Clarify whom a child is referring to if people are identified by relationship rather than by actual name. Never make assumptions.
- Allow children to use media (pictures, dolls, etc.) to communicate with the interviewer. Suggest changing media if the child becomes agitated.
- Minimize the number of professionals who interview the child. Frequent repetitions can be draining for the child and may reduce the reliability of a disclosure.

Social workers should approach child interviews with particular sensitivity and a keen understanding of cognitive, social, and emotional development. Cultural factors may also influence how the interview is conducted and how the child responds. As with any forensic interview, the goal is a simple one: to ascertain the truth.

Legal challenges have recently questioned the ability of social workers to conduct interviews in the school setting without a search warrant, court order, or parental consent. In *Camreta v. Greene* (2011), a suspected victim of child sexual abuse was interviewed on school premises; the girl's mother subsequently brought suit, claiming the interview had violated the Fourth Amendment's protection against unreasonable search and seizure. The district court found in favor of the social worker, but the Court of Appeals for the Ninth Circuit reversed, concluding that the interview had indeed been unconstitutional because it was conducted in the absence of both a warrant and parental consent. The case was appealed to the U.S. Supreme Court, which declined to consider the Fourth Amendment issue—leaving the circuit court decision in favor of the parent intact. NASW filed an *amicus* brief in this case, emphasizing the importance of using multidisciplinary teams and having safe interviewing spaces in order to protect children from additional trauma during child abuse investigations. NASW has expressed concern that the decision in *Camreta v. Greene* may interfere with the use of best practice approaches by social workers, hindering their ability to perform their jobs and protect the children they work with (Morgan & Khan, 2011; NASW, 2011).

When a child abuse investigation is complete, the worker makes a determination concerning the validity of the maltreatment report, categorizing the results as follows:

- *Substantiated* or *founded*. The results of the investigation support the criteria for child abuse and neglect found in the applicable state statute
- *Indicated* or *reason to suspect*. The report cannot be substantiated under state law, but there is nonetheless reason to suspect abuse or neglect
- *Not substantiated* or *unfounded*. The report cannot be substantiated under state law and the investigation suggests no reason to suspect maltreatment

Different states categorize investigation results differently. In Virginia, for example, the category of *reason to suspect* was eliminated in 1995. Findings are now limited to *founded* or *unfounded*. States also vary in the standard of proof required to conclude that a report is *substantiated*. Missouri, for example, made it more difficult to substantiate a report of child maltreatment in 2004 when it went from requiring *probable cause* to requiring a *preponderance of the evidence*. *Probable cause* requires only a reasonable belief that a child was abused or neglected, whereas a *preponderance of the evidence* requires it to be more likely than not that the maltreatment occurred (Missouri Department of Social Services, 2008).

Assessment and Response

Following this initial investigation, the worker must determine whether the child can remain safely in the home and whether the family is in need of services. The following guidelines are recommended (Downs et al., 2009, p. 128):

- Child safety should be the primary consideration.
- Services should be child focused and family centered.
- Services should be provided in the child's home if the child can remain there safely.
- Services should aim to enhance the child's well-being and improve the ability of parents to meet the child's needs.
- Services should be culturally sensitive and culturally responsive.

In order to ensure that the safety of the child is not compromised, the worker must conduct an assessment of the family to determine whether the child can remain in the home. The goal of preserving the family must be balanced against any immediate safety risks to the child (Crosson-Tower, 2009). As a result of the assessment, workers may develop a safety plan with the parents that will allow the child to remain in the home, develop a voluntary plan for the family to receive agency services to support the child at home, or decide that it is unsafe for the child to remain in the home. In the latter case, the worker may conduct an *emergency removal*. This entails collaborating with the agency's legal counsel to file an abuse/neglect petition within 72 hours (Clement, 1997; Downs et al., 2009). If the worker does not believe emergency removal is necessary, the worker has 45 days to file a petition with the appropriate court (Clement, 1997).

Placement in Out-of-Home Care

Generally speaking, unless and until parental rights are terminated, reunification remains the goal for families with a child in an out-of-home placement. This preference for reunification was clearly established by the Adoption Assistance and Child Welfare Act of 1980, following reports that children were languishing in foster care even though it was designed to be a temporary solution. Reunification is seen as having a less detrimental effect on children than alternative placements outside the home (Goldstein, 1999). This is supported by research revealing that children in foster care experience poorer mental health outcomes than their counterparts in the general population, are seven times more likely to have substance abuse problems, and are five times more likely to experience posttraumatic stress disorder (Pecora et al., 2003).

In addition to the state bearing the burden of proof in cases of abuse and neglect, the 1980 act required that CPS agencies make reasonable efforts to preserve or reunite the family by providing an appropriate array of services. According to the U.S. Supreme Court in *Suter v. Artist M.* (1992), however, this does not mean that parents have a right to sue if reasonable efforts have not been made; it means only that states must submit a plan to demonstrate reasonable efforts in order to receive federal funding. Exceptions to the reasonable efforts requirement apply when parental rights have been terminated in relation to a child's sibling; when the parent has been convicted of murder or voluntary manslaughter of another child; or when the parent has subjected the child to certain aggravated circumstances, including sexual abuse (Ramsey & Abrams, 2003).

When it is determined that a child cannot safely remain in the home, the child is placed in an out-of-home setting. The goal is to offer a family-like environment whenever possible (Crosson-Tower, 2009). Although the CPS agency chooses the out-of-home placement for the child, it is the court's role to monitor this placement and ensure that it is in the child's best interests (Goldstein, 1999). The social worker determines the available placement options and decides which will most effectively meet the child's needs. This placement may be with other relatives, friends, foster parents, or in an institution (such as a group home or residential treatment facility); placements that offer minimal disruption for the child are favored (Goldstein, 1999; Ramsey & Abrams, 2003). In 2009, 20.8% of those identified as child abuse victims were placed in foster care (U.S. DHHS, 2010).

Family Foster Care

More than 400,000 children are in foster care in the United States (U.S. DHHS, 2011b). Foster care providers are licensed by the state and receive a monetary stipend to provide for the child's needs. Under these foster care arrangements, the foster parents make day-to-day decisions for the child, but the state retains legal custody and the right to alter the child's placement arrangements. Consequently, a child may be removed from a foster home at the state's discretion in order to be reunified with the parent or may be placed in another foster home. Placement with extended family—kinship care—is often the least disruptive option for the child because many children have established relationships with these caregivers. Both the Adoption Assistance and Child Welfare Act of 1980 and the Indian Child Welfare Act support the use of kinship care in out-of-home placements for children (Goldstein, 1999). More recently, the Fostering Connections to Success Act of 2008 established new federal support for kinship families by requiring that relatives be notified when a child is in need of care, providing federal funding for kinship caregivers through Guardian Assistance Programs, and authorizing federal funding for kinship navigator systems to assist relative caregivers in identifying available community resources (Child Welfare League of America, 2009). Regardless of whether children are placed with family or in nonrelative care, foster care is intended to be temporary, with the goal of reunification or another permanent option such as adoption (Ramsey & Abrams, 2003).

Institutional Care

Institutional care includes residential treatment, group homes, shelter facilities, and hospitals. Institutional care is considered to be a more restrictive option than family foster care and is thus less desirable. Children in institutional settings are typically those who previously experienced unsuccessful placements in family foster homes or who have specialized needs that are difficult to handle in a family setting (Crosson-Tower, 2009). The focus of institutional care is on rehabilitation for the child, with staff acting as a therapeutic family. As with other foster care placements, the goal is for the child to be reunified with his or her family or placed for adoption (Crosson-Tower 2008).

Transitioning Out of Care

Although out-of-home care is intended to be short term and temporary, many children remain in foster care until age 18 without ever achieving a permanent living situation. According to the U.S. Census Bureau, of the approximately 500,000 children in the foster care system in the United States, an estimated 24,000 *age out* of care each year and attempt to live independently (Gardner, 2008). These youth, who often leave the child welfare system with no family to fall back on, face increased risks for victimization, poverty, incarceration, mental illness, substance abuse, unwanted pregnancy, and homelessness (Wald & Martinez, 2003). Through funds made available under the Foster Care Independence Act of 1999 (P.L. 106-169), agencies are able to provide teenagers in care with independent living services aimed at preparing them for a successful transition to adulthood. Examples of these programs and services include healthy relationship building and self-esteem; daily living skills; budgeting and financial management; assistance in obtaining a high school diploma; employment services, job placement, and retention; career exploration; vocational training or preparation for postsecondary education; healthy living activities (smoking avoidance, substance abuse and pregnancy prevention); mentoring; crisis intervention (money for rent, utilities, and food); and financial, housing, and other appropriate supports (Missouri Department of Social Services, 2009). States and localities vary in the number and type of independent living programs and services they provide. The Foster Care Independence Act also allows states to provide Medicaid coverage to youth aging out of care, extended room and board payments to youth ages 18–21 who are leaving the foster care system, and adoption incentive payments to states that increase the number of children adopted from foster care.

Going to Court

Allegations of child abuse and neglect may trigger both civil and criminal processes. In the civil process, dependency courts (also known as family courts, juvenile courts, or domestic relations courts) determine whether or not the child has been maltreated and what will happen as a result. The goal is not to punish the perpetrator, but rather to ensure the safety and best interests of the child (Goldstein, 1999; Ramsey & Abrams, 2003). All alleged cases of abuse and neglect for which a petition is filed are heard through this civil process.

In some cases, criminal charges are also filed. These cases are handled through criminal courts and are concerned with determining the guilt or innocence of the alleged perpetrator. The goal is the protection of society as a whole (Goldstein, 1999). Criminal charges most often are filed against perpetrators when children have been severely injured or killed as a result of maltreatment or in cases of sexual abuse (Crosson-Tower, 2009). These proceedings are separate from civil proceedings and, like any other criminal case, require that the government prove its case *beyond a reasonable doubt*. The specific criminal charges brought are based on the severity and outcome of the alleged abuse and may include murder, manslaughter, or assault and battery. Some states also recognize as crimes the aggravated abuse of children, unreasonable corporal punishment, and child endangerment (Goldstein, 1999; Ramsey & Abrams, 2003).

Every case, whether civil or criminal, requires the court to reconcile the respective rights and interests of the state (on behalf of the child) and the parents (or other alleged perpetrators of abuse). On one hand, our legal system purports to give parents wide-ranging discretion in raising their children—and our culture prizes privacy within the nuclear family. On the other hand, we have committed ourselves to safeguarding the well-being of vulnerable children. This tension is often on display in child welfare cases, especially when unfamiliar cultural norms or unusual family traditions have resulted in allegations of maltreatment.

Although states are empowered to intervene when children are believed to be at risk, the U.S. Supreme Court has made clear that they have no affirmative responsibility to do so under the Constitution. In the landmark 1989 case of *DeShaney v. Winnebago County Department of Social Services,* a 4-year-old child was brutally beaten by his father over a period of several years. Repeated reports to CPS went unheeded. The child consequently sustained severe brain damage, leaving him unable to live a normal life. The Court found that under the 14th Amendment, the state agency had no duty to protect children even from known, ongoing abuse; the provision was designed to safeguard citizens from government wrongs, not from each other.

RECOVERED MEMORY SYNDROME

Since the 1980s, a topic of considerable controversy has been the phenomenon of recovered memory—that is, memories of childhood abuse that are "recovered" during adulthood either spontaneously or in the course of therapy. The debate centers on whether or not traumatic experiences can actually be forgotten and later retrieved, the accuracy and credibility of recovered memories, and the role of therapy in influencing recollections of childhood abuse.

Recovered memory is both a clinical issue and a legal one. It becomes a legal issue when clients who recover repressed memories bring suit against their alleged perpetrators. Some of these cases are successful; others are not. In *Anonymous v. Vella* (2006), for example, a jury awarded the 33-year-old plaintiff $1.75 million in a case against her father, a Baptist minister. She alleged that he had repeatedly sexually abused her from ages 3 to 12. He was found guilty following expert testimony supporting the validity of repressed memory claims.

Lawsuits can also be brought against clinicians by clients or alleged perpetrators. In *Ramona v. Isabella* (1994), a 19-year-old college student charged her father with child sexual abuse based on memories recovered during therapy. He, in turn, sued the therapist for implanting false memories via hypnosis and sodium amytal ("truth serum") during his daughter's treatment for bulimia. The father was acquitted and the jury awarded him $500,000 in damages.

A final legal issue raised by recovered memory cases concerns the relevant statutes of limitations for child abuse and neglect—that is, how long can a plaintiff wait before bringing the alleged perpetrator to court? As of 2003, a total of 42 states had revised their statutes of limitations to apply what is called the *discovery rule*. Under this rule, the statute of limitations begins to run when the victim recalls the abuse, rather than when the act of abuse actually occurred. Some states also apply the discovery rule when plaintiffs were aware of the abuse during childhood but connected the abuse to subsequent psychological harm only as adults (Goldstein, 1999).

As a clinical issue, it is important to recognize that no test or instrument can confirm whether or not a recovered memory is accurate. Clients seeking treatment should be alerted to the associated risks, including the possibility that they may never know whether or not their memories are true. Therapists should avoid using retrieval techniques unless absolutely necessary for the client's benefit and unless specifically trained in the methods employed. Finally, therapists involved in recovered memory cases often must testify in court, whether in an action against the alleged perpetrator or in defending against a malpractice suit (Madden & Parody, 1997). It is important to be conversant with the research literature on recovered memory to understand both sides of the debate.

The Players

Every case that goes to court represents a contest between opposing parties. In civil child welfare cases, at least three important parties are involved: the CPS agency, the parent or other alleged perpetrator, and the *guardian ad litem* for the child. All parties are entitled to constitutional due process protections including notice, legal counsel, the right to present evidence, and the right to confront and cross-examine witnesses (Crosson-Tower, 2009).

The Agency

The CPS worker, assisted by the agency's legal counsel, files a petition of abuse and/or neglect. This is what triggers the involvement of the court. The agency social worker then plays a number of different roles throughout the course of child dependency proceedings. These include providing testimony to support the allegations in the petition, developing a family treatment plan to be adopted by the court, providing written and oral updates on the family's progress toward meeting the case plan goals, demonstrating that reasonable efforts have been made to preserve the family unit, recommending specific out-of-home placements when appropriate, monitoring and supporting reunification, and offering evidence to support the agency's recommendations (Downs et al., 2009).

The Parents

Parents may represent themselves or request legal counsel. If they cannot afford counsel, they may apply for representation by a public defender. Any attorney representing the parents is under an ethical obligation to represent the parents' interests, even if they differ from the interests of the child or family (Vandervort, 2008). Parents may choose to testify during the proceedings but may also exercise their Fifth Amendment right against self-incrimination and remain silent (Ramsey & Abrams, 2003). If the court finds the child to be abused or neglected, the court may order the parents to participate in services or in the case plan submitted by the CPS agency.

Guardian Ad Litem

Under the Child Abuse and Prevention Treatment Act as amended in 2003 (section 106 [b][2][xiii]), children in a child abuse and neglect proceeding are entitled to a *guardian ad litem* (GAL) to serve as an independent advocate for the child's interests. The GAL is included in all proceedings involving the alleged maltreatment of the child (Goldstein, 1999) and is responsible for conducting an independent investigation, including meeting with the child and family, in order to protect the child's interests throughout the case (Child Welfare Information Gateway, 2006b). Some states permit only attorneys to serve as GALs, whereas others permit the role to be filled by members of other professional disciplines (including social workers) or by special advocates appointed by the court, known as court-appointed special advocates (CASAs). Since 1973, community members have been recruited and trained to look out for the interests of children in abuse and neglect proceedings as CASA volunteers (Clement, 1997). Today, there is an extensive network of local and state CASA programs throughout the country. In 2011, more than 77.000 CASA volunteers served 234,000 children (National CASA Association, 2012).

The Proceedings

A case enters the court through the filing of an abuse, neglect, or dependency petition by the CPS agency. What follows is a series of legal steps. These are depicted in Figure 6.2 and described next.

FIGURE 6.2   Court Process

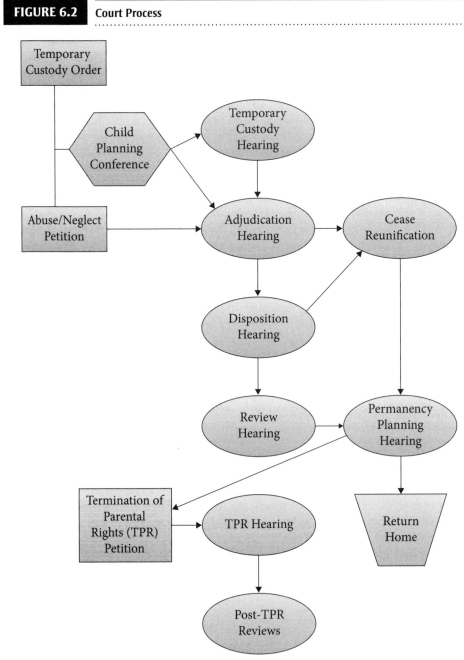

Source: North Carolina Administrative Office of the Courts (n.d.).

Temporary/Emergency Custody Hearing

This hearing allows the judge to decide whether or not a child should remain in custody following an emergency removal from the home (Crosson-Tower, 2008). Judges will also inquire about the needs of the child, available placements for the child, and the locations of parents and other relatives. It is generally held within 72 hours after removal and involves testimony from the CPS worker regarding the situation that resulted in the child being removed.

Adjudication Hearing

At the adjudication hearing, which usually occurs within 60 days after the filing of the initial petition, facts and circumstances surrounding the abuse and neglect allegations are presented to the court. The judge must determine if the child is abused, neglected, or dependent (as defined by the applicable state statute), justifying government intervention with the family. The CPS agency (representing the state) has the burden of proof and must demonstrate that the child has been maltreated according to the state's abuse, neglect, and dependency laws. Most states require only a preponderance of the evidence, although some require the higher standard of clear and convincing evidence. At this point, the judge can either dismiss the petition and the child is returned to or remains with the family, or he or she can issue a finding of abuse, neglect, or dependency and assert jurisdiction over the child (Goldstein, 1999).

Disposition Hearing

The disposition hearing may immediately follow adjudication or may occur shortly thereafter. In any case, it is recommended that it occur within 30 days. The purpose of the disposition hearing is twofold: to make a custodial decision for the child and to adopt a case plan to guide the family in addressing the issues leading to the child's abuse or neglect (Crosson-Tower, 2009; Goldstein, 1999). In making a custodial decision, the judge may order that the child remain at home or decide that out-of-home placement is necessary. In the former instance, the agency social worker would provide information about available in-home family supports; in the latter, he or she would identify possible out-of-home placements for the child including available relatives, friends, and foster parents. Federal guidelines (P.L. 96-272) favor the least restrictive placement environment for children. Federal law also prioritizes placing children with relatives, assuming they meet all relevant child protection standards (42 U.S.C. 671[a][19]). Meanwhile, court-filed case plans, developed jointly by the family and the CPS worker, identify what the family needs to do to end court intervention and/or achieve reunification. Case plans often include behavioral goals for parents as well as rehabilitative services that will be provided to the family. Once adopted, the case plan becomes an order of the court (Goldstein, 1999).

Review Hearings

Review hearings are held periodically to assess the parent's treatment progress and determine whether the child can safely be returned home. Under the Adoption Assistance and Child Welfare Act of 1980 (P.L. 96-272), states are required to review each case at least every 6 months when a child is in a temporary setting, although some states review cases more frequently. During these hearings, the agency reports on its efforts to reunify the family and updates the court regarding the family's treatment progress. Illustration 6.1 contains a sample progress report. This is the kind of report a social worker might prepare for a review hearing.

ILLUSTRATION 6.1

Sample Progress Report

FAMILY COURT
CHILD ABUSE AND NEGLECT DOCKET

In the Matter of: Allan Smith   DOB: 6/18/08
Case Number: 08-7779
Parents: Richard and Grace Smith
Hearing Date: 12/05/08
Progress Report for Review Hearing

History

Grace gave birth to Allan on 6/18/08 at Jones County Hospital. Allan showed signs of drug withdrawal from birth and Grace tested positive for opiates on the day of his birth. Grace admitted to having a substance abuse problem and using opiates while pregnant with Allan. Upon investigation, Richard also admitted to having a substance abuse problem. On June 30, 2008, Richard and Grace left Allan in the home unattended with no adult present. A police report indicates that they were at the home of a known drug dealer at this time. Following this incident and their refusal to engage in substance abuse counseling, the court ordered temporary custody of Allan to Jones County Children Services.

Placement

Allan was placed in the home of paternal aunt, Shirley Smith, and remains in this placement. Caseworker has visited Allan in the home on a monthly basis since his initial placement. Allan appears happy and comfortable in their home. He smiles and laughs when playing with Shirley. Shirley is retired and is able to provide for Allan's daily care. Allan continues to show signs of withdrawal and engages in self-soothing behavior. Shirley ensures that Allan attends all of his doctor's appointments, including a visit to a neurologist last month. The neurologist reported that Allan is no longer having withdrawal-induced seizures. Shirley keeps Richard and Grace notified of Allan's appointments and also offers to provide them with transportation.

Progress

- Richard and Grace continue to work on their case plan goals. Grace engaged in services at Meadowbrook Recovery Services on September 3rd. Since then, she has attended 50% of her scheduled sessions. Grace reports that she has transportation problems on the days she does not make it to these appointments. Caseworker has provided Grace with a bus pass to alleviate this problem. Grace's progress reports from her treatment at Meadowbrook Recovery Services are attached to this report. These reports indicate that Grace continues to express a desire to abuse substances. She has tested positive for opiates on 3 occasions between September and December.

- Richard has not engaged in substance abuse counseling. Richard scheduled an assessment appointment at Meadowbrook Recovery Services on September 10th but did not attend. Richard reports to caseworker that he does not believe that he has a substance abuse problem and described his drug use as "recreational." Richard has not completed a substance abuse test that caseworker requested.

- Both Richard and Grace express a desire to regain custody of Allan. They have both engaged in parent mentor services. The agency parent mentor reports that both parents fully participate in parent mentor sessions and has also observed positive interactions between parents and Allan.

- Richard and Grace have attended regular visits with Allan in Shirley's home. They visit for 3 hours, three times a week, and occasionally on the weekends. Shirley reports that Richard and Grace attend regularly but that at times they are distracted. Shirley reports that at some visits, Grace will spend more than half of the visit talking on the phone to friends. Caseworker has also observed Grace's disengagement in visits and spoken to Grace about ways to make the visits more natural for both her and Allan.

Recommendations

We recommend Allan remain in the temporary custody of Jones County Children Services and remain placed in the home of paternal aunt, Shirley Smith. There is concern that Richard and Grace continue to have substance abuse problems that interfere with their ability to safely supervise Allan. It is also concerning that Grace does not engage during her visits with Allan. We recommend that they continue to work on their case plan goals including continuing their work with the parent mentor, fully engaging in substance abuse counseling, and fully engaging in visits with Allan.

Permanency Hearing

Permanency reviews are held for the court to examine case progress and make a determination regarding a permanent plan for the child. Options for permanency include reunification with parents, terminating parental rights, adoption, legal guardianship, placing a child with a relative or close family friend, and agreeing to another planned permanent living arrangement. Federal law requires that a permanency hearing be held within 12 months of a child's entering foster care (P.L. 105-89).

Termination of Parental Rights (TPR)

A termination of parental rights (TPR) hearing occurs when the agency decides that it will no longer seek to reunify a child with the family. The agency must file a TPR petition with the court outlining specific facts supporting the petition. At the hearing, the judge decides whether to terminate parental rights, which has the effect of permanently severing all legal ties between the parent and child (Goldstein, 1999; Ramsey & Abrams, 2003). Grounds for TPR petitions vary from state to state and are defined in each state's statutes. General requirements include a prior adjudication of maltreatment and the parents' failure to comply with the treatment plan (Clark & Estin, 2000). The court must also find that termination is in the child's best interests. Under the Adoption and Safe Families Act, parental rights may be terminated because of abandonment or prior abuse of a sibling. If a child has been in out-of-home care for 15 of the past 22 months, states must initiate TPR proceedings, although there are some exceptions. TPR is considered to be so significant a deprivation of parental rights that the U.S. Supreme Court requires the government to prove its case by *clear and convincing evidence (Santosky v. Kramer*, 1982), a higher standard than is typical in civil proceedings.

Post-Termination Placement Reviews

The purpose of post-termination placement reviews is for the court to review the agency's progress in achieving a permanent placement for the child. It may examine the appropriateness of the permanency planning goal, the appropriateness of the child's current placement, and the adequacy of the agency's efforts to arrange an adoption or other permanent care. The caseworker's tasks include reporting on what actions have been taken to achieve permanency, progress in eliminating permanency barriers, and timelines for actually attaining permanency for the child (State Court Administrative Office, 2008).

Children as Witnesses in Court

In both civil and criminal proceedings, children may be called to testify in court regarding allegations of abuse and neglect. The issue of children as witnesses raises two important considerations: the competence of a child to take the stand and provide reliable testimony and the need to protect children within the judicial process (Schneider & Brinig, 2000).

It is essential that the child's testimony be reliable and accurate because it remains an important source of evidence in determining the validity of an abuse allegation. This serves the best interests of the child as well as the interests of the court (Schneider & Brinig, 2000). It is important to recognize that, legally, age alone is not considered an absolute determinant of competency. According to the Supreme Court in *Wheeler v. United States* (1895), "there is no precise age which determines the question of competency. This depends on the capacity and intelligence of the child, his appreciation of the difference between truth and falsehood, as well as of his duty to tell the former" (p. 524). As a result, all children are deemed competent to testify unless and until their competency is challenged (Goldstein, 1999). Once challenged, the court determines the child's competency using essentially the same criteria enunciated in *Wheeler* more than a century ago: whether the child can distinguish between the truth and a lie, appreciate the meaning of taking an oath, and understand the potential consequences of lying on the stand (Myers, 1998). In addition, the child must demonstrate sufficient memory and intelligence, as well as an adequate ability to observe, recall, and communicate information. Methods of ascertaining the competency of child witnesses vary depending on the judge, the court, and the jurisdiction. Most, however, use one or a combination of the following (Bourg Carter, 2009):

- The judge appoints a forensic mental health professional to assess the child's competence to testify.
- The child is brought to the courtroom and questioned by the attorneys and/or the judge about competency-related matters.

- The judge reviews the child's sworn statement and/or deposition.
- Testimony related to witness competency is taken from those who are familiar with the child's abilities or from those who interviewed the child about the alleged incident(s).

When a child is found competent to testify, additional issues come into play. In criminal proceedings, the Constitution's Sixth Amendment protects the right of the accused to confront his or her accuser. When the accused is an alleged perpetrator and the child is a victim, the prospect of testifying may have serious consequences for the emotional health of the child. Because the state has an interest in safeguarding the child's physical and psychological well-being, the judicial system has developed strategies to meet the child's needs while simultaneously satisfying the defendant's constitutional right to confrontation. These include limiting face-to-face confrontation, age-appropriate examinations, and permitting the child to testify out of court.

Limiting face-to-face confrontation reduces the trauma that can be associated with children facing an alleged perpetrator (Ramsey & Abrams, 2003) and may result in more accurate and comprehensive testimony. If the state can demonstrate that there is a compelling interest to protect the child victim from face-to-face confrontation, the court will allow the use of videotaped testimony from the child, one-way closed circuit television, or two-way closed circuit television (Clark & Estin, 2000; Ramsey & Abrams, 2003). In *Coy v. Iowa* (1988), the Supreme Court struck down the use of a screen that provided a visual barrier between two 13-year-old victim witnesses and the alleged perpetrator, finding that it violated the confrontation clause. Two years later, in *Maryland v. Craig* (1990), the Court upheld the use of one-way, closed-circuit television for the testimony of a 6-year-old child in a sexual abuse case, noting the emotional distress that courtroom testimony might cause the child and the detrimental effect it might have on his ability to communicate clearly.

Courts may also require that the examination of the child be age appropriate (Goldstein, 1999) in an effort to ensure that the child understands the content of the attorneys' questions and feels as comfortable as possible in the courtroom. The judge can enforce this by encouraging attorneys to use age-appropriate language and a suitable tone during their interactions with child witnesses, as well as by intervening when attorneys are not approaching the examination of the child as they should. Lawyers and social workers often prepare children for court appearances by bringing them into the courtroom ahead of time, allowing them to get the feel of the witness stand, and explaining who will be present and what will transpire on the day of the trial.

Finally, courts may admit children's out-of-court statements under exceptions to the hearsay rule contained in the Federal Rules of Evidence (Goldstein, 1999; Ramsey & Abrams, 2003). Most courts, for example, will accept out-of-court statements that constitute excited utterances (unplanned comments made in reaction to a startling event), statements made for the purpose of medical diagnosis or treatment, prior consistent statements, statements of present bodily sensations or present sense impressions, and fresh complaints of rape (Goldstein, 1999). In *Idaho v. Wright* (1990), however, the Supreme Court ruled that the admission of statements a child made to a pediatrician about her own and her sister's abuse violated the alleged perpetrator's rights under the confrontation clause. In this case, the Court found insufficient reason to consider the statements trustworthy.

Summary and Conclusion

Child maltreatment is a social problem of enormous proportions that can have devastating physical, behavioral, and emotional consequences. Although a number of child welfare laws have been enacted by Congress over the past several decades, child maltreatment remains an issue that is largely addressed state by state. The reporting of suspected maltreatment triggers a complex legal process that ultimately determines the fate of children and their families. Social workers and others in child welfare agencies are intimately involved in these proceedings, along with judges, attorneys, and *guardians ad litem*. In addition to the civil process that ensures the safety of the child, charges against the alleged perpetrator may also be filed in criminal court. Experts continue to wrestle with the issue of how to safeguard children who testify in these proceedings while respecting the defendant's constitutional rights.

Sample Case

Following is a child maltreatment case from New York that raises some important policy and practice issues. After you read the case, try briefing it in order to synthesize the important information. Then consider the questions that appear at the end of the case.

DUMPSON V. DANIEL M.
New York Law J., Oct. 16, 1974, at 17

Judge Rigler.

This neglect action has been commenced pursuant to article 10 of the Family Court Act. A preliminary hearing on Aug. 18, 1974, resulted in an order directing temporary removal of three children from the respondent's home. Nuadiazio, Achuzian and Ekenediliz M. were placed with the Commissioner of Social Services pending further fact-finding proceedings which were held before this court on Sept. 9, 1974.

According to the petition, the respondent-father has administered excessive corporal punishment to his seven-year-old son, Ekenediliz. It was alleged that on March 7, 1974, the respondent struck the child repeatedly with his hands, a belt, and his feet, when summoned to P.S. 221 to discuss his son's behavior in school. Furthermore it is alleged that on June 5, 1974, the child suffered a cut lip and bruises because of respondent's use of excessive corporal punishment. The preliminary hearing resulted in a determination that, based on these allegations, all of the respondent's children should be removed pending further inquiry. This fact-finding hearing dealt only with the allegations as to the child Ekenediliz.

Testimony at the hearing revealed the following. The respondent is a thirty-four year old native of Nigeria who settled in the United States in 1968. He drives a taxi part time and attends Brooklyn College where he is taking courses to prepare himself for a career in engineering. His wife is thirty-five years old and teaches high school chemistry and biology in the New York City school system. She is the mother of two of the four children in the family. The respondent's first wife, from whom he is divorced and who resides in Africa, is the mother of Ekenediliz. Both the respondent and his present wife live with the four children in the same household.

It appears that the respondent had received approximately nine letters from his son's teacher at P.S. 221 about the child's school behavior. On March 7, 1974, the respondent visited the school and asked to speak with Ekenediliz's teacher. When informed that she was out to lunch, he spoke with Mrs. G., an assistant principal at P.S. 221. According to Mrs. G., she told Mr. M. about the difficulty Ekenediliz's teacher was having with him in the classroom. The child was present during this discussion. Suddenly, the respondent struck the child repeatedly with his fists, his belt and also kicked him while the boy lay on the ground. Mrs. G. stated that when she tried to restrain Mr. M., he struck her also. Later, the respondent apologized to Mrs. G. after he regained his composure. Mrs. G. reported this incident to B.C.W. The respondent denied striking Mrs. G. but admitted striking his son with his hands and his belt. He denied kicking the child.

Mr. M. stated to the court that he struck his son because according to his culture pattern this type of punishment was necessary and appropriate. In Nigeria according to the respondent if a child misbehaves in school and causes shame to the family, the parent has the duty to punish immediately and in any manner he sees fit. On cross-examination, the respondent testified that he was angered also by his son's lack of respect while he was talking with Mrs. G. When asked how the child exhibited a lack of respect during the conversation, the respondent stated "Ekenediliz was looking at Mrs. G.'s face while we were talking about him."

On redirect, Mr. M. briefly discussed Nigerian child-rearing and disciplinary practices as well as cultural attitudes towards the judicial process. For example, he related that in his country, if a villager is summoned to court for any reason, he cannot return home until he has purified himself by way of a special cleansing ritual. No matter what the reason, it is a cause for embarrassment and shame if one has to appear in court. Mr. M. told the court that he was ashamed just to have to be in the courtroom.

As to the incident of June 5, 1974, the respondent denied hitting his son. Mr. M. said that he discovered the bruises and welts on his son's body. When he asked his son why he was hurt, the boy allegedly told his father than some boys in school had beaten him up while he was returning home. Mr. M. informed the court that when he accompanied his son to school the next day, his son was unable to identify any of the boys who allegedly struck him. In an aside, Mr. M. added that he does not approve of some of the children in his neighborhood because they are a bad influence on his own children. At times the respondent has kept his son home after school to protect him from what he considers undesirable association.

When the court interposed a few questions, the respondent stated that he considered his son's bad behavior in school a bad reflection on the family, and that in his judgment, he applied the appropriate punishment in order to stop any further negative school reports. It was obvious to the court that the respondent was very upset that his children have been away from him since August. He said that he loved his children and cared very much about their welfare. Eventually, after almost one hour on the witness stand, the respondent broke down and was unable to continue. After a ten-minute recess, Mrs. M. as called to the stand.

Respondent's wife testified that she believed her husband was a good father and that other than the incident at P.S. 221, she never saw him beat the children. As for the June incident, she said that her husband had punished the boy that day, but that there were no bruises or welts on his body, at least not because of anything she saw him do to the child. She denied telling a DSS worker that the boy told her that his father had beaten him and caused the bruises. Mrs. M., a native of Barbados, was a lucid and articulate witness. She admitted that her husband struck the children when they did something wrong but that she understood why he behaved this way—it was the way he was raised at home. She remarked that although she did not agree with him on how to discipline his children, she rarely, if ever, interfered.

The facts described above present interesting considerations for the Family Court. Our society is becoming increasingly more mobile each year, especially in large urban areas. As judges, we hear cases involving people from all walks of life and from many different countries. All people have similar problems but not all of them seek to solve them in the same manner. It is in this context that the court must decide the issue of neglect raised in this proceeding. While recognizing individual and cultural differences, this court has the obligation to apply the law equally to all men.

One of the grounds upon which a finding of neglect can be made under article 10 of the Family Court Act is contained in section 1012 subdivision (f)(i)(B):

(B) In providing the child with proper supervision or guardianship, by reasonably inflicting or allowing to be inflicted harm, or a substantial risk thereof, including the infliction of excessive corporal punishment...

The sole issue for determination herein is whether the respondent's conduct constitutes excessive corporal punishment as would warrant a finding of neglect under the statute. We think that it does.

This case is a perfect illustration of somewhat unorthodox childrearing practices as evidence of neglect. In a society as culturally amorphous as our own, it is incumbent upon all members of society to be tolerant and understanding of customs that differ from their own. Officially, corporal punishment is viewed with some disdain when applied to very young children. Nevertheless, this court is aware that most parents use some form of corporal punishment in disciplining their children. While the commonly accepted definition of corporal punishment means some type of applied bodily force, there is no doubt that pummeling with the fists, striking with a belt, and kicking with the feet, satisfy the elements of even the most conservative definition of corporal punishment. The court finds the testimony of the school and agency personnel credible. Moreover, the respondent admitted hitting his child, not only once but on several occasions. Although the respondent's wife did not come out and say so, she hinted that often she questioned or had doubts about her husband's concept of appropriate punishment for the children.

What we have here is not a mean, vindictive, or disturbed parent, but rather a man who honestly believes that he is acting in the best interests of his children. The concept "best interests of the child" is a broad term subject to much difference of opinion. Courts have applied this rather vague standard to neglect, abuse, custody, permanent neglect and guardianship cases. Often it has become a vehicle for the court to substitute its own judgment for that of the parent in determining what is best for the child. Fortunately, we do not have to wrestle with that problem. Any reasonable man knows that it is not in the best interests of a child for its parent to punish in the manner we have seen here. While we are sympathetic and understanding of the respondent's motives, we must conclude that motive is irrelevant when we are confronted with the type of punishment this seven-year-old boy has received.

The Family Court Act uses the terms "excessive" corporal punishment, thereby implying that the Legislature recognized that the prudent use of corporal punishment would not constitute neglect under section 1012. We find that the respondent was guilty of inflicting excessive corporal punishment on March 7, 1974. Furthermore, evidence seems to indicate that this was not the first nor only time the respondent has inflicted excessive corporal punishment.

The issue of unorthodox childrearing practices is not new to the Family Court (see, *Matter of Kevin Sampson*, 37 A.D.2d 668 [3rd Dept. 1971], aff'd per curiam 29 NY2d 900 [1972]. *In re Watson, et al.*, 95 N.Y.S.2d 798 [Dom.Rel.Ct., Kings Co., 1950], and *Matter of Elwell*, 55 Misc.2d 252 [Fam. Ct., Dutchess Co. 1967] regarding diverse religious practices (see, *Matter of Ronald Currence*, 42 Misc.2d 418 [Fam.Ct., Kings Co., 1963] regarding different attitudes towards education. In each of these cases, neglect was found on the theory that while a parent has rights with regard to his child, those rights may be limited. The right of the child to welfare, protection, and care is superior to the right of the parent to get out of the child what the parent conceives as his right to demand and enforce.

An article 10 proceeding is not a device for recrimination against parents who use unorthodox childrearing practices. The court is impressed with the sincerity of the respondent's beliefs, and it is satisfied that the respondent loves his children, is concerned about them, and wishes them returned. As stated before, this is not the typical neglect case and it is in that context that the court finds the child Ekenediliz neglected in a limited legal sense. The facts establish that the respondent and his family need counseling, and the court in the discharge of its duty and responsibilities must try to provide the respondent and his children with some form of treatment. A finding of neglect in this matter is not meant to cast any negative overtones on the respondent's ability to function as a parent in any other respect (*Matter of Santos v. Goldstein*, 16 A.D.2d 755 [1st Dept., 1962]). Rather, it is to enable the court to get the M. family the type of assistance they need so that the respondent and his children may be reunited.

Accordingly, the endorsement of September 9, 1974, is to continue until a future hearing. Three of the M. children are paroled to the parents with a temporary order of protection directed at the respondent not to physically punish any of these three children. The remand of Ekenediliz to the commissioner is not to be disturbed. B.C.W. will report on the three children paroled to the parents and the commissioner is to produce the child Ekenediliz before the court (at a future hearing).

Questions

1. What were the important facts of this case? What was the court trying to decide? What decision did it reach? How did it reach its conclusion?

2. The evidence in this case suggests that Mr. M. struck his son with his fists and his belt and kicked him. The court describes this behavior as unacceptable corporal punishment. Mr. M. describes it as appropriate discipline. Is there a difference between discipline and abuse? If so, what do you think it is? How does the court make this distinction?

3. The Commonwealth of Virginia describes the difference as follows: "Unlike discipline, abuse isn't a learning process. It is designed to stop behavior through inflicting pain. It doesn't teach alternative correct behavior." This definition suggests that the perpetrator's motive is an important consideration. Do you agree? How would Mr. M. have fared under this definition?

4. Courts typically accept the proposition that parents can use *reasonable* force that they *reasonably* believe is necessary for the child's control, teaching, or education. Judge Rigler states, "Any reasonable man knows that it is not in the best interests of a child for its parents to punish in the manner we have seen here." What do you think is meant by the term *reasonable*? How might it be measured?

5. What did the court decide should happen to Mr. M's children? Do you think this was an appropriate outcome? Why or why not?

6. How does the court address the fact that Mr. M., a Nigerian immigrant, comes from a culture with child-rearing norms different from our own? Did it affect the outcome of the case?

7. Do you believe that cultural norms should be taken into consideration in cases of child abuse and neglect? If so, how? If not, why not?

8. The United Nations Committee on the Rights of the Child asserts that physical punishment violates a child's right to dignity, physical integrity, and equal protection under the law (Bennett, 2005). This sentiment is echoed by the National Association of Social Workers, which, in 1990, adopted a policy statement opposing corporal punishment. Meanwhile, 26 countries have passed laws prohibiting all physical punishment of children (Global Initiative, 2010). Would you be in favor of the United States passing such a law? What would be its advantages? Its disadvantages?

CHAPTER 6 PRACTICE TEST

The following questions will test your application and analysis of the content found within this chapter. For additional assessment, including licensing-exam type questions on applying chapter content to practice behaviors, visit **MySearchLab**.

1. American child welfare policy
   a. requires that children be removed from home at the first sign of risk.
   b. requires that agencies make reasonable efforts to preserve or reunite families.
   c. recognizes the benefits to children of institutional care.
   d. could be characterized as "holistic" in nature.

2. You are a child protective services worker investigating a maltreatment complaint. You appear at the child's school and ask to interview her alone. The principal calls the child's parents, who argue that you are legally prohibited from interviewing the child without their consent. Which of the following is true?
   a. Parents who are accused of malpractice forfeit their constitutional rights.
   b. If you have the child's consent, the parent's consent is unnecessary.

   c. Although courts have upheld child interviews at school without parental consent, you would be wise to secure a warrant.
   d. You are on stronger legal ground if you interview the child alone at home, even over the parents' objection.

3. Termination of parental rights
   a. requires proof by a preponderance of the evidence.
   b. requires proof by clear and convincing evidence.
   c. requires proof beyond a reasonable doubt.
   d. permits the parent to retain custody of the child while sacrificing other legal rights.

4. The role of a guardian *ad litem* is to
   a. explain difficult concepts to the court.
   b. advocate for the parent's interests.
   c. protect the child's interests.
   d. represent the agency's interests.

5. Describe the role of the social worker in child welfare proceedings. What kinds of court appearances are required? What would the social worker's role be in those proceedings?

6. Whose interests must be balanced when child victims need to testify in court? Discuss the various strategies that have been employed to reconcile these interests. Which have the courts upheld? Which have they not?

MYSEARCHLAB CONNECTIONS

Reinforce what you learned in this chapter by studying videos, cases, documents, and more available at **www.MySearchLab.com**.

Watch these Videos

* Relinquishing Custody
  * *How do you think the needs of children and youth with mental illness should be addressed within the child welfare system?*

Read these Cases/Documents

Δ Crisis and Kinship in Foster Caser
  * *How does the child welfare worker's dual role in protecting the child and supporting the family make establishing trust more difficult? How can this be overcome?*

Explore these Assets

* Techniques for Generalist Practice: Family Preservation Model (or Home Based-Model), The
* Website: Child Welfare Information Gateway
* Website: Children's Rights

Research these Topics

* clergy as mandated reporters
* courtroom dogs
* safe haven laws

Assess Your Knowledge

Go to **MySearchLab** to test your knowledge of key topics in this chapter with topic-specific quizzes. Conclude your assessment by completing the chapter exam.

---

* = CSWE Core Competency Asset   Δ = Case Study

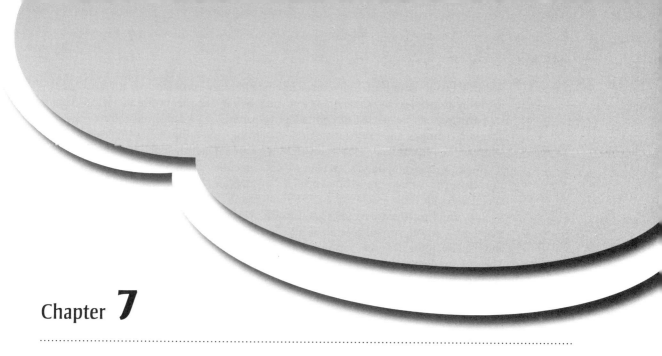

Chapter **7**

Adoption

Adoption is the process by which parental rights and obligations transfer from one party, typically the birth family, to another, the adoptive family. Adoption grants full legal family membership to the child who is adopted, giving the child a new and permanent legal identity.

Background

Adoption, in its broadest meaning, has existed since ancient times. In many early civilizations, it was a way for adoptive parents to have a male heir (Crosson-Tower, 2001). As sensitivity to the needs of dependent children grew, communities turned to informal means of finding stable environments for children who could not be raised by their biological parents. Children who were orphaned or homeless, or whose parents were too poor to care for them, were often housed in orphanages. Alternatively, extended family members assumed responsibility for children whose parents lacked the physical, mental, or emotional capacity to provide appropriate care or had died (Grotevant, Perry, & McRoy, 2007). These arrangements continue to exist across the world today. Although the United States has moved away from housing children in orphanages, informal care by family members remains common.

The modern era has witnessed the emergence of formal legal procedures governing the adoption process. Mississippi, Texas, and Massachusetts are believed to have been the first states to enact adoption laws in the mid-1800s. The Massachusetts statute, in particular, is considered to have been a precursor to contemporary adoption law; it embodied the following principles: (1) Written consent must be obtained from the biological parent, (2) participation is expected of both adoptive parents, (3) a judge must decree that the adoption is proper, and (4) the biological relationship is consequently completely severed (Crosson-Tower, 2001). By 1929, every state in the union had an adoption statute in place.

Today, we see adoption as a way in which a parentless child becomes part of a family. Because social workers are so often involved in adoption, it is important to recognize that adoption is ultimately a legal event and to understand the processes that define it.

Like child maltreatment (discussed in Chapter 6), adoption is largely a function of state law; however, several federal laws have come to play an important role in defining and regulating the adoption process. Some of these also apply to children in foster care. They are summarized here:

- **Adoption Assistance and Child Welfare Act of 1980 (P.L. 96–272):** Established the first adoption assistance program under Title IV-E of the Social Security Act. Requires states to have a plan for providing adoption assistance payments to facilitate the adoption of children with special needs. States must also engage in permanency planning, including adoption if it is in the best interests of the child.
- **Multiethnic Placement Act of 1994 (P.L. 103–382):** Prohibits state agencies from delaying, denying, or otherwise discriminating against adoption placements on the basis of the prospective adoptive parent's race, color, or ethnicity. Requires states to develop strategies to recruit adoptive families that reflect the racial and ethnic diversity of children available for adoption. A provision permitting the consideration of race and ethnicity in matching children with adoptive parents was later repealed.
- **The Adoption and Safe Families Act of 1997 (P.L. 105–89):** Provides funding for pre-adoption and post-adoption services. Authorizes incentive payments and technical assistance to states to facilitate adoptions and limits the time permitted for family unification so that adoption can occur more quickly.
- **Intercountry Adoption Act of 2000 (P.L. 106–279):** Implements the U.S. signing of the Hague Convention treaty (described later in this chapter).
- **Fostering Connections to Success and Increasing Adoptions Act of 2008 (P.L. 110–351):** Allows for kinship guardianship in place of formal adoption. Expands eligibility for adoption assistance payments, and doubles incentive amounts for adopting children with special needs and older children. Requires agencies to make reasonable efforts to keep siblings together in adoptive placements.

To put these laws into perspective, it is helpful to envision adoption as part of a holistic system that also includes *family support services* (designed to prevent child abuse and neglect), *child protective services* (designed to respond to allegations of child maltreatment), *family preservation services* (designed to prevent removal of children from home), *foster care* (designed to provide temporary, out-of-home placements), and *reunification* (designed to return children safely to their original families). Since the enactment of the Adoption Assistance and Child Welfare Act of 1980, American child welfare policy has put a premium on seeking a permanent living arrangement for every child and minimizing stays in out-of-home care. The favored outcome is to strengthen and preserve the family unit so the child can remain there or return there in safety. If this cannot be achieved, some other permanent arrangement is pursued; the most common include adoption and guardianship with another family member. In the case of older youth, the emphasis often shifts to preparation for living independently, although efforts to secure adoptive parents or guardians for these youth have intensified in response to growing evidence that, absent a consistent adult in their lives, they are more likely to face significant social, financial, and emotional disadvantages.

This chapter describes various types of adoption, the adoption process, access to adoption records, and problems that can arise in adoption. Highlighted sections address adoption under the Indian Child Welfare Act (ICWA) and special considerations in adoption placements including race, religion, and sexual orientation. The chapter closes with a sample case on the adoption rights of unmarried fathers. Although adults can also be the subjects of adoption, the focus here is on the adoption of children. Note that the terms *biological parent* and *birth parent* are used interchangeably, as are *biological family, birth family*, and *family of origin*.

Types of Adoption

Adoptions can be categorized in several ways. First, we can look at them in terms of the relationship between the child and the adoptive parent. Children can be adopted by a non-relative (a *stranger adoption* or *unrelated adoption*) or by someone having a blood tie to the child (a *relative adoption* or *kinship adoption*). Unrelated adoptions are the more common type. In these adoptions, an agency recruits and screens prospective adoptive parents, matches available children with potential placements, and provides follow-up support. Alternatively, the biological and adoptive parents can be connected through an intermediary, or they may contact each other directly to arrange for the adoption. In a kinship adoption, the child is adopted by a member of his or her extended family—typically a grandparent, uncle, aunt, or cousin. This can be accomplished through a public or private agency, an intermediary, or by direct placement. The court must finalize all adoptions, regardless of type. For many years, kinship adoptions were discouraged in the United States, although informal kinship arrangements were common. More recently, research has extolled the virtues of placing children with family members when their parents cannot raise them; such an arrangement enhances the child's sense of stability, continuity, and identity, and results in a range of improved health and mental health outcomes (Sakai, Lin, & Floes, 2011) Compared to their nonrelative counterparts, relatives who seek to adopt reflect a wider range of incomes and ages (Zinn, 2009).

We can also categorize adoptions based on the status of the adoptive parents, for example, *single-parent* adoptions and *couple* adoptions, either of which may involve a *same-sex* adoption. All states permit single-parent adoptions, with single women comprising 28% of public adoptions and single men comprising 3% (Administration for Children and Families, 2011b). Single parents are more likely than couples to adopt older children, children of color, and children with disabilities. There are also *stepparent* and *second-parent* (or *co-parent*) adoptions, the former involving adoption by a spouse and the latter involving adoption by an unmarried partner. These adoptions most often occur in the context of remarriage or in same-sex unions, respectively. For example, one of the early cases to consider a second-parent adoption was the New York case of *Matter of Adoption of Evan* (1992). One partner in a lesbian couple had a child by artificial insemination and her partner sought to share legal parenting rights through adoption. The child's *guardian ad litem* (aptly named Sylvia Law) and two social work experts recommended in favor of the adoption, citing the partners' long-term, committed relationship and the strong bond between the child and each of the women. The court agreed, although other courts have gone the other way. Stepparent adoptions are the most common type of adoption in the United States (Child Welfare Information Gateway, 2008). Aside from finalization by the court, they do not require the involvement of the government or of an adoption agency.

Adoptions may be further categorized based on how they are achieved. In the United States, the options include *public agency adoptions, private agency adoptions, independent adoptions,* and *direct placement adoptions.* These options are illustrated in Figure 7.1. Although public agencies sometimes serve children who are voluntarily relinquished by their parents, they most often serve children who become available subsequent to termination of parental rights and the child's placement in foster care. According to the Administration for Children and Families (2011a), the number of children waiting to be adopted has been steadily decreasing over the past decade. In 2010, a total of 107,011 children were in foster care waiting to be adopted, 27,000 fewer than 8 years prior. The average age of a child adopted out of the foster care system was 6.4 years (Administration for Children and Families, 2011b). Children ages 8 and older, children of color, sibling groups, and children with disabilities are especially in need of adoptive families (Child Welfare Information Gateway, 2010a). Children in foster care can be adopted by relatives, strangers, or their foster parents. State law determines the eligibility requirements for adoptive parents; in many instances, they are less restrictive than those of private agencies. Adoptions by both family members and foster parents are becoming more common. Between 2000 and 2010, the number of children adopted

FIGURE 7.1   **Adoption Options**

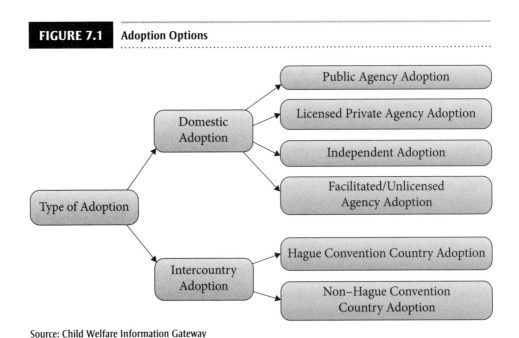

Source: Child Welfare Information Gateway

from foster care by relatives increased from 21% to 32% (Administration for Children and Families, 2011b), whereas a majority (54%) of children adopted from foster care are now adopted by their foster parents (Child Welfare Information Gateway, n.d.). Although adoption by foster parents was long discouraged, agencies now recognize that it can provide consistency for a child who has already adjusted to the foster home and bonded with the foster parents. Public agency adoptions have distinct advantages. First, there is generally little or no cost to the adoptive parent. Second, the children awaiting adoption are often in dire need and are harder to place than those served by private agencies; adoption, therefore, can provide such a child with a much-needed opportunity for family, love, and security. Finally, social workers in public agencies provide services and support throughout the adoption process. These agencies are comparatively stable, and adoption placements are less risky, given that agency operations are subject to government oversight. They also, of course, have some disadvantages. Many children being adopted from foster care have experienced significant trauma; parenting these children can be particularly challenging. Not all prospective adoptive parents are equipped to deal with these children's special needs.

Private agency adoptions can occur through both licensed and unlicensed agencies. Licensed agencies are required to comply with state standards; unlicensed agencies are not. Private agencies typically serve younger children whose parents voluntarily relinquish them for adoption. These agencies have the advantage of allowing the birth parents to play a role in selecting the adoptive parents and may allow them to negotiate the role they will play (if any) in the child's life after the adoption is completed. In addition, the prospective adoptive parents often pay the costs associated with carrying the pregnancy to term. The adoptive parents, meanwhile, have the opportunity to learn about the child's social and medical history and to have ongoing contact with the birth parent if they so choose. Nevertheless, there are some disadvantages. Eligibility criteria may be more restrictive, with agencies giving preference to applicants of certain ages, religious affiliations, sexual orientations, incomes, or family types. In addition, many prospective adoptive parents are wary of private adoptions because of the potential for birth parents to change their minds at the last minute (Stein, 2004). Unlicensed private agencies can pose particular risks because they are unregulated by state authorities.

Private adoptions can also be arranged by intermediaries such as physicians, attorneys, or professional facilitators (*independent adoptions*) or by direct contact between the parties (*direct placement adoptions*). Not all states permit these adoptions, and in many states the birth parents' written consent to relinquish the child must be approved by the court. Otherwise, the legal process in these instances is straightforward; it requires only that the court finalize the adoption (Stein, 2004). Independent and direct placement adoptions have the advantage of being less bureaucratic than the alternatives; they often can be completed more quickly and with less intrusion into the private lives of the birth parents and the adoptive family (Daly & Sobol, 1994). They also typically allow the child to be placed directly from the hospital after birth. On the other hand, these adoptions entail considerable risk. Some people who advertise themselves as adoption facilitators may be inexperienced or untrustworthy. And there is always a possibility that the birth mother will change her mind. Although states that permit independent and direct placement adoptions have laws that address the provision and revocation of consent, there are fewer safeguards in these types of adoptions than in those facilitated by public or licensed private agencies.

Finally, there are *domestic adoptions* and *international adoptions.* In 2002, U.S. courts approved a total of 130,269 domestic adoptions and 21,063 international adoptions (Abrams, Cahn, Ross, & Meyer, 2009). Most of the material in this chapter pertains to domestic adoptions. A separate section, toward the end of the chapter, specifically addresses international adoptions.

The Adoption Process

Each state in the United States defines its own legal process for adoption and has jurisdiction only over those adoptions that take place within its borders. Many children, however, are placed in adoptive homes outside their home state. In 2002, there were approximately 14,000 such children (Abrams et al., 2009). In order to facilitate adoption placements across state lines and to ensure the appropriateness of adoptive families and homes, all 50 states have joined the Interstate Compact on the Placement of Children (ICPC). This compact requires cooperation between those agencies placing children out of state and the agencies in the state receiving them (Freundlich, 1999).

Both the adoptive parents and the child must be eligible for an adoption to be legal. A child becomes eligible if his or her biological parents have died, their parental rights have been terminated, or they have voluntarily consented to the adoption. Adoptive parents are eligible if they meet the state's eligibility requirements or the eligibility criteria established by the agency involved; eligibility is also premised on the results of a comprehensive family assessment.

For parents working with an agency, the adoption process typically begins with orientation and training. These services are designed to acquaint the parents with the agency's rules and procedures while they begin to consider they type of child they feel best equipped to raise. Before an adoption can be approved, every state requires the completion of a *home study*, which includes an in-depth assessment of the adoptive family, usually conducted by a social worker. This family assessment is one of the most vital steps in the adoption process. It employs a multifaceted approach to evaluate the prospective parents and to prepare them for the possibility of adopting a child.

The specifics of how a family assessment is conducted and what it entails may vary by state and by agency. Generally speaking, a series of meetings is held between the agency social worker and the prospective parents. These meetings are an important source of information; they provide an opportunity to explore each parent's strengths and any limitations and allow the worker to better understand the prospective parents, their expectations, and their family life. At least one meeting is held in the prospective parents' home. During this *home visit,* the worker checks to be sure that basic health, safety, and licensing standards are met; the worker also observes the living space planned for the child and gets a sense of how an adopted child will be incorporated into the physical household.

Family members are also asked to provide the agency with important personal documents including birth certificates, marriage licenses, divorce decrees, driving records, credit reports, mental health evaluations, results of physical health examinations, and verification of income. The applicants must undergo both criminal and child abuse background checks. They will also be asked to submit three or four character references and to complete an autobiographical statement. The statement should reflect on their personal history and their thoughts or concerns regarding adoption. In assessing the parents' suitability for adoption, the worker considers the following:

- The family's motivation to adopt
- The type of child the family is best prepared to parent
- The family's expectations regarding adoption
- The family's education and experience related to adoption and child rearing
- The stability of the marriage relationship
- The potential impact of any health issues
- Any family criminal history
- The family's financial status
- The suitability of the family's living arrangements

In some instances, an assessment is also conducted with the child. This occurs most often with children awaiting adoption from the foster care system. Like the family assessment, this assessment is usually conducted by a social worker. It is designed to help the foster care agency make the best placement match possible, while affording the prospective parents an opportunity to acquire information about the child they are interested in adopting. A child assessment typically seeks to shed light on the following:

- The child's desire to be adopted
- The child's attitude toward his or her birth parents
- The child's physical and mental health
- The impact of any abuse or neglect on the child's development
- The child's current family relationships
- The child's needs in a future family

This information is ascertained through interviewing the child, talking with the child's caregivers and acquaintances, and reviewing relevant records (Child Welfare Information Gateway, 2006).

The actual home study report completed by the social worker is based on the results of the family assessment and (if relevant) the child assessment. It aims to evaluate the parents' suitability for adoption, drawing on the information gathered during meetings with the family, documentation submitted by the prospective parents, and observations from the home visit. It typically includes a description of the applicant's family background, education and employment, relationships with significant others, daily routine, neighborhood, and religious beliefs (Child Welfare Information Gateway, 2010b), as well as the social worker's conclusion and recommendation regarding the advisability of adoption. Three outcomes are possible:

- **The adoption request is approved.** The approval typically specifies the maximum number of children permitted, their age range, sex, and any special needs the agency believes the parents can handle.
- **The adoption request is deferred.** The family is deemed not yet ready or qualified to adopt.
- **The adoption request is denied.** The family fails to meet the applicable laws regulating adoption, or the worker believes the family cannot provide a safe, permanent home for a child.

Once the agency has approved the family for adoption, the parents await the availability of a child. After the child has been placed with the family, the social worker continues to visit the home and assist the family in adjusting to the adoption. Each state's laws determine how much time must elapse between the placement of the child in the adoptive home and the court's finalization of the adoption; this probationary period can last between 3 months and a year. In Virginia and the District of Columbia, for example, adoptions typically take 6 months to be finalized; in Alabama, it may take only 90 days (Adoption Advisor, n.d.; District of Columbia Adoption Laws, 2011; Infant Adoption Training Initiative, n.d.). Finally, informed by the home study and the social worker's recommendation, the court makes a determination as to whether or not the adoption is in the child's best interests. If it is, the adoption becomes legal and a new birth certificate is issued (Stein, 2004).

SPECIAL CONSIDERATIONS IN ADOPTION PLACEMENTS

Among the most controversial aspects of adoption policy are the roles that race, religion, and sexual orientation should play in placement decisions.

For much of U.S. history, adoption placements sought to maximize similarities between adoptive parents and children. This led to prioritizing matches along racial, ethnic, and religious lines. The issue of race in adoption decisions has been the subject of a long-standing debate, not only within legislatures and the public, but also within the social work profession. Prior to the civil rights movement, segregation laws in the South often prohibited interracial adoption. After these laws were found to be unconstitutional, interracial (or *transracial*) adoptions increased dramatically. In 1972, the National Association of Black Social Workers (NABSW) decried this trend, arguing that transracial adoptions robbed minority children of their heritage through what it termed "cultural genocide." Agencies came to recognize the benefits of same-race placements, although by the 1990s, a new problem had emerged. Children of color were languishing in foster care, awaiting available same-race parents. It was with this in mind that Congress passed the Multiethnic Placement Act, which explicitly permitted agencies to consider race as a factor in choosing adoption placements but prohibited delaying adoption or discriminating against prospective adoptive parents on the basis of race. The former provision was subsequently repealed. As it stands now, race may not be a consideration in selecting adoptive homes.

The realities of supply and demand continue to drive transracial adoption; in public agency adoptions, children of color are disproportionately represented among those awaiting adoption, whereas prospective adoptive parents are disproportionately White. Although transracial adoptions historically involved placing African American children with White adoptive parents, today they most often involve Hispanic children, more than one-third of whom are placed with non-Hispanic families. Caucasian children remain least likely to be adopted transracially. Overall, transracial adoptions increased from 11.6% in 1997 to 16.9% in 2003 (Hansen & Pollack, 2007). Meanwhile, their advantages and disadvantages continue to be hotly debated.

Religious matching, like race matching, has engendered controversy. Some maintain that it is preferable for the religious backgrounds of the adoptive parent and child to be similar, especially when a child is old enough to have already established his or her own religious beliefs. Others contend that this practice discriminates against some prospective adoptive parents and violates the Constitution's prohibition against establishment of religion. Each state's laws determine what role religion plays in adoption placements; these laws have often been challenged in court. Courts generally permit religion to be considered in the placement of a child as long as it is not the deciding factor. Most agree that the adoptive parents' religious affiliation might be relevant to a child's best interests, but it is the child's best interests overall that must prevail. As with race matching, courts have disallowed holding out for a same-religion parent if doing so results in a child with special needs not being placed at all. When an adoptive parent of the same religion as the child is available, however, religion can be considered in determining the best interests of the child.

The most recent debate involves adoption by same-sex couples. As with religion, federal law is silent and state law controls. Twenty-eight states and the District of Columbia currently permit adoptions by lesbians, gay men, and bisexual individuals; not all of them have enacted statewide policies, however, nor do any address adoption by transgender individuals or families (Human Rights Campaign, 2010). These adoptions can involve a single parent adoption, joint adoption by a couple, or second-parent adoption by the nonbiological parent in a same-sex couple.

At this time, only a few states expressly prohibit these adoptions. Arkansas effectively prohibits gay men and lesbians from adopting by restricting adoption to married couples. Utah prohibits adoption by unmarried cohabitants but allows single persons to adopt regardless of sexual orientation. Mississippi bans gay couples from adopting but allows gay singles to adopt. A number of state laws prohibiting adoptions by lesbians, gay men, or bisexuals have recently been, or are in the process of being,

repealed. This includes laws in New Hampshire and Florida, for example (Almanzar, 2008; Averett, Nalavany, & Ryan, 2009).

Research continues to assess the impact on children of being adopted into gay and lesbian households; both proponents and critics of these adoptions have cited scholarly findings to bolster their views. In 2002, the American Psychiatric Association adopted a resolution in support of gay adoption which states, "Numerous studies over the last three decades consistently demonstrate that children raised by gay or lesbian parents exhibit the same level of emotional, cognitive, social, and sexual functioning as children raised by heterosexual parents.... Optimal development for children is based not on the sexual orientation of the parents, but on stable attachments to committed and nurturing adults" (APA, 2002. p.1). NASW, meanwhile, has consistently engaged in legislative and legal advocacy to support laws that legitimize same-sex adoption. Although privacy concerns make it impossible to know with certainty how many of these adoptions occur, a 2007 survey estimates that lesbians and gay men have adopted approximately 65,500 children (Gates, Badgett, Macomber, & Chambers, 2007).

Consent and Revocation of Consent

Courts are not allowed to proceed on adoption petitions until written consent has been secured from all relevant parties. This generally includes both biological parents. Under most state laws, the parents cannot validly consent until after the child is born and a specified number of hours, days, or weeks has elapsed. When the adoption involves an older child (usually between ages 10 and 14), the child's consent is also required (Abrams & Ramsey, 2000; Krause & Mayer, 2007). The general rule that both biological parents are required to give consent in an adoption proceeding has several exceptions. For example, consent is not required when a biological parent is deceased, when a court has deemed a parent mentally incompetent, or when parental rights to the child have been terminated (Abrams & Ramsey, 2000).

Consent cases are not always straightforward. The courts have wrestled, for example, with how unmarried fathers should be treated. In 1972, the U.S. Supreme Court decided the landmark case of *Stanley v. Illinois*. The case concerned an unmarried couple who lived together for 18 years and produced three children. When the mother died, the children were automatically removed from the father's custody. The father objected, noting that he had never been declared unfit, and that other parents (including married fathers and unwed mothers) could not be deprived of their children under the state's law without a showing of unfitness. The U.S. Supreme Court agreed and concluded that the state's law violated the equal protection clause of the 14th Amendment, thus vindicating the right of unmarried fathers to their children. Although this case was not actually about adoption, its principle informed a string of adoption cases that followed. Most of these cases have relied on a footnote in the *Stanley* opinion that explicitly addresses adoption; it drew what has become an important distinction between the rights of unwed fathers who quickly demonstrate their interest in caring for the child and those who do not. The sample case at the end of this chapter, *Robert O. v. Russell K.,* explores this issue further.

Other difficult consent cases involve stepparents. The typical case involves a stepparent seeking to adopt his or her spouse's child over the objection of the other biological parent. Most states give the courts broad discretion to override the birth parent's objection under these circumstances—or at least allow courts to dispense with the birth parent's consent when they deem the stepparent adoption to be in the best interests of the child (Wadlington & O'Brien, 1998).

Of course, the thorniest legal issues concern birth parents who consent to an adoption and subsequently change their minds. We call this *revocation*. In all 50 states, adoptions become legal and permanent once a court issues the final adoption decree. However, in many states, the biological parents have a limited window of opportunity to revoke their consent before the decree is issued. In Alabama, for example, a birth parent can revoke consent for any reason within 5 days after his or her initial written consent is provided. Alaska allows revocation of consent within 10 days, as do Arkansas, the District of Columbia, Minnesota, and Tennessee. Other states give the birth parents even more latitude; examples include 21 days in Vermont, 30 days in Maryland, and 60 days in Delaware (Price, 2004). Still other states permit revocation at any time prior to the court's issuance of the final adoption decree (McDermott, 1993). In each case, the court must determine whether revoking the birth parent's consent is in the best interests of the child.

Each state's laws also articulate the circumstances under which consent can be revoked for cause. Nearly half of all states allow revocation when there is strong evidence of fraud, duress, undue influence, coercion, or misrepresentation. Revocation may also occur if the adoptive parents and birth parents mutually agree, or if the court finds that revoking the adoption would be in the child's best interests. Some states (e.g., California) put limits on when this can occur; others (including Georgia, Iowa, Kansas, and North Dakota) do not stipulate a time frame (Price, 2004).

Consent laws do what all laws do: They attempt to balance competing interests. At the same time that we do not want biological parents to make rash decisions they might later regret, we do not want to leave adoptive parents and children hanging. The goal is to reconcile the needs of the various parties by allowing some opportunity for the birth parents to revoke their consent, without disrupting adoption arrangements any more than necessary.

Open Adoptions and Access to Adoption Records

Adoptions also vary in terms of the amount of contact and communication that occur between the adoptive and biological families. Openness occurs on a continuum. At one end of the spectrum are *confidential* adoptions in which no identifying information is shared with the parties and no contact between them occurs. On the other end of the spectrum are *fully disclosed* adoptions, which are characterized by the routine exchange of letters, photographs, and telephone calls and may include face-to-face visits between the birth and adoptive families. In the middle are *mediated open adoption*s in which birth parents and adoptive families maintain communication through an attorney, adoption agency, or other authorized intermediary.

In the United States, confidential adoptions were traditionally the norm. The idea of adoption was to create a new family that could pass as the child's "natural" family. Children's physical traits were matched as closely as possible to the traits of the adoptive parents to lessen the chance that outsiders would detect that the child had been adopted. Secrecy was maintained for the benefit of the relinquishing parents, to avoid the stigma of their having given up a child and to help them move on with their lives. It was also thought to benefit the adoptive parents and child, who could settle into their new life without disruption or interference. The trend, however, has moved toward openness in adoptions, especially when a child is voluntarily placed by his or her birth parent into an adoptive family. It has become quite common for the birth and adoptive parents to meet once or twice before the adoption takes place and to maintain communication for a mutually agreed-upon period of time following the adoption. It is less common for birth and adoptive families to continue to visit each other after the placement occurs (Atwood, 2007a). These issues become more complicated when a child is not relinquished voluntarily but is removed from his or her birth parents following the involuntary termination of parental rights (Grotevant et al., 2007).

Some states have created legal statutes to formalize agreements between birth and adoptive parents. These written agreements are known as *enforceable contact agreements* or ECAs. They are binding contracts that establish the type and amount of contact an adoptive family will maintain with a birth family and vice versa. Because they are monitored by a court, one party can seek a court order to force compliance if the other party is not meeting the terms of the agreement (LeCheminant, 2007). In 2007, these binding contracts between adoptive parents and birth parents were recognized in 18 states. Three additional states recognize nonbinding open adoption agreements.

Opinions vary within the social work community regarding the virtues of open adoptions. Some argue that their potential to undermine the parenting authority of the adoptive parents can be harmful to the new family unit. Ongoing visits, in particular, can interfere with the adoptive family's efforts to achieve and maintain stability. There is a reason, they argue, for the historical practice of secrecy. The adoptive family can function best when ties between the child and the birth parent are thoroughly and permanently severed—not just legally, but socially as well (LeCheminant, 2007). On the other side are those who argue that open adoptions provide children with important opportunities to feel complete and to understand the circumstances that led to their adoption. Contact with birth families can also provide children with a link to their heritage and ancestry and can increase the number of supportive adults who love them (Craft, 2011). A major longitudinal study begun in the 1980s suggests that the level of openness in adoptions is not significantly related to children's identify formation, self-esteem, or socio-emotional adjustment. The researchers also found that the need for communication between the adoptive family and birth family changes over time. Based on their findings, they recommend that procedures regulating contact between adoptive families and birth families, including ECAs, be completely voluntary and amenable to renegotiation as the child matures (Grotevant et al., 2007).

Closely related to the issue of openness in adoption is that of access to adoption records. Once the court finalizes an adoption, and a new birth certificate is issued, the original birth certificate and all relevant court documents are *sealed*. If the records remain sealed, the birth parents may never know the identity or whereabouts of their child or of the adoptive parents, and the adoptive family may never know the identity or whereabouts of the birth family. The information in the adoption record can be shared under two circumstances: (1) The birth parents, adoptive parents, and adoptee all consent to disclosure, or (2) a court order is issued for *good cause* (ofen involving a specific need for the birth parent's medical history). The rationale for secrecy in adoption records is the same one that underlies confidentiality in the adoption process: concern for the privacy of the parties and the finality of the adoption decree. This emphasis on confidentiality is reinforced by the fact that adoption proceedings are not open to the public, and adoption records are exempt from Freedom of Information Act (FOIA) requests. Although the prevailing policy is to protect the privacy of the parties, most states either mandate or permit adoptive families to have access to the child's medical and genetic history in order to safeguard the child's health and well-being. Some allow adult adoptees to have access to additional, nonidentifying information including the birth parent's age, race, nationality, religious affiliation, and interests. The birth parent's actual identity, however, remains under seal. Bucking the trend are a handful of states, including Alaska, where adult adoptees have an unfettered right to access their original birth certificates (Abrams et al., 2009; Fair, 2008).

As with the question of openness in adoption, there are wide-ranging views about how adoption records should be treated. Most people agree that the information should be made available when both the adult adoptee and the birth parent consent (Atwood, 2007b). Beyond that, controversies remain. Many adult adoptees believe that they should be entitled to have complete access to everything in their adoption records, whether or not the birth parent consents. Keeping the record secret, they argue, implies that there is something shameful about being adopted. And if adoption is supposed to create a family unit that is just as legitimate as other families, why would we permit those who are not adopted to have access to their birth information while denying it to those who are? Advocates for open records see this unequal treatment as a violation of civil rights.

On the other side are arguments for maintaining secrecy. Mandating open adoption records deprives birth parents of their right to personal privacy. Birth parents might prefer that the adoption remain confidential for a number of reasons: They might want to control the timing of a potential contact with their child; they might not want the information to become known to a spouse, other family members, or friends; they might fear that disclosure would require them to relive a painful experience that led to the adoption in the first place; or they might simply believe it is best for the child not to have access to the adoption information (Atwood, 2007b).

In an effort to find a happy medium, some states have created *mutual consent registries* or *search and consent* processes. Both are designed to help connect adult adoptees with their birth parents. The registries provide a mechanism for adoptees and birth parents to communicate their interest in receiving information about each other. If both express a desire for identifying information, contact information, or access to the sealed adoption record, then both are provided with the requested information. Search and consent processes are similar, but the state takes a more active role. An adoptee can request that the state locate his or her birth parents and seek their consent to release identifying information. Note that in both scenarios, the birth parents retain the right to choose whether or not to keep the adoption information private, and no information is shared without the consent of both parties (Fair, 2008).

A number of states that allow access to their adoption records have been challenged in court by birth parents seeking to keep those records sealed. In *Doe v. Sundquist* (1999), the Tennessee Supreme Court upheld a state law permitting adoptees age 21 and older to have access to their adoption records. The law also provided for a *contact veto* under which the birth parent could prevent unwanted contact with his or her child, despite the disclosure of identifying information. The birth parents argued that the law violated their rights to familial privacy, reproductive privacy, and privacy regarding nondisclosure of personal information. However, the court found no violation under the state's constitution. This was true even though it was applied retroactively to adoptions in which confidentiality had been assured.

Annulment and Wrongful Adoption

What happens if a couple adopts a child but later discovers that the agency lied, or neglected to tell them, about the child's medical condition or special needs? Or the adoption just is not working out as planned? Can the adoptive parents cancel the adoption? For obvious reasons, public policy has an interest in avoiding the disruption of adoption placements; maintaining a stable family situation is considered to be in the child's best interests. Narrow exceptions have been drawn, however, which allow the court to *abrogate* the adoption through *annulment*. Any party to the adoption may petition the court to dissolve the adoption; the best interests of the child will guide the court's decision. Because courts are disinclined to disturb an adoption once finalized, they require a truly compelling justification. An annulment might be considered, for example, when the agency failed to divulge the child's full medical and familial history and a disability or medical condition later becomes apparent. Another possibility is if the relationship between the adoptive parents and the child is so poor that neither is benefiting from it—or the adoptive parents can no longer properly care for the child. Although it happens rarely, if the court grants an annulment, the child is either returned to the birth parents or to the child welfare agency and the original birth certificate is reinstated (Krause & Meyer, 2007).

More common than annulment petitions are suits for *wrongful adoption*. In this case, the adoptive parents are seeking financial compensation rather than reversal of the adoption. A wrongful adoption suit, even if successful, leaves the adoptive family intact. Most often, these suits are brought when the adoption agency either intentionally or negligently misleads the adoptive parents by misrepresenting information that might have impacted their adoption decision (Emmanel, 2010). As discussed in Chapter 5, all material information must be shared in order to have valid informed consent—and adoption is premised on the informed consent of the parties. If a wrongful adoption suit is successful, the court may order punitive damages—that is, a financial award that goes above and beyond compensating the adoptive parents for their actual loss (Abrams et al., 2009).

Wrongful adoption claims became a viable remedy with the 1986 Ohio Supreme Court case *Burr v. Board of County Commissioners of Stark County*; prior to that time, the only recognized remedy for a wrongful adoption was annulment. The Court in *Burr* ruled that an agency is liable for punitive damages if it deliberately misinforms the adoptive parents of the child's familial or medical history, preventing the parents from making an informed decision about whether to adopt the child. The California Court of Appeals similarly ruled that adoptive parents could claim punitive damages when an adoption agency intentionally misrepresents the health of the prospective adoptee (*Michael J. v. County of Los Angeles Department of Adoptions*, 1988).

Although these first successful wrongful adoption lawsuits involved intentional deceit by the adoption agency, courts have more recently found adoption agencies to also be liable if they are negligent, or neglectful, in sharing information about the adoptive child's health. The Wisconsin Supreme Court decided the first such case, *Meracle v. Children's Service Society*, in 1989. The grounds for wrongful adoption were further expanded a few years later (*M.H. & J.L.H. v. Caritas Family Services*, 1992) when the Minnesota Supreme Court held that an adoption agency is liable if it only partially discloses information relevant to an adoption. The court stated that once the adoption agency begins to disclose information about the adoptee's history, it has a duty to ensure that the disclosure is complete. Numerous other courts subsequently reached the same conclusion. The Appellate Court of Illinois, for example, ruled that adoption agencies may be liable if they fail to disclose all available information about the potential adoptee that the adoptive parents request (*Roe v. Catholic Charities*, 1992). The ability to claim damages for wrongful adoption reaffirms the rights of the adoptive parents in the adoption process (Fields, 1996). Although it places a greater burden on the state, many believe that burden is justified by the importance of the parents' right to receive all available information regarding the child's history so they can make an informed adoption decision (Emmanel, 2010).

ADOPTION UNDER THE INDIAN CHILD WELFARE ACT (ICWA)

A glaring exception to the prohibition against considering race and ethnicity in making adoption placements is the Indian Child Welfare Act of 1978 (ICWA). ICWA was enacted as a response to the common, and often unwarranted, removal of Native American children from their tribal homes and families. It established minimum standards to ensure the protection of parental rights and to safeguard the interests of the child in maintaining ties to his or her heritage and culture. Although Congress passes numerous laws that impact the Native American community, laws pertaining to the termination of parental rights, foster care placements, and adoption of Indian children are governed by ICWA, superseding the state laws that would otherwise be applicable (Hollinger, 1993; Stein, 2004). Under the law, preference is given to placing children with extended family members, tribal members, or other Native American homes rather than with non–Native American parents.

ICWA has a dual mandate to both maintain tribal integrity and protect the best interests of the child. Unfortunately, these goals sometimes conflict. Such was the case in *Mississippi Choctaw Indians v. Holyfield*, decided by the U.S. Supreme Court in 1989. This case involved a couple who left their reservation and went to another county to give birth to twins, specifically because they wanted the twins to be adopted outside their tribe. When the tribe challenged the adoption, the Mississippi Supreme Court affirmed its legitimacy. On appeal, however, the U.S. Supreme Court reversed. Under ICWA, tribal

courts are vested with exclusive jurisdiction for proceedings concerning any Indian child "who resides
or is domiciled within the reservation of such tribe"
(1978, Sec. 1911[a]). The case turned on the meaning
of the term *domiciled*. The parents argued that the
children were never domiciled on the reservation
because they were born more than 200 miles away;
the Supreme Court, however, read *domicile* to mean
the place where the parents lived, which in this case
was the reservation. The case was remanded so that
the tribal court could decide whether or not to vacate
the adoption of the now 3-year-old twins. The rights
of the tribe were found, under the Court's reading of
ICWA, to supersede those of the adoptive parents
and perhaps of the child.

Despite the Court's holding in *Choctaw*, thousands of Native American children are adopted each
year by families who have no ties to the child's tribal
community. This phenomenon raises many of the
same issues raised by transracial and international
adoptions, although they are addressed through significantly different policies.

International Adoption

Americans began adopting from other countries in significant numbers following World
War II. The subsequent wars in Korea and Vietnam continued to fuel American sympathy
for children left orphaned or displaced and international adoptions grew rapidly. Today,
the United States adopts more children internationally than all other countries in the
world combined; in fact, approximately two-thirds of all children adopted internationally are adopted by U.S. citizens (Bartholet, 2007b). Countries placing children for adoption are referred to as *sending countries*. Table 7.1 identifies the top 10 sending countries,
and the number of children adopted from each, from 2005 to 2009 (U.S. Department of
State, 2010a). In fiscal year 2010, China again continued to head the list with 3,401 children
placed for adoption in United States. It was followed by Ethiopia (2,513), Russia (1,082),
South Korea (863), and Ukraine (445) (U.S. Department of State, 2010b). Fluctuations
in adoption are largely attributable to the political dynamics impacting various sending
countries, causing them to restrict or suspend their international adoptions. In July 2011,
for example, India implemented a temporary freeze on new applications, and Ethiopia
closed many of its orphanages, greatly restricting the opportunity for Americans to adopt
Ethiopian children (U.S. Department of State, 2011).

International adoptions follow a distinctly different process than domestic adoptions.
These adoptions are subject to U.S. law as well as to the laws and regulations of the foreign country from which the parents are adopting. Just as there is a different process in
every state in domestic adoptions, every sending country has its own process. Most prospective adoptive parents elicit the help of an international adoption agency in navigating
the various requirements involved in completing an adoption. Like domestic adoptions,
intercountry adoptions generally require a family assessment, home visit, and extensive
documentation sufficient to demonstrate to the foreign government that the prospective
adoptive parents can provide a safe and healthy home for a child.

Broadly speaking, intercountry adoptions are of two types: *Hague adoptions* and *non–
Hague adoptions*. Hague adoptions occur between countries that are party to the Hague
Convention on Protection of Children and Co-operation in Respect of Inter-country

TABLE 7.1   **Top 10 Sending Countries, Fiscal Years 2005–2009**

	FY 2009	FY 2008	FY 2007	FY 2006	FY 2005
1	China 3,001	Guatemala 4,122	China 5,453	China 6,492	China 7,903
2	Ethiopia 2,277	China 3,911	Guatemala 4,727	Guatemala 4,135	Russia 4,631
3	Russia 1,586	Russia 1,857	Russia 2,303	Russia 3,702	Guatemala 3,783
4	South Korea 1,080	Ethiopia 1,724	Ethiopia 1,254	South Korea 1,373	South Korea 1,628
5	Guatemala 756	South Korea 1,065	South Korea 938	Ethiopia 731	Ukraine 824
6	Ukraine 610	Vietnam 748	Vietnam 828	Kazakhstan 588	Kazakhstan 755
7	Vietnam 481	Ukraine 490	Ukraine 613	Ukraine 463	Ethiopia 442
8	Haiti 330	Kazakhstan 380	Kazakhstan 547	Liberia 353	India 323
9	India 297	India 308	India 411	Colombia 344	Colombia 287
10	Kazakhstan 295	Colombia 306	Liberia 314	India 319	Philippines 268

Source: http://adoption.state.gov/news/total_chart.html

Adoption. Approximately 75 countries are signatories to this treaty, including China, Guatemala, India, France, Italy, Spain, Australia and the United Kingdom (U.S. Department of State, 2010a). The convention was ratified by the United States in 1994 and was implemented in 2008. Its purpose is to regulate international adoptions by establishing minimum standards to safeguard the interests of children, adoptive parents, and birth parents. The hope is that it will prevent the instances of child abduction, bribery, and parental coercion that have sometimes characterized intercountry adoptions.

The U.S. Immigration and Nationality Act (INA) stipulates the eligibility criteria regarding who can be adopted. Children adopted from a country that is party to the Hague treaty (a *convention country*) must meet different standards than children adopted from a *nonconvention country*. Any child can be adopted from a convention country as long as both parents provide irrevocable written consent. Children adopted from nonconvention countries are ineligible for adoption if they have two living birth parents, regardless of consent (U.S. Department of State, 2010a).

There are both similarities and differences in the adoption process, as well. All Hague adoptions require that the prospective adoptive parents work with an adoption service provider (usually an adoption agency) that is accredited by the U.S. Department of State. The parents then complete a home study and compile a dossier of documentation meeting the foreign country's adoption requirements. Every sending country requires different documentation. This documentation must be notarized, authenticated by designated state authorities within the United States, and submitted to the State Department and/or the consulate of the foreign country involved in the adoption. An application is then made to U.S. Citizenship and Immigration Services (USCIS), which determines the prospective parents' eligibility to adopt. Once the USCIS application is approved, the parents submit their paperwork to the country from which they seek to adopt. In a non–Hague adoption, the parents complete the foreign adoption first, then apply to be found eligible in the United States.

The information the prospective adoptive parents receive about the child they are going to adopt is called a *referral*. In most situations, the child referral will include pictures, medical information, and basic socio-biological information. Referral information varies greatly depending upon the age of the child, the country from which the child is being adopted, and the amount of information available about the child's past.

For a Hague adoption, the prospective adoptive parents apply for eligibility by completing an application; once the application is approved, they can adopt the child according to the foreign country's adoption process. For both Hague and non–Hague adoptions, the last step before returning home is applying for a visa to allow the child to enter the United States. The type of visa depends on a number of factors, including whether it is a Hague adoption or a non–Hague adoption, the foreign country's adoption process, and whether or not both parents are present in the foreign country to complete the adoption. Like all immigrants to the United States, children adopted abroad must be screened by a physician approved by the U.S. State Department (U.S. Department of State, 2010a).

All children who are adopted internationally are eligible to become U.S. citizens. Under the Child Citizenship Act of 2000 (P.L. 106-395), some internationally adopted children can gain U.S. citizenship immediately upon entering the United States, with no naturalization process necessary, depending on the type of visa issued (U.S. Department of State, n.d.). For other children, however, readoption is required. This process requires the state government to legally recognize the foreign-born child placed in the United States as a child by adoption.

Intercountry adoption has both proponents and critics. Its advocates argue that adopting internationally is a win-win; it rescues needy children abroad from lives of destitution and neglect, while filling a void for U.S. parents who yearn for a child but cannot find one (especially one without special needs) through domestic adoption. Opponents, on the other hand, bemoan the fact that international adoptions separate children from their countries and cultures of origin (Bartholet, 2007a). Another concern is that these adoptions fuel child trafficking, and that they tear children from low-income mothers in order to place them with wealthier and more advantaged ones. Meanwhile, little is done to improve the local conditions in which these mothers and children subsist.

Summary and Conclusion

Adoption laws and processes have evolved in an effort to balance the interests of three distinct parties: the birth parents, the adoptive parents, and the child or adult adoptee. Social workers engaged in adoption may find themselves working with each of these as individuals, couples, families, or groups in search of information and support. Although the experience of adoption has profound social and emotional aspects, it ultimately is a legal process that permanently severs the biological relationship and replaces it with a new one. Types of adoptions include those secured through public agencies, private agencies, intermediaries, and direct contact between the parties. Both domestic adoptions and international adoptions are governed by strict rules and procedures, including the completion of a home study and the collection of extensive documentation. State laws regulate the granting and revoking of consent to adopt, as well as who may have access to adoption records. The law has also evolved to provide adoptive parents with legal recourse when adoptions are premised on faulty or misleading information. Many aspects of adoption law continue to engender controversy.

Sample Case

This case from New York considers the right of an unmarried father to veto the mother's decision to place their child for adoption. Read the case carefully and then answer the questions that follow.

ROBERT O. v. RUSSELL K.
604 N.E.2D 99 (1992)

Simons, Judge.

Petitioner, an unwed father, seeks to vacate a final order approving the adoption of his son. He contends that the mother or the State had a duty to ensure he knew of the birth and that their failure to do so denied him his constitutional rights. Inasmuch as petitioner failed to take any steps to discover the pregnancy or the birth of the child before first asserting his parental interest 10 months after the adoption became final, we conclude he was neither entitled to notice nor was his consent to the adoption required. We, therefore, affirm. ***

In December 1987, petitioner Robert O. and Carol A. became engaged and petitioner moved into Carol's home. Disagreements arose, however, and in February 1988, petitioner moved out and terminated all contact with Carol. At that time Carol was pregnant but she did not tell petitioner, apparently because she believed he would feel she was trying to coerce him into marriage. Over the next few weeks, Carol approached her friends, respondents Russell K. and his wife Joanne K., and obtained their agreement to adopt her child. On October 1, 1988, Carol gave birth to a boy, who was delivered to respondents upon her discharge from the hospital. Carol later executed a judicial consent and, in May 1989, the adoption was finalized....

Between the time Carol and petitioner separated in March 1988 and January 1990, petitioner made no attempt to contact Carol although she continued to live in the same house and, as the courts below found, did nothing to conceal her whereabouts or her pregnancy. In January 1990, petitioner and Carol reconciled and subsequently married. In March 1990—nearly 18 months after the birth and 10 months after the completed adoption—Carol informed petitioner that the child had been born. In a belated effort to meet the statutory requirements for notice and consent, petitioner reimbursed Carol for her medical expenses, filed with the Putative Father Registry, and commenced this proceeding to vacate the adoption.***

Petitioner concedes that the applicable statutes do not require notice to one in his position or require his consent to the adoption. Domestic Relations Law § 111-a (2) provides the father of a child born outside wedlock can qualify for notice of an adoption proceeding in any one of several ways....As petitioner notes, these actions generally presume that the father knows he has a child before the adoption is finalized and he had no such knowledge.

Petitioner contends that because these New York laws fail to require notice and consent from a father in his position, they deny biological fathers a constitutional liberty interest. He maintains that before an adoption is finalized, the courts must be required to resolve the factual issue of who the biological father is and determine whether he has had sufficient opportunity to establish a relationship with the child, in part by requiring the mother to testify as to paternity....

The nature of the constitutional interest possessed by unwed fathers has been addressed previously by both the Supreme Court and this Court....The guiding principle has been that the biological connection between father and child is not sufficient, in and of itself, to create a protected interest for the father. Only if the unwed father "grasps the opportunity" to form a relationship with his child will the inchoate right created by biology blossom into a protected liberty interest under the Constitution....

Manifestly, the unwed father of an infant placed for adoption immediately at birth faces a unique dilemma should he desire to establish his parental rights. Any opportunity he has to shoulder the responsibility of parenthood may disappear before he has a chance to grasp it, no matter how willing he is to do so. Accordingly, we have acknowledged that in some instances the Constitution protects an unwed father's *opportunity* to develop a relationship with his infant son or daughter. This constitutional right to the opportunity to develop a qualifying relationship does not extend to all unwed fathers or arise from the mere fact of biology. The right exists only for the unwed father who manifests his willingness to assume full custody of the child and does so promptly.

To conclude that petitioner acted promptly once he became aware of the child is to fundamentally misconstrue whose timetable is relevant. Promptness is measured in terms of the baby's life not by the onset of the father's awareness. The demand for prompt action by the father at the child's birth is neither arbitrary nor punitive, but instead a logical and necessary outgrowth of the State's legitimate interest in the child's need for early permanence and stability....

During the first months of his son's life, the petitioner's only connection to the infant was biological. That he now asserts that he was willing to be a custodial parent, had he only known, adds nothing to his argument, even if we accept the dubious proposition that a willingness so abstract and amorphous has some legal significance....No one...prevented petitioner from finding out about Carol's pregnancy. His inaction, however regrettable and with whatever unfortunate consequences, was solely attributable to him. *** [W]e reaffirm today, that opportunity becomes protected only if grasped.

Titone, Judge (concurring).

I agree that due process does not require the unraveling of a 10-month-old adoption at the behest of a biological father whose identity was unknown and unknowable at the time the adoption became final, but I cannot agree that in all circumstances "biology alone is not enough to warrant constitutional protection." Additionally, I cannot agree with the majority's reliance on the purported fault of this biological father in "failing to take any steps to discover the pregnancy or the birth of the child" until after the child was adopted....

At the heart of my disagreement with the majority is the unrealistic burden that its rationale imposes on the multitude of men who, in this age of sexual permissiveness, have intimate relationships with women to whom they are not married. Because of the biological characteristics of the parties to these relationships, it is the women, rather than the men, who are in the unique position to discover whether a pregnancy has resulted. Further, in most instances, it is the women, rather than the men, who hold the exclusive power to decide whether or not the other progenitor is to be informed of the pregnancy's existence. The man who has not been told of the pregnancy has few, if any avenues of recourse.

Indeed, although the majority has not hesitated to assign blame to petitioner because of what it terms his "inaction," it has not even begun to identify just what it is that petitioner might have done to fulfill his responsibilities in these circumstances. Does the majority mean to suggest that all men who engage in sexual intercourse with women to whom they are not married must remain in regular contact with them even after their relationships have terminated in order to ascertain whether there has been a pregnancy? Must they also make inquiries in the community or pursue alternative sources of information in order to definitively rule out the possibility that the relationship may have produced a child?

I would submit, most respectfully, that a rule which places the onus on the man to investigate whether a woman with whom he is no longer intimate has become pregnant is simply out of step with modern mores....Moreover, a rule that requires men to foist continued contact on women with whom they are no longer involved overlooks women's interest in preserving their own privacy after the relationship has been terminated....

Although petitioner is innocent of any untoward neglect and, in fact, had a constitutionally cognizable interest in a parental relationship with his biological child, that interest does not outweigh the State's countervailing interest in ensuring the finality of adoptions and, thus, it was not entitled to constitutional protection....

While the State must make every effort to protect the rights of biological parents in adoption proceedings, there also must come a point where the matter is deemed irrevocably closed, so that the parties can go forward with their lives, secure in the certainty that their legal and familial status can no longer be disturbed....

If petitioner's position were to be embraced by the Court, the critical goal of finality could never be achieved for the substantial number of children whose biological fathers have not been apprised of their existence. Such children—as well as their adoptive families—would be forever relegated to a state of legal limbo in which their familial relationship would remain subject to the possibility that their biological fathers might suddenly learn of their birth and appear to reclaim them. Clearly, such a result is one that cannot be tolerated in a legal system that concerns itself with humane values....

In sum, petitioner's situation is an unfortunate one, since, through no real fault of his own, he has been deprived of "the blessings of the parent-child relationship" and even the opportunity of developing such a relationship. However, his dilemma was created not by any institutionalized mechanism or unrealistic legal barrier imposed by the State, but rather by Carol A.'s . . . perfectly understandable decisions to keep her pregnancy secret from him and to surrender their child without disclosing his identity. In these circumstances, the interests petitioner may have had in his role as a biological father are more than out-weighed by society's overriding interest in ensuring the finality of his child's adoption....I concur in the Court's decision to affirm.

Questions:

1. The father in this case, Robert O., is seeking to have an adoption decree reversed because he was never given an opportunity to either consent or object to the adoption. What exactly is he claiming that the state should have done differently?

2. The court in this case denied the father's petition. Why? According to the court, are there any circumstances under which an unmarried father would have the right to have a say in whether or not his child is placed for adoption? If so, what would those circumstances be?

3. The majority opinion and the concurring opinion agree that, in this case, the father's petition should be rejected. They disagree, however, on whether the father is to blame for his plight. What do you think? Why?

4. Under the court's decision, it is perfectly acceptable for a woman to have a child, never inform the child's father, and then put the child up for adoption without his consent. Are you comfortable with this approach? Why or why not?

5. If you were responsible for crafting a policy that balances the interests of the child and each of the unmarried parents, what might it look like? Whose consent would be required for adoption? Under what circumstances? If you are unable to do justice to everyone's interests, whose interests do you think should prevail? Why?

CHAPTER 7 PRACTICE TEST

The following questions will test your application and analysis of the content found within this chapter. For additional assessment, including licensing-exam type questions on applying chapter content to practice behaviors, visit **MySearchLab**.

1. Adopting a child from foster care is most likely to involve a(n)
   a. direct placement adoption.
   b. independent adoption.
   c. private agency adoption.
   d. public agency adoption.

2. Your client, who is adopted, is interested in locating and meeting her birth parents. Your state has a mutual consent registry. This means that she can
   a. receive information about her medical history only.
   b. receive identifying information about her birth parents if they request information about her.
   c. receive information about her birth parents, but not access to sealed birth records.
   d. request that the state locate her parents and seek their consent to meet with her.

3. Your neighbor adopted a child who, it turns out, has serious mental health issues that were never disclosed by the agency. Can your neighbor have the adoption annulled?
   a. Yes, if she can prove that the agency intentionally withheld the information.
   b. Yes, if she can prove the agency mistakenly failed to provide the information.
   c. Yes, if she can demonstrate that it would be in the child's best interests.
   d. No, once an adoption is final it can never be dissolved.

4. Most transracial adoptions today involve
   a. African American children placed in Caucasian homes.
   b. Caucasian children placed in non-Caucasian homes.
   c. Hispanic children placed in non-Hispanic homes.
   d. Native American Indian children placed in Caucasian homes.

5. The four major types of adoptions are public agency, private agency, independent, and direct placement. What are the advantages and disadvantages of each?

6. Although very popular, international adoptions have come under some criticism. What are the arguments in favor of them? What are the arguments against them?

MYSEARCHLAB CONNECTIONS

Reinforce what you learned in this chapter by studying videos, cases, documents, and more available at www.MySearchLab.com.

Watch these Videos

⋆ Institution Care/Adoption and Foster Care: Nathan Fox

- *What special challenges do adoptions of children from insitututions pose? How can these challenges be addressed?*

Read these Cases/Documents

Δ Adoption Records Controversy, The

- *Whose rights must be balanced in deciding how to approach the confidentiality of adoption records? How do you think the law should go about balancing those rights?*

Δ Boyds, The

- *What special challenges do court-mandated clients pose in treatment? What special challenges do international adoptions pose?*

Research these Topics

- social work and race matching in adoption
- second parent adoption by same-sex couples
- guardianship as an alternative to adoption

Assess Your Knowledge

Go to **MySearchLab** to test your knowledge of key topics in this chapter with topic-specific quizzes. Conclude your assessment by completing the chapter exam.

⋆ = CSWE Core Competency Asset   Δ = Case Study

Child Custody

Social workers practicing with children and families may be involved in child custody actions that arise from divorce, child abuse and neglect, or delinquency. Child maltreatment and delinquency are addressed in chapters 6 and 11, respectively; the focus of this chapter is child custody pursuant to divorce.

Although biological parents are generally afforded wide latitude in raising their children, courts are empowered to assign a change in custody under the principle of *parens patriae*—the doctrine that allows the government to intervene to safeguard the interests of those who are vulnerable (Clement, 1997; Downs, Moore, & McFadden, 2009). Although the vast majority of child custody disputes are resolved by the parties without legal intervention, some custody cases do in fact reach the courts. Social workers can play an indispensible role in these proceedings by serving as fact witnesses, expert witnesses, or child custody evaluators. Social workers also work with many families undergoing divorce; in addition to providing concrete services and emotional support, we can help these families navigate the complex legal terrain involved in custody determinations.

This chapter discusses the various types of custody, the historical development of different approaches to custody decision making, how custody decisions are made today, and issues regarding visitation. A special section highlights what social workers should know about conducting child custody evaluations. The chapter ends with a sample case depicting some of the difficulties in deciding custody cases.

Types of Custody

Most parents in divorce cases voluntarily agree to a custody arrangement; in about 5% of cases, however, the parents are unable to agree and the determination is made by a judge. In order to assist in this determination, the court will generally encourage the parents to select an evaluator (often a social worker) who will make a recommendation to the court; if the parents cannot agree on an evaluator, the judge will appoint one. Custody determinations are made at the trial court level and are governed by state law. A substantial change of circumstances is needed to modify an existing custody order (Krause & Meyer, 2007). Custody decisions are often exceedingly painful and difficult; they inevitably result in the dissolution of a family, with the child being separated from one of his or her parents.

Although the term *custody* is commonly used, some courts regard this term as unnecessarily adversarial and refer instead to "allocating parental responsibilities" or "parenting plans following divorce" (Downs et al., 2009, p. 168). Regardless of what it is called, the court will make two determinations: who will have physical custody of the children and who will have legal custody.

Physical custody involves having the actual, physical right to be with the child and to make all day-to-day decisions. The parent with physical custody is the parent with whom the child lives. If *sole physical custody* is awarded, then the child will live primarily with one parent and may have visitation with the other. In cases of *shared* or *joint physical custody*, the child will spend a significant amount of time living with each of the parents. With *split physical custody,* the children are divided between the parents; for example, one child might live with the mother while the other two live with the father.

Legal custody involves having the right to make long-term decisions regarding the child's health, welfare, education, and religious upbringing. Legal custody may be awarded to one parent (*sole legal custody*) or shared by both parents (*joint legal custody*) meaning that both share decisions. With *split legal custody,* decision making for different children are made by different parents.

Let's consider a fairly typical example: Jon and Jane are getting divorced. They have four children: Jim, Judy, Josh, and Jeff. The parents cannot reach agreement regarding who should have custody of the children so they go before a judge. The judge awards joint legal custody to both parents and awards sole physical custody to Jon. This means that although both parents will have a voice in making decisions affecting the children's lives, the children will live with Jon and he will handle day-to-day decisions such as what they eat for dinner and what they wear to school.

Joint custody emerged in the mid-1970s as a strategy to keep both parents involved in their children's lives after divorce. It has since become commonplace and often is the preferred solution to custody disputes when the parents are able to cooperate in raising their children. Custody awards to fathers have also increased significantly, although custody arrangements continue to favor mothers. Data from the 1970s through the 1990s show women being granted sole custody of children approximately 85% of the time and men approximately 10%; in the remainder of cases, custody was joint or split or was awarded to a third party (Kelly, 1994). In the years since, the proportion of men being awarded sole custody has stayed the same while the incidence of joint custody has increased (LawFirms.com, 2012).

Historical Approaches to Custody

The history of child custody arrangements dates back to English common law in the 1600s. During that time, divorces were rare and when they did occur, children were seen as the father's property. This idea persisted in the United States from its founding until the 1800s. The perceived primacy of the father is well articulated in this quote from an 1842 Mississippi opinion (*Foster v. Alston*, p. 463):

> We are informed by the first elementary books we read, that the authority of the father is superior to that of the mother. It is the doctrine of all civilized nations. It is according to the revealed law and the law of nature, and it prevails even with the wandering savage, who has received none of the lights of civilization.

Tender Years Doctrine

In the mid-19th century, a new idea emerged that switched the custodial preference from the father to the mother. Known as the *tender years doctrine,* it asserted that young children—typically those younger than age 7—should be placed with their mothers unless it can be shown that the mother is unfit (Clement, 1997; Krause & Meyer, 2007). The rationale, of course, was that mothers tend to be more nurturing and generally are responsible for tending to the young child's day-to-day needs. However, as more mothers made their way into the workforce, and the women's movement of the 1970s took hold, household dynamics changed. Courts were often faced with two-career couples and stereotypes about maternal roles became less and less acceptable. In 1981 (*Ex Parte Devine*), the Alabama Supreme Court concluded that the tender years presumption constituted sex discrimination in violation of the 14th Amendment's equal protection clause. In that case, a father contested the award of the couple's two young children to the mother. Both parents had been found to be equally fit to raise the children; both were well educated and gainfully employed. Each parent was believed to have positive attributes that might make them the better parent, and each had some shortcomings that raised questions about their relative suitability. In keeping with Alabama law, however, the trial court had automatically granted custody to the mother. The state supreme court, in reversing, concluded that the Constitution requires that custody decisions be based on the individual facts of the case, rather than on gender stereotypes and assumptions. Permissible considerations include the following:

- Age and sex of the children
- The children's emotional, social, moral, material, and educational needs
- The respective home environments offered by the parents
- Age, character, stability, and mental and physical health of each parent
- Capacity and interest of each parent in providing for the children's needs
- Relationship between the children
- Potential effect on the children of changing the existing custodial arrangement
- Preference of each child
- Recommendations of expert witnesses or evaluators
- Available alternatives

At the time this case was heard, 22 states had a tender years presumption similar to Alabama's. Although most states have since abolished the presumption, many judges continue to believe that young children should be placed with their mothers.

Primary Caretaker Standard

As reliance on the tender years doctrine began to fade, some jurisdictions adopted the *primary caretaker* or *primary parent* approach: "When both parents seek custody of a child too young to express a preference, and one parent has been the primary caretaker of the child, custody should be awarded to the primary caretaker absent a showing that that parent is unfit to be the custodian" (*Pikula v. Pikula*, 1985, p. 712). The logic behind the primary caretaker standard is the belief that a child's emotional attachment is most often established through repeated, daily interactions with the parent who performs various nurturing and caretaking activities. The case of *Kennedy v. Kennedy* (1985) is a good illustration of how this doctrine has been applied. The court originally hearing the custody dispute between the parties granted split custody, with the father having sole custody of the three older children and the mother having temporary custody of the youngest child. The Minnesota Court of Appeals remanded the case, ordering the court to consider which parent was the primary caretaker. According to the court, the primary caretaker is the parent most often responsible for

- Planning and preparing meals
- Bathing, grooming, and dressing the child
- Purchasing, cleaning, and caring for the child's clothing
- Ensuring proper medical care including transporting the child to the doctor
- Arranging for the child's social activities
- Arranging for babysitting or day care
- Putting the child to bed at night and waking the child in the morning
- Disciplining the child
- Supporting the child's education

On remand, the trial court found that the mother was the primary caretaker of the youngest child (5-1/2 months old), but that neither parent could be considered the primary caretaker in relation to the three older children (ages 4, 6, and 11). So as not to disturb the existing custody arrangement, the court awarded the parents joint legal custody of all four children, while continuing to vest physical custody of the three older children with the father and physical custody of the youngest child with the mother.

The primary caretaker standard was meant to address the gender bias inherent in the tender years presumption. Rather than rely on gender stereotypes, it mandates an examination of each parent's role in caring for the child. Critics have argued, however, that its emphasis on homemaker duties simply perpetuates discrimination under a different guise. It appears to disadvantage the breadwinner, who is more often the father in traditional family relationships, and provides an incentive for women to stay home with their children. Many also question the doctrine's underlying assumption: Is being the primary caretaker an acceptable proxy for the psychological bond between parent and child? In time, most jurisdictions agreed that although identifying the primary parent is important, it should be only one consideration among many that determine the custody of a child (Krause & Meyer, 2007).

Psychological Parent Standard

While the courts were experimenting with these various approaches to custody, Goldstein, Freud, and Solnit (1973) published a provocative book in which they advanced yet another possible basis for deciding custody disputes: the *psychological parent standard.* Essentially, this approach seeks to apply psychoanalytic theory to child custody cases (notice that one of the coauthors is Anna Freud—youngest child of Sigmund Freud and an eminent child psychologist in her own right). Rather than confining the debate to which biological parent would be the better custodian, the psychological parent standard jettisoned the idea that biological ties are necessarily primary and urged instead that courts focus on who would best meet the emotional needs of the child. The authors drew on the literature of the time to assert that children are in many ways different from adults: Their needs change over time as they mature; they have a different sense of time than adults and are less able to tolerate separation or delay; they experience life's ups and downs more profoundly than adults; they suffer from loyalty conflicts when the adults they love do not love each other; and they are more affected by their day-to-day interactions with adults than by the fact of a biological relationship. The authors agreed that parents should have the right to raise their children without government interference, but they noted that if and when custody becomes an issue, the adult with whom the child is emotionally connected (the psychological parent) should prevail. In determining the strength of that bond, the court should consider children's need for continuity and their sense of time. Most often, therefore, custody would rest with the adult who has been with the child the longest and/or most recently.

One advantage of this standard is that it appears to be more gender neutral than others the courts have entertained, although in traditional households, mothers remain more likely than fathers to be involved with the child day-to-day. Its most controversial aspect, of course, is that it gives no advantage to birth parents over others. For example, if a biological parent needing hospitalization were to temporarily relinquish custody of his or her child to a family friend, the importance of continuity would weigh in favor of the child remaining with the friend rather than returning to the biological parent. The logic is that even a separation that seems relatively brief to an adult is likely to seem lengthy to a child; thus, restoring the child to the biological parent would disrupt the child's sense of stability. The psychological parent standard brought important attention to the emotional impact of separation, and motivated courts to look at prospective custody arrangements through the child's eyes. Much of the theoretical underpinning of the psychological parent idea has been reinforced by modern attachment theory—although we now understand that children can (and often do) form emotional bonds with more than one adult.

Best Interests of the Child

The one constant that characterizes the modern era of custody law is the principle that the needs of the child should supersede those of the parents. As early as 1925, the *best interests of the child* standard began to gain support (Ricks, 1984). It remains the predominant standard governing custody decisions today. Laws in every state reinforce the primacy of the child's best interests and articulate factors to be considered in making custody awards. Nonetheless, actually determining what would be in a child's best interests is often more art than science; judges exercise enormous discretion in making this subjective but far-reaching determination.

Current Trends

Currently, all states and the District of Columbia have adopted statutes requiring courts to consider the best interests of the child whenever specific decisions are made regarding child custody and placement. Under the standard, courts take into consideration an array of factors with the ultimate safety and well-being of the child being paramount (Child Welfare Information Gateway, 2008).

Defining the Best Interests of the Child

Judges rely on the statutory definition of *best interests* outlined in each state's law. Although there is no uniform definition, most states articulate similar overarching goals: maintaining family integrity, keeping children in their home of origin, protecting the child's health and safety, making timely decisions promoting permanence, and ensuring the provision of proper care and guidance (Child Welfare Information Gateway, 2008).

A number of states, including Kentucky (K.R.S. §§ 403.010 to 403.350) and Minnesota (M.S.A. §§ 518.002 to 518.66) have adopted the language contained in the Uniform Marriage and Divorce Act, which mandates the following considerations:

> (1) the wishes of the child's parents as to custody, (2) the wishes of the child as to his or her custodian, (3) the interaction and interrelationship of the child with the parents, siblings, and any other person who may significantly affect the child's best interests, (4) the child's adjustment to the home, school, and community, and (5) the mental and physical health of all individuals involved.

The specific items delineated in other state statutes vary, but most reinforce similar themes. For example, the Connecticut statute reads as follows (Conn. Gen. Stat. Ann. § 45a-719):

> "Best interest of the child" shall include, but not be limited to, a consideration of the age of the child, the nature of the relationship of the child with his or her caretaker, the length of time the child has been in the custody of the caretaker, the nature of the relationship of the child with the birth parent, the length of time the child has been in the custody of the birth parent, any relationship that may exist between the child and siblings or other children in the caretaker's household, and the psychological and medical needs of the child. The determination of the best interests of the child shall not be based on a consideration of the socioeconomic status of the birth parent or the caretaker.

Additional factors included in some state laws are, for example, the sincerity of each parent's request, any family history of abuse, prior involvement of each parent in the child's life, the demands of parental employment, and prior voluntary abandonment or surrender of custody of the child. Contrary to the Connecticut law just cited, some states specifically include the financial status of the parents or, as in Maryland, "the material opportunities affecting the future life of the child."

The variation among statutes highlights the reality that "best interests of the child" will be understood, interpreted, and applied differently in different states, and by different judges within a single state. Even when the list of considerations seems exhaustive, how each is weighted in any given case is left to the discretion of the judge. Although this flexibility has advantages, it also may result in inconsistent outcomes.

Inconsistency has also raised confounding jurisdictional issues when custody cases cross state lines. The Uniform Child Custody Jurisdiction and Enforcement Act (UCCJEA) was introduced in 1997 as a response to these issues. It has since been adopted by all 50 states and the District of Columbia. The act addresses interstate divorce, separation, and paternity and vests jurisdiction over custody matters in the home state of the child. It was designed as a strategy to deter parental kidnapping and to promote uniform enforcement in cases involving interstate child custody and visitation (Aaby, 2009; Hoff, 2001).

The Nexus Test

Given the inherent subjectivity of custody determinations, it is not surprising that courts have often been influenced by parental characteristics or behaviors regarded as titillating or unconventional. Custody decisions have historically mirrored societal prejudices. In the landmark case of *Palmore v. Sidoti* (1984), the U.S. Supreme Court addressed the issue of race in custody determinations. A Caucasian couple divorced and the mother was awarded sole custody of their infant daughter. The mother later began cohabiting with an African American man, at which point the father sued for custody. The Florida court awarded custody to the father, arguing that living in a mixed-race household would be harmful to the child, subjecting her to stigma and discrimination. The U.S. Supreme Court reversed. In a unanimous opinion, it concluded that removal of the child from the mother's custody under these circumstances violated the 14th Amendment's equal protection clause.

Many of the cases debated by the courts involve the sexual orientation or sexual behavior of the parents. In 1974, the New York Supreme Court considered a case (*Feldman v. Feldman*) in which the lower court had transferred custody of a couple's two children, ages 6 and 9, from the mother to the father, even though the children had lived continuously with the mother since their birth. The court found the change of custody warranted by the best interests of the child, noting the mother's dubious morals: She had dated a married man and had advertised in *Screw Magazine*, soliciting other couples for "fun and games." The New York Supreme Court was clear that "the mother's private sex life in no way involved or affected the children" and was therefore irrelevant to her suitability as a parent.

Twelve years later, in *M.A.B. v. R.B.* (1986), the New York Supreme Court reached a similar conclusion when the father's sexual orientation was at issue. In this case, the mother sought to relocate out of state with her children, and the father sued to oppose the relocation and seek sole custody of the oldest child. The child at issue apparently had experienced chronic difficulties both at home and at school. After entering therapy, he went to live with his father where by all accounts he made wonderful progress. The mother's primary objection was the father's sexual orientation. Their separation and divorce had apparently been triggered by his admission to being gay, and following the divorce, he had chosen to live with a male partner. In finding the father's sexual orientation irrelevant to the custody determination, the court relied on what it called the *nexus test*. Under the nexus test, parental characteristics and behaviors may be considered only if the evidence shows that they have a clear connection to the child's well-being. In this case, the court found no factual support for the mother's contention that the father's sexual orientation adversely affected the child. Courts in a number of states have used the nexus test to reach the same conclusion. When the parent's "moral fitness and reputation" is included in the statutory definition of best interests, however, sexual orientation is likely to continue to be a source of controversy and concern.

The nexus test is a useful tool in separating relevant from irrelevant considerations in regard to custody. It reinforces the importance of looking closely at the facts of each case and avoiding assumptions about what is best for the child. In addition to race, sexual orientation, and sexual behavior, it has been applied to religion and disability. Some urge that it also be applied to gender identity, including transgender status (Carter, 2006). In each case, the principle is the same: These factors cannot be considered in making custody determinations absent direct evidence of harm to the child. Unfortunately, not all courts apply the nexus test; parental characteristics related to religion and sexual orientation, in particular, continue to be treated by some courts as an automatic barrier to custody.

CONDUCTING CHILD CUSTODY EVALUATIONS

Social workers are often called upon to conduct child custody evaluations. This is a forensic role designed to assist the court in making a proper determination regarding what custody arrangement is best for the child. As with any forensic evaluation, a child custody evaluation must be based on objective evidence and must be conducted in conformity with the highest professional standards. Professional ethics suggest that you consent to serve as an evaluator only when both parents have agreed to hire you or the court appoints you. If you are asked to conduct an evaluation involving a client with whom you already have a therapeutic relationship, the NASW Code of Ethics, which prohibits dual relationships, would require you to inform the court and withdraw.

A child custody evaluation should be based on four sources of information: observation, interviews, psychological testing, and a home study. First, it is important to *directly observe* the child or children interacting with each of the parents (Lewis, 2009). In order to avoid advantaging or disadvantaging either parent, try to spend an equal amount of time with each. The types of observations should also be as similar as possible. They can be unstructured (watching informal interactions) or structured (story time, mealtime, separation and reunion, etc.). Your focus should be on the relationship between each child and each parent. Specifically, you will want to

observe the following (Baerger, Galatzer-Levy, Gould, & Nye, 2002, p. 65):

- How each parent expresses love, affection, and support
- How each parent disciplines the children or provides structure
- Each parent's capacity to understand and respond to the children's cues
- Each parent's capacity to recognize the child as a separate individual
- Each parent's enjoyment of and confidence in the parenting role
- Each parent's sense of frustration or inadequacy in the parenting role
- The children's responses to each parent's behavior

Observations should be videotaped whenever possible; the parents' consent is required. You should also be taking notes that capture your observations in neutral terms with as little interpretation as possible.

Interviews should be conducted with each of the children and each of the parents. You might want to meet with them in various combinations: the children together and then separately, and each of the parents with each of the children. You might also want to meet with both parents jointly so you can evaluate the quality of their interaction, and then meet with each individually so they feel at liberty to speak freely. Remember that these are forensic interviews; therefore, all of the information discussed in Chapter 3 is relevant here. Your goal in these interviews is to gain an understanding of each parent's role as part of the family unit, including strengths and weaknesses and attitudes toward child rearing, marriage, and each other. In keeping with the nexus test, stay away from extraneous factors that have no bearing on actual parenting capacity. Be familiar with your state's child custody law and focus on those items enumerated under the definition of "best interests of the child." Because your goal is to be able to compare the two parents, be sure to examine the same competencies for each one, during the same time frame, based on the same sources. Typically, a semi-structured interview allows for the best balance of uniformity and flexibility. Because most parents emphasize the positives in relation to themselves and the negatives in relation to their partner, it is critical that you also interview various *collaterals,* including older children, stepparents, potential stepparents, grandparents, boyfriends and girlfriends, caregivers, neighbors, friends, coaches, scout leaders, teachers, doctors, mental health professionals, and social service providers—essentially anyone who has had contact with the children and family and might be able to shed light on what would be best for the child.

Psychological tests should never be relied on, in and of themselves, but only as a supplement to other sources of information. They typically include personality inventories and standardized instruments that can help the evaluator assess parenting knowledge and ability. Examples include the Parent Competency Study (PCS), Bricklin Perceptual Scales

(BPS), Ackerman-Scoendorf Scales for Parent Evaluation for Custody (ASPECT), and Perception of Relations Test (PORT). It is essential that you be trained in the specific instrument you intend to use; otherwise, you must have another trained professional administer the test and interpret its results. Limit your findings to the legal issue at hand, and remember that your conclusions must be confirmed by data from other sources.

Finally, it is important to conduct a *home study* for each parent. The goal is to observe the children's physical living environment and to get a sense of their experience and behavior in each home setting. Be careful to maintain an open mind about routines, behaviors, or expectations that may seem unusual to you; remember that there are many cultural variations in the lives of families and households.

Based on the data collected, a report is prepared and submitted to the court, both parents, and both attorneys. The report should share the data from your evaluation and relate the information to the relevant scholarly literature and to the factors enumerated in the state's definition of "best interest of the child." You will want to identify the strengths and weaknesses of each parent in relation to meeting the children's needs. Finally, your recommendation should specify which (if any) is the preferred custodian and what type of custody arrangement (sole, joint, or split) would be best, based on your expert professional judgment.

Social workers make excellent child custody evaluators. By combining their understanding of family relationships and child development with an understanding of the law, they can serve as an invaluable asset to the courts in making difficult decisions about what is best for struggling families and children.

Legal Presumptions

Although all states weigh the best interests of the child, some states have adopted legal preferences or presumptions that tilt the scales in particular directions. Under a legal *preference*, when both parties are equally qualified to assume custody of the child, preference is given to a particular party. For example, if a father and mother are equally suitable custodians, a preference might be given to placing an infant with the mother. Under a *presumption,* custody automatically is awarded to a particular party without weighing the parties' relative virtues at all. Presumptions are *rebuttable,* however; this means they can be superseded by a showing that the favored custodian is unfit or that placement with that custodian would be contrary to the child's best interests. Many states have a legal presumption in favor of the biological parent. Typically, when a custody dispute is between two birth parents, the best interests of the child determine custody. However, when the dispute is between a birth parent and a third party (e.g., an adoptive parent, in-law, or family friend), custody is awarded to the birth parent unless there is clear and convincing evidence that the birth parent is unfit.

A number of states have presumptions in favor of joint legal and/or physical custody. In other words, rather than considering all possible custody arrangements and then choosing the one that best meets the child's interests, joint custody is automatically awarded unless the court finds that it would be detrimental to the child. In some states (including Connecticut, Michigan, and Minnesota), the presumption is triggered when both parents agree to joint custody. In Iowa, the presumption is triggered if one of the parents requests it. In Florida, the presumption is in favor joint custody, period; the same is true for legal custody in New Hampshire. On the other hand, several states expressly indicate the absence of a preference or presumption in favor of any particular custody arrangement; these states include Alaska, Arizona, New Jersey, and California.

A growing number of states recognize a presumption against custody with a parent who has perpetrated domestic violence. As of 2005, there were 24 such states and territories (Bolotin, 2008). This means that instead of a history of domestic violence being one consideration among many that determine what is in the child's best interests, the court automatically awards custody to the nonoffending parent. Other types of presumptions include favoring the primary caretaker (West Virginia) and favoring a spouse who has been abandoned (Utah). Nebraska's law makes a point of specifying that the state permits no preferences on the basis of the parent's sex or the child's sex or age.

As social workers who may become involved in child custody cases, it is important to know how the state makes its custody decisions, including how it defines the best interests of the child and whether any preferences or presumptions exist. It is also important to consider whether or not these presumptions are desirable. Are there factors that are so crucial to a child's well-being that they should automatically decide a custody case—or is it better to consider an array of factors and weigh each of them in making a determination? Under what circumstances, if at all, does a presumption in favor of joint custody make sense?

Rights to Visitation

Visitation, the temporary custody of a child for a defined period of time, is considered the right of every fit noncustodial parent (Abrams, Cahn, Ross, & Meyer, 2009). Courts frequently rely on the assessments of social workers when making decisions regarding visitation (Cohen & Shnit, 2001). When granting visitation rights, courts may base their decision on what they consider to be in the best interest of the child or on the right of parents to make decisions regarding their children.

Visitation Rights of Biological Parents

The Uniform Marriage and Divorce Act of 1970 states, "A parent not granted custody of the child is entitled to reasonable visitation rights unless the court finds, after a hearing, that visitation endangers seriously the child's physical, mental, moral, or emotional health." Most state statutes pertaining to child custody include language granting the noncustodial parent reasonable visitation. If a court determines that unsupervised visitation with a noncustodial parent could risk harming the child, it may order that all visitation be supervised by a third party. Supervised visitation is often ordered when there is evidence of physical or sexual abuse, substance abuse, or mental illness on the part of the noncustodial parent. Supervised visitation may take place in a specialized agency visitation center, in a mental health professional's office, a public location, or in a private home. Social workers often are called upon to oversee supervised visitations (Abrams et al., 2009).

In some situations, custodial parents attempt to interfere with the visitation rights of the noncustodial parent by preventing telephone contact, Internet communication, or planned visits between the child and the parent. Judicial sanctions for violating a visitation order can last indefinitely until the parent complies and can include fines or incarceration (Krause & Meyer, 2007).

Perhaps the most famous example of interference was the case of *Morgan v. Foretich* (1988). That case, which captured national headlines throughout the late 1980s, involved a divorced woman who was awarded custody of her young daughter and her ex-husband who was awarded liberal visitation. Both were highly educated and successful professionals. The following year, the mother returned to court, alleging that the father was molesting the child and seeking to have the visitation order revised. The court found insufficient evidence to do so. The mother subsequently hid the child and refused to allow visitation by the father. She was held in contempt and briefly jailed, after which visitation resumed and gradually expanded. When the judge later ordered a 2-week, unsupervised visit with the father, the mother again refused to make the child available and was again sent to jail where she remained for nearly 2 years. The child could not be found. It was later revealed that the child had been living under an assumed name with her grandparents in New Zealand. Although many doubted the mother's account, others shared her conviction that visitation might have exposed the child to harm. As this case demonstrates, risk can be difficult to assess, and courts take very seriously the right of parents to have access to their children. Custody cases can be extremely complicated, and that complication extends beyond the custody award itself to the visitation issue as well.

Cases also arise when one parent sabotages the relationship between the child and the other parent. In *Usack v. Usack* (2005), the court suspended a noncustodial mother's child support obligation after finding that the father had deliberately pitted the children against her, thus interfering with her visitation rights.

Third-Party Visitation

In some circumstances, individuals other than the child's biological parents seek to establish visitation with the child. Every state has some provision for third-party visitation by nonparents; typically, these nonparents must have strong ties demonstrated by living with the child or providing care and affection as a parent would (Abrams et al., 2009). Nonparents can petition for visitation in cases involving divorce, legal separation, custody, or the death of a parent. Third-party visitation provisions are sometimes controversial because they challenge the closely held notion that parents have the exclusive right to control who has contact with their children (Keith, 2002).

As is true with most legal determinations, issuing third-party visitation orders requires the court to balance different interests: the parents' right to make decisions concerning their children, and the children's interest in maintaining strong ties with other important people in their lives. More and more often, those people are the children's grandparents. A leading case on this topic, *Troxel v. Granville* (2000), concerned a mother who had separated from the children's father. During the separation, his parents had visited the children regularly. After the husband's suicide, however, the mother asked the grandparents to limit their visits to once per month. The grandparents went to court, seeking formal visitation rights. The state's statute afforded visitation rights to any person, under any circumstances, when it was considered to be in the child's best interests. The mother challenged the law, claiming that it violated her right under the 14th Amendment to make decisions regarding the care, custody, and control of her children. The U.S. Supreme Court agreed. Although most statutes are drafted more narrowly than the Washington state statute in this case, the Court's decision was significant in that it reaffirmed the fundamental right of parents to raise their children.

Nonparents who are eligible for visitation rights vary by state. Most are family members including grandparents, siblings, and great-grandparents. Half the states include stepparents in their third-party visitation statutes (Hans, 2002). In Wyoming, only grandparents and primary caretakers have the right to petition for visitation (*M.B.B. v. E.R.W.*, 2004). Similarly, Pennsylvania courts have ruled that siblings are ineligible for visitation rights if not specifically granted them by statute (*Ken R. v. Arthur Z.*, 1996). On the other hand, the New Jersey Supreme Court has ruled that siblings have the same right to visitation as other third parties (Abrams et al., 2009). Social workers should be aware of the third-party visitation laws, regulations, and court decisions in the state in which they practice.

Summary and Conclusion

Child custody cases can arise in a variety of contexts, but they most often occur in the context of divorce. The various types of custody include physical custody and legal custody. Over the years, the courts have applied different standards to determine who should have custody of minor children. These include the tender years presumption, the primary caretaker standard, the psychological parent standard, and the best interests of the child standard. All states are currently guided by the best interests of the child, which each state's statute defines for that state. Judges retain considerable discretion in making custody determinations; the nexus test, however, requires that only factors directly impacting the child's well-being be considered. States have enacted a number of preferences and presumptions that tip the scales for or against particular custodians. In addition to awarding custody, courts routinely award visitation; the right to visitation, however, must be weighed against the parent's right to control the upbringing of his or her child.

Sample Case

This is a colorful case that was decided by the Iowa Supreme Court according the best interests of the child standard. Read it carefully and then consider the questions that follow.

PAINTER v. BANNISTER
140 N.W.2d 152 (1966)

Stuart, Justice.

We are here setting the course for Mark Wendell Painter's future. Our decision on the custody of this seven-year-old boy will have a marked influence on his whole life. The fact that we are called upon many times a year to determine custody matters does not make the exercising of this awesome responsibility any less difficult. Legal training and experience are of little practical help in solving the complex problems of human relations. However, these problems do arise and under our system of government the burden of rendering a final decision rests upon us. It is frustrating to know we can only resolve, not solve, these unfortunate situations.

The custody dispute before us…is between the father, Harold Painter, and the maternal grandparents, Dwight and Margaret Bannister. Mark's mother and younger sister were killed in an automobile accident on December 6, 1962. . . . The father, after other arrangements for Mark's care had proved unsatisfactory, asked the Bannisters to take care of Mark. They went to California and brought Mark to their farm home near Ames in July 1963. Mr. Painter remarried in November 1964 and about that time indicated he wanted to take Mark back. The Bannisters refused to let him leave and this action was filed in June 1965. Since July 1965 he has continued to remain in the Bannister home under an order of this court staying execution of the judgment of the trial court awarding custody to the father until the matter could be determined on appeal. For reasons hereinafter stated, we conclude Mark's better interests will be served if he remains with the Bannisters.

Mark's parents came from highly contrasting backgrounds. His mother was born, reared and educated in rural Iowa. Her parents are college graduates. Her father is agricultural information editor for the Iowa State University Extension Service. The Bannister home is in the Gilbert community and is well kept, roomy and comfortable. The Bannisters are highly respected members of the community. Mr. Bannister has served on the school board and regularly teaches a Sunday school class at the Gilbert Congregational Church. Mark's mother graduated from Grinnell College. She then went to work for a newspaper in Anchorage, Alaska, where she met Harold Painter.

Mark's father was born in California. When he was two and one-half years old, his parents were divorced and he was placed in a foster home. Although he has kept in contact with his natural parents, he considers his foster parents, the McNellys, as his family. He flunked out of a high school and a trade school because of a lack of interest in academic subjects, rather than any lack of ability. He joined the navy at 17. He did not like it. After receiving an honorable discharge, he took examinations and obtained his high school diploma. He lived with the McNellys and went to college for two and one-half years under the G. I. bill. He quit college to take a job on a small newspaper in Ephrata, Washington, in November 1955. In May 1956 he went to work for the newspaper in Anchorage which employed Jeanne Bannister.

Harold and Jeanne were married in April 1957. Although there is a conflict in the evidence on the point, we are convinced the marriage, overall, was a happy one, with many ups and downs as could be expected in the uniting of two such opposites.

We are not confronted with a situation where one of the contesting parties is not a fit or proper person. There is no criticism of either the Bannisters or their home. There is no suggestion in the record that Mr. Painter is morally unfit. It is obvious the Bannisters did not approve of their daughter's marriage to Harold Painter and do not want their grandchild reared under his guidance. The philosophies of life are entirely different. As stated by the psychiatrist who examined Mr. Painter at the request of Bannisters' attorneys: "It is evident that there exists a large difference in ways of life and value systems between the Bannisters and Mr. Painter, but in this case there is no evidence that psychiatric instability is involved. Rather, these divergent life patterns seem to represent alternative normal adaptations."

It is not our prerogative to determine custody upon our choice of one of two ways of life within normal and proper limits and we will not do so. However, the philosophies are important as they relate to Mark and his particular needs.

The Bannister home provides Mark with a stable, dependable, conventional, middle-class, middle-western background and an opportunity for a college education and profession, if he desires it. It provides a solid foundation and secure atmosphere. In the Painter home Mark would have more freedom of conduct and thought with an opportunity to develop his individual talents. It would be more exciting and challenging in many respects, but romantic, impractical and unstable.

Little additional recitation of evidence is necessary to support our evaluation of the Bannister home. It might be pointed out, however, that Jeanne's three sisters also received college educations and seem to be happily married to college graduates.

Our conclusion as to the type of home Mr. Painter would offer is based upon his Bohemian approach to finances and life in general. We feel there is much evidence which supports this conclusion. His main ambition is to be a free-lance writer and photographer. He has had some articles and picture stories published, but the income from these efforts has been negligible. At the time of the accident, Jeanne was willingly working to support the family so Harold could devote more time to his writing and photography. In the ten years since he left college he has changed jobs seven times. He was asked to leave two of them; two he quit because he did not like the work; two because he wanted to devote more time to writing and the rest for better pay. He was contemplating a move to Berkeley at the time of trial. His attitude toward his career is typified by his own comments concerning a job offer:

"About the Portland news job, I hope you understand when I say it took guts not to take it; I had to get behind myself and push. It was very, very tempting to accept a good salary and settle down to a steady, easy routine. As I approached Portland, with the intention of taking the job, I began to ask what, in the long run, would be the good of this job: 1, it was not really what I wanted; 2, Portland is just another big farm town, with none of the stimulation it takes to get my mind sparking. Anyway, I decided Mark and myself would be better off if I went ahead with what I've started and the hell with the rest, sink, swim or starve."

There is general agreement that Mr. Painter needs help with his finances. Both Jeanne and Marilyn, his present wife, handled most of them. Purchases and sales of books, boats, photographic equipment and houses indicate poor financial judgment and an easy come easy go attitude. He dissipated his wife's estate of about $4300, most of which was a gift from her parents and which she had hoped would be used for the children's education.

The psychiatrist classifies him as "a romantic and somewhat of a dreamer." An apt example is the plan he related for himself and Mark in February 1963: "My thought now is to settle Mark and myself in Sausalito, near San Francisco; this is a retreat for wealthy artists, writers, and such aspiring artists and writers as can fork up the rent money. My plan is to do expensive portraits ($150 and up), sell prints ($15 and up) to the tourists who flock in from all over the world."

The house in which Mr. Painter and his present wife live, compared with the well-kept Bannister home, exemplifies the contrasting ways of life. In his words "it is a very old and beat-up and lovely home." They live in the rear part. The interior is inexpensively but tastefully decorated. The large yard on a hill in the business district of Walnut Creek, California, is of uncut weeds and wild oats. The house "is not painted on the outside because I do not want it painted. I am very fond of the wood on the outside of the house."

The present Mrs. Painter has her master's degree in cinema design and apparently likes and has had considerable contact with children. She is anxious to have Mark in her home. Everything indicates she would provide a leveling influence on Mr. Painter and could ably care for Mark.

Mr. Painter is either an agnostic or atheist and has no concern for formal religious training. He has read a lot of Zen Buddhism and "has been very much influenced by it." Mrs. Painter is Roman Catholic. They plan to send Mark to a Congregational Church near the Catholic Church, on an irregular schedule.

He is a political liberal and got into difficulty in a job at the University of Washington for his support of the activities of the American Civil Liberties Union in the university news bulletin.

There were "two funerals" for his wife. One in the basement of his home in which he alone was present. He conducted the service and wrote her a long letter. The second at a church in Pullman was for the gratification of her friends. He attended in a sport shirt and sweater.

These matters are not related as a criticism of Mr. Painter's conduct, way of life or sense of values. An individual is free to choose his own values, within bounds, which are not exceeded here. They do serve however to support our conclusion as to the kind of life Mark would be exposed to in the Painter household. We believe it would be unstable, unconventional, arty, Bohemian and probably intellectually stimulating.

Were the question simply which household would be the most suitable in which to rear a child, we would have unhesitatingly chosen the Bannister home. We believe security and stability in the home are more important than intellectual stimulation in the proper development of a child. There are, however, several factors which have made us pause.

First, there is the presumption of parental preference, which, though weakened in the past several years, exists by statute. . . . We have a great deal of sympathy for a father who, in the difficult period of adjustment following his wife's death, turns to the maternal grandparents for their help and then finds them unwilling to return the child. There is no merit in the Bannister claim that Mr. Painter permanently relinquished custody. It was intended to be a temporary arrangement. A father should be encouraged to look for help with the children from those who love them without the risk of thereby losing the custody of the children permanently. This fact must receive consideration in cases of this kind. However, as always, the primary consideration is the best interest of the child and if the return of custody to the father is likely to have a seriously disrupting and disturbing effect upon the child's development, this fact must prevail.

Second, Jeanne's will named her husband guardian of her children and, if he failed to qualify or ceased to act, named her mother. The parent's wishes are entitled to consideration.

Third, the Bannisters are 60 years old. By the time Mark graduates from high school they will be over 70 years old. Care of young children is a strain on grandparents and Mrs. Bannister's letters indicate as much.

We have considered all of these factors and have concluded that Mark's best interest demands that his custody remain with the Bannisters. Mark was five when he came to their home. The evidence clearly shows he was not well adjusted at that time. He did not distinguish fact from fiction and was inclined to tell "tall tales.".…He was very aggressive toward smaller children, cruel to animals, not liked by his classmates and did not seem to know what was acceptable conduct. As stated by one witness: "Mark knew where his freedom was and he didn't know where his boundaries were." In two years he made a great deal of improvement. He now appears to be well disciplined, happy, relatively secure and popular with his classmates, although still subject to more than normal anxiety.

We place a great deal of reliance on the testimony of Dr. Glenn R. Hawks, a child psychologist. The trial court, in effect, disregarded Doctor Hawks' opinions, stating: "The court has given full consideration to the good doctor's testimony, but cannot accept it at full face value because of exaggerated statements and the witness's attitude on the stand." We, of course, do not have the advantage of viewing the witness's conduct on the stand, but we have carefully reviewed his testimony and find nothing in the written record to justify such a summary dismissal of the opinions of this eminent child psychologist.

Doctor Hawks is head of the Department of Child Development at Iowa State University. However, there is nothing in the record which suggests that his relationship with the Bannisters is such that his professional opinion would be influenced thereby. Child development is his specialty and he has written many articles and a textbook on the subject. He is recognized nationally, having served on the staff of the 1960 White House Conference on Children and Youth and as consultant on a Ford Foundation program concerning youth in India. He is now educational consultant on the project "Head Start." He has taught and lectured at many universities and belongs to many professional associations. He works with the Iowa Children's Home Society in placement problems. Further detailing of his qualifications is unnecessary.

Between June 15 and the time of trial he spent approximately 25 hours acquiring information about Mark and the Bannisters, including appropriate testing of and "depth interviews" with Mark. Doctor Hawks' testimony covers 70 pages of the record and it is difficult to pinpoint any bit of testimony which precisely summarizes his opinion. He places great emphasis on the "father figure" and discounts the importance of the "biological father." "The father figure is a figure that the child sees as an authority figure, as a helper, he is a nutrient figure and one who typifies maleness and stands as maleness as far as the child is concerned."

His investigation revealed: "the strength of the father figure before Mark came to the Bannisters is very unclear. Mark is confused about the father figure prior to his contact with Mr. Bannister." Now, "Mark used Mr. Bannister as his father figure. This is very evident. It shows up in the depth interview, and it shows up in the description of Mark's life given by Mark. He has a very warm feeling for Mr. Bannister."

Doctor Hawks concluded that it was not for Mark's best interest to be removed from the Bannister home. He is criticized for reaching this conclusion without investigating the Painter home or finding out more about Mr. Painter's character. He answered:

"I was most concerned about the welfare of the child, not the welfare of Mr. Painter, not about the welfare of the Bannisters. Inasmuch as Mark has already made an adjustment and sees the Bannisters as his parental figures in his psychological makeup, to me this is the most critical factor. Disruption at this point, I think, would be detrimental to the child even though Mr. Painter might well be a paragon of virtue. I think this would be a kind of thing which would not be in the best interest of the child. I think knowing something about where the child is at the present time is vital. . . . The thing I was most concerned about was Mark's view of his own reality in which he presently lives. If this is destroyed I think it will have rather bad effects on Mark." . . .

Doctor Hawks stated: "I am appalled at the tremendous task Mr. Painter would have if Mark were to return to him because he has got to build the relationship from scratch. There is essentially nothing on which to build at the present time. Mark is aware Mr. Painter is his father, but he is not very clear about what this means. In his own mind the father figure is Mr. Bannister. I think it would take a very strong person with everything in his favor in order to build a relationship as Mr. Painter would have to build at this point with Mark."

It was Doctor Hawks' opinion "the chances are very high [Mark] will go wrong if he is returned to his father." This is based on adoption studies which "establish that the majority of adoptions in children who are changed, from ages six to eight, will go bad, if they have had a prior history of instability, some history of prior movement. When I refer to instability I am referring to where there has been no attempt to establish a strong relationship." Although this is not an adoption, the analogy seems appropriate, for Mark who had a history of instability would be removed from the only home in which he has a clearly established "father figure" and placed with his natural father about whom his feelings are unclear.

We know more of Mr. Painter's way of life than Doctor Hawks. We have concluded that it does not offer as great a stability or security as the Bannister home. Throughout his testimony he emphasized Mark's need at this critical time is stability. He has it in the Bannister home.

Other items of Doctor Hawks' testimony which have a bearing on our decision follow. He did not consider the Bannisters' age anyway disqualifying. He was of the opinion that Mark could adjust to a change more easily later on, if one became necessary, when he would have better control over his environment.

He believes the presence of other children in the home would have a detrimental effect upon Mark's adjustment whether this occurred in the Bannister home or the Painter home.

The trial court does not say which of Doctor Hawks' statements he felt were exaggerated. We were most surprised at the inconsequential position to which he relegated the "biological father." He concedes "child psychologists are less concerned about natural parents than probably other professional groups are." We are not inclined to so lightly value the role of the natural father, but find much reason for his evaluation of this particular case.

Mark has established a father-son relationship with Mr. Bannister, which he apparently had never had with his natural father. He is happy, well-adjusted and progressing nicely in his development. We do not believe it is for Mark's best interest to take him out of this stable atmosphere in the face of warnings of dire consequences from an eminent child psychologist and send him to an uncertain future in his father's home. Regardless of our appreciation of the father's love for his child and his desire to have him with him, we do not believe we have the moral right to gamble with this child's future. He should be encouraged in every way possible to know his father. We are sure there are many ways in which Mr. Painter can enrich Mark's life.

For the reasons stated, we reverse the trial court and remand the case for judgment in accordance herewith.—Reversed and remanded.

Questions

1. Notice that this custody dispute is between a biological parent and the child's grandparents. Who had custody of Mark at the time the case was decided? Is this important? Why? How did this custody arrangement come about in the first place? Does that matter?

2. What do we know about the Bannisters? What do we know about Mr. Painter? Which of the many facts the court shares do you think should be weighed most heavily?

3. Apply the nexus test to the facts of this case. Which items recounted by the court should be considered irrelevant to the custody determination? Why? Do you think the court's treatment of the facts reflects any biases? Explain.

4. Who was the expert witness in this case? What is the basis for his testimony? What is the problem with observing only one of the parties in a custody dispute?

5. Who would have been awarded custody in this case under a tender years presumption? A primary caretaker standard? A psychological parent standard? Explain.

6. Who *was* awarded custody of Mark? Do you agree that this was the right decision? Why or why not? You might find it interesting to know that after a couple of visits to California, Mark expressed a desire to live with his father. This time, the Bannisters did not object and the court eventually awarded custody to Mr. Painter.

CHAPTER 8 PRACTICE TEST

The following questions will test your application and analysis of the content found within this chapter. For additional assessment, including licensing-exam type questions on applying chapter content to practice behaviors, visit **MySearchLab**.

1. In a custody suit concerning David, age 10, the court awards shared legal custody to both parents and sole physical custody to the mother. Which of the following is true?

   a. David will spend alternate weeks living with each of his parents.

   b. David's mother can make all major medical decisions regarding David's health.

   c. Both parents must have input into deciding which middle school David will attend.

   d. Both parents must have input into deciding on David's weekend plans.

2. Jill and Bob are divorcing; at issue is the custody of their daughter, Harmony. Under the nexus test, which of the following factors is LEAST likely to be relevant to the custody determination?

   a. Jill was raised on a commune.

   b. Bob is in excellent physical health.

   c. Harmony has been living with Jill since the couple separated 2 years ago.

   d. Bob's job requires that he travel regularly.

3. Tiffany, a client in your private practice, is facing a custody battle with her ex-husband George. You have been working with Tiffany for many years, and she feels you know her better than anyone. She asks you to complete a child custody evaluation that she can present to the court as evidence to support her claim. You should

   a. comply with Tiffany's request because you believe she is a terrific mother.

   b. comply with Tiffany's request because you do not want to lose her as a client.

   c. decline because you have doubts about Tiffany's parenting skills.

   d. decline because your therapeutic relationship with Tiffany could compromise your objectivity.

4. Standardized psychological tests

   a. can be used as the basis for custody decisions.

   b. must be supplemented by other relevant information.

   c. can substitute for interviews with collaterals.

   d. can be administered only if ordered by the court.

5. What is a legal presumption? How does it differ from a preference? Identify some of the presumptions that various states have adopted and share your opinion regarding whether such presumptions are or are not a good idea.

6. When families break up, noncustodial parents and extended family members often seek visitation rights. How have the courts responded to this issue?

MYSEARCHLAB CONNECTIONS

Reinforce what you learned in this chapter by studying videos, cases, documents,
and more available at **www.MySearchLab.com**.

Read these Cases/Documents

Δ Divorce, Remarriage and Stepparenting
   • *In your opinion, are laws that create a presumption in favor of joint custody a good idea? Why or why not?*

Δ Alternative Dispute Resolution: A Central Texas Center
   • *What would be the advantages of handling child custody disputes through mediation rather than in court?*

Research these Topics

• model standards for conducting child custody evaluations

Assess Your Knowledge

Go to **MySearchLab** to test your knowledge of key topics in this chapter with topic-specific quizzes. Conclude
your assessment by completing the chapter exam.

⋆ = CSWE Core Competency Asset   Δ =Case Study

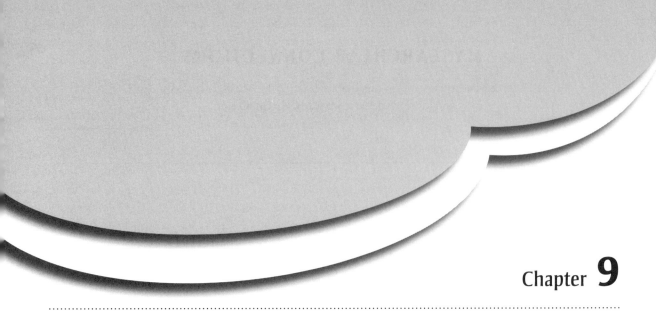

Domestic Violence

The National Center for Victims of Crime (2012) defines domestic violence as "the willful intimidation, assault, battery, sexual assault or other abusive behavior perpetrated by one family member, household member, or intimate partner against another." It is important to note, however, that there is no uniform definition of domestic violence. What constitutes domestic violence as a legal matter varies widely from state to state. This chapter provides background information on domestic violence (also called *intimate partner* violence), examines historical trends and the current state of the problem, and discusses efforts to protect victims and prosecute abusers. Although survivors of domestic violence can be both men and women, approximately 85% are female (Lapidus, Martin, & Luthra, 2009). Consequently, the pronoun *she* will be used with the understanding that it is meant to apply to all domestic violence cases. Similarly, the terms *victim* and *survivor* will be used interchangeably to refer to those who are on the receiving end of domestic abuse.

Background

The fight against domestic violence in the United States, begun by a small group of activists in the 1970s, has gained considerable ground over the past 40 years. Closely tied to the broader women's movement, the "battered women's movement" emerged from the fundamental belief that every woman deserves a life free of rape, physical and sexual abuse, and unwanted pregnancy. The first domestic violence shelter was founded in Minnesota in 1974. Because the early shelters were shrouded in secrecy, the urgency of the issue was largely shielded from view. Domestic violence often went unrecognized by the criminal justice system; police response was extremely limited and intervening in domestic disputes was considered a waste of resources. Gradually, awareness of domestic violence as a pressing social problem grew. Policy reforms took root within police departments and prosecutions of perpetrators increased.

In 1994, in recognition of the severity of domestic violence, the Violence Against Women Act (VAWA) was enacted, establishing domestic violence as an issue of national importance. VAWA is a legislative package that developed new programs and standards by which to prosecute violent crimes against women and to meet their needs as survivors of abuse. An Office on Violence against Women (OVW) was established as part of the U.S. Department of Justice in order to implement VAWA and related legislation. OVW administers financial and technical assistance to facilitate the creation of programs, policies, and practices aimed at ending domestic violence, dating violence, sexual assault, and stalking. VAWA was reauthorized in 2000 and 2005, reinforcing the original guidelines and adding new programs. These new programs focus on, among other things, educating court personnel, developing community protocols for addressing violence by and against teenagers, protecting child witnesses, providing victims with stable housing, and providing resources to organizations in communities of color. The reauthorizations also improved protections for battered immigrants, sexual assault survivors, and victims of dating violence. Since 1994, OVW has awarded more than $3 billion in grant funds to state, tribal, and local governments; nonprofit victim service providers; and universities (U.S. Department of Justice, 2010c). As of this writing, another reauthorization of VAWA is pending.

Incidence and Trends

Domestic violence is a costly and devastating crime. Approximately 26% of women and 8% of men report having been abused or victimized in some way by an intimate partner, including an average of 1.3 million women and 835,000 men who are physically assaulted each year (Lapidus et al., 2009; Tjaden & Theonnes, 2000). Women between the ages of 20 and 24 are at the greatest risk for nonfatal intimate partner violence, whereas those age 12-15 and those older than age 50 are at the lowest risk. Both males and females who are separated from their domestic partners, followed by those who are divorced, are at much greater risk of victimization than those of other marital statuses. Women of all races are more or less equally vulnerable to intimate partner violence, although people with annual incomes below $25,000 have been found to be at higher risk than those earning more than $50,000 a year (Domestic Violence Resource Center, 2011). Studies consistently show that at least 50% to 60% of women receiving public benefits have experienced physical abuse by an intimate partner at some point during their adult lives, compared to 22% of the general population; in some studies, the rate is as high as 82% (American Bar Association, 2010). Finally, people residing in urban areas are at about 20% greater risk than those living in suburban or rural areas (Domestic Violence Resource Center, 2011).

Increased recognition has been given to domestic violence among adolescents and young adults. Studies suggest that date rape accounts for almost 70% of sexual assaults reported by high school and college-age women (Domestic Violence Resource Center, 2011). Approximately 20% of high school students report having been physically or sexually abused by a dating partner (Silverman, Raj, Mucci, & Hathaway, 2001), and 80% report knowing someone their age who has been physically or sexually assaulted or threatened with physical abuse (Liz Claiborne Inc., 2009).

In 2005 alone, 1,181 women and 329 men were reportedly killed by an intimate partner (Bureau of Justice Statistics, 2012). Intimate partners are responsible for approximately 33% of female deaths by murder and 4% of male deaths by murder. Among African American women ages 15-34, homicide at the hands of a current or former intimate partner is the most common cause of death (American Bar Association, 2010; Rennison, 2003). Access to firearms plays a significant role in intimate partner homicide; abusers with ready access to handguns are five times more likely to kill their partners (Campbell et al., 2003). Aside from its personal costs, domestic violence has a significant impact on health care, mental health, job loss, and housing. Domestic violence accounts for 15% of total crime costs in the United States, the equivalent of approximately $67 billion annually (Lemon, 2009).

The research is filled with conflicting and confusing data, so all figures should be viewed cautiously. Because of the shame and privacy associated with domestic violence, and the fact that most data result from self-report, accuracy is difficult to achieve. Nonetheless, these statistics do provide a general sense of the enormity of the problem and of the various factors most associated with risk. They are a helpful starting point for both policy and practice.

Types of Abuse

Domestic violence includes physical abuse, sexual abuse, emotional abuse, financial abuse, and actions or threats designed to influence or control another person. This includes any behaviors that intimidate, manipulate, humiliate, isolate, frighten, terrorize, coerce, blame, hurt, injure, or wound a person with whom one shares an intimate relationship, including a husband, wife, same-sex partner, boyfriend, or girlfriend. The various types of domestic violence are summarized in Table 9.1. Although some groups are at higher risk than others, domestic violence can happen to anyone regardless of race, age, sex, sexual orientation, or religion. It affects people of all socioeconomic backgrounds and education levels. Domestic violence occurs in approximately 30% of all relationships, whether they are heterosexual or same-sex relationships or partners who are married, living together, or dating (Hines & Malley-Morrison, 2005).

The Dynamics of Domestic Violence

At one time, any investigation into who instigated a domestic dispute was regarded as a form of blaming the victim. We know now that violence is not always one-sided, and that exploration into the dynamics of abuse is critical to understanding and defusing the situation and achieving justice for the victim. Multiple factors are associated with domestic violence, including personal characteristics of the perpetrator and the victim; whether either has a history of abuse or violence; power dynamics and patterns in the couple's relationship; and cultural contexts including gender roles, religion, race, and class (Mills, 2008).

TABLE 9.1	Types of Domestic Abuse

Type of Abuse	Definition
Physical/Terroristic	Includes physical actions, such as hitting, slapping, shoving, grabbing, pinching, biting, hair pulling, etc. Also includes denying a partner medical care or forcing alcohol and/or drug use.
Sexual	Coercing or attempting to coerce any sexual contact or behavior without consent. Sexual abuse includes, but is not limited to, marital rape, attacks on sexual parts of the body, forcing sex after physical violence has occurred, or treating one in a sexually demeaning manner.
Emotional	Undermining an individual's sense of self-worth and/or self-esteem. This may include, but is not limited to, constant criticism, diminishing one's abilities, name-calling, or damaging one's relationship with his or her children.
Economic	Making or attempting to make an individual financially dependent by maintaining total control over financial resources, withholding one's access to money, or forbidding one's attendance at school or employment.
Psychological	Causing fear by intimidation; threatening physical harm to self, partner, children, or partner's family or friends; destruction of pets and property; and forcing isolation from family, friends, or school and/or work.
Stalking	A course of harassing conduct directed at a specific person that places him or her in fear for his or her safety.

Source: U.S. Department of Justice (2010a).

Abusers may use violence as a form of communication. They experience a need for release and for control, but the only way they know to express it is through violence. They are often able to manage their anger in the workplace and other public settings and are violent only toward their partners in private. Victims, meanwhile, live in fear. They are afraid of what will happen if they leave the relationship or report the abuse to authorities; this leads to underreporting and failure to press charges, allowing the cycle of abuse to continue (Hines & Malley-Morrison, 2005; Mills, 2008). Research shows that young women with a history of family aggression, physical or mental health issues, and substance use are at significantly higher risk for victimization. Characteristics associated with perpetrators include substance use, impulsivity, antisocial behaviors and beliefs, and a family history of violence or mental illness. Relationship factors associated with a high risk of domestic violence include communication problems, marital dissatisfaction, cohabitation, and separation or divorce. Domestic violence is linked to environmental factors, as well; it occurs most often in impoverished neighborhoods and where social support systems are lacking (Hines & Malley-Morrison, 2005) .

BATTERING IN SAME-SEX COUPLES

Domestic violence occurs in same-sex couples, just as it does among heterosexual couples. Research suggests that 20% to 33% of same-sex couples experience domestic violence; this rate is comparable to the rate among heterosexuals (Dugan & Hock, 2006). It is also equally likely that an arrest will be made when same-sex abuse has occurred (Hirschel, 2008).

Domestic violence within same-sex relationships presents different challenges because it involves some complicating dynamics. Although most states now have gender-neutral laws regarding eligibility for protective orders, they are not universally available to those in same-sex relationships. Except where these laws explicitly reference lesbian, gay, bisexual, or transgender (LGBT) victims, their applicability may be left up to interpretation. The inability to obtain a civil protective order makes it significantly more challenging for a person in a violent same-sex relationship to feel safe or to leave the abuser.

Weak nondiscrimination laws may afford LGBT individuals fewer legal protections in relation to employment, housing, marriage, and children. As a result, these survivors may face a greater risk of loss as a result of abuse or when leaving a violent partner. Many LGBT victims lack confidence in law enforcement. In communities with a history of police brutality against sexual minorities or of indifference toward those suffering abuse, victims are less likely to come forward. Isolation can also be a significant factor among LGBT individuals. Stigma and fear of rejection lead many to withhold information about the nature of their relationships from family, friends, and the larger community. This can make it especially difficult to find needed support and assistance.

LGBT victims are more likely to face dual arrest. Law enforcement officers may have difficulty identifying the primary aggressor and may end up arresting both the victim and the perpetrator. LGBT couples are 10 to 30 times more likely to experience dual arrest than heterosexual couples, and lesbian couples are twice as likely as gay male couples to experience dual arrest (Hirschel, 2008). In addition to dual arrest, failure to identify the primary aggressor may lead to no arrest being made, further jeopardizing the victim's safety.

Organizations committed to assisting survivors of domestic violence are increasingly sensitive to the needs of LGBT clients. Social workers can use their cultural competence to assist the service delivery system in accommodating same-sex victims and can continue to advocate for nondiscrimination measures that protect their legal rights.

The Cycle of Violence

Domestic violence in a relationship follows a pattern that has been described as the *cycle of violence*, which consists of three phases: tension, explosion (or battery), and honeymoon (see Figure 9.1). Each stage is characterized by changes in both the perpetrator and the victim. The *tension* stage involves an escalation of negative emotions in the abuser, including jealousy and a need for control. In this stage, the abuser will often accuse, criticize, and demand things from the victim. The victim reacts to these behaviors by trying to placate the abuser. Unfortunately, this is usually an impossible feat, leading inevitably to the explosion phase. In the *explosion* phase, the abuser's behavior becomes threatening. It is in this phase that the act of violence occurs, be it physical or emotional. The victim may respond to the abuser by begging or by agreeing to do anything to make the violence stop. This leads to the *honeymoon* phase in which the abuser uses remorse tactics to regain the victim's trust. The abuser will often be on his or her best behavior and promise to change. The victim responds by feeling guilty about what happened, thinking that the abuser needs him or her, and offering forgiveness. Unfortunately, the honeymoon phase soon gives way to a repetition of the tension phase and the cycle begins again.

FIGURE 9.1   The Cycle of Violence

Tension Building
The abuser becomes jealous,
controlling, critical,
or demanding.

Explosion or Battery
There is an outburst of physical,
verbal, or emotional abuse that
may include hitting, biting, shoving,
stabbing, or threats of violence.

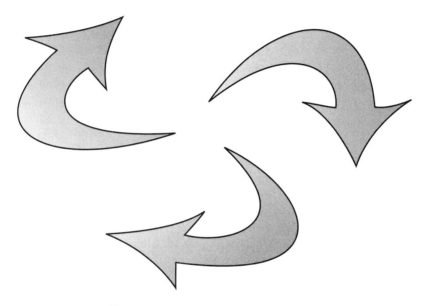

Honeymoon
The abuser apologizes, sends gifts, rationalizes
the behavior, and promises not to do it again.

STALKING AND CYBERSTALKING

Stalking is a form of violence that most often occurs between intimate partners or former intimate
partners. It is defined as a pattern of repeated and
unwanted attention, harassment, contact, or any
other course of conduct directed at a specific person
that would cause a reasonable person to feel fear.
According to the Stalking Resource Center (2012):

- 6.6 million people are stalked annually in the
  United States

- 1 in 6 women and 1 in 19 men have been victims
  of stalking in their lifetime

- A majority of victims know their stalker; 66%
  of female victims and 41% of male victims are
  stalked by an intimate partner

- 1 in 4 victims reports being stalked through the
  use of some form of technology (such as e-mail or
  instant messaging).

- 10% of victims report being monitored with global positioning systems (GPS), and 8% report being monitored through video or digital cameras, or listening devices.

Stalking is a fear-inducing course of conduct that can take numerous forms, including repeated, unwanted, intrusive, and frightening communications; repeatedly leaving or sending unwanted gifts or items; following or waiting for the victim at places she frequents; making threats to harm the victim or someone close to her; damaging or threatening to damage the victim's property; spreading information or rumors about the victim; and obtaining personal information about the victim by hiring a private investigator, going through the victim's garbage, and so on (U.S. Department of Justice, 2010b).

All states have laws that address stalking; they define the proscribed behaviors and specify the legal consequences. As technology has advanced, a new form of stalking has emerged called *cyberstalking*, which involves the use of the Internet, email, texting, or other electronic communication to control, intimidate, threaten, or frighten the victim. Although the goals of stalking and cyberstalking are similar, cyberstalking can be even more pernicious because images or messages can be widely disseminated very quickly, the perpetrator can be at a great geographical distance from the victim, the perpetrator can easily remain anonymous, and the perpetrator can easily impersonate the victim. Because cyberstalking can transcend state lines, it can create jurisdictional issues around prosecution (Goodno, 2007).

Authorities have created the distinct categories of cyberstalking, cyberharassment, and cyberbullying to capture variations that have entered the landscape. Cyberstalking involves using electronic media to engage in threatening or malicious behavior that poses a credible danger to the victim; 34 states cover cyberstalking in their laws. *Cyberharassment* refers to electronic communication designed to torment the victim that is not considered to pose a credible threat of violence; 38 states have laws that cover cyberharassment. Finally, *cyberbullying* refers to harassment among minors that occurs within the school context; 34 states have laws that cover cyberbullying (National Conference of State Legislatures, 2011).

Harassment is believed to be a particular problem on college campuses. One study found that 10% to 15% of college students had received email or instant messages that were threatening, insulting, or harassing. More that 50% of students had received unwanted pornography. Lesbian, gay, bisexual, and transgender students were more likely than heterosexual students to receive harassing messages from strangers. Only about 7% of students reported the harassing behaviors to authorities (Finn, 2004).

A recent study in England found that cyberstalking (defined as harassment through social networking sites, email, or cell phones) is now more common than face-to-face stalking. The study also revealed some interesting differences in the profiles of these stalking incidents. Unlike with traditional stalking, perpetrators of cyberstalking were more likely to be complete strangers or casual acquaintances of the victim. Also, nearly 40% of the victims were male. Twenty percent of the sample (including most of the teenage victims) had been stalked on social networking sites, 16% on blogging forums, and 4% through online dating sites. Approximately one-third of those surveyed reported experiencing clinical symptoms of posttraumatic stress disorder; men expressed anxiety about the possible damage to their reputations and women feared physical violence against them or their families (McVeigh, 2011).

Although traditional stalking is more likely to involve intimate partners or former intimate partners, the rapid increase in cyberstalking in all its forms is cause for additional alarm. Social workers should be attuned to the risks and consequences so they can better assist clients and advocate for relevant policy change.

Effects on Child Witnesses

Intimate partner violence can have profound negative consequences not only for the victim of the abuse, but for child witnesses as well. Because of the psychological effects that result from witnessing abuse, child witnesses are often considered secondary victims; the trauma they experience is not unlike the trauma that results from being a direct victim of maltreatment (Stiles, 2002). A study conducted in 2003 found that more than 15 million children in the United States lived in families where intimate partner violence had occurred at least once in the past year, and 7 million children lived in families where the violence was considered severe (Whitfield, Anda, Dube, & Felittle, 2003). A census taken on a single day in 2011 revealed more than 25,000 children (and more than 40,000 adults) seeking refuge from domestic violence in shelters or transitional housing, or receiving related nonresidential services (National Network to End Domestic Violence, 2012). Children may be direct witnesses to domestic violence, seeing or hearing abusive incidents as they happen—or they may simply live in a household where abuse occurs. Either way, they suffer harm. They are more likely to develop cognitive or language problems, stress-related physical ailments, and hearing and speech problems. They are also at risk for school-related problems including difficulty concentrating, poor academic performance, and difficulty interacting with peers. Children who witness abuse may also suffer from guilt and self-blame. They may believe that they are responsible for the abuse or that they should have stopped it. These children live in fear of further abuse and often develop stress-related disorders. They may have difficulty sleeping or eating and may regress developmentally and emotionally. Children who witness abuse often develop low self-esteem and withdraw or become avoidant around others (Stiles, 2002).

The immediate effects of expose to violence often diminish over time, but its impact can continue through adulthood. Adults who witnessed domestic violence as children may suffer from depression, anxiety, or posttraumatic stress disorder. Men who witnessed domestic violence as children are more likely to batter their partners as adults (UNICEF, 2006).

Protecting the Victims

The primary tool used to protect potential victims from domestic abuse is a *protective order*, which is a type of restraining order. It is issued to deter a perpetrator from engaging in harmful or threatening behavior, and it carries legal consequences for the perpetrator if violated. In the past, protective orders against a violent partner were limited to marital and family relationships. In many states, they have been expanded to include cohabitating, dating, or same-sex couples (Dalton & Schneider, 2001).

Eligibility for Protective Orders

Protective orders are available only to those who are covered by the state's definition of domestic violence; it is therefore important to know how your particular state law is drafted. In every state, protective orders are available to family and household members of the perpetrator. In Maine, for example, this includes couples who live together or have a sexual relationship. Virginia includes parents, children, stepparents, stepchildren, siblings, grandparents, and grandchildren, whether or not they live together; in-laws who live in the same home; cohabitants and those who have cohabited in the past year and their children; and persons who have a child in common, whether or not they live together. Virginia is one of 12 states, however, that do not include dating relationships. The vast majority of states now include same-sex couples, although few of these states explicitly reference them; instead, they are covered through the use of gender-neutral language. By contrast, Louisiana's law explicitly restricts coverage to heterosexual couples who are currently living together or have previously lived in the same household. Montana, North Carolina, and South Carolina likewise do not include same-sex couples in their definitions of domestic abuse. Virginia's law is silent on the topic, but same-sex couples are unlikely to qualify (Domestic Violence and Sexual Assault Data Resource Center, 2011).

Under federal law, protective orders issued in one state must be accorded "full faith and credit" in all other states (18 U.S.C. Sec. 2265). In other words, once a civil protective order is filed, it must be honored in all states regardless of where it was obtained. If a victim who was issued a protective order in Maryland is vacationing in Florida, for example, and the perpetrator follows her there and thus violates the order, Florida authorities would be required to enforce the order as if it had been issued in their state.

Obtaining a Protective Order

Protective orders can be issued in two circumstances. First, if the perpetrator is arrested, the court can issue a restraining order prohibiting him from having contact with the victim until the case has made its way through the system. This can occur with or without the victim's consent or cooperation. Second, the victim herself can initiate the process of securing an order of protection. This is done in a local civil court and does not require any action or involvement on the part of law enforcement.

To obtain a civil protective order, the victim (*petitioner*) completes paperwork (a *petition* or *order for protection*) at the courthouse in the county where he or she lives, the county where the abuser lives, the county where the abuse happened, or the county where the victim and abuser have had other family court cases heard. No lawyer is required, but assistance can be requested from court staff or a legal advocate. Supporting evidence (photographs, letters, recordings, police reports, etc.) substantiating the violence or threat of violence may also be submitted. Typically, the victim will be interviewed by a judge or magistrate who has the authority to issue a temporary restraining order (*ex parte order*) if the victim needs immediate protection. The judge may also issue a *vacate order* that requires the perpetrator to leave the couple's shared home. These orders become effective as soon as the abuser is notified and provided with a copy.

In most cases, a formal hearing will be held within 14 days after an application for a standard protective order is filed or 7 days following the issuance of an *ex parte* order. Both the victim and the perpetrator (often represented by counsel) attend the hearing at which each has the opportunity to share his or her side of the story in court. Witnesses and evidence may be presented as well. At the conclusion of the hearing, the court will either grant or deny the protective order request. Protective orders typically last for one year but can be extended if the threat continues or violations occur.

Civil protective orders generally order the abuser to stay away from the petitioner. More specifically, they may order some or all of the following (Lapidus et al., 2009):

- The abuser cannot molest, assault, harass, threaten, or abuse the petitioner.
- The abuser must stay away from petitioner's home, job, church, and so on.
- The abuser must have no contact with the petitioner.
- The abuser must leave shared living space.
- The abuser must turn in firearms to police.
- The victim may be given temporary custody of shared children.
- Visitation rights/child support requirements may be outlined.
- The abuser must complete counseling or a batterers' intervention program.

In some cases, a mutual protective order is entered against both the victim and the abuser. Although this type of order increases the likelihood that no contact will ensue, it is rarely used because it labels both parties as abusers and often creates barriers for the victim in future legal proceedings. Furthermore, mutual protective orders cannot be honored in other states unless each party also files a civil protective order against the other and both are deemed abusers by the court (Lapidus et al., 2009).

Although not common, it is possible to obtain a protective order without ever having a hearing. Under these circumstances, however, the terms of the protective order are much more limited in scope. The victim can only ask the court to (1) order the abuser not to harm, threaten, or contact the victim or their children; (2) order the abuser out of the home; (3) order the abuser to stay away from the victim's place of employment; and (4) order that the perpetrator refrain from making changes to the family's insurance coverage. Once the perpetrator is served with the protective order, he or she has the right to request a hearing to challenge the issuance of the order.

Victims who receive protective orders are required to have them handy at all times. Thirty-six states also require that protective orders be entered into the National Protection Order Registry. This electronic system is designed to help protect victims by making information readily available to law enforcement and the criminal justice community (Lapidus et al., 2009). If a victim wants to reinstate contact with the abuser, the protective order can be changed or dismissed by completing a form in the county where the order was issued. Most courts also require the petitioner to make a court appearance. If the victim resumes contact with the perpetrator without the judge's having dismissed the protective order, the victim can be found in violation of the order and fined.

Effectiveness of Protective Orders

Although protective orders are commonly issued in domestic violence cases, they are not admissible as evidence of abuse in court (Dalton & Schneider, 2001). More importantly, they cannot guarantee the safety of the victim. Social workers must help clients understand that although protective orders are a helpful tool, they should never be considered a substitute for a sound safety plan.

The effectiveness of protective orders continues to be debated. In one study, however, 86% of the women who received a protective order indicated that the abuse subsequently stopped or was greatly diminished (American Bar Association, 2010; Ptacek, 2001). Victims without protective orders are at higher risk for abuse, are more often involved with alcohol and drugs, and are more likely to be assaulted or injured. Some research suggests that the effectiveness of protective orders may depend on their specific stipulations. For example, protective orders that prohibit all contact with the victim are more likely to be effective than those that prohibit only abusive contact. Similarly, longer-term protective orders are more effective than temporary ones, especially when they are accompanied by criminal prosecution of the abuser (National Institute of Justice, 2009).

Prosecuting the Perpetrators

Traditionally, law enforcement personnel could not legally make a warrantless arrest in domestic violence cases unless the officer actually witnessed an act of violence or had probable cause to believe that a felony had taken place. Because simple assault and battery is a misdemeanor charge, police were often unable to arrest the perpetrator at the scene. Much has changed, however, leading to increases in perpetrator arrests.

Arrest

The major catalyst for reexamining traditional arrest policies was *Thurman vs. City of Torrington* (1984). That case involved a woman whose estranged husband repeatedly attacked her and threatened her and her son over a period of 8 months. Each time she reported his actions to police, however, they refused to take her complaint. In one instance, a police officer stood watching while her husband screamed threats at her and broke her car windshield while she sat inside; she later sought a warrant for her husband's arrest and was told that the only officer who could help her was away on vacation. At another point, officers assured her that her husband would be arrested, but no arrest took place; instead, the husband appeared at her home and stabbed her repeatedly in the chest, neck, and throat. After the stabbing, police at the scene saw him holding the bloody knife; they stood by while he continued to kick her in the head and threaten her. He was eventually arrested. The court concluded that the police department had violated her constitutional rights by treating her differently from other crime victims because the perpetrator here was her husband.

In response to the ruling in *Thurman*, the U.S. attorney general recommended that arrest be the standard police response to domestic violence. All 50 states now allow for warrantless arrests in domestic violence cases. Another barrier remained, however. Victims often resisted interference by the police or chose not to press charges; without the victim's cooperation, an officer had no choice but to leave the scene without making an arrest. This led to the adoption of *mandatory arrest* policies, which require that the officer make an arrest, regardless of the victim's wishes, if the officer has probable cause to believe that domestic violence has occurred. Twenty-one states and the District of Columbia have adopted mandatory arrest policies (American Law and Legal Information, 2010). Arrest rates are 97% higher in states with mandatory arrest policies than in states with *discretionary arrest* policies (Hirschel, 2008). Mandatory arrest has given rise to new concerns, however. It is often difficult to determine whether abuse has taken place and, if it has, who the primary aggressor was. In order to avoid having the victim mistakenly arrested, many jurisdictions have initiated training to help law enforcement officers recognize victim self-defense, assess fear of the abuser, examine injuries and evidence of abuse, and consider past histories of violence (Mills, 2008). Instead of mandatory arrest policies, six states (Arkansas, California, Massachusetts, Montana, North

Dakota, and Tennessee) have adopted *preferred arrest* policies. As the name suggests, law enforcement officers are encouraged to make an arrest when there is probable cause to believe domestic violence has occurred, but an arrest is not required. Arrest rates in states with preferred arrest policies are 177% higher than in states with discretionary arrest policies (Hirschel, 2008).

The increased involvement of law enforcement in domestic violence cases appears to have had an impact on victim safety. According to the U.S. Department of Justice, 60% of domestic victimizations were reported to police between 1998 and 2002; although still far from adequate, this represents an increase over reporting in previous years (U.S. Department of Justice, 2005). Arrests are made in approximately half of all domestic violence cases reported (Hirschel, 2008), and 90% of abusers adjudicated in interstate domestic violence cases are convicted. Among domestic violence abusers convicted of felony assault, 45% are sent to prison with a sentence of more than 2 years (American Bar Association, 2010; American Law and Legal Information, 2010).

Underreporting of victimization remains a serious problem, but it is easy to understand. Many victims fear the potential consequences of the perpetrator's arrest, including family breakdown, financial hardship, and loss of a parent for their child. Many fear reprisal by the abuser; others want to keep the abuser from getting into trouble. Many victims, particularly men, are anxious to keep these matters private. As social workers who encounter family violence, we are in a position to help victims explore their feelings about the abuse and determine a safe course of action.

Prosecution and Conviction

The prosecution of domestic violence defendants varies considerably from jurisdiction to jurisdiction. On average, 63.8% of cases are prosecuted nationwide (Klein, 2008.) The vast majority of domestic violence defendants are prosecuted for misdemeanor assault. It is important to keep in mind that not all prosecutions go to trial; many are resolved through plea agreements or are simply dismissed.

Domestic violence cases can be difficult to prosecute. Relatively little physical evidence is available, so the victim's testimony is heavily relied upon. In many cases, the victim may decline to appear in court or to take the stand against the abuser. Beginning in the 1980s, a number of jurisdictions implemented *no-drop* policies under which prosecutors can bring domestic violence cases to trial even if the victim declines to appear in court or to testify. Research suggests that prosecutors in no-drop jurisdictions end up screening out approximately 30% of domestic violence cases, but they pursue the remaining cases by bringing them to trial. Those cases that do go to trial generally end in conviction (Klein, 2008).

Sentencing and Recidivism

Defendants in domestic abuse cases very often reabuse. Research suggests that law enforcement intervention in domestic violence cases has a strong deterrent effect, regardless of who makes the report, whether an arrest occurs, and whether the perpetrator is prosecuted (Felson, Ackerman, & Gallagher, 2005; Klein, 2008) This involvement can include not only making arrests, but also providing informational pamphlets, taking statements from witnesses, and assisting victims in obtaining protective orders.

It seems that what makes the biggest difference in whether or not a defendant re-abuses is the severity of the sentence. Sentences including incarceration, work-release programs, probation, and electronic monitoring result in lower recidivism rates than fines or suspended sentences (Klein, 2008). Because most domestic violence defendants are prosecuted for misdemeanors, however, jail time is rare. Instead, the perpetrator typically faces a minimum of 3 years of probation and must participate in a batterer intervention program. If jail time is permitted at all, it is usually suspended and is reconsidered if the abuser violates the terms of probation. Probation often requires the defendant to undergo drug testing, substance abuse treatment, and anger management counseling. Even offenders convicted of felony assault do not necessarily face incarceration. Depending on the specific case, they may instead be required to pay restitution for the victim's hospital bills or complete several years of supervised probation (National Institute of Justice, 2009; Tayak, 2010).

In order to impose an informed and appropriate sentence in domestic violence cases, the National Council of Juvenile and Family Court Judges recommends that the following factors be taken into account: the facts of the case, the defendant's criminal history, any prior abusive behavior, drug or alcohol use, mental health status, prior and pending court contacts, children living in the home, impact of the violence on the victim, and the outcome the victim desires (Herrell & Hofford, 1990). Social workers can assist attorneys in ensuring that all pertinent information is available to the court when these sentencing decisions are made.

As mentioned previously, defendants in domestic violence cases are often mandated to participate in batterer intervention programs. These programs provide services to address underlying issues and change behavior patterns that could lead to further abuse. Although batterer intervention programs vary, most use a group approach to treatment. Standard programs are at least 26 weeks long, but programs of 52 weeks or longer are often preferred, given the cyclical nature of domestic violence. In addition to educating perpetrators about various forms of abuse and strategies for managing anger, topics may include gender roles, socialization, the nature of violence, power and control, and the effects of domestic violence on children and on victims. Social workers (or others) who provide these services are required to submit monthly reports to the court, describing the perpetrator's progress (National Institute of Justice, 2009; Tayak, 2010).

Not surprisingly, compliance with these programs is generally quite low, and evidence concerning their effectiveness is mixed. Research shows that after completion of batterer intervention programs and other court recommendations, approximately 41% of abusers reoffend within 2 years. Nearly 70% of reassaults occur within 6 months, and approximately 20% of abusers repeatedly reassault their victims (American Bar Association, 2010).

Domestic Violence Courts

As attention to domestic violence cases has increased, some jurisdictions have established specialized courts, dockets, or processes for handling them. This approach appears to be effective in increasing the responsiveness of the justice system to complaints of domestic abuse. Dedicating all or part of a court to domestic violence sends a message to the community and to victims of abuse that specialized help is available and that the abuser will face consequences (Advocates for Human Rights, 2010; Weber, 2000).

Specialized courts have several advantages. To begin with, the same group of judges or prosecutors deals with all domestic violence cases. This allows them to develop expertise on domestic violence, become familiar with treatment resources, and handle cases more consistently. Dedicated courts or prosecution teams may also be able to process cases more quickly; this reduces the opportunity for victims to recant and for perpetrators to reoffend while awaiting resolution of the case. Judges and prosecutors who consistently deal with domestic violence cases may also see repeat offenders; knowing the details of the case and the history of the parties may result in more appropriate penalties and increased accountability (Weber, 2000).

Some systems hear civil and criminal cases in the same court. This combination allows victims to take all necessary legal action in one place. For example, an integrated court might allow a victim to testify in a domestic violence prosecution and arrange for child support payments at the same time. Judges and prosecutors who hear both the civil and criminal sides of a case may have a more holistic view of the family situation and may make better informed decisions.

In some courts, victims of abuse are provided with support through specialized staff or units. Specialized staff in courts may include case managers, resource specialists, or witness assistants who accompany the victim to court. Specialized support units may help victims file protective orders, provide referrals to community services, coordinate scheduling, and share information (Fritzler & Simon, 2000; Weber, 2000).

Battered Women as Defendants

In some highly publicized cases, battered women have been put on trial for assaulting or killing their abusers. Historically, some of these women relied on the insanity defense, claiming that their mental state at the time of the crime kept them from distinguishing between right and wrong. Other defendants claimed that they acted in self-defense, but they often had difficulty proving that they perceived themselves to be in immediate danger, that they used force proportionate to the force used against them, and that they attempted to avoid conflict before resorting to violence. Relying on any defense was usually fruitless because of the widespread cultural disapproval of women who act violently, misconceptions about domestic violence, and laws derived from the male experience (Dalton & Schneider, 2001).

Beginning in the 1970s, state courts began to recognize the legal rights of women to protect themselves and their children. In *State v. Wanrow* (1977), for example, the Washington Supreme Court reversed the conviction of a woman who shot a man after he attacked her son and a friend's daughter. The court recognized that self-defense may mean something different to a woman than to a man and concluded that the jury should approach the case from the perspective of the defendant. Although traditionally it would have been unacceptable for a woman to commit violence under any circumstances, the court upheld the applicability of self-defense to women acting to protect themselves and their children.

A breakthrough case was heard by the New Jersey Supreme Court in 1982. *State v. Kelly* was the first case to allow the use of expert testimony on battered woman syndrome (BWS). BWS, first identified by Lenore Walker (the same person responsible for describing the cycle of violence), is a psychological condition experienced by victims of consistent or severe domestic abuse. Considered a type of posttraumatic stress disorder, BWS helps explain why many victims of abuse react and behave the way they do. In the *Kelly* case, the court ruled that expert testimony on BWS was admissible because of its relevance to understanding why the defendant believed homicide was the only way she could protect herself from her abuser.

Other cases involve battered women who are coerced by their abusers into engaging in criminal conduct. *People v. Romero* (1992) involved a couple that was convicted of second-degree robbery. The woman claimed that she participated in the crimes because she was afraid that if she did not, her abusive partner would kill her. In appealing her conviction, she argued that she was denied effective assistance of counsel because her lawyer failed to present expert testimony on BWS. The court concluded that if expert testimony on BWS is relevant to a defendant's credibility in a homicide case, it is equally relevant when a victim claims her participation in a crime resulted from an abusive relationship.

In 2006, the U.S. Supreme Court considered a case with similar facts. *Dixon v. United States* involved a woman who claimed that her abusive boyfriend had coerced her into illegally purchasing guns for him. The question before the Court was who has the burden of proof to demonstrate duress; was it up to her to prove that she was being coerced or up to the government to prove that she was not? A majority of the Court sided with the state, concluding that the defendant has the burden of proving duress. At the time, 26 states required their prosecutors to disprove duress in such cases. This was a blow to domestic violence victims, who now have the burden of proving the role of abuse in their behavior in order to establish their innocence.

Although numerous courts have ruled that expert testimony on BWS is relevant to cases involving battered woman defendants, it is less clear whether an expert on BWS must be paid for by the state. The Tenth Circuit Court of Appeals concluded that a defendant's due process rights were violated when the trial court denied a woman's request for funds to hire an expert in BWS for her defense. This decision was at odds with decisions in other states, including Georgia, Kansas, Mississippi, Montana, and Tennessee (Dalton & Schneider, 2001).

Summary and Conclusion

Although social workers and other advocates have made great strides in preventing and responding to domestic violence, much remains to be accomplished. Given the impact of domestic violence on victims, their children, and the larger community, its incidence is unacceptably high. Social workers involved with families experiencing domestic violence must be aware of the legal dimensions of both protecting victims and prosecuting perpetrators. Social workers can assist victims in obtaining protective orders, developing safety plans, and securing needed resources and services. They can also assist attorneys when perpetrators go to trial. They may serve as expert witnesses to help the court understand the dynamics of domestic violence and the behavior of both victims and abusers. And they may also be involved with batterer intervention programs, providing therapeutic services to offenders. Survivors of domestic violence face fear and intimidation; social workers can be a vital resource in helping them navigate the legal system and ensuring outcomes that protect their safety.

Sample Case

The case that follows examines the intersection of culture and domestic violence. Read the case and consider the questions that follow.

STATE v. VUE
606 N.W.2d 719 (2000)

Facts

Appellant and M.V. are Hmong immigrants who came to the United States from Laos in the late 1970s. They were never legally married, but lived as husband and wife from 1980 through the mid-to-late 1990s, when their relationship deteriorated. In February 1998, M.V. obtained an order for protection against appellant.

On June 5, 1998, M.V. reported appellant to the police, claiming he had raped her four times in four separate incidents occurring between February and May 1998. Appellant was arrested and charged with four counts of criminal sexual conduct, four counts of violating an order for protection, and one count of pattern of harassing conduct.

Before jury selection, the court and counsel had a preliminary discussion on the state's plan to introduce expert testimony on Hmong culture. The prosecutor noted that the jury pool's responses to questionnaires showed a poor understanding of Hmong culture. The prosecutor sought to introduce expert testimony to provide context for the jury's determinations of witness credibility, but said the expert would not comment on the case itself. The prosecutor described the scope of the proposed testimony and added that it could help explain M.V.'s delay in coming forward and rebut the defense theory that the allegations were rooted in M.V.'s jealousy of appellant's second wife. The defense objected to the proposed testimony, and the court took the matter under advisement.

At trial, M.V. testified about the clan structure of Hmong society, the hierarchy of leadership within the clan, and the role of Hmong women in choosing a husband. She said it was inappropriate in Hmong culture for individuals with family or clan-related problems to seek help from outside the clan and that she was being treated as an outcast for having reported her husband to the police. She claimed appellant had been threatening and abusive to her throughout their marriage and had forced her to have sex with him hundreds of times. She said she did not report the rapes earlier because of Hmong social pressure and because appellant said he would kill her if she did.

During a break in the state's case-in-chief, the court held a voir dire examination of the proposed expert witness, a white Minneapolis Park Police officer, and a hearing on the defense motion to exclude his testimony. On direct and cross-examination, the officer described his interest in and personal and professional exposure to Hmong culture.

The prosecutor said the officer would testify to the following: a general history of the Hmong in America; the clan system and the hierarchy within the clans; assimilation issues facing the Hmong in America; Hmong-Americans' attitudes toward the American criminal justice system; the traditional system for resolving family and clan-related problems; issues with going outside the clan for help; the role and position of women in Hmong culture; and male-female relations in traditional marriages.

In allowing the testimony, the court compared it to expert testimony on battered woman syndrome, noted it was being offered to promote a complete understanding of the evidence, and found it would be helpful to the jury.

As an example of a conflict between Hmong culture and the American legal system, the officer described a traditional marriage practice in which men "kidnap" young girls. Among other generalized statements, the state's expert testified that Southeast Asian victims are generally reluctant to report crimes. Speaking of Hmong culture, he testified in part:

> Well, as I indicated it is a male-dominated culture, very clearly. It's not the only culture that's male dominated, I might add, but it's very clear in Hmong culture. Women are to be obedient, to be silent, to suffer rather than to tell. Domestic abuse is a very private situation. I'm not even so sure if the abuse is shared with other women. I think it's kept very much internal.

On cross-examination, the officer stated that "male-dominance" was "fairly universal in the Hmong culture." In addition, the defense counsel asked and the expert responded as follows:

> Q: Are you suggesting that what male dominance really means is abuse?
>
> A: I have seen evidence—second hand, I might add, maybe third hand, not first hand or I would have to act as a police officer—of male aggression within the Hmong community to keep the female in her place.
>
> Q: Are you saying that that is a general trait or are you saying that all Hmong traditional males are abusive?
>
> A: I've been around long enough to know that you can never make a statement that says all of anything will happen all of the time. I think there are patterns that can be identified over time and that that pattern is disturbing in the Hmong culture.

Issue

Did the district court abuse its discretion in admitting expert testimony on aspects of Hmong culture?

Analysis

Appellant argues the expert testimony was inadmissible cultural stereotyping calculated to appeal to cultural and racial prejudice. He claims it (1) lacked foundation, (2) was irrelevant and unduly prejudicial, and (3) violated public policy and his state and federal constitutional rights to a fair trial, the presumption of innocence, due process, and equal protection. We agree.

Generally, admission of expert testimony rests within the district court's discretion and will not be reversed absent clear error.... Minn. R. Evid. 702 sets the basic standard for admission of expert testimony:

> If scientific, technical, or other specialized knowledge will assist the trier of fact to understand the evidence or to determine a fact in issue, a witness qualified as an expert by knowledge, skill, experience, training, or education, may testify thereto in the form of an opinion or otherwise.

But, along with the bare bones provisions of Minn. R. Evid. 702, a district court may consider the offered expert testimony under a balancing test embodied in Minn. R. Evid. 403:

> Although relevant, evidence may be excluded if its probative value is substantially outweighed by the danger of unfair prejudice, confusion of the issues, or misleading the jury, or by considerations of undue delay, waste of time, or needless presentation of cumulative evidence.

In criminal trials in particular, courts must be cautious when ruling on the admissibility of expert testimony. This is necessary to guard against the expert's "potential to influence a jury unduly" with his court-recognized "special knowledge" and to "ensure that the defendant's presumption of innocence does not get lost in the flurry of expert testimony."

In this case, the primary issue at trial was whether M.V. consented to the sexual contact with appellant. Both sides addressed her delay in bringing the allegations. The prosecutor offered the testimony of a park policeman to bolster M.V.'s story by "explaining" why a Hmong immigrant who had been raped by her husband would be reluctant to go to the police.

There is little in this record suggesting cultural testimony was necessary. The complainant was a grown woman; she was bilingual and educated; and she had been in the United States for many years. A lay jury would not have had trouble understanding or believing her testimony simply because she was Hmong. It is patronizing to suggest otherwise. The expert testimony itself confirmed the lack of relevancy to this case and to this victim. The transcription shows the following questions and answers:

Q: Are you saying then—and this is what I'm leading up to, Lieutenant—that all of the Hmong people in Minnesota are following the same cultural trends?

A: I would not say that all Hmong follow the same cultural trends, but I would say that the Hmong culture that I've observed is slower to change than other cultures that I've observed.

Q: Would you say that language is one reason why, at least in your observations, there has been a slower cultural change?

A: I would strongly agree that, *particularly among older Hmong citizens where English is nonexistent or very difficult at best*. I would say that the isolation that comes from not being able to go to a mall and shop and exchange normal conversation with shopkeepers or other people in society has kept Hmong women, in particular older Hmong women, prisoners in their homes. (Emphasis added.)

Thus, the "expert's" cultural testimony emphasized the barriers on reporting "among older Hmong citizens where English is nonexistent or very difficult at best." This is not our case.

Further, the credentials of this Minneapolis Park Police officer to give expert opinions on Hmong culture are suspect. The record shows that the officer's contact with Hmong culture arose primarily from personal experience with family friends, that his exposure to Hmong culture as a police officer was limited, and that he had little or no academic training involving Hmong culture.

While we acknowledge there is no formal requirement to qualifying as an expert under Minn. R. Evid. 702, the informal nature of this officer's familiarity with Hmong culture brings his qualifications to be an expert into doubt.

The "expert" testimony was inherently prejudicial. It went far beyond describing Hmong cultural practices that would help explain the alleged victim's behavior, if such testimony was needed. The testimony included generic statements about "male-dominance" in Hmong culture and directly implied a generalized perceived pattern of abuse of Hmong females by Hmong males.

While some of these statements could conceivably be relevant to a complainant's reluctance to come forward, their probative value, if any, is based on generalizations that appellant is part of a "guilty class" of spouse-abusers, and the victim is part of a "victim class" of abused women. By asserting that Hmong men tend to abuse their wives, the expert testimony directly implied to the jury that because the defendant was Hmong, he was more likely to have assaulted his wife. It is self-evident that this is highly prejudicial. It is impermissible to link a defendant's ethnicity to the likelihood of his guilt.

Our criminal code is supposed to be blind to the array of cultures present in the State of Minnesota. The state wants it that way when cultural testimony goes against them. The state conceded at oral argument that it would object, in a statutory rape case or a domestic abuse trial, if defense counsel attempted to introduce expert evidence showing the charged conduct was permissible in the defendant's culture. For instance, marriage to young women under the age of 14 is acceptable in many cultures, including Hmong. The prosecutor stated she would object to that as irrelevant, if offered by a defense attorney. But here the state urges the same kind of cultural evidence be allowed to bolster a case against appellant.

We conclude the prejudicial effect of the expert testimony about Hmong males' tendency to dominate and abuse their wives, and the tendency of Hmong wives not to want to report assaults, far outweighed any probative value. We find the district court abused its discretion in qualifying the expert and admitting his testimony. ***

Admitting expert testimony always risks that the expert's opinions will inordinately influence the jury. The record shows appellant's conviction was based on disputed testimonial evidence. The outcome of the trial depended on whom the jury believed. By implying appellant's Hmong descent made him a probable spouse-abuser, the improper testimony clearly implied a conviction should be forthcoming. In view of the severe risk of prejudice it posed, we cannot escape the conclusion that the improper testimony strongly influenced the jury's decision to convict.

We reverse and remand for a new trial.

Decision

The district court improperly allowed expert testimony on Hmong culture. The testimony was speculative, conjectural, and its prejudicial effect far outweighed any possible probative value.

Questions

1. Who was the expert witness in this case? What were his qualifications?
2. What do you suppose the prosecutor hoped to achieve by calling him as a witness?
3. Early in the opinion, the court describes two standards for deciding whether to admit expert testimony: the "basic standard for admission" and the "balancing test." What

does each one say? Which did the court use? If the other one had been used, would the outcome have been any different?

4. The state suggests that the expert's testimony here is analogous to testimony regarding battered woman syndrome. Do you agree? Why or why not?

5. If you were the judge, would you have allowed expert testimony explaining the cultural factors underlying the victim's delay in reporting the abuse? Would you have allowed expert testimony on male domination in Hmong relationships?

6. Do you think it is ever appropriate for cultural norms be considered in the context of a legal proceeding? Might they be instructive—or are they necessarily unfair?

CHAPTER 9 PRACTICE TEST

The following questions will test your application and analysis of the content found within this chapter. For additional assessment, including licensing-exam type questions on applying chapter content to practice behaviors, visit **MySearchLab**.

1. Protective orders
   a. can guarantee a victim's safety.
   b. are enforceable only in the state in which they are issued.
   c. are inadmissible in court as evidence of abuse.
   d. are available in every state to same-sex couples.

2. In jurisdictions with "no drop" policies
   a. it is mandatory for police to make an arrest at the scene.
   b. prosecutors can bring cases to trial even if the victim declines to testify.
   c. domestic violence is considered a felony.
   d. protective orders continue in force until the victim chooses to terminate them.

3. Battered woman syndrome
   a. is a defense to homicide.
   b. explains why victims of abuse behave the way they do
   c. must be established by an expert paid for by the state.
   d. has never been ruled admissible by the courts.

4. Cyberstalking
   a. has never been linked to posttraumatic stress disorder.
   b. is less dangerous than traditional forms of stalking.
   c. is less likely to target men as victims.
   d. is explicity prohibited by law in a majority of states.

5. What are domestic violence courts? What are their advantages over traditional civil and criminal courts?

6. Describe the unique problems faced by victims of domestic violence in same-sex relationships.

MYSEARCHLAB CONNECTIONS

Reinforce what you learned in this chapter by studying videos, cases, documents, and more available at **www.MySearchLab.com**.

Read these Cases/Documents

Δ Faith Harper
- *How might race, ethnicity, or immigration status affect one's experience as a perpetrator or victim of domestic violence? How could the law be more helpful in addressing these differences?*

Explore these Assets

- Website: Justice Information Center (NCJRS): Family Violence

Research these Topics

- the politics of reauthorizing VAWA
- power and control in LGBT relationships

Assess Your Knowledge

Go to **MySearchLab** to test your knowledge of key topics in this chapter with topic-specific quizzes. Conclude your assessment by completing the chapter exam.

---

* = CSWE Core Competency Asset   Δ = Case Study

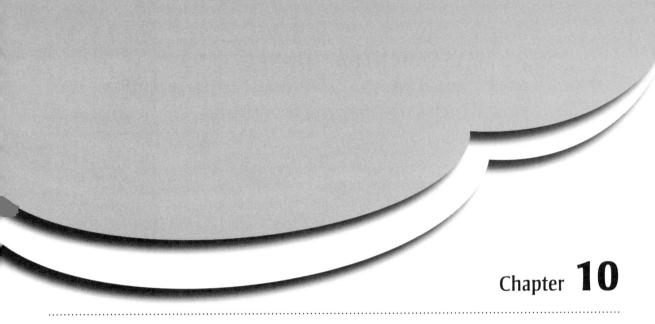

Chapter **10**

Older Adults

The demographics of the United States are changing rapidly; the population is becoming increasingly diverse and adults are living longer. This chapter examines current trends in aging, focusing on important legal and social policy concerns including adult protection, age discrimination, the legal rights of grandparents, and competency and guardianship. A special section is devoted to the controversy of physician-assisted suicide, and a sample case is provided concerning employment discrimination.

It is important for social workers to be conversant with the law in these areas because many of the employment opportunities for social workers over the coming decade will involve working with older adults. According to the U.S. Department of Labor (2009), "the growing elderly population and the aging baby boom generation will create greater demand for health and social services, resulting in rapid job growth among gerontological social workers." Although many older adults remain healthy, vibrant, and active, some will face biopsychosocial challenges including cognitive and physical changes; loss of identity or purpose; increased isolation; and barriers to health care, mental health care, and housing (NASW, 2010). Although we must consider the needs of all older adults, we can be of particular value to those who experience abuse, exploitation or discrimination, or who find themselves in need of increased physical, emotional, social, or financial support.

Background

According to the Administration on Aging (AOA, 2012), in 2009 approximately 39.6 million Americans, or one out of every eight, were 65 or older. This is equivalent to 12.9% of the entire U.S. population. Census projections through 2050 (depicted in Figure 10.1) indicate that between 2010 and 2030, we will continue to see increasing numbers of older adults in the United States. This is attributable in part to members of the "baby boom" generation (the large cohort of individuals born following World War II) turning 65. It is estimated that there will be 55 million older adults in 2020 and 72.1 million in 2030, more than twice the number there were in 2000. In addition, the proportion of older adults who are people of color is projected to increase by 160% between 2010 and 2030, dwarfing the 59% increase projected for Whites. Demographers anticipate an equally dramatic change among the oldest segment of the population, those ages 85 and older. This group is projected to grow by 19% between 2010 and 2020, from 5.5 million to 6.6 million (AOA, 2011).

The aging of the population is not a phenomenon limited to the United States; it is a global reality. According to the United Nations Department of Economic and Social Affairs (2009), in the year 2045, older adults will outnumber children, worldwide, for the first time ever. Those older than age 60 are projected to comprise 22% of the world's population at that time, compared to 11% in 2009 and 8% in 1950: "In absolute terms, the number of older persons has more than tripled since 1950 and will almost triple again by 2050" (p. 47). The fastest growing segment of the global population is those ages 80 and older. The United Nations cautions that this could constitute the biggest crisis in the coming century because of the increased burden on working-age adults to support an aging population, along with increased risks for the elderly, including social isolation and economic deprivation.

| **FIGURE 10.1** | Older Adult Population Trends: 1900–2050 |

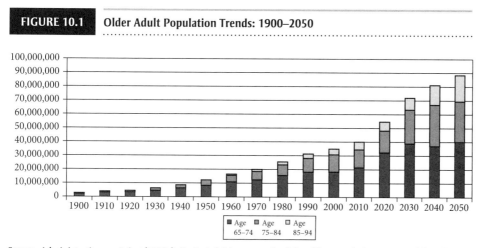

Source: Administration on Aging (2010a). Projected future growth of the older population. Retrieved from http://www.aoa.gov/AoARoot/Aging_Statistics/future_growth/future_growth.aspx#age

Population Characteristics

Recognizing and addressing the needs of older adults requires a more refined understanding of who they are. According to the U.S. Administration on Aging (2012):

- Older women outnumber older men by approximately 5.5 million
- 3.5 million or 9% of older adults live at or below the federal poverty line
- 78.9% of older adults live in metropolitan areas
- 1.5 million or 4.1% live in institutional settings
- 11.3 million or 29.3% of noninstitutionalized older adults live alone
- Minorities comprise 20% of the older adult population

Many of these characteristics hold true worldwide. According to the Centers for Disease Control (2006), the largest projected increases in the older adult population will occur in developing countries. Older women are expected to outnumber older men, particularly among the oldest-old (age 80 and older). Because older men are more likely than older women to be married, older women will encounter special challenges, particularly if they are in ill health. Finally, illiteracy among older adults remains high in much of the world, especially among women. In some regions, an estimated one-third of men age 65 and older and nearly 60% of women of the same age cannot read or write. This has important implications for quality of life, because educational attainment among older adults is positively correlated with both good health and higher socioeconomic status (United Nations, 2009).

Implications for Policy and Practice

Older adults are a diverse population that includes individuals with differing abilities, family and social supports, living situations, genders, ages, cultures, socioeconomic statuses, and levels of physical and mental acuity (Ginsberg & Miller-Cribbs, 2005). The fact that the aging process affects everyone differently creates challenges in meeting the needs of older adults through social policy. Most of the federal policy responses to aging address the income and health care concerns of older adults. According to the Social Security Administration (2010), these major federal programs include the following:

- **Social Security:** Provides a pension to retirees age 62 and above. In most cases, a minimum of 10 years of employment is required for eligibility. In 2010, the average Social Security payment for a retired worker was $1,164 per month. Current workers and employers contribute equally to the fund, which is used to support current retirees. Benefits are also available for family members of retired and deceased workers and for people with disabilities.
- **Medicare:** Provides eligible retirees with health benefits, including hospital insurance, coverage for doctors' visits and outpatient services, and a prescription drug plan.
- **Supplemental Security Income (SSI):** Provides income support to low-income older adults and people with disabilities. Unlike Social Security, it does not require a work history but rather is financed from general revenues. In 2010, the average benefit for an individual was $674 per month.
- **Medicaid:** Provides health insurance coverage to low-income, older adults who lack the required work history to qualify for Medicare. Eligibility for Medicaid varies by state, and in some cases it is possible to be eligible for both Medicare and Medicaid.

The one federal policy that aims to meet the needs of older adults more comprehensively is the Older Americans Act (OAA), originally passed in 1965. The OAA established a national Aging Services Network that includes the federal Administration on Aging, 56 State Agencies on Aging, and 629 Area Agencies on Aging. The OAA also established a number of important programs on the federal, state, and local levels to help older adults maintain their quality of life, including low-cost, home-delivered meals; senior centers and adult day care; and transportation services. Finally, the OAA serves to coordinate the array of resources available to older adults and ensures the availability of advocacy on their behalf through a Long-Term Care Ombudsman Program (Administration on Aging, 2010b; Ginsberg & Miller-Cribbs, 2005)

As the population of older adults continues to grow and individuals, families, communities, the nation, and the world feel its effects, the role of social workers will become increasingly vital. Social workers will be needed to

- Work directly with older adults by providing case management and delivering services
- Provide support to families and friends who serve as caregivers to older adults
- Provide support to older adults who serve as caregivers for their grandchildren
- Provide support in health care decision making, including decisions involving end-of-life care
- Advocate on behalf of older adults in agencies, health care facilities, and public policy

One of the most significant changes brought about by the aging boom is that family members have become more involved in caregiving for older relatives (Richardson & Barush, 2006). The term *family caregiver* can refer to the family of origin, extended family, friends, partners, or other individuals who provide support to an older adult and whose primary relationship with them is not based on a financial or professional agreement. Family caregivers take on multiple roles, including providing emotional, social, financial, and spiritual support; assisting with decision-making and future planning; helping with physical tasks; and negotiating with health care and social service providers (NASW, 2010). Although many families are choosing to be involved in the care of their loved ones, caregiving can be stressful, resulting in depression, loneliness, difficulty sleeping, and role conflict issues. Family caregivers are often asked to put their own personal well-being on hold; their sacrifices go without financial compensation and they are often underappreciated (National Alliance for Caregiving, 2009).

Policy makers and communities have responded to these needs in a variety of ways. First, respite care and adult day services provide loved ones with temporary relief from full-time caregiving responsibilities. Second, policies including the Family and Medical Leave Act, enacted in 1993, provide workers with up to 12 weeks of unpaid leave to care for a dependent family member. Finally, the National Family Caregiver Support Program, authorized as part of the Older Americans Act, provides informal caregivers with information, training, counseling, and respite care as they seek to meet the needs of the growing older adult population (Richardson & Barush, 2006).

In 2010, NASW released *Standards for Social Work Practice with Family Caregivers of Older Adults* in an effort to educate social workers about family caregiving and ensure quality service provision in this expanding field. Social workers have a key role to play in alleviating the stress that comes with family caregiving. This might include helping identify and access community resources, including housing, hospice services, and support groups. It might also include providing conflict resolution or family counseling in order to assist older adults and their family caregivers in recognizing and balancing their respective needs. Social workers must maintain a working knowledge of theory, practice, policy, research, and evaluation methods related to aging and use this information consistently in their practice with family caregivers and older adults (NASW, 2010).

Adult Protection

Unfortunately, not all caregivers have the best interests of older adults at heart. The need for adult protective services (APS) first gained attention in the late 1950s, when the National Council on Aging responded to growing concerns about the vulnerability of the older adult population. Specifically, it identified the growing numbers of incapacitated and isolated older persons who lacked appropriate caregivers. The Older Americans Act was passed in 1965, and by 1974, all states had passed laws to protect older adults from mistreatment. A 1978 amendment to OAA required that long-term care facilities provide an ombudsman to investigate complaints of abuse (McClennen, 2010). In March 2010, Congress passed the Elder Justice Act as part of comprehensive health care reform. The Elder Justice Act authorizes dedicated funding for APS agencies and funds demonstration projects to test new ways of improving their effectiveness; provides grants to support the Long-Term Care Ombudsman program, including enhanced training; creates an Elder Justice Coordinating Council to coordinate public and private efforts to combat elder abuse; and creates a national program of criminal background checks for people seeking employment in nursing homes and other long-term care facilities (Elder Justice Coalition, 2010).

The National Center on Elder Abuse (NCEA) identifies three broad categories of elder abuse. *Domestic abuse* refers to maltreatment that occurs in the elder's home, or in the home of a caregiver, and is perpetrated by someone who has a special relationship with the elder (a spouse, sibling, child, friend, or caregiver). *Institutional abuse*, on the other hand, refers to abuse that occurs in residential facilities for older persons, such as nursing homes, foster homes, group homes, or board and care facilities. Perpetrators of institutional abuse usually are paid caregivers, staff, or professionals who have a legal or contractual obligation to provide older adults with care and protection. *Self-neglect* or *self-abuse* includes behaviors on the part of an older adult that threaten his or her own health or safety. It generally manifests itself in an older person's refusal or failure to seek adequate food, water, clothing, shelter, or medication; maintain appropriate personal hygiene; or take reasonable safety precautions (NCEA, 2007). Although these definitions serve as a helpful guideline, specific legal definitions vary from state to state (Richardson & Barusch, 2006).

Elder abuse can take the form of physical abuse, sexual abuse, psychological abuse, neglect, and financial abuse. Although state definitions vary, *physical abuse* generally refers to the nonaccidental use of force resulting in bodily injury, pain, or impairment. *Sexual abuse* entails nonconsensual sexual contact of any kind with an older person. *Psychological abuse* refers to the willful infliction of mental intimidation or emotional distress through verbal or nonverbal conduct. *Neglect* refers to the failure to provide food, medical care, or other necessities. Lastly, *financial abuse* refers to exploitation through the unauthorized use of funds, property, or resources of an older person (National Committee for the Prevention of Elder Abuse, 2008).

The rate of older adult abuse in the United States is difficult to determine with accuracy, because many people are reluctant to report it. Although estimates vary considerably, it appears that 1–2 million adults age 65 and older (5% of persons in that age group) are victims of abuse or neglect each year (Bonnie & Wallace, 2003). According to a 2004 survey using data from 19 states, the largest number of substantiated reports are for self-neglect (37.2%), followed by caregiver neglect (20.4%), psychological or verbal abuse (14.8%), financial exploitation (14.6%), physical abuse (10.7%), and sexual abuse (1%) (Teaster et al., 2006). Elder abuse is typically perpetrated by someone close to the victim; in fact, an estimated 90% of elder abuse incidents are committed by family members (National Council on Aging, n.d.). Figure 10.2 shows a breakdown of confirmed perpetrators of elder abuse as reported by the National Association of Adult Protective Services Administrators (NAAPSA) in 2001. As the figure indicates, the most common perpetrators are adult children of the victim followed by the victim's spouse. Spousal abuse in older adult relationships can occur as either ongoing abuse from earlier in the relationship or as domestic violence that begins during old age (Straka & Montminy, 2006). Older adults may also enter into new relationships late in life that become abusive.

FIGURE 10.2   **Perpetrators in Elder Abuse Cases**

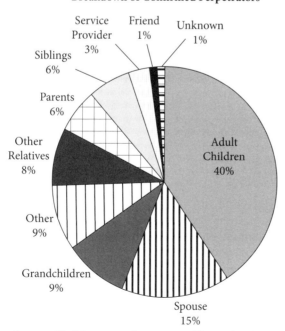

Breakdown of Confirmed Perpetrators

Reporting and Investigating Elder Abuse

NCEA, directed by the Administration on Aging, coordinates the reporting of elder abuse. NCEA has a national hotline number that can be used to report elder abuse, neglect, and exploitation and provides contact information for local APS agencies. State laws vary in their definitions of elder abuse and in their reporting requirements. Most states identify specific professionals as mandated reporters (the most common being social workers, doctors, dentists, nurses, law enforcement personnel, and mental health providers), whereas others use more general language that requires reporting by anyone working with older adults for compensation (McClennen, 2010). National data show that most reports come from family members, followed in descending order by social services staff, friends and neighbors, self-report, long-term care facility staff, law enforcement, nurses or nurses' aides, home health staff, and physicians. Less frequently identified were the abusers themselves, municipal agents, postal service workers, utility workers, and hospital discharge planners (Teaster et al., 2006).

Most researchers agree that elder abuse is vastly underreported. Studies suggest that only 1 in 14 incidents of domestic abuse (not including incidents of self-neglect) and 1 in 25 incidents of financial abuse actually come to the attention of authorities (Pillemer & Finkelhor, 1988; Wasik, 2000). In a 2003 study involving interviews with 5,000 adults older than age 60, approximately 12.5% acknowledged having been mistreated in the previous year and only 31% of those mistreated had reported the abuse (Acierno, Hernandez-Tejada, Muzzy, & Steve, 2009).

Responsibility for investigating and responding to the mistreatment of older adults rests with state and local APS agencies. The aim of APS is to ensure the safety and well-being of older adults. Goals typically include stopping the abuse, neglect, or exploitation while restricting the victim's liberty as little as possible; assisting the victim in remaining at home as long as it is safe and appropriate to do so; restoring the elder's independent functioning to the greatest extent possible; and arranging for an out-of-home placement when necessary (Virginia Department of Social Services, 2008). The role of APS caseworkers includes the following:

- Receiving and evaluating reports
- Investigating reports
- Determining if services are needed
- Providing an array of services if the adult agrees to accept assistance
- Making a disposition
- Notifying the mandated reporter that the report has been investigated

When a report is received, the APS worker performs a sort of triage; she determines the urgency of the call. Every case involves a face-to-face interview with the alleged victim in order to determine the validity of the maltreatment report. In an emergency, the worker (usually accompanied by law enforcement) is permitted to enter the home without a court order. If the victim needs immediate protection, an *ex parte protection order* can be sought from the court and the perpetrator can be temporarily removed pending a hearing before a judge, usually held within 30 days. In nonemergency situations, the APS worker can enter the elder's home with his or her consent or can obtain a search warrant from the court. The court can also issue a restraining order to prohibit the alleged perpetrator from coming near the victim and his or her resources (Roby & Sullivan, 2000).

Responding to Elder Abuse

Based on the investigation, the APS worker makes a determination regarding the validity of the maltreatment allegation. Although states vary in the options they employ, typical dispositions include the following:

- **Needs protective services:** There is evidence of maltreatment requiring the provision of services to protect the older adult.
- **Need no longer exists:** The alleged perpetrator no longer has access to the older adult or the older adult has been removed from the situation or has died.
- **Unfounded:** Insufficient evidence exists to establish *by a preponderance of the evidence* that abuse, neglect, or exploitation occurred.

The finding of a substantiated or founded case sets in motion a civil process designed to protect the victim. The perpetrator may also be charged with a criminal offense. Unlike in the case of child maltreatment, no specialized courts exist to adjudicate the maltreatment of older adults. These cases are brought in regular civil or criminal court. To protect the interests of older adult victims, courts can appoint a *guardian ad litem* who investigates the older adult's life situation and the circumstances surrounding the abuse and makes a recommendation to the court. The court may also appoint a lawyer to represent the older adult's legal interests during court proceedings (Roby & Sullivan, 2000).

When services are needed, a plan is developed with the older adult that identifies appropriate interventions; the least restrictive alternatives are favored. The APS worker often serves as a case manager, coordinating a wide array of services that can include medical care, nutrition assistance, legal assistance, mental health treatment, recreation, substance abuse services, income support, housing or institutional placement, transportation, job training, homemaker services, financial services, and home health care (McClennen, 2010). Regular updates are provided to the court until the case is closed.

Special Challenges for Social Workers

Unlike vulnerable children, competent adults are legally entitled to make decisions on their own behalf. They remain in charge of their own lives unless and until they voluntarily delegate this responsibility to someone else or a court does so for them. This can present ethical challenges for those working with older adults. For example, although social workers in many states are mandated reporters of elder abuse, we are also bound by our Code of Ethics to honor client self-determination. We may suspect that an older person is being mistreated, but he or she may not want to have the abuse reported. As with any difficult professional decision, it is important to seek supervision, consult with colleagues, be conversant with the applicable state laws, and document the rationale for our actions.

Investigating and responding to elder abuse must include an assessment of the older adult's decision-making capacity, including his or her ability to participate in the development of the case plan and to consent to receipt of services. This should be done as early in the process as possible. Determining decision-making capacity can be tricky, especially because an older person can be competent at some times and for some purposes but not others. Social workers involved with older adults must assess specific abilities and disabilities, including their ability to understand and process relevant information, make rational decisions in their own self-interest, appreciate consequences, and communicate their desires. An older person's capacity may be impaired by dementia and can also be affected by poor nutrition, depression, the effects of medication, or time of day. If a client is found to lack capacity, it is important to identify the underlying cause because many of these contributing factors can be remedied. Table 10.1 illustrates the interplay between the client's capacity to consent to services and the role of the service provider. If it is unclear whether or not an older adult is capable of making the decisions called for, Nerenberg (2008) advises weighing the risk of continued maltreatment against the potential harm or loss of liberty associated with intervention. If the services contemplated are minimally invasive and the risk of continued violence is great, the worker should err on the side of caution and intervene. This should be done only after conducting a more comprehensive evaluation, seeking consultation, and documenting the decision-making process and rationale. This is not to suggest, of course, that all clients who refuse help do so because they lack decision-making capacity. Competent older adults may choose to decline services out of fear, shame, pride, or distrust. Although workers must honor their wishes, it is recommended that efforts be made to establish rapport, build trust, and seek consent for more modest interventions such as telephone contact or visits by community volunteers (Nerenberg, 2008).

Another challenge for social workers stems from the fact that abuse or neglect may be hard to detect among older adults because it can be masked by illness, frailty, or dementia. Social isolation, along with underreporting, can also make identifying mistreatment more difficult. Some people fail to report suspected elder abuse because they are reluctant to interfere in family matters, especially ones involving possible financial exploitation. Others are influenced by stereotypes that depict older adults as senile, incompetent, or dependent. Once abuse, neglect, or exploitation is detected, older adults may face multiple barriers to receiving appropriate services. Unlike survivors of intimate partner violence, for example, older adults may lack access to emergency shelters (McClennen, 2010). Limitations

TABLE 10.1	**Ability to Consent and Worker's Role**
Capable and Consenting	When capable clients consent to help, their worker's role is to provide them with information and help them evaluate their options. Workers must be willing to accept clients' choices, even if they disagree with them.
Capable and Nonconsenting	When capable clients refuse help, those working with them have to respect their wishes.
Incapable and Consenting	Some clients who are deemed incapable of making decisions nonetheless consent to services. Although providing services to them raises ethical questions, most agencies respect these clients' wishes to the degree that they seem reasonable and appropriate.
Incapable and Nonconsenting	When clients who lack capacity refuse needed services, and the potential consequences of failure to act are serious, involuntary interventions such as protective custody or guardianship may be needed.

Source: Adapted from *Elder Abuse Prevention: Emerging Trends And Promising Strategies* by Lisa Nerenberg. Copyright © 2007 by Lisa Nerenberg. Reproduced with permission of SPRINGER PUBLISHING COMPANY, Inc. via Copyright Clearance Center.

in health or functioning may also make it difficult for an older person to leave his or her current living situation. Older women experiencing spousal abuse often have been socialized to abide by traditional values that encourage subordination to the male head of the household and discourage leaving the marital relationship. Finally, financial constraints may keep older women in violent relationships because they may not have any employment history and may experience ageism in the workplace (Straka & Montminy, 2006).

Age Discrimination

In many ways, society's view of older adults has changed in recent years. We speak of *healthy aging* and *aging in place* as laudable goals for growing old gracefully. As people live longer, we recognize that many remain vital and active well into their later years. We expect older adults to maintain their involvement in society, including continued employment. In 2000, approximately 18.4 million workers in the labor force were age 55 and older. By 2015, this number is projected to reach 31.9 million (U.S. General Accounting Office, 2001). Mandatory retirement laws requiring the termination of workers at a specific age (usually 65) were commonplace in the United States during the 1960s and 1970s and still exist in much of Europe. In 1978, Congress banned mandatory retirement before age 70, and in 1986, it abolished mandatory retirement entirely (von Wachter, 2009). Unfortunately, older adults may continue to face barriers securing and retaining employment because of age discrimination. Social workers, both as advocates and service providers, are in a unique position to respond to this problem (Mon-Barak & Tynan, 1993).

The Age Discrimination in Employment Act (ADEA)

In 1967, the U.S. Congress passed the Age Discrimination in Employment Act (ADEA, P.L. 90-202) in an effort to protect older adults from discrimination in the workplace. The ADEA was modeled, in large part, on Title VII of the Civil Rights Act of 1964, which prohibits discrimination on the basis of race, color, religion, sex, and national origin. Specifically, the ADEA protects employees and job applicants older than age 40 from discrimination in hiring, firing, promotion, layoff, compensation, benefits, job assignments, and training (Equal Employment Opportunity Commission, 2008). The legislation has undergone numerous changes since 1967, but its goal remains to "promote employment of older persons based on their ability rather than age; to prohibit arbitrary age discrimination in employment; and to help employers and workers find ways of meeting problems arising from the impact of age on employment" (ADEA, Sec. 621[b]).

The ADEA applies to both public and private employers with 20 or more employees. If employers have fewer than 20 employees, they may still be subject to state laws prohibiting age discrimination. Part-time employees are not considered in this calculation but are covered by the ADEA if the employer has more than 20 full-time employees. (Tennessee Employment Law Center, 2010).

The main question posed by the ADEA is when distinctions based on age are justified. Under the Act, employers are permitted to discipline or discharge an employee for good cause, regardless of age. They may also take age into account if it is a characteristic that is reasonably necessary for the particular job (i.e., it constitutes a *bona fide occupational qualification* or *BFOQ*). Examples might include hiring a younger, rather than an older, actor to play a young character in a movie, or setting age limits for pilots in the interest of public safety. Courts generally interpret the protections of the ADEA broadly and permissible BFOQ defenses narrowly, meaning that employers are faced with an especially heavy burden to justify age-related employment decisions. Some observers note that judges tend to approach age discrimination claims with particular empathy, because many are themselves age 40 or older (Zachary, 2000).

Pursuing an ADEA Claim in Court

The majority of cases brought to court alleging age discrimination under the ADEA involve claims of improper termination. In contrast, only 10% of claims allege age discrimination in hiring. Before initiating a suit in court, a complaint must be filed with the Equal Employment Opportunity Commission (EEOC) or the appropriate state agency. The employer is then required to file a response to the complaint and provide supporting documents. The EEOC may then conduct an investigation of the claim that includes interviewing witnesses and subpoenaing records. After its investigation, the EEOC can file a lawsuit against the employer or it can issue a "right to sue letter" permitting the employee to pursue the case in court. The employee then has 90 days to file his or her case.

In order for a case to be heard by the court, it must be brought within the applicable statute of limitations: 3 years from the date of an alleged willful violation or 2 years from the date of an alleged nonwillful violation. The employee has the burden of proving that he or she was the subject of discrimination. One option is to offer direct proof that the employment decision was based solely on age. Alternatively, the employee can offer circumstantial evidence by mounting a *prima facie* case, meaning that "on the face of it" or "at first sight" it appears that age discrimination occurred. The idea here is that the employee must produce enough evidence for the court to infer that the employment decision was based on an illegal, discriminatory criterion. This would typically involve showing that age was one of the determining factors, even if not the only one, motivating the employment decision. To make out a *prima facie* case under the ADEA (as interpreted by the U.S. Supreme Court in *O'Connor v. Consolidated*, 1996), the employee must demonstrate by a *preponderance of the evidence* that

- The employee is in the age group protected by the law.
- The employee was discharged or demoted.
- At the time of the discharge or demotion, the employee was performing at a level that met the employer's legitimate expectations.
- Following the discharge or demotion, the employer replaced the employee with a younger person who had comparable qualifications.

Once a successful *prima facie* case is made, there is a legal presumption that age discrimination occurred. In other words, the court accepts the explanation presented by the employee unless the employer can prove otherwise. The burden of proof then shifts to the employer, who has the opportunity, in rebuttal, to articulate a legitimate, nondiscriminatory reason for the action taken against the employee. If the employer fails to do so, the court will rule in favor of the employee. If the employer is successful in doing so, the burden then shifts back to the employee who must show that the reason articulated by the employer is a mere pretext and that age is the more likely explanation.

In a controversial decision (*Gross v. FBL Financial Services, Inc.,* 2009), a majority of the Supreme Court (Justices Thomas, Scalia, Roberts, Alito, and Kennedy) held that when "mixed motives" are involved (i.e., when age is one of several motivating factors for the disputed employment action), the employee has the burden of proving that "but for" age, the employment action would not have been taken. The employer can defend against the claim by proving that the same action would have occurred regardless of the employee's age. Justice Kennedy had previously advanced the "but for" argument in his dissent in an earlier case involving sex discrimination under Title VII of the Civil Rights Act of 1964 (*Price Waterhouse v. Hopkins*, 1989), but the majority of the Court rejected it. This time, he was successful. By embracing this approach to "mixed motive" cases, the Court in *Gross* substantially narrowed the opportunities for victims of age discrimination to seek redress. As a result of this case, those experiencing workplace discrimination based on age will have to meet a higher threshold of proof than those bringing discrimination claims based on race, color, sex, religion, or national origin.

Even more complicated than cases in which direct, deliberate discrimination is alleged (*disparate treatment*) are cases of unintentional discrimination (*disparate impact*). *Smith v. City of Jackson* (2005) involved a citywide plan to institute pay raises for all city workers. A group of older police officers objected to the specifics of the plan under which employees with fewer than 5 years of service were granted proportionately greater increases than those with 5 or more years on the force. They claimed that because of their age, they would be unfairly disadvantaged by the policy because they were more likely than younger workers to exceed the 5 years and to receive the smaller raises. The question for the Supreme Court was whether the ADEA applies to situations involving disparate impact—that is, situations in which a policy inadvertently affects older workers differently than it does younger ones. In this particular case, the Court found that the police officers had failed to demonstrate the policy's disparate impact on older workers but affirmed that disparate impact claims, like claims of disparate treatment, are covered by the ADEA.

Implications for Social Work

Social workers are in a position to see, firsthand, the challenges faced by older adults in the workplace. It is important that we be involved, as both practitioners and advocates, in promoting the continued employment of older adults and in recognizing and responding to instances of discrimination. Mor-Barak and Tynan (1993) propose the following action steps for social workers:

- Promote hiring of older workers through drawing employers' attention to the strengths of older workers.
- Provide victims of age discrimination with support and refer them for legal assistance.
- Help managers understand the nation's changing demographics and how current programs and practices affect older workers and their families.
- Link older adult job seekers with employers; assist them with preparing resumes, rehearsing for interviews, and responding to discrimination.
- Advise companies on work arrangements and training programs for older adults.
- Counsel and support older workers and their families to promote continued participation in the labor force.

In addition, social workers need to be aware of the changing interpretations of employment discrimination law and advocate for policies that protect older workers.

Grandparents Raising Grandchildren

For many older adults, one of the by-products of today's increased life expectancy is the increased duration of grandparenthood (Richardson & Barush, 2006). Grandparents continue to assume diverse roles in family and society, including providing care to grandchildren, nieces, nephews, and other child relatives (Generations United, 2009; Richardson & Barush, 2006). The number of grandparent-headed households with grandchildren more than doubled between 1970 and 2000, increasing from 2.2 million to 5.8 million (Letiecq, Bailey, & Porterfield, 2008). According to the U.S. Census Bureau (2009), more than 6 million grandparents have grandchildren living with them; 2.5 million of these grandparents are responsible for meeting their grandchildren's basic needs. This phenomenon reflects an increase in births to unmarried teen mothers, a high divorce rate, parental death or incapacity from HIV/AIDS, parental alcohol and drug use (particularly methamphetamine use), abuse or neglect, and abandonment, all of which may result in children being left parentless or in the custody of parents who are unable to fulfill the parenting role (Tremblay, Barber, & Kubin, 2006). Other circumstances giving rise to grandparents raising grandchildren include parental death, mental illness, incarceration, military service, and children experiencing difficulty living with their biological parents. The length of time that grandparents remain the primary caregivers for grandchildren varies. As Figure 10.3 illustrates, most grandparents who assume primary caregiving responsibilities, regardless of their age, do so for 5 years or more.

This trend presents several challenges for social workers, who increasingly encounter multigenerational families in the course of their practice (Richardson & Barusch, 2006). Approximately 450,000 or 20% of grandparent-headed families live in poverty. In addition, research suggests that children cared for by grandparents suffer higher rates

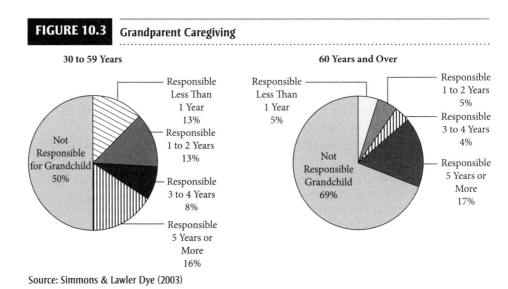

FIGURE 10.3   Grandparent Caregiving

Source: Simmons & Lawler Dye (2003)

of physical, mental, and emotional problems than do other children, probably as a result of the same issues that caused them to be living with grandparents (Generations United, 2009). Grandparent caregivers, too, have complex social, financial, and legal needs, regardless of whether they are raising children through informal arrangements or as the result of a court order (Wallace, 2001).

Legal and Policy Considerations

Grandparent caregivers have one of four statuses: (1) They may be informal caregivers; (2) they may have court-ordered custody or guardianship; (3) they may provide kinship foster care through the child welfare system while the state retains legal custody of the child; or (4) they may adopt the children, giving them the same legal rights and responsibilities as birth parents (Wallace, 2001).

Unlike birth parents, grandparents do not automatically have a fundamental constitutional right to a permanent relationship with the relative child. When conflicts arise, grandparents' rights are subordinated to the interests of the parents. Through the legal system, however, grandparents may be able to achieve the authority to act as substitute parents and to access public benefits, including Temporary Assistance to Needy Families (TANF), SSI, Social Security, and Medicaid (Wallace, 2001).

The majority of grandparents provide informal care to grandchildren without the involvement of the child welfare system (Generations United, 2009; Letiecq et al., 2008). Those who do have child welfare involvement, however, may either be informal caregivers or kinship foster parents. An estimated 2 million children receive informal care from grandparents, usually in an effort to keep them out of the formal foster care system. Meanwhile, nearly one-fourth of children in foster care are cared for by relatives, most often grandparents. Grandparents may assume formal responsibility for a grandchild by several means. A parent can create a *power of attorney* granting the grandparent or other adult the authority to make specific decisions regarding the child, for example, to seek medical care for the child or to enroll the child in school. A grandparent may also seek *legal custody* of a grandchild by petitioning the Juvenile and Domestic Relations Court. A custody award does not sever the child's other family relationships, including those of the parent; custody awards can also be reversed at a later date. *Adoption* of the grandchild by the grandparent is the least common alternative; unlike an award of custody, it results in the grandparents becoming the legal parents of the child. Regardless of the legal status of the relationship, children often come into grandparent care as a result of a family crisis; both the grandparent caregiver and the child may need a great deal of support (Generations United, 2009; Letiecq et al. 2008; Wallace, 2001).

A number of federal policies address the specific needs of grandparents raising children. The child welfare system, recognizing the importance of cultural and familial ties, has implemented policies favoring kinship placements (Richardson & Barusch, 2006). The Adoption and Safe Families Act (ASFA) of 1997 encourages states to give preference to relatives when placing a child in foster care. The Act also allows states to waive certain foster care requirements for relatives under certain circumstances (Letiecq et al., 2008). In addition, the U.S. Supreme Court, in *Miller v. Youakim* (1979), held that states must make the same payments to relatives caring for children in foster care that they make to nonrelative foster parents, providing they meet all applicable foster care licensing standards (Wallace, 2001; Warren, 2001).

The National Family Caregiver Support Program (NFCSP), which is part of the Older Americans Act, authorizes funds to assist grandparents age 55 and older who are raising their grandchildren. These funds may be used to provide the following types of support: information for caregivers about services, respite care, assistance to caregivers in gaining access to services, individual counseling and the formation of support groups, and supplemental services (Generations United, 2009; Richardson & Barusch, 2006). More recently, the Fostering Connections to Success and Increasing Adoptions Act of 2008 expanded access to services and financial supports for grandparents raising grandchildren (Generations United, 2009). The following provisions affect grandparent caregivers:

- **Kinship Navigator Programs:** The Act authorizes funding for states to establish kinship navigator programs. These programs are designed to provide information for relative caregivers about available programs and services, including public benefit programs, local support groups, and respite care programs.
- **Subsidized Guardianship Programs:** The Act allows states to use federal Title IV-E funds to establish kinship guardianship programs (as an alternative to traditional foster care) when relatives commit to permanently caring for a child.
- **Mandated Notification of Relatives:** States are required to exercise due diligence in notifying grandparents and other adult relatives within 30 days of a child's removal from home, in order to increase the opportunity for family placements.
- **Waiver of Non-Safety Licensing Standards:** States may waive nonsafety licensing requirements, on a case-by-case basis, for relatives seeking to be foster parents.

Despite these and other efforts to encourage and assist grandparents raising children, little systematic response exists outside the child welfare system. Many grandparents avoid involvement with the child welfare system and consequently miss out on available benefits. Although they are the most common among grandparent caregivers, those in these informal arrangements are the least likely to receive assistance and services from the state. Instead, they are often left to discover the complex legal, financial, emotional, and policy implications of their situation only haphazardly (Letiecq et al., 2009).

At best, services available for grandparents raising grandchildren remain scarce and often unavailable. Housing assistance, in particular, continues to fall short. Federally subsidized senior housing units may not meet the needs of grandparent-headed families, and children are often excluded. Although there have been successful housing initiatives for grandparents raising grandchildren in certain areas of the country, most are in the start-up phase (Wallace, 2001). The U.S. Department of Housing and Urban Development (2009) completed a congressionally mandated study on intergenerational housing needs. The LEGACY Act of 2003 (P.L. 108-186), which called for the study, also authorized several demonstration projects designed to make supportive housing available to intergenerational households. This includes funding for retrofitting existing units and developing new units to serve this population, as well as providing services to meet the special needs of older adults, children, and intergenerational families.

Social workers should understand the various legal options available to grandparents who wish to raise their grandchildren, as well as the benefits and services that may be available to assist them. As advocates, program developers, and administrators, we need to ensure that our service system includes appropriate supports and interventions to help these households be healthy, stable, and successful.

Competency, Guardianship, and End of Life

As people live longer, many will experience the limitations of compromised health and ability. Decisions about how to cope with these later years, including end-of-life issues, will become an important consideration for many families. This portion of the chapter addresses key legal issues that adults may face in later life, including guardianship and the preparation of health care directives. A special section addresses the controversial issue of physician-assisted suicide. It should be noted that many of these issues are not the exclusive domain of older adults, but rather are equally relevant to those of all ages facing serious health or mental health challenges or a terminal illness.

As social workers, our work with older adults and their families is likely to include not just the delivery of services, but initiating, facilitating, and mediating sensitive discussions around competency and end-of-life care. These discussions often include where one wants to spend the final months before death, the lifestyle and degree of self-sufficiency one desires, and the acceptability of medical and technological interventions to sustain life. It is important for social workers to understand these issues so that we can educate families about their options and assist them as they grapple with these difficult and often painful decisions.

Competency and Guardianship

In some cases, older adults may become incapacitated from illness or disability, compromising their ability to care for themselves. In these situations, social workers must work with both the individual and the family to determine what actions should be taken. One option is adult guardianship. *Guardianship* involves the legal authorization of a surrogate decision maker for those judicially determined to be incapable of making decisions on their own behalf (American Bar Association, 2009). Rooted in the legal doctrine of *parens patriae*, guardians (or *conservators*) were originally appointed to preserve the estates of incompetent individuals, rather than to make personal decisions on their behalf. Although guardianship protects individuals who might otherwise be vulnerable to abuse, it also interferes with fundamental rights and client autonomy (Crampton, 2004).

In most states, guardians are appointed by the probate court. The proceedings are initiated by the filing of a petition and include a hearing before a judge. All states require that the older adult be notified prior to the hearing; some require that the nearest relative receive notice as well. Additional due process rights, although recommended by the American Bar Association, have not been universally implemented. These include representation by legal counsel, the right to be present at the hearing, the right to call and cross-examine witnesses, and the right to appeal. Two determinations are required for guardianship: a finding of legal incapacity and a finding that the appointment of a guardian is necessary. Traditionally, determinations of incapacity were based on diagnostic labels such as depression or dementia (Roy, 2003). Today, however, they typically involve considerations of functionality and cognition. The American Bar Association (2006) recommends that they be premised on an assessment of the individual's medical condition, cognition, everyday functioning, values and preferences, risk and level of supervision, and opportunities to enhance capacity through treatment, services, or accommodations. Although laws vary by state, they generally require a *sufficient showing* that the person in question is unable to make rational life decisions and that a guardian is needed to protect the individual's health, well-being, or financial interests. Judges retain considerable discretion in determining legal competency based on the evidence and testimony presented.

The various types of guardianship involve differing levels of decision-making authority. *Plenary guardians* are empowered by the court to make both financial and health care decisions on behalf of the elderly individual. *Guardians ad litem* are given temporary authority to represent an older adult during legal proceedings. *Limited guardianship* applies when an older adult is deemed competent for some purposes but not others; the court will empower a guardian to make decisions only under certain circumstances. Finally, *voluntary guardianship* refers to when the older adult chooses to relinquish decision-making authority; this type of guardianship can typically be discontinued if and when the older person believes that a guardian is no longer necessary (University of Miami, 2009). With plenary guardianship, the possible scope of decision making is vast. It can include decisions about financial matters (making large purchases or gifts, selling off property or other assets), medical and surgical interventions (sterilization, life support, undergoing chemotherapy, taking psychotropic drugs) and decisions about living arrangements (relocating, entering a nursing home or other facility). Recognizing that "incompetence is neither total nor static for many individuals" (Dickson, 1995, p. 208), many states have moved away from plenary guardianship and toward various forms of limited guardianship. For example, the court may appoint a *guardian of the estate* to deal only with financial matters or a *guardian of the person* to deal with nonfinancial concerns.

Guardians can be *public* or *private*. Public guardians are public officials or publicly funded organizations that assume guardianship responsibilities. Private guardians can be either professional or lay individuals who perform guardianship functions on a volunteer basis or for pay. Although the level of oversight varies enormously from state to state, guardians are supervised by state and local courts and are generally required to submit reports to the court on an annual basis (Bovbjerg, 2006).

Social workers may face conflicts when involved in guardianship cases as they try to both empower clients and protect their best interests. Although guardianship may be necessary, it seriously curtails an older individual's autonomy and eliminates many of his or her basic rights. People under guardianship in many states lose their right to vote, to sign contracts, to buy or sell real estate, to marry or divorce, and to make medical decisions (Bovbjerg, 2006). A less drastic alternative to guardianship is a *durable power of attorney,* which is a legal assignment of responsibility in which a *principal* authorizes an *agent* to act for him or her in certain matters. The principal has considerable flexibility in defining the scope of the agent's authority; it can be broad or narrow, ranging from managing all of the principal's income to selling a particular stock. Federal benefit programs also allow for the appointment of a *representative payee* who is authorized to receive the benefit checks and spend the money on behalf of the actual recipient. Unlike guardianship, no finding of incapacity is required for the assignment of a representative payee; in fact, these appointments are made by the agency that administers the benefit program rather than by the court.

The negative aspects of guardianship can be ameliorated by helping clients think ahead and designate in writing who should handle their affairs when they are no longer able to do so. This may necessitate raising and discussing the issue with family members and friends. In the event that these discussions become contentious, social workers and others can act as neutral facilitators or mediators.

End-of-Life Care

Advance directives are legal documents in which adults express their wishes regarding end-of-life care. Although different states use different terminology, the term *advance directive* is generally regarded as an umbrella term encompassing more specific legal arrangements, including living wills, health care proxies, and "do not resuscitate" orders. The Patient Self-Determination Act of 1991, part of the Omnibus Budget Reconciliation Act of 1990 (P.L. 101-508), requires health professionals to question patients about advance directives when they enter hospitals receiving reimbursement under Medicare or Medicaid. Many patients lack information regarding end-of-life options. Social workers play an important role in educating clients about the importance of making their wishes known. They can also help identify individual and family needs and advocate for the client's preferences (Richardson & Barusch, 2006). Advance directives promote client self-determination and empower older individuals to maintain some control during the final period of their lives. NASW (2009) recommends that "decisions regarding end-of-life care should be considered at numerous junctures over the course of one's life, not just when diagnosed with a terminal illness or faced with an acute, life-ending event" (p. 114).

Living wills are advance directives that express the patient's wishes regarding specific medical treatments, including the administration of specific medications, the use of extraordinary life-sustaining measures (including feeding tubes, respiratory support, and CPR), and the withdrawal of life support (Richardson & Barusch, 2006). The document should also identify the circumstances under which these provisions become effective. A living will is often paired with a *durable health care proxy,* which specifies who should make medical decisions on the patient's behalf in the event that the patient is unable to do so. Health care proxies are considered "durable" because, unlike some other legal documents, they remain in effect even if the individual is incapacitated (Dickson, 1995). *Do not resuscitate (DNR) orders* instruct health care professionals not to administer CPR. DNR orders are narrow in their scope; they simply let health care professionals know that the individual does not want life-preserving treatment if his or her heart or breathing stops. DNR orders are generally put in the patient's medical chart and are accepted by health care professionals and hospitals in all states (American Academy of Family Physicians, 2009).

Although state laws vary, it generally is not necessary to obtain the services of an attorney in order to create an advance directive. Forms are easily available from most doctors and health departments and they can be accessed online (American Academy of Family Physicians, 2009). Alternatively, the individual can simply write down his or her wishes. Once signed and properly witnessed, these advance directives become legally valid. They should be reviewed periodically to be sure that they continue to accurately reflect the individual's wishes regarding end-of-life care. A sample advance directive appears in Illustration 10.1.

In general, before an advance directive can be implemented, two physicians must determine that the individual is unable to make medical decisions and that he or she meets the conditions laid out in the document. This also applies before a health care proxy can begin making decisions. In the event that the individual regains the ability to make medical decisions, the health care proxy's authority is terminated (National Hospice and Palliative Care Organization, n.d.).

ILLUSTRATION 10.1

Sample Living Will

STATE OF RHODE ISLAND
CHAPTER 23-4.11
RIGHTS OF THE TERMINALLY ILL ACT
DECLARATION

I, _____, being of sound mind willfully and voluntarily make known my desire that my dying shall not be artificially prolonged under the circumstances set forth below, so hereby declare:

If I should have an incurable or irreversible condition that will cause my death and if I am unable to make decisions regarding my medical treatment, I direct my attending physician to withhold or withdraw procedures that merely prolong the dying process and are not necessary to my comfort, or to alleviate pain.

This authorization (check only one):

includes ____
does not include ____

the withholding or withdrawal of artificial feeding.

Signed this _____ day of _____, _____

_____
Signature of Declarant

_____
Address

The Declarant is personally known to me and voluntarily signed this document in my presence. I am not related to the Declarant by blood or marriage.

_____   _____
Witness   Witness

_____   _____
Address   Address

It is important to note that an advance directive that is valid in one state may not be valid in other states. Therefore, it is advisable that persons wishing to complete advance directives who spend time in multiple states complete advance directives for all of the

PHYSICIAN ASSISTED SUICIDE

Individuals with a terminal illness sometimes express a desire to die. "Although prevailing practice encourages the person with terminal illness to acknowledge the inevitability of death and to discuss related feelings, indications that a person wants to die can produce confusion and fear in professionals and family members alike" (Van Loon, 1999, p. 260). Although these expressions may be linked to depression or suicidal ideation, they may also be a coping mechanism, an indication of a rational choice to die, or a spiritually based acceptance of death. In certain states, individuals may choose to end their lives through physician-assisted suicide. A physician provides the patient with lethal drugs that aid in an individual's suicide. Physician-assisted suicide should be distinguished from *euthanasia,* in which it is the physician, not the patient, who administers the lethal medication in order to accelerate death. Physician-assisted suicide is also different from *terminal sedation*, in which the doctor administers the medication and the goal is to relieve suffering, not achieve death.

Oregon was the first state to legalize physician-assisted suicide by passing the Oregon Death with Dignity Act in 1997, which was upheld by the U.S. Supreme Court (*Gonzales v. Oregon*) in 2006. Other states have followed suit, despite earlier Supreme Court decisions affirming state bans on physician-assisted suicide in New York (*Vacco v. Quill*, 1997) and Washington (*Washington v. Glucksberg*, 1997). In 2008, the state of Washington passed a ballot initiative legalizing physician-assisted suicide, and in 2009 the Montana Supreme Court, in *Baxter v. Montana*, ruled that nothing in the state's laws prohibits terminally ill Montanans from choosing aid in dying. In all other states, physician-assisted suicide remains illegal and may be prosecuted as form of

manslaughter or as its own criminal act (Frolik & Kaplan, 2006).

Physician-assisted suicide is highly controversial. On one hand, it allows terminally ill individuals to avoid a potentially painful, prolonged death and, as some contend, to die with dignity. On the other, it may be rashly considered, stem from temporary feelings of depression and despair, or be motivated by concern for others' needs rather than one's own. In order to protect patients who seek to die, a thorough assessment is essential. The Oregon Act requires the following:

- Patients must be terminally ill and have 6 months or less to live.
- The patient must orally request a prescription and then wait 15 days.
- A physician determines if the patient has the capacity to make the decision and if the decision is voluntary.
- The physician's diagnosis and prognosis are confirmed by another attending physician.
- Physicians can stop the procedure if they believe the individual is suffering from a psychiatric illness or depression.
- The patient must sign a written request, witnessed by two individuals.
- The patient must again orally request medication.

These measures aim to ensure that physician-assisted suicide is carefully planned and rationally chosen. Social workers should be familiar with their state's laws concerning physician-assisted suicide. NASW encourages social workers to discuss all end-of-life options with a client, including physician-assisted suicide (where it is legal) and, if they are comfortable doing so, to be present with the client or family when the procedure occurs.

states in which they regularly spend time. It should also be noted that emergency medical technicians (EMTs) are required to do what is necessary in order to stabilize the patient and cannot honor advance directives.

Recommendations for Social Workers

Preferences regarding end-of-life care are highly personal; they are complex medical, spiritual, and psychosocial determinations that reflect closely held values. NASW does not take a position concerning the morality of end-of-life decisions, but it affirms the right of any individual to direct his or her care wishes at the end of life. Social workers often work with clients who express a desire to talk about their thoughts and feelings regarding dying and death. Social workers play an important role in assessing statements made by clients expressing their desire to die and in providing appropriate knowledge, compassion, and skill; they also can intervene with medical professionals to ameliorate pain and suffering. Social workers can explore and assess all of these issues with clients and can educate and direct them to appropriate resources such as pain management, palliative care, or hospice care (NASW, 2009).

Because social workers play a role in assisting clients and families as they confront and prepare for the possibility of death and dying, it is essential that they be familiar with state laws and procedures regarding advance directives, including living wills, durable health care proxies, and DNR orders. In addition, social workers must use sensitivity and cultural competence in addressing the psychosocial issues that accompany the end of life. Those facing terminal illness are likely to experience significant anxiety, depression, and stress (Richardson & Barusch, 2006). Metzger and Kaplan (2001, p. 7) provide a best-practice framework for social workers involved in end-of-life care:

- Pain and other physical symptoms should be alleviated and comfort maximized by medical care that conforms to best-practice standards and is consistent with the person's values and preferences.
- The physical and emotional environment should be as pleasant and supportive as possible and include time spent with loved ones and other people of choice.
- Dying people and their families should be cared for in a manner that respects their inherent dignity.
- Dying people should be able to exercise personal control to the extent that they desire and is feasible.
- Dying people who wish to do so should be able to explore issues of meaning and spirituality with support from others.

(Source: From *Transforming Death In America: A State Of The Nation Report.* Copyright © 2001 by the Robert Wood Johnson Foundation. Reprinted with permission by the Robert Wood Johnson Foundation.)

Social workers are often the most appropriate professionals to initiate conversations about adult guardianship and advance directives. It is important that clients thoughtfully consider the various options available to them in the event that aging necessitates entrusting their care to another person. By planning for the possibility of incapacitation, medical emergency, or death, clients can maximize self-determination and autonomy. Social workers must advocate for the safety of vulnerable older adults, including the provision of quality end-of-life care.

Summary and Conclusion

Across the globe, the population is aging. Demographers project a 36% increase in the number of U.S. older adults between 2010 and 2020 alone. The aging population is also becoming more diverse. More and more of us will encounter older adults as part of our social work practice. It is important that we understand the legal issues that older adults may face. Some will encounter abuse, neglect, or exploitation. Social workers have a role in reporting suspected mistreatment, investigating and assessing reports, and responding to elder abuse by ensuring the safety of victims and making necessary services available. Other older adults may experience workplace discrimination. The Age Discrimination in Employment Act prohibits discrimination based on age. Subsequent court decisions have outlined the procedures for bringing cases to court and have defined how these cases are decided. With the increase in life expectancy has come an increase in the number of grandparents raising grandchildren. Policies define various legal statuses of grandparent caregivers and provide them with varying degrees of assistance. Finally, adults who face incapacitation or terminal illness have legal options for expressing their wishes and directing their care, including guardianship, durable power of attorney, living wills, health care proxy, and DNR orders. Social workers are well suited to educate families about these options and assist them in planning for the future.

Sample Case

Following is the U.S. Supreme Court's opinion in a case concerning the Age Discrimination in Employment Act (ADEA). It was brought by a group of former and current employees between the ages of 40 and 50 (old enough to be covered by the ADEA, but treated disadvantageously under a company policy). Included are excerpts from the majority opinion and from two dissenting opinions. After you read the case, try briefing it in order to synthesize the important information. A case brief includes the following parts: (1) case name and citation, (2) facts, (3) issue, (4) holding, (5) rationale, and (6) summary of concurring/ dissenting opinions. Then consider the questions that appear at the end of the case.

GENERAL DYNAMICS LAND SYSTEMS, INC. V. CLINE
540 U.S. 581 (2004)

Justice Souter delivered the opinion of the Court.

The Age Discrimination in Employment Act of 1967 (ADEA or Act), 81 Stat. 602, 29 U.S.C.§ 621 *et seq.*, forbids discriminatory preference for the young over the old. The question in this case is whether it also prohibits favoring the old over the young. We hold it does not.

In 1997, a collective-bargaining agreement between petitioner General Dynamics and the United Auto Workers eliminated the company's obligation to provide health benefits to subsequently retired employees, except as to then-current workers at least 50 years old. Respondents (collectively, Cline) were then at least 40 and thus protected by the Act... but under 50 and so without the promise of the benefits. All of them objected to the new terms, although some had retired before the change in order to get the prior advantage, some retired afterwards with no benefit, and some worked on, knowing the new contract would give them no health coverage when they were through.

Before the Equal Employment Opportunity Commission (EEOC or Commission) they claimed that the agreement violated the ADEA, because it "discriminate[d against them]…with respect to…compensation, terms, condition, or privileges of employment, because of [their] age," §623(a)(1). The EEOC agreed, and invited General Dynamics and the union to settle informally with Cline.

When they failed, Cline brought this action against General Dynamics, combining claims under the ADEA and state law. The District Court called the federal claim one of "reverse age discrimination," upon which it observed, no court had ever granted relief under the ADEA. It dismissed on reliance on the Seventh Circuit's opinion in *Hamilton v. Caterpillar Inc.*, 966 F.2d 1226 (1992), that "the ADEA 'does not protect…the younger against the older,'" *id.*, at 1227.

A divided panel of the Sixth Circuit reversed, with a majority reasoning that the prohibition of §623(a)(1), covering discrimination against "any individual…because of such individual's age," is so clear on its face that if Congress had meant to limit its coverage to protect only the older worker against the younger, it would have said so. The court acknowledged the conflict of its ruling with earlier cases, including *Hamilton and Schuler v. Polaroid Corp.*, 848 F.2d 276 (1988) (Breyer, J), from the First Circuit…. ***

We granted certiorari to resolve the conflict among the Circuits…and now reverse. ***

Congress chose not to include age within discrimination forbidden by Title VII of the Civil Rights Act of 1964….Instead it called for a study of the issue by the Secretary of Labor who concluded that age discrimination was a serious problem….The report contains no suggestion that reactions to age level off at some point, and it was devoid of any indication that the Secretary had noticed unfair advantages accruing to older employees at the expense of their juniors.

Congress then asked for a specific proposal…which the Secretary provided in January 1967….Extensive House and Senate hearings ensued. ***

The testimony at both hearings dwelled on unjustified assumptions about the effect of age on ability to work….The hearings specifically addressed higher pension and benefit costs as heavier drags on hiring workers the older they got….The record thus reflects the common facts that an individual's chances to find and keep a job get worse over time; as between any two people, the younger is in the stronger position, the older more apt to be tagged with demeaning stereotype. Not surprisingly, from the voluminous records of the hearings, we have found (and Cline has cited) nothing suggesting that any workers were registering complaints about discrimination in favor of their seniors.

Nor is there any such suggestion in the introductory provisions of the ADEA, 81 Stat. 602….The findings stress the impediments suffered by "older workers…in their efforts to retain…and especially to regain employment," *id.*, §2(a)(1)….The statutory objects were "to promote employment of older persons based on their ability rather than age; to prohibit arbitrary age discrimination in employment; [and] to help employers and workers find ways of meeting problems arising from the impact of age on employment." *Id.*, §2(b). ***

Such is the setting of the ADEA's core substantive provision, §4 (as amended, 29 U.S.C. §623), prohibiting employers and certain others from "discriminat[ion]…because of [an] individual's age, "whenever (as originally enacted) the individual is "at least forty years of age but less than sixty-five years of age," §12, 81 Stat. 607. The prefatory provisions and their legislative history make a case that we think is beyond reasonable doubt, that the ADEA was concerned to protect a relatively old worker from discrimination that works to the advantage of the relatively young.

Nor is it remarkable that the record is devoid of any evidence that younger workers were suffering at the expense of their elders, let alone that a social problem required a federal statute to place a younger worker in parity with an older one. Common experience is to the contrary, and the testimony, reports, and congressional findings simply confirm that Congress used the phrase "discrimina[tion]…because of][an] individual's age" the same way that ordinary people in common usage might speak of age discrimination any day of the week.***

This same, idiomatic sense of the statutory phrase is confirmed by the statute's restriction of the protected class to those 40 and above. If Congress had been worrying about protecting the younger against the older, it would not likely have ignored everyone under 40.…The enemy of 40 is 30, not 50.…Even so, the 40-year old threshold was adopted over the objection that some discrimination against older people begins at an even younger age.…Thus, the 40-year threshold makes sense as identifying a class requiring protection against preference for their juniors, not as defining a class that might be threatened by favoritism toward seniors. ***

The Courts of Appeals and the District Courts have read the law the same way, and prior to this case have enjoyed virtually unanimous accord in understanding the ADEA to forbid only discrimination preferring young to old. The very strength of this consensus is enough to rule out any serious claim of ambiguity, and congressional silence after years of judicial interpretation supports adherence to the traditional view. ***

We see the text, structure, purpose, and history of the ADEA, along with its relationship to other federal statutes, as showing that the statute does not mean to stop an employer from favoring an older employee over a younger one. The judgment of the Court of Appeals is Reversed.

Justice Scalia, dissenting

The Age Discrimination in Employment Act of 1967 (ADEA), 29 U.S.C. §621-634, makes it unlawful for an employer to "discriminate against any individual with respect to his compensation, terms, conditions, or privileges of employment, because of such individual's age." §623(a)(1). The question in this case is whether…the ADEA prohibits an employer from favoring older over younger workers when both are protected by the Act, *i.e.,* are 40 year of age or older.

The Equal Employment Opportunity Commission (EEOC) has answered this question in the affirmative. In 1981, the agency adopted a regulation which states, in pertinent part: "It is unlawful in situations where this Act applies, for an employer to discriminate in hiring or in any other way by giving preference because of age between individuals 40 and over. Thus, if two people apply for the same position, and one is 42 and the other 52, the employer may not lawfully turn down either one on the basis of age, but must make such decision on the basis of some other fact." 29 C.F.R. §1625.2(a) (2003). This regulation represents the interpretation of the agency tasked by Congress with enforcing the ADEA.

The Court brushes aside the EEOC's interpretation as "clearly wrong." I cannot agree with the contention upon which that rejection rests. ***

Because §623(a) "does not unambiguously require a different interpretation, and …the [EEOC's] regulation is an entirely reasonable interpretation of the text," I would defer to the agency's authoritative conclusion. I respectfully dissent.

Justice Thomas, with whom Justice Kennedy joins, dissenting.

This should have been an easy case. The plain language of 20 U.S.C. §623(a)(1) mandates a particular outcome: that the respondents are able to sue for discrimination against them in favor of older workers. ***

The plain language of the ADEA clearly allows for suits brought by the relatively young when discriminated against in favor of the relatively old. The phrase "discriminate…because of such individual's age," 29 U.S.C. §623(a)(1), is not restricted to discrimination because of relatively *older* age. If an employer fired a worker for the sole reason that the worker was under 45, it would be entirely natural to say that the worker had been discriminated against because of his age. ***

As the ADEA clearly prohibits discrimination because of an individual's age, whether the individual is too old or too young, I would affirm the Court of Appeals. Because the court resorts to interpretive sleight of hand to avoid addressing the plain language of the ADEA, I respectfully dissent.

Questions

1. What's the legal question that the Court was deciding here?

2. Six of the nine Supreme Court justices supported the majority opinion, concluding that the ADEA does not protect younger workers (those age 40–49) against favoritism shown to those age 50 and older. How did the Court reach this conclusion? What did it base its decision on?

3. The two dissenting opinions reach the opposite conclusion. What was the basis for their interpretation?

4. Both sides cannot be right. Which side's reasoning did you find more convincing? Why?

5. As a policy matter, which outcome would you favor? Why?

6. In a section of his dissent not reprinted here, Justice Thomas draws an analogy between age discrimination and race discrimination. He points out that when the Civil Rights Act was enacted in 1964, it was commonly understood as an effort to protect African Americans from employment discrimination. Yet, in the intervening years, the Supreme Court has held that the Civil Rights Act protects all races, including Whites who are unfairly disadvantaged relative to people of color. Does this analogy make sense to you? Can there be "reverse discrimination" against younger people relative to their elders? If so, do you think it is a serious enough social problem to warrant protection under federal law?

7. Given what you know about the ADEA, how would you have decided this case? What social work principles can you bring to bear in making your decision?

CHAPTER 10 PRACTICE TEST

The following questions will test your application and analysis of the content found within this chapter. For additional assessment, including licensing-exam type questions on applying chapter content to practice behaviors, visit **MySearchLab**.

1. Most older adults
   a. are minorities.
   b. are women.
   c. live in poverty.
   d. live in nursing homes.

2. Most founded reports of adult mistreatment involve
   a. caregiver neglect.
   b. financial exploitation.
   c. self-neglect.
   d. physical abuse.

3. John is a 55-year-old man who was recently fired from his job with an advertising agency. He wants to sue for age discrimination. Which of the following is true?
   a. He must first file a complaint with the Equal Employment Opportunity Commission (EEOC).

   b. The Age Discrimination in Employment Act (ADEA) only covers employees age 60 and older.
   c. The agency bears the initial burden of proving that it fired John for legitimate, nondiscriminatory reasons.
   d. No statute of limitations restricts when John must file his claim.

4. Matilda knows that she needs to step up and take care of her grandson, Mikey. Mikey's mother, age 16 and a crack addict, is in no position to raise him. If Matilda wants to be sure she is entitled to all of the same legal rights and responsibilities as a birth parent, which of the following should she pursue?
   a. becoming an informal caregiver
   b. court-ordered guardianship
   c. kinship foster care
   d. adoption

5. When an older adult's capacity to make her own decisions or handle her own affairs begins to decline, what legal options are available to her? Describe what these various options entail and when each might be desirable.

6. Discuss some of the ethical challenges involved in social work with older adults.

MYSEARCHLAB CONNECTIONS

Reinforce what you learned in this chapter by studying videos, cases, documents,
and more available at **www.MySearchLab.com**.

Watch these Videos

* Grandmothers Raising Grandchildren
  * *What policies and services could help support grandparents who are raising their grandchildren? What policies and services could help support the children in these families?*
* Successfully Aging-Thelma
  * *What factors contribute to successful aging? How can social workers promote successful aging? How can law and policy?*

Read these Cases/Documents

Δ Volunteer Experiences with the Neighbors Helping Neighbors Program
  * *How can communities come together to support their older adult members?*

Explore these Assets

* Website: AARP
* Website: Administration on Aging

Research these Topics

* cultural competence and older adults
* ethical issues in end-of-life decision-making

Assess Your Knowledge

Go to **MySearchLab** to test your knowledge of key topics in this chapter with topic-specific quizzes. Conclude your assessment by completing the chapter exam.

---

* = CSWE Core Competency Asset   Δ = Case Study

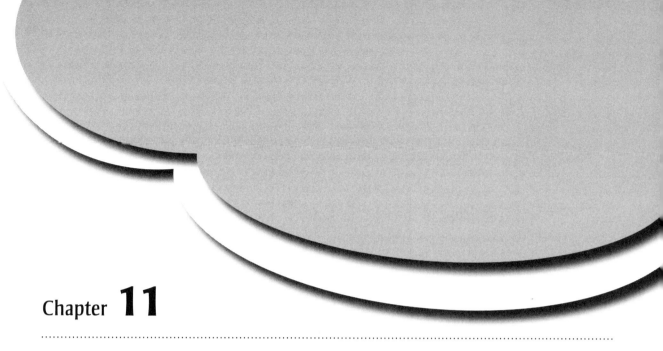

Chapter **11**

Juvenile Justice

In addition to hearing cases involving child maltreatment and child custody, family courts (also called *juvenile courts* or *juvenile and domestic relations courts*) hear cases involving juvenile offenders. Offenses committed by juveniles can be categorized either as status offenses or as delinquency. *Status offenses* are those acts that are unlawful only because juveniles commit them; examples include runaway, truancy, and underage drinking. *Delinquency*, on the other hand, refers to offenses that are unlawful for both juveniles and adults.

The purpose, mission, and characteristics of the juvenile justice system—and its relationship to the adult criminal justice system—have changed considerably over time. The Juvenile Justice Delinquency and Prevention Act of 1974 (JJDPA) is the major federal law that affects juvenile offenders and provides financial support for state improvements to the juvenile justice system. Its goals include keeping children and adult offenders separate, deinstitutionalizing status offenders, and addressing the disproportionate involvement of minority youth in the juvenile justice system (Center for Children's Law and Policy, 2010).

This chapter reviews the evolution of the juvenile justice system, the constitutional protections afforded juvenile offenders, and the players and procedures that comprise the juvenile justice process. Special sections highlight the potential impact of recent brain research on our understanding of juvenile offenders and the controversial issue of trying juveniles as adults. A sample case explores the issue of juvenile confessions.

Background

In order to fully understand America's changing approach to juvenile justice, we begin by examining the scope of juvenile court jurisdiction and the historical trends in juvenile crime. The evolution of the juvenile justice system in many ways reflects these phenomena.

The Scope of the Juvenile Court

As is true with child maltreatment and child custody, the details of juvenile justice law are largely determined by the states. Each state plays a fundamental role in defining the purpose of its juvenile courts, the offenses that will be addressed through the juvenile justice system, and the upper and lower age limits of juvenile court jurisdiction.

How each state regards the purpose of its juvenile justice system is reflected in its state statutes on juvenile delinquency. In developing these statutes, states attempt to reconcile the sometimes conflicting interests of the juvenile and the larger community. At least 17 states include what have been called *balanced and restorative justice* (BARJ) clauses in their laws. These states aim to balance three concerns: public safety, accountability to victims and the community, and the needs of juvenile offenders as they seek to become productive and law-abiding citizens. Another nine states derive their purposes from the Standard Juvenile Court Act, which dates back to 1959. These states emphasize providing juvenile offenders with "care, guidance, and control" in order to satisfy both the best interests of the child and the best interests of the community. Six additional states use a configuration dating from the 1960s that puts special emphasis on rehabilitation. These clauses identify several purposes of the juvenile court, including providing juveniles with care, supervision, and protection rather than punishment, and ensuring that all parties are free to exercise their legal rights. Finally, at least six states have "get tough" statutes that emphasize accountability and punishment, and three states have statutes that frame the purpose of their juvenile justice systems exclusively in terms of the best interests of the child (Griffin, 2008a).

In most states (38 plus the District of Columbia), the juvenile court has jurisdiction over youth younger than age 18. In 10 states (Georgia, Illinois, Louisiana, Massachusetts, Michigan, Missouri, New Hampshire, South Carolina, Texas, and Wisconsin), it has jurisdiction over youth younger than 17, and in three states (Connecticut, New York, and North Carolina), it has jurisdiction over youth younger than 16. The majority of states do not specify the youngest age at which children are subject to the court's jurisdiction. Of those that do, however, the most common minimum age is 10. A few states include even younger children in their juvenile courts: The minimum age is 8 in Arizona; 7 in Maryland, Massachusetts, and New York; and 6 in North Carolina (Snyder & Sickmund, 2006).

Not all youth who fall within the designated age range are actually tried and sentenced in the juvenile court. Every state requires or allows certain juveniles to be prosecuted as adults. Usually, the juvenile court judge makes the decision; however, in a few states, prosecutors decide whether to file the case in adult court or in juvenile court. In 29 states, neither the judge nor the prosecutor has total discretion; the law explicitly requires that certain types of cases be tried in criminal, rather than juvenile, court. Where discretion does exist, a hearing is required before a juvenile can be waived to adult court. State laws identify criteria that must be met and factors that the judge must consider in determining whether this transfer from juvenile to adult court should take place. In Virginia, for example, these factors include (Virginia Code Sec. 16.1-269.1):

- The juvenile's age
- The seriousness and number of alleged offenses
- Whether the juvenile can be retained in the juvenile justice system long enough for effective treatment and rehabilitation
- The appropriateness and availability of the services and dispositional alternatives in both the criminal justice and juvenile justice systems for dealing with the juvenile's problems
- The record and previous history of the juvenile
- Whether the juvenile has previously absconded from the legal custody of a juvenile correctional entity
- The extent, if any, of the juvenile's degree of mental retardation or mental illness
- The juvenile's school record and education
- The juvenile's mental and emotional maturity
- The juvenile's physical condition and physical maturity

Generally, these *discretionary waiver* hearings require proof by a preponderance of the evidence that the youth is not "amenable to treatment" (based on a consideration of the factors enumerated) and therefore should not be processed through the juvenile court, but rather should be prosecuted as an adult "in the interests of justice" (NASW, 2010, p. 7). In at least six states, the higher burden of "clear and convincing evidence" applies (Griffin, Torbet, & Szymanski, 1998).

In some states, instead of being entirely discretionary, there is a presumption that certain juveniles should be waived to criminal court. In these *presumptive waiver* cases, the court begins by assuming that the juvenile should be treated as an adult, and the juvenile must convince the court otherwise. Often, this presumption depends on the seriousness of the crime. In Alaska, for example, youth charged with certain violent felonies face a presumption in favor of waiver regardless of their age. In other states, the youth's age triggers the presumption; in New Hampshire, for example, a 15-year-old would presumptively be waived to adult court, whereas a 13-year-old who committed the identical offense would be treated as a juvenile. In some states, the presumption hinges on whether the juvenile has a prior history of offending (Griffin, Addie, Adams, & Firestine, 2011).

Finally, approximately 15 states have *mandatory waiver* (or *automatic transfer*) laws that require certain juveniles to be treated as adults, period. Typically, these juveniles meet some combination of criteria based on their age and the seriousness of the crime (Griffin, et al., 2011). In Illinois, for example, youth age 15 or older are automatically treated as adults under the law if they are charged with first-degree murder, aggravated criminal sexual assault, armed robbery with a firearm, aggravated vehicular hijacking committed with a firearm, aggravated battery with a firearm, or unlawful use of a weapon on school grounds (Bostwick, 2010). There is no opportunity for the judge, the prosecutor, or the juvenile to argue that the case should be heard in juvenile court because the law specifically excludes these youth from the state's definition of "delinquent minor" for purposes of juvenile court jurisdiction.

State laws may combine these various provisions by identifying which cases fall within the juvenile court and which cases are subject to discretionary waiver, to presumptive waiver, or to mandatory waiver. As more and more cases involving younger and younger juveniles are transferred to criminal court, the issue of trying and punishing juveniles as adults has become increasingly controversial. A special section later in the chapter highlights this controversy in light of both recent research and social work values.

Incidence and Trends

Although juvenile justice policies and operations vary from state to state, certain national data are collected annually. These data typically reflect the number of arrests made by law enforcement and the number of cases that are handled by the juvenile court. The statistics are largely organized around types of crimes; the most common categories are property crimes, drug crimes, crimes against persons, and crimes disrupting public order (Sickmund, 2003). Sometimes data are reported using the Juvenile Violent Crime Index (which includes the four crimes of murder/nonnegligent manslaughter, forcible rape, robbery, and aggravated assault), and the Juvenile Property Crime Index (which includes the four crimes of burglary, larceny/theft, motor vehicle theft, and arson). Many of the existing measures include Hispanics under "White," complicating efforts to analyze the data by race and ethnicity.

According to the Office of Juvenile Justice and Delinquency Prevention, in 2008, there were 2.11 million arrests of youth younger than age 18. Juveniles accounted for 16% of all arrests for violent crimes and 26% of all arrests for property crimes. Females accounted for 30% of all juvenile arrests, including 17% of those for violent crimes, 36% of those for property crimes, and 44% of those for larceny and theft. Youth younger than age 15 were responsible for more than one-fourth of both juvenile violent crimes (27%) and juvenile property crimes (29%). As we have seen in relation to other phenomena, young people of color are disproportionately charged. For example, although Black youth comprise only 16% of those ages 10–17, in 2008 they were implicated in 52% of juvenile violent crime arrests and 33% of juvenile property crime arrests (Puzzanchera, 2009).

The current juvenile crime rate is relatively low, especially compared to the rate in the 1990s. Between 1989 and 1998, the number of juvenile court cases increased by 44%, with arrests for many crimes peaking in the early part of the decade. Caseloads increased for juveniles of all ages, with 65% of juvenile crimes being committed by youth age 15–17 and 10% being committed by children younger than age 12. The case rate also increased during this time period for both boys and girls, with an 83% increase in female cases and a 35% increase in male cases. Not surprisingly, African American youth were disproportionately represented in the juvenile justice system: They had contact with the system at twice the rate of White youth and, if convicted of delinquency, were more likely to be held in a juvenile facility (Sickmund, 2003). The spike in juvenile crime during the late 1980s and 1990s contributed significantly to the get tough attitudes that have taken hold of the juvenile justice system since then (Kurlychek & Johnson, 2004). This trend is discussed more fully later.

Following the late 1990s, striking reductions were seen in the occurrence of both violent crimes and property crimes. Juvenile arrests declined by a total of 33% between 1997 and 2008. In 2009, the rate of violent juvenile crime hovered around 12%, approximately half of what it was two decades earlier (Puzzanchera & Adams, 2011). In 2008, the juvenile arrest rate for murder was 74% lower than at its peak in 1993; arrests for rape were at their lowest since 1980; arrests for aggravated assault, which had doubled between 1980 and 1994, were at their lowest in 20 years; and arrests for robbery were 46% lower than at their peak in 1995. Similarly, the arrest rate for property crimes in 2008 was 49% lower than at its peak in 1991. Although arrests declined for both male and female juveniles between 1999 and 2008, the declines for males were more pronounced. Both boys and girls had fewer arrests for aggravated assault, burglary, motor vehicle theft, weapons violations, and drug/alcohol violations, but more arrests for robbery. Arrests for simple assault, larceny/theft, vandalism, driving under the influence, and disorderly conduct decreased for boys but increased for girls (Puzzanchera, 2009).

History and Philosophy of the Juvenile Justice System

Today's juvenile court system is the product of a unique philosophy about the distinctive nature of childhood and adolescence, tempered by increasing concerns for public safety. What follows is a summary of the milestones that have characterized and shaped the development of the juvenile court.

The Early History of the Juvenile Court

Until the early 19th century, the American legal system treated youth who broke the law in much the same way it treated adults. Under common law, children as young as age 7 could be tried and sentenced in criminal court (Bilchik, 1999). As new ideas about childhood and adolescence found their way onto the world stage (beginning in the 16th century in Europe and the 19th century in the United States), the appropriateness of the criminal justice system for youthful offenders came under scrutiny. At the same time, urbanization, immigration, and industrialization created a slew of new social problems that were regarded by reformers as contributors to juvenile crime.

As part of the larger Progressive movement, the first juvenile court was established in Cook County, Illinois, in 1899. Like other reforms of the time, including the first child labor laws and the establishment of public education, the juvenile reform movement was predicated on the recognition that childhood and adolescence are distinct phases of human development and that children are deserving of protection. Juvenile crime was increasingly viewed as the result of internal processes and environmental circumstances that were amenable to change; as a result, the approach to juvenile offenders shifted from one of punishment to one of reform. Social workers were integral to the development of the juvenile justice system. Jane Addams, known for her role in the settlement house movement, actively supported the establishment of the juvenile court. Another social worker, Julia Lathrop, pushed for legislative reforms aimed at improving the conditions in juvenile holding facilities. Unfortunately, the initial operationalization of the juvenile court had its downside as well. The system was often used as a tool for social control by upper- and middle-class "child savers" who sought to "Americanize" immigrant children, reinforce parental authority over unruly offspring, intervene in the lives of impoverished families, and separate "good" from "bad" children (Feld, 2003).

Unlike the criminal court, the juvenile court was conceived as a benevolent institution in which the judge would reform wayward children "as a wise and merciful father handles his own child" (Mack, 1909, p. 453). From its initial inception well into the 20th century, it was guided by four primary objectives:

- **Rehabilitative Ideal:** The juvenile court was premised on the notion that youth, unlike adults, are still malleable and amenable to change. In place of legal fact finding and punishment, the juvenile justice system was rooted in the investigation, diagnosis, and "cure" of delinquent behavior.
- **Procedural Informality:** The formal, adversarial legal proceedings that characterized adult criminal court were regarded as counterproductive. They were replaced with flexible rules under which the judge could do what was necessary to set the youth on the proper path.
- **Individualization:** The judge was afforded tremendous discretion in determining each child's need for treatment. Each youth's background and circumstances were considered in determining the appropriate consequence for the offending behavior.
- **Separation of Juvenile and Adult Offenders:** In recognizing that juveniles are fundamentally different from adults and that they need protection and care, the notion of a separate juvenile court included trying, sanctioning, and housing juveniles separately from adults.

Consistent with these underpinnings, juvenile proceedings were shielded from the public, records were sealed, and names were withheld in order to minimize the stigma of youthful indiscretions and facilitate a fresh start as adults. The language used in the juvenile court system reflected its effort to distinguish itself from its adult counterpart. Juveniles are *held in custody* rather than arrested, police file a *petition* rather than filing charges, a *hearing* is held rather than a trial, and a *disposition* is entered rather than a sentence. Although many of these features remain, the system itself has undergone enormous changes since its earliest formulation.

Constitutional Rights for Juveniles

Because the juvenile court had jurisdiction not just over juvenile crime but also over abuse, neglect, and noncriminal offenses, the proceedings were considered "civil" rather than "criminal," and the legal protections afforded adults were dismissed as unnecessary. All of this changed drastically in 1967 with the Supreme Court case of *In re Gault. Gault* forced a recognition that the reality of the juvenile court had fallen woefully short of its promise. Instead of leading to rehabilitation as contemplated, juvenile proceedings (marked, as they were, by judicial discretion and the absence of legal safeguards) often resulted in blatantly unfair consequences for youth.

Fifteen-year-old Gerald Gault was a prime example. He was adjudicated delinquent after making prank telephone calls ("of the irritatingly offensive, adolescent, sex variety") to a neighbor while on probation for a previous offense (being in the company of a boy who stole a wallet from a woman's purse). Gerald was arrested on the basis of the neighbor's verbal complaint without any notice to his parents, was taken into custody, and was released several days later without any explanation as to why he had been detained or why he had been released. Following a hearing at which the neighbor failed to appear, for which no written transcript was produced, and from which no appeal was permitted, Gerald was sentenced to the state industrial school (basically a juvenile detention center) until age 21—a total of 6 years. Had an adult committed the identical offense (using vulgar, abusive, or obscene language in the presence of a woman or child), the penalty would have been a fine of between $5 and $50 or imprisonment for a maximum of 2 months. Gerald brought suit under the 14th Amendment, claiming that he had been deprived of his liberty without due process of law. After cataloging the shortcomings of the juvenile court system, Supreme Court Justice Abe Fortas observed that under the then-current system, children were receiving the worst of both worlds: They were neither getting the legal protections afforded adults nor were they getting the rehabilitation the juvenile court movement had promised. In making its decision, the Supreme Court kept intact the principle of processing and treating juveniles separately from adults and retained the "civil" nature of the proceedings, but it concluded that the Constitution requires numerous legal safeguards for delinquency proceedings to be fair. Those safeguards, which apply during the adjudication phase (when guilt or innocence is determined), include the following:

- Timely notice of the specific charges
- Right to the assistance of counsel
- Right to confront and cross-examine witnesses
- Right against self-incrimination

Subsequent decisions resulted in additional rights for juveniles. For example, the Court in *In re Winship* (1970) concluded that a finding of delinquency requires proof beyond a reasonable doubt; this is the highest standard of proof, previously reserved for adult criminal convictions. The Supreme Court argued that although juvenile proceedings are civil in nature, the risk to liberty is too great to depend on a mere preponderance of the evidence. A few years later, in *Breed v. Jones* (1975), the Court ruled that the prohibition against double jeopardy applies to juveniles as well as adults; a youth cannot be adjudicated delinquent and then transferred and tried in adult court for the same offense. Meanwhile, community-based programs, diversion, and deinstitutionalization policies for juveniles flourished—reflecting the new attention to juveniles' rights. Lawsuits challenged conditions in juvenile institutions. Congress passed the Juvenile Justice and Delinquency Prevention Act of 1974. Although some differences between juveniles and adults remain (juveniles have no right to a transcript or to an appeal, as well as no right to a jury trial), *Gault* and the cases that followed have narrowed the differences between juvenile court and criminal court proceedings. With each set of rights conferred, the juvenile court process began to look more and more like the traditional criminal court. On the one hand, advocates applauded the legal protections for juvenile offenders; on the other, they expressed concern that the heart of the juvenile justice system (rehabilitation and individualization) might be lost. These concerns were validated by several additional decisions in which the Supreme Court permitted the press to disclose the identities of youthful offenders (*Oklahoma Publishing Company v. Oklahoma City*, 1977; *Smith v. Daily Mail Publishing Company*, 1979) and upheld the constitutionality of keeping youth in preventive detention while awaiting trial (*Schall v. Martin*, 1984).

The Modern Era: Getting Tough

The trend toward narrowing the differences between the juvenile and criminal court systems got a boost in the late 1980s and 1990s as the public reacted to reports of dramatically increased juvenile crime (Kurlychek & Johnson, 2004). Public outrage, captured by the mantra "If you're old enough to do the crime, you're old enough to do the time," led to sweeping reform of juvenile justice policies. Between 1992 and 1997, nearly every state amended its laws to allow juveniles to be tried and sentenced as adults. A total of 45 states made it easier to transfer juveniles to the criminal justice system; 31 states gave juvenile and criminal courts expanded sentencing options; 47 states modified or removed confidentiality protections for juvenile records and proceedings; and 22 states increased the role of victims in the juvenile justice process (Snyder & Sickmund, 2006). This trend has continued, with children at younger and younger ages being tried as adults for less and less serious crimes. As a result, approximately 250,000 juveniles are prosecuted, sentenced, or incarcerated as adults each year (Campaign for Youth Justice, 2011). As one observer notes, the juvenile justice system has transformed from one resembling a social service agency to a scaled-down version of the criminal justice system (Feld, 2003).

Although as social workers we applaud the increased vigilance in protecting juveniles' rights that was introduced by the *Gault* case and its progeny, the same cannot be said for the harsh treatment of young offenders that has dominated the past several decades. According to its policy statement on juvenile justice and delinquency prevention, "NASW recommends that the processing and treatment of children and youths who enter the juvenile justice system be differentiated from the treatment of adults through every phase of contact, including prevention, early intervention, formal diversion, detention, probation, residential care, incarceration, and post-release care" (NASW, 2009, p. 210). On the bright side, there is reason to believe that the get tough era may be undergoing a reversal. Between 2005 and 2010, nearly half the states considered or passed legislation to reduce the number of juveniles in the adult criminal justice system. These efforts have taken a variety of forms. Here are a few examples (Campaign for Youth Justice, 2011):

- In 2010, Virginia passed a law creating a legal presumption that children being tried as adults should await trial in juvenile detention centers rather than in adult jails. In order to overcome the presumption, a judge must find that the child is a safety or security threat.
- In 2007, Connecticut raised the upper age limit for youth under its juvenile court jurisdiction from 16 to 18. As a result, 16- and 17-year-olds are now treated as juveniles rather than automatically being prosecuted as adults.
- In 2010, Utah passed a *reverse waiver* law permitting an adult court judge with jurisdiction over a child to transfer the case back to juvenile court if doing so would be in the child's best interests. A total of 10 states have made changes to their transfer laws.
- In 2005, Washington State eliminated mandatory minimum sentences for juveniles tried as adults.

Underlying many of these changes are recent scientific discoveries in adolescent brain development that have led both courts and legislatures to conclude that juvenile offenders are less blameworthy than once thought and more open to rehabilitation. This approach is epitomized by two U.S. Supreme Court cases: *Roper v. Simmons* (2005), which declared it unconstitutional to apply the death penalty to juveniles, and *Graham v. Florida* (2010), which declared it unconstitutional to sentence juveniles to life in prison without the possibility of parole.

THE ADOLESCENT BRAIN

Recent research on brain development suggests that critical parts of the human brain are still developing during the adolescent years (American Bar Association, 2004) and that the brains of adolescents are fundamentally different from the brains of adults (Righmer, 2005). These scientific findings are critical to our understanding of juvenile crime and the blameworthiness of youthful offenders. They have already begun to influence both legislative and judicial policy.

Of particular interest here is the prefrontal cortex, which is the portion of the brain involved in moral reasoning. Often referred to as the "CEO" of the brain, it governs the ability to plan, inhibit impulses, and consider consequences. This part of the brain undergoes drastic changes during adolescence, beginning its maturation around age 17 and continuing into the 20s. In fact, the prefrontal cortex is the last part of the brain to develop. Research also suggests that dopamine, a neurotransmitter involved in the functions of memory, concentration, and problem solving, is not at its most effective state during adolescence (Coalition for Juvenile Justice, 2006). The more primitive parts of the brain develop first, including the amygdala, which is responsible for emotions and gut reactions. As a result, adolescents often misinterpret emotional cues, have difficulty resisting impulses, and behave irrationally under stress (Rightmer, 2005). This leaves adolescents more vulnerable to taking risks and less able to use reasoned judgment.

This brain research has been used to argue that the legal line we draw between juveniles and adults, at age 18, is out of step with biological reality. If the juvenile brain is not yet fully developed, then we cannot consider juveniles to be as blameworthy as adults when they engage in unacceptable or dangerous behavior. This argument was a significant part of the rationale in *Roper v. Simmons*, in which the U.S. Supreme Court found it unconstitutional to impose the death penalty on juveniles. Many states are embracing this new understanding of brain development as they consider trying fewer juvenile offenders as adults. Some advocates argue that juveniles should have a "presumption of diminished capacity" (Aronson, 2009); others argue that juvenile court jurisdiction should continue to age 22 (Rightmer, 2005).

Although the research surrounding brain development seems to provide a powerful reason to view juvenile offenders as less blameworthy than adults, some in the scientific community are uncertain as to what role these findings should actually play in the juvenile justice debate. They caution that this research is still in its early stages and should not be used to inform major policy decisions until it is more fully tested and better understood (Aronson, 2009).

Juvenile Court Proceedings

As with any legal process, involvement in the juvenile justice system includes a number of distinct steps and decision points. Social workers may be involved at numerous stages and in numerous capacities.

The vast majority of youth (approximately 83%) enter the juvenile justice system as a result of an encounter with law enforcement (Puzzanchera, Adams, & Sickmund, 2010). Social service agencies, victims, probation officers, schools, and parents can also refer youth. Many youth never reach the juvenile justice system because they are screened out, either on the street or at the police station. These youth may be counseled and released to their parents or diverted to various community programs. Other youth, however, are processed through the juvenile or criminal courts. In 2008, 22% of juveniles were released after their initial arrest, 66% were processed through the juvenile court, 10% were waived to criminal court, and 2% were referred to a child welfare agency (Puzzanchera, 2009).

Although there are variations among state processes, Figure 11.1 depicts a fairly typical process. If formal charges are filed, a *detention hearing* takes place to determine where the youth will remain until the case goes to court. Most juveniles are released to their parents; however, they may be placed in pretrial detention if they are deemed likely to commit another offense, have a history of running away, or pose a serious threat of

FIGURE 11.1   Juvenile Justice System Flowchart

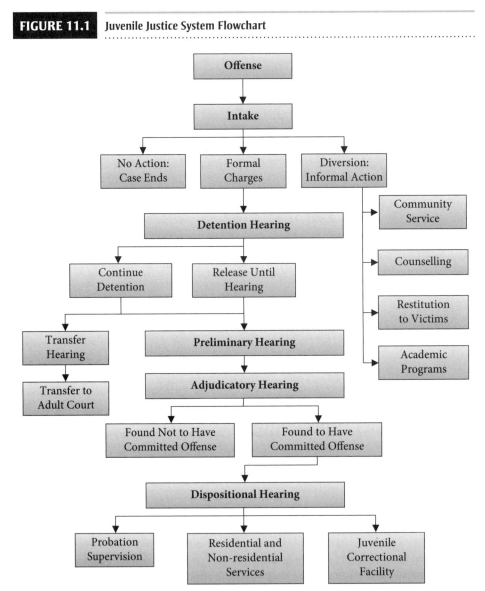

Source: Juvenile Justice System Flowchart. Reprinted with permission of the Center on Juvenile and Criminal Justice.

immediate danger to themselves or others. Boys and older youth are most likely to be detained (Puzzanchera et al., 2010). Next, the case will proceed to either a *transfer hearing* (if the child is eligible to be tried in adult court) or a *preliminary hearing.* At the preliminary hearing, the judge informs the child and his or her parents of the charges and determines whether or not the child has a lawyer so that one can be appointed if necessary. The next step, usually within 60 days, is the *adjudicatory hearing.* This is when the judge hears all of the evidence, the witness statements, and the facts of the case and determines whether or not the youth is guilty of the offense. Between 1985 and 2007, the number of cases in which the juvenile being adjudicated was found to be delinquent increased by 97% (Puzzanchera et al., 2010). Following adjudication, those youth who are not found delinquent are released or referred for services or treatment. Those who are found to be delinquent are scheduled for a *disposition hearing,* at which sentencing occurs. Disposition options include commitment to a juvenile correctional facility, placement in a residential facility, outpatient services, or supervised probation. Probation remains the most common sanction imposed by juvenile courts, comprising 56% of all dispositions (Puzzanchera et al., 2010). In making a disposition determination, judges rely heavily on both the social study and the probation officer's recommendation. A *social study* describes the youth's family background, past and present behavior, health and mental health history, and social and emotional needs. This information assists the judge in making the most appropriate decision for the individual child.

Social workers most often become involved in delinquency cases as probation officers or as treatment professionals. They work for courts, residential facilities, juvenile detention facilities, and agencies that provide mental health or social services to court-involved youth and their families. Social workers also work with families who request court intervention to help manage their children's behavior. All states allow for the filing of what are variously called *CHINS* (Child in Need of Services) or *PINS* (Person in Need of Supervision) petitions. When a child repeatedly runs away, constantly disobeys, regularly misses school, or refuses to follow school rules, the court can place the child in an alternative living arrangement, require that the child meet specific rules or conditions, or maintain court supervision. This action follows a hearing before a judge. Every state has guidelines regarding how long a CHINS petition can remain in effect; once a petition is entered, however, only the court can dismiss it.

Waiving Constitutional Rights

Earlier in the chapter, we discussed the legal rights that children are entitled to in juvenile court proceedings. A body of law has emerged surrounding the competency of juveniles to waive these legal rights. This might include the right to have an attorney present, the right to withhold consent to a search, or the right to remain silent. Whatever right is at issue, a waiver is legally valid only if it is made *knowingly, intelligently, and voluntarily.* The question at issue is whether and how a child's age is relevant to this requirement.

One type of case concerns the provision of *Miranda* warnings; these are the warnings (ubiquitous on television procedural dramas) that inform suspects of their legal rights. Under the law, *Miranda* warnings are required when a suspect is *in custody.* The legal test for determining whether someone is in custody is whether, considering the circumstances surrounding the interrogation, a reasonable person would feel at liberty to leave.

In the 2004 U.S. Supreme Court case *Yarborough v. Alvarado*, a 17-year-old youth and an accomplice were convicted of first-degree murder and attempted robbery. The youth's lawyer sought to suppress his confession because he had not been read his *Miranda* rights. Whether *Miranda* was required depends on whether or not the youth was in custody when he was questioned. The U.S. Supreme Court's role was to decide whether the lower court had reasonably applied the law when it found that *Miranda* warnings were unnecessary because the youth was not in custody.

A few facts: After suspecting Alvarado of participating in the crime, the police instructed his parents to bring him to the station. They put him in a small room with a single detective who questioned him for 2 hours while his parents waited in the lobby. The detective told him that he was a suspect and repeatedly urged him to tell the truth about what had happened, focusing on the need to bring his accomplice to justice. Although the detective never told him that he was free to leave, she did offer him the opportunity to take a break, which he declined. Eventually, Alvarado admitted to his role in the crime. The pivotal legal question was whether Alvarado's age and inexperience should have been considered in determining whether a reasonable person in his position would have felt free to get up and leave. A five-member majority of the Supreme Court concluded that this determination should be made based on objective factors, not subjective factors such as age and experience. Four members of the Court disagreed, arguing that no one would have felt free to leave under these circumstances, let alone a 17-year-old; they considered age to be an important consideration.

This question again came before the U.S. Supreme Court in 2010. This time the majority of the Court went the other way. In *J.D.B. v. North Carolina*, a 13-year-old student was removed from his seventh grade classroom by a uniformed police officer; he was escorted to a closed-door conference room where two police officers and two school administrators questioned him for 30–45 minutes. His grandmother, who was his legal guardian, was never contacted; he was never read his *Miranda* rights; and he was never told that he was free to leave the room. After being pressed by the investigator, urged to tell the truth, and threatened with juvenile detention, J.D.B. confessed to being involved in two home break-ins. His public defender subsequently challenged the admissibility of the confession on the grounds that J.D.B. had not been read his rights. The trial court ruled against him, concluding that J.D.B. had not been in custody and his statements were voluntary. The court of appeals and the state supreme court affirmed. The U.S. Supreme Court, however, reversed. Justice Sonia Sotomayor, writing for the Court's 5-member majority, concluded that a child's age must be considered in determining whether or not *Miranda* warnings are required. She argued that a reasonable child may feel pressured to submit to questioning by police when a reasonable adult in the same situation would realize that he or she was free to go.

Although these cases turn on the necessity of delivering *Miranda* warnings, they raise another question as well. How effective are these *Miranda* warnings for juveniles, even when they are given? Research suggests that most juveniles agree to waive their rights, but a significant number do not fully understand those rights or the consequences of waiving them. In one interesting study, Grisso (1980) empirically tested juveniles' understanding of the *Miranda* warnings. After the rights were read, the subjects were asked to paraphrase them, define some of the key words, indicate whether a rewording of each warning was correct, and demonstrate their understanding of the function and significance of the rights conveyed by the warnings. The study found that juveniles younger than age 15 were unable to understand their rights and the implications of waiving them. These findings are consistent with other empirical studies that have found that understanding varies with age (Feld, 2006; Goldstein, Condie, Kalbeitzer, Osman, & Geier, 2003). In one study, 96% of 14-year-olds were unable to fully understand their rights or what it meant to waive them (Ferguson & Douglas, 1970).

Child advocates and attorneys have found this issue to be of great concern. A number of remedies have been suggested, including developing a simplified *Miranda* warning for juveniles, requiring that a juvenile's level of comprehension be assessed before an interrogation begins, requiring that a parent or other adult be present during interrogation, and requiring that an attorney be present during interrogation. Requiring that a parent be present may not solve the problem; they often encourage their children to tell the truth even when it is against the child's legal self-interest. The American Bar Association favors the last option, arguing that every juvenile should have an absolute, non-waivable right to counsel when interrogated.

The question of a juvenile's competence to waive his or her legal rights has also been raised in the context of consent. *In re J.M.* (1992) involved a 14-year-old who was traveling on a bus from New York City to Washington, D.C. A police officer boarded the bus to check for drugs and weapons. He asked J.M. if he could search his bag. The boy consented but nothing was found. He then asked J.M. if he would mind if he patted him down; J.M. stayed in his seat but raised his arms. The officer patted him down and found a plastic bag containing crack cocaine. The question before the court was whether this search and seizure were constitutional under the Fourth Amendment. That, in turn, depends on whether J.M.'s consent was voluntary. The majority on the D.C. Court of Appeals concluded that age and immaturity might well affect the ability of a child to legally consent and must be considered in determining whether the search was voluntary. The court clarified that age does not automatically render consent invalid, nor is there a presumption that a juvenile's consent is involuntary. Rather, the court must make explicit findings regarding the effects of age and immaturity on the voluntariness of consent in each individual case.

TRYING JUVENILES AS ADULTS

Beginning in the 1990s, public opinion shifted noticeably in the direction of trying juvenile offenders in criminal courts rather than juvenile courts, particularly if they had committed violent crimes (Witt, 2003). This movement was fueled by a dramatic increase in juvenile crime and reflected the widely held sentiment that if children can commit adult crimes, then they should face adult punishments (Kurlychek & Johnson, 2004).

Many states began enacting changes aimed at making it easier to transfer juvenile offenders to the adult criminal court system. These changes included lowering the legal age for allowable transfers, expanding the crimes eligible for transfer, allowing prosecutors greater discretion in transfer decisions, and eliminating some of the factors that judges were required to consider before allowing a transfer to occur (Redding, 2003). Lost in the race to treat juvenile offenders more severely was an understanding of the dynamics behind the surge in juvenile crime. For example, research shows that more than 83% of serious crimes were committed by only 5% of juveniles (Institute for Youth Development, 1998)—and that more than 90% of juveniles arrested for violent crimes were no longer dangerous by the time they were young adults.

Research on the success of these get tough measures has also been unconvincing. There is no evidence, for example, that the threat of transfer to adult court deters youth from committing crimes or lowers offending rates (Redding, 2003). In fact, youth transferred to the adult criminal justice system are more likely to re-offend, re-offend sooner, and commit more violent crimes than those retained in the juvenile justice system (Centers for Disease Control and Prevention, 2007).

Juveniles tried in criminal court receive harsher sentences than their counterparts in juvenile court; they also receive harsher sentences than non-juveniles (young adults) who are tried in criminal court. One study found that juveniles tried in adult court received sentences averaging 18 months, whereas non-juveniles charged in the same courts received sentences averaging only 6 months. Some believe that judges view the transfer of a juvenile into the adult court system as an aggravating factor, leading them to issue particularly severe sentences (Kurlychek & Johnson, 2004). In addition to receiving harsher sentences, the outcomes for juveniles facing adult punishments can be tragic. Juveniles held in adult prisons and jails are eight times more likely than their peers in juvenile facilities to commit suicide, five times more likely to be sexually assaulted, and twice as likely to be attacked with a weapon or beaten by staff (Redding, 2003).

The ongoing quandary of how to protect the public from serious crime while protecting youthful offenders remains the subject of great debate. In a book entitled *Rethinking Juvenile Justice* (Scott & Steinberg, 2008), the authors propose what they call a developmental model of juvenile justice policy. The model recommends the following reforms: (1) Offenders younger than age 10 should be diverted from the juvenile justice system entirely; (2) offenders age 10–15 should be handled within the juvenile justice system, regardless of the offense; (3) violent recidivists older than age 15 should be eligible for transfer to adult court, based on a case-by-case assessment; and (4) all offenders between the ages of 15 and 25 who are not violent recidivists should be sentenced as juveniles. This model is meant to reflect our current understanding of adolescent development, including the recent research on the adolescent brain discussed earlier. Along with other recommended changes to the current system, it should be used as a catalyst for discussion and innovation.

As social workers, we believe in the possibility of change. Children, regardless of the crimes they commit, should be treated fairly, afforded safe conditions and appropriate services, and provided with the opportunity to have meaningful futures. Although we also have a responsibility to the larger society, we should keep in mind the conclusion of the Centers for Disease Control and Prevention (2007, p. 10) that the "use of transfer laws and strengthened transfer policies is counterproductive to reducing juvenile violence and enhancing public safety."

Social Workers and the Juvenile Justice System

Social workers have many opportunities to become involved with the juvenile justice system. Social work, for example, is good preparation for those considering careers as probation officers or correctional treatment specialists. According to the Bureau of Labor Statistics (2009), job growth for these positions is expected to be greater than the average between now and 2018, and job prospects are projected to be excellent. State or local governments, courts, and prisons employ these professionals. The work may involve developing treatment plans for youth on probation, monitoring their behavior, evaluating their progress, providing individual and family therapy, providing substance abuse treatment, and teaching coping skills and anger management. It also involves frequent contact with the court, including drafting presentencing reports (social studies), making sentencing recommendations, and testifying as a fact witness.

Many social workers are involved in efforts to prevent delinquent behavior through their role as school social workers or through community agencies that offer mentoring, home visiting, parenting education, bullying prevention, or after-school activities. Others work with court-involved youth through community-based organizations offering community service or restitution; facilitating victim-offender counseling; or conducting trainings in victim empathy, conflict resolution, or anger management. Many youth who have problems with the law also face substance abuse and/or mental health challenges. According to Cocozza and Skowyra (2000), one in every five youth in the juvenile justice system has serious mental health problems, often with a co-occurring substance abuse disorder. Social workers are often involved in the treatment of these youth, either in outpatient settings or residential facilities.

As advocates, we have an obligation to ensure that juveniles' rights are safeguarded and to press for laws that respect their ability to overcome adversity and become responsible adults. Social workers can also engage in research to develop "screening, assessment, treatment and aftercare protocols to help ensure that the vision of the first juvenile court is honored" (NASW, 2010, p. 4). Most important, we should be leaders in the effort to reform the juvenile justice system so that it reflects social work values and promotes social justice.

Summary and Conclusion

Social workers have a long history of involvement with juvenile justice. Important reforms introduced at the turn of the 20th century reflected the recognition that children are profoundly different from adults. This thinking was epitomized by the first juvenile court, which embodied several important principles: rehabilitation, procedural informality, individualization, and separation of juveniles from adult offenders. Another wave of reforms in the 1960s and 1970s focused on equipping juveniles with many of the same legal rights enjoyed by adults. This led to a narrowing of the differences between the juvenile justice system and the adult criminal justice system. Growing juvenile crime rates in the 1990s led many states to enact get tough policies that allowed increasing numbers of juveniles to be tried and sentenced as adults. Since 2005, a number of states have begun to reverse those policies, in keeping with recent U.S. Supreme Court decisions. Questions remain about the competency of juveniles to waive their legal rights. Social workers have an important role to play in the prevention of delinquency, the treatment of juvenile offenders, advocacy, research, and protecting juveniles' legal rights.

Sample Case

This New Jersey case provides another example of the issues surrounding the competency of children to waive their right against self-incrimination. Be sure to consider the questions that follow.

STATE IN INTEREST OF S.H.
293 A.2d 181 (1972)

Proctor, J.

A juvenile delinquency complaint in the Mercer County Juvenile and Domestic Relations Court charged that the appellant, S.H., age 10, caused the drowning of B.R., age 6, by pushing him into a canal.... On March 17, 1970, three boys, E.J., age 7, W.W., age 8, and B.R. were returning to school in Trenton after lunch. A short distance from the school S.H. approached the boys, accused them of beating up his sister, and asked for some money. The boys denied beating up his sister and refused to give him any money. S.H. then punched W.W. in the face and took B.R. by the coat into an adjacent alley. The two other boys continued to school. B.R. did not return to school or to his home that evening.

The following day, March 18, the Trenton Police Department began a missing person's investigation of B.R. That morning Sergeant John Girman, along with two patrolmen, went to the school S.H. attended. At 11:00 A.M. in the presence of the vice-principal they spoke to S.H. He was not a suspect at this time, as the police did not know whether or not B.R. was the victim of foul play. S.H. was being questioned because the police had information that he was one of the last persons to see B.R. S.H. told the police that he had seen B.R. on Brunswick Avenue with W.W. and E.J. He said they were approached by a boy named Leroy who hit one or both of the older boys and took B.R. away with him. S.H. said he then went to school. After the questioning, S.H. returned to class.

That same day, after speaking to W.W. and E.J., the police returned to S.H.'s school at 1:00 P.M. and asked to see the boy again. They questioned him as to the identity of Leroy. After describing Leroy, S.H. suddenly began to cry and said Leroy threw B.R. into the canal. He agreed to show the police the place where Leroy had thrown the boy. Shortly thereafter the police and fire departments along with S.H. went to the canal and he showed them the place where Leroy pushed B.R. into the water. He also told them B.R. floated down the canal, and he pointed out the spot where he last saw him go under. At 3:30 P.M. B.R.'s body was discovered about 300 feet from where S.H. said he saw Leroy push the boy into the water.

After the body was found, S.H. told the police he would take them to Leroy's house. They arrived at the address S.H. gave them about 4:45 P.M., where he identified a certain boy as Leroy. Investigation showed that the boy was not named Leroy, was in school at the time of the episode and was in no way involved.

Thereafter, at about 5:00 P.M., the police took S.H. to the first precinct Trenton Police Station. After discussing the matter with other policemen, Sergeant Girman concluded a homicide had occurred, and S.H. was a prime suspect.

When S.H. arrived at the police station, his father was already there. However, the police told Mr. H. he was not needed at that time, and he left the station and went home.

Sergeant Girman turned S.H. over to Detective Purdy of the Juvenile Bureau of the Trenton Police Department. The detective took the boy to a room on the second floor usually used to interrogate adults. Alone in the room with S.H., the detective read the boy his *Miranda* rights from a card, explaining what they meant as he went along. According to the detective, he spent about 10 minutes explaining the *Miranda* rights. . .

The entire interrogation lasted about 90 minutes.

About 6:30 P.M., after the interrogation was completed, the police picked Mr. H. up at his house and brought him to the station house. He was taken to a second floor room where he found four policemen. S.H. was brought in by Detective Purdy from the adjoining room where the questioning had taken place. The detective then asked S.H. to tell his father what he had told him during the interrogation. The boy complied.

At the hearing the State called Mr. H. and asked him what S.H. had told him in the presence of the police. Defense counsel objected to the State's use of the father to testify against his son. The objection was sustained. The State then put Detective Purdy back on the stand to relate what S.H. told his father. Purdy told the court that S.H. said, "I walked the boy down by the railroad crossing. And we got by the creek (canal) and, I mean by the water, and I pushed him in." . . . This testimony was admitted over defense counsel's objection.

The State rested, and after motions of defense counsel were heard and denied the defense rested without calling any witnesses.

On this appeal appellant contends his confession was the product of police coercion, and therefore its admission into evidence violated the due process clause of the Fourteenth Amendment. In a juvenile case where a serious offense is charged, before the confession of an accused can be received in evidence against him the State has the burden of establishing that the accused's will was not overborne and that the confession was the product of a free choice. We are not satisfied the State has borne its burden of proving that this confession was voluntarily made and that the fundamental fairness requirement of due process has been met.

The circumstances under which the station house interrogation was conducted showed a complete disregard for the well-being of the accused juvenile. Placing a young boy in the "frightening atmosphere" of a police station without the presence of his parents or someone to whom the boy can turn for support is likely to have harmful effects on his mind and will. . . . Not only was S.H. interrogated in the police station, but he was isolated in a room with a detective for a period of 90 minutes. The State's proofs account for only 10 minutes of this period, that used to give and explain the *Miranda* warnings. There is nothing in the record to show what occurred during the remaining 80 minutes except Detective Purdy's testimony of what the boy told him about the episode (the same story which he told his father in the presence of the police). More significant is the action of the police in sending the father away from the police station before questioning the boy. We emphasize whenever possible and especially in the case of young children no child should be interviewed except in the presence of his parents or guardian. . . . That the police allowed Mr. H. to be present immediately after the interrogation in order to secure a separate confession in no way detracts from our conclusion. This second confession was merely a reprise of what the boy told Detective Purdy when he was secluded alone with him in the room and at best was nothing more than the tainted product of the coercion which produced the first confession. . . . The conduct of the police in sending Mr. H. home from the police station when he had appeared in the interest of his son without more may be sufficient to show that the confession was involuntary. In light of the other circumstances, however, we need not pursue this point.

In reaching our conclusion as to the voluntariness of the confession, we have taken into consideration that the police gave S.H. the *Miranda* warnings and that he purportedly waived his rights. We think this factor, however, was of little or no significance in the present case. Recitation of the *Miranda* warnings to a boy of 10 even when they are explained is undoubtedly meaningless. Such a boy certainly lacks the capability to fully understand the meaning of his rights. Thus, he cannot make a knowing and intelligent waiver of something he cannot understand. However, questioning may go forward even if it is obvious the boy does not understand his rights if the questioning is conducted with the utmost fairness and in accordance with the highest standards of due process and fundamental fairness. Such was not the case here.

Upon consideration of the totality of the circumstances under which the appellants' confession was obtained, we cannot say it convincingly appears that his confession was voluntarily made. In view of the appellant's age, the oppressive environment of the police station where the questioning was conducted, the lengthy period of interrogation (the nature of which is only partially explained) and the cavalier treatment of the father in sending him home when his boy most needed him, we cannot say the State has met its burden of proving the confession of appellant was obtained by methods consistent with due process. We therefore hold that his confession was improperly admitted in evidence....

The judgment of the trial court is modified in accordance with this opinion.

Questions

1. Note that unlike in the cases discussed earlier in the chapter, S.H. was read his *Miranda* rights. Nonetheless, the court found his confession to be inadmissible. Why?

2. The government had the burden of proof to show that the confession was knowing, intelligent, and voluntary. What evidence to that effect did it produce? Can you think of other ways that the voluntariness of a juvenile confession might be demonstrated?

3. Do you agree with the court's holding in this case? Why or why not?

4. Do you think that the law should ever allow 10-year-olds to waive their rights? What about 13-year-olds? 17-year-olds? If no, why not? If yes, which rights? Under what circumstances?

5. S.H. was ultimately found guilty of manslaughter. The social study submitted during sentencing disclosed that he had an I.Q. "within the mild defective range of intelligence" and that he functioned "severely behind the norm for his chronological age" (*State in Interest of S.H*, 1972). If this information had been revealed earlier, do you think the court would have considered it relevant to a determination of whether S.H.'s confession was admissible? Explain.

CHAPTER 11 PRACTICE TEST

The following questions will test your application and analysis of the content found within this chapter. For additional assessment, including licensing-exam type questions on applying chapter content to practice behaviors, visit **MySearchLab**.

1. One of the striking facts about juvenile crime is that
   a. arrests of girls now exceed those of boys.
   b. the juvenile crime rate continues to escalate.
   c. the majority of property crimes in the United States are committed by juveniles.
   d. youth of color are disproportionately arrested and charged.

2. The landmark Supreme Court case of *In re Gault* afforded youth in the juvenile justice system a number of important legal rights, including the right to a(n)
   a. appeal.
   b. attorney.
   c. jury trial.
   d. transcript of the proceedings.

3. In order for a juvenile to be tried as an adult in states with discretionary waiver policies, the judge must find by at least a preponderance of the evidence that the youth
   a. has previously been tried as an adult.
   b. is a danger to self or others.
   c. is not amenable to treatment.
   d. lacks remorse for his or her actions.

4. Zelda, age 12, is being questioned in connection with a neighborhood burglary. After several grueling hours, she confesses to the crime. Her lawyer objects to the introduction of her confession on the grounds that, because of her age, it was not
   a. clear and convincing.
   b. consistent with the best interests of the child.
   c. knowing, intelligent, and voluntary.
   d. within the hearsay exception.

5. Describe the "rehabilitative ideal" that personified the original juvenile court. What was its underlying philosophy? What were its key characteristics?

6. Discuss how recent research on brain development has impacted our understanding of juvenile culpability. How have the courts responded to these findings?

MYSEARCHLAB CONNECTIONS

Reinforce what you learned in this chapter by studying videos, cases, documents, and more available at **www.MySearchLab.com**.

Watch these Videos

* MS 13: Gang Life
  * *How do you think members of gangs like MS 13 should be treated within the justice system? Should they be tried as juveniles or as adults? Or is there a new and different model that you would recommend?*

Read these Cases/Documents

Δ Travis: A Case of Working with Children in Juvenile Detention
  * *What array of sentencing and treatment options do you think should be available to juvenile offenders?*

Research these Topics

* girls and the juvenile justice system
* treatment of juvenile offenders in other countries

Assess Your Knowledge

Go to **MySearchLab** to test your knowledge of key topics in this chapter with topic-specific quizzes. Conclude your assessment by completing the chapter exam.

---

* = CSWE Core Competency Asset   Δ = Case Study

Chapter **12**

....

Criminal Justice

Familiarity with the criminal justice system is critical for social workers. Many have clients who have been involved with the justice system, whereas others, including forensic specialists, may work in correctional settings. All of us should be committed to remedying the social injustices that permeate our criminal laws and their application, including discrimination against people of color and those in poverty. This chapter discusses crime rates and trends; characteristics of offenders and victims; and issues in law enforcement, trial, and corrections. A special section highlights the controversy surrounding restoration of voting rights for felons, and the sample case addresses the issue of prisoners' rights.

Background

....

The criminal justice system is composed of three major units: law enforcement, the courts, and corrections. *Law enforcement* is responsible for arresting people who break the law; the *court system* is responsible for determining the guilt of those arrested; and the *correctional system* implements and oversees their sentences. All told, the criminal justice system at the federal, state, and local levels has a huge footprint, costing taxpayers billions of dollars each year.

From a legal standpoint, *crime* is defined as any act that is against the law. Legal scholars classify crimes into two categories: *mala in se* and *mala prohibita*. *Mala in se* crimes are those understood by most members of society to be inherently evil; they are banned in almost every society. These include, for example, murder, rape, arson, assault, and robbery.

Mala prohibita crimes are crimes only because our laws have defined them as such; there is nothing inherently evil about them. Examples include drug use, prostitution, and gambling. In some societies, these acts may be legal, whereas in others they constitute crimes (Popple & Leighninger, 2005).

Crime statistics can be very confusing. A number of different government agencies collect crime data, but the sources of their information and their definitions of crimes, victims, and perpetrators can vary. Comprehensive data on the intersection of race and crime are particularly lacking; many agencies report information on only Blacks and Whites, whereas some include Blacks, Whites, Asian Americans, and Native Americans. Hispanics are rarely identified separately; they are generally included in the "White" category, limiting our insight into the experience of Hispanics in the criminal justice system. With these limitations in mind, some basic statistics follow.

In 2008, an estimated 4.9 million violent crimes were committed in the United States; this includes rapes and sexual assaults, robberies, aggravated assaults, and simple assaults. There were also 16.3 million property crimes, including burglaries, motor vehicle thefts, and household thefts, and 137,000 personal thefts, including pickpocketing and purse snatching. These numbers reflect both reported and unreported victimizations ascertained through victim surveys (Rand, 2009). White-collar crimes, which are often ignored in discussions of the criminal justice system, cost taxpayers more than $300 billion per year. These include fraud, insider trading, embezzlement, computer crimes, and identity theft. Table 12.1 identifies the estimated number of actual arrests for various crimes in 2009. Excluding traffic crimes, more than 13.8 million arrests were made, including 581,765 for violent crimes and 1,728,285 for property crimes. Most common were drug- and alcohol-related crimes, with the total number of drug abuse and driving under the influence (DUI) arrests exceeding 3 million.

Males account for nearly three-fourths of all arrests, including 81.2% of arrests for violent crimes and 62.6% of arrests for property crimes. Blacks account for 28.3% and Whites for approximately 61% (FBI, 2010a). Although crimes occur in every jurisdiction in the country, the rates of both violent crime and property crime are highest in the South and lowest in the Northeast, with the Midwest and West falling in between (FBI, 2010b). Violent crime rates are also highest in metropolitan cities and lowest in nonmetropolitan areas, while property crime rates are highest in the surrounding cities outside of metropolitan areas and are lowest in nonmetropolitan counties (FBI, 2010c). Low-income households are particularly likely to experience property crimes. Nationally, both violent crime rates and property crime rates have been declining since 1999. These rates are at their lowest levels since 1973 when such data were first collected. Between 1999 and 2008, overall violent crime fell by 41% and property crime fell by 32% (Rand, 2009). In 2010, crime rates fell particularly sharply; the victimization rate for violent crime dropped 13% (three times the average annual decrease seen in 2001–2009) and the rate for property crimes dropped 5% (twice the average annual decrease seen in 2001–2009) (Truman, 2011).

Victims of crime are most likely to be male, Black, between the ages of 12 and 24, and poor. Women are more likely than men to be victims of rape or sexual assault; however, men experience higher rates of victimization for all other violent crimes. Males represent 77% of homicide victims and nearly 90% of homicide offenders. Native Americans experience victimization at more than five times the rate of Asians, twice the rate of Blacks, and

TABLE 12.1   Estimated Number of Arrests, 2009

Violent Crimes	
Aggravated assault	421,215
Robbery	126,725
Forcible rape	21,407
Murder and nonnegligent homicide	12,418
Property Crimes	
Larceny-theft	1,334,933
Burglary	299,351
Motor vehicle theft	81,797
Arson	12,204
Other (Selected)	
Drug abuse violations	1,663,582
Driving under the influence	1,440,409
Other assaults	1,319,458
Disorderly conduct	655,322
Drunkenness	594,300
Liquor laws	570,333
Vandalism	270,439
Fraud	210,255
Weapons	166,334
Offenses against the family and children	114,564
Curfew and loitering law violations	112,593
Stolen property	105,303
Runaways	93,434
Forgery and counterfeiting	85,844
Sex offenses (except rape and prostitution)	77,326
Prostitution and commercialized vice	71,355
Vagrancy	33,388
Gambling	10,360

Source: FBI (2010). Estimated number of arrests 2009—Crime in the United States. Retrieved from http://www2
.fbi.gov/ucr/cius2009/data/table_29.html

2-1/2 times the rate of Whites. Blacks are six times more likely than Whites to be victims of a homicide and have the highest rate of involvement as both victims and offenders in homicides that are drug related (Fox & Zawitz, 2010).

People commit crimes for a variety of reasons, and numerous theories seek to explain criminal behavior. Property crimes are often committed for material gain and are usually planned in advance. Violent crimes are more often impulsive, stemming from a desire for revenge, power, or control. Criminal behavior has been linked to social factors, including drug and alcohol use, peer influence, the availability of handguns, poverty, and abuse. Violent crime has also been correlated with biological factors, including unusual patterns in brain chemistry (high levels of dopamine and low levels of serotonin) and hormonal activity (high levels of testosterone and low levels of cortisol).

Law Enforcement

The first formal city police department in the United States was formed in Boston in 1838. Today, there are policing agencies at the federal, state, county, and local levels. Federal law enforcement agencies are charged with enforcing specific laws. These agencies include the Federal Bureau of Investigation (FBI); the U.S. Marshalls; the Bureau of Alcohol, Tobacco, Firearms and Explosives (ATF); and Immigration and Customs Enforcement (ICE). State law enforcement agencies enforce traffic laws, conduct highway patrol, and provide emergency medical services. County law enforcement agencies serve the unincorporated areas within a county and assist city police departments. Local police agencies make up the majority of law enforcement. They range in size from the New York City Police Department, which has 40,000 full-time officers and 10,000 civilian employees, to rural police departments, which may have only one part-time officer. City police provide their local communities with traffic enforcement, radio communications, narcotics and vice control, patrol and peacekeeping, crime prevention, fingerprint processing, property and violent crime investigation, accident and death investigation, and search and rescue services. Civilians are often hired into metropolitan police departments to assist with law enforcement activities, bringing the number of employees in local law enforcement up to 580,000 nationwide (Siegel, 2010).

Stop and Frisk

In 1968, the U.S. Supreme Court decided an important case called *Terry v. Ohio*. The case involved a police officer in Cleveland who observed three men on the street who were acting suspiciously. Believing that their behavior was consistent with the planning of a burglary, the officer stopped them and patted down the outside of their coats to see if they were armed. He had no warrant. In its opinion, the Supreme Court upheld the officer's actions, finding that there was no violation of the men's constitutional rights. The Court distinguished this circumstance from a traditional "search and seizure" (discussed later) for which a warrant is required. According to the Court, temporarily detaining someone for the purpose of protecting the officer or public safety is permitted if the officer has a *reasonable suspicion* that the person has committed, is committing, or is about to commit a crime, and a reasonable belief that the person may be armed and dangerous. The goal must be to ensure immediate safety rather than to gather evidence of a crime. Reasonable suspicion requires more than a mere hunch but less than the *probable cause* required in the typical search for evidence. The law pertaining to what is often called *stop and frisk* has been extended to traffic stops as well.

To determine whether a stop is legal, the court examines the *totality of the circumstances* as experienced by both the officer and the suspect. Factors to consider include the stop's duration, location, invasiveness, and whether the suspect feels free to walk away. Courts have found stops to be legally justified based on the following (Stevens, 2003):

- The suspect does not seem to fit the time or place.
- The suspect fits a description of a wanted person on a flyer.
- The suspect is acting strangely, emotional, angry, frightened, or intoxicated.
- The suspect is loitering, hanging out, or looking out for something.
- The suspect is running away or engaging in furtive movements.
- The area is a high-crime area (not sufficient by itself).

Not every stop involves frisking for weapons or drugs. To be justified in conducting a frisk, the officer must believe that the suspect is armed and dangerous. A frisk allows an officer to pat down only the outer clothing; on the basis of that limited contact, the officer must determine whether the suspect is in possession of contraband.

Racial profiling is closely tied to stop and frisk. *Racial profiling* is defined as "the targeting of individuals and groups by law enforcement officials, even partially, on the basis of race, ethnicity, national origin, or religion, except where there is trustworthy information, relevant to the locality and timeframe, that links persons belonging to one of the aforementioned groups to an identified criminal incident or scheme" (Amnesty International USA, 2004, p. v). It is easy to imagine that stereotypes about, or experience with, a particular racial group could inform an officer's reasonable suspicion. The justifications listed here seem to invite such judgments. In fact, stop and frisk policies have led to discriminatory treatment of racial and ethnic minorities in numerous communities, making racial profiling a serious problem.

A study of the New York Police Department (NYPD) in 2006 found that 85% of those stopped were minorities; 55% were Black and 30% were Latino. Of the 508,540 people stopped, only 6% were arrested and only 1.5% were found to be in possession of weapons—suggesting that nearly 9 out of 10 people stopped were innocent of any crime. The study also found that police officers used force in connection with these stops 50% more often with Blacks than with Whites. People of color were also frisked more often than Whites; frisks occurred with 45% of Blacks and Latinos who were stopped, compared to 29% of Whites (Gelman, Fagan, & Kiss, 2007). The disparities in New York's application of its stop and frisk policy were confirmed by an independent research study analyzing stops involving 125,000 pedestrians over a 15-month period (Ridgeway, 2007). A class action lawsuit is pending (Rudolf, 2012).

In Philadelphia, only 8.4% of people subjected to stop and frisk in 2009 were arrested. African Americans, who comprise 44% of the city's population, accounted for 77% of those stopped (American Civil Liberties Union [ACLU], 2010). A settlement agreement was recently reached in a lawsuit filed by the ACLU against the city of Philadelphia. Under the terms of the agreement, the city will collect and electronically post data related to police stop and frisks, institute training to help law enforcement officers meet civil rights requirements, provide closer supervision of stop and frisk actions, and create a racial profiling monitoring system within the police department (ACLU, 2011a).

Nationally, approximately 32 million Americans report having been victims of racial profiling; this is equivalent to nearly the entire population of Canada. Victims include men and women; people in every age group and of every socioeconomic status; and residents of urban, suburban, and rural neighborhoods. Although racial minorities including African Americans and Hispanics continue to experience racial profiling at alarming rates, people appearing to be from the Middle East and immigrants are increasingly experiencing harassment. Those testifying at public hearings organized by Amnesty International USA reported having been targeted by police when walking, driving, at airports, at shopping malls, at home, and while traveling to places of worship (Amnesty International USA, 2004).

Racial profiling has unfortunate consequences. Its victims suffer humiliation, fear, depression, helplessness, and anger. It reduces trust in law enforcement, making people less likely to cooperate in investigations or seek help from police. It divides neighborhoods, reinforces segregation, and reduces domestic security (Amnesty International USA, 2004). Racial profiling practices are a clear violation of several international treaties that the United States has ratified; these include the United Nations Charter, the Universal Declaration of Human Rights, the International Convention on Civil and Political Rights, and the International Convention on the Elimination of All Forms of Racial Discrimination. Legislation banning racial profiling has been introduced in the U.S. Congress, most recently as the End Racial Profiling Act of 2011 (ERPA) sponsored by Sen. Ben Cardin (D-MD) and Rep. John Conyers (D-MI). As of 2004, bills prohibiting racial profiling had also been passed in 23 states. Meanwhile, lawsuits continue to be filed with the hope of curbing discriminatory stop and frisk policies and practices.

Search and Seizure

Law enforcement must maintain a delicate balance between protecting the rights of the innocent and apprehending the guilty. When a crime is committed, various methods are used to gather the evidence needed for a criminal prosecution. Nearly every investigation involves searching for incriminating evidence, seizing that evidence, and introducing it during a criminal trial. The ability of law enforcement to engage in *search and seizure* is regulated by the U.S. Constitution's Fourth Amendment, which reads as follows:

> The right of the people to be secure in their persons, houses, papers, and effects, against unreasonable searches and seizures, shall not be violated, and no warrants shall issue, but upon probable cause, supported by oath or affirmation, and particularly describing the place to be searched, and the persons or things to be seized.

Under the Fourth Amendment, a search must be *reasonable* and, in most circumstances, must be authorized by a warrant. A *search warrant* is a court order issued by a judge or magistrate that authorizes law enforcement officers to conduct a search of specified premises for specified objects. To obtain a warrant, there must be *probable cause*—that is, a reasonable belief, based on fact, that a crime has been committed and that the person, place, or object to be searched and/or seized is linked to the crime with a reasonable degree of certainty (Siegel, 2010).

The requirement for a warrant is triggered when a person other than a private citizen, most often a police officer, seeks to invade a person's privacy in order to conduct a search. Whether the search is permissible depends on whether, according to objective societal standards, the search would violate a *reasonable expectation of privacy*. For example, a warrant would routinely be required before searching a person's private home but would not be required to search a public street, an abandoned lot, or a field—locations that few people would expect to be private.

Once a warrant is issued, it must be executed within the time frame specified. Law enforcement officers are required to *knock and announce* their presence and their purpose before entering the premises, unless doing so is likely to threaten the officers' safety or result in evidence being destroyed; in these cases, a *no-knock* warrant is permitted. Property damage must be kept to a minimum, and only a minimum amount of force may be used. This applies to executing arrest warrants as well as searches. An exception occurs when an officer comes across contraband or evidence not listed in the warrant that is in *plain view*; in this instance, seizure is constitutionally permissible.

The warrant requirement has several exceptions. Warrantless searches are permitted in cases of emergency (*exigent circumstances*), stop and frisk (discussed earlier), search incident to a lawful arrest, automobile searches, searches based on plain view (mentioned earlier), crimes committed in the officer's presence, and consent searches.

A *consent search* occurs when the Fourth Amendment's warrant requirement is waived when a subject voluntarily grants permission for the search to occur. This can be done orally or nonverbally. For example, in *Schneckloth v. Bustamonte* (1973), a suspect who was stopped by police assisted them by opening the trunk and glove compartment of his car; the U.S. Supreme Court concluded that his behavior constituted the required consent. In certain cases, third parties may consent to a search. The general rule is that anyone with common authority or control over the premises or items identified in the warrant has the legal right to consent. For example, if someone other than the subject has his or her name on a lease, has a key, or serves as the landlord of a rented property, that person can consent as long as no one else is there and no one objects. In *Georgia v. Randolph* (2006), however, the U.S. Supreme Court made it clear that one resident cannot grant permission over the objection of another. In that case, a woman called police claiming that her estranged husband had absconded with their child. She invited the police into her home to conduct a search, but the husband arrived and refused consent. The police conducted the search over his objection and found cocaine. The Supreme Court ruled the warrantless search unconstitutional.

Although we usually think of search and seizure as involving a hands-on investigation for concrete property, its definition goes well beyond that. In *Katz v. United States* (1967), the U.S. Supreme Court found the FBI guilty of violating the Fourth Amendment when it attached an eavesdropping device to the outside of a telephone booth. The Court concluded that the suspect had a reasonable expectation of privacy in the phone booth and that the Fourth Amendment applies not only to tangible items but to the recording of oral statements as well. More recently, the Supreme Court considered a different type of surveillance. In *Kyllo v. United States* (2001), police used thermal imaging technology to measure heat emissions from a suspect's home that were consistent with the type of high-intensity lamps used to grow marijuana. The Court concluded that this qualified as a search under the Fourth Amendment and therefore required a warrant. A final example of nontraditional search and seizure is drug testing. In *Ferguson v. City of Charleston* (2001), the U.S. Supreme Court concluded that the Medical University of South Carolina conducted an illegal search and seizure when it tested non-consenting pregnant women for cocaine and used the positive test results as evidence in criminal prosecutions.

Arrest and Interrogation

Of the crimes brought to the attention of police, 20% result in an arrest (Neubauer & Fradella, 2011). To make an arrest, the officer must have probable cause. This standard, like the standard for search and seizure, derives from the Fourth Amendment. Once a person is arrested, he or she is taken into custody by the police. Anyone taken into custody has certain legal rights of which they must be apprised. The requirement that suspects be formally advised of their rights stems from the 1966 case of *Miranda v. Arizona*. Although the exact wording may vary, the following recitation of rights is typical:

> You have the right to remain silent. Anything you say can and will be used against you in a court of law. You have the right to an attorney. If you cannot afford an attorney, one will be provided for you. Do you understand the rights I have just read to you? With these rights in mind, do you wish to speak to me?

Miranda warnings must be given as soon as an individual is taken into custody, before interrogation begins. If that person does not understand the *Miranda* warnings for reasons including a language barrier, intellectual disability, or age, he or she may not be questioned without an attorney. If translation into another language is provided, the provision of *Miranda* warnings is typically recorded. Once a person being interrogated chooses to invoke his or her *Miranda* rights and requests an attorney, no further questioning can proceed until counsel is present. Invoking these rights can occur at any point before or during an interrogation. The person in custody can, of course, choose to waive his or her rights and talk to the police or sign a confession. To be valid, a waiver must be *knowing, voluntary, and intelligent.* The burden is on the government to show that the person was aware of his or her rights and the waiver was voluntary.

Considerable controversy has surrounded the requirement that *Miranda* warnings be given. Although many applaud its role in protecting a suspect's constitutional rights, some critics question its effectiveness and others bemoan the number of cases that are lost because of *Miranda*. The stiffest challenge came in 1999 when the Fourth Circuit Court of Appeals ruled that confessions are valid as long as they are voluntarily given, regardless of whether or not the suspect was *Mirandized.* The U.S. Supreme Court, by a margin of 7–2, reversed that decision and reaffirmed the necessity of giving the *Miranda* warnings (*Dickerson v. U.S.*, 2000). New concerns have since emerged regarding the applicability and advisability of issuing *Miranda* warnings in cases of suspected terrorism.

The Courts

Prosecutors make the decision regarding whether or not to bring a case to trial; this is known as *prosecutorial discretion*. The sufficiency of the evidence collected by law enforcement is an important factor in deciding which cases to pursue. Prosecutors may also consider the seriousness of the case, the potential cost of a trial, the wishes of the victim, the likelihood of success, the level of public outrage or media scrutiny, and whether diversion to treatment or rehabilitation might be more appropriate in the particular case. When the decision to prosecute is believed to be discriminatory, the person who is charged may bring a case claiming *selective prosecution*. Because courts tend to defer to prosecutors' decisions, however, these cases are rarely successful.

In many states, once the presence of probable cause is confirmed at a *preliminary hearing*, the case then goes before a *grand jury*. If the grand jury indicts, the case proceeds to *arraignment*, at which the defendant issues a plea. Between 90% and 95% of cases involve *plea bargains*, whereby the defendant pleads guilty in exchange for a lesser sentence and a trial is avoided altogether. In those cases that do proceed to trial (following a plea of *not guilty*), two out of three defendants are convicted (Neubauer & Fredella, 2011).

The U.S. Supreme Court decided an interesting case in 2010. *Padilla v. Kentucky* concerned a commercial trucker from Honduras. He was a legal permanent resident, had served in the war in Vietnam, and had lived in the United States for more than 40 years. Arrested for transporting marijuana, he pled guilty after his attorney advised him that a conviction would have no effect on his immigration status. In fact, the attorney was wrong; the crime with which he was charged is a deportable offense under federal immigration law. The Court ruled that the defendant had been deprived of his constitutional right to effective assistance of counsel and that, under the Sixth Amendment, attorneys must inform their clients about the collateral consequences of a plea decision.

Rights of the Defendant

Criminal defendants have a number of important legal rights during trial. They include:

- The right to an impartial judge
- The right to an impartial jury
- The right to be tried only if competent
- The right to subpoena and confront witnesses
- The right to counsel
- The right to a speedy and public trial

Several of these issues have been, or will be, discussed in other chapters. Central to this chapter is an understanding of the right to counsel.

Having an attorney has become indispensable to justice in the United States. Despite the myriad laws designed to ensure equity in judicial outcomes, the quality of legal representation continues to make a difference. Through a series of landmark decisions, the U.S. Supreme Court has defined the right of people living in poverty to have access to legal counsel. The first was the 1932 case of *Powell v. Alabama*. Nine illiterate African American youth (who came to be known as the Scottsboro boys) were tried, without counsel, on trumped up charges for the rapes of two White women. Despite the lack of evidence, all were convicted and eight were sentenced to death. The Court ruled that, in the interests of justice, even defendants who cannot afford to hire lawyers are constitutionally entitled to be represented; counsel must be provided for them free of charge. The right to counsel was later expanded beyond death penalty cases to all state criminal cases involving felonies (*Gideon v. Wainwright*, 1963), and then to misdemeanor proceedings involving a potential loss of liberty (*Argersinger v. Hamlin*, 1972). This right to counsel applies throughout the criminal justice process, from initial appearance to appeal.

The right to counsel can be waived, and a defendant can choose to represent him- or herself at trial. This is called proceeding *pro se*. Judges will generally encourage representation by counsel but will allow self-representation if they are satisfied that the choice is being made knowingly, voluntarily, and intelligently—and that the individual is competent to proceed. The judge will often require that the defendant have *stand-by counsel* to serve in a consulting and advisory capacity. The judge can terminate a defendant's right to proceed *pro se* if the defendant disrupts or interferes with the smooth operation of the trial.

The right to have an attorney does not guarantee the quality of representation. Although egregious shortcomings may constitute ineffective assistance of counsel, the only actual requirement is that defense attorneys demonstrate *reasonable competence*. For people living in poverty, the right to counsel is of critical importance. Although people who hire their own attorneys and people represented by appointed counsel are equally likely to be convicted, indigent defendants are incarcerated at significantly higher rates (Rachlin, 2007).

The Exclusionary Rule

In order to discourage law enforcement officers from exceeding the bounds of the law in their zeal to secure evidence, a 1914 case, *Weeks v. United States*, established the exclusionary rule. Simply put, the *exclusionary rule* prohibits evidence that is illegally obtained from being introduced in a criminal trial. The *Weeks* case applied the exclusionary rule only to federal cases; it was extended to state criminal trials in *Mapp v. Ohio* (1961). The law now recognizes three exceptions to the exclusionary rule. A *good faith* exception applies when police seize evidence based on a warrant they believe is valid but which is later found to be defective. The *independent source* exception allows evidence to be introduced in court if a warrant was issued but was not presented at the scene. The *inevitable discovery* exception permits evidence obtained through an unlawful search or seizure if it can be established, to a very high degree of probability, that the evidence would inevitably have been discovered by other means.

The *fruit of the poisonous tree* doctrine is an extension of the exclusionary rule. Under this doctrine, any secondary evidence obtained as a result of the initial Fourth Amendment violation is also inadmissible in court. For example, if police illegally secure a confession and the suspect mentions having a storage shed where physical evidence is subsequently found, the physical evidence would be considered fruit of the poisonous tree; neither the confession nor the evidence would be admissible in court.

Although the exclusionary rule was established to protect criminal defendants from law enforcement abuses and to incentivize police to abide by the law, it remains extremely controversial. Police violations of citizens' rights are a significant problem; one study found that nearly one-third of police searches conducted in a medium-size city were performed unconstitutionally, and the illegal conduct rarely reached the attention of the courts (Gould & Mastrofski, 2004). Proponents of the exclusionary rule argue that it is necessary to curb the overzealous pursuit of evidence and to safeguard the rights of the citizenry; it also is consistent with our country's system of checks and balances between the judicial branch (courts) and the executive branch (police). Critics are concerned that too many cases are thrown out on technicalities, rendering our criminal justice system ineffective and reducing public confidence in the courts. The United States is the only country to apply the exclusionary rule in order to protect persons from illegal searches and seizures.

Corrections

Once a defendant is convicted, a sentencing hearing is held at which the punishment for the crime is determined. Criminal punishment serves four purposes: incapacitation, deterrence, retribution, and rehabilitation. The idea behind *incapacitation* is that an offender is unable to commit any crimes while detained in a secure facility; the public is thus protected when we take an offender off the streets. The idea behind *deterrence* is that seeing other people punished, and knowing that punishment is possible, will dissuade people from committing crimes in the first place. *Retribution* involves "getting even" or "seeing justice done." It satisfies the public's need to know that people who are guilty will not get away with their crimes. Each of these justifications for punishment has its critics. They argue, for example, that incapacitation (with the exception of the death penalty) does not eliminate future crime so much as postpone it, that most criminals are not deterred by the possibility of future punishment, and that retribution by the state is morally indefensible. The final justification for punishment is rehabilitation. Although considerable doubt has been cast on the effectiveness of many rehabilitative approaches, the new focus on *evidenced-based corrections* suggests that there are indeed rehabilitative strategies that can be effective in reducing recidivism. These include therapeutic interventions that are intensive and multimodal, provide rewards for pro-social behavior, match the abilities and learning styles of the offender, and can be implemented in the offender's natural environment (Neubauer & Fradella, 2011). A few examples are provided later in this chapter. Other evidence-based and promising practices have been identified by the U.S. Department of Justice and can be accessed online at www.crimesolutions.gov.

Sentencing

A number of factors affect the type of sentence that is issued. These are enunciated in each state's criminal code and typically include the severity of the offense, the offender's prior criminal record, the use of violence or weapons, and whether the crime was committed for monetary gain. Many states also allow victim impact statements. We know, of course, that more subjective factors often influence sentencing outcomes as well. Lower-income defendants are more likely to get longer sentences than their more affluent counterparts, probably because they are less likely to have high-quality legal representation. The youngest and oldest defendants are treated more leniently than those in the middle part of the age spectrum. Women are treated more harshly in the early phases of the process (arrest, bail, etc.) but more generously when it comes to sentencing (Siegel, 2010). The impact of race on sentencing is well documented. More than 60% of prison inmates are racial or ethnic minorities, and nearly two-thirds of prisoners with life sentences are non-White (Quigley, 2010). One-third of African American males born today will likely spend some time during their lives in jail, and nearly 1 in 10 African American males in their 20s is already in prison. African Americans are incarcerated at six times the rate of Whites, and Latinos are incarcerated at nearly double the rate of Whites (Viglione, Hannon, & DeFina, 2011). In a recently published study of 12,158 Black women in North Carolina imprisoned between 1995 and 2009, researchers found that those who were light skinned served 12% less time than those who were darker skinned (Viglione et al., 2011). This suggests that discriminatory sentencing continues to occur and that it occurs at an even deeper level than previously recognized.

In some instances, these disparities in sentencing result from bias on the part of individual judges; in others, they result from the sentencing laws themselves. Different treatment of convictions involving crack and powdered cocaine, for example, led African Americans to receive disproportionately stiffer sentences. Although this particular disparity has been remedied in the law, approximately 75% of those in prison for drug offenses are people of color (Quigley, 2010). Both women and minorities have been disadvantaged by the increased use of mandatory sentencing schemes, including *three strikes* laws that mandate life in prison upon the conviction of a third serious crime.

Institutional Corrections

The *correctional system* is responsible for the supervision of those who are convicted and sentenced for criminal behavior. Although social workers should be familiar with all aspects of the criminal justice system, understanding the correctional system is perhaps most important of all. It is estimated that 7.3 million people (or 1 out of every 31 adults in the United States) are under some form of correctional supervision by the criminal justice system. This includes 1 out of every 18 men and 1 out of every 89 women (Perlin & Dlugacz, 2009).

We usually think of corrections as composed of two major categories: *institutional corrections* and *community corrections*. With total correctional spending estimated at $68 billion in 2008, it is far less expensive to manage offenders in the community than to house them in prison or jail. The average reported inmate cost is $79 per day, or nearly $29,000 per year. The average cost of managing an offender in the community ranges from $3.42 per day to $7.47 per day, or about $1,250–$2,750 per year (Pew Center on the States, 2009).

There are several different types of correctional institutions. *Jails* are correctional facilities that are administered by local law enforcement; they typically house inmates who are sentenced to 1 year or less. *Prisons* are run by the state or federal government and typically hold prisoners who are sentenced for more than 1 year (Dolgoff & Feldstein, 2009). Crimes are of two basic types: *Misdemeanors* are less serious offenses and are usually punishable by a fine and/or no more than 1 year in jail, whereas *felonies* are more serious offenses and are usually punishable by 1 year or more in prison. In addition to imprisonment, institutional corrections can carry out *shock incarceration*, whereby the offender is sentenced to jail or prison for a limited time (usually 1–3 months) and then released on probation, or *boot camps*, which involve a short-term regimen of military-style discipline (Neubauer & Fradella, 2011).

Between 1980 and 2002, the total number of inmates in the United States quadrupled to more than 2 million, representing the highest incarceration rate in the world. This increase is commonly attributed to the enactment of stricter drug laws and high rates of substance abuse and dependence. Drug convictions represent one of the largest categories of convictions in both state and federal prisons. Some states have also abolished parole, leading to more offenders being concentrated in prisons for longer periods of time (Maschi, Bradley, & Ward, 2009). Many of those currently imprisoned are serving time for minor offenses as a result of mandatory sentencing laws. It is estimated that about 5% of the American population, or more than 13 million people, will serve a prison sentence at some point during their lives (Siegel, 2010).

Men comprise the overwhelming majority of prisoners; however, women are the fastest growing segment of the prison population. In the past 20 years, the incarceration rate for Black women has increased by 571%, compared to 131% for Hispanic women and 75% for White women. Female inmates are most likely to be younger than age 30, members of a minority group, unmarried, and unemployed or underemployed. Class also plays a role in incarceration. Only 60% of male inmates and 40% of female inmates report being employed full time prior to their incarceration, and one-third of all prisoners in the United States had annual incomes of less than $5,000 prior to their arrests (Maschi et al., 2009). Similarly, only about one-third of inmates have completed a high school education, compared to approximately 80% of the general population (Siegel, 2010).

Community Corrections

Community corrections involve sanctions including probation, fines, home confinement and electronic monitoring, restitution, and community service. *Probation* is by far the most common alternative to imprisonment, as depicted in Figure 12.1. Approximately 4 million adults are on probation; this represents a 200% increase in less than 20 years (Neubauer & Fradella, 2011). Although judges have discretion in ordering probation, they are most likely to do so when the best interests of both the public and the offender are unlikely to be served by incarceration. State laws provide guidelines for ordering probation and typically restrict it to certain types of crimes or offenders. The terms of probation can vary enormously and often include making contact with a probation officer on a regular basis. In some instances, a judge may order *intensive supervision* probation, which involves meeting with the probation officer multiple times per week or even daily, unannounced home visits, and/or random drug screening. If the terms of any probation agreement are violated, the judge can instate different conditions or revoke the probation entirely and require the offender to serve time in jail.

FIGURE 12.1   **Adult Correctional Populations, 1980–2009**

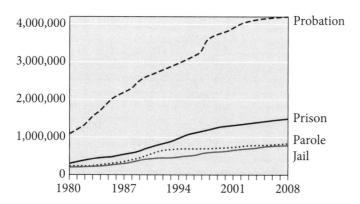

Source: Bureau of Justice Statistics (n.d.). Correctional population trends chart. Retrieved from http://bjs.ojp .usdoj.gov/content/glance/corr2.cfm

Fines are most often the sanction of choice for first-time offenders. They are ordered (either alone or in combination with other sentences) between 45% and 85% of the time, depending on the court. Questions have been raised about the fairness of levying fines as a criminal penalty because doing so directly disadvantages those who lack the ability to pay. *Home confinement* (also known as "house arrest") and *electronic monitoring* (use of an electronic surveillance device attached to a person or vehicle) represent other alternatives. Most often, they provide enhanced supervision for offenders who would otherwise be sentenced to probation; occasionally, they are provided as a final opportunity for offenders to prove they can remain in the community before incarceration is ordered. The terms of these arrangements vary considerably; as technology advances, the options for electronic monitoring continue to expand. *Restitution* involves requiring the offender to compensate the victim monetarily; this is typically restricted to cases involving property crimes. *Community service* is also referred to as *symbolic restitution.* Here, the offender repays the victim indirectly by doing work that benefits the entire community. Although it may be of great value to the public, evidence of its effectiveness in reducing recidivism is mixed (Neubauer & Fradella, 2011). Many jurisdictions lack mechanisms for coordinating and monitoring sentences involving community service, and some are unwilling to assume the potential liability risks.

FELONY CONVICTIONS AND VOTING RIGHTS

One of the consequences of being convicted of a felony is the loss of one's right to vote. In all but two states, Maine and Vermont, citizens with felony convictions are prohibited either permanently or temporarily from voting (Project Vote, 2010). In those states that deprive felons of their voting privileges, all but Kentucky and Virginia provide an avenue for voting rights to be restored.

In 13 states plus the District of Columbia, voting rights are restored as soon as the offender has completed his or her sentence, even if it is followed by probation or parole. In 5 states, voting rights are reinstated only after the offender has completed parole. In 18 states, voting rights are restored upon the completion of the offender's sentence, parole, and probation. The remaining 10 states have more complicated provisions under which different rules apply to different types of offenders. In Arizona, for example, a first-time offender can vote after completing probation and paying additional fines. After a second offense, however, only a judge can grant restoration of voting rights after a minimum waiting time of 2 years. In Delaware, people convicted of selected serious offenses are permanently disenfranchised; however, those who commit lesser offenses can apply for restoration of their rights after probation, parole, paying a fine, and waiting a minimum of 5 years. In Wyoming, first-time offenders can apply to have their voting rights reinstated after probation, parole, fines, and a 5-year waiting period, but violent offenders or recidivist offenders must appeal directly to the governor. In the most restrictive states, Kentucky and Virginia, only a pardon from the governor can restore a felon's voting privileges (Project Vote, 2010).

As a result of these policies, approximately 4.7 million felons in the United States are ineligible to vote, 74% of whom are living in the community on probation or parole. Of those who do seek to reclaim their voting rights, approximately 1.5 million are denied (Mauer & Kansal, 2005). Others are unsuccessful because they lack information about their voting status, they are discouraged by long waiting periods, or they cannot afford to pay required fines. Exclusion of persons with felony records from the democratic process has serious implications for individuals, communities, and society at large. Given the disproportionate number of convicted felons who are people of color and people living in poverty, many voices are silenced through these policies—particularly those from communities that lack political power and are heavily dependent on government benefits, services, and resources.

If offenders have any hope of reintegrating into the community once they have served their time, it is essential that they be permitted to participate in the electoral process. Recognizing this, NASW "supports the full restoration of voting rights for all ex-felons who have completed their sentences" (NASW, 2009, p. 354). Other recommendations include repealing laws that permanently disenfranchise felons, requiring transparency in the restoration process, eliminating waiting periods, requiring corrections staff to educate felons and assist them in reinstating their rights, and establishing a presumption of restoration (Mauer & Kansal, 2005; Project Vote, 2010).

Legal challenges to felony voting rights laws have been brought under the equal protection clause. Although the U.S. Supreme Court has declined to apply strict scrutiny (*Richardson v. Ramirez*, 1974), the Court has clarified that state felony disenfranchisement laws that reflect purposeful race discrimination are unconstitutional (*Hunter v. Underwood*, 1985). Additional challenges have been brought under the Voting Rights Act of 1965. Results among the various circuit courts have varied. Meanwhile, a bill consistent with NASW's position was introduced in the 111th Congress by Sen. Russ Feingold (D-WI) and Rep. John Conyers (D-MI). Now part of the Voting Opportunity and Technology Enhancement Rights Act of 2011, it was reintroduced by Rep. Conyers in the 112th Congress.

Social workers must work with those reentering the community to inform them of their status, assist them in seeking restoration of their rights as citizens, and advocate for policy change at the state and national levels.

Prisoners' Rights

Historically, prisoners were assumed to have forfeited their civil rights as part of the punishment for their offense. Abiding by what was known as the *hands-off doctrine*, state and federal courts rarely intervened in the prison system; the prevailing belief was that correctional professionals were in the best position to navigate the complexities of these institutions and make appropriate decisions. This began to change in the 1960s, when the deplorable conditions inside many of the nation's correctional facilities were revealed to the public, and prisoners became increasingly militant in pursuit of their constitutional rights. The composition of the U.S. Supreme Court also favored reform; it was the same Court that instituted *Miranda* warnings and the exclusionary rule. In 1972, the ACLU National Prison Project was created; together with the NAACP Legal Defense Fund, it remains a major engine behind efforts to ensure safe and humane prison conditions through education, advocacy, and litigation.

As the law evolved, prisoners were recognized as having a number of important constitutional rights. These include freedom of speech, freedom of religion, freedom to marry, equal protection and due process, the right to have access to the courts, and protection from cruel and unusual punishment (Branham, 2005). Many of these rights, though recognized by the courts, are in practice quite restricted; generally speaking, they must give way to the legitimate objectives of the correctional system.

The First Amendment, for example, confers (among others) the rights to freedom of speech and freedom of religion. Prison policies limiting free speech have been upheld, however, when correctional officials demonstrate that the communication would create a security concern. Examples include regulations prohibiting inmates from receiving hardbound books mailed from outside the prison (*Bell v. Wolfish*, 1979) and inmate-to-inmate correspondence (*Turner v. Safley*, 1987). In 2012, however, an injunction was successfully obtained against a South Carolina detention center that, ostensibly for safety reasons, prohibited inmates from having access to publications containing staples (including, for example, *Time* and *Newsweek* magazines and *Prison Legal News*) and publications containing pornography (defined sufficiently broadly to include the *Washington Post*, which advertises swimsuits) (U.S. Department of Justice, 2012). As for freedom of religion, the Supreme Court has recognized that inmates must be afforded reasonable opportunities to practice their religion, but religious practices can be restricted if they interfere with security or are costly or logistically difficult to accommodate. Although some prisoners have successfully asserted the right to a special diet, for example, most courts have upheld regulations that prohibit inmates from growing beards (Branham, 2005).

The right to have access to the courts has enjoyed somewhat more protection. For example, inmates have the right to challenge the conditions of their confinement, contest the legality of their convictions, and resolve civil disputes including divorce and child custody. As articulated by the U.S. Supreme Court, inmates must be provided with meaningful access to the courts (*Bounds v. Smith*, 1997). This includes being permitted to file legal documents while incarcerated and having private conversations with attorneys. Inmates must also be afforded access to adequate law libraries or be provided with adequate assistance from people trained in the law. On the other hand, the Prison Litigation Reform Act (PLRA) enacted in 1996 made enforcement of these rights more difficult. Under the PLRA, prisoners must thoroughly exhaust the prison grievance process before filing a suit in federal court; they cannot file lawsuits for mental or emotional injury unless they can also show physical injury; they must pay their own fees; and courts can penalize prisoners who bring frivolous cases (ACLU, 2002).

The Constitution's right to due process entitles inmates to certain procedural safeguards in connection with disciplinary proceedings (*Wolff v. McDonnell*, 1974) and certain transfers, for example, from a prison to a mental hospital (*Vitek v. Jones*, 1980). The equal protection clause has been held to prohibit racial segregation of prisoners (*Johnson v. California*, 2005) and to require the equal treatment of female inmates.

Finally, the Eighth Amendment, which prohibits cruel and unusual punishment, has been used to address the conditions of confinement more broadly. Courts have placed limits on how inmates can be disciplined, resulting in the reduced use of corporal punishment and solitary confinement. Prison officials who inflict physical harm on inmates can be held liable if they act maliciously and their actions are without penological justification. Sexual contact between prisoners and corrections staff is expressly prohibited in federal prisons and in 27 states. Nonetheless, an estimated 12% to 20% of inmates are sexually assaulted while incarcerated. Prison gangs are also a common source of prison violence; often organized along racial or ethnic lines, they use violence and intimidation to maintain control over other inmates (Fleisher & Decker, 2001). The failure of prison authorities to protect inmates from one another amounts to cruel and unusual punishment only if officials act with deliberate indifference in the face of a significant risk of harm. The same standard has been applied to the failure to treat an inmate's serious medical needs (*Estelle v. Gamble*, 1976) and the failure to prevent a prisoner's suicide (*Jacobs v. West Feliciana Sheriff's Department*, 2000).

One of the current issues regarding inmate health and safety concerns the practice of shackling pregnant inmates during labor and postpartum recovery. Several states, including Hawaii, Rhode Island, Idaho, and Nevada, have recently passed laws banning the practice; the Virginia Department of Corrections has agreed to implement regulations prohibiting it, though the state legislature declined to pass a law during its 2012 session that would have prohibited the practice. Meanwhile, many states continue to subject female prisoners to this dangerous and degrading treatment (National Women's Law Center, 2010). In 2005, an interesting challenge was launched against a Wisconsin law barring physicians from providing transgender inmates with medically necessary hormone therapy or sex reassignment surgery. The Inmate Sex Change Prevention Act was struck down by a federal district court in 2010 and was recently found to be a violation of the Eighth Amendment by the U.S. Court of Appeals for the Seventh Circuit (*Fields v. Smith*, 2011).

Prisoners also have a right under the Eighth Amendment to reasonable care, including the provision of necessary food, clothing, and shelter. In 2011, nearly 12,000 prisoners in California joined a hunger strike to draw attention to unsatisfactory treatment (Lavender, 2011). Meanwhile, concerns over the growing number of older adults who are incarcerated has led one state, Louisiana, to introduce legislation that permits those age 60 and older to be considered for parole.

Overcrowding is one of the most serious threats to achieving safe and humane conditions, and it is closely tied to the adequacy of attention paid to the health and mental health needs of prisoners. In a stunning 2011 ruling, the U.S. Supreme Court upheld a lower court's order requiring California to reduce its prison population—which was nearly double its intended capacity—by more than 30,000 inmates over the following 2 years. The Court bemoaned the alarming impact overcrowding had on prisoner health, mental health, and safety, noting, for example, that as many as 200 inmates were being housed in a gymnasium and as many as 54 inmates shared a single toilet. Also detailed were the substantial risk for transmission of infectious diseases, wait times for medical attention that ranged from 5 hours to 17 months and resulted in numerous patient deaths, lack of appropriate medical equipment, failure to meet basic sanitation standards, and rampant chaos. California's prisons also experienced a suicide rate approaching an average of one per week, nearly 80% higher than the national average. This was reportedly due to a severe shortage of treatment beds and chronic understaffing (*Brown v. Plata*, 2011).

Providing Treatment

California is not alone in housing substantial numbers of inmates with mental health problems. In a nationwide study of more than 25,000 federal prisoners, state prisoners, and local inmates, more than half reported having a mental health problem as defined by recent history or current symptoms (James & Glaze, 2006). Mental health problems are closely associated with violence and past criminal activity. In the study just referenced, 44% of jail inmates and 61% of state prisoners with mental health problems had committed past or current violent offenses; one-fourth had served three or more prior sentences. Approximately 25% of inmates with mental health problems reported past physical or sexual abuse.

In addition to those with mental health problems, inmates with substance abuse problems are overrepresented in the nation's correctional system. Of the 2.3 million inmates incarcerated in the United States, 65% percent or 1.5 million inmates meet the Diagnostic and Statistical Manual of Mental Disorders (DSM-IV) criteria for substance abuse or dependence. Another 458,000 inmates who do not meet the DSM criteria have histories of substance abuse, were under the influence of alcohol or other drugs at the time of the offense, committed their offense to get money to buy drugs, were incarcerated for an alcohol or drug law violation, or shared some combination of these characteristics. Combined, these two groups comprise 85% of the population in the U.S. correctional system. Only 11% of the inmates who meet the criteria for abuse or dependence receive any treatment during their incarceration (National Center on Addiction and Substance Abuse, 2010).

Given that one of the goals of the correctional system is rehabilitation, the paucity of treatment services is both ironic and deplorable. The constitutional requirements for the provision of reasonable care establish only a bare minimum, and the right to treatment is considered violated only in cases of blatant disregard for serious illness. The Supreme Court has affirmed other rights of substance abusers in relation to incarceration, however. For example, in *Robinson v. California* (1962), the Court held that it is cruel and unusual punishment to incarcerate someone because of the "illness" of drug addiction if they have not committed a criminal offense. In *Tapia v. United States* (2011), the Court ruled that it is likewise constitutionally impermissible to impose a sentence or determine the length of a sentence based on a prisoner's need for rehabilitation. In that case, the district court had sentenced the defendant to the maximum allowed under the Sentencing Guidelines, plus 3 years' supervised release, in order to allow him enough time to complete a recommended 500-hour drug treatment program offered by the Bureau of Prisons. The Supreme Court found this to be a violation of his Eighth Amendment rights.

Although far from adequate, most correctional facilities do provide some form of treatment for inmates with mental health and/or substance abuse problems. To address mental health, they may provide individual or group therapy, education, and vocational counseling. Programs focus on helping inmates work toward better controlling their emotions, improving communication skills, managing life issues, and maintaining social relationships. Anger management programs are common in correctional facilities because of the links among anger, poor impulse control, and violent criminal behavior. Mental health treatment is often combined with drug treatment and sex offender programs (Siegel, 2010).

The most intensive type of substance abuse treatment provided in some state prisons is known as the therapeutic community (TC); it is a form of residential treatment, lasting 12–18 months, in which participants are isolated from the rest of the general prison population. The primary goal is to change the negative patterns of behavior, thinking, and feeling that are often implicated in drug use (Inciardi, Martin, & Butzin, 2004). The therapeutic community typically involves three successive stages: incarceration, work release, and parole (or other form of community supervision). The ultimate goal is to reduce recidivism by teaching social responsibility and emphasizing desired behavior (National Institute on Drug Abuse, 2008). The approach has been found to be most effective with participants who complete the full program and engage in the aftercare component. Separating participants from the rest of the prison population allows them to maintain some distance from drugs, violence, and other characteristics of the prison atmosphere that make rehabilitation difficult.

As discussed in Chapter 1, drug courts have evolved as an alternative for low-risk criminal offenders. Their purpose is to place first-time nonviolent offenders into treatment rather than into jail or prison (Siegel, 2010). Under the drug court model, legal, court, and treatment professionals work together to identify potential participants, develop treatment plans, provide appropriate services, and monitor and report on their progress. Drug courts embody five essential features: integration of alcohol and drug case processing, a nonadversarial courtroom environment, random drug testing, close judicial monitoring through regular status hearings, and sanctions and rewards for infractions and achievements (Frescoln, 2009).

In response to reports that inmates who experience religious conversions while incarcerated are less likely to re-offend, some states have opened faith-based correctional facilities focused on religious teachings; these began in 2003 under Governor Jeb Bush of Florida. Many of these programs incorporate faith-based principles along with mentoring, life skills training, and other kinds of treatment. Although much research remains to be done, they show some success in the short term, but their benefits are not often sustained (Siegel, 2010).

Most correctional facilities provide some form of educational or vocational programming. Some prisons allow inmates to obtain a high school diploma or a GED; other institutions provide classroom education staffed by certified teachers. These programs are often underfunded and poorly administered. Vocational training programs are available in most institutions. In the federal system, inmates are able to work in the Federal Prison Industries where they are taught to produce goods and services, including clothing, electronics, automobile components, and office furniture. Unfortunately, inmates often have difficulty translating this experience into post-release employment (Siegel, 2010).

Prisoner Reentry

Each year, approximately 175,000 individuals go unsupervised into the community after serving their maximum sentence (Siegel, 2010). Within 3 years of being released, more than 40% of inmates are returned to prison; this number has remained relatively stable since the mid-1990s (Pew Center on the States, 2011). A significant number of inmates (more than 500,000 per year) are released on parole. Parole can be granted as a result of good behavior, to relieve overcrowded prison conditions, or because a sentence has been commuted. If the conditions of the parole are violated, the offender is sent back to prison to serve the remainder of his or her sentence.

Many factors contribute to how well an inmate copes upon reentering society. More than 75% of offenders report using drugs or alcohol during the first year following their release. Most inmates leave prison with no savings. Many ex-offenders have little employment experience, and only an estimated one-third of prisoners receive any vocational or educational training while in prison. Those with a criminal record are prohibited from working in certain occupations, including child care, nursing, education, and security, and many employers are reluctant or unwilling to hire people who have served time in prison or jail. Lack of opportunity for lawful employment often leads former inmates to engage in illegal activity. In addition, they face enormous barriers to finding housing, including high start-up costs, a dearth of affordable options, and laws that prohibit ex-felons with drug convictions from accessing public housing. Although some former prisoners have homes awaiting them, many inmates are unable to maintain ties with family while incarcerated and lack support when they return to the community. For those former prisoners with children, especially women, there may be additional barriers to reunification; often children are removed to state custody while a parent is incarcerated, and the parent must meet the court's requirements to be reunited with the child. Having a criminal record increases the likelihood of being deemed an unfit parent, making resumption of custody less likely (Maschi et al., 2009).

Recognition of how our lack of attention to prisoner reentry affects the likelihood of recidivism has led to passage of important federal legislation. The Second Chance Act of 2008 authorizes grants to government agencies and nonprofit organizations for the provision of reentry services, including employment assistance, substance abuse treatment, housing, family programming, mentoring, and victim support (National Reentry Resource Center, n.d.). Helping prisoners reintegrate into the community is a fertile area of practice for social workers who are adept at identifying and meeting individual and family needs, as well as coordinating the complex array of services required for success (Wheeler & Patterson, 2008). Social workers within correctional settings can begin the planning process, identifying potential challenges, strengths, and resources, and helping to transition inmates to appropriate providers in the community. Social workers in the community can help ensure that those reentering get a foothold in the economy, and that their health, mental health, social, and spiritual needs are adequately addressed.

Summary and Conclusion

A significant segment of the U.S. population has experience with the criminal justice system. Most striking is the disproportionate representation of racial and ethnic minorities and people living in poverty. The criminal justice system is composed of three parts: law enforcement, the courts, and corrections. Relevant issues in law enforcement include detention by police, racial profiling, search and seizure, and interrogation. In court, criminal defendants have a number of constitutional rights; they also benefit from the exclusionary rule, which requires suppression of illegally obtained evidence. The correctional system includes the administration of both institutional and community sentences. The United States has the highest incarceration rate in the world. The U.S. Supreme Court has established that a number of constitutional rights apply to prisoners, although many of those rights are restricted in practice. Treatment programs for prisoners with mental health and substance abuse needs are available in most facilities but are woefully inadequate. Social workers should understand the workings of the criminal justice system so they can assist clients who are involved with the courts. They also must advocate for greater equity and humane treatment.

Sample Case

The case that follows is an extremely important one, relating to the rights of prisoners. Read the case and carefully consider the questions that follow.

FARMER V. BRENNAN
511 U.S. 825 (1994)
Justice Souter delivered the opinion of the Court.

A prison official's "deliberate indifference" to a substantial risk of serious harm to an inmate violates the Eighth Amendment. This case requires us to define the term "deliberate indifference," as we do by requiring a showing that the official was subjectively aware of the risk.

. . . Petitioner, who is serving a federal sentence for credit card fraud, has been diagnosed by medical personnel of the Bureau of Prisons as a transsexual, one who has "[a] rare psychiatric disorder in which a person feels persistently uncomfortable about his or her anatomical sex," and who typically seeks medical treatment, including hormonal therapy and surgery, to bring about a permanent sex change. For several years before being convicted and sentenced in 1986 at the age of 18, petitioner, who is biologically male, wore women's clothing (as petitioner did at the 1986 trial), underwent estrogen therapy, received silicone breast implants, and submitted to unsuccessful "black market" testicle-removal surgery. . . . Petitioner's precise appearance in prison is unclear from the record before us, but petitioner claims to have continued hormonal treatment while incarcerated by using drugs smuggled into prison, and apparently wears clothing in a feminine manner, as by displaying a shirt "off one shoulder. . . . " The parties agree that petitioner "projects feminine characteristics."

The practice of federal prison authorities is to incarcerate preoperative transsexuals with prisoners of like biological sex, and over time authorities housed petitioner in several federal facilities, sometimes in the general male prison population but more often in segregation. While there is no dispute that petitioner was segregated at least several times because of violations of prison rules, neither is it disputed that in at least one penitentiary petitioner was segregated because of safety concerns.

On March 9, 1989, petitioner was transferred for disciplinary reasons from the Federal Correctional Institute in Oxford, Wisconsin (FCI-Oxford), to the United States Penitentiary in Terre Haute, Indiana (USP-Terre Haute). . . . [P]enitentiaries are typically higher security facilities that house more troublesome prisoners than federal correctional institutes. . . . [P]etitioner was placed in the USP-Terre Haute general population. Petitioner voiced no objection to any prison official about the transfer to the penitentiary or to placement in its general population. Within two weeks, according to petitioner's allegations, petitioner was beaten and raped by another inmate in petitioner's cell. Several days later, after petitioner claims to have reported the incident, officials returned petitioner to segregation to await, according to respondents, a hearing about petitioner's HIV-positive status.

. . . [T]he complaint alleged that respondents either transferred petitioner to USP-Terre Haute or placed petitioner in its general population despite knowledge that the penitentiary had a violent environment and a history of inmate assaults, and despite knowledge that petitioner, as a transsexual who "projects feminine characteristics," would be particularly vulnerable to sexual attack by some USP-Terre Haute inmates. This allegedly amounted to a deliberately indifferent failure to protect petitioner's safety, and thus to a violation of petitioner's Eighth Amendment rights. Petitioner sought compensatory and punitive damages, and an injunction barring future confinement in any penitentiary, including USP-Terre Haute. ***

The Constitution "does not mandate comfortable prisons," but neither does it permit inhumane ones, and it is now settled that "the treatment a prisoner receives in prison and the conditions under which he is confined are subject to scrutiny under the Eighth Amendment." In its prohibition of "cruel and unusual punishments," the Eighth Amendment places restraints on prison officials, who may not, for example, use excessive physical force against prisoners. The Amendment also imposes duties on these officials, who must provide humane conditions of confinement; prison officials must ensure that inmates receive adequate food, clothing, shelter and medical care, and must "take reasonable measures to guarantee the safety of the inmates."

In particular, as the lower courts have uniformly held, and as we have assumed, "[p]rison officials have a duty . . . to protect prisoners from violence at the hands of other prisoners." . . . Being violently assaulted in prison is simply not "part of the penalty that criminal offenders pay for their offenses against society."

It is not, however, every injury suffered by one prisoner at the hands of another that translates into constitutional liability for prison officials responsible for the victim's safety. Our cases have held that a prison official violates the Eighth Amendment only when two requirements are met. First,…[f]or a claim…based on a failure to prevent harm, the inmate must show that he is incarcerated under conditions posing a substantial risk of serious harm.

[S]econd, . . . [t]o violate the Cruel and Unusual Punishments Clause, a prison official must have a "sufficiently culpable state of mind." In prison-conditions cases that state of mind is one of "deliberate indifference" to inmate health or safety. . . . The parties disagree . . . on the proper test for deliberate indifference, which we must therefore undertake to define. ***

We hold . . . that a prison official cannot be found liable under the Eighth Amendment for denying an inmate humane conditions of confinement unless the official knows of and disregards an excessive risk to inmate health or safety; the official must both be aware of facts from which the inference could be drawn that a substantial risk of serious harm exists, and he must also draw the inference. . . . [A]n official's failure to alleviate a significant risk that he should have perceived but did not, while no cause for commendation, cannot under our cases be condemned as the infliction of punishment. ***

Under the test we adopt today, an Eighth Amendment claimant need not show that a prison official acted or failed to act believing that harm actually would befall an inmate; it is enough that the official acted or failed to act despite his knowledge of a substantial risk of serious harm. . . .

Nor may a prison official escape liability for deliberate indifference by showing that, while he was aware of an obvious, substantial risk to inmate safety, he did not know that the complainant was especially likely to be assaulted by the specific prisoner who eventually committed the assault.***

In addition, prison officials who actually knew of a substantial risk to inmate health or safety may be found free from liability if they responded reasonably to the risk, even if the harm ultimately was not averted. . . . ***

The judgment of the Court of Appeals is vacated, and the case is remanded for further proceedings consistent with this opinion. ***

Justice Blackmun, concurring.

. . . I join the Court's opinion, because it . . . sends a clear message to prison officials that their affirmative duty under the Constitution to provide for the safety of inmates is not to be taken lightly. [P]rison officials may be held liable for failure to remedy a risk so obvious and substantial that the officials must have known about it. . . .

The horrors experienced by many young inmates, particularly those who, like petitioner, are convicted of nonviolent offenses, border on the unimaginable. Prison rape not only threatens the lives of those who fall prey to their aggressors, but is potentially devastating to the human spirit. . . .

The fact that our prisons are badly overcrowded and understaffed may well explain many of the shortcomings of our penal systems. But our Constitution sets minimal standards governing the administration of punishment in this country . . . and thus it is no answer to the complaints of the brutalized inmate that the resources are unavailable to protect him from what, in reality, is nothing less than torture.

Questions

1. What do you consider to be the important facts in this case? Who was the plaintiff? What happened?

2. The Court is trying to balance the rights of a prisoner against the practicalities of administering a prison. What test did the Court enunciate for determining when correctional officials are responsible for violence perpetrated by one inmate against another?

3. Can you come up with an example of another scenario that you think would meet this test? How easy or difficult is it to apply?

4. Do you think the Court struck the right balance here? Should it be easier or harder for prisoners to hold prison officials responsible for violence perpetrated by one inmate against another? Explain.

CHAPTER 12 PRACTICE TEST

The following questions will test your application and analysis of the content found within this chapter. For additional assessment, including licensing-exam type questions on applying chapter content to practice behaviors, visit **MySearchLab**.

1. Stop and frisk laws have been associated with
   a. injuries to law enforcement officers.
   b. racial profiling.
   c. reduced recidivism.
   d. successful prosecution.

2. Allison and her friends were camping at a state park near her home. Shortly after midnight, police arrived. They searched Allison's open cooler and found marijuana. Allison's lawyer is seeking to exclude the evidence, claiming that the search violated her Fourth Amendment rights because it was conducted without a warrant. Whether or not Allison wins will depend on whether she
   a. had a reasonable expectation of privacy in the cooler.
   b. has had previous drug convictions.
   c. lied to the police about the presence of drugs.
   d. was given *Miranda* warnings.

3. Which of the following correctly describes the prison population in the United States?
   a. It is one of the smallest in the world.
   b. People with mental health and substance abuse problems are disproportionately represented.
   c. Those from impoverished backgrounds and those from affluent backgrounds serve sentences of comparable length.
   d. White women are the fastest growing segment of the prison population.

4. The Sixth Amendment guarantees all criminal defendants the right to
   a. legal counsel only during the adjudication phase of the process.
   b. no legal counsel.
   c. quality legal counsel.
   d. reasonably competent legal counsel.

5. Discuss the four purposes of criminal punishment. What criticisms have been leveled against each of them? Which holds the most promise? Why?

6. What are the implications of laws that deprive convicted felons of their right to vote? How do these laws fit with social work values?

MYSEARCHLAB CONNECTIONS

Reinforce what you learned in this chapter by studying videos, cases, documents, and more available at **www.MySearchLab.com.**

Read these Cases/Documents

Δ Incarcerated Women
  • *How can legal professionals and social workers collaborate in assisting people who are incarcerated?*

Explore these Assets

• Website: National Criminal Justice Reference Service
• Website: National Institute of Justice

Research these Topics

• victim impact statements
• racial disparities and three-strikes laws

Assess Your Knowledge

Go to **MySearchLab** to test your knowledge of key topics in this chapter with topic-specific quizzes. Conclude your assessment by completing the chapter exam.

---

* = CSWE Core Competency Asset   Δ = Case Study

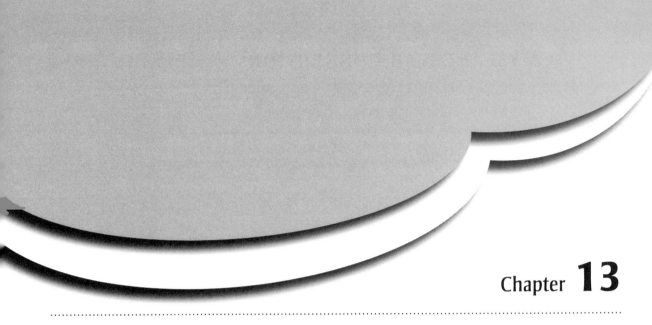

Chapter **13**

Death Penalty

The death penalty remains a highly controversial issue that has moral, social, legal, and practical implications. Some argue that life is sacred and should not be subject to termination by the state. Others think that certain crimes are so heinous that the only reasonable response is the death penalty. In a 2010 public opinion poll, 64% of Americans supported the use of the death penalty, down from 80% in 1994. When asked to choose between life without the possibility of parole and the death penalty, however, life in prison was favored, 49% to 46% (Gallup, 2012). The National Association of Social Workers has adopted a policy position against the death penalty because of its disproportionate application to people of color and the lack of respect it shows for human life (NASW, 2009). This chapter provides a brief history of the death penalty, discusses arguments commonly made for and against it, explains how the courts have applied the Constitution's 8th and 14th Amendments to the issue, and examines legal exceptions to the death penalty. Special sections highlight disproportionality in applying the death penalty and the role of forensic social workers in death penalty mitigation.

Background

The death penalty, considered the ultimate criminal sentence because of its finality, has been applied in this country since its inception and is currently legal in 33 states. The federal government and the military also apply the death penalty to certain crimes (Death Penalty Information Center [DPIC], 2012a). Specific crimes that are eligible for the death penalty vary from state to state and have varied throughout history as well. In general, the only crimes that can legally result in the death penalty today are crimes against the government and crimes that result in the death of the victim.

Understanding the 8th and 14th Amendments

Historically, the Supreme Court has considered death penalty cases under the Constitution's Eighth Amendment, which prohibits the use of "cruel and unusual" punishment. In analyzing these cases, the Court determines whether the punishment is *cruel* by examining whether or not it is proportional to the offense; it determines whether it is *unusual* by examining how frequently the punishment is imposed. Over the years, various cases have established that the basis for these judgments can change over time. In determining whether a punishment is cruel and unusual, the Court refers to "the evolving standards of decency that mark the progress of a maturing society" (*Trop v. Dulles*, 1958, pp. 100–101). In other words, what is considered cruel and unusual at one point in time might not be considered so at another point in time. Fluctuations in death penalty law attest to how interpretations of the Eighth amendment have varied, at least in part because of changes in public norms and perceptions of morality.

The 14th Amendment's equal protection clause requires that groups of people who are similarly situated be treated similarly under the law. The law cannot discriminate based on characteristics such as sex, race, or national origin without an acceptable justification. A more detailed explanation of the equal protection clause appears in Chapter 16. Although the 14th Amendment has only occasionally been the basis for death penalty cases, it has figured prominently in a few important decisions when the imposition of the death penalty disproportionately affected certain groups.

History of the Death Penalty in the United States

Few American policies have undergone the recurrent reversals that have characterized the history of the death penalty. Influenced by the practice in Europe, the original colonists brought the death penalty with them to the New World. In its early years, executions were conducted in a public setting, and the death penalty was mandatory for certain crimes. In 1863, it became discretionary. Like the use of the death penalty itself, the fight to reform it has early roots. Thomas Jefferson introduced a bill to limit the death penalty to cases involving murder or treason; his effort was defeated by only a single vote (DPIC, 2012b), and it took until the late 20th century for his vision to be realized.

The 20th century marked the beginning of what has been called the Abolition Movement, a movement aimed at eradicating the death penalty entirely. As a part of this movement, six states completely eliminated the death penalty between 1907 and 1917, although five of them reinstated it years later because of fears brought on by World War II. Public opinion once again turned away from the death penalty in the United States in the 1950s, with opposition reaching an all-time high in 1966 (DPIC, 2012b). This was clearly reflected in the U.S. Supreme Court's reconsideration of the death penalty in the 1972 case of *Furman v. Georgia*.

The *Furman* decision was the first by the Supreme Court to pose a serious challenge to the death penalty. It was heard in conjunction with two similar cases, *Jackson v. Georgia* and *Branch v. Texas*. All three cases involved African American defendants and White victims. *Furman* involved a defendant who had been sentenced to death on murder charges;

the other two cases involved rape. The Court's 5–4 decision, which is only six sentences long, concluded that the death penalty as applied in these cases violated both the Eighth Amendment's ban on cruel and unusual punishment and the 14th Amendment's equal protection clause. The reasoning behind the decision, however, varied from justice to justice. In fact, every single one of the justices authored a separate opinion in the case. Two justices found the death penalty to be unconstitutional per se because it was degrading to human dignity and offended contemporary values. Others alluded to the arbitrary application of the death penalty and its disproportionate use with defendants who were poor and socially disadvantaged. Still others raised concerns about its ineffectiveness as a deterrent to crime. Despite the lack of a uniform rationale, the decision had an enormous impact: All 40 states that permitted the death penalty at the time halted their executions. What the Court perhaps did not anticipate was the backlash that followed; the decision was deeply unpopular among the states and fueled a resurgence of grassroots support for the death penalty (Jacobs & Kent, 2007). Figure 13.1 depicts the fluctuations in public opinion that have driven these repeated reversals in our death penalty laws.

Four years later, in 1976, the *Furman* decision was put to the test in *Gregg v. Georgia.* This case involved a defendant who picked up two hitchhikers traveling cross-country, then robbed them and shot them at close range. The Georgia death penalty statute at issue had been amended in the aftermath of the *Furman* decision to address some of the Supreme Court's concerns. The new law included an automatic appeals process in death penalty cases, required the state supreme court to identify decisions with similar outcomes whenever a capital sentence was imposed, and required that juries consider both the facts and the character of the defendant (positive/mitigating factors and negative/aggravating

FIGURE 13.1   **The Death Penalty and Public Opinion, 1957–2007**

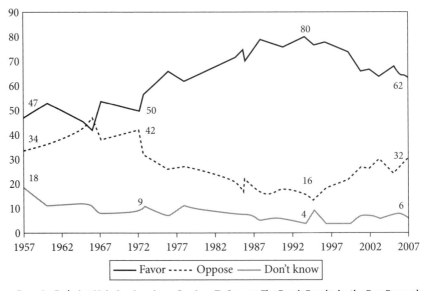

Source: From *An Enduring Majority: Americans Continue To Support The Death Penalty* by the Pew Research Center's Forum on Religion & Public Life, September 23, 2011. Copyright © 2011 by the Pew Research Center, http://pewforum.org. Reprinted with permission.

factors) in recommending a death sentence. Because this statute was so different from the statute that led to the *Furman* decision, the Supreme Court was left to decide whether the death penalty, regardless of how it is crafted and applied, necessarily runs afoul of the Eighth Amendment. It held that the death penalty could indeed be constitutional, as long as it is neither inhumane nor disproportionate to the offense. It also concluded that a strongly worded statute could address equal protection concerns under the 14th Amendment by ensuring that the death penalty's imposition is neither arbitrary nor capricious. Although a state need not replicate Georgia's law exactly, the Court in *Gregg* did express its approval for (1) instituting separate proceedings for determining guilt and imposing sentencing, (2) limiting jury discretion, and (3) providing an automatic right to appeal. Although specific aspects of the death penalty have been challenged in recent years, the constitutionality of the death penalty overall has not been challenged since *Gregg v. Georgia*. The criteria articulated in that case are still in force today.

The Death Penalty Today

Following the reinstatement of the death penalty in 1976, the number of executions in the United States gradually increased, topping out in 1999 with a total of 98. Since then, the United States has experienced a gradual decline in the use of the death penalty, with a total of 37 executions occurring in 2008. Use of the death penalty also varies by state. Texas has imposed the death penalty far more often than any other state, having completed 483 executions since 1976. Following Texas is Virginia, where 109 executions have taken place since 1976 (DPIC, 2012c). Since 1976, Texas and Virginia together have accounted for more executions than the entire West, Midwest, and Northeast combined (DPIC, 2012d). Texas was also the site of the most recent execution in July 2012 (DPIC, 2012e). At the other end of the spectrum are Kansas and New Hampshire, neither of which has had an execution since reinstating their death penalties in 1994 and 1991, respectively (Amnesty International, 2010a). For the 34 death penalty states (those where the death penalty is legal), Table 13.1 details when the

TABLE 13.1 **States with the Death Penalty**

State Name	Year of Death Penalty Reinstatement	Number of Executions Since Reinstatement of the Death Penalty	Current Death Row Population	Primary Method(s) of Execution	Exonerations from Death Row Since Reinstatement of the Death Penalty
Alabama	1976	44	200	Lethal injection, electrocution	6
Arizona	1973	23	129	Lethal injection, gas chamber	8
Arkansas	1973	27	43	Lethal injection, electrocution	0

State Name	Year of Death Penalty Re-instatement	Number of Ex-ecutions Since Reinstatement of the Death Penalty	Current Death Row Population	Primary Method(s) of Execution	Exonerations from Death Row Since Reinstatement of the Death Penalty
California	1974	13	690	Lethal injection, gas chamber	3
Colorado	1975	1	3	Lethal injection	0
Connecticut	1973	1	10	Lethal injection	0
Delaware	1974	14	19	Lethal injection, hanging	0
Florida	1972	69	403	Lethal injection, electrocution	23
Georgia	1973	46	108	Lethal injection	5
Idaho	1973	1	18	Lethal injection	1
Indiana	1973	20	17	Lethal injection	2
Illinois	1974	12	15	Lethal injection, electrocution	20
Kansas	1994	0	10	Lethal injection	0
Kentucky	1975	3	36	Lethal injection, electrocution	1
Louisiana	1973	28	84	Lethal injection	8
Maryland	1975	5	5	Lethal injection, gas chamber	1
Mississippi	1974	10	60	Lethal injection, gas chamber	3
Missouri	1975	67	52	Lethal injection, gas chamber	3
Nebraska	1973	3	11	Lethal injection	1
Nevada	1973	12	78	Lethal injection	1
New Hampshire	1991	0	1	Lethal injection, hanging	0
North Carolina	1977	43	169	Lethal injection	8
Ohio	1974	36	176	Lethal injection	5
Oklahoma	1973	92	86	Lethal injection, electrocution, firing squad	10

(continued)

| TABLE 13.1 | States with the Death Penalty *(continued)* |

State Name	Year of Death Penalty Re-instatement	Number of Executions Since Reinstatement of the Death Penalty	Current Death Row Population	Primary Method(s) of Execution	Exonerations from Death Row Since Reinstatement of the Death Penalty
Oregon	1978	2	33	Lethal injection	0
Pennsylvania	1974	3	225	Lethal injection	6
South Carolina	1969	42	63	Lethal injection, electrocution	2
South Dakota	1979	1	3	Lethal injection	0
Tennessee	1974	6	92	Lethal injection, electrocution	2
Texas	1979	451	342	Lethal injection	11
Utah	1973	6	10	Lethal injection, firing squad	0
Virginia	1975	106	16	Lethal injection, electrocution	1
Washington	1975	4	9	Lethal injection, hanging	1
Wyoming	1977	1	1	Lethal injection, gas chamber	0

Source: Amnesty International USA. (2010a). Executions by state. Retrieved from http://www.amnestyusa.org/our-work/issues/death-penalty/us-scheduled-executions/executions-by-state; Death Penalty Information Center. (2012g). Methods of execution. Retrieved from http://www.deathpenaltyinfo.org/methods-execution

death penalty was reinstated, how many executions have taken place, the size of the death row population, and how many have been exonerated.

Whites comprise the majority of those executed overall, although persons from minority racial groups are disproportionately represented. In addition, more than 98% of inmates on death row are male (Prison Policy Initiative, 2003). Although women account for 1 in 10 arrests for murder, only about 1 in 100 is actually executed (DPIC, 2012f). More information about the disproportionate application of the death penalty is highlighted elsewhere in this chapter.

Death Penalty Crimes

One of the issues that the U.S. Supreme Court has repeatedly revisited is whether or not the death penalty is constitutional when applied to crimes that do not result in the death of the victim. In *Coker v. Georgia* (1977), the Supreme Court heard the case of a convicted felon who, after escaping from prison, committed rape in the course of an armed robbery. The Court held that applying the death penalty to cases of rape was a violation of the Eighth Amendment's ban on cruel and unusual punishment. Many states, however, continued to apply the death penalty in cases of child rape, a crime widely considered to be especially heinous. This, too, was put to the test in *Kennedy v. Louisiana* (2008), a case involving a man who was convicted of brutally raping his 8-year-old stepdaughter. In a controversial 5–4 decision, the Court concluded that punishing child rape by imposing the death penalty violates the Eighth Amendment. Taken together, the *Coker* and *Kennedy* cases suggest that the death penalty is permissible only for crimes that result in the victim's death.

Although the Supreme Court has set broad parameters, state laws vary in the specific crimes they deem deserving of capital punishment. Missouri, for example, includes all defendants convicted of first-degree murder. California identifies specific crimes that are death penalty eligible; these include sabotage, intentional train wrecking, treason, fatal assault by a prisoner incarcerated for life, and perjury resulting in the execution of an innocent person. Other states only impose the death penalty if the first-degree murder conviction is accompanied by *aggravating factors*. The number of aggravating factors required in order to impose the death penalty varies by state as well. Indiana requires that 16 aggravating factors be present for a defendant to be eligible for the death penalty; Kansas requires eight; other states require that only one aggravating circumstance be met. Examples of aggravating factors from around the country include the following:

- The murder was especially heinous, atrocious, or depraved (California).
- The defendant knowingly created a grave risk of death for one or more persons in addition to the victim (Florida).
- The murder was committed by intentionally discharging a firearm into an inhabited dwelling (Indiana).
- The defendant caused or directed another to commit murder, or the defendant procured the commission of the offense by payment, promise of payment, or anything of pecuniary value (Maryland).
- The murder was committed to avoid or prevent arrest, to effect an escape, or to conceal the commission of a crime (Nebraska).
- The defendant, with the intent to kill, murdered an employee of the Corrections and Criminal Rehabilitation Department (New Mexico).
- The defendant was involved in acts of terrorism resulting in the death of another person (Oklahoma).
- The defendant has been convicted of, or committed, a prior murder, a felony involving violence, or other serious felony (South Dakota).
- The defendant is a future danger (Virginia).

The fact that a crime makes one eligible for the death penalty does not mean that the death penalty is necessarily imposed. The jury makes the actual sentencing recommendation. During the sentencing phase of a capital trial, in addition to hearing evidence of aggravating factors (weighing in favor of the death penalty), the jury also hears *mitigating* evidence. These are factors that weigh in favor of a more lenient sentence: life in prison without the possibility of parole, rather than execution. Mitigation evidence, and the role of forensic social workers in preparing mitigation reports, is highlighted elsewhere in this chapter.

Forms of Execution

States also vary in the methods of execution that they employ. The most common method today is lethal injection, but other execution methods, including the electric chair and the gas chamber, remain legal in certain states (DPIC, 2010). For example, Florida uses lethal injection and electrocution as its primary methods, Missouri uses lethal injection and poison gas, and until 2009 Idaho used both lethal injection and firing squad. Other methods, although not commonly used, may be employed if requested by the inmate (Clark County Prosecutors Office, 2008; see Table 13.1). Although lethal injection has been widely adopted because it is believed to be more humane than the alternatives, concerns about this method have persisted. Despite continued controversy and a temporary moratorium on its use, the U.S. Supreme Court affirmed its constitutionality in the 2008 case of *Baze v. Rees*. This is consistent with prior decisions that found death by firing squad (1878) and use of the electric chair (1890) to be consistent with the Eighth Amendment. In point of fact, no challenge to any specific method of capital punishment has ever been successful before the Supreme Court.

DISPROPORTIONALITY AND THE DEATH PENALTY

One of the most serious criticisms of the death penalty in the United States is that it is disproportionately applied to racial and ethnic minorities. According to the American Civil Liberties Union (ACLU, 2003a), people of color have accounted for 43% of total executions since 1976 and comprise 55% of those currently awaiting execution. Of the 18 people on federal death row in 2003, 16 were African American, Hispanic, or Asian. Between 1995 and 2000, 80% of all cases recommended for the federal death penalty involved people of color. Even after review by the attorney general, 72% of the cases approved for death penalty prosecution involved minority defendants. Research in Pennsylvania, controlling for the severity of the crime, found that African American defendants are 3.9 times more likely than White defendants to face the death penalty (Deiter, 1998). Minorities comprise 70% of death row inmates in Pennsylvania, 72% in Louisiana, 80% in Colorado, and 86% in the U.S. military (ACLU, 2003a).

In addition to people of color disproportionately facing execution, the death penalty is disproportionately applied in cases in which the victim is White. The U.S. Government Accountability Office (1996) indicates that the most reliable predictor of whether an offender will receive the death penalty is the race of the victim. Between 1976 and 1990, 76% of murders resulting in the death penalty were murders in which the victim was White. Research studies in Maryland and New Jersey confirmed disproportionate use of the death penalty in cases in which the victim was white (Amnesty International 2010b). Examining all homicide cases between 1993 and 1997 in North Carolina, researchers found that the odds of being sentenced to the death penalty were 3.5 times greater if the victim was White than if the victim was African American (Unah & Boger, 2001).

Nationally, racial bias is perhaps most apparent when examining capital cases in which the defendant is one race and the victim is another. As of

2002, there were 12 death penalty cases in which the defendant was White and the victim was Black, and 178 death penalty cases in which the defendant was Black and the victim was White. A study of prosecutions in Georgia during the 1980s revealed that the death penalty was sought in 70% of cases involving Black defendants and White victims, but in only 15% of cases involving White defendants and Black victims (ACLU, 2003b). In Virginia, Black defendants charged with raping and murdering White victims were sentenced to death in nearly every case, whereas Black defendants charged with raping and murdering Black victims were sentenced to death in only 28.6% of cases (ACLU of Virginia, 2003).

Addressing this issue has led to controversy in both the legislatures and the courts. In 2009, North Carolina became the second state (after Kentucky in 1998) to pass a Racial Justice Act allowing judges to consider whether racial bias played a role in the decision to seek or impose the death penalty. The U.S. House of Representatives has twice passed a national Racial Justice Act, but both times the legislation failed in the Senate. Introduction of these bills was prompted by the Supreme Court's decision in *McCleskey v. Kemp* (1987), which concluded that a showing of racial bias in a death penalty case requires more than a reliance on studies of racial disparity; it requires evidence of race discrimination in the individual case.

The National Association of Social Workers recognizes that the death penalty continues to be differentially applied to people who are poor, disadvantaged, of limited mental or emotional capacity, and from minority racial and/or ethnic groups. This is one reason why NASW opposes the death penalty. Research evidence has consistently supported this concern over time. Our commitment to social and economic justice demands that as long as the death penalty continues to be legal, it must be applied even-handedly, absent bias or prejudice.

Arguments For and Against the Death Penalty

Given that the death penalty is a social issue that often sparks heated debate, it is not surprising that multiple arguments have been presented both for and against its use. The courts have relied on a number of these arguments in making death penalty decisions. As you review them, think about which of them reflect, or conflict with, basic social work values.

Arguments Supporting the Death Penalty

The *deterrence* argument, described in Chapter 12, is often used in defense of the death penalty. It relies on the idea that criminals rationally weigh possible costs and benefits before committing serious crimes, and that stiff punishments serve as a significant disincentive (Stolzenberg & D'Alessio, 2004). Especially relevant in the death penalty context are the ideas of *incapacitation* and *general deterrence*. Capital punishment is the ultimate form of incapacitation, because it keeps the perpetrator forever off the streets. In terms of *general deterrence*, it tests the notion that the harsher the punishment we inflict on some, the more it serves as a disincentive to others.

Empirical evidence regarding the validity of the deterrence argument is inconclusive. Although a majority of criminologists believe that the death penalty does little to deter crime, some researchers have found an inverse relationship between executions and murder rates: the higher the number of executions, the lower the murder rate (Stolzenberg & D'Alessio, 2004). For example, in analyzing murder rates between 1933 and 1969, Ehrlich (1975) concluded that for every execution conducted, eight murders were deterred. Although widely regarded as the most compelling evidence for the deterrence argument, Ehrlich's research has since been criticized as biased and methodologically poor by many top criminologists (e.g., Radelet & Akers, 1996). In fact, most empirical evidence in the research finds no relationship between executions and murder rates. In particular, there is very little evidence to suggest that the death penalty is any more effective in deterring crime than a sentence of life in prison. In a poll of top criminologists, nearly 90% stated that, based on their knowledge of the literature, the death penalty does not have a deterrent effect on crime (Radelet & Akers, 1996).

Another argument in favor of the death penalty is that it provides for *retribution;* that is, death is a just punishment for particularly heinous crimes including the taking of a life. This idea is reflected in the notion of "an eye for an eye"—those who murder others do not deserve to live. Advocates for the death penalty believe it offers closure for victims of violent crimes and their families, as well as a sense of justice that would not be equally achieved by a sentence of life in prison. On a societal level, they argue that removing people who commit vile crimes from society promotes public safety and allows justice to prevail (Pataki, 1997). The validity of the retribution argument cannot be studied empirically because it is grounded in moral judgment. Research suggests, however, that it enjoys considerable popular support within the United States (Radelet & Akers, 1996).

Proponents also argue that imposing the death penalty on the worst criminal offenders saves the criminal justice system money by not having to house and provide for inmates for the remainder of their lives. This is countered by the argument, equally valid, that appeals in death penalty cases greatly extend inmates' time on death row, resulting in high court costs and making the death penalty no more financially feasible than life in prison. A final argument is that the death penalty serves an important function in the criminal justice system; it is used as a bargaining chip (Messerli, 2009). By having the threat of the death penalty on the table, prosecutors can persuade defendants to accept lesser sentences as part of a plea agreement; this keeps the case out of court, cutting down on costs and allowing those affected by the crime to avoid the added trauma of a trial.

Arguments Against the Death Penalty

An argument sometimes voiced by opponents of the death penalty is the *brutalization* argument. Rooted in social learning theory, it postulates that repeated exposure to violence generates more violence. While this argument is often used to advocate for less violence in the media, it has also been applied in the context of the death penalty. The idea is that when the government executes a prisoner, it models violent behavior to its citizens; when we condone the use of capital punishment, we are teaching individuals that in some circumstances it is acceptable to kill for retribution (Cochran & Chamlin, 2000). As is true with deterrence theory, there is little empirical evidence supporting the brutalization argument (Stolzenberg & D'Alessio, 2004). Cochran and Chamlin (2000), however, disagree. They believe that both theories have merit. According to their research, executions are positively correlated with certain types of murders (consistent with brutalization theory) and negatively correlated with others (consistent with deterrence). Specifically, they conclude that the death penalty tends to deter murders associated with the commission of a felony (e.g., an armed robbery gone awry) but encourages murders resulting from argument-based disputes (e.g., domestic violence cases). Future research will no doubt continue to explore the merits of this and other arguments.

Another basis for opposing the death penalty is the belief that it violates the inherent *sanctity of life*. This argument is consistent with many religious traditions and with the Universal Declaration of Human Rights (General Assembly of the United Nations, 1948). Advocates for social justice, including NASW, have embraced a similar argument: that capital punishment *undermines human dignity and the worth of the individual* (NASW, 2009). In fact, the United States is now part of a minority of world nations that imposes the death penalty. As of 2012, 141 countries have abolished the death penalty, whereas only 57 retain it (Amnesty International, 2012). Although China conducts more executions that the rest of the world combined, the United States ranks fifth in the number of executions committed, following behind Iran, North Korea, and Yemen (Amnesty International, 2011). In fact, a number of other countries—including Canada, Mexico, and South Africa—resist extraditing criminals to the United States because they regard our use of the death penalty as a human rights violation (Dieter, n.d.). Some Americans argue that this *international disapproval* negatively impacts our standing in the world.

A number of additional arguments stem from concerns about how the death penalty is administered. The first is that its use is often *arbitrary*. In other words, two people convicted of the identical crime could end up being given different sentences: One could get the death penalty and the other, life in prison. Second, as data suggest, it is *disproportionately applied* to racial minorities and those who are socially and economically disadvantaged. Finally, assessing guilt or innocence remains an inexact science; as a result, people who are in fact innocent may be put to death for crimes they did not commit. As this *innocence* argument suggests, "it is better that ten guilty persons escape, than one innocent suffer" (Blackstone, 1979, p. 358). Although supporters of the death penalty point out that today's technology renders this outcome increasingly unlikely, others are persuaded by repeated headlines revealing wrongful convictions. The Innocence Project, a nonprofit legal clinic based in New York, has been working since 1992 to help exonerate those convicted of crimes they did not commit. Using DNA evidence, their work has resulted in 251 post-conviction exonerations, 17 of which involved individuals on death row (Innocence Project, n.d.).

Legal Exemptions to the Death Penalty

Since the mid-1980s, the U.S. Supreme Court has decided several cases that questioned the constitutionality of applying the death penalty to special groups of people. Although the Court's reasoning varied somewhat from case to case, each case involved people with vulnerabilities the Court viewed as rendering them less blameworthy for their crimes. This section focuses on people with mental illness, people with intellectual disabilities, and juveniles—all of whom have merited exemptions from capital punishment.

Mental Illness and the Death Penalty

In 1986, the U.S. Supreme Court decided in *Ford v. Wainwright* that executing the criminally insane violates the Eighth Amendment's ban on cruel and unusual punishment. The case involved a defendant (Ford) who began to show signs of a mental disorder while serving a prison sentence for murder. He exhibited paranoid delusions, including a belief that he was Pope John Paul II. He insisted that the Ku Klux Klan had conspired to bury people within the prison and that prison officials were capturing and torturing his female relatives. After extensive interviews, his psychiatrist concluded that Ford "had no understanding of why he was being executed, made no connection between the homicide of which he had been convicted and the death penalty, and indeed sincerely believed that he would not be executed because he owned the prisons and could control the Governor through mind waves" (p. 399). The appeal of his death sentence reached the Supreme Court, which held that executing Ford would violate the Eighth Amendment. In reaching its decision, the Court concluded that applying the death penalty to persons with mental illness fails to satisfy any of the goals of the justice system: It has no retributive value because the defendant lacks an appreciation for his or her impending execution, it has no deterrent value because it provides no relevant example to others, and it offends humanity.

The important point here is that, according to the Court in *Ford*, having a mental illness, in and of itself, does not render one ineligible for the death penalty. To be incompetent for execution defendants must be "unaware of the punishment they're about to suffer and why they are about to suffer it" (p. 422). The Court also found that Florida's procedure for determining competency—a 30-minute evaluation by a panel of three psychiatrists—was constitutionally insufficient. A hearing is required to ensure that the defendant has an opportunity to challenge the findings of a competency determination.

In 2007, the Court reexamined the *Ford* decision in *Panetti v. Quarterman*. In this case, a man with a documented history of severe hallucinations and delusions took his estranged wife and child hostage and killed his estranged wife's parents. He was tried in a Texas court and sentenced to death despite his clear history of severe mental illness. He requested a competency hearing regarding his eligibility to be executed, but it was denied. Reaffirming its earlier holding in *Ford*, the Court held that the denial of that hearing was a clear constitutional violation.

Although the Supreme Court has been consistent in protecting the criminally insane from capital punishment, many people with severe mental illness continue to be put to death because they are found to be legally competent for execution. In a 2009 report, the ACLU argues that individuals with severe mental illnesses face serious barriers at every point of interaction with the criminal justice system leading to a death sentence. Beginning with the initial police interrogation, people with mental illnesses are more vulnerable. They may be more likely than others to offer false confessions or may have difficulty understanding their *Miranda* rights. The definition of competence to stand trial is easily satisfied; even people suffering from severe hallucinations or delusions may be deemed competent. Furthermore, these defendants may distrust their attorneys, side effects from medication may adversely affect their demeanor during trial, and they are more likely than other defendants to waive their right to an appeal. Although checks are in place to alleviate some of these issues, they are inadequate to protect all death penalty defendants who suffer from mental illnesses.

Intellectual Disabilities and the Death Penalty

Historically, the Supreme Court rejected the notion that executing people with intellectual disabilities was barred by the Eighth Amendment. In the 1989 case of *Penry v. Lynaugh*, a defendant with the mental capacity of a 6-year-old and the social development of a 9- or 10-year-old was sentenced to death after beating and raping a woman and then stabbing her to death with a pair of scissors. The Court concluded that evidence of Penry's intellectual disability (then referred to as mental retardation) could be considered a mitigating factor by the jury, but it did not automatically render him ineligible for the death penalty. Looking at "evolving standards of decency," a 5–4 majority of the Court found no national consensus to support a finding that executing people with intellectual disabilities was cruel and unusual punishment.

Thirteen years later, in 2002, the U.S. Supreme Court again considered the constitutionality of executing people with intellectual disabilities in *Atkins v. Virginia*. This time, by a 6–3 margin, the Court held that such executions indeed constitute cruel and unusual punishment in violation of the Eighth Amendment. To support its conclusion that the practice was now *unusual,* the Court noted that since its earlier decision, an additional 17 states had enacted legislation barring the execution of persons with intellectual disabilities. In the remainder of states, the practice was highly uncommon. The consistency and direction of change were regarded as demonstrating a national consensus against executing people with intellectual disabilities. As for it being *cruel,* the Court noted that people with intellectual disabilities should be considered less culpable because of their limitations in reasoning, judgment, and impulse control. Given their reduced culpability, the goals of the justice system (deterrence and retribution) would not be served by their execution. In addition, they could not merit the most extreme form of punishment available; the death penalty would necessarily be excessive. Finally, the Court recognized that those with intellectual disabilities face a special risk of wrongful execution; they make poor witnesses, are more likely to give false confessions, and are less likely to be able to assist their attorneys.

Although the Supreme Court has banned the use of the death penalty with people who are intellectually disabled, many vulnerable individuals remain unprotected. The definition of intellectual disability is left to each state, along with the process for determining who will evaluate the defendant's status and on what basis. Generally speaking, an intellectual disability involves significant limitations in both intellectual functioning and adaptive behavior, with the onset occurring before age 18 (American Association of Intellectual and Developmental Disabilities, 2010). Some observers have raised concerns about state laws that use a specific IQ score to distinguish between normal and impaired intellectual functioning. They argue that defining intellectual disability based on an arbitrary score excludes many people whose limitations may be equally significant. Thus, in a state that defines intellectual disability using an IQ score of 70 or lower, a defendant with an IQ of 70 would be spared the death penalty whereas someone with an IQ of 71 might be executed (ACLU, 2003b). The variation among states is also problematic. Many states, such as Kentucky, Maryland, and North Carolina, draw the line at an IQ of 70. Illinois draws the line at 75. Arkansas has no firm cutoff, but it does have a rebuttable presumption of intellectual disability for an IQ of 65; in other words, it is assumed that a defendant with an IQ of 65 or less has an intellectual disability unless the prosecution provides evidence to the contrary. Given these variations, a defendant with an IQ of 75 would be protected in Illinois, for example, but would be subject to the death penalty in Idaho. Finally, most states require that the disability originate before age 18, but others, including Utah, Maryland, and Indiana, include those disabilities originating before age 22 (DPIC, 2010).

Including the requirement that the intellectual disability be diagnosed before adulthood prevents individuals from faking an intellectual disability in order to avoid or lessen punishment, but it also creates important limitations (ACLU, 2003b). The causes of intellectual disabilities vary but include developmental disorders, brain abnormalities, and traumatic brain injuries (Centers for Disease Control and Prevention, n.d.). The fact that intellectual disabilities can result from traumatic brain injuries suggests that onset could occur at any point in a person's life. Under most state laws, however, a person with essentially the same symptoms as someone with a diagnosed intellectual disability would not receive the same protection from the death penalty if the symptoms resulted from a brain injury occurring during adulthood.

A final concern relates to the failure of some states to require that trained professionals conduct assessments for intellectual disability. Many states are silent regarding who counts as a "qualified examiner." Of those that do address the issue, the required qualifications vary. Many states require a licensed psychiatrist or psychologist. South Dakota explicitly includes "licensed psychiatric social workers" (i.e., "clinical" social workers). New York's law affords more latitude by requiring a psychiatrist, psychologist or "other trained individual." Florida simply includes "experts in the field of intellectual disabilities." Washington State's law is quite specific; it requires a licensed psychiatrist or psychologist "who is an expert in the diagnosis and evaluation of intellectual disabilities." In some states, such as Arizona, the court appoints the evaluator; in Utah, at least two mental health experts are required. In Georgia, the evaluator is chosen and paid for by the defendant. In Nevada, the prosecution selects the evaluator. In some states, the judge makes the determination of intellectual disability before the trial begins; in others, the jury makes it during sentencing.

Despite these variations and concerns, there is no question that the Supreme Court's decision in *Atkins* is enormously significant. In addition to protecting those with intellectual disabilities from the death penalty, it paved the way for the recent exemption of juveniles from capital punishment in the United States.

Juveniles and the Death Penalty

The Supreme Court began limiting the application of the death penalty to juvenile offenders in the 1988 case of *Thompson v. Oklahoma*. In that case, a 15-year-old boy (Thompson) participated in the murder of his former brother-in-law. He was waived to adult court and, taking into consideration the particularly brutal nature of the crime, the jury sentenced him to death. On appeal, Thompson's attorney argued that executing a 15-year-old violated the Eighth Amendment's ban on cruel and unusual punishment. The U.S. Supreme Court agreed. In reaching its conclusion, the Court argued that executing 15-year-olds was unusual; 18 states had set the minimum age for death penalty eligibility at 16 and no one under the age of 16 had been executed in any state since 1948. In addition, the Court added juveniles to those groups thought to have diminished culpability for their actions. The Court noted that executing juveniles does little to achieve the goals of the death penalty in that, like executing people with mental illness or intellectual disabilities, it is unlikely to deter other criminals and it has little retributive value.

The following year, the Supreme Court heard another challenge to the death penalty, this time concerning the constitutionality of executing 16- and 17-year-olds. In that case (*Stanford v. Kentucky*, 1989) the Supreme Court, by a vote of 5–4, upheld the constitutionality of applying the death penalty to juveniles age 16 and older. Justice Sandra Day O'Connor was the swing vote in both cases; her switching sides accounts for the difference in the two outcomes. As a result of these two cases, the death penalty line was drawn at age 16 until the issue again came before the Supreme Court in the 2005 case of *Roper v. Simmons.*

Roper v. Simmons involved a 17-year-old boy who was convicted of a gruesome premeditated murder, tried as an adult, and sentenced to death. In this case, the Supreme Court agreed that the execution of any juvenile under 18 violates the Eighth Amendment. The Court once again referred to the evolving standards of decency in determining whether executing juveniles was cruel and unusual. The 5–4 majority identified 30 states that had banned the execution of juveniles and noted that even where the practice was legal, it was rare. According to the Court, there was no longer a national consensus in favor of the juvenile death penalty. The Court also noted that the United States was the only country in the world that continued to sanction the juvenile death penalty, and that it was one of only two countries (the other being Somalia) that had failed to ratify the U.N. Convention on the Rights of the Child, which expressly prohibits capital punishment for crimes committed by juveniles younger than age 18. As it did in the *Atkins* case with regard to intellectual disabilities, the Court argued in *Simmons* that juvenile offenders are less culpable for their crimes than are adults. Specifically, the Court recognized three important ways in which juveniles differ from adults: (1) their comparative immaturity, (2) their susceptibility to outside influences, and (3) their amenability to further development and change. Because they are less blameworthy, imposing the death penalty on juveniles fails to satisfy the aims of deterrence and retribution. It is also disproportionate because the most severe punishment should be reserved for those offenders "whose extreme culpability makes them the most deserving of execution" (p. 568). NASW contributed to an *amicus* brief in the *Simmons* case, arguing for elimination of the juvenile death penalty largely on the basis of recent scientific findings regarding adolescent brain development. These findings and their implications are highlighted in Chapter 11.

SOCIAL WORKERS AND MITIGATION

Social workers can play an important role in ensuring that capital defendants are spared the death penalty. They do this by serving as *mitigation specialists.* The sentencing process in capital cases includes a presentation to the jury of *aggravating factors* (those that weigh in favor of a death sentence) and *mitigating factors* (those weighing in favor of life in prison, rather than death). Social workers are among those forensic experts who may be called upon to provide mitigation evidence. The evidence is developed through the preparation of a comprehensive life history of the defendant. The idea is to complete a social history that gives the jury insight into the defendant's background and character and identifies reasons why the defendant's life should be spared. Research suggests that these life histories can be vital in guiding jury sentencing decisions (Schroeder, 2003).

Every state defines, by statute, what will be considered mitigating evidence. Some states enumerate specific considerations. Colorado, for example, identifies the following factors (Code Section 18-1.3-1201[4]):

- Defendant's age at the time of the crime

- Defendant's emotional state at the time of the crime
- Defendant's capacity to appreciate the wrongfulness of his behavior
- Defendant was under duress
- Defendant's participation in the crime was relatively minor
- Defendant could not reasonably have anticipated that his behavior would result in someone's death
- Defendant has no prior convictions
- Defendant cooperated with law enforcement
- Defendant was under the influence of drugs or alcohol
- Defendant believed his behavior was morally justified
- Defendant is not a continuing threat to society

Compare this to Oklahoma's law under which mitigating circumstances are defined simply as (1) circumstances that may extenuate or reduce the degree of moral culpability or blame or (2) circumstances in which fairness, sympathy or mercy may lead jurors individually or collectively to decide against imposing the death penalty (Code Section OUJI-CR 4-78).

In the 1978 case of *Lockett v. Ohio*, the U.S. Supreme Court made it clear that states must permit the introduction of any and all mitigating evidence in death penalty cases; consequently, states that enumerate specific mitigating circumstances must also include a "catch all" statement in their definitions. The Colorado statute, for example, concludes with the phrase "any other evidence which in the court's opinion bears on the question of mitigation" (Code Section 18-1.3-1201[4]).

Completing a life history as part of a mitigation investigation can take between 200 and 500 hours and typically involves compiling information stretching back three generations. Preparation may include interviewing the client, various relatives, and others in the client's life (employers, teachers, clergy, etc.); preparing a timeline of the client's development, experiences, and behavior; conducting psychosocial assessments, IQ tests, or personality tests; and examining the client's medical and mental health history, substance abuse history and treatment, school records, social service records, military service records, juvenile and criminal charges, employment and training history, incarceration record, immigration experiences, religious training, and participation in sports or other recreational activities.

The mitigation specialist, who serves as part of the defense team, then uses these data to draw conclusions about the influences in the client's life and patterns in the client's behavior. These conclusions are presented within a theoretical framework that helps the jury understand who the defendant is and how the defendant ended up at this point in his or her life. Whether the emerging theme is a history of abuse or repeated systemic failures, the life history helps humanize the defendant (Schroeder, 2003). The hope is that as a result, the jury might regard the defendant as less blameworthy and therefore undeserving of death.

Compiling a life history requires the use of an ecological approach in which the entire client system is examined in order to identify both the negative and positive factors that have shaped the client's experience and behavior. Social workers are especially well suited to this role because of our experience with multidimensional assessment. Social work case management, casework, and mediation skills can also be helpful in the mitigation process (Schroeder, Guin, Pogue, & Bordelonm, 2006). Given the significant weight given to mitigation evidence in the sentencing phase of capital trials, social workers who serve as mitigation specialists have an important role to play and much to offer.

Summary and Conclusion

The death penalty is an issue that continues to capture the interest of the public and the courts. Its history in the United States has been characterized by repeated reversals as it gained and lost and regained favor over time. The social work profession, consistent with its concern for human dignity and social justice, opposes the death penalty. Of particular concern is the mounting evidence that those who are marginalized in society are disproportionately likely to be executed. Today, 16 states prohibit the use of the death penalty, and many others impose it only infrequently. Undoubtedly, the controversy surrounding the constitutionality, morality, and advisability of the death penalty will continue to occupy the American landscape. Social workers must collaborate with others seeking the vindication of civil and human rights through reform of death penalty laws. In the meantime, as practitioners, social workers can help protect defendants from the reach of the death penalty by serving as mitigation specialists in capital trials.

Sample Case

The following is a relatively recent case concerning the applicability of the death penalty to child rape. Try briefing the case and answering the questions that follow.

KENNEDY v. LOUISIANA
128 S.Ct. 2641 (2008)

Justice Kennedy delivered the opinion of the Court.

…Patrick Kennedy, the petitioner here, seeks to set aside his death sentence under the Eighth Amendment. He was charged by the respondent, the State of Louisiana, with the aggravated rape of his then-8-year-old stepdaughter. After a jury trial petitioner was convicted and sentenced to death under a state statute authorizing capital punishment for the rape of a child under 12 years of age. This case presents the question whether the Constitution bars respondent from imposing the death penalty for the rape of a child where the crime did not result, and was not intended to result, in death of the victim. We hold the Eighth Amendment prohibits the death penalty for this offense. The Louisiana statute is unconstitutional.***

Petitioner's crime was one that cannot be recounted in these pages in a way sufficient to capture in full the hurt and horror inflicted on his victim or to convey the revulsion society, and the jury that represents it, sought to express by sentencing petitioner to death. At 9:18 a.m. on March 2, 1998, petitioner called 911 to report that his stepdaughter, referred to here as L. H., had been raped. He told the 911 operator that L. H. had been in the garage while he readied his son for school. Upon hearing loud screaming, petitioner said, he ran outside and found L. H. in the side yard. Two neighborhood boys, petitioner told the operator, had dragged L. H. from the garage to the yard, pushed her down, and raped her. Petitioner claimed he saw one of the boys riding away on a blue 10-speed bicycle.

When police arrived at petitioner's home between 9:20 and 9:30 a.m., they found L. H. on her bed, wearing a T-shirt and wrapped in a bloody blanket. She was bleeding profusely from the vaginal area. Petitioner told police he had carried her from the yard to the bathtub and then to the bed. Consistent with this explanation, police found a thin line of blood drops in the garage on the way to the house and then up the stairs. Once in the bedroom, petitioner had used a basin of water and a cloth to wipe blood from the victim. This later prevented medical personnel from collecting a reliable DNA sample.

L. H. was transported to the Children's Hospital. An expert in pediatric forensic medicine testified that L. H.'s injuries were the most severe he had seen from a sexual assault in his four years of practice. . . . The injuries required emergency surgery. . . .

Eight days after the crime, and despite L. H.'s insistence that petitioner was not the offender, petitioner was arrested for the rape. . . . About a month after petitioner's arrest L. H. was removed from the custody of her mother, who had maintained until that point that petitioner was not involved in the rape. On June 22, 1998, L. H. was returned home and told her mother for the first time that petitioner had raped her. And on December 16, 1999, about 21 months after the rape, L. H. recorded her accusation in a videotaped interview with the Child Advocacy Center.

The State charged petitioner with aggravated rape of a child under La. Stat. Ann. §14:42 and sought the death penalty. . . . The jury unanimously determined that petitioner should be sentenced to death. The Supreme Court of Louisiana affirmed. . . .

We granted certiorari.***

The Eighth Amendment, applicable to the States through the Fourteenth Amendment, provides that "[e]xcessive bail shall not be required, nor excessive fines imposed, nor cruel and unusual punishments inflicted." The Court explained in *Atkins*, and *Roper* that the Eighth Amendment's protection against excessive or cruel and unusual punishments flows from the basic "precept of justice that punishment for [a] crime should be graduated and proportioned to [the] offense." Whether this requirement has been fulfilled is determined not by the standards that prevailed when the Eighth Amendment was adopted in 1791 but by the norms that "currently prevail." The Amendment "draw[s] its meaning from the evolving standards of decency that mark the progress of a maturing society." This is because "[t]he standard of extreme cruelty is not merely descriptive, but necessarily embodies a moral judgment. The standard itself remains the same, but its applicability must change as the basic mores of society change."...

Evolving standards of decency must embrace and express respect for the dignity of the person, and the punishment of criminals must conform to that rule. As we shall discuss, punishment is justified under one or more of three principal rationales: rehabilitation, deterrence, and retribution. It is the last of these, retribution, which most often can contradict the law's own ends. This is of particular concern when the Court interprets the meaning of the Eighth Amendment in capital cases. When the law punishes by death, it risks its own sudden descent into brutality, transgressing the constitutional commitment to decency and restraint.

For these reasons we have explained that capital punishment must be limited to those offenders who commit "a narrow category of the most serious crimes" and whose extreme culpability makes them "the most deserving of execution."

...Based both on consensus and our own independent judgment, our holding is that a death sentence for one who raped but did not kill a child, and who did not intend to assist another in killing the child, is unconstitutional under the Eighth and Fourteenth Amendments.***

...The evidence of a national consensus with respect to the death penalty for child rapists, as with respect to juveniles, mentally retarded offenders, and vicarious felony murderers, shows divided opinion but, on balance, an opinion against it. Thirty-seven jurisdictions—36 States plus the Federal Government—have the death penalty. As mentioned above, only six of those jurisdictions authorize the death penalty for rape of a child. Though our review of national consensus is not confined to tallying the number of States with applicable death penalty legislation, it is of significance that, in 45 jurisdictions, petitioner could not be executed for child rape of any kind. That number surpasses the 30 States in *Atkins* and *Roper*...that prohibited the death penalty under the circumstances those cases considered. *** These statistics confirm our determination from our review of state statutes that there is a social consensus against the death penalty for the crime of child rape.***

It must be acknowledged that there are moral grounds to question a rule barring capital punishment for a crime against an individual that did not result in death. These facts illustrate the point. Here the victim's fright, the sense of betrayal, and the nature of her injuries caused more prolonged physical and mental suffering than, say, a sudden killing by an unseen assassin. The attack was not just on her but on her childhood....We cannot dismiss the years of long anguish that must be endured by the victim of child rape.

It does not follow, though, that capital punishment is a proportionate penalty for the crime....Consistent with evolving standards of decency and the teachings of our precedents we conclude that, in determining whether the death penalty is excessive, there is a distinction between intentional first-degree murder on the one hand and non-homicide crimes against individual persons, even including child rape, on the other. The latter crimes may be devastating in their harm, as here, but "in terms of moral depravity and of the injury to the person and to the public," they cannot be compared to murder in their "severity and irrevocability."

Our decision is consistent with the justifications offered for the death penalty. *Gregg* instructs that capital punishment is excessive when it is grossly out of proportion to the crime or it does not fulfill the two distinct social purposes served by the death penalty: retribution and deterrence of capital crimes.

The goal of retribution, which reflects society's and the victim's interests in seeing that the offender is repaid for the hurt he caused, does not justify the harshness of the death penalty here. In measuring retribution, as well as other objectives of criminal law, it is appropriate to distinguish between a particularly depraved murder that merits death as a form of retribution and the crime of child rape....In considering whether retribution is served, among other factors we have looked to whether capital punishment "has the potential ... to allow the community as a whole, including the surviving family and friends of the victim, to affirm its own judgment that the culpability of the prisoner is so serious that the ultimate penalty must be sought and imposed." In considering the death penalty for non-homicide offenses this inquiry necessarily also must include the question whether the death penalty balances the wrong to the victim.

It is not at all evident that the child rape victim's hurt is lessened when the law permits the death of the perpetrator. Capital cases require a long-term commitment by those who testify for the prosecution, especially when guilt and sentencing determinations are in multiple proceedings. In cases like this the key testimony is not just from the family but from the victim herself. During formative years of her adolescence, made all the more daunting for having to come to terms with the brutality of her experience, L. H. was required to discuss the case at length with law enforcement personnel. In a public trial she was required to recount once more all the details of the crime to a jury as the State pursued the death of her stepfather.... Society's desire to inflict the death penalty for child rape by enlisting the child victim to assist it over the course of years in asking for capital punishment forces a moral choice on the child, who is not of mature age to make that choice.

There are, moreover, serious systemic concerns in prosecuting the crime of child rape that are relevant to the constitutionality of making it a capital offense. The problem of unreliable, induced, and even imagined child testimony means there is a "special risk of wrongful execution" in some child rape cases. This undermines, at least to some degree, the meaningful contribution of the death penalty to legitimate goals of punishment....

Similar criticisms pertain to other cases involving child witnesses; but child rape cases present heightened concerns because the central narrative and account of the crime often comes from the child herself. She and the accused are, in most instances, the only ones present when the crime was committed....Although capital punishment does bring retribution, and the legislature here has chosen to use it for this end, its judgment must be weighed, in deciding the constitutional question, against the special risks of unreliable testimony with respect to this crime.

With respect to deterrence, if the death penalty adds to the risk of non-reporting, that, too, diminishes the penalty's objectives. Underreporting is a common problem with respect to child sexual abuse. The experience of the *amici* who work with child victims indicates that, when the punishment is death, both the victim and the victim's family members may be more likely to shield the perpetrator from discovery, thus increasing underreporting. As a result, punishment by death may not result in more deterrence or more effective enforcement.

In addition, by in effect making the punishment for child rape and murder equivalent, a State that punishes child rape by death may remove a strong incentive for the rapist not to kill the victim....Each of these propositions, standing alone, might not establish the unconstitutionality of the death penalty for the crime of child rape. Taken in sum, however, they demonstrate the serious negative consequences of making child rape a capital offense. These considerations lead us to conclude, in our independent judgment, that the death penalty is not a proportional punishment for the rape of a child.***

In most cases justice is not better served by terminating the life of the perpetrator rather than confining him and preserving the possibility that he and the system will find ways to allow him to understand the enormity of his offense. Difficulties in administering the penalty to ensure against its arbitrary and capricious application require adherence to a rule reserving its use, at this stage of evolving standards and in cases of crimes against individuals, for crimes that take the life of the victim....The judgment of the Supreme Court of Louisiana upholding the capital sentence is reversed.

Questions

1. In this case, the Supreme Court of Louisiana concluded that the rape of a child is a sufficiently heinous crime to incur the death penalty. The U.S. Supreme Court disagreed. Which position do you agree with? What crimes do you believe are

deserving of the death penalty? What criteria should govern how we identify such crimes?

2. The National Association of Social Workers (NASW) submitted an *amicus brief* in this case that was cited in the Court's opinion. Which side do you suppose the brief supported? Why? If you were charged with writing the NASW brief, what arguments would you make?

3. How would you summarize the policy arguments made by the Court? Do you think they have merit? Why or why not?

4. In his dissenting opinion (not reprinted), Justice Scalia takes issue with the majority's use of statistics. He also argues that the policy arguments made by the majority are simply "not pertinent to the question of whether the death penalty is cruel and un-usual punishment." Do you agree? Why or why not?

CHAPTER 13 PRACTICE TEST

The following questions will test your application and analysis of the content found within this chapter. For additional assessment, including licensing-exam type questions on applying chapter content to practice behaviors, visit **MySearchLab**.

1. The U.S. Supreme Court has ruled that the death penalty is unconstitutional when applied to which of the following?

   a. juveniles

   b. parents of young children

   c. people in poverty

   d. people with physical disabilities

2. Which of the following is TRUE regarding race and the death penalty?

   a. It is disproportionately applied when both the victim and the perpetrator are Black.

   b. It is disproportionately applied when the victim is Black and the perpetrator is White.

   c. It is disproportionately applied when the victim is White.

   d. There is no evidence-based research confirming racial disparities in the application of the death penalty.

3. Most legal challenges to the death penalty have been brought under the Eighth Amendment. In analyzing these cases the court looks at

   a. equal protection under the law.

   b. evolving standards of decency.

   c. freedom of association.

   d. the right against self-incrimination.

4. Social workers who perform mitigation assessments

   a. assist with jury selection in capital cases.

   b. conduct life histories that attempt to humanize the defendant.

   c. identify aggravating factors that weigh in favor of the death sentence.

   d. work with victims to draft victim impact statements.

5. Discuss the major arguments for and against the death penalty. Which are most consistent with social work values? Explain.

6. In recent years, the U.S. Supreme Court has found the death penalty to be unconstitutional in relation to several specific groups of defendants. Who are they? What has the Court's reasoning been in excluding these groups from the reach of the death penalty? Can you think of any other groups that might fit within the Court's rationale in the future?

MYSEARCHLAB CONNECTIONS

Reinforce what you learned in this chapter by studying videos, cases, documents, and more available at **www.MySearchLab.com.**

Explore these Assets

- Interactive Case Study: Race and the Death Penalty

Research these Topics

- exoneration using DNA evidence
- the death penalty and foreign nationals

Assess Your Knowledge

Go to **MySearchLab** to test your knowledge of key topics in this chapter with topic-specific quizzes. Conclude your assessment by completing the chapter exam.

⋆ = CSWE Core Competency Asset   Δ = Case Study

Chapter **14**

....

Health

The quest for good health transcends age, culture, sex, and geography. As the world population ages, both the promotion of good health and the treatment of disease become focal points for research, innovation, service delivery, and policy. This chapter examines the meaning of health, both in the United States and abroad, and explores several health-related issues of relevance to social work including reproductive rights, HIV/AIDS, and human genetics. A special section highlights the controversy surrounding conscience clauses, and a sample case examines the issue of fetal rights.

Background
....

What does it mean to be healthy? In 1945, the United Nations began the creation of a global health agency. Founded in 1948 and called the World Health Organization (WHO), it included the following definition of health in its constitution: Health is a state of "complete physical, mental, and social well-being and not merely the absence of disease or infirmity" (World Health Organization, 2010). This was a departure from the traditional disease model that focused exclusively on treatment, and it opened up new possibilities for a more holistic approach emphasizing prevention.

This holistic view of health took root in the Western world during the 1960s and 1970s. Scholars and observers increasingly recognized the impact of environment, biology, lifestyle choice, and health care delivery on the maintenance of good physical, social, and psychological health (Irvine, Elliott, Wallace, & Crombie, 2006; Wolinsky, 1980). This was consistent with social work's biopsychosocial and spiritual perspective (NASW, 2005). Meanwhile, in 1979, the U.S. surgeon general released a report, "Health Promotion and Disease Prevention," which revealed that the general health of the American population lagged behind that of other developed nations despite soaring expenditures on health care (Irvine et al., 2006). This led to the creation of the Healthy People Initiative, which is now in its third decade of setting 10-year goals for health improvement. Figure 14.1 illustrates the framework for Healthy People 2020.

Health Disparities

Health disparities are defined as "differences in the incidence, prevalence, mortality, and burden of diseases and other adverse health conditions that exist among specific population groups in the United States" (Hofrichter & Bhatia, 2010, p. 372). Factors that may lead to disparities in health include biological variations among ethnic groups or between sexes; environmental factors such as exposure to disease or toxic substances; and social factors including income, level of education, and access to adequate health care services (Dolgoff, 2007; Hofrichter & Bhatia, 2010). Many health disparities are avoidable inequities that have profound social justice implications. Poor health takes its toll on the individual, family, community, and society by causing human suffering, stressing relationships, and reducing productivity.

One area in which race and sex disparities are apparent is life expectancy. As Figure 14.2 suggests, White women live the longest at an average of 80.5 years, whereas

FIGURE 14.1   **Healthy People 2020 Framework**

Healthy People 2020

A society in which all people live long, healthy lives

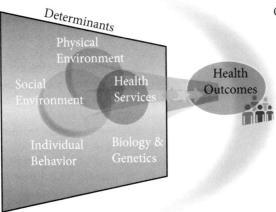

Overarching Goals:

- Attain high quality, longer lives free of preventable disease, disability, injury, and premature death.
- Achieve health equity, eliminate disparities, and improve the health of all groups.
- Create social and physical environments that promote good health for all.
- Promote quality of life, healthy development, and healthy behaviors across all life stages.

Source: http://www.healthypeople.gov/2020/Consortium/HP2020Framework.pdf

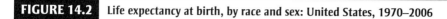

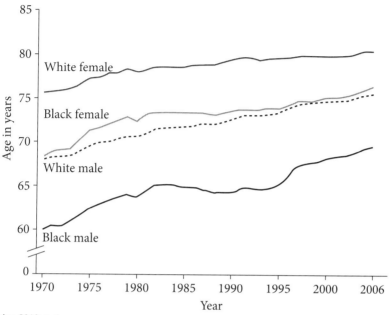

| FIGURE 14.2 | Life expectancy at birth, by race and sex: United States, 1970–2006 |

Source: Arias, 2010, p. 4

African American women live an average of 76.1 years; for White men, life expectancy is 75.3 years, and for African American men it is 69 years. African American men also experience the highest death rates in every age group. Research shows that if the mortality gap between African Americans and Whites were eliminated, an estimated 84,000 African American lives would be saved in a single year (Williams, 2007).

The most common cause of death for all racial and ethnic groups is chronic disease, with heart disease and cancer ranking either first or second for all groups. Stroke is the third most common cause of death for all groups except for Hispanics, for whom it ranks fourth, and for American Indians/Native Alaskans, for whom it ranks seventh. There is a large disparity between African Americans and Whites in the incidence of cardiovascular disease, which is mostly due to the prevalence of hypertension in the African American community. Whites are most often hospitalized for acute myocardial infarction, whereas African Americans, Hispanics, and American Indians/Native Alaskans are most often hospitalized for chronic heart failure. Research shows that many of these hospitalizations could be avoided if preventive care were more readily available. Overall, American Indians/Native Alaskans, African Americans, and Hispanics report more unhealthy days than do Asian Americans and Caucasians (Williams, 2007).

In terms of sex differences, men are more than twice as likely as women to die in automobile accidents and approximately four times more likely than women to die by suicide. Men, along with younger people, are also most likely to engage in binge drinking (Centers for Disease Control and Prevention, 2011b).

Social Determinants of Health

Although biological factors and individual behavior are important contributors to health, social and environmental conditions also determine health status. These aspects of health are especially important because they are amenable to change and often reflect serious lapses in social and economic justice. The term *social determinants of health* refers to unequal access to health resources, differential vulnerability on the part of certain population groups, and differential exposure to risk (Blas, Sommerfeld, & Kurup, 2011). The Centers for Disease Control and Prevention (CDC) monitor many of these conditions and their relationship to health disparities within the U.S. population. Poor air quality, for example, contributes to premature death, lung cancer, respiratory illness, childhood asthma, and cardiovascular disease. It is more pronounced in urban areas, where racial and ethnic minorities are more likely to be concentrated. Similarly, inadequate or unhealthy housing conditions contribute to infectious diseases, chronic health conditions, injuries, and developmental delays. In 2009, African Americans, Hispanics, and American Indians/Native Alaskans were approximately twice as likely as Caucasians to have inadequate housing (CDC, 2011b).

Education is a strong determinant of both future employment and income. Low income, in turn, is correlated with many adverse social and environmental conditions. The recent housing bust and ongoing economic recession have disproportionately affected people of color, exacerbating these disparities even further. Between 2005 and 2009, the racial wealth gap doubled, wiping out much of the progress made by people of color over the past 20 years. During that brief span, Hispanic wealth declined by 66% and African American wealth declined by 53%, whereas White wealth declined by only 16%. White Americans average 20 times the net worth of African Americans and 18 times the net worth of Latinos (Jordan, 2011). The consequences can be seen in rates of infant mortality (infants born to African American women are up to three times more likely to die than those born to mothers of other races); new HIV infections (which are disproportionately high within all minority groups except Asians/Pacific Islanders); teen pregnancy (birth rates are three times higher among Hispanic youth than Whites and 2.5 times higher among African American youth than Whites); and smoking (rates decline significantly with increased income and education across all races).

These disparities also extend to prevention and early intervention, including seeking appropriate medical care. Whites are more likely than both Blacks and Hispanics to be vaccinated against the flu and to be screened for colorectal cancer; the use of both preventive measures increases with education and household income (CDC, 2011b). Having insurance coverage is also a factor in successfully controlling health conditions and receiving treatment.

Environmental disasters can have devastating health consequences for the people who live in affected areas. One of many examples is Hurricane Katrina, which resulted in contaminated water and toxic fumes, causing hundreds to suffer from infected sores, vomiting, and asthma; its health effects are still being felt. Low-income neighborhoods and those populated by people of color are disproportionately the sites of hazardous waste dumping and toxic product production; the term *environmental racism* has emerged to describe this phenomenon. In recent years, the Environmental Protection Agency has responded by committing itself to environmental justice; the problem, however, is a global one (Bullard, 2002).

Access to Health Care

Under U.S. law, there is no constitutional right to receive health care or for the government to pay for the care of its citizens. Generally speaking, the Constitution protects individuals from government interference with their rights rather than conferring rights upon them. There are a few exceptions, notably when a person is in state custody; this explains, for example, the right of institutionalized people to receive treatment. The American approach to health care is at odds with international treaties and conventions that regard health care as a basic human right. These include the Universal Declaration of Human Rights (UDHR) and the International Covenant on Economic, Social, and Cultural Rights (ICESCR).

In the absence of government-provided health care, an insurance-based system has developed in the United States. Health insurance has become an indispensable asset in the equitable distribution of health resources; those lacking health insurance are at increased risk for poor health and premature death. Of those Americans who are insured, nearly 30% receive health care through Medicare or Medicaid, approximately 58.5% receive health insurance through their employers, and approximately 8.2% purchase their own private insurance policies (U.S. Census Bureau, 2009). These sources of coverage, however, comprise a fragmented system that is enormously costly yet leaves many people vulnerable. Private plans often limit reimbursements and have high deductibles and co-pays, putting them beyond the reach of many individuals and families. One study of bankruptcy filers with significant medical debt found that approximately 80% had some form of health insurance yet still were unable to pay (Jacoby, Sullivan, & Warren, 2001). These payment systems also restrict coverage for certain health conditions, resulting in insufficient care for some patients. Publicly funded plans have narrow eligibility criteria, and access to care may be impeded because not all physicians accept payment from these programs (Furrow, Greaney, Johnson, Jost, & Schwartz, 2008). Likewise, managed care organizations may threaten access to needed services by limiting patients to a particular network of providers and controlling the approval of health care expenditures (Furrow et al., 2008). Case law has established that private physicians are not required to accept every patient seeking care (*Williams v. United States*, 2001), but neither can a physician unilaterally stop treating a patient because of lack of payment (*Ricks v. Budge*, 1937).

Perhaps the most serious problem is that, as of 2009, 15.4% of the population (a total of 46.3 million people) remained uninsured—including 7.3 million children younger than age 18. Adults between the ages of 19 and 29 are the group least likely to carry insurance; although they comprise 20% of the population, they comprise 30% of the uninsured (Karger & Stoesz, 2008). People of color and people living in poverty are disproportionately represented among those without health insurance; families with incomes below 200% of the federal poverty level are at the greatest risk of being uninsured. Low-wage workers, those in small businesses, and part-time workers are also at increased risk (NASW, 2009b). In 2008, almost 1.1 million part-time workers lost their health insurance (U.S. Census Bureau, 2009). Even among those with health insurance, minority groups are more likely than dominant groups to be enrolled in "lower end" health plans that provide less adequate reimbursement and impose stricter limits on covered services (NASW, 2009b).

Studies show that adults younger than age 65 without insurance have a 40% higher risk of death than those who are insured (Wilper et al., 2009). Individuals without insurance and those on Medicaid who are diagnosed with cancer are 1.6 times more likely to die within five years of their diagnosis than those with private insurance (Ward, Halperin,

Schrag, Cokknides, DeSantis, Brandi, Siegel, Stewart, & Jemal, 2008). Health status is inevitably compromised for people who lack insurance because they are less likely to receive adequate preventive care, early diagnosis of disease, and timely therapeutic intervention.

Federal Legislation

A number of important federal programs provide or finance health care for many Americans:

- **Medicare:** Provides health insurance for people older than age 65, people younger than age 65 with certain disabilities, and people of any age with end-stage renal disease. Part A helps cover the costs of hospital care, skilled nursing facilities, hospice care, and home health care; Part B helps cover doctors' services, outpatient care, and preventive care; and Part D helps cover the cost of prescription drugs. Medicare covers approximately 14.3% of the U.S. population.
- **Medicaid:** Provides health benefits for certain low-income individuals and families. Each state sets its own eligibility and service guidelines within the strictures of federal law. Covered populations include pregnant women, children, low-income older adults, and people with disabilities. Medicaid covers approximately 14.1% of the U.S. population.
- **Children's Health Insurance Program (CHIP):** Uses federal funds to help states insure low-income children who are ineligible for Medicaid but cannot afford private insurance.
- **V.A. Health Care:** Provides for the health care needs for America's veterans. The Veterans Health Administration (VHA) oversees a network of hospitals, clinics, nursing homes, and counseling centers at approximately 1,400 sites.
- **Indian Health Service:** Provides health care services to the country's 564 federally recognized tribes, serving approximately 1.9 million people.

In 2010, Congress passed the Patient Protection and Affordable Care Act (ACA, P.L. 111-148), commonly referred to as *health care reform*. The goals of this legislation include increasing the affordability and availability of health insurance and reducing the number of people who are uninsured (NASW, 2011). The law is highly complex and many of its provisions will not be implemented until at least 2014. Among the reforms included are ending lifetime and most annual limits on care, allowing youth to stay on their parents' insurance until age 26, providing some patients with preventive services free of charge, increasing care coordination, and prohibiting the denial of coverage to people with pre-existing conditions. Every American will be required to purchase health insurance; state exchanges will be created to facilitate comparison and choice among plans.

The ACA has been controversial since its inception, having been passed on a largely party-line vote by congressional Democrats early in the Obama administration. Lawsuits challenging the new law's constitutionality proliferated. Most focused on the requirement that every American purchase health insurance or face a fine (the so-called *individual mandate*). Results of these lower court cases were mixed, leading the U.S. Supreme Court to take up the case (*National Federation of Independent Business v. Sebelius*) in 2012. In an unexpected turn of events, a 5-member majority of the Court declared nearly all of the law constitutional. Specifically, Chief Justice John Roberts joined justices Ginsburg, Breyer, Sotomayor, and Kagan in upholding the individual mandate as a legitimate exercise of

Congress's taxing power. A majority of the Court also upheld the law's required Medic-aid expansion, with the exception of a provision that would have penalized states with the complete withdrawal of federal Medicaid funds if they failed to comply. Social work-ers have been strong supporters of the ACA because it expands preventive care, increases health care accessibility, invests in public health and provider training, and moves us closer to universal coverage.

Reproductive Rights

One of the greatest, most enduring controversies in the field of health pertains to re-productive rights. As a result of religious tradition or other personal convictions, many Americans, including many social workers, wrestle with these issues. The National As-sociation of Social Workers affirms the right of individuals, without government inter-ference, to make their own decisions about sexuality and reproduction (NASW, 2009a). Before turning to issues concerning contraception and abortion—which involve the right to refrain from procreation—we begin by examining the right *to* procreate.

The Right to Procreation

The United States has a long and unfortunate history of restricting childbearing. The first compulsory sterilization law was passed in Indiana in 1907. By the 1930s, more than half the states had such laws. In 1927, the U.S. Supreme Court decided a famous case called *Buck v. Bell*. It involved an 18-year-old woman with an intellectual disability whose mother and daughter were similarly disabled. In upholding the Virginia law permitting steriliza-tion of the so-called feeble minded, Justice Oliver Wendell Holmes wrote for an eight-member majority, "Three generations of imbeciles are enough" (*Buck v. Bell*, 1927, p. 207). To this day, the case has never been explicitly overturned, although Virginia's law was fi-nally repealed in 1974.

The tide turned with another Supreme Court decision, this time in 1942. It concerned a man named Jack Skinner who was convicted first for stealing chickens and twice later for armed robbery. He was deemed a three-time loser and ordered to undergo a vasectomy under Oklahoma's Habitual Criminal Sterilization Act. In keeping with *Buck v. Bell*, the idea was to protect society from future generations of misfits—in this instance, chicken thieves and robbers. At the time Skinner's appeal was heard by the Supreme Court, Americans had become aware of the horror of Nazi policies under which thousands of people were sterilized in order to cleanse the gene pool and breed a superior race. The Court found the Oklahoma law unconstitutional and recognized a fundamental right to reproduce (*Skinner v. Oklahoma*, 1942).

Although *Skinner* was a hugely important case, forced sterilization continued to be fairly widespread. More than 30 years later, the Fourth Circuit Court of Appeals heard a case called *Walker v. Pierce* (1977) in which an obstetrician was requiring Medicaid recipi-ents to undergo a tubal ligation if they were delivering a third or subsequent child. The Court affirmed his right to do so. The dissenting opinion quotes a witness as saying,

> He came in and he hadn't examined me or anything. I was laying on the table. And, he
> said, "Listen here young lady." He said, "This is my tax money paying for something

like this." He said, "I am tired of people going around here having babies and my tax money paying for it." He said, "So, if you don't want this done, you go and find yourself another doctor." (p. 614)

Research has revealed that throughout the 1970s, the Indian Health Service (which is part of the U.S. government) had sterilized one-fourth of the Native American population of childbearing age without their informed consent (Lawrence, 2000). As of 1992, 14 states still authorized sterilization. North Carolina was among them. Between 1929 and 1974, it sterilized nearly 7,600 men, women, and children—some as young as 10. Like other states, it sterilized those considered to be undesirable drains on society: criminals, people with intellectual disabilities, and low-income illiterate women. In early 2012, North Carolina became the first state to agree to compensate its victims and establish a pool to fund mental health services for those victims still alive (James & Hutchison, 2012). Recently, a Virginia legislator urged his state to follow suit by compensating the approximately 8,000 poor, uneducated, mentally ill, physically disabled, intellectually disabled, and homeless citizens whom it had allowed to be forcibly sterilized between 1924 and 1979—a period during which an estimated 65,000 forced sterilizations had occurred nationwide (Vozzella, 2012). Although the idea of forced sterilization seems shocking to our modern sensibilities, the coercive use of birth control has been used more recently toward similar ends.

The Right to Contraception

The first U.S. law restricting access to contraception was the Comstock Act of 1873, named after its major proponent, the 29-year-old secretary of the New York Society for the Suppression of Vice. Similar laws proliferated until a successful U.S. Supreme Court challenge in 1965. *Griswold v. Connecticut* ushered in the modern era of case law concerning access to contraception. At the time, Planned Parenthood was operating a medical clinic in New Haven, Connecticut. The city's district attorney reluctantly followed up on a complaint by a neighbor who objected to the clinic's operation. The clinic's director, Estelle Griswold, was arrested, tried, and fined $100. This turned out to be fortuitous; the Supreme Court had previously refused to hear a challenge to the Connecticut birth control law because no one had actually been penalized for breaking it. Now opponents of the law, including Ms. Griswold, had a case that would qualify. When the Court did consider the case, the Yale Law School professor who argued for Griswold relied on the *Skinner* decision as precedent. The Court ruled that it is unconstitutional for the government to regulate sexual conduct within marriage. The Court carved out a right to privacy that, although not explicit in the Bill of Rights, was said to emanate from those rights and give them meaning. This right to privacy, which includes sexual conduct between married partners, was recognized as being implicit in the Constitution.

The right to use contraception was extended to single adults 7 years later in *Eisenstadt v. Baird* (1972) and to minors a short time later in *Carey v. Population Services International* (1977). In each of these cases, the Court emphasized that the constitutional right to privacy is not absolute; it can be superseded by a compelling interest on the part of the government. As is often the case, the courts engage in a balancing test: the interests of the state versus the privacy rights of the individual. In terms of contraception, the state's declared interest was in deterring promiscuity. The debate about whether access to contraceptives

promotes promiscuity is still alive and well, often surfacing in discussions of sex education. Meanwhile, a number of states continue to regulate minors' access to contraception.
According to the Guttmacher Institute (2011), 21 states allow minors unfettered access to
contraceptive services, and another 25 permit only certain minors to consent to services
under certain circumstances. These include youth who are married, are parents, have
previously been pregnant, need contraception to avert a health hazard, or have reached a
specified minimum age.

Access to contraception, although legal, is often curtailed in practice. Funding for family planning services under Title X is 61% lower in constant dollars today than it was in
1980. Some employer-provided health care plans exclude contraceptives from coverage.
The Food and Drug Administration (FDA) has limited the sale of emergency contraceptives, and some states allow pharmacists and other health care providers to refuse to honor
birth control prescriptions (Center for Reproductive Rights, 2011). In a recent blow to
reproductive rights advocates, the secretary of Health and Human Services (HHS) publicly overruled an FDA recommendation that emergency contraception be made available
over-the-counter to women of all ages (Harris, 2011). Meanwhile, rules issued by HHS require that new insurance plans under the Affordable Care Act provide contraceptives free
of charge, although an exemption is included for certain religious employers.

The Right to Abortion

In 1962, a television personality named Sherri Finkbine—29 years old, married with
four children, and pregnant—discovered that the anti-nausea medication she was taking
was in fact thalidomide. Thalidomide had been causing an epidemic of deformed infants
in England and West Germany. After seeing pictures of these babies, and fearing that her
own child might be severely deformed, she sought an abortion. When news of her decision hit the media, the hospital refused to terminate her pregnancy. She filed suit and
proceeded to have the abortion in Sweden. As it turns out, her fears were well founded;
the fetus had no legs and only one arm. Although public opinion was sympathetic to her
position, her doctor refused to continue treating her, she was fired from her job, and her
husband was suspended from his position as a high school teacher. Ms. Finkbine lost
her case in court, but the publicity surrounding her personal journey brought the abortion
issue to the fore (Irons, 2006).

Meanwhile, the 1960s and early 1970s saw the rise of the women's movement, providing additional momentum to the abortion debate. The American Civil Liberties Union adopted a platform supporting abortion rights, physicians joined in the cause, and between
1967 and 1971, 17 states revised their laws. All of this culminated in the 1973 Supreme Court
decision of *Roe v. Wade*.

The woman at the center of this case (Jane Roe, whose real name was Norma
McCorvey) was a surprising choice for a plaintiff. She came from a broken home, had
dropped out of high school, was raped at an early age, and spent much of her childhood
in reform schools. She became pregnant for the first time at age 16, married the father,
and moved from Texas to California. When he found out she was pregnant, he beat
her. She made her way back to Texas, got a job at a lesbian bar, and then had the baby,
whom her mother took and raised out of state. She had a second child after a brief affair
and voluntarily relinquished custody to the father. Two years later, while working for a
traveling circus, she discovered that she was pregnant again and returned to Texas. Her

doctor was appalled when she said she did not want the baby, and he referred her to a lawyer to help her arrange an adoption. That lawyer put her in touch with a colleague who had been looking for a woman who might be willing to challenge the Texas abortion statute (Irons, 2006). That statute permitted abortion only to save the life of the mother. Roe claimed that she wanted an abortion but could not afford to travel to a jurisdiction where abortion was legal. She brought a *class action* suit on behalf of all women who faced the same situation.

The *Roe v. Wade* decision is not nearly as straightforward as most people believe. The Court engaged in a balancing test, considering the woman's right to privacy (as established in the contraception cases), the state's interest in protecting the mother's health, and its interest in protecting potential life (the fetus). According to the Court's analysis, each of these rights becomes compelling at a different point during the pregnancy. During the first 3 months, the mother's privacy right prevails; around the end of that first trimester, the mother's health becomes compelling; and at the point of viability (when the fetus can live outside the mother, around 28 weeks into gestation), protecting the fetus becomes the compelling concern. Based on this timeline, the court devised the following formulation:

- **First trimester:** The state cannot regulate or prohibit abortion.
- **Second trimester:** The state can regulate abortion in the interest of promoting the mother's health but cannot prohibit abortion.
- **Third trimester:** The state can both regulate and prohibit abortion, unless it is necessary to save the life or health of the mother.

There have been many criticisms of the Court's holding in this case. Aside from ideological and policy concerns, legal scholars have taken issue with the Court's analysis. The Court maintained that under the law a fetus is not considered a person; instead, it used the point of viability as its touchstone. Viability, however, may be a moving target; as technology advances, the point of viability may occur earlier and earlier in the pregnancy. It is also unclear how the Court reached its conclusion that the constitutional right to privacy encompasses abortion. Critics point out that the Court's opinion devotes 12 pages to the history of abortion, 12 pages to a discussion of the medical facts, and only two paragraphs to legal precedent.

Court observers have detailed the drama that occurred behind the scenes as *Roe v. Wade* was being considered. It was in fact a political compromise. Initially, three justices wanted to unequivocally recognize a woman's constitutional right to abortion. Two others agreed that the Texas law should be invalidated, not because it interfered with women's reproductive freedom but because it interfered with physician discretion. Two justices supported the Texas law. As discussed in Chapter 2, the chief justice sided with the majority (against his own conviction) so that he could assign the writing of the opinion; he assigned it to the justice who he believed would make the holding as narrow as possible. He also ordered a rehearing that delayed the court's decision until two new justices could join the Court, and until President Nixon (a staunch abortion opponent) was sworn into office (Irons, 2006). An initial draft of the Court's opinion that prohibited any regulation of abortion during the first 6 months was unable to attract a majority; some justices wanted more regulation to be permitted and others wanted less. To win over his colleagues, Justice Blackmun (author of the majority opinion) devised the trimester scheme. The final vote was 7–2.

Since *Roe v. Wade*, the Court has repeatedly upheld the fundamental constitutional right to abortion, while chipping away at its original protections. In *Planned Parenthood v. Danforth* (1976), the Court ruled that the abortion decision belongs to the woman alone, and that her husband has no rights in relation to abortion. In *Webster v. Reproductive Health Services* (1989), the Court reaffirmed the basic holding of *Roe* but upheld restrictions on where and by whom abortions could be performed. In *Planned Parenthood v. Casey* (1992), the Court ruled that a state can regulate abortion as long as the regulation does not place substantial obstacles in the path of a woman seeking an abortion before viability; under this new *undue burden* test, a requirement for spousal notification was struck down but a 24-hour waiting period, a parental consent requirement, and a requirement for informed consent were upheld. Finally, in *Gonzales v. Carhart* (2007), a 5–4 majority of the Court upheld a ban on late-term abortion. This was the first time the Supreme Court had prohibited a specific abortion procedure; it was widely viewed as signaling a more activist stand toward scaling back abortion rights.

Despite the endurance of *Roe v. Wade*, restrictions on the right to abortion make realizing that right difficult for many women. States continue to implement regulations on where, when, by whom, and under what circumstances abortions can be performed. In the first half of 2011, for example, Maryland issued draft regulations requiring abortion clinics to apply for state licenses, and Virginia passed legislation requiring clinics to meet the same standards as hospitals; this potentially includes everything from staffing and equipment to architectural requirements. Opponents of the new law believe it could cause 80% of the state's abortion clinics to close. Kansas has followed Virginia's lead with a bill requiring abortion clinics to meet the same standards as hospitals and outpatient surgical centers; it would also ban distance prescriptions (via web cam) for RU-486 emergency contraceptives. Meanwhile, 34 states currently require pre-abortion counseling (10 of them mandate coverage of "fetal pain" and 20 mandate coverage of the emotional consequences of abortion). Twenty-nine states require waiting periods before an abortion can be performed, usually 24 hours. Twenty-six states require parental consent before minors can have an abortion, and 20 require parental notification (National Conference of State Legislatures, 2011). Low-income women face particularly difficult hurdles. The Hyde Amendment has long made federal Medicaid funding for abortion unavailable. That debate played out again in relation to the recently enacted health care reform legislation (the Affordable Care Act), which likewise prohibits the use of federal funds for abortions. A total of 32 states permit coverage of abortion under their state Medicaid programs when the mother's life is at risk or the pregnancy resulted from rape or incest; this means, of course, that 18 states do not.

CONSCIENCE CLAUSES

In the aftermath of the U.S. Supreme Court's 1973 decision in *Roe v. Wade,* several states enacted what have come to be called *conscience clauses*. These are statutes or regulations that permit health care professionals to refuse to perform abortions on the basis of their religious, moral, or ethical convictions.

These conscience clauses currently exist in at least 46 states.

Similar laws have emerged that permit pharmacists to refuse to fill prescriptions for contraceptives (Miller, 2006). Some states, including Mississippi, even permit pharmacists to refuse to refer customers to other pharmacies that would be willing to fill their prescriptions. This is particularly problematic for low-income women and women in remote areas who would essentially be deprived of their constitutional right to contraception enunciated in *Griswold v. Connecticut* and its progeny.

Conscience clauses have not been limited to physicians and pharmacists. In 2010, Idaho enacted the Freedom of Conscience for Health Care Professionals Act, which specifically includes social workers. Under its provisions, a social worker cannot be required to counsel, advise, perform, dispense, or assist in any health care services that violate his or her religious, moral, or ethical principles (Malamud, 2010). This means that clients could be left to make critical life decisions without the benefit of complete information about their legal options. The Idaho chapter of NASW opposed the legislation, believing it would be a disservice to clients and run counter to our professional obligations under the Code of Ethics.

Similar regulations were introduced on a national scale. In the final days of the George W. Bush administration, the Department of Health and Human Services issued draft regulations under which workers in health care settings—from doctors to social workers to janitors—could refuse to provide services, information, or advice to patients on subjects such as contraception, family planning, blood transfusions, and even vaccination if they were morally opposed to doing so. In fact, the rules were so broadly worded that some feared they could lead to refusal to fill prescriptions for HIV medications or denial of services to racial or sexual minorities. Fortunately, President Obama rescinded the measure during his first days in office (Social Workers and Conscience Clauses, 2010).

Despite the rescission of the federal rules, conscience clauses continue to proliferate at the state level. In 2009, a Texas physician who identified herself as an evangelical Christian refused to prescribe birth control pills to a single woman based on her moral objections to premarital sex. That same year in California, a doctor refused, on moral grounds, to treat a lesbian patient seeking *in vitro* fertilization. The second of these cases went to court, where the patient prevailed; according to the judge, if a treatment is provided to some patients, it must be provided to all. This was distinguished from issues such as abortion or contraception for which the treatment itself is the source of the moral objection.

In addition to health care professionals, the logic of conscience clauses has been applied to students receiving education and training. In 2010, a student was dismissed from a graduate counseling program at Eastern Michigan University after refusing to assist gay clients in her field practicum, claiming that it violated her religious beliefs. She sued. The court dismissed the case, noting that the American Counseling Association's Code of Ethics explicitly states that counselors may not discriminate and that all counselors must respect client diversity. Although the university prevailed in this particular case, other states, such as Arkansas, passed legislation protecting students in counseling and social work programs from disciplinary actions that would penalize them for refusing to work with clients or in environments that go against their religious beliefs and values (Provider Refusal and Conscience Clause Controversies, 2011).

As social workers bound by the NASW Code of Ethics, we have a duty to put our clients' interests ahead of our own; discrimination is unsupportable, even if it stems from the provider's personal belief system. The best solution is to be aware of our personal values and to avoid practicing in environments where we know we will be unable to comprehensively meet client needs. If a conflict does arise, we must be diligent in ensuring that clients are referred to practitioners who are willing and able to provide them with the full range of relevant information, advice, and services.

Protecting the rights of providers at the expense of client needs is a dangerous precedent. The right to health care is meaningless if it cannot be exercised. Values including informed consent, client self-determination, and freedom from discrimination deserve our active protection.

Alternative Methods of Reproduction

The availability of nontraditional methods of reproduction, including *in vitro* fertilization, has raised countless legal issues. For example, in *Davis v. Davis* (1992), the Tennessee Supreme Court considered who should have custody of seven embryos that a couple (Mary Sue and Junior) had arranged to cryogenically preserve (freeze) before the deterioration of their marriage. In a tongue-in-cheek column, humorist Ellen Goodman suggested that perhaps joint custody should be awarded, with the embryos' time being equally divided between one parent's freezer and the other (Goodman, 1989, p. A-33). Amazingly, that is essentially what the state court of appeals actually did! It awarded the parents joint custody of the frozen ova. The decision was overruled, however, by the state supreme court, which, after determining that each party's interests should be weighed on a case-by-case basis, found in Junior's favor. In the two decades or so since the *Davis* case, surprisingly few states have enacted legislation to address these kinds of occurrences, although a number of suits have been brought.

Another example of nontraditional reproduction is surrogacy, in which a woman carries and delivers a child for another couple. Although the early surrogacy cases surfaced in the 1980s, surrogacy has seen a resurgence in popularity in light of several high-profile celebrities whose children have been born using surrogates, including Sarah Jessica Parker and Matthew Broderick, Ricky Martin, Kelsey Grammer, and Neil Patrick Harris. The most famous surrogacy case, *In Re Baby M*, was heard by the New Jersey Supreme Court in 1988. In that case, the court found the surrogacy contract entered into by the parties to be invalid. It concluded that the contract violated state laws pertaining to baby selling and termination of parental rights, and that it offended public policy by ignoring the rights of the biological mother (surrogate) and discounting the best interests of the child. The *Baby M.* case, which was not decided until the child in question was nearly 2 years old, dominated headlines for months. At the time, no states had surrogacy laws in place. Today, approximately half of the states have them, although they vary in their specifics. Some, such as Arizona and New Jersey, make all surrogacy contracts unenforceable. Others, such as Kentucky, only prohibit agreements under which the surrogate is compensated. Florida permits surrogacy only when the intended mother is infertile. New Hampshire and Virginia restrict who can act as a surrogate and require advance judicial approval of all surrogacy agreements. Many states that address surrogacy allow only married couples to hire surrogates, thereby excluding gay men and lesbians. Finally, some states have intentionally avoided passing surrogacy laws because of the difficult ethical, religious, and moral questions the issue raises.

HIV/AIDS

Although HIV/AIDS no longer monopolizes American headlines as it did in the 1980s and 1990s, it remains a significant threat to public health. In 2009, the rate of new AIDS cases diagnosed in the District of Columbia was the highest in the nation: 119.8 per 100,000 people, compared to a national rate of 11.2. The lowest rate, 1.1, was in Vermont (CDC, 2011a). HIV/AIDS is also a topic of particular concern to social workers because of the social and psychological dimensions of the illness. Unlike other diseases—even other communicable diseases—HIV/AIDS carries with it an indelible and potentially debilitating stigma.

Approximately 1 million people in the United States are currently living with HIV. Although the number of those living with the disease continues to grow, the number of new infections each year has remained relatively stable. The CDC estimates that 56,300 Americans are infected with HIV annually, and that more than 18,000 people with AIDS die each year. Men who have sex with men (MSM) remain the population most severely affected by HIV; they are the only risk group in the United States for which new HIV infections have increased since the early 1990s. MSM account for more than half (53%) of all new HIV infections in the United States each year, as well as nearly half (48%) of people living with HIV (CDC, 2010a). The rate of new HIV diagnoses among MSM in the United States is more than 44 times that of other men and more than 30 times that of women. Heterosexuals account for 31% of annual new HIV infections, and 28% of people living with HIV contracted the disease through heterosexual contact. As a group, women account for 27% of annual new HIV infections and 25% of those living with HIV. Intravenous (IV) drug users represent 12% of annual new HIV infections and 19% of those living with HIV (CDC, 2010a).

To put this in perspective, it is important to note that HIV has disproportionately impacted the developing world, with 90% of infections occurring in developing countries (WHO, 2012). East Africa and Southern Africa persist as the regions most heavily impacted by the HIV/AIDS epidemic. In 2009, 34% of all individuals with HIV lived in 10 countries in Southern Africa (UNAIDS, n.d.). Southeast Asian countries have relatively low rates of HIV infection (AVERT, n.d.); in all of Asia, an estimated 4.9 million people were living with HIV in 2009. The number of people infected in the Pacific region is small, and the number of new infections has decreased, although the number of those living with HIV in this region has almost doubled since 2001. The HIV epidemic is comparatively small in Latin America and the Caribbean, hovering near 1% in most countries, although social stigma may keep many of those infected from self-identifying. The only regions where the prevalence of HIV continues to increase are Eastern Europe and Central Asia, where the number of people living with HIV has almost tripled since 2000 (UNAIDS, n.d.).

Brief History

Some describe the history of HIV/AIDS as occurring in three waves. The first wave began in 1980 when the first cases surfaced. They were mysterious, deadly, and believed to be a rare cancer. More than 80% of people died within 2 years of diagnosis. In this early stage, there was no understanding of what caused the disease or how it was transmitted. It was referred to as "gay-related immune disorder" or GRID. Social workers were active on the front lines of this new epidemic; we helped infected clients locate housing, prepare advance directives and wills, and find meaning as they faced the possibility of death (Strug, Grube, & Beckerman, 2002).

In the second wave, two events occurred that significantly changed the course and treatment of the disease. First, the human immunodeficiency virus (HIV) was identified in 1984. Second, AZT was introduced in 1986, and its use became widespread, creating new hope for those with HIV and their loved ones. This period also marked a transition in risk groups, with IV drug users, their sexual partners, and heterosexual women and their children being diagnosed more frequently (Strug et al., 2002). Between 1986 and 1990, the number of HIV positive women in the United States increased by 600%. In 1992, infections from heterosexual contact outpaced infections resulting from IV drug use for the first time. Also during this period, the most significant increase in incidence was among African Americans. Mother-fetus transmission was recognized as a problem; approximately 30% of newborns tested positive for HIV, a majority of those being African American and Hispanic. Other stigmatized groups including inmates, prostitutes, and homeless people also had high rates of transmission. The second wave posed dilemmas for social workers as they grappled with difficult issues; these included the right of infected women to reproductive choice, the right of social workers to know their clients' HIV status, the right of sexual partners to be informed of a client's HIV status, and the ethics of mandatory HIV testing (Strug et al., 2002).

The third wave began in 1996 with the introduction of protease inhibitors, which resulted in a dramatic reduction in AIDS-related mortality and markedly improved the quality of life for many HIV-positive people. The perception of the illness changed from that of a terminal illness to a chronic one. Problems remained, however. Some people were unable to tolerate the medications and others became resistant to the drugs. People with limited resources often had difficulty accessing the drugs because of their high cost, and many who obtained them were unable to adhere to the strict regimens required. During this time, HIV continued to spread among low-income people of color. Hispanic and African American women were infected at a rate three times greater than Whites. African Americans and Latinos accounted for 70% of all new AIDS cases in the United States. In 1999, the number of new cases among Hispanics was three times the number among Whites.

Today, people of color continue to be at higher risk for HIV infection. Socioeconomic status has become a greater predictor of HIV transmission than it was in the past. HIV prevalence in the country's poorest urban neighborhoods is four times the national average (CDC, 2010b). Meanwhile, prevention efforts successfully reduced mother-to-fetus transmission of HIV from 896 cases in 1992 to 38 cases in 2006 (CDC, 2006).

Legal Protections for People with HIV/AIDS

In addition to their health concerns, people with HIV face two significant hurdles, each of which results in large part from the particular stigma associated with the disease. One issue concerns the right to keep one's HIV status private, and the other concerns protection from discrimination. In addition, courts have grappled with the issue of whether and when a person with HIV should be held criminally responsible for transmitting the disease.

Many of the early cases before the courts concerned the right of a person with HIV/AIDS to keep his or her health status private. In the 1977 case of *Whalen v. Roe*, the U.S. Supreme Court confirmed the existence of a constitutional right to privacy in one's medical records. The Court of Appeals for the Second Circuit interpreted this right as encompassing the health status of those with HIV (*Doe v. City of New York*, 1994); other courts, however, have not uniformly followed suit.

Even when a constitutional right is recognized, it is not absolute. When it comes to protected health information, courts weigh the individual's interest in maintaining privacy against society's interest in disclosure. In *Doe v. Borough of Barrington* (1990), a man who was arrested notified the arresting officer of his HIV-positive status; the officer, in turn, informed another officer, who told the man's neighbors. One of the neighbors, an employee of the local school district, contacted the media and other parents who had children at the school. A panic ensued. Nineteen children were removed from school by their parents the next day and reports appeared in the newspaper and on television, mentioning the man by name. The man's wife and children sued the police officers and the city for violating their rights. The court found in the wife's favor, concluding that her privacy interest was substantial and that the state advanced no compelling interest by disclosing the information.

A different conclusion was reached in a Pennsylvania case decided the same year. *Application of Milton S. Hershey Medical Center* concerned a medical resident who contracted HIV from a cut through his surgical glove. As soon as he was tested, he voluntarily withdrew from the residency. The two hospitals where he had been working, however, identified nearly 500 patients who had been treated by the doctor in the course of his residency; they sought to notify these patients of the possibility of transmission, naming the doctor in question and disclosing his HIV status. They also planned to notify other physicians and staff at the hospitals. The doctor objected. In determining whether the hospitals had a compelling justification for disclosing the information, the court noted that the risk of transmission was approximately 1 in 48,000. This, they concluded, was sufficient to override the doctor's privacy interests. Federal guidelines now recommend that health care workers with HIV notify their patients; not all state laws, however, follow this policy. How to reconcile the competing interests of privacy and public health remains controversial.

Mandatory HIV testing is another area of controversy; without informed consent, testing may constitute an unconstitutional search and seizure under the Fourth Amendment. Again, the courts conduct a balancing test, weighing the expectation of privacy against the risk of transmission. Mandatory testing has been upheld for members of certain occupations, including Foreign Service workers, firefighters, military personnel, and federal prisoners (Stein, 1998). For groups whose risk of transmission is very low, courts have been less tolerant of mandatory testing. Although blood tests are considered routine in medicine, the stigma associated with the AIDS epidemic has led to stiffer informed consent requirements for HIV testing. Meanwhile, with the advent of successful regimens to reduce the incidence of fetal transmission, the issue of prenatal testing has moved to the forefront of the debate. In 1999, the Institute of Medicine recommended routinely testing all pregnant women for HIV, suspending requirements for mandatory counseling and written informed consent. The U.S. Public Health Service, however, declined to adopt these recommendations. Its 2001 guidelines (like most state laws) urge physicians to encourage prenatal testing but continue to require specific informed consent (Wolf & Lo, 2001).

A significant breakthrough in the law's treatment of people with HIV/AIDS occurred as a result of their being covered by the Americans with Disabilities Act (ADA). The ADA, enacted in 1990, is an overarching civil rights law that protects people with disabilities against discrimination in employment, access to public services and programs (including transportation), and places of public accommodation (including lodging, restaurants, shopping centers, retail stores, health care providers, and hospitals). The ADA applies to both public and private entities. Under the ADA, a *disability* is defined as (1) a physical or mental impairment that substantially limits one or more major life activities, (2) a record of such impairment, or (3) being regarded as having such an impairment. In other words, this would include people actually diagnosed with AIDS (if the disease substantially limits a major life activity), people whose medical records mistakenly identify them as having AIDS, and people thought to have AIDS even if it is untrue. This definition recognizes that discrimination is sometimes based on false information or speculation, not just on facts. In addition to having a disability, the claimant has to be *otherwise qualified*. In an employment setting, for example, this might include having the requisite training and skills. Finally, the employer or service provider is under an obligation to make *reasonable modifications* to accommodate the disabled person unless those modifications would fundamentally alter the nature of the service, program, or activity.

The U.S. Supreme Court has decided several important cases that have clarified how HIV/AIDS fits into the protections of the ADA. In a 1987 employment discrimination case, the Court ruled that contagious diseases (in this instance, tuberculosis) meet the definition of disability even though they are not what we might traditionally think of as a physical or mental impairment. However, people with contagious diseases may be excluded from coverage if their condition poses a *direct threat* to the health or safety of others (*School Board of Nassau County v. Arline*, 1987). This exception to the general requirement for inclusion was the Court's way of trying to balance the rights of people with disabilities against the need to protect the public health. The ruling was put to the test in a 1988 case involving a special education teacher who was relieved of his classroom teaching responsibilities because he had AIDS. In keeping with the *Arline* decision, the Ninth Circuit Court of Appeals recognized AIDS as a covered disability; in addition, the court concluded that removing the teacher from the classroom would be a violation of the ADA because there was no significant risk of transmission and therefore no direct threat (*Chalk v. United States*, 1988).

The U.S. Supreme Court considered a more complicated scenario in *Bragdon v. Abbott* (1998). This case involved a patient whose dentist refused to treat him in the office because he had HIV. In a 5–4 decision, the Court concluded that a person with HIV, although asymptomatic, meets the definition of disability under the ADA. The dentist was found to have violated the patient's rights because, given the objective medical evidence available at the time, the patient's condition was not considered a direct threat,

Even if someone is considered to pose a direct threat, *reasonable modifications* must be made in order to eliminate the threat or render it insignificant. In doing so, however, there is no requirement that one fundamentally alter the nature of the policy or program. In 1999, the Fourth Circuit considered how far a retail business must go in making reasonable modifications to accommodate a person with AIDS. A karate school refused to admit a 12-year-old boy with AIDS into its regular classes but offered instead to accommodate him by providing private lessons. The boy's father sued, claiming that the studio was discriminating in violation of the ADA. The court found that the boy's health condition posed a direct threat to other students and to instructors. Central to their conclusion was the fact that the school's curriculum included a heavy emphasis on sparring and traditional Japanese-style fighting, which often resulted in bloody abrasions. This in turn meant that blood from one student could easily end up on another student's hands, uniform, or mouth, thereby posing a significant risk of transmission. The court next considered the school's obligation to make reasonable modifications that would allow the boy to safely participate. The court concluded that the school was not required to abandon its mission and make its curriculum less combat oriented; its offer of private lessons was considered to be a sufficiently reasonable modification under the law (*Montalvo v. Radcliffe*, 1999).

Suppose medication keeps the disease from substantially limiting a major life activity by, for example, allowing a person with AIDS to continue to work? In a 1999 case, *Sutton v. United Air Lines*, the U.S. Supreme Court ruled that whether or not a person qualifies as having a disability must be determined by taking into account any mitigating or corrective measures. Although the case concerned plaintiffs with impaired eyesight, it has clear implications for people with HIV/AIDS. Under the Court's ruling, if taking medication could keep the disease from substantially limiting a major life activity, then a person with HIV/ AIDS would not be protected from discrimination under the law. Fortunately, this interpretation was explicitly reversed by amendments to the ADA enacted by Congress in 2008. As it stands now, with the exception of ordinary eyeglasses or contact lenses, mitigating or corrective measures may *not* be taken into account in determining whether an individual has a covered impairment; we look at the effect of the impairment in its original, unaltered state. The amendments also specify that impairments that are episodic, or in remission, must be considered disabilities if they substantially limit a major life activity while in their active state.

Prosecuting People with HIV/AIDS

In keeping with the law's dual mission of protecting people with HIV/AIDS and safeguarding the public health, many states have enacted laws that criminalize behaviors on the part of those with HIV/AIDS that put others at risk. Thirty-six states and territories have laws specifically criminalizing nondisclosure of HIV status, exposure, or transmission of HIV, and other states prosecute under broader criminal statutes. According to the Center for HIV Law and Policy (2011), there were 121 arrests and prosecutions of people with HIV/AIDS between 2008 and 2011. The vast majority, however, involved consensual sexual contact or behaviors such as spitting or biting that pose no significant transmission risk. These defendants are often sentenced to substantial jail time, even when no transmission actually occurred. Although little controversy surrounds the very small number of cases in which the infected individual intentionally transmits the disease, many believe that transmission through carelessness or accident or the mere failure to disclose one's status should not be criminalized.

In 2006, the California Supreme Court pushed the envelope unusually far by ruling that people who do not even know they are HIV-positive can be guilty of negligent transmission (*John B. v. The Superior Court of Los Angeles County*). The case concerned a newly married couple, both of whom contracted HIV shortly after their honeymoon. Each accused the other of transmitting the disease, although the husband later admitted to having slept with men before he entered the marriage. According to the court, given the totality of the circumstances, he should have known he might be infected and therefore had an obligation to inform his wife of the possibility of exposure. Under this ruling, people can be held criminally responsible for withholding information, exposing someone to the virus, or transmitting the disease without even knowing that they are HIV-positive.

An increasing number of countries around the globe have begun to aggressively prosecute people with HIV/AIDS who are believed to put others at risk. Several international bodies have articulated their opposition to this trend. These include the United Nations Programme on HIV/AIDS (UNAIDS), the United Nations Development Programme (UNDP), and the UNAIDS Reference Group on HIV and Human Rights. They recommend that only acts committed with the specific intention of harming others be considered criminal, and that these be covered by existing criminal laws rather than by specific laws targeting people with HIV/AIDS. There is no credible evidence that criminalizing negligent or reckless exposure or transmission is effective in reducing the spread of HIV. Furthermore, attempting to do so undermines important prevention efforts, promotes fear and stigma, and often results in punishing people who are undeserving of criminal sanctions. This includes those who are unaware of their HIV status, who are ignorant of how the disease is transmitted, whose behavior entailed an insignificant risk of transmission, who disclosed their status to their partner (or thought their partner knew), who failed to disclose because of fear of violence or discrimination, whose partner knew and agreed to the risk, or who attempted to reduce the risk by practicing safer sex. Instead of criminalization, these organizations urge countries around the globe to focus on pursuing the achievement of public health goals through the implementation of evidence-based prevention and treatment strategies (Open Society Institute, 2008).

Social Work and HIV/AIDS

Social workers have played, and will continue to play, a major role in the primary prevention of HIV/AIDS by helping uninfected persons who are at risk decrease or eliminate risky behaviors, including unsafe sex and the sharing of hypodermic syringes. Social workers also play an important role in secondary prevention, including helping people who are already infected manage complex medical regimens, maintain good health, and avoid spreading the virus to others (Strug et al., 2002). Finally, social workers serve as advocates for medical and psychosocial support services for infected clients and family members, as well as for policies that minimize stigma, bias, and discrimination.

Undoubtedly, the profession will continue to be confronted with a range of ethical dilemmas regarding clients' need for confidentiality on the one hand and our duty to warn on the other. Consistent with the guidelines discussed in Chapter 5, many social workers apply a *Tarasoff* analysis to these cases. Meanwhile, laws in every state detail the obligations of health care professionals to report communicable diseases to state or local public health authorities. It is important to know what requirements are applicable in your state.

Human Genetics

Social work has long had a close association with advancements in the field of genetics (NASW, 2003). The most important development in human genetics was the Human Genome Project, established in 1990 under the U.S. Department of Energy. Its purpose is to identify the genes within human DNA while gaining insight into the role they play in the human population. The hope is that this knowledge will be helpful in the search for cures to genetic disorders and diseases (Furrow et al., 2008). Although still underway, the project has already contributed to important breakthroughs in DNA testing and stem cell research, both of which have engendered controversy.

In 2003, NASW published Standards for Integrating Genetics into Social Work Practice. Because social workers are often the first to provide psychosocial services to individuals and families with genetic disorders, we must be knowledgeable about the implications of genetic testing and genetic research. We must also understand the legal ramifications of having access to genetic information and the potential it carries for discrimination.

DNA

Advances in genetics have made it possible to identify an individual's DNA. This has allowed the justice system to identify criminals, solve crimes, and successfully prosecute cases (Duncan, 2008; Guyer & Collins, 1995). As its use has become more widespread, however, important concerns have surfaced. Given the high cost of DNA testing, many criminal defendants are unable to afford an independent genetics expert to retest the DNA for trial. Many law enforcement officers lack a proper understanding of DNA evidence encountered at the crime scene. Juries may not understand DNA evidence well enough to render informed verdicts; this means that even faulty DNA evidence can be seen as accurate and truthful (Koehler, 2001). The increased reliance on DNA evidence may also infringe on the civil liberties not just of criminal defendants but also of all citizens. For example, former New York City mayor Rudolph Giuliani proposed that all newborn babies have their DNA tested and recorded in a database that the justice system could later access (Duncan, 2008). This raises serious ethical concerns. Social workers should be educated about the limitations of DNA evidence and help clients understand the implications of its use in court. We also must be vigilant in ensuring that civil liberties are protected against the unjustified and ill-advised use of genetic information.

The use of genetic mapping and sequencing in criminal trials is only one aspect of what has evolved from the study of the human genome. The ability to identify an individual's genetic markers has also enabled medical professionals to offer genetic testing aimed at identifying possible genetic disorders (Guyer & Collins, 1995). Many prospective parents seek genetic testing before conceiving, or during pregnancy, in order to determine whether they risk passing on a genetic predisposition to conditions such as Tay-Sachs or Huntington's disease. Having this information can allow them to make better-informed decisions about childbearing and child rearing; it can help them prepare to address symptoms that may surface in themselves or their children.

Although the availability of this information can be a tremendous benefit, it has significant drawbacks as well. Many people seek genetic testing because a family member has exhibited symptoms of an illness, yet they often are ill prepared for the news that they carry a risk for disease. This recognition can create overwhelming anxiety or depression, particularly if the illness in question is potentially fatal. For those whose symptoms are dormant, it can also generate constant worry about whether, and when, the disease will become manifest. Counseling by professionals who are trained in genetic counseling is crucial as clients adjust to the realities of possible illness and make decisions about their own futures and those of their offspring. Social workers can help clients explore their options, address their concerns, and make decisions about sharing genetic information with family members who may be similarly affected.

Apart from the emotional repercussions of genetic testing, a second concern is that the results will become part of the client's medical file. This opens the door to genetic discrimination. Several studies have documented the concerns of people at risk of genetic disorders who experienced or feared being refused insurance, denied jobs, or released from employment (Klitzman, 2010; Lapham, Kozma, & Weiss, 1996). The U.S. government has meanwhile enacted the Genetic Information Nondiscrimination Act (P.L. 110-233), which prohibits insurance companies and employers from discriminating based on genetic information. Even though these protections are not perfect, they are a good beginning; social workers should strive to ensure that these and other safeguards are maintained and routinely enforced.

One of the most recent innovations is do-it-yourself genetic testing. A fascinating legal battle has been unfolding between the American Civil Liberties Union (ACLU) and Myriad Genetics over the patenting of specific genes—in this instance, those associated with breast and ovarian cancer. A federal district court invalidated the patents in 2010, but the court of appeals reversed that holding in 2011—rejecting the Obama administration's argument that isolated

DNA should not be patented. The case may well reach the U.S. Supreme Court. Meanwhile, home genetic testing remains extremely costly and out of reach for most Americans. Although wider availability would ensure greater privacy and reduce the risk of genetic discrimination, it might also result in fewer people having the benefits of counseling and support.

Stem Cell Research

Continued advances in the field of genetics have also led to the controversial issue of stem cell research. Stem cells have been found to have enormous reparative and curative properties; they can be differentiated into a number of cell types, making cures possible for a wide range of currently intractable diseases (Bongso & Richards, 2004). Of the various types of stem cells, those harvested from human embryos hold the most promise; they can potentially become hundreds of different cell types depending on their treatment in the lab. They are also the most controversial, however, because their use requires the destruction of human embryos considered by many to be human lives. Numerous efforts have been made to try to balance these pro-life concerns against the potential for prolonging life by curing disease. In the mid-1990s, Congress passed a law that prohibited the use of federal funding to create embryos for research purposes. During the next administration, President George W. Bush expanded the allowable scope of federal funding for stem cell research (Annas, 2010). In 2009, President Barack Obama issued an executive order that opened up federal funding for human embryonic stem cell research even further. The controversy, of course, continues.

Summary and Conclusion

Health care is a vast field of practice that touches on every aspect of social work concern. Consistent with social work's bio-psycho-social-spiritual perspective, the World Health Organization has endorsed a holistic view of health. In the United States, as elsewhere, health disparities remain. People of color and people living in poverty are significantly more likely to suffer from an array of debilitating health conditions. Social conditions contribute to these inequities, as do barriers to accessing and affording health care services. Although the Patient Protection and Affordable Care Act is positioned to ameliorate some of these problems, many of its central provisions have yet to be implemented. Among the specific health-related issues of interest to social work are reproductive rights, HIV/AIDS, and human genetics. Social workers should be familiar with the legal issues in each of these arenas so we can better assist clients in making sound decisions and advocate successfully for policies that respect social justice and civil liberties.

Sample Case

Following is an abbreviated version of the court's opinion in a 1991 Florida case. Consider the court's arguments and then answer the questions that follow.

JOHNSON v. FLORIDA
578 So.2d 419 (1991)

Dauksch, J.

This is an appeal from two convictions for delivery of a controlled substance to minors.

It was established by the evidence that appellant consumed cocaine knowing that the cocaine would pass to her soon-to-be-born fetus. Upon the birth of her children it was medically determined that each of them had received some of the cocaine into their bodies. A qualified witness testified that some of the cocaine left the mother and was received by the child after birth but before the umbilical cord was cut. Under Florida law a person comes into being upon birth. . . .

Section 893.13 (1)(c), Florida Statutes (1989) says:

> Except as authorized by this chapter, it is unlawful for any person 18 years of age or older to deliver any controlled substance to a person under the age of 18 years, or to use or hire a person under the age of 18 years as an agent or employee in the sale or delivery of such a substance, or to use such a person to assist in avoiding detection or apprehension for a violation of this chapter.

The question is whether the acts of appellant violate the statute. Logic leads us to say that appellant violated the statute.

Appellant voluntarily took cocaine into her body, knowing it would pass to her fetus and knowing (or should have known) that birth was imminent. She is deemed to know that an infant at birth is a person, and a minor, and that delivery of cocaine to the infant is illegal. We can reach no other conclusion logically.

We have spent the necessary time and effort considering the many arguments of appellant and her supporters who argue the mother's rights to her body and the analogies to the abortion cases. We have also considered the appellant's assertion that the Florida legislature declined to pass a child abuse statute which forbade similar conduct. We have considered other arguments, such as what pregnant mothers might resort to if they know they may be charged with this crime; we were singularly unimpressed with those latter arguments.

This appellant on two occasions took cocaine into her pregnant body and caused the passage of that cocaine to each of her children through the umbilical cord after birth of the child, then an infant person. The statute was twice violated.

Convictions affirmed.

W. Sharp, Judge, dissenting.

. . . The state's theory of the case was that Johnson "delivered" cocaine . . . to her two children via blood flowing through the children's umbilical cords in the sixty-to-ninety second period after they were expelled from her birth canal but before their cords were severed. . . . Because I conclude that section 893.113(1)(c) was not intended to apply to these facts, I would vacate the convictions and remand for entry of a judgment of acquittal. ***

I submit there was no medical testimony adequate to support the trial court's finding that a "delivery" occurred here during the birthing process, even if the criminal statute is applicable. *** However, in my view, the primary question in this case is whether section 893.13(1)(c) was intended by the Legislature to apply to the birthing process.***

In 1987, a bill was proposed to broaden the definition of "harm" [in the child abuse and neglect statute] to include physical dependency of a newborn infant upon certain controlled drugs. However, there was a concern among legislators that this language might authorize criminal prosecutions of mothers who give birth to drug-dependent children. The bill was then amended to provide that no parent of a drug-dependent newborn shall be subject to criminal investigation solely on the basis of the infant's drug dependency. . . .

From this legislative history, it is clear that the Legislature *considered* and *rejected* a specific statutory provision authorizing criminal penalties against mothers for delivering drug-affected children. . . . In light of this express legislative statement, I conclude that the Legislature never intended for the general drug delivery statute to authorize prosecutions of those mothers who take illegal drugs close enough in time to childbirth that a doctor could testify that a tiny amount passed from mother to child in the few seconds before the umbilical cord was cut. Criminal prosecution of mothers like Johnson will undermine Florida's express policy of "keeping families intact" and could destroy the family by incarcerating the child's mother when alternative measures could protect the child and stabilize the family. ***

There can be no doubt that drug abuse is one of the most serious problems confronting our society today. Of particular concern is the alarming rise in the number of babies born with cocaine in their systems as a result of cocaine use by pregnant women. Some experts estimate that as many as eleven percent of pregnant women have used an illegal drug during pregnancy, and of those women, seventy-five percent have used cocaine. Others estimate that 375,000 newborns per year are born to women who are users of illicit drugs.

It is well-established that the effects of cocaine use by a pregnant woman on her fetus and later on her newborn can be severe. On average, cocaine-exposed babies have lower birth weights, shorter body lengths at birth, and smaller head circumferences than normal infants. Cocaine use may also result in sudden infant death syndrome, neural-behavioral deficiencies as well as other medical problems and long-term developmental abnormalities. . . .

Florida could possibly have elected to make *in utero* transfers criminal. But it chose to deal with this problem in other ways. One way is to allow evidence of drug use by women as a ground for removal of the child to the custody of protective services, as was done in this case. Some states have responded to this crisis by charging women with child abuse and neglect. . . . However, prosecuting women for using drugs and "delivering" them to their newborns appears to be the least effective response to this crisis. Rather than face the possibility of prosecution, pregnant women who are substance abusers may simply avoid prenatal or medical care for fear of being detected. Yet the newborns of these women are, as a group, the most fragile and sick, and most in need of hospital neonatal care. . . . Prosecution of pregnant women for engaging in activities harmful to their fetuses or newborns may also unwittingly increase the incidence of abortion. ***

In summary, I would hold that section 893.13(1)(c) does not encompass "delivery" of an illegal drug derivative from womb to placenta to umbilical cord to newborn after a child's birth. If that is the intent of the Legislature, then this statute should be redrafted.

Questions

1. Does the ruling of the majority in this case surprise you? As you read the statutory language the court is relying on, does it seem to encompass the facts of this case? What does the intent of the statute appear to be?

2. What are the main arguments behind the dissenting opinion? Do you find them persuasive? Why or why not?

3. This issue presents a conflict between a mother's rights and the rights of a fetus. How do you suppose those rights can be reconciled? How would you have ruled in this case? Why?

4. If you agree with the majority's ruling, how would you answer the policy concerns articulated by the dissent? If you disagree with the majority's view, what policies would you favor to reduce drug use during pregnancy?

5. If NASW had submitted an *amicus* brief in the case, which side do you think it would support? What arguments do you think it would make? How can social work values inform this difficult issue? You might find it interesting to know that this case was appealed to the Florida Supreme Court the following year. That court reversed the ruling you just read, borrowing nearly verbatim from the dissenting opinion.

CHAPTER 14 PRACTICE TEST

The following questions will test your application and analysis of the content found within this chapter. For additional assessment, including licensing-exam type questions on applying chapter content to practice behaviors, visit **MySearchLab**

1. Isabelle, a low-income mother of four, is 11 weeks pregnant. She has been agonizing over this pregnancy and recently came to the conclusion that she cannot afford to raise another child. She decides to seek an abortion. Her husband, Sam, has religious objections to abortion and wants her to carry the pregnancy to term. Under the law, which of the following is true?

   a. If Isabelle seeks an abortion, the cost will be covered by Medicaid.

   b. Isabelle can obtain a legal abortion because she is in her first trimester.

   c. Isabelle can obtain a legal abortion at any time during her pregnancy.

   d. Sam can veto the abortion because, when couples disagree, the law protects the life of the fetus.

2. Mandatory HIV testing

   a. has been upheld for people in occupations with a high risk of transmission.

   b. is always permissible because it protects public safety.

   c. is never permissible because it is done without informed consent.

   d. is routinely performed on pregnant women.

3. The disproportionately high infant mortality rate among African Americans is an example of

   a. environmental racism.

   b. social determinants of health.

   c. the effects of globalization.

   d. unintended consequences of the Affordable Care Act.

4. Helen applies for a job as a lifeguard at the local community center. When she discloses that she has AIDS, her interview is abruptly terminated and another candidate is offered the job. Helen decides to sue under the Americans with Disabilities Act. Which of the following is correct?

   a. She will lose because AIDS is not a covered disability.

   b. The community center will win if it can show that her disability poses a direct threat to the health or safety of others.

   c. The community center can be required to cancel all its swimming classes and permit only accomplished swimmers to use the pool, in order to minimize the risk that Helen's AIDS might pose.

   d. She will win if she can show that she worked as a lifeguard before contracting AIDS.

5. What are the primary benefits and problems associated with conscience clauses? Craft an argument in response to these policies that draws on social work values.

6. Discuss the ethical issues related to genetic testing. How are these issues relevant to social work practice?

MYSEARCHLAB CONNECTIONS

Reinforce what you learned in this chapter by studying videos, cases, documents,
and more available at **www.MySearchLab.com**.

Watch these Videos

* AIDS in Black America
  * *What explains the disproportionate impact of HIV/AIDS on the African American community? How should it be addressed?*
* 2010 Health Care Legislation, The (2010)
  * *How did the U.S. Supreme Court rule on the constitutionality of the Affordable Care Act? What was their reasoning? What do you think the implications will be?*
* Vaccines: Mandatory Protection (2007)
  * *What are the controversies surrounding mandatory vaccines?*

Read these Cases/Documents

Δ Genetic Research
  * *How would you use the NASW Code of Ethics in arguing against genetic testing? In arguing in favor of it? Which do you think is the stronger argument? Why?*

Δ HIV
  * *How would you use the NASW Code of Ethics to argue in favor of upholding an HIV-positive client's right to confidentiality? How would you use it to argue in favor of warning the client's sexual partners? Which do you think is the stronger argument? Why?*

Explore these Assets

* Interactive Case Study: Comparing Health Systems
* Website: Collaborative on Health and the Environment, The
* Website: Society for Social Work Leadership in Healthcare

Assess Your Knowledge

Go to **MySearchLab** to test your knowledge of key topics in this chapter with topic-specific quizzes. Conclude your assessment by completing the chapter exam.

---

* = CSWE Core Competency Asset   Δ = Case Study

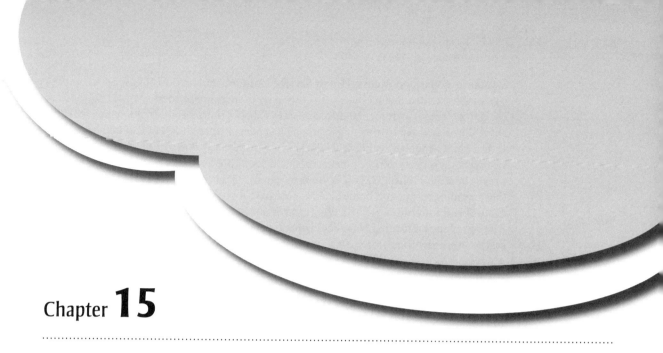

Chapter **15**

....

Mental Health

Understanding the law in relation to mental health is critical for social workers. Many social workers work specifically with clients suffering from mental illness; others encounter clients with mental illness in the course of providing a broad array of services to individuals, families, and communities. Advocates and policy experts advance the rights of people with mental illness to have access to appropriate services and to be free from discrimination. Forensic specialists work with the courts to assess the mental health status of criminal defendants and to provide mental health services to those in prisons and jails. This chapter provides a brief history of America's response to mental illness; discusses the legal bases for the right to receive and to refuse treatment; and explores the processes of civil commitment, determining competency to stand trial, and qualifying for the insanity defense. Special sections highlight the use of mental health advance directives and the civil commitment of convicted sex offenders. The sample case provides insight into the use of expert testimony when mental status is an issue at trial.

Background

....

Approximately 26.2% of Americans age 18 and older, or more than one in four adults, suffers from a mental disorder. Of these, nearly 45% suffer from two or more disorders simultaneously, and approximately 6% suffer from a serious mental illness (Kessler, Berglund, Demler, Jin, & Walters, 2005). Many adults also experience both mental illness and another co-occurring disorder, most commonly substance abuse. According to the

Substance Abuse and Mental Health Services Administration (SAMHSA, 2005), 30% to 50% of those with a mental illness also have a co-occurring disorder.

Among adults with mental disorders, fewer than 4 in 10 receive treatment (SAMHSA, 2010). There is also a treatment gap among juveniles. Although 15% of parents sought help with a child's mental health problem in 2005–2006, only 10% of the children received treatment—5% in the form of medication and 5% in the form of non-medication alternatives (Simpson, Cohen, Pastor, & Reuben, 2008). Older adults are at particular risk; of those residing in nursing homes, nearly 67% have a mental disorder (Centers for Disease Control and Prevention [CDC], 2009). Rates are also especially high within the military. Among soldiers returning from deployment, 20% of active duty personnel and 42% of reservists were identified as needing mental health treatment (National Institute on Alcohol Abuse and Alcoholism [NIAAA], 2011).

Common Mental Health Conditions

Mental disorders are identified and defined in the *Diagnostic and Statistical Manual* (DSM), published by the American Psychiatric Association. Most social workers receive training in the DSM, and clinical social work practitioners routinely use it; reimbursement for mental health diagnosis and treatment is premised on the categorization of illnesses contained in the DSM. Courts also rely on expert testimony concerning the DSM when considering the mental status of people involved in legal proceedings. Among the mental disorders social workers encounter most frequently are the following:

- **Mood disorders.** These include depressive disorders and bipolar disorders. Approximately 9.5% of the adult population in the United States has a mood disorder (NIMH, 2012). Mood disorders are more common among Caucasian adults than among either African Americans or Hispanics (National Institute of Mental Health [NIMH], 2010). The various forms of depression affect approximately 19 million Americans each year. Major depressive order is the single most debilitating mental disorder, affecting approximately 6.9% of the U.S. population (World Health Organization, 2008). Women are 70% more likely than men to experience major depressive disorder (NIMH, 2010). Of those who commit suicide each year, 90% have a diagnosable mental disorder, most often major depressive disorder or substance abuse (Moscicki, 2001). Bipolar disorders affect approximately 2.6% of the adult population in a given year; 82.9% of these cases are considered severe. The onset of bipolar disorders most commonly occurs between the ages of 15 and 25. These disorders involve periods of mania or hypomania, interspersed with periods of depression (NIMH, 2010).
- **Anxiety disorders.** These include agoraphobia, generalized anxiety disorder, obsessive compulsive disorder, panic disorder, posttraumatic stress disorder, social phobias, and specific phobias. According to estimates, 18.1% of adults suffer from anxiety disorders in a given year. Women are 60% more likely than men to experience an anxiety disorder over their lifetime, and anxiety disorders are more common among Caucasians than among people of color. In approximately 75% of cases, symptoms first surface before age 22. More than 25% of 13- to 18-year-olds suffer from anxiety disorders, and the average age of onset is 11 (NIMH, 2010).

- **Eating Disorders.** Eating disorders, which include anorexia nervosa, binge eating, and bulimia, affect approximately 2.7% of teenagers, significantly more girls than boys (NIMH, 2010). Eating disorders have the highest mortality rate of any mental disorder (National Association of Anorexia Nervosa and Associated Disorders, 2011).

- **Personality Disorders.** Approximately 9.1% of adults are diagnosed with personality disorders. Although difficult to define, they encompass enduring patterns of behavior that differ markedly from generally accepted expectations within one's cultural context. The most common types are borderline personality disorder and antisocial personality disorder.

- **Psychotic Disorders.** Psychotic disorders are severe, chronic, and highly debilitating conditions affecting approximately 1.1% of the adult population (Nemade & Dombeck, 2009). The most common psychotic disorder is schizophrenia. Schizophrenia is a complex constellation of disorders that may be marked by delusions, visual or auditory hallucinations, illogical thinking, impaired contact with reality, and blunted affect or emotion. Even though it affects a relatively small proportion of the population, its costs are enormous, estimated at $62.7 billion per year (Wu et al., 2005).

- **Attention Deficit Hyperactivity Disorder (ADHD) and Pervasive Developmental Disorders.** These are part of a larger category of disorders usually first diagnosed during infancy, childhood, or adolescence. ADHD is characterized by difficulty staying focused and paying attention, difficulty controlling behavior, and hyperactivity. It is one of the most common childhood disorders, continuing through adolescence into adulthood in 30% to 65% of cases (American Academy of Child and Adolescent Psychiatry, 2010). ADHD is believed to affect two to three times more boys than girls. The most common pervasive developmental disorder is autism. Its symptoms, which appear along a spectrum ranging from more to less severe, include deficits in social interaction and communication. It is estimated that one in every 110 eight-year-olds has an autism spectrum disorder.

In addition to these disorders, social workers often encounter clients with substance abuse disorders, adjustment disorders, impulse control disorders, sexual disorders, and conduct disorders. An exhaustive examination is beyond the scope of this text; all, however, are detailed in the DSM and social workers diagnosing and treating clients with mental disorders should be properly trained in its use.

We often talk about clients with *serious mental illness* (SMI). By this, we mean a mental disorder that negatively affects one or more facets of a person's everyday life. According to the National Institute of Mental Health (2012), approximately 6% of Americans are affected by an SMI. Figure 15.1 depicts the incidence of SMI by sex, age, and race.

In 2003, fewer than half of all adults with serious mental illness were receiving treatment; the likelihood of accessing treatment increased with age, and women were more likely than men to be engaged in treatment. Of those needing treatment who did not receive it, more than 45% cited cost or insurance issues as the reason. As for adolescents, approximately 5.1 million youth between the ages of 12 and 17 received treatment for a serious mental illness in 2003; approximately 9.1% were hospitalized (SAMHSA, 2004).

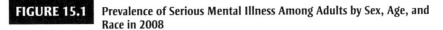

FIGURE 15.1   Prevalence of Serious Mental Illness Among Adults by Sex, Age, and Race in 2008

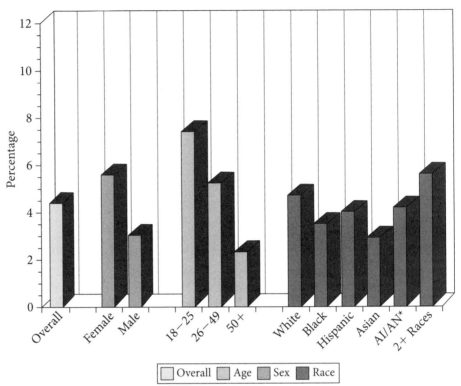

*AI/AN = American Indian/Alaska Native

Source: http://www.nimh.nih.gov/statistics/SMI_AASR.shtml

Untreated mental illness can have serious consequences for individuals, families, and communities. These include unemployment; homelessness; substance abuse; incarceration; and episodes of violence, victimization, and suicide (Treatment Advocacy Center, 2011). Often these conditions are interconnected. For example, 20% to 25% of people who are homeless in the United States suffer from a serious mental illness; mental illness has been identified as the third most common cause of homelessness for single adults. More than half of those who are mentally ill and homeless also suffer from a substance abuse disorder (National Coalition for the Homeless, 2009). Similarly, more than half of U.S. prisoners suffer from a mental disorder (James & Glaze, 2006), and 65% meet the criteria for substance abuse or dependence (National Center on Addiction and Substance Abuse, 2010). These conditions have enormous economic costs in addition to their human toll. Serious mental illness alone is estimated to cost the treasury $316 billion each year, including $193.2 billion in lost earnings (Insel, 2008).

Historical Overview

Awareness of mental illness has existed for at least the past 2,000 years. In the course of history, people with mental illness have at some times been regarded as demons from whom society needed protection, and at other times as deserving of protection themselves. Beginning in the 18th century, asylums became the most common solution to housing people with mental illness in Europe and the Americas. These institutions featured horrifying conditions and little treatment. They were primarily a vehicle for moving people off the streets and instituting a measure of social control. In the mid-19th century, Dorothea Dix began to use institutionalization as a way of taking care of people with mental illness. Following her lead, treatment became more humane and psychiatric hospitals proliferated. By the mid-20th century, large state hospitals dominated the field of mental health.

The return of large numbers of troops showing signs of "battle fatigue" (now known as post-traumatic stress disorder) following World War II brought mental health to the forefront of the public's attention, and people began to recognize the role of social and economic factors in mental illness (Popple & Leighninger, 2005). Congress created the National Institute of Mental Health (NIMH), which, together with the increased availability of psychotropic drugs, ushered in a new era of releasing patients from hospitals in order to care for them in the community (Mechanic, 2008). This deinstitutionalization movement was bolstered by a 1963 federal law mandating the creation of community mental health centers nationwide, and it led to a steep decline in hospitalizations.

Although community-based treatment continues to be the preferred approach, it has suffered from chronic underfunding, leaving many people with mental illness without support. As discussed in Chapter 12, people with mental illness are also overrepresented in prisons, partially as a result of too few inpatient hospital beds and inadequate community resources. In 2003, the President's New Freedom Commission on Mental Health conducted a comprehensive review of mental health in America and issued a set of recommendations for moving forward. The goals and recommendations contained in the commission's report are outlined in Illustration 15.1. These findings and recommendations are in the process of being implemented by the states and represent a shared vision of the future for mental health care.

Most of the federal legislation governing mental health today applies to people with health care needs or disabilities more broadly. This includes Medicare, Medicaid, the Children's Health Insurance Program, and the Americans with Disabilities Act, all of which are summarized in Chapter 14. The Mental Health Parity Act, enacted in 1996, was a particularly important milestone in mental health care coverage; it requires large group insurance plans to treat mental health and substance abuse services the same way they treat medical and surgical services in terms of coverage, treatment limits, co-payments, and deductibles. The requirement for parity was substantially expanded under the Patient Protection and Affordable Care Act of 2010. All insurance plans available through the new state exchanges, including those purchased by individuals and small businesses, are required to treat mental health and physical health care similarly. This could potentially improve coverage for millions of additional consumers of mental health services. The law also promotes integration of medical and mental health care in order to promote wider access to services.

ILLUSTRATION 15.1

President's New Freedom Commission on Mental Health Goals

GOAL 1: AMERICANS UNDERSTAND THAT MENTAL HEALTH IS ESSENTIAL TO OVERALL HEALTH.

- Advance and implement a national campaign to reduce the stigma of seeking care and a national strategy for suicide prevention.

- Address mental health with the same urgency as physical health.

GOAL 2: MENTAL HEALTH CARE IS CONSUMER AND FAMILY DRIVEN.

- Develop an individualized plan of care for every adult with a serious mental illness and child with a serious emotional disturbance.

- Involve consumers and families fully in orienting the mental health system toward recovery.

- Align relevant Federal programs to improve access and accountability for mental health services.

- Create a Comprehensive State Mental Health Plan.

- Protect and enhance the rights of people with mental illnesses.

GOAL 3: DISPARITIES IN MENTAL HEALTH SERVICES ARE ELIMINATED.

- Improve access to quality care that is culturally competent.

- Improve access to quality care in rural and geographically remote areas.

GOAL 4: EARLY MENTAL HEALTH SCREENING, ASSESSMENT, AND REFERRAL TO SERVICES ARE COMMON PRACTICE.

- Promote the mental health of young children.

- Improve and expand school mental health programs.

- Screen for co-occurring mental and substance use disorders and link with integrated treatment strategies.

- Screen for mental disorders in primary health care, across the life span, and connect to treatment and supports.

GOAL 5: EXCELLENT MENTAL HEALTH CARE IS DELIVERED AND RESEARCH IS ACCELERATED.

- Accelerate research to promote recovery and resilience, and ultimately to cure and prevent mental illnesses.

- Advance evidence-based practices using dissemination and demonstration projects and create a public-private partnership to guide their implementation.

- Improve and expand the workforce providing evidence-based mental health services and supports.

- Develop the knowledge base in four understudied areas: mental health disparities, long-term effects of medications, trauma, and acute care.

GOAL 6: TECHNOLOGY IS USED TO ACCESS MENTAL HEALTH CARE AND IN-
FORMATION.

- Use health technology and telehealth to improve access and coordination of mental health care, especially for Americans in remote areas or in underserved populations.

- Develop and implement integrated electronic health record and personal health information systems.

Source: President's New Freedom Commission on Mental Health, 2003, pp. 24–25.

Civil Commitment

People with mental illness can be treated in a variety of settings, ranging from inpatient care in a psychiatric facility to outpatient therapy in the community. When hospitalization is required, they can seek care voluntarily or may be committed against their will. Involuntary commitment, also called *civil commitment*, accounts for approximately 12% of psychiatric hospitalizations. It is a serious matter because it results in a loss of liberty and can be stigmatizing for years to come. When we have someone civilly committed, we are making a judgment that our concern for their safety or the safety of others supersedes their rights to informed consent and self-determination. Unlike in the vast majority of civil cases that require only a preponderance of the evidence, civil commitment requires clear and convincing evidence that the criteria for commitment are met (*Addington v. Texas,* 1979).

Legally, what allows us to hospitalize someone without his or her consent is the doctrine of *parens patriae.* We previously discussed this idea in the context of maltreatment; it is the doctrine under which the government, acting in a parenting role, is empowered to protect those who are vulnerable. The government's *police power,* meanwhile, is what empowers it to take action to keep its citizens safe. Civil commitment laws are an attempt to find the delicate balance between respecting the civil liberties of people with mental illness and protecting the public from potential harm.

Criteria for Commitment

Each state has its own laws that govern civil commitment. Until the 1970s, the procedures for commitment were relatively relaxed. As advocates pressed for greater rights for people with mental illness, however, many laws were amended to make it more difficult to commit people without their consent. During the past few years, many of those same laws were once again amended to make civil commitment easier. Spurred in large part by the 2007 massacre at Virginia Tech in which a young man with mental illness killed 32 people and himself, the goal was to prevent other potential acts of violence.

Generally speaking, civil commitment is permissible when it can be demonstrated by clear and convincing evidence that the person has a mental illness and is a danger to him or herself or to others. This standard evolved from a 1975 U.S. Supreme Court case, *O'Connor v. Donaldson*. In that case, a man who was experiencing delusions was committed to a state hospital where he remained, without any discernable treatment, for 15 years. When he was finally released at age 62, he filed suit against the hospital administrator for violation of his constitutional rights. The administrator claimed to have kept Donaldson confined for his own good, but the Court ruled that mental illness alone is insufficient justification for keeping a person institutionalized against his or her will; the person must also be dangerous or must be receiving treatment to alleviate the mental disorder. In Donaldson's case, neither was true; according to the Court, his constitutional rights had indeed been violated.

Today, all states require dangerousness as part of their definition of who may be involuntarily committed. What constitutes a danger, how imminent it must be, how severe it must be, and what alternatives must first be explored, however, are questions often left to interpretation. The District of Columbia's commitment statute is one of the most succinct:

> If the Court or jury finds that the person is mentally ill and, because of that mental illness, is likely to injure himself or others if not committed, the Court may order the person's commitment to the Department or to any other facility, hospital, or mental health provider that the Court believes is the least restrictive alternative consistent with the best interests of the person and the public. (D.C. Code Ann. § 21-545[b][2])

An example of a more detailed statute is presented in Illustration 15.2. It is important to be familiar with the commitment criteria in your state. Social workers are often in a position to initiate civil commitment proceedings; they also provide expert testimony on whether the criteria for commitment are met.

The Commitment Process

In every state, a *commitment hearing* is required before a person with a mental illness can be involuntarily committed. In a typical scenario, a law enforcement officer, mental health professional, or family member files a petition to have someone committed. A law enforcement officer transports the person to a hospital where an evaluation is conducted. If there is probable cause to believe the person meets the state's criteria for commitment, the court will issue a *temporary detention order* that allows the person to be detained (in what is often called a *precommitment hold*) until the hearing; under most state laws, this hearing must take place within 2 to 5 days. In some cases, if the person cannot remain safely in the community prior to an evaluation, a judge or magistrate may issue an *emergency custody order* that allows the person to be taken into custody immediately.

The commitment hearing, although considered civil in nature, involves many of the safeguards required in criminal proceedings. These include the right to timely notice, the right to counsel (including appointed counsel if the person cannot afford an attorney), the right to be present at the hearing and to testify, the right to present evidence, and the right to cross-examine witnesses. Most states also require that the court consider the evaluation of an independent examiner, most often a psychiatrist, psychologist, or social worker who is specially trained and certified. The evaluation generally consists of a mental status examination, an assessment of the person's medical and psychiatric

ILLUSTRATION 15.2

Arkansas Standard for Involuntary Commitment

A person shall be eligible for involuntary admission if he or she is in such a mental condition as a result of mental illness, disease, or disorder that he or she poses a clear and present danger to himself or herself or others;

(1) As used in this subsection, "a clear and present danger to himself or herself" is established by demonstrating that:

(A) The person has inflicted serious bodily injury on himself or herself or has attempted suicide or serious self-injury, and there is a reasonable probability that the conduct will be repeated if admission is not ordered;

(B) The person has threatened to inflict serious bodily injury on himself or herself, and there is a reasonable probability that the conduct will occur if admission is not ordered;

(C) The person's recent behavior or behavior history demonstrates that he or she so lacks the capacity to care for his or her own welfare that there is a reasonable probability of death, serious bodily injury, or serious physical or mental debilitation if admission is not ordered; or

(D) (i) The person's understanding of the need for treatment is impaired to the point that he or she is unlikely to participate in treatment voluntarily; (ii) The person needs mental health treatment on a continuing basis to prevent a relapse or harmful deterioration of his or her condition; and (iii) The person's noncompliance with treatment has been a factor in the individual's placement in a psychiatric hospital, prison, or jail at least two times within the last forty-eight months or has been a factor in the individual's committing one or more acts, attempts, or threats of serious violent behavior within the last forty-eight months; and

(2) As used in this subsection, "a clear and present danger to others" is established by demonstrating that the person has inflicted, attempted to inflict, or threatened to inflict serious bodily harm on another, and there is a reasonable probability that such conduct will occur if admission is not ordered. (Ark. Code Ann. § 20-47-207[c])

INVOLUNTARY COMMITMENT OF CONVICTED SEX OFFENDERS

Sex crimes are considered by many to be among the most egregious offenses addressed by the criminal justice system. As a result of the high recidivism rate among sex offenders, Americans fear the prospect of allowing them to return to the community once they have served their sentences. One solution that has gained considerable traction is to permit the involuntary mental health commitment of sex offenders at the end of their incarceration period. Twenty-one states currently have such policies in place (Kumar, 2011).

The U.S. Supreme Court ruled on the constitutionality of this approach in the 1997 case of *Kansas v. Hendricks*. Hendricks, a sexually violent pedophile, claimed that committing him to a mental health facility would violate his due process rights and constituted double jeopardy because he had already served his criminal sentence. The Court ruled against him on the due process claim, noting that the commitment law required evidence of both past violent sexual behavior and an intent to continue offending. In rejecting his double jeopardy claim, the Court reasoned that involuntary commitment constitutes a civil proceeding, not a form of criminal punishment. The Supreme Court has upheld the involuntary civil commitment of sex offenders in other cases, as well (*Kansas v. Crane*, 2002; *Seling v. Young*, 2001; *United States v. Comstock*, 2010).

Although this solution is effective in helping the public feel safe, many advocates believe that the involuntary commitment of sex offenders is unacceptable. First, it is inconsistent with the purpose of involuntary civil commitment which is treatment, not punishment. Second, involuntary commitment is reserved for individuals found to be dangerous to themselves or others, a criterion that is difficult to prove in the case of recently released sex offenders who may not reoffend (Mental Health America, 2011). Third, as more and more sex offenders are committed, the cost of continuing to confine them keeps rising; current estimates place the cost at approximately $100,000 per offender, per year. Given the current economic climate, many states are now questioning their ability to continue this practice (Kumar, 2011).

From a social work standpoint, there are serious flaws in this approach. Without an individualized finding that released sex offenders are a danger to themselves or others, committing them represents a violation of civil liberties. It should be a priority for us, along with other mental health and criminal justice professionals, to identify efficacious treatments so that those who have served their sentences can safely take their place in the community.

history, medication history, substance abuse evaluation and screening, review of the detention facility's records, an assessment of the person's capacity to consent to treatment, a discussion of the person's treatment preferences, and consideration of alternatives to involuntary hospitalization. Based on this evidence, the examiner determines the person's fit with the criteria for involuntary commitment and offers a recommendation concerning placement, care, and treatment. In addition to submitting a report, the examiner is often called to testify as an expert witness. Courts tend to place great weight on the findings and recommendations of the examiner. At the conclusion of the commitment hearing, the judge may order involuntary commitment or may dismiss the case. In some states, there is an additional option for assisted outpatient treatment (described next). When hospitalization is ordered, it is typically for an initial period of 30 to 45 days, after which the necessity for continued commitment must be determined and periodically reviewed.

Assisted Outpatient Treatment

One of the more recent trends in mental health law has been the widespread adoption of *assisted outpatient treatment* (AOT), also referred to as *mandatory outpatient treatment* or *involuntary outpatient treatment*. Currently, 44 states and the District of Columbia provide for this option in their state laws; the exceptions are Connecticut, Maryland, Massachusetts, Nevada, New Mexico, and Tennessee (Advocacy Treatment Center, 2011). The purpose of these laws is to allow courts to mandate treatment for those who are at risk of escalating or recurrent episodes of dangerousness, who are unable to voluntarily engage in treatment, and for whom hospitalization is deemed unnecessary. Some states apply a single set of criteria to both involuntary inpatient commitment and AOT, requiring the least restrictive alternative. Others have separate criteria that govern AOT. Here, as an example, is the law from Georgia:

> "Outpatient" means a person who is mentally ill and:
> (A) Who is not an inpatient but who, based on the person's treatment history or current mental status, will require outpatient treatment in order to avoid predictably and imminently becoming an inpatient;
> (B) Who because of the person's current mental status, mental history, or nature of the person's mental illness is unable voluntarily to seek or comply with outpatient treatment; and
> (C) Who is in need of involuntary treatment. (Ga. Code Ann. § 37-3-1 [12.1])

Here is another example, this one from Illinois:

> "Person subject to involuntary admission on an outpatient basis" means:
> (1) A person who would meet the criteria for admission on an inpatient basis … in the absence of treatment on an outpatient basis and for whom treatment on an outpatient basis can only be reasonably ensured by a court order mandating such treatment; or
> (2) A person with a mental illness which, if left untreated, is reasonably expected to result in an increase in the symptoms caused by the illness to the point that the person would meet the criteria for [inpatient] commitment, and whose mental illness has, on more than one occasion in the past, caused that person to refuse needed and appropriate mental health services in the community. (405 Ill. Comp. Stat. 5/1-119.1)

Assisted outpatient treatment is controversial. Some see it as a welcome alternative to inpatient mental health commitment that can help prevent future dangerous acts. Others believe that those who fail to meet the criteria for inpatient civil commitment should be entitled to live freely in the community; they also note that AOT statutes in some states have disproportionately been applied to people of color, particularly African Americans (Israel, 2011). Constitutional challenges have gone both ways, with court in New York upholding its AOT statute (*In re K.L.*, 2004) and court in New Mexico striking its statute down (*Protection and Advocacy System v. City of Albuquerque*, 2008). Social workers who evaluate people with mental illness for civil commitment must be aware of the options that exist within their states so that their recommendations can accurately reflect the needs of the person in question while maximizing their civil liberties. More research is needed to assess the efficacy of AOT as well as its impact on equity and civil rights.

The Right to Receive and Refuse Treatment

In response to our long history of using psychiatric hospitals as dumping grounds for those considered socially undesirable, a body of law has developed that articulates a right to treatment. Perhaps the most pivotal case on this topic is *Wyatt v. Stickney* (1972). The case, originally filed in 1970, was initiated in response to the layoff of nearly 100 employees at Bryce Hospital in Alabama. Twenty of these were mental health professionals including psychiatrists, psychologists, and social workers. As a result, the ratio of staff to patients became grossly inadequate. The judge concluded that the hospital was within its rights to fire the employees; however, he believed that an important legal issue existed regarding the minimum treatment requirements for people committed to state mental health facilities. Describing conditions at the hospital, a former U.S. attorney on the case explained, "There was one ward with nothing on it but old people. Beds were touching one another and they were simply warehoused. There was a cemetery in the back, but no records. Someone would die—they would merely dump them in an unmarked grave and that was the end of it" (Carr, 2004, p. 2).

The named plaintiff in the case, Ricky Wyatt, was a 15-year-old boy who had been committed to the hospital because he was a "juvenile delinquent" who had acted out at a children's group home. Although not mentally ill, it was believed that commitment to the hospital might make him behave. He described the hospital's inhumane conditions, including being forced to sleep on a wet floor in a dark cell-like room and being heavily medicated to keep him out of trouble. At the time, Alabama ranked last in the country for spending on mental health and intellectual disabilities: the equivalent of 50 cents per patient per day. The judge decried the unacceptable conditions at Bryce Hospital and ruled that involuntarily committed patients "unquestionably have a right to receive such individual treatment as will give each of them a realistic opportunity to be cured or to improve his or her mental condition" (*Wyatt v. Stickney*, 1971, p. 784). He gave the hospital 6 months to implement standards for adequate patient treatment. Two additional mental hospitals with equally abysmal conditions were added to the case. When the hospitals reported back to the court 6 months later, the judge found their efforts deficient. The court subsequently issued a set of standards that, in its judgment, constituted minimum requirements under the Constitution's due process clause. It further specified that a hospital's lack of funds was not an acceptable justification for failure to implement the standards.

These standards, which appear in an appendix to the court's opinion, address a wide range of considerations, including the right of patients to

- Be deemed competent to manage their own affairs
- Have visitation and telephone communication
- Send sealed mail without restriction
- Be free from unnecessary or excessive medication
- Be free from physical restraint or isolation
- Not be subjected to experimental research
- Not to be subjected to unusual or hazardous treatment procedures without consent
- Receive prompt and adequate medical treatment
- Wear their own clothes and keep their own personal possessions
- Have regular physical exercise

- Be outdoors at regular and frequent intervals
- Engage in religious worship
- Interact with members of the opposite sex

In addition, the standards address the need for privacy, the minimum size of a residential unit, requirements for toilets and showers, day rooms and dining facilities, housekeeping, bedding, heating, air conditioning, ventilation, fire and safety standards, nutritional standards, professional staff and staffing ratios, individualized treatment plans, patient records, therapy, post-hospitalization planning, and special requirements for children and youth. In deference to safety concerns, many of these patient rights can be suspended in an emergency. Alabama continued to make incremental reforms to its mental health system for many years; the *Wyatt* litigation continued until 2004.

Although *Wyatt* was not a U.S. Supreme Court case, it nonetheless had a huge impact on the *right to treatment* nationwide; many states used it as a model in developing their own laws and articulating patient rights. With *Wyatt v. Stickney*, the push for mental health rights took its place beside the civil rights movements addressing race, sex, and sexual orientation that had helped define an era.

An example is *Dixon v. Gray*, a right to treatment case originally brought in 1974 by patients in the District of Columbia seeking alternatives to the city's single, problem-ridden psychiatric hospital. Under an agreement with the court, the D.C. government agreed to create an array of community-based treatment options, create an additional 300 housing units, provide job counseling, and decrease the number of youth in private treatment facilities. After 37 years of receivership, during which a court-appointed monitor oversaw the District's mental health system, the parties finally reached a settlement (Levin, 2012).

Complementing a right to treatment for people with mental illness is the *right to refuse treatment.* If you look carefully at the standards articulated by the court in the *Wyatt* decision, several actually pertain to refusing treatment; these include the right to be free from unnecessary and excessive medication, the right to be free from physical restraint or isolation, and the right not to be subjected to unusual or hazardous treatment procedures in the absence of consent. There was a time when it was not unusual to force patients in mental hospitals to undergo lobotomies, electroconvulsive therapy (ECT), or aversive conditioning. In recent years, the right to refuse treatment has centered more on medication. As the use of psychotropic drugs became more common, their negative side effects became more apparent; some of these side effects were permanent and debilitating.

The right to refuse treatment is related to the right to informed consent. This means that the patient must be competent when refusing treatment and must make an informed decision. As with informed consent, exceptions include emergencies and situations where the patient poses an immediate danger to him or herself or to others (Epright, 2010).

The central case that laid the groundwork for a right to refuse treatment is *Rennie v. Klein* (1978). The case concerned a New Jersey man who was suicidal and suffered from paranoid schizophrenia and depression. He was in and out of mental hospitals over a period of years. In the course of these hospitalizations, a large assortment of psychotropic drugs was administered in the hope of successfully treating his condition. As a result, he endured side effects including blurred vision, dry mouth, low blood pressure, uncontrollable tremors, worm-like movements of the tongue, and dulled senses, some of which could result in permanent damage. During his 12th hospitalization, Rennie instituted a suit in federal district court to keep the doctors from requiring him to take any more antipsychotic medications. The court held that people who are civilly committed do have a constitutional right to refuse medication, but that right can be overridden based on four considerations: (1) whether the patient poses a physical threat to patients and staff at the institution, (2) whether the patient has the capacity to decide on his or her particular treatment, (3) whether any less restrictive treatments exist, and (4) the risk of permanent side effects from the proposed treatment.

The U.S. Supreme Court considered the right to refuse treatment in a somewhat different context in *Sell v. United States* (2003). The question was whether it is constitutionally permissible for the state to force a criminal defendant to take antipsychotic drugs in order to render him or her competent to stand trial. The Court ruled that it is permissible, but only if all of the following conditions are met:

- The treatment is medically appropriate.
- It is substantially unlikely to have side effects that could undermine the fairness of the trial (e.g., by sedating the defendant, interfering with his or her communication, preventing timely reactions to trial developments, or diminishing the ability to express emotion).
- There are no less intrusive alternatives.
- It is substantially likely to render the defendant competent.

Both *Rennie* and *Sell* recognize a limited constitutional right to refuse treatment because, as always, the court is trying to balance competing interests. In *Rennie*, the patient's interests in privacy and bodily integrity are weighed against the government's interest in safeguarding public safety. In *Sell*, the defendant's interests in privacy and bodily integrity are weighed against the government's interest in a fair and speedy trial.

Over the past decade, a number of courts have considered whether it is constitutional to medicate people against their will in order to make them competent for execution under the death penalty. Although none of these cases has reached the U.S. Supreme Court, lower courts have affirmed the state's right to override defendants' refusal of treatment.

MENTAL HEALTH ADVANCE DIRECTIVES

While advance directives have been used to guide patients' end-of-life care decisions for several decades, the use of mental health advance directives (or *psychiatric advance directives*) is relatively new. Mental health advance directives are legal documents "allowing a consumer to direct his or her psychiatric treatment in the event that he or she becomes unable to make or communicate decisions about that treatment" (National Resource Center on Psychiatric Advance Directives [NRCPAD], 2011).

For people with a mental illness that interferes with rational decision making, a mental health advance directive can ensure that they retain a degree of self-determination even when the illness is acute.

There are various types of mental health advance directives. An *instructional directive* enables consumers to delineate which treatments they would or would not like to receive while they are incapable of making treatment decisions. A *proxy directive* allows consumers to appoint an alternate decision maker to make decisions on their behalf in the event that they are unable to do so. A *hybrid directive* combines aspects of the instructional and proxy directives. A *Ulysses directive* is perhaps the most useful type for people with mental illnesses that are episodic in nature and result in impaired insight. It "enables them prospectively to bind themselves to treatment and override, in advance, their refusals during acute episodes of their illnesses" (Sheetz, 2007, p. 403). Mental health advance directives can identify warning signs and symptoms, convey consent to specific interventions (including involuntary hospitalization), and document refusal to undergo specific treatments.

In accordance with the Patient Self-Determination Act of 1990, publicly funded health facilities in every state are required to advise patients of their right to prepare an advance directive (Backlar, McFarland, Swanson, & Mahler, 2001). Although the legislation was originally intended to apply to living wills and health care directives, it also covers mental health advance directives (Swartz, 2008). A total of 25 states have passed laws specifically authorizing mental health advance directives; several other states permit limited mental health treatment decisions to be made through general advance directives (Backlar et al., 2001).

Supporters of mental health advance directives assert that they allow for better decision making, enhanced self-efficacy, and more effective treatment. They also note that consumers, their families, and mental health providers all find them to be valuable.

Opponents, however, worry that mental health advance directives prioritize consumers' past decisions over their current wishes and represent a form of paternalism. They also argue that treatment providers and others may inadvertently coerce consumers into incorporating certain decisions in their mental health advance directives (Sheetz, 2007).

Although research suggests that fairly widespread support for mental health advance directives exists "in concept," questions persist regarding their actual implementation (Backlar et al., 2001; Swanson, Van McCrary, Swartz, Van Dorn, & Elbogen, 2007). These include whether an assessment establishing competency should be required at the time a mental health advance directive is created, how competency should be determined, whether advance directives can or should allow for refusal of all psychiatric treatment, under what conditions the consumer's wishes can be overridden by a clinician, and under what conditions the consumer can revoke a mental health advance directive that is in place (Sheetz, 2007; Swanson et al., 2007). Other concerns relate to whether mental health directives are readily accessible when needed and how best to ensure that they are honored (Backlar et al., 2001; Wang, 2007).

As social workers, we should be aware of the role that mental health advance directives can play in the lives of our clients. We are in an excellent position to provide education and to ensure that these advance directives are properly created and implemented and that the wishes of our clients with mental illness are respected.

Competency to Stand Trial

Our discussion of involuntary commitment has so far focused on a civil process, but social workers may also assume forensic roles in relation to the criminal justice process. One example involves assessing defendants for competency to stand trial.

The requirement that one must be competent in order to stand trial derives from the 14th Amendment's due process clause: no person may be deprived of liberty without due process of law. Due process requires fairness. Here, the idea is that it is unfair to prosecute people who cannot understand or meaningfully participate in the proceedings against them.

The key question in competency is what the client's mental state is *at the time of trial.* Being deemed incompetent is not the same as being acquitted; it means that the trial is delayed until the person regains the mental capacity for meaningful participation in the proceedings. The question of competency can be raised at any point during the trial. The defendant has the burden of proving that he or she is incompetent by a preponderance of the evidence. Once the issue is raised, the judge will order that a mental health expert evaluate the defendant and present a recommendation to the court. Although it is the court that determines whether or not the defendant is competent, the expert's recommendation is usually given considerable weight. In some states, social workers are among the experts qualified by law to evaluate defendants regarding competency to stand trial.

Defining Competency to Stand Trial

Competency has different definitions in different legal contexts. Prior to the late 1950s, courts determined competency to stand trial by determining whether a defendant was oriented to person, place, and time. This approach changed as the result of a U.S. Supreme Court case, *Dusky v. United States* (1960); today's state laws reflect the standards laid out in the *Dusky* decision.

Milton Dusky began to experience severe panic attacks while in the U.S. Navy at age 18. His agitation increased over the next several years, during which he was hospitalized several times for suicidal ideation. Dusky was diagnosed with anxiety and alcoholism; he was also hostile and homicidal, had fantasies of beating his ex-wife, and had periods in which he felt like he was "somebody else" and did not know where he was. He was so confused that his teenage son moved in with him in order to help. It was a chaotic household, with his son's various friends constantly coming and going. After an episode in which Dusky's son let the landlord's dog out of the house and it was killed, Dusky and his son were evicted; Dusky began taking tranquilizers and drinking more heavily—as much as two pints of vodka per day.

One night, Dusky and two of his son's friends (ages 14 and 16) picked up a 15-year-old girl on the pretext of giving her a ride to her friend's house. Instead, they drove across state lines to a deserted country road; both boys raped her and Dusky attempted rape but was unsuccessful. The following night, Dusky and one of the boys were arrested. Dusky was indicted on kidnapping charges and was tried in federal court. His attorney requested a mental health evaluation. Following a 4-month period of assessment and treatment, the psychiatrist testified that Dusky was competent to stand trial because he was oriented to time, place, and person (meaning he knew what day and year it was, that the judge was the judge, and that his lawyer was his lawyer). He also mentioned, however, that Dusky, who had been diagnosed with schizophrenia, would be unable to assist in his defense because his mental illness confused his thinking. Two other psychiatrists testified as well: One believed he was not competent to stand trial but could become competent if he remained hospitalized and stayed off the tranquilizers. The other reported that Dusky was currently agitated, anxious, and hostile; that he was experiencing delusions and hallucinations; and that he believed he was being framed. Despite the doctors' testimony, the court found Dusky competent to stand trial because he was oriented to person, place, and time. He was convicted and sentenced to 45 years in prison.

The case was appealed to the U.S. Supreme Court, which reversed the lower court's ruling. The Court ordered a new competency evaluation and a new trial. Dusky was again found to be competent—but this time, in addition to being oriented, he was able to remember the events of the crime, was able to consult with his attorney, and understood the proceedings against him. He was again found guilty and was sentenced to 20 years.

The takeaway message from the *Dusky* case is that incompetency requires more than disorientation. Having a mental illness is necessary, but not sufficient. In order to stand trial, defendants must be able to (1) understand the proceedings against them and (2) assist in their own defense. Unless they are capable of both, they will be considered incompetent to stand trial.

Conducting a Competency Assessment

Although there are standardized instruments that can assist in determining competency to stand trial, conducting an assessment is far more involved. An assessment generally has three steps: (1) determining whether the defendant has a mental disorder, (2) determining whether that mental disorder impairs the defendant's ability to understand the proceedings and to communicate with counsel, and (3) using that information to determine the defendant's fitness to stand trial under the state's law.

In order to make these determinations, the evaluator typically begins by contacting both the prosecuting and defense attorneys to determine why the competency issue was raised and what evidence was offered. To gain a comprehensive understanding of the defendant's condition, relevant records should be collected and reviewed; these include the defendant's mental health history, the police report for the crime, any other existing court records, and psychological test results. A clinical assessment can be useful in helping the evaluator determine whether the defendant is currently exhibiting symptoms and how those might be related to his or her ability to meet the criteria for competency. Finally, specialized measurement instruments are often used to assess the defendant's psycho-legal abilities. Before interviewing the defendant, it is important to be sure he or she understands the limits to confidentiality; consent to record the interview should be requested from both the defendant and his or her attorney.

Measurement instruments used in assessing competency to stand trial represent a single source of information about the defendant and should never be considered dispositive in and of themselves. The evaluator must be trained in the specific instrument being used. Most are designed as structured interviews; they take about 30 minutes and can be administered in jails, courts, community mental health centers, or other outpatient settings. Some are designed to be completed in writing by the defendant. They usually address the defendant's general mental health status as well as what are called *socio-legal* competencies (those specific to the legal process). Some of the available instruments include the following:

- MacArthur Competence Assessment Tool–Criminal Adjudication (MacCAT-CA)
- Computer-Assisted Determination of Competency to Proceed (CADCOMP)
- Competency Screening Test (CST)
- Competency Assessment Instrument (CAI)
- Interdisciplinary Fitness Interview (IFI)
- Fitness Interview Test-Revised (FIT-R)

Illustration 15.3 provides an example of interview questions contained in the FIT-R.

Illustration 15.3

Sample Competency Questions from the FIT-R

The FIT-R is an instrument commonly used in the United States and Canada to help assess competency to stand trial. Selected sample questions follow:

ABILITY TO UNDERSTAND THE NATURE OF THE PROCEEDINGS
- Can you tell me how you came to be here (in jail)?
- Did you say anything to the police? What do you think they might do with that information?
- What are you charged with? How serious is that charge?
- What is the job of your lawyer? The prosecutor? The judge? The jury?
- What questions would you ask your lawyer before you decide whether or not to plead guilty?

ABILITY TO UNDERSTAND THE POSSIBLE CONSEQUENCES OF THE PROCEEDINGS
- If you are found guilty, what are the possible sentences the judge could give you?
- How can you explain your way out of these charges?
- What do you think your chances are to be found not guilty?
- Do you have to abide by the court's decision?

ABILITY TO COMMUNICATE WITH COUNSEL
- What will you do if you disagree with your lawyer about how to handle your case?
- Do you understand the consequences of being found incompetent to stand trial?
- What do you think would happen if you spoke out, interrupted the court proceedings, or moved around in the courtroom without permission?

The evaluator rates each response and uses this feedback to reach a conclusion about whether the defendant meets the legal criteria for competency to stand trial. The instrument is designed to weed out those who are clearly competent so that a more rigorous evaluation can be completed with those about whose competence there is doubt.

Source: Roesch, R., Zapf, P.A., & Eaves, D. (2006). *Fit-R: Fitness interview for assessing competency to stand trial.* Sarasota, FL: Professional Resource Press.

The last step in the assessment process is to submit a written report to the court. Each state has specific requirements for the report's content and format. In Virginia, for example, the report must describe "the defendant's capacity to understand the proceedings against him; his ability to assist his attorney; and his need for treatment in the event he is found incompetent but restorable, or incompetent for the foreseeable future" (Virginia Code Sec. 19.2-169.1). It is also helpful to describe the defendant's mental status and how it impairs his or her court-related competencies, because a causal link is required between the two. As with any forensic report, it is important to recount the process you undertook and to discuss the facts on which your conclusions are based.

Remember that to be competent, both prongs of the test must be met. If the defendant is *either* unable to understand the proceedings *or* unable to assist counsel, he or she will be judged incompetent. What happens to people deemed incompetent to stand trial? They are committed for mental health treatment until competency is restored, at which point the case can be re-filed. In most cases, with the help of medication, this occurs within a matter of months. Can a defendant be held indefinitely if he or she is unable to regain competency? According to the U.S. Supreme Court in *Jackson v. Indiana* (1972), the answer is no. The Court, in that case, ruled that someone who is detained solely because of incompetency to stand trial can be held only long enough to determine whether there is a substantial probability of regaining competency in the foreseeable future. If there is not, either commitment proceedings must be initiated or the defendant must be released.

The sample case at the end of this chapter provides a vivid example of how difficult it can be to determine whether a defendant is really incompetent to stand trial or is manipulating the court by feigning incompetency.

The Insanity Defense

Whereas competency to stand trial involves a determination of the accused's mental state at the time of trial, the insanity defense (also referred to as *not guilty by reason of insanity,* NGRI) turns on the defendant's mental state *at the time the crime was committed.* Under our judicial system, someone may be found guilty of a crime only if there is both an illegal act (*actus reas*) and criminal intent (*mens rea*). We do not hold people criminally responsible who are incapable of forming the required intent. It is this idea that gave rise to the insanity defense.

Defining the Insanity Defense

In 1962, the American Law Institute proposed a model law with the following standard for legal insanity:

> A person is not responsible for criminal conduct if at the time of such conduct as a result of mental disease or defect he (or she) lacks substantial capacity either to appreciate the criminality/wrongfulness of his (or her) conduct or to conform his (or her) conduct to the requirements of the law. (Sec. 4.01)

By the early 1980s, this standard had been adopted by all federal courts and a majority of state courts. Then, in 1981, the country was rocked by an assassination attempt on President Ronald Reagan. The assailant was John Hinckley. As a young man, Hinckley had become obsessed with actress Jodie Foster. As his mental health deteriorated, he joined the American Nazi Party and began to accumulate guns. He moved 17 times during the 6 years following his high school graduation. He tried to contact Jodie Foster while she was attending college at Yale University; when he finally spoke to her, he was disappointed by her response. Desperate to impress her, he traveled to Washington, D.C., and fired six shots at the president. Although Reagan—who took a bullet in the chest—recovered from his injuries, Press Secretary James Brady suffered extensive neurological damage. At trial, Hinckley's lawyers raised the insanity defense, laying out their client's history of maladjustment, anxiety, obsession, and mental instability. The trial lasted more than 7 weeks; nearly half a million dollars was spent on mental health experts, most of it by the prosecution. After 3 days of deliberations, the jury found Hinckley not guilty by reason of insanity; he was committed to a psychiatric hospital for treatment.

The public reacted strongly to Hinckley's acquittal and the fact that he would never serve a day in jail. In the weeks following the verdict, 26 bills were introduced to modify the law pertaining to the insanity defense. This resulted in several important changes. First, the federal courts adopted a new standard, which eliminated the part of the earlier standard addressing the "capacity to conform one's conduct to the requirements of the law" (often called the *irresistible impulse* test). Second, numerous states shifted the burden of proof from the prosecution to the defense. Third, many states also amended their standard of proof to require clear and convincing evidence. These changes were designed to make it more difficult for criminal defendants to make out a successful insanity plea.

Where does that leave us? Current federal law now deems a defendant NGRI if, as a result of severe mental disease or defect, he or she was unable to appreciate the nature and quality or the wrongfulness of his or her acts. This is also the definition contained in most state laws, although 18 states have retained the irresistible impulse test. Note that, either way, mental illness in and of itself is not a defense; it is necessary for a finding of NGRI, but not sufficient.

The Process

When defendants offer an insanity defense, the evidence they provide typically includes an evaluation by a mental health professional. Which mental health professionals are qualified to conduct such an evaluation is a matter of state law, although many states now include social workers along with psychiatrists and psychologists. A 1985 U.S. Supreme Court case, *Ake v. Oklahoma*, reinforced the importance of having access to a mental health professional for these purposes. The case involved a man who was charged with murder and malicious wounding. After being found incompetent to stand trial and subsequently regaining competency (with the help of huge quantities of Thorazine), he went to trial and raised the insanity defense. No evidence was offered to support his defense because no one had evaluated his mental condition at the time the crime was committed, and he could not afford to hire a mental health expert to do so at the time of trial. The jury was instructed to presume that Ake was sane at the time of the offense unless he presented enough evidence to raise a reasonable doubt. Absent any testimony on his behalf, Ake was found guilty and sentenced to death. He initiated suit, claiming that an indigent defendant who raises the insanity defense has a constitutional right to receive a psychiatric evaluation at the state's expense. Although he lost in both the district court and the circuit court, the Supreme Court took his side. It recognized that psychiatrists have become indispensible in helping the jury render an informed judgment and that, without one, the risk of wrongful conviction is extremely high. The Court thus proceeded to rule that when the insanity defense is raised and a defendant cannot afford access to a psychiatrist, one must be provided at the state's expense.

Contrary to what people think, the insanity defense is infrequently raised and even less frequently successful. Battling experts, coupled with doubts about the validity of many psychological tests, make it difficult to meet the burden of proof. The insanity defense is raised in only about 1% of criminal cases—and of these, only one-fourth result in acquittals. Many people are also under the misapprehension that defendants found NGRI get off "scot-free" and are simply released back into the community. In fact, although they do avoid a prison term, these defendants are involuntarily committed—sometimes for longer than their incarceration might have been. In a closely divided U.S. Supreme Court case, *Jones v. United States* (1983), a defendant charged with stealing a jacket was found not guilty by reason of insanity and was committed to a psychiatric facility. This misdemeanor offense, had he been convicted, would have been punishable by a maximum of 1 year in prison. Jones argued that because he was found *not* guilty, his confinement in the hospital should similarly be limited to 1 year. The Court disagreed. According to the majority opinion, the purpose of a mental health commitment following an NGRI finding is to rehabilitate the defendant; it has nothing to do with punishment. The purpose of incarceration for those found guilty, on the other hand, is punishment for the offense. Because their purposes are entirely different, there is no reason why a mental health commitment cannot last longer than a criminal sentence stemming from the same offense.

Once committed pursuant to an insanity defense, the process resembles the one we discussed earlier in relation to civil commitment. There is an initial detention period (usually 30 to 45 days) at which point the defendant is reevaluated. Based on the findings (danger to self or others due to mental disease or defect), the person can be released or recommitted. His or her status must be reviewed again at regular intervals, usually once a year for the first 5 years and every other year thereafter.

Conducting the Evaluation

The insanity defense turns on the defendant's mental state at the time of the offense. Making this determination can be extremely tricky, because it requires evaluating in the present a condition that existed in the past. Given how slowly the wheels of justice turn, it is possible that weeks, months, or years may have elapsed between the commission of the crime and the NGRI evaluation. The best option, if possible, is to collect information about how the person was functioning at the time of the offense. Remember that this is a forensic evaluation that must be premised on objective evidence. This might include police reports from the incident in question, witness statements about the crime and the defendant's behavior, any statement made by the defendant to police, and any additional communication between the defendant and other relevant parties. The evaluator should also interview the defendant and hear his or her account of what transpired, focusing on thoughts, feelings, and perceptions, and the explanation offered for committing the crime (Swerdlow-Freed, 2003). It is also critical to know the state's criteria for NGRI, because they determine the questions that need to be answered.

In the event that adequate information from the time of the offense is not available, the next best approach would be to try to determine the defendant's mental state prior to commission of the crime. This is especially helpful if the client has a history of mental illness or instability. Sources of evidence might include medical records, hospital or outpatient treatment records (such as intake assessments, progress notes, medication logs, and discharge summaries), psychological test results, jail or prison records, and anything pertaining to the defendant's criminal justice history. In addition to interviewing the defendant, interviews should be conducted with friends, family members, and acquaintances who can comment on the defendant's thought processes and behaviors.

Finally, if it is impossible to retrieve sufficient information either from the time leading up to the offense or from the time surrounding the offense itself, the evaluator should assess the defendant's mental health status at the time of trial. This is the weakest type of evidence because there has been so much opportunity for change. If the defendant has been in jail, for example, the added trauma might be an intervening variable affecting his or her mental status. Other possible influences (both good and bad) include the administration of medication, deterioration of the defendant's mental condition over time, manipulation based on awareness that the defense is being raised, and coaching from the defendant's attorney or others.

Finally, the evaluator prepares a report for the court that provides an expert opinion drawn from the clinical interview, observations, defendant history, psychological testing, and relevant documents (Swerdlow-Freed, 2003). Like other forensic reports, it should include the following:

- Who commissioned the evaluation
- Date and place of the evaluation
- Time spent preparing the report
- List of materials reviewed and interviews conducted
- Relevant statutory requirements that have to be met
- Summary of background information collected
- Diagnostic impression
- Detailed account of how the diagnosis was reached
- Explanation of the correlation between defendant's behavior at the time of the offense and the symptoms of his or her mental illness

Alternatives to NGRI

Considerable controversy still surrounds the idea of NGRI. Many in the public decry the fact that an insanity defense can result in an acquittal. As a result, states have experimented with other models. In the aftermath of the Reagan assassination attempt (described earlier), some states simply eliminated the insanity defense; as of 2012, four states (Idaho, Kansas, Montana, and Utah) do not recognize it (Arnold, 2012). The problem with that, of course, is that it contravenes one of the basic premises of our legal system: that people whose mental illness keeps them from appreciating the wrongfulness of their conduct should not be held criminally responsible. Other states instituted an alternative known as *guilty but mentally ill* (GBMI). This is used when the defendant clearly committed the crime and is obviously mentally ill, but the mental illness does not rise to a level that would absolve him or her of criminal responsibility. Unlike with NGRI, a finding of GBMI results in a criminal sentence, just like any other guilty verdict. The court, however, must order that mental health treatment be provided while the defendant is incarcerated. Unlike with NGRI, once the defendant is considered "cured," he or she is not released but is required to serve out the rest of his or her sentence. Proponents of GBMI see it as a valuable compromise; it is an intermediate verdict that protects the public while providing mentally ill defendants with treatment. Critics, including the American Psychological Association, argue that it has done nothing to reduce the number of NGRI verdicts and that it misleads jurors; it provides them with an easy out, absolving them of making the hard choices regarding who is and is not deserving of criminal punishment. In addition, the scarcity of resources in prisons and jails often makes the requirement for treatment virtually meaningless (Melville & Naimark, 2003; Public Broadcasting System, 2011). As of 2012, six states allow GBMI verdicts (Arnold, 2012).

Summary and Conclusion

Mental health challenges are surprisingly common. Research suggests that as many as one in four adults suffers from a mental disorder. Over the course of history, our treatment of people with mental illness has become more humane; much remains to be done, however, as evidenced by the goals established by the President's New Freedom Commission. The Patient Protection and Affordable Care Act of 2010 (ACA) promises improvements in access to care. Social workers are often involved in legal actions involving people with mental illness. Civil commitment requires a determination of whether a person is a danger to him or herself or to others and requires hospitalization. An evaluation to determine competency to stand trial examines whether a criminal defendant's mental condition renders him or her unable to meaningfully participate in the proceedings and aid in his or her own defense. An evaluation in support of the insanity defense attempts to establish whether, at the time a crime was committed, the defendant's mental condition impaired his or her ability to understand the wrongfulness of his or her actions. Whether or not social workers are permitted to conduct these evaluations is specified in each state's laws.

Sample Case

The following case, decided by a California appeals court in 1982, documents the twists and turns involved in making a determination concerning competency to stand trial. Because the details here are so important, edits have been kept to a minimum. After reading the case, consider the questions that follow.

PEOPLE v. KURBEGOVIC
138 Cal. App. 3d 731 (1982)

Younger, J.

Muharem Kurbegovic, the self-proclaimed "Alphabet Bomber," was convicted of twenty-five felonies, including seven arsons, three murders and eight charges based on injuries resulting from the bombing of Los Angeles International Airport. We affirm the judgment.

The Facts

The Crimes ***

In the early morning hours of November 9, 1973, three residences were burned by an arsonist. Their owners were Allan G. Campbell, a municipal court judge, and Marguerite Justice and Emmet McGaughey, two members of the Los Angeles Police Commission. It took only 19 minutes to drive from house to house, so it was possible for one person to have set all three fires.

Seven months later, an arson device was placed in the gas tank of Commissioner McGaughey's car, and he received two strange telephone calls. In the first, the person on the other end made sounds of heavy breathing, without saying anything, but in the second, a male caller said he was from the S.L.A. and that the date for Mr. McGaughey's execution was set within 30 days.

On June 16, 1974, nine postcards, each with a small metal disc under the stamp, got caught in the cancelling machine in the Palm Springs Post Office. The postcards were addressed to the justices of the United States Supreme Court, and each bore a picture of Bob Hope on one side of the card and his signature on the other.

On July 4, 1974, fires were set using gasoline at three apartment buildings in Santa Monica and Marina del Rey. KFWB, an all-news radio station, received a telephone call from a man identifying himself as Isaiak Rasim, a "field commander in the Symbionese Liberation Army," stating that in celebration of the Fourth of July and recognition of the S.L.A., he had set the three fires by means of "bombs."

The next day, a security guard at the Los Angeles Times found the first of several tapes to be connected over the coming weeks with appellant, in the planter box in the lobby. It purported to be from Rasim, who now claimed to be "Chief Military Officer" of "Aliens of America" and claimed that deadly nerve gas had been mailed to each Supreme Court justice under a postcard stamp.

On August 6, a bomb exploded in a locker at the Los Angeles International Airport, and shrapnel-like pieces of metal and broken glass showered the terminal, killing three men. A fourth man had his right leg blown off and several other persons suffered injuries. Late that night, Conrad Casler, city editor of the Los Angeles Herald-Examiner, received a telephone call claiming credit for the bombing. The caller identified himself as Rasim and claimed that the bombing was done by "Aliens of America," correctly giving the publicly undisclosed locker number "T 225" as the location of the bomb.

Over the next several days, Mr. Casler received further telephone calls from the same man, who, on each occasion, used the code number "T 225." During these telephone conversations, the caller spoke further of a group he called "Aliens of America." The first bomb, he explained, was placed at the airport because the letter "A" in the word "airport" was the first letter in "Aliens of America."

Another cassette message was found, this time announcing a bomb at the Greyhound Bus depot. The depot was evacuated and police removed one of the largest bombs in the history of Los Angeles from the locker designated by the caller. Casler was again called and told the bomber had chosen the depot because the letter "L" in the word "locker" was the second letter in "Aliens of America." The caller stated that ultimately a series of bombs placed at different locations would spell out "Aliens of America."

Muharem Kurbegovic

Appellant was born in 1943 in Sarajevo, Yugoslavia. His mother may have been mentally ill and he claims to have suffered headaches as a child. After studying engineering at universities in Europe, he immigrated to Los Angeles in 1967 via Canada.

Between 1967 and 1974, he moved between various engineering jobs as a result of the cyclic nature of high-technology industries. He was mute at work, but was viewed as very bright, an excellent engineer and a personable coworker. He communicated articulately in writing.

In the late 1960's, appellant began telling friends of a plan to become rich by opening a dance hall, but he was denied a business license by the police commission.

His employment also was to relate circumstantially to the later crimes of the "Alphabet Bomber": Appellant had worked, for example, at Dynatech Industries and a tank of the type used by that firm became a part of the Greyhound Bus terminal bomb. While at Dynatech, he also learned how to purchase explosive chemicals from Erb and Gray Company by posing as a representative of a customer (he selected Hughes Aircraft). He also had numerous conversations about bomb construction and related matters with at least one coworker, Stephen Smith, including one in which Kurbegovic asked how Smith would undertake a scheme to demand $10 million after setting off a bomb, in exchange for not setting off a second.

Various witnesses tied appellant to parts of the bombs from both the airport and Greyhound terminal, and by August 20, 1974, Kurbegovic was a suspect. A surveillance began that followed him to an apartment, ultimately proving to be his own. Later the same day, appellant left with a box in his hand and drove to the Santa Monica beach area where he parked his car. Officer Robert Sauter observed Kurbegovic sitting in his car with papers in his hand and his lips moving. The appellant then returned home.

That evening, Kurbegovic left his apartment and drove to Hollywood, wearing a red wig, glasses and a green coat. He parked his car and walked to a Carl's Jr. restaurant, entering the restroom. After remaining for a few minutes, he walked out of the restaurant. Officer Curtis Hagel thereafter went into the restroom and found a tape cassette wrapped in green paper. The officers listened to the tape in the police car and it was very similar to the others described above.

Moments later, appellant returned, ordered a cup of coffee and went into the restroom for a second time. Officer Hagel followed Kurbegovic into the restroom and arrested him.

After his arrest, Kurbegovic never spoke.

Officers then searched appellant's apartment. Detective McCree, a police bomb specialist, smelled the odor of nitrobenzene (the explosive in the Greyhound bomb) as he entered and, inside, located live pipe bombs and explosive materials.

Other items found inside of the apartment included books on arson, explosives and germ and chemical warfare, a gas mask, documents relating to the denial of his business permit, records of his misdemeanor arrest, newspaper articles on the airport bombing, green paper towels, a tape recorder, a document entitled "Alien Manifesto" (which corresponded to the tape recording recovered at the Carl's Jr.), a rental agreement for the apartment with Kurbegovic's name on it, mechanical timers, tubes, wigs and two receipts for the purchase of chemicals from Erb and Gray for Hughes Aircraft.

We are required to review a jury's finding that appellant, a complex, intelligent, frightening and highly disturbed man, was competent to stand trial, and the court's determination that he be allowed to represent himself. Those issues will each be separately addressed; various others are discussed in a fourth section.

While appellant's actual jury trial (as opposed to the competency hearing) is mentioned on occasion herein below, no issue has been raised in this appeal which requires, or would even be illuminated by, a summary of it, beyond the factual presentation…taken from both the trial and competency hearing records.

Competence to Stand Trial

Competency Hearings

1. The Prior Hearings, 1974–1978

Shortly after his arrest in 1974, the judge scheduled to preside expressed a doubt as to appellant's competency to stand trial, as defined by Penal Code section 1367: "A person cannot be tried or adjudged to punishment while such person is mentally incompetent. A defendant is mentally incompetent for purposes of this chapter if, as a result of mental disorder or developmental disability, the defendant is unable to understand the nature of the criminal proceedings or to assist counsel in the conduct of a defense in a rational manner."

Pursuant to section 1369 a jury trial on the competency issue was held and, in January of 1975, the jury determined that appellant was competent to stand trial, but the court granted a judgment notwithstanding the verdict and found appellant not competent. . . .

In October of 1976, appellant was once again returned to court certified as competent by the superintendent of Atascadero State Hospital, but this time the jury returned a verdict that appellant was not competent and he was returned to Atascadero.

2. The 1979–1980 Hearing

In November of 1978, appellant was returned to court and criminal proceedings reinstated. But the court again declared a doubt concerning appellant's competency to stand trial, so a third competency hearing was commenced in early 1979…. [T]he focus of appellant's first and most significant contention on appeal is on the finding of competence based on that verdict.

Appellant, who was represented by counsel at the competency hearing, called two witnesses from Atascadero State Hospital, Roger Pittenger and Dr. Linda Pendleton, and his former attorney, Gerald Chaleff.

a. The Pittenger Testimony   Mr. Pittenger was program director for the intensive psychiatric program at Atascadero and a licensed psychiatric technician, who first encountered appellant in 1975.

According to Mr. Pittenger, "staffings" in September 1976 and December 1977 had resulted in consensus opinions that appellant was competent. While the clinical director at Atascadero overruled the 1977 conclusion in a letter to the superior court, Pittenger still agreed with the staff.

During 1978, however, Pittenger had observed symptoms of paranoid schizophrenia (inability to tolerate denials of request, threatening and degrading remarks, and increased attention to numerology) and concluded appellant was, by then, incompetent to stand trial. A December 1978 report noted appellant's asserted plan to prove scientifically to the jury that he was the Messiah, and opined that appellant's grandiose legal strategy represented a major problem in appellant's potential for cooperation with defense counsel.

While Pittenger understood appellant's strategy to be contrary to the purpose of a trial, the possibility that appellant was malingering occurred to him, and he thought some symptoms exaggerated. For example, from the time of his admission to Atascadero until shortly before he was first certified competent in 1976, appellant maintained that he was being charged with public masturbation, which Pittenger doubted he really believed.

Mr. Pittenger was aware that the two psychiatrists who had contact with appellant at Atascadero—Drs. Schumann and Estess—were of the opinion that, aside from appellant's mental disorder, there was some feigning or exaggeration of symptoms.

Approximately two years before the 1979 competency proceedings, appellant told Pittenger that if he could convince a jury three or four times that he was incompetent, the charges would have to be dismissed. To Pittenger's knowledge, appellant never stated to a member of the Atascadero staff before his certification of competency in September 1976 that he was a Savior or Messiah.

b. The Pendleton Testimony   Linda Pendleton, Ph.D., was a staff psychologist for the intensive psychiatric program at Atascadero State Hospital, and, in her opinion, appellant was competent to stand trial as of December 1977.

By 1978, however, Dr. Pendleton had concluded that appellant was incompetent because of his belief that he was the Messiah, his belief that his legal strategy should be to convince a jury of that and the very poor quality of his relationship with his attorney.

Dr. Pendleton admitted that a paranoid schizophrenic may be competent to stand trial, and can exaggerate his symptoms and be deceitful. She further testified that it is possible, though rare, for a paranoid schizophrenic to simulate incompetence and to "turn off" faked delusional material to give the impression that medication is stopping the delusions.

While she testified that, in looking for feigning mental illness symptoms, motivation should be examined, Dr. Pendleton knew of no motive for appellant to fake. She could not be shaken by cross-examination in her belief that appellant was not faking, because appellant, to her, seemed so consistent and earnest. She acknowledged that he was highly intelligent and that she had advised him that his notion of being the Messiah was a delusion characteristic of someone who is schizophrenic. This latter conversation was when he complained to her of being denied access to textbooks on schizophrenia.

In short, the jury obviously concluded appellant was "using" and manipulating a well-meaning but naive psychologist to the hilt.

During her testimony, Dr. Pendleton was confronted with evidence that supported such a conclusion by the trier of fact. In 1976, for instance, a letter was sent by appellant to Mr. Bozanich, the prosecutor:

Dear Pal:

After this jury finds me incompetent as they will do, no god under the sun can beat my N.G.I. plea.

Savior my ass, best possible way to beat a murder rap is to play a Savior.

"A" is one, "B" is two, "C" is three. But, really:

"A" stands for "ass."

"B" stands for "Bozanich."

And "C" stands for "Chaleff" [his then attorney].

"D" stands for "destiny."

So it is destiny of two of you legal nutheads to kiss my ass.

I wonder if I could apply for enrollment at UCLA Law School.

Whenever a defendant in murder case gives prosecutor convicting evidence, where previously prosecutor didn't have anything but circumstantial evidence, there are only two possibilities:

Defendant is insane or a fisherman. During questioning of [psychiatrist] Coburn you have become a fish.

Keep this note and frame it. It is worth million times your diploma.

Alphabet Bomber

Dr. Pendleton saw the letter as evidence of schizophrenia, rather than evidence that appellant was faking incompetency.

Dr. Pendleton acknowledged she had heard appellant state that he had fooled a prior jury, but did not feel this statement was "necessarily inconsistent" with a diagnosis of chronic paranoid schizophrenia and she testified that she would need "more information" to be able to determine whether it supported competency or incompetency.

Evidence that appellant had feigned muteness at work for years did not alter Dr. Pendleton's opinion on the validity of Kurbegovic's symptoms; she stated she would consider the possibility that she had been fooled only if she became aware of some change in his behavior.

Interestingly, Dr. Pendleton testified that she never had a serious doubt that appellant understood the nature of the proceedings and the charges against him.

c. The Chaleff Testimony   Mr. Chaleff testified (pursuant to waiver of the attorney-client privilege) that he represented appellant from shortly after his arrest until March 1977, a period which included his first two competency trials. Appellant had consistently refused to discuss facts relating to the charged offenses, and, at times, claimed to believe he was charged with public masturbation.

In late 1974 Chaleff felt appellant was incompetent to stand trial. Although he later, on occasion, thought appellant was "putting me on," he concluded that appellant, although mentally ill, believed he was manipulating everyone.

In Chaleff's last prehearing discussion with appellant, the latter's belief that the purpose of the competency trial was to find him to be the Messiah was more fixed than previously, and, although then aware that he was charged with very serious offenses, he was unable to rationally assist in the preparation of his defense. Chaleff had no doubt that appellant believed he was the Messiah, though at some point appellant mentioned the "ping pong ball thing," according to which, if appellant had enough competency hearings, the system would "lose him" and he would be let go. Chaleff told appellant this was not the case.

d. Appellant's Testimony   The appellant also testified. He was aware of the charges against him and was able to briefly outline them, and he was aware that the "obvious purpose of these proceedings" was to determine whether he was competent or incompetent to stand trial. He also indicated that the proceedings had a "special purpose," namely, to determine whether or not he was the "Messiah," and he explained his intent to convince the jury that he was incompetent to stand trial. He explained his method of presenting as much evidence as he could to support his Messiah proposition to the jury as follows:

"Let's assume that I have committed all the crimes that I'm charged with. It's theoretically in my interests not to go to trial. And it is theoretically in my interests to do whatever I can to be found incompetent to stand trial. Now, the most beautiful way, the smoothest way for that in my circumstances to prove that I'm incompetent to stand trial is to present, come up with some kind of evidence that I'm a Messiah. And the more such evidence that I would present that I'm a Messiah, the deeper that a jury would believe that I'm insane and incompetent to stand trial."

In line with this defense, appellant described the sort of attorney he would like representing him:

"I want someone who is willing to and able to cooperate within rational terms and from the standpoint of defense counsel, the rational thing is to prove I am incompetent to stand trial and to do it by the root of proving that I am a Messiah, the most brilliant line of defense in this particular case. Now, whether I am Messiah or not is irrelevant. And if I am a Messiah, God will force the jury to accept the proposition that I am. If I am not, my legal interests will be perfectly protected."

Appellant saw it as his attorney's job to help him overtly try to prove himself the Messiah, hence, implicitly incompetent, while at the same time protecting his legal rights.

Appellant also testified that, when he had appeared in 1975 in front of Judge Keene, he attempted to portray "the typical insane person" by asking about his dead father and by stating that his head was a hydrogen bomb filled with "heavy water." He did not believe what he told the judge but put on "a big show" so he would be sent back to Atascadero as incompetent.

He explained that, during the three years before his arrest, he played mute at his place of employment but talked elsewhere. He was also mute when he went to see a doctor to inquire about a 4-F Selective Service classification, because he was aware that aliens were subject to the draft.

Appellant explained his attempts to deceive a number of psychiatrists: He told one, for example, that he was charged with public masturbation and that he thought he was talking to Hitler. Appellant did not believe this, but wanted the psychiatrist to believe he was incompetent.

He explained his 1976 "ping-pong" motion (whereby he would be found incompetent and returned to Atascadero, then stop being a Messiah so he would be returned to court, at which time he would again become a Messiah, be found incompetent, etc.). The motion had raised a "due process" claim that if competency could not be determined and if he could prove that he was not a danger to himself or others, he should be released.

Appellant had termed his own writings "crap," and characterized a document entitled "The Holy Word" as "something I wanted others to think I believed in 1976." Most of it was a "put-on," a fact he revealed neither to Chaleff nor to the psychiatrists with whom he spoke in 1976. He admitted he had said a lot of things in the last four years and it was hard to keep it all straight, but it was the prosecutor's problem, not his, to separate the "wheat" from the "chaff."

e. The People's Witnesses   The prosecution called several people who had known and worked with appellant. The first was Keith Nelson, the president of Dynatech Industries, appellant's employer in the late 1960s. He testified appellant had been a good employee and was very bright; after he was laid off, Nelson told him that if there was more work he would like to have him back. Until his arrest, appellant was mute in his contacts with Nelson, but he did not do anything suggesting he was mentally ill, such as claiming to be the Messiah or speaking of a group such as "Aliens of America."

Joseph Durfee, of Wintec Products, hired appellant in 1969. Although appellant was mute, he was quick and was a good engineer, and some of appellant's designs and drawings undoubtedly went into the Apollo program, with which Wintec was involved. Several months before appellant's arrest, Durfee appeared as a witness on appellant's application for citizenship, and spent several hours with him waiting for a hearing. He saw nothing about appellant's behavior on that date which was different from before, and, aside from muteness (which appellant linked to a frightening incident of his mother's with the Yugoslavian secret police), appellant exhibited no mental abnormality prior to his arrest.

Mr. Durfee's wife, Verona, recalled that appellant came to their home on a number of occasions, and she visited him in the county jail in October 1974. Appellant never exhibited signs of mental illness in Mrs. Durfee's presence.

Allan Bell hired Kurbegovic in 1972 for RPM Industries, where he remained until August 1974. Appellant seemed brilliant and appeared to "know his engineering," but did not speak. On one or two occasions, appellant conversed with Bell over the telephone by Morse code. On other occasions, he communicated through notes in a very expressive manner. Bell had never heard of any claims by appellant to be the Messiah, nor had he heard of the "Aliens of America."

Joseph Sampietro worked with and thought highly of appellant at RPM for about one and one-half years ending in August 1974, and never suspected there was anything wrong with his mental health.

Stephen Smith was an employee of McCulloch Corporation and its subsidiary RPM for five or six years, ultimately as manager of engineering, and was appellant's supervisor for about one year before appellant was laid off several days before his arrest.

Smith considered Kurbegovic a friend and they had spent considerable time discussing matters which could later appear significant, but he never questioned appellant's mental health or his grasp of objective reality or heard him claim to be a prophet or Savior.

In their conversations, Smith testified, both were critical of the "involvement of religious beliefs into government," and they theorized that "something very akin to paranoia" probably influenced the followers of "cultish religions."

Smith and appellant discussed the movie "The Sting." When Smith stated to appellant that the most interesting part of the movie was that the audience itself was "conned" by the scenario unfolding on the screen, appellant responded that the movie would not have done well in Yugoslavia, "because everything in Yugoslavia was layer after layer after layer of deception," and that the popularity of the movie in America testified to the naiveté of Americans.

On a number of occasions Smith and appellant discussed the subject of a person playing a religious leader in order to make money; they felt that many present and past religious leaders were involved in this activity.

Smith had told appellant of his previous experience in trying to influence a school board on an issue. Although Smith could do very little as an individual, he found that by writing letters claiming to be from a "taxpayers' concerned group" he gained access to newspaper and television publicity.

In October or November 1976, before appellant's second competency trial, Smith met with appellant at the request of the latter's attorney. Appellant, who was, by then, speaking, stated something to the effect that he was godlike or a Savior, and that Smith was his science prophet, according to appellant's "theory of numbers."

What appellant told Smith was entirely different from anything before, but Smith detected a "snickering attitude," and he concluded that appellant did not believe the material he was presenting to Smith, but rather was using him as a "sounding board" to see "if the script would work." Smith relied on his prior experience with appellant in coming to this conclusion.

Discussion

The trial court and jury's task in "competency to stand trial" proceedings and insanity plea situations is to weigh the evidence and determine whether a given individual is "competent" and/or "sane" for the law's purposes, not merely to decide whether or not he is "mentally ill" in some sense. Our task, on appeal, is to determine whether the evidence "view[ed] in the light most favorable to the verdict," supports their finding. ***

The Witnesses' Testimony ***

The appellant presented three witnesses (other than himself). Taking them in reverse order, we can see why the jury could have given little weight to Chaleff's testimony, as he was equivocal on the issue of whether Kurbegovic was malingering or at least "making up" some symptoms. Chaleff plainly had his doubts and those doubts were communicated to the jury.

On turning to Pittenger, it must be noted that the People never did (and do not on appeal) concede his expertise on the competency to stand trial issue. While a licensed technician, he had essentially no academic background and the jury, instructed to consider the qualifications of the witnesses, could properly have discounted his testimony due to his lack of "credentials."

More significantly, however, Pittenger was impeached on the issue of appellant's potential for malingering, and could well have been seen by the jury as a victim of his own circular reasoning: He simply could not square an individual's trying to prove nonsense with any conclusion other than incompetency. His own notion that it would not be in Kurbegovic's interest to try to prove himself the Messiah in front of a jury led him to believe that appellant's professed desire to do just that was the equivalent of inability to cooperate with counsel. In fact, the jury was presented with evidence, including the letter to Bozanich from appellant, that such a tactic was exactly what the defendant had in mind— the cynical and completely calculated espousal of the Messiah theory to convince the jury of his incompetence.

The jury could, on the evidence before it, conclude—and its verdict makes it clear that it did conclude—that Pittenger was simply fooled.

But, if the evidence permitted the jury to find that Pittenger got cleverly manipulated, it plainly allowed it to find that Dr. Pendleton was massively taken in—sufficiently to make her testimony completely unpersuasive. Her denial of the significance of evidence such as the letter to Bozanich, for example, encouraged the jury to infer that she had simply made up her mind and that nothing was going to change it.

The record is replete with other evidence that Dr. Pendleton had become an increasingly certain captive of her own earlier diagnoses, to the point of being an advocate for Kurbegovic's assertion of incompetency. . . .

Kurbegovic as a Defendant

. . .[T]he record is replete with evidence of Kurbegovic's intelligence. All his former acquaintances and, in fact, the doctors themselves, confirm the view one gets from even skimming the 25,000-page record: Appellant was a man of education and great intellectual resources.

We do not, of course, hold that intellect is, in and of itself, the critical factor...but it is one which the jury can logically consider when evaluating whether an individual is trying to deceive it. . . . Kurbegovic was adept at doing just that, such as by feigning muteness in his workplace for years, without one reported slipup, while being able to speak at will. . .

Kurbegovic...left a trail of evidence suggesting he was not only competent but very capable of manipulating those around him such as by falsely claiming to believe himself a religious leader or a spokesman for a radical group. Putting that trail together with the letter to Bozanich and appellant's own testimony that he fooled at least one judge (Keene) and jury (the second), the jury had a basis to believe appellant had manipulated Dr. Pendleton and Mr. Pittenger and that he was trying to manipulate them. They were confirmed in their view by the appellant's own assertion that the "obvious purpose of these proceedings is to determine whether I am competent or incompetent to stand trial" and his letter to Judge Light just before the competency hearing (admitted in evidence) in which he stressed a desire to be found not competent to go to trial and his ability to cooperate with a particular attorney of his choice.

While the jury's verdict, on this record, appears equivalent to a finding that Kurbegovic was consciously malingering, that would not necessarily be the only basis for its finding him competent. In what, at first, appears to be a bizarre discussion, a New York court, three decades ago, made the good point that even sincerely believed delusions do not, in all cases, equal incompetency to stand trial. The court pointed to examples, in the modern world, of men claiming divine powers who were not only competent for courtroom purposes but, indeed, highly effective. . . .

A properly instructed jury, relying on substantial evidence, determined that appellant was competent to stand trial, and we are given no substantial basis for overturning that determination. ***

The judgment of conviction is affirmed.

Questions

1. The issue in this case is whether the defendant, Kurbegovic, is competent to stand trial. What did the juries in his previous hearings decide? What did this court decide?

2. One of the witnesses was a licensed psychiatric technician, Mr. Pittenger. Did he believe Kurbegovic was incompetent, or did he think he was faking it?

3. A second witness was Dr. Pendleton, a psychologist. Did she believe Kurbegovic was incompetent or did she think he was faking it?

4. A third witness was Mr. Chaleff, Kurbegovic's former attorney. What was his conclusion?

5. Consider the letter from Kurbegovic to Mr. Bozanich, the prosecutor. As you read the letter, does it seem to you that Kurbegovic is incompetent or do you think he is faking it?

6. What do you make of Kurbegovic's "ping-pong" theory?

7. In your opinion, is Kurbegovic savvy and manipulative or delusional?

8. How is it possible for so many observers to have such disparate opinions? What does that suggest about the capacity of mental health experts to draw conclusions about competency to stand trial?

9. The court mentions several times that Kurbegovic is highly intelligent. Should this be relevant to a determination of his competency? How do you think information about a defendant's intelligence might influence a jury's verdict?

10. Even if we believe that Kurbegovic is mentally ill, what would you conclude about his ability to understand the proceedings against him? His ability to assist his attorney in mounting a defense? Do you believe that Kurbegovic meets the criteria for competency to stand trial?

CHAPTER 15 PRACTICE TEST

The following questions will test your application and analysis of the content found within this chapter. For additional assessment, including licensing-exam type questions on applying chapter content to practice behaviors, visit **MySearchLab**.

1. Which of the following is TRUE regarding the treatment of mental illness?
   a. Eating disorders have the lowest mortality rate of all mental disorders.
   b. Mood disorders are more common among African Americans and Hispanics than among Caucasians.
   c. More than half of all adults with serious mental illness go untreated.
   d. The majority of people who are homeless suffer from a serious mental illness.

2. Mrs. Wise is concerned about her husband. He is sleeping a lot, has little appetite, and shows little interest in his work or his hobbies. She takes him to a psychiatrist who diagnoses depression. Mrs. Wise worries about her ability to take care of him and seeks to have him committed to a psychiatric facility. He objects. Which of the following is TRUE?
   a. She can have him committed because he has a diagnosed mental illness.
   b. She cannot have him committed because he is not a danger to himself or others.
   c. She does not need his consent for psychiatric hospitalization because the doctors believe it would be temporary.

   d. She could have him committed only if she could prove, by a preponderance of the evidence, that he is dangerous.

3. Defendants found incompetent to stand trial
   a. are considered to be "not guilty."
   b. are committed to a psychiatric facility until they regain competency.
   c. cannot be forcibly medicated in order to stand trial.
   d. must prove, by clear and convincing evidence, that they were legally insane at the time the offense was committed.

4. When conducting a forensic evaluation for purposes of an insanity defense,
   a. it is important to assess the defendant's current mental state.
   b. it is important to assess the defendant's mental state at the time of the crime.
   c. only documentary (written) evidence can be considered in formulating an opinion.
   d. the evaluator should take every opportunity to advocate for the defendant's innocence.

5. What are mental health (or "psychiatric") advance directives? How can they benefit clients with mental illness? What safeguards would you recommend to ensure that they are used properly?

6. Considerable controversy surrounds the involuntary commitment of sex offenders who have finished serving their sentences. Present the arguments for and against this policy and discuss how you think social work values apply.

MYSEARCHLAB CONNECTIONS

Reinforce what you learned in this chapter by studying videos, cases, documents, and more available at **www.MySearchLab.com**.

Read these Cases/Documents

Δ Mental Health Services Consumers
- *How do consumers experience the mental health service system? What reforms would you recommend to address their concerns?*

Explore these Assets

- Website: Bazelon Center for Mental Health Law
- Website: SAMHSA's National Mental Health Information Center

Research these Topics

- Jared Loughner and the Tucson shootings
- veterans and PTSD

Assess Your Knowledge

Go to **MySearchLab** to test your knowledge of key topics in this chapter with topic-specific quizzes. Conclude your assessment by completing the chapter exam.

---

* = CSWE Core Competency Asset   Δ = Case Study

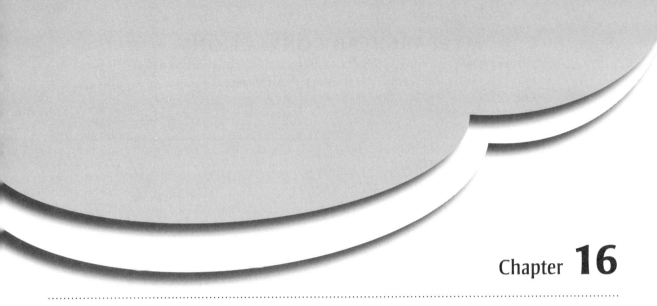

Chapter **16**

Legal Rights of Racial and Ethnic Minorities

Discrimination against racial and ethnic minorities continues to plague American society and societies throughout the world. As social workers, we have an ethical obligation to confront our own prejudices, combat discrimination, and actively value diversity. Over the past 50 years, the United States has adopted important measures to prohibit discrimination in many areas of public life. The U.S. Constitution has also been used to remedy discrimination. This chapter presents background information on racial minorities in the United States, summarizes the major federal laws that seek to address discrimination, and explains the equal protection clause of the 14th Amendment and how it has been applied over time to cases involving racial and ethnic minorities. Finally, the chapter examines how courts have approached discrimination in relation to employment, housing, and education. The topic of hate crimes is highlighted, and a sample case involving "reverse discrimination" is presented for analysis.

Background

For centuries in America, legal mandates promoted racism against Native Americans, African Americans, Asian Americans, and Latinos. Ethnic groups including certain European immigrant populations and American Jews also suffered discrimination in the form of xenophobia and anti-Semitism. Manifested throughout history as slavery,

368

internment camps, American Indian reservations, Jim Crow laws, immigration exclusion, segregation, and other measures, discrimination has kept racial and ethnic minorities from enjoying equal treatment in relation to property ownership, voting rights, citizenship, criminal justice, education, housing, employment, and other economic and social opportunities.

Demographics and Trends

The ethnic and racial composition of the United States is far more diverse in the 21st century than it was previously. Racial and ethnic minorities comprise almost 41% of the total U.S. population: 16% are Hispanic or Latino; 13% are Black or African American; and 5% are Asian. The remainder includes American Indians and Alaska Natives, Native Hawaiians and other Pacific Islanders, other races, and those of two or more races (U.S. Census Bureau, 2011). As a point of comparison, at the turn of the 20th century, minorities comprised less than 13% of the total population (Hobbs & Stoops, 2002). Although Caucasians remain the largest racial group, the number of minorities has steadily grown since the 1970s, with an increasing number of U.S. cities becoming home to more minorities than Whites.

As shown in Figure 16.1, racial and ethnic minorities continue to be concentrated in certain parts of the country. In addition, specific groups are concentrated in specific regions: Hispanics, Asian Americans, and Pacific Islanders are heavily concentrated in the West, whereas African Americans live primarily in the South. Whites are fairly evenly spread throughout the various regions (Hobbs & Stoops, 2002).

FIGURE 16.1 Percentage Minority by State in 2000

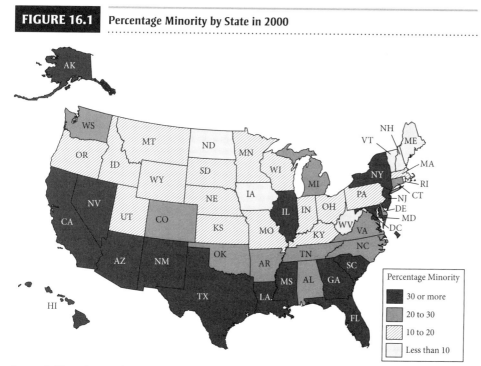

Source: Hobbs and Stoops (2002).

Racial and ethnic minorities are disproportionately poor. Although Caucasians make up the largest number of people in poverty, only 10% of Caucasians are poor, compared to 25% of African Americans and 20% of Hispanics (Katel, 2008). Socioeconomic status in turn is correlated with other social indicators. In 2009, for example, 32.4% of Hispanics, 21% of African Americans, 17.2% of Asians, and 12% of Caucasians lacked health insurance coverage (DeNavas-Walt, Proctor, & Smith, 2010).

Census Bureau projections indicate that by the year 2050, racial and ethnic minorities will comprise slightly more than half of the U.S. population: 30.3% of the population is projected to be Hispanic, 11.8% Black, 7.6% Asian, less than 1% American Indian and Alaska Native, less than 1% Native Hawaiian and other Pacific Islander, and 3% of two or more races (U.S. Census Bureau, 2008). This trend is largely a result of immigration and births to new immigrants, especially among Asians and Hispanics. Between 1980 and 2000, the Hispanic population alone doubled in size and is expected to triple between 2008 and 2050 (Stein, 2008).

How these trends will impact the financial, political, social, and legal status of racial and ethnic minorities remains to be seen. Some believe these demographic shifts will enable people of color to secure a more prominent place in the mainstream of American society; others believe that Whites will continue to dominate. As it is, Whites and minorities have markedly different perceptions of how much progress our country has made toward achieving a color-blind society. The election of the first African American president, Barack Obama, was surely a high-water mark. Meanwhile, however, the wealth gap between races in the United States is the largest ever recorded. As Figure 16.2 indicates, the bursting of the housing bubble and subsequent recession resulted in unprecedented losses for racial minorities, with the median net worth of Black and Hispanic households plummeting by more than half. This left the typical Black household with a net worth of $5,677 and the average Hispanic household with a net worth of $6,325, while the average White household—despite its losses—retained a net worth of $113,149 (Kochlar, Fry, Taylor, Velasco, & Motel, 2011).

FIGURE 16.2   **Percentage Change in Median Net Worth of Households, 2005–2009**

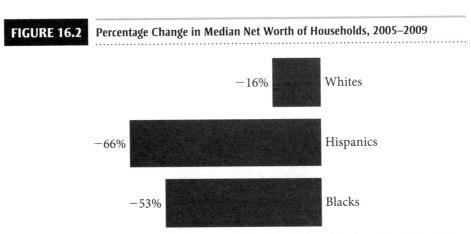

Source: From *Wealth Gaps Rise to Record Highs Between Whites, Blacks, Hispanics* by Paul Taylor, Richard Fry and Rakesh Kochhar, from Pew Research Center website, July 26, 2011. Copyright © 2011 by the Pew Research Center Social & Demographic Trends Project. Reprinted with permission. http://pewsocialtrends.org/2011/07/26/wealth-gaps-rise-to-record-highs-between-whites-blacks-hispanics/

Brief History

As a result of their small population size and limited access to power, minorities have traditionally faced disadvantages relative to their counterparts in the dominant culture. However, there have been a number of noteworthy efforts throughout our history to prevent race discrimination and address its consequences. Congress established the Freedmen's Bureau in 1865 as a temporary federal agency designed to supervise and manage all matters regarding newly freed slaves and other minority populations. Although its educational services continued until 1872, most of the bureau's work was completed by 1869. In addition to educational services, the bureau's purview included social services, food aid, legal assistance, political activities, family reunification, and labor relations.

A year after the bureau's creation, Congress overrode a presidential veto and enacted the Civil Rights Act of 1866. The act declared all persons born in the United States, regardless of race or ethnicity, to be U.S. citizens entitled to the benefits and responsibilities granted to White citizens under law. Although it did not protect the rights of minorities in practice, the Civil Rights Act of 1866 was the first federal law to prohibit race discrimination.

The civil rights movement of the 1950s and 1960s marked the first time since the late 19th century that the federal government assumed a major role in securing equal rights for racial minorities. The landmark Civil Rights Act of 1964 (CRA) prohibits discrimination on the basis of race, color, national origin, religion, and sex in various realms, including education, employment, public accommodations, and government services. The Civil Rights Act served as a catalyst for a number of antidiscrimination laws that followed, including the Voting Rights Act of 1965, the Age Discrimination in Employment Act of 1967, and the Fair Housing Act of 1968. It also became a model for later civil rights struggles, including those for gay rights and disability rights.

Out of these advances in civil rights came a federal policy known as *affirmative action*. Initially referenced in Executive Order 10925 in 1961, it recognizes the necessity of taking active measures to ensure equal opportunity for women and racial minorities. The idea is that our historical legacy of discrimination has created ongoing disadvantages for certain groups that cannot be rectified by simply ceasing to discriminate. Affirmative action policies are designed to counteract that legacy by providing racial minorities and women with a level playing field; they aim to facilitate equal opportunity in the present in order to offset the discrimination faced by women and minorities in the past.

HATE CRIMES

The U.S. government defines a hate crime as a "criminal offense against a person or property motivated in whole or in part by an offender's bias against a race, religion, disability, ethnic origin, or sexual orientation" (Federal Bureau of Investigation [FBI], n.d.). Since the initial hate crimes legislation was enacted in the 1960s, subsequent legislation has expanded the penalties for committing hate crimes, broadened the demographic groups covered, and increased the government's responsibilities. The Hate Crimes Statistics Act of 1990 required the attorney general to collect statistics regarding crimes motivated by bias, including information on the victims, the perpetrators, and the types of crimes committed (FBI, 2008). The Violent Crime Control and Law Enforcement Act of 1994 increased the penalties for hate crimes committed against individuals participating in certain federally protected activities, including voting and attending school. Most recently, the Matthew Shepard and James Byrd Jr. Hate Crimes Prevention Act of 2009 extended criminal prosecution to hate crimes targeting "actual or perceived gender, sexual orientation, gender identity, or disability." The law also eliminated the requirement that a victim be engaged in a federally protected activity, broadened federal authority to investigate hate crimes, and required the FBI to track crimes against transgender individuals.

Of the 6,624 hate crime incidents reported in 2010, 47.3% were motivated by racial bias, 20% were motivated by religious bias, 19.3% were motivated by sexual orientation bias, and 12.8% were motivated by bias against a particular ethnicity or national origin. African Americans, Jews, gay men, and Hispanics were particularly common targets. Intimidation accounted for 46.2% of crimes against persons, and vandalism accounted for 81.1% of crimes against property (FBI, 2011).

The FBI's hate crime statistics permit a general understanding of which groups are being targeted, but the accuracy of the data is questionable. Many victims choose not to report hate crimes, officials often lack the training necessary to accurately identify them, and local agency reporting is inconsistent. In 2009, 47 cities with populations greater than 100,000 reported no hate crimes (Pellegrinelli, 2010). Most experts believe that the numbers reported are substantially lower than the actual numbers of hate crimes committed.

Social workers' commitment to social justice requires that we advocate for the continued strengthening of hate crimes laws. At the same time, we must work with individuals, groups, and communities to promote tolerance, cultural understanding, and peaceful conflict resolution. Cultivating our own respect for diversity and serving as role models is an excellent place to start.

The Equal Protection Clause

Legal challenges to race discrimination are brought in three primary ways. The first involves suits under the Civil Rights Act of 1964, briefly described earlier. The second involves suits under Sec. 1983 of the U.S. Code, which allows individuals to recover monetary awards as a result of a civil rights violation. The third involves challenging a law's conformity with the Constitution. Most of the discussion in this chapter centers on constitutional challenges involving the 14th Amendment.

Levels of Scrutiny

The 14th Amendment to the U.S. Constitution contains several clauses that are extremely important in addressing issues relevant to social work interests. It is the 14th Amendment that defines who is a U.S. citizen, a topic discussed further in Chapter 19. The 14th Amendment is also home to the *due process* clause, which has been discussed previously in relation to juvenile justice, criminal justice, and reproductive rights. A third important provision of the 14th Amendment is the *equal protection* clause. The equal protection clause is surprisingly brief and straightforward. It states the following: "[No state shall] deny to any person within its jurisdiction the equal protection of the laws." This seemingly simple statement has undergone more than a century of interpretation by the courts, and its meaning continues to evolve.

The equal protection clause originated in 1868 during the Reconstruction period; its purpose was to bring newly freed African American slaves into the mainstream of American society by affording to them the same constitutional rights enjoyed by the dominant culture. The basic idea of equal protection is that people who are similarly situated must be treated similarly under the law. If, for example, I run a red light and you run a red light, the law should treat us the same way—even if I have blue eyes and you have brown eyes. If the law treated us differently, allowing only blue-eyed people to be ticketed, I might argue that the law is unconstitutional because it violates the equal protection clause.

In reality, many laws distinguish between groups of people with different characteristics, and they are not all unconstitutional. For example, in many states, only those who are at least 16 years old can obtain a driver's license. The rationale behind the law is that a certain degree of maturity is necessary to handle the responsibilities of driving a car. Notice that the law is substituting a classification (people age 16 and older) for a case-by-case determination of maturity. Most classifications are imperfect; they can be *over-inclusive* (restricting the rights of more people than necessary) or *under-inclusive* (restricting the rights of fewer people than they should). In most cases, the court will uphold legal distinctions between groups if doing so is "rationally related to a legitimate government interest." This is called the *rational basis test* or *minimal scrutiny*.

Let us return to the example of having to be 16 to get a driver's license. The government's interest in applying this rule is to promote public safety. Most people would agree that this is a *legitimate government interest.* The next question is whether there is a *rational relationship* between requiring a minimum age for a driver's license and promoting public safety. If the answer is yes (which it undoubtedly is), then the distinction the law is drawing based on age is constitutional.

When the distinction the law draws between groups is based on race or national origin (in other words, people of one race are treated differently from people of another), a much stronger justification is required. Because the court is skeptical that such distinctions are ever warranted, the government must show that it is "necessary to achieve a compelling government interest." This standard, called *strict scrutiny*, is very difficult to meet. When the court applies strict scrutiny to its examination of a law, the law is almost always struck down.

Table 16.1 depicts these two levels of scrutiny and their legal requirements. Although this approach to evaluating the constitutionality of a law under the equal protection clause seems very technical, it has enormous ramifications for the life opportunities afforded people of color in our society. As you read about important civil rights cases in this chapter and those that follow, see if you can understand how the court uses these levels of scrutiny in conducting its analysis.

TABLE 16.1   **Levels of Scrutiny under Equal Protection Analysis**

Level of Scrutiny	Government Purpose	Relationship of Classification to Purpose
Minimal scrutiny	Legitimate	Rationally related
Strict scrutiny	Compelling	Necessarily related

Explicit Discrimination

The equal protection clause was put to the test as early as 1879. In *Strauder v. West Virginia*, a Black man accused of murder asked for his case to be removed to federal court because Blacks in his home state, West Virginia, were barred from serving on juries or grand juries. The lower court denied his request, but the U.S. Supreme Court reversed. Noting that the purpose of the 14th Amendment was to give Blacks all the same legal rights enjoyed by Whites, the Court ruled that the Constitution affords the right to a jury selected without discrimination. Although the *Strauder* decision represents an important enunciation of the equal protection clause's application to race discrimination, the Court's opinion reflects the prevailing views of the time. In describing the 14th Amendment, the Court wrote:

> This is one of a series of constitutional provisions having a common purpose; namely, securing to a race recently emancipated, a race that through many generations had been held in slavery, all the civil rights that the superior race enjoy. . . . The colored race, as a race, was abject and ignorant, and in that condition was unfitted to command the respect of those who had superior intelligence. Their training had left them mere children, and as such they needed the protection which a wise government extends to those who are unable to protect themselves. (p. 306)

It is also interesting to note that the Court had no problem with the state restricting jury service to men, landowners, and those with certain educational qualifications. The judges of that time could never have fathomed how the reach of these civil rights laws would expand in the generations to come.

In *Strauder*, the Supreme Court struck down a state law that explicitly discriminated against members of a minority group, concluding that it was unconstitutional. The Court reached the opposite conclusion in a now infamous case from 1944, *Korematsu v. United States*. The historical context for this case is World War II. The attack on Pearl Harbor by Japan in 1941 had set off widespread panic throughout the United States. In response, President Roosevelt issued an executive order requiring all Japanese Americans in certain parts of the West Coast to abide by a curfew that confined them to their homes between 8:00 p.m. and 6:00 a.m. He also issued an evacuation order that required relocation to what were essentially concentration camps. These evacuation orders gave people one week to dispose of their property and report to assembly centers from which they were transported to internment camps. Within a single year, more than 110,000 people were imprisoned in these camps. Most were native-born American citizens. They were never charged with crimes or given a hearing.

This was not the first time the United States had discriminated against Asian Americans. The 1882 Chinese Exclusion Act resulted in the suspension of immigration from China. The Immigration Act of 1924 disallowed immigrants from Japan and prohibited those Japanese in the country from being naturalized; California also barred them from owning or leasing land.

Following the attack on Pearl Harbor, three important test cases were brought to challenge the constitutionality of the curfew and evacuation orders. The plaintiff in the first was a man named Gordon Hirbayashi; he was an American-born Quaker in his 20s, living in Seattle. After obeying the evening curfew for more than a month, Hirbayashi decided to defy the order. He was eventually tried in a Seattle court and convicted after only 10 minutes of deliberation (Irons, 2006).

The second case involved another young man, Min Yasui, who was also an American citizen. After volunteering for the army reserves and officer's training, he became a lawyer and went to work for the Japanese consulate in Chicago. When World War II broke out, he returned home to Oregon and tried to enlist in the army. He was told he was unacceptable for service and was ordered off the base. Yasui decided to defy the curfew law but was not successful in getting caught; he finally went to police headquarters and convinced them to arrest him. Yasui was tried in Portland and convicted; they gave him the maximum penalty allowed (Irons, 2006).

Fred Korematsu brought the third test case. Of the three, he was the only one who was not trying to get arrested. In fact, he tried to evade the evacuation order by changing his name, altering his I.D. card, and undergoing plastic surgery. Acting on a tip, however, the police found and arrested him in May 1942 while he was waiting to meet up with his girlfriend. He later agreed to accept legal assistance from the American Civil Liberties Union (ACLU) and to serve as a test case. Korematsu was tried in San Francisco and, like Hirbayashi and Yasui, he was found guilty. He was released on bail. As he left the courtroom, a military police officer took him into custody and transported him to a race track where his parents were being held in horse stalls, awaiting transfer to an internment camp in Utah (Irons, 2006).

All three men appealed their cases to the circuit court; all three lost. The U.S. Supreme Court agreed to hear their cases and, in 1943, decided the first two: *Hirbayashi v. United States* and *Yasui v. United States*. The high Court unanimously upheld their curfew convictions. Meanwhile, members of the Court were hoping that the government would end the internment program before they had to decide the *Korematsu* case, making it moot. In fact, the Interior Department (the federal agency overseeing the camps) had urged President Roosevelt to close them in 1943; however, the president wanted to hold off until after the 1944 election. As it happens, the Supreme Court heard arguments in *Korematsu* in October 1944, President Roosevelt won his second term in November, and the Court announced its decision one day after the camps were finally closed (Irons, 2006). By a vote of 6–3, Korematsu lost his case and the Court upheld the constitutionality of the evacuation order.

This was a highly unusual outcome, given that the Court applied strict scrutiny. As mentioned earlier, this is the standard used when laws treat people differently on the basis of race or national origin; to pass muster, the law must be necessary to achieve a compelling government interest. The Court reasoned that the evacuation order was necessary to protect the United States from espionage and sabotage; that it had to cover everyone of Japanese ancestry because it was impossible to distinguish between those who were and were not loyal; and that it was about military necessity, not discrimination.

The dissenting justices argued that this was racism, pure and simple. In an eloquent defense of the equal protection clause, one of the dissenting judges wrote, "If any fundamental assumption underlies our system, it is that guilt is personal and not inheritable. . . . But here is an attempt to make an otherwise innocent act a crime merely because this prisoner is the son of parents as to whom he had no choice, and belongs to a race from which there is no way to resign" (*Korematsu v. United States*, 1944, p. 243).

In the 1970s, Japanese Americans began a grassroots campaign asking the U.S. government to pay reparations for those who had been forced into internment camps. Their efforts were successful, and in 1988, Congress awarded $20,000 to those Japanese Americans who had been held in the camps, along with a national apology. Meanwhile, a professor at the University of California at Berkeley discovered that the government had knowingly withheld important information from the Supreme Court when it was considering the *Hirbayashi*, *Yasui*, and *Korematsu* cases. Included were two intelligence memos from the Justice Department saying that there was no existing evidence of disloyalty on the part of Japanese Americans and that no overt acts of treason had been committed. In 1985, federal courts in San Francisco, Portland, and Seattle ordered new trials and reversed the convictions of Hirbayashi, Yasui, and Korematsu. In 1988, President Clinton awarded Korematsu the Presidential Medal of Freedom.

Discriminatory Purpose

In the 1960s, the U.S. Supreme Court decided another landmark civil rights case, *Loving v. Virginia* (1967). This case concerned a Black woman who married a White man in Washington, D.C. Upon their return to Virginia, they were convicted of violating a statute called the Racial Integrity Act that banned interracial marriage. They were sentenced to a year in prison, which would be suspended for 25 years if they left the state. They moved to D.C., and in 1963, their case came to the attention of the ACLU, which filed suit on their behalf under the 14th Amendment. Although the lower court upheld the state law, a unanimous Supreme Court struck it down as a violation of the equal protection clause. Unlike the laws in *Strauder* and *Korematsu*, this law was considered to be neutral in the way it was drafted; in other words, it applied equally to both Whites and Blacks (neither was permitted to marry someone of a different race). The Court applied strict scrutiny and found that although neutral on its face, the statute's purpose was racist and it was therefore unconstitutional.

To recap, if a law explicitly treats people of different racial or ethnic groups differently, there must be an exceedingly good reason. It must meet the requirements of strict scrutiny—a standard that nearly always results in the law being declared unconstitutional. The *Korematsu* case is a glaring exception to that rule. If a statute is not explicitly discriminatory and is written in a racially neutral way, such as the one at issue in *Loving*, the law is nonetheless unconstitutional if its purpose is racist.

Discriminatory Impact

What about a policy that is neutral on its face and does not have a racist purpose, but it has a discriminatory effect? An example is the U.S Supreme Court case of *Washington v. Davis* (1976) in which the D.C. Police Department required an exam as part of its hiring process and four times more Blacks than Whites failed the exam. When two African Americans challenged the test, the district court ruled in favor of the city. On appeal, the circuit court reversed and ruled in favor of the plaintiffs. The Supreme Court, by a vote of 7–2, upheld the constitutionality of the test. Its reasoning was that absent intent to discriminate, the fact that different races are impacted differently is insufficient to constitute a violation of the equal protection clause. Here, there was evidence that the police force had made a concerted effort to recruit African American officers, and no racist motive could be found. Interestingly, because the test at issue was neutrally written, the Court applied minimal scrutiny instead of the usual strict scrutiny; if the Court had applied strict scrutiny, the test most likely would have been invalidated.

The question of how we treat laws that are not obviously discriminatory but impact different racial groups differently is a complex one. Although a showing of disparate impact does not render a law unconstitutional under the equal protection clause, it is treated very differently under the Civil Rights Act of 1964. How a case is brought can make an enormous difference.

Affirmative Action

As mentioned earlier, the idea of affirmative action is to remedy the past effects of race and sex discrimination by directing opportunities to individuals based on their membership in a historically disadvantaged group. The idea is that simply stopping discrimination in the present is not sufficient, because centuries of discrimination have left women and minorities handicapped to compete. Affirmative action policies are designed to put them on an equal footing. The original justification for affirmative action is beautifully captured by this 1965 quote from President Lyndon B. Johnson:

> Freedom is not enough. You do not wipe away the scars of centuries by saying "now you are free to go where you want, do as you desire, and choose the leaders you please." You do not take a man who for years has been hobbled by chains, liberate him, bring him to the starting line of a race, saying, "you are free to compete with all the others," and still justly believe you have been completely fair. Thus it is not enough just to open the gates of opportunity. All our citizens must have the ability to walk through those gates. This is the next and more profound stage of the battle for civil rights. We seek not just freedom but opportunity—not just legal equity but human ability—not just equality as a right and a theory, but equality as a fact and as a result. (Johnson, 1965)

Affirmative action policies proliferated during the late 1960s and throughout the 1970s as educational institutions and businesses sought to increase their diversity. These policies attracted considerable opposition, however, which reached a tipping point in the 1980s and became enshrined in the Supreme Court's approach to analyzing the cases that came before it. One example is *City of Richmond v. Croson* (1989). In this case, a challenge was brought against a minority set-aside program requiring contractors for city projects to subcontract at least 30% of the amount of their contracts to minority business enterprises. The Supreme Court struck down the program, applying strict scrutiny. This was significant because strict scrutiny traditionally had been used only when laws disadvantaged racial minorities—not when laws were designed to help them. Discrimination, the Court reasoned, was discrimination; it did not matter if the person disadvantaged was part of the majority or of the minority. The Court also reasoned that findings of widespread race discrimination in the contracting industry were irrelevant. To justify the use of affirmative action, the city would have to show that there was discrimination against minority contractors specifically in Richmond's contracting industry. In an even harsher concurring opinion, Justice Scalia argued that only specific individual bidders who had actually been discriminated against should be able to benefit from the set-aside.

The dissenting opinion argued that Richmond's efforts were laudable, not unconstitutional, and that strict scrutiny was appropriate only when a law is racist—not when it seeks to remedy racism. In fact, the *Croson* case was only one in a long line of cases that thrust affirmative action into legal jeopardy. The same continues to be true in education. The watershed case that first recognized "reverse discrimination" under the equal protection clause, *Regents of the University of California v. Bakke*, appears as the sample case at the end of this chapter.

Rights in Employment

Along with the Constitution's equal protection clause, the most important law to safeguard the employment rights of minorities is the Civil Rights Act of 1964 (CRA). Title VII of the CRA prohibits employment discrimination based on race, color, religion, sex and national origin; it also prohibits discrimination based on stereotypes or assumptions about a group's traits, intelligence, or abilities. In its current form, the act applies to private employers; employment agencies; labor unions; educational institutions; and federal, state, and local governments. It addresses discriminatory practices in recruitment, hiring, compensation, work assignment, training, promotion, benefits, discipline, termination, and layoffs. It also protects against hostile work environments that permit ethnic slurs, racial jokes and symbols, derogatory comments, and physical segregation based on membership in a protected group.

The EEOC

Title VII also created the Equal Employment Opportunity Commission (EEOC), which monitors employment discrimination, processes complaints under the Act, and implements strategies to reduce employment discrimination.

If an employee believes that he or she has been the victim of discrimination in the workplace, the first step is to file a claim with the EEOC; this must be done within 45 calendar days of when the discriminatory act occurred. The burden of proving the validity of the allegation lies with the complainant. Once the charge is filed and the employer has been notified of the complaint, the EEOC initiates an investigation. In conducting its investigation, the EEOC has the right to request information, conduct interviews, review relevant documents, and visit the facility where the alleged discrimination took place. Once the investigation is complete, the claim may take one of several paths:

- **Settlement:** The EEOC can seek to settle a complaint at any stage of the investigation if the charging party and the employer express an interest in doing so. If settlement efforts are not successful, the process continues.
- **Mediation:** Mediation is an informal and confidential means of dispute resolution, conducted by a neutral facilitator. A charge may be referred to the EEOC's mediation program as an alternative to the investigation if both the charging party and the employer agree to do so. If mediation is unsuccessful, the EEOC moves forward with its formal investigation.
- **Conciliation:** Whereas mediation seeks to reach a settlement through agreement, conciliation resolves the dispute through seeking concessions or reparations. If conciliation is undertaken, the parties involved meet separately with a conciliator who then communicates information between them and attempts to broker a deal.

- **Litigation:** Neither the EEOC nor the charging party is permitted to go to court unless conciliation, mediation, or settlement has been attempted and an agreement could not be reached, or an agreement was made but not honored. If this is the case, the EEOC can either file suit in the federal courts or opt to take no further action. If the EEOC decides not to sue, it will issue a notice closing the case. Once closed, the complainant has 90 days in which to file a lawsuit on his or her own behalf.
- **Dismissal:** A charge may be dismissed at any point if, in the EEOC's best judgment, further investigation will not establish a violation of the law. Once a charge is dismissed, the claimant has 90 days in which to file a lawsuit on his or her own behalf.

If the case ends up going to court, the claimant will be seeking to demonstrate one of two things: either that the employer treated him or her disadvantageously because of race or national origin (*disparate treatment*) or that the employer's policies or practices resulted in disproportionately negative consequences for people of a particular race or national origin (*disparate impact*). The process for pursuing these allegations is described next.

Proving Disparate Treatment

The process for litigating a case under Title VII is fairly complex. When the issue is *disparate treatment*—a person is alleging that he or she was treated differently because of his or her race—the plaintiff has the burden of making out a *prima facie* case of discrimination.

As discussed earlier in the context of age discrimination (Chapter 10), this requires an initial showing that, on the face of it, discrimination appears to have taken place. This is most often accomplished by providing circumstantial evidence demonstrating the following (*McDonnell Douglas Corp. v. Green*, 1973):

- The plaintiff belongs to a racial minority.
- The plaintiff applied and was qualified for a job the employer was trying to fill.
- Though qualified, the plaintiff was rejected.
- Thereafter, the employer continued to seek applicants with the plaintiff's qualifications.

The same logic applies regardless of whether the plaintiff is challenging a hiring decision or some other employment action such as promotion, advancement, training, or pay. Once the plaintiff has presented an acceptable *prima facie* case, the burden of proof shifts to the employer. The employer must show that there is a nondiscriminatory explanation for the action. For example, if the employee was fired, the employer might provide evidence that the employee was chronically absent or demonstrated poor job performance. If no credible explanation is forthcoming, the plaintiff will prevail. On the other hand, if the employer offers a nondiscriminatory explanation, the burden shifts back to the plaintiff to prove that the explanation is merely a pretext.

Occasionally, the employer has a policy or employment practice that is admittedly discriminatory—for example, a French restaurant that hires only French chefs. Once the plaintiff establishes a *prima facie* case, the restaurant could argue that being French in this instance is a *bona fide occupational qualification* (BFOQ). BFOQs are discriminatory employment practices that are reasonably necessary to the normal functioning of a business's operations (Willborn, Schwab, Burton, & Lester, 2007). They are permissible defenses to employment discrimination in relation to age, sex, religion, and national origin, but never in relation to race.

Another defense is that the challenged practice or policy is consistent with a voluntarily implemented affirmative action plan. Here, the burden of proof is on the plaintiff to prove that the plan is invalid. This can be done by showing that a documented plan does not exist, that the defendant has previously discriminated against protected groups, that the plan precludes opportunities for members of majority groups, or that the plan has remained in place even after the company has met its diversity goals (Levinson, 2011).

Proving Disparate Impact

Unlike the equal protection clause of the Constitution, Title VII of the Civil Rights Act has been used to invalidate laws that impact people of different races differently. In *Griggs v. Duke Power Co.* (1971), hiring and promotion policies relegated all African Americans to the lowest-paying positions. Advancement within the company was premised on the results of two aptitude tests and required a high school diploma. African American applicants and employees were disproportionately excluded from better-paying positions as a result. The U.S. Supreme Court invalidated the policies as a violation of Title VII, concluding that neither of the requirements was shown to bear any relationship to successful job performance; instead, their actual purpose appeared to be ensuring the perpetuation of the company's long-standing preference for White employees.

As with disparate treatment cases, *disparate impact* claims begin with the plaintiff establishing a *prima facie* case. This is usually accomplished through the use of statistics demonstrating that the policy or practice has had a disproportionate adverse effect on racial or ethnic minorities. The EEOC, Department of Labor, Department of Justice, and Civil Service Commission have all adopted a uniform definition of just how disparate the impact must be in order to constitute an acceptable showing. They use a quantitative approach called the *80 percent rule*. The idea is that the selection rate for any racial group's applicants must be equal to at least 80% of the selection rate for the group with the most favorable outcome. So if 60% of White applicants passed a particular qualifying test, at least 48% of every other group's applicants should have passed the test. If only 30% of African American applicants passed, for example, this would be considered a disparate impact because it constitutes only half the passing rate for Whites rather than the minimum 80% (Society for Human Resource Management, 2011).

Once a *prima facie* case is established, the burden of proof shifts to the defendant. He or she can counter the data produced by the plaintiff or assert that the disputed practice or policy is a business necessity. For example, requiring a certain skill might disadvantage a particular minority group, but it might be justified because it is necessary to ensure safety on the job (EEOC, 2010). If the defendant's argument appears to be valid, the burden shifts back to the plaintiff to prove that the employer could have implemented an alternate practice that would meet its needs without disadvantaging racial or ethnic minorities.

In 2009, the U.S. Supreme Court considered a case in which the city of New Haven sought to remedy a case of disparate impact (*Ricci v. DeStefano*, 2009). As part of its process for determining eligibility for promotion among its firefighters, the city required an exam. A total of 118 candidates took the exam; of those who passed and were otherwise eligible for immediate promotion, 17 were White, 2 were Hispanic, and none were Black.

Fearful of being sued for discrimination on the basis of these racially skewed outcomes, the city invalidated the test results and none of the candidates was promoted. Two of the firefighters who had passed, one White and one Hispanic, brought a Title VII suit against the city claiming reverse discrimination. A closely divided Court (5–4) ruled in their favor. This outcome is consistent with the shift in views regarding affirmative action that was discussed in relation to the equal protection clause; earlier cases routinely upheld affirmative action policies, but more recent ones have struck them down.

Rights in Housing

Discrimination in housing has far-reaching effects. It creates barriers to home ownership, limits housing choice, perpetuates segregation, and interferes with educational and employment opportunities (Turner et al., 2002). Disparities in housing-related health conditions are especially pronounced in inner cities and rural areas. African Americans, who are more likely than Whites to live in old, poorly maintained housing, face twice the risk Whites do of contracting childhood lead poisoning. Roach infestation has been associated with asthma, another condition that disproportionately affects people of color. The U.S. Supreme Court has made it clear that adequate housing is not a fundamental constitutional right, despite its social importance (*Lindsey v. Normet*, 1972).

Prior to the establishment of federal laws prohibiting housing discrimination, racial and ethnic minorities were routinely subjected to discriminatory practices that limited where they could live and perpetuated segregation. Housing covenants, for example, were a popular method of housing discrimination. These covenants, which were written into the property deed, barred the sale or rental of properties to people of certain races, ethnicities, or religions. Although the Supreme Court ruled in 1917 that the government could not pass laws preventing Blacks from buying or occupying housing in "White" neighborhoods, it left intact the right of private citizens to do so. The case of *Shelley v. Kraemer* in 1948 challenged this ruling. It involved an African American couple with six children who moved to the St. Louis area from Mississippi. They unwittingly purchased a home that was covered by a restrictive racial covenant originally signed in 1911, and were consequently evicted. With the help of the National Association for the Advancement of Colored People (NAACP), the case reached the U.S. Supreme Court. Armed with voluminous social science statistics and supported by *amicus* briefs from 15 diverse religious, racial, and ethnic organizations—as well as the U.S. Department of Justice—Shelley and his family prevailed. A unanimous Court determined that property owners indeed have the right to adopt restrictive covenants, but the courts cannot constitutionally enforce them. Although the Court's ruling fell short of actually invalidating restrictive covenants, it rendered them virtually useless.

Even with the reduction in restrictive covenants, housing remained racially divided throughout the 1960s. In 1967, fewer than 20% of Americans lived in integrated neighborhoods (Clark, 1995). Segregated housing for racial and ethnic minorities was perpetuated through the use of other discriminatory strategies, including racial steering and redlining. Racial steering occurs when real estate agents guide potential homebuyers toward or away from certain neighborhoods based on the potential homebuyer's race. Redlining involves lenders refusing to loan money or extend credit to persons living in racially dense areas (U.S. Department of Housing and Urban Development [HUD], 2008). Although these practices are now unlawful, instances of redlining and racial steering are occasionally still reported to HUD today.

Zoning laws have also been used to limit housing opportunities for racial and ethnic minorities. In 1977, the Supreme Court considered such a case (*Village of Arlington Heights v. Metropolitan Housing Development Corporation*). The Metropolitan Housing Development Corporation (MHDC) had contracted with a Chicago suburb to build federally subsidized, racially mixed, low- and moderate-income housing. The local planning commission, however, denied the MHDC's application for a zoning permit. The MHDC and several minority members brought suit, arguing that the denial was discriminatory because it would have a disproportionately negative impact on African Americans. The Court upheld the planning commission's decision, concluding that despite the disparate impact, there was no showing of discriminatory intent.

Perhaps the most important case in housing rights was heard by the Supreme Court in 1968. In *Jones v. Mayer*, a private developer in St. Louis refused to sell a home to Jones because he was African American. The Court ruled, for the first time ever, that federal law bans discrimination not just by public entities but also in the private housing market. The case was brought under a law derived from the 13th Amendment; in an expansive interpretation, the Court concluded that Congress's power to eliminate "the badges and incidents of slavery" extends to the prohibition of all discrimination, both public and private.

The Civil Rights Act of 1964 barely addressed housing discrimination, but the problem was addressed through Title VIII of the Civil Rights Act of 1968. Commonly known as the *Fair Housing Act*, this is the federal law that prohibits housing discrimination on the basis of race, color, national origin, sex, family composition, and disability. Covering most forms of housing, from private homes and apartment buildings to condominium developments, the Act bans discrimination involving refusing to rent, sell, or negotiate for housing; establishing different terms, conditions, or privileges for the sale or rental of a home; and providing different housing services or facilities. In addition, the Fair Housing Act prohibits discrimination in advertising and mortgage lending practices and makes it illegal to threaten, coerce, intimidate, or interfere with any person exercising a fair housing right (HUD, 2002). The Act was further strengthened by passage of the 1974 Equal Credit Opportunity Act, which prohibits credit discrimination on the basis of race, color, national origin, religion, sex, marital status, age, or use of public assistance. This means that banks, lenders, and other creditors may not discriminate against people seeking financial assistance to purchase homes or other goods.

HUD administers the Federal Housing Act and other federal laws that prohibit housing discrimination; it is responsible for receiving and investigating complaints. In 2010, nearly 29,000 complaints of housing discrimination were filed with public and private organizations (National Fair Housing Alliance, 2011). In 2008, more than half of all complaints received by HUD and Fair Housing Assistance Program agencies nationwide alleged discrimination on the basis of race (38%), national origin (13%), and color (2%). After disability, race is the basis for the majority of housing discrimination complaints each year (HUD, 2008). Minorities continue to be subject to considerable discrimination in rental and sales markets, especially in large metropolitan areas. Prospective African American and Hispanic homebuyers often experience steering by real estate agents and receive little help in assessing their lending options. Asian Americans and Pacific Islanders experience similar discrimination when seeking financial assistance.

FIGURE 16.3   Diversity Experienced in Each Racial/Ethnic Group's Typical Neighborhood in a Metropolitan Area

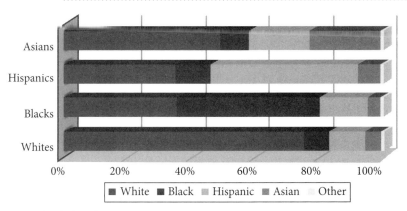

Source: Logan and Stults (2011).

Although neighborhood segregation has decreased significantly since the 1960s, Whites continue to live in neighborhoods with minimal minority representation. As Figure 16.3 depicts, Whites in metropolitan areas live in neighborhoods that are up to 75% White (Logan & Stults, 2011). In contrast, minorities residing in metropolitan areas live in somewhat more diverse neighborhoods. Blacks and Hispanics live in neighborhoods with high minority representation but low White representation; Asians, on the other hand, tend to live in neighborhoods where minorities and Whites are more equally represented.

Rights in Education

Historically, racial and ethnic minorities have often been denied equal rights in the realm of education. Even today, the right to education is apparent in many controversies, including affirmative action, de facto school segregation, and bilingual education.

School Desegregation

Plessy v. Ferguson, an 1896 case, established the principle of *separate but equal* that dominated public education in the United States for more than 50 years. Beginning in the 1930s, a series of challenges was successfully brought against states that failed to accommodate African Americans in graduate and professional programs that were substantially equal to those attended by Whites. These cases laid the groundwork for one of the best-known Supreme Court cases of all time, *Brown v. Board of Education* (1954). The *Brown* case (along with five others that were heard at the same time) was selected in part because it involved a school district where Black and White schools were of relatively equal quality; the idea was to isolate the segregation issue, forcing the Court to confront the question of whether segregation of public schools, in and of itself, is permissible under the Constitution. A unanimous Supreme Court ruled that "separate educational facilities are inherently unequal" and are thus in violation of the equal protection clause. Rather than basing its argument on the quality of education, the Court's rationale emphasized the psychological impact of segregation on African American schoolchildren. The Court maintained that separation solely on the basis of race creates a sense of inferiority that undermines motivation and educational development. In a follow-up decision the following year (known as *Brown II*), the Court ordered that schools be desegregated "with all deliberate speed" (*Brown v. Board of Education*, 1955). This inexact standard was employed as a nod to anticipated resistance in the South and was agreed to by the justices as part of the compromise that led to its unanimous decision.

To no one's surprise, implementation of the *Brown* decision was slow in coming, as numerous school districts—particularly those in the South—dragged their feet. By 1964, 10 years after the decision, only half of the southern school districts had desegregated; in the Deep South, less than 1% of Black children attended integrated schools (Vieira, 1990). Meanwhile, the Court continued to hear additional cases regarding *de jure* (legally sanctioned) segregation. A variety of state tactics designed to evade *Brown's* desegregation order were struck down.

The question remained, however, how to light a fire under school districts that had done little since the *Brown* decision to unify their schools. In a North Carolina case, *Swann v. Charlotte-Mecklenberg Board of Education* (1971), the U.S. Supreme Court ruled that once a violation of the equal protection clause is established, the federal courts are empowered to develop and enforce a desegregation plan rather than leaving it in the hands of the local school board to comply. In that same case, the Court clarified that school districts do not have to achieve a perfect racial balance; they are even permitted to have a small number of single-race schools, as long as they continue to strive for the greatest possible degree of desegregation given the practicalities of the situation. The Court also upheld the use (within limits) of racial quotas, racial gerrymandering, and school transfers as strategies to achieve desegregation.

In some ways, the more difficult issue is the constitutionality of *de facto* (unintentional) segregation. Where residence patterns, changing demographics, or other "fortuitous" factors result in racial segregation, the Court has declined to find a constitutional violation. In his searing dissent to a Supreme Court ruling supporting this conclusion, Justice Douglas noted with skepticism that seemingly innocent school segregation is often the result of intentional discrimination in other realms. He quoted the U.S. Commission on Civil Rights as follows:

> The current situation we face, in which most minority group children attend school in isolation from children of the majority group, is *not* accidental or purely *de facto*. In many cases, it has resulted in whole or in substantial part from an accumulation of governmental actions. Thus the categorical distinction between *de jure* and *de facto* segregation is not as clear-cut as it would appear. . . . The Government has a moral as well as legal responsibility to undo the segregation it has helped to create and maintain. (*Spencer v. Kugler*, 1972, p. 1027)

Finally, in *Board of Education of Oklahoma City v. Dowell* (1991), the Supreme Court signaled its intention to step back from its enforcement role in school desegregation. Oklahoma City had been under a court order to desegregate its schools through mandatory busing. The remedy proved successful, and the court's order was lifted 5 years later. Seven years after that, the city suspended its mandatory busing program, and a motion was made to reopen the case. The Supreme Court declined, ruling that the court may terminate its jurisdiction over a case after a reasonable period of compliance. In his dissent, Justice Thurgood Marshall argued that the court's jurisdiction should continue until the effects of prior segregation are fully eliminated; he added that 15 years of compliance after 65 years of forced segregation was not enough.

Affirmative Action

One of the most controversial issues concerning the education rights of racial minorities is affirmative action. Throughout the 1960s and 1970s, many universities in the United States implemented plans to remedy the vestiges of past discrimination by adopting admissions policies designed to level the playing field for women and minorities. Supporters of affirmative action argue that it is a necessary strategy in ensuring equal opportunity and that it contributes to the educational mission by increasing diversity. Opponents argue that affirmative action engenders reverse discrimination and further stigmatizes minorities by promoting the idea that they are unable to succeed on their own merit. Interestingly, the latter theory has been dispelled by at least one empirical study (Onwuachi-Willig, Houh, & Campbell, 2008).

After a decade or more of consistently being upheld by the courts, affirmative action in higher education was turned on its head by the Supreme Court's decision in *Regents of the University of California v. Bakke*. This case (which appears as the sample case at the end of this chapter) was the first in which the Court upheld a White plaintiff's claim of reverse discrimination under the equal protection clause. Following the *Bakke* decision, the notion of reverse discrimination captured the American imagination, leading to widespread public disapproval of affirmative action in university admissions. What was left unclear was just how an educational institution could fashion a policy that would be constitutionally acceptable. Two Supreme Court cases decided on the same day in 2003 muddied the waters even further.

In *Grutter v. Bollinger*, the Court upheld an admissions policy at the University of Michigan Law School that gave extra consideration to members of racial minority groups as part of an individualized review process that considered multiple factors; special consideration was given for other characteristics as well, including being an athlete, a legacy applicant, and a White graduate from a predominantly Black high school. In *Gratz v. Bollinger*, the Court reached the opposite conclusion, striking down the admissions policy at the University of Michigan's undergraduate College of Literature, Science, and the Arts. Under that approach, students received points based on their grade point average, test scores, legacy status, leadership, and race. A total of 100 points qualified a student for admission; members of an underrepresented minority group were automatically given 20 points.

Drawing a conclusion from this mix of cases is difficult. The safest course of action seems to be to consider a variety of admissions criteria but not to assign any of them a specific value. What we can say with certainty is that the Supreme Court's guidance in this area has been inconsistent to date.

Students with Limited English Proficiency

The fastest-growing population in today's public schools is children from immigrant families; they comprise 10.6% of public school enrollment through the 12th grade (Calderón, Slavin, & Sanchez, 2011). Many of these students are classified as *English language learners* or students with *limited English proficient* (LEP), a demographic that increased by 105% during the 1990s (Callahan, Wilkinson, Muller, & Frisco, 2009). Limited English proficiency has been associated with disparities in academic achievement, including poorer academic performance, lower test scores on standardized instruments, lower graduation rates, and lower college enrollment rates (Calderón et al., 2011; Callahan, 2005; Callahan et al., 2009). In addition, LEP students complete less math and science coursework than their English-speaking peers (Callahan, Wilkinson, & Muller, 2008). In addition to facing language barriers, LEP students disproportionately attend schools that are poorly funded, overcrowded, segregated, and serve large numbers of students living in poverty (Li, 2007).

The Bilingual Education Act of 1968 was the first indication that Congress recognized "the special educational needs of the large numbers of children of limited English-speaking ability in the U.S." (McDonald & Powell, 1998, p. 69). The goal of the Bilingual Education Act was to promote school attendance for low-income, non-English-speaking children and to guarantee that they have the same access to educational opportunities as other students. Bilingual education programs facilitate LEP students' entry into standard classes by initially teaching content in their native language and gradually transitioning to instruction in English. Many consider bilingual education essential in guaranteeing that LEP students have equal access to education (Li, 2007).

The case of *Lau v. Nichols* (1974) involved a challenge to the San Francisco Unified School District, home to 2,856 students of Chinese ancestry with limited English proficiency of whom only 1,000 received English language instruction. The Supreme Court ruled that the school system must take affirmative steps to help LEP students overcome language barriers. It declined to consider the case on 14th Amendment equal protection grounds, instead relying on the Civil Rights Act of 1964. According to Justice Douglas,

> Basic English skills are at the very core of what these public schools teach. Imposition of a requirement that, before a child can effectively participate in the educational program, he must already have acquired those basic skills is to make a mockery of public education (p. 566).

A Fifth Circuit case, *Castañeda v. Pickard* (1981), was brought by Mexican American children and their parents against a school district in Texas. Among many other claims of discrimination, they argued that the bilingual education program being offered them was inadequate. Without prescribing specific techniques or approaches, the court articulated the following evaluative criteria to be used in determining whether the school's program is meeting the needs of LEP students:

- It is based on sound educational theory or principles.
- It follows through with the practices, resources, and personnel necessary for effective implementation.
- It yields positive results after a reasonable trial period.

In recent years, there has been a significant push for English-only education in public schools. California adopted such a requirement in 1998 through Proposition 227 (Li, 2007). Additional ballot measures mandating English-only education passed in Arizona in 2000 and Massachusetts in 2002. The National Association of Social Workers opposes any legislation that promotes English-only agendas, recognizing that "to limit or deny language as an extension of culture is to reject that aspect of human beings that helps to define them" (NASW, 2009, p. 216).

Many believe that the No Child Left Behind Act of 2002 (NCLB) has adversely affected LEP students' access to bilingual education. Following its enactment, the Bilingual Education Act was renamed the English Language Acquisition, Language Enhancement, and Academic Achievement Act, and the Office of Bilingual Education was renamed the Office of English Language Acquisition, Language Enhancement, and Academic Achievement for Limited-English-Proficient Students (Li, 2007). Although the NCLB does not eliminate bilingual education programs outright, it discourages bilingual education by emphasizing and rewarding the acquisition of English over the acquisition of subject matter content (Mitchell, 2005). Many advocates argue that this overemphasis on English language acquisition has perpetuated the achievement gap between LEP and English-proficient students.

Summary and Conclusion

Important strides have been made in recognizing equal rights for racial and ethnic minorities, both under the 14th Amendment's equal protection clause and under the Civil Rights Act of 1964. Nonetheless, minority status continues to be associated with adverse socioeconomic conditions. When cases are brought under the equal protection clause, the Supreme Court applies strict scrutiny—a tough standard that most laws are unable to meet. Beginning in the 1980s, the Court applied this same standard to affirmative action policies designed to benefit historically disadvantaged groups, striking them down as unconstitutional. Title VII of the Civil Rights Act prohibits discrimination in employment. Claims must be filed with the Equal Employment Opportunity Commission before a lawsuit can be initiated. The Supreme Court has also decided cases related to housing, ruling that federal law applies to both public and private acts of discrimination. Barriers to equal educational opportunity include school segregation and failure to provide instruction for students with limited English proficiency. In recent years, the Supreme Court has also upheld claims of reverse discrimination in university admissions. Social workers can make a difference on all of these fronts by ensuring that clients know their rights, helping them pursue discrimination claims, and advocating for systems change that respects and values diversity.

Sample Case

As mentioned earlier, this case was an important turning point in the Supreme Court's approach to affirmative action. Read the case and consider the questions that follow.

REGENTS OF THE UNIVERSITY OF CALIFORNIA v. BAKKE
438 U.S. 265 (1978)

Mr. Justice Powell announced the judgment of the Court.

This case presents a challenge to the special admissions program of the petitioner, the Medical School of the University of California at Davis, which is designed to assure the admission of a specified number of students from certain minority groups. ***

The Medical School of the University of California at Davis opened in 1968 with an entering class of 50 students. In 1971, the size of the entering class was increased to 100 students, a level at which it remains. No admissions program for disadvantaged or minority students existed when the school opened, and the first class contained three Asians but no blacks, no Mexican-Americans, and no American Indians. Over the next two years, the faculty devised a special admissions program to increase the representation of "disadvantaged" students in each Medical School class. The special program consisted of a separate admissions system operating in coordination with the regular admissions process.

Under the regular admissions procedure . . . [c]andidates whose overall undergraduate grade point averages fell below 2.5 on a scale of 4.0 were summarily rejected. About one out of six applicants was invited for a personal interview. Following the interviews, each candidate was rated on a scale of 1 to 100 by his interviewers and four other members of the admissions committee. . . . The ratings were added together to arrive at each candidate's "benchmark" score.

The special admissions program operated with a separate committee, a majority of whom were members of minority groups. . . . [T]he applications . . . were rated by the special committee in a fashion similar to that used by the general admissions committee, except that special candidates did not have to meet the 2.5 grade point average cutoff applied to regular applicants. About one-fifth of the total number of special applicants were invited for interviews. . . . Following each interview, the special committee assigned each special applicant a benchmark score.

Allan Bakke is a white male who applied to the Davis Medical School in both 1973 and 1974. In both years Bakke's application was considered under the general admissions program. . . . In both years, applicants were admitted under the special program with grade point averages, MCAT scores, and benchmark scores significantly lower than Bakke's.

*** The parties . . . disagree as to the level of judicial scrutiny to be applied to the special admissions program. . . . The special admissions program is undeniably a classification based on race and ethnic background. To the extent that there existed a pool of at least minimally qualified minority applicants to fill the 16 special admissions seats, white applicants could compete only for 84 seats in the entering class, rather than the 100 open to minority applicants. Whether this limitation is described as a quota or a goal, it is a line drawn on the basis of race and ethnic status.

. . . The guarantee of equal protection cannot mean one thing when applied to one individual and something else when applied to a person of another color. If both are not accorded the same protection, then it is not equal.

Nevertheless, petitioner argues that the court below erred in applying strict scrutiny to the special admissions program because white males, such as respondent, are not a "discrete and insular minority" requiring extraordinary protection from the majoritarian political process. This rationale, however, has never been invoked in our decisions as a prerequisite to subjecting racial or ethnic distinctions to strict scrutiny. . . . Racial and ethnic distinctions of any sort are inherently suspect and thus call for the most exacting judicial examination. ***

Over the past 30 years, this Court has embarked upon the crucial mission of interpreting the Equal Protection Clause with the view of assuring to all persons "the protection of equal laws" in a Nation confronting a legacy of slavery and racial discrimination. Because the landmark decisions in this area arose in response to the continued exclusion of

Negroes from the mainstream of American society, they could be characterized as involving discrimination by the "majority" white race against the Negro minority. But they need not be read as depending upon that characterization for their results. . . .

Petitioner urges us to adopt for the first time a more restrictive view of the Equal Protection Clause and hold that discrimination against members of the white "majority" cannot be suspect if its purpose can be characterized as "benign." The clock of our liberties, however, cannot be turned back to 1868. . . .

The concepts of "majority" and "minority" necessarily reflect temporary arrangements and political judgments. As observed above, the white "majority" itself is composed of various minority groups, most of which can lay claim to a history of prior discrimination at the hands of the State and private individuals. . . . There is no principled basis for deciding which groups would merit "heightened judicial solicitude" and which would not. . . . Those whose societal injury is thought to exceed some arbitrary level of tolerability then would be entitled to preferential classifications at the expense of individuals belonging to other groups. . . . As these preferences began to have their desired effect, and the consequences of past discrimination were undone, new judicial rankings would be necessary. The kind of variable sociological and political analysis necessary to produce such rankings simply does not lie within the judicial competence—even if they otherwise were politically feasible and socially desirable. ***

. . . The special admissions program purports to serve the purposes of: (i) "reducing the historic deficit of traditionally disfavored minorities in medical schools and in the medical profession," (ii) countering the effects of societal discrimination; (iii) increasing the number of physicians who will practice in communities currently underserved; and (iv) obtaining the educational benefits that flow from an ethnically diverse student body. It is necessary to decide which, if any, of these purposes is substantial enough to support the use of a suspect classification.

If petitioner's purpose is to assure within its student body some specified percentage of a particular group merely because of its race or ethnic origin, such a preferential purpose must be rejected not as insubstantial but as facially invalid. Preferring members of any one group for no reason other than race or ethnic origin is discrimination for its own sake. This the Constitution forbids.

The State certainly has a legitimate and substantial interest in ameliorating, or eliminating where feasible, the disabling effects of identified discrimination. The line of school desegregation cases, commencing with Brown, attests to the importance of this stated goal and the commitment of the judiciary to affirm all lawful means toward its attainment. In the school cases, the States were required by court order to redress the wrongs worked by specific instances of racial discrimination. That goal was far more focused than the remedying of the effects of "societal discrimination," an amorphous concept of injury that may be ageless in its reach into the past.

We have never approved a classification that aids persons perceived as members of relatively victimized groups at the expense of other innocent individuals in the absence of judicial, legislative, or administrative findings of constitutional or statutory violations. . . . Hence, the purpose of helping certain groups whom the faculty of the Davis Medical School perceived as victims of "societal discrimination" does not justify a classification that imposes disadvantages upon persons like respondent, who bear no responsibility for whatever harm the beneficiaries of the special admissions program are thought to have suffered.

Petitioner identifies, as another purpose of its program, improving the delivery of health-care services to communities currently underserved. It may be assumed that in some situations a State's interest in facilitating the health care of its citizens is sufficiently compelling to support the use of a suspect classification. But there is virtually no evidence in the record indicating that petitioner's special admissions program is either needed or geared to promote that goal. . . .

The fourth goal asserted by petitioner is the attainment of a diverse student body. This clearly is a constitutionally permissible goal for an institution of higher education. Academic freedom, though not a specifically enumerated constitutional right, long has been viewed as a special concern of the First Amendment. The freedom of a university to make its own judgments as to education includes the selection of its student body. . . .

Thus, in arguing that its universities must be accorded the right to select those students who will contribute the most to the "robust exchange of ideas," petitioner invokes a countervailing constitutional interest, that of the First Amendment. In this light, petitioner must be viewed as seeking to achieve a goal that is of paramount importance in the fulfillment of its mission.

It may be argued that there is greater force to these views at the undergraduate level than in a medical school where the training is centered primarily on professional competency. But even at the graduate level, our tradition and experience lend support to the view that the contribution of diversity is substantial. . . . Physicians serve a heterogeneous population. An otherwise qualified medical student with a particular background—whether it be ethnic, geographic, culturally advantaged or disadvantaged—may bring to a professional school of medicine experiences, outlooks, and ideas that enrich the training of its student body and better equip its graduates to render with understanding their vital service to humanity.

Ethnic diversity, however, is only one element in a range of factors a university properly may consider in attaining the goal of a heterogeneous student body. . . . As the interest of diversity is compelling in the context of a university's admissions program, the question remains whether the program's racial classification is necessary to promote this interest.

It may be assumed that the reservation of a specified number of seats in each class for individuals from the preferred ethnic groups would contribute to the attainment of considerable ethnic diversity in the student body. But petitioner's argument that this is the only effective means of serving the interest of diversity is seriously flawed. . . . The diversity that furthers a compelling state interest encompasses a far broader array of qualifications and characteristics of which racial or ethnic origin is but a single though important element. . . .

The experience of other university admissions programs, which take race into account in achieving the educational diversity valued by the First Amendment, demonstrates that the assignment of a fixed number of places to a minority group is not a necessary means toward that end. An illuminating example is found in the Harvard College program. . . . In such an admissions program, race or ethnic background may be deemed a "plus" in a particular applicant's file, yet it does not insulate the individual from comparison with all other candidates for the available seats. The file of a particular black applicant may be examined for his potential contribution to diversity without the factor of race being decisive when compared, for example, with that of an applicant identified as an Italian-American if the latter is thought to exhibit qualities more likely to promote beneficial educational pluralism. Such qualities could include exceptional personal talents, unique work or service experience, leadership potential, maturity, demonstrated compassion, a history of overcoming disadvantage, ability to communicate with the poor, or other qualifications deemed important. In short, an admissions program operated in this way is flexible enough to consider all pertinent elements of diversity in light of the particular qualifications of each applicant, and to place them on the same footing for consideration, although not necessarily according them the same weight. Indeed, the weight attributed to a particular quality may vary from year to year depending upon the "mix" both of the student body and the applicants for the incoming class.

This kind of program treats each applicant as an individual in the admissions process. The applicant who loses out on the last available seat to another candidate receiving a "plus" on the basis of ethnic background will not have been foreclosed from all consideration for that seat simply because he was not the right color or had the wrong surname. It would mean only that his combined qualifications, which may have included similar nonobjective factors, did not outweigh those of the other applicant. . . .

In summary, it is evident that the Davis special admissions program involves the use of an explicit racial classification never before countenanced by this Court. It tells applicants who are not Negro, Asian, or Chicano that they are totally excluded from a specific percentage of the seats in an entering class. No matter how strong their qualifications, quantitative and extracurricular, including their own potential for contribution to educational diversity, they are never afforded the chance to compete with applicants from the preferred groups for the special admissions seats. At the same time, the preferred applicants have the opportunity to compete for every seat in the class. . . .

When a State's distribution of benefits or imposition of burdens hinges on ancestry or the color of a person's skin, that individual is entitled to a demonstration that the challenged classification is necessary to promote a substantial state interest. Petitioner has failed to carry this burden. For this reason, that portion of the California court's judgment holding petitioner's special admissions program invalid under the Fourteenth Amendment must be affirmed. ***

Mr. Justice Marshall

*** While I applaud the judgment of the Court that a university may consider race in its admissions process, it is more than a little ironic that, after several hundred years of class-based discrimination against Negroes, the Court is unwilling to hold that a class-based remedy for that discrimination is permissible. In declining to so hold, today's judgment ignores the fact that for several hundred years Negroes have been discriminated against, not as individuals, but rather solely because of the color of their skins. It is unnecessary in 20th-century America to have individual Negroes demonstrate that they have been victims of racial discrimination; the racism of our society has been so pervasive that none, regardless of wealth or position, has managed to escape its impact. The experience of Negroes in America has been different in kind, not just in degree, from that of other ethnic groups. It is not merely the history of slavery alone but also that a whole people were marked as inferior by the law. And that mark has endured. The dream of America as the great melting pot has not been realized for the Negro; because of his skin color he never even made it into the pot. ***

It is because of a legacy of unequal treatment that we now must permit the institutions of this society to give consideration to race in making decisions about who will hold the positions of influence, affluence, and prestige in America. For far too long, the doors to those positions have been shut to Negroes. If we are ever to become a fully integrated society, one in which the color of a person's skin will not determine the opportunities available to him or her, we must be willing to take steps to open those doors. I do not believe that anyone can truly look into America's past and still find that a remedy for the effects of that past is impermissible. ***

Mr. Justice Blackmun

*** At least until the early 1970's, apparently only a very small number, less than 2%, of the physicians, attorneys, and medical and law students in the United States were members of what we now refer to as minority groups. In addition, approximately three-fourths of our Negro physicians were trained at only two medical schools. If ways are not found to remedy that situation, the country can never achieve its professed goal of a society that is not race conscious. I yield to no one in my earnest hope that the time will come when an "affirmative action" program is unnecessary and is, in truth, only a relic of the past. . . . Then persons will be regarded as persons, and discrimination of the type we address today will be an ugly feature of history that is instructive but that is behind us. ***

It is somewhat ironic to have us so deeply disturbed over a program where race is an element of consciousness, and yet to be aware of the fact, as we are, that institutions of higher learning, albeit more on the undergraduate than the graduate level, have given conceded preferences up to a point to those possessed of athletic skills, to the children of alumni, to the affluent who may bestow their largess on the institutions, and to those having connections with celebrities, the famous, and the powerful. ***

I, of course, accept the propositions that (a) Fourteenth Amendment rights are personal; (b) racial and ethnic distinctions where they are stereotypes are inherently suspect and call for exacting judicial scrutiny; (c) academic freedom is a special concern of the First Amendment; and (d) the Fourteenth Amendment has expanded beyond its original 1868 concept and now is recognized to have reached a point where . . . it embraces a "broader principle." This enlargement does not mean for me, however, that the Fourteenth Amendment has broken away from its moorings and its original intended purposes. Those original aims persist. And that, in a distinct sense, is what "affirmative action," in the face of proper facts, is all about.

I am not convinced, as MR. JUSTICE POWELL seems to be, that the difference between the Davis program and the one employed by Harvard is very profound or constitutionally significant. The line between the two is a thin and indistinct one. . . . The cynical, of course, may say that under a program such as Harvard's one may accomplish covertly what Davis concedes it does openly. . . .

I suspect that it would be impossible to arrange an affirmative-action program in a racially neutral way and have it successful. To ask that this be so is to demand the impossible. In order to get beyond racism, we must first take account of race. There is no other way. And in order to treat some persons equally, we must treat them differently. We cannot—we dare not—let the Equal Protection Clause perpetuate racial supremacy.

Questions

1. How exactly did the medical school's special admissions program work? According to Bakke, how did it disadvantage him?

2. What level of scrutiny did the Supreme Court apply? What does this level of scrutiny require?

3. The university identified four purposes for its special admissions program. What are they? Did the Court find any of them compelling? Why did the Court conclude that the medical school's program violated the equal protection clause?

4. What kind of admissions program does the Court recommend? In what significant ways does it differ from the one the Court is rejecting?

5. Do you agree with Justice Powell that "the guarantee of equal protection cannot mean one thing when applied to one individual and something else when applied to a person of another color"? Or is there a difference between providing special opportunities to Whites and providing special opportunities to members of historically disadvantaged groups?

6. Is Justice Marshall correct that we have not yet become a color-blind society? Or do you think the need for affirmative action has passed?

7. What does Justice Blackmun mean when he says, "In order to get beyond racism, we must first take account of race. . . . And in order to treat some persons equally, we must treat them differently." Do you agree or disagree? Why?

CHAPTER 16 PRACTICE TEST

The following questions will test your application and analysis of the content found within this chapter. For additional assessment, including licensing-exam type questions on applying chapter content to practice behaviors, visit **MySearchLab**.

1. Which of the following does Title VII of the Civil Rights Act protect against?

   a. Ben, an American Indian, is routinely subjected to racial slurs on the job from both colleagues and upper management.

   b. Mary, an employee at a private investment firm, is overlooked for a promotion because she is a lesbian.

   c. Peter, a middle-aged man, discovers that he is being paid less than his younger counterparts.

   d. Sarah is convinced that she was laid off from her job as an elementary school teacher because of her recent struggle with cancer.

2. Which of the following forms of housing discrimination involves refusing to extend loans or credit to people living in racially dense neighborhoods?

   a. racial steering

   b. redlining

   c. restrictive covenants

   d. zoning laws

3. Which of the following is true of limited English proficient (LEP) students?

   a. School systems are under no legal obligation to help them overcome language barriers.

   b. They are less likely to graduate than other students.

   c. They do best when required to study exclusively in English.

   d. They outperform other students in math and science.

4. When a court considers a case of racial discrimination under the equal protection clause, it applies

   a. minimal scrutiny.

   b. intermediate scrutiny.

   c. strict scrutiny.

   d. the rational basis test.

5. Describe the process involved in pursuing a claim of employment discrimination under Title VII of the Civil Rights Act.

6. Discuss the Supreme Court's decision in *Korematsu v. United States*. What does it say about how we regard racial and ethnic minorities when our national security is threatened? Can you draw any more recent parallels?

MYSEARCHLAB CONNECTIONS

Reinforce what you learned in this chapter by studying videos, cases, documents,
and more available at **www.MySearchLab.com.**

Watch these Videos

⋆ Supreme Court: No Race-based Admissions (2007)

- *How can local school districts insure that their schools are racially integrated? What strategies are and aren't legally permissible?*

⋆ Trials of Racial Identity in Nineteenth Century America

- *Historically, what was the role of the legal system when it came to issues of race? How would you describe its role today?*

Read these Cases/Documents

Δ Plessy v. Ferguson (1896)

- *What reasoning did the majoirty of the Supreme Court use in concluding that "separate but equal" was Consitutionally acceptable? What reasoning did Justice Harlan use in his dissent to reach the opposite conclusion?*

Explore these Assets

- Website: National Urban League
- Website: The National Association of Black Social Workers (NABSW)

Research these Topics

- racial harassment

Assess Your Knowledge

Go to **MySearchLab** to test your knowledge of key topics in this chapter with topic-specific quizzes. Conclude your assessment by completing the chapter exam.

⋆ = CSWE Core Competency Asset   Δ= Case Study

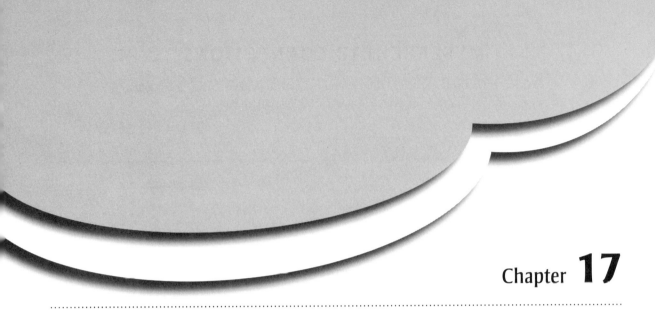

Legal Rights of Women

As we have seen, both the U.S. Constitution and federal laws, including the Civil Rights Act of 1964, have been used to help ensure the equal treatment of racial and ethnic minorities. Despite these efforts and the progress that has resulted from them, many inequities remain. This chapter discusses the legal rights of another group that, although not a minority, has nonetheless experienced a history of discrimination in the United States: women. The chapter begins with a brief history and then discusses sex discrimination under the equal protection clause, and women's legal rights in employment and education. A special section highlights the issue of same-sex education, and the sample case addresses the rights of women who are pregnant.

Background

Brief History

The fight for equal rights for women has a long and complex history. The "women's movement" represents a centuries-long process of seeking equal treatment through political, legal, and social reform. It is generally divided into two periods of activity. The first wave spanned the years 1840 to 1920 and was marked by the increased involvement of women in the antislavery (or *abolitionist*) movement (Becker, Bowman, & Torrey, 2001). The abolitionist movement was important in the early stages of the women's movement because it presented women with an egalitarian framework for social change, as well as a forum for espousing their beliefs. As women became more socially and politically active, they began to realize that confronting the wrongs of slavery was inextricably linked to obtaining equal rights for all people, including themselves. The women's movement gained momentum and, in 1869, the National Women's Suffrage Movement began its fight to enfranchise women under the Constitution. Although the fight for women's voting rights lasted another 52 years, the interim period, known as the Progressive Era, was marked by notable accomplishments related to improving policies and conditions for low-income women, working-class women, and immigrants.

The ratification of the 19th Amendment in 1920 granted voting rights to women and ushered in the second wave of the women's movement. This period was marked by the continued growth and development of a feminist ideology, as well as the expansion of public supports for women in the areas of welfare, maternal and child health, and citizenship rights for immigrants' wives (Becker et al., 2001). Legislative milestones including the Equal Pay Act of 1963 and the Civil Rights Act of 1964 have helped enshrine women's rights in law. There were, however, significant setbacks, including the failure of the Equal Rights Amendment to be incorporated into the Constitution.

Summary of Federal Laws

Sex discrimination cases can be brought as challenges under the U.S. Constitution (usually the *equal protection clause* of the 14th Amendment) or under specific federal and state laws. The two major federal laws most relevant to sex discrimination are the following:

- **Civil Rights Act of 1964.** Prohibits discrimination on the basis of race, color, religion, sex, and national origin; it also prohibits discrimination based on stereotypes or assumptions about a group's traits, intelligence, or abilities. Provisions that are most relevant to women include Title VII, which addresses employment discrimination, and Title IX, which prohibits discrimination in educational programs and activities.
- **Equal Pay Act of 1963.** Prohibits discrimination on the basis of sex in the payment of wages.

Sex and the Equal Protection Clause

As with race and national origin, the equal protection clause of the 14th Amendment has played a prominent role in relation to discrimination on the basis of sex. Sex, however, has proven to be a more difficult subject for the courts in many ways. First, as discussed previously, the original purpose of the 14th Amendment was to bring the newly freed African American slaves into the mainstream of American society; applying it to women represented a significant expansion of that original intent. Second, because there are indeed some actual physical differences between the sexes, the courts must determine under what circumstances it is permissible for the law to treat them differently.

The Early Cases

Historically, the courts' treatment of men and women reflected what was known as the *separate spheres doctrine*. Men were thought to belong to the public sphere of the working world, whereas women were thought to belong to the private sphere of family life. The courts traditionally upheld differential treatment of men and women on the basis of either their physical characteristics or their respective roles within the family. A good example is *Bradwell v. Illinois* (1873). This case concerned a woman who had learned law from her husband and qualified for the Illinois state bar. She was nonetheless denied admission because she was a married woman. The U.S. Supreme Court sided with the state, arguing in essence that women have the same rights as men to pursue an occupation—but for women that occupation is wife and mother. A concurring opinion captured this well (p. 141):

> The civil law, as well as nature herself, has always recognized a wide difference in the respective sphere and destinies of man and woman. Man is, or should be, woman's protector and defender. The natural and proper timidity and delicacy which belongs to the female sex evidently unfits it for many of the occupations of civil life ... the paramount destiny and mission of woman are to fulfill the noble and benign offices of wife and mother. This is the law of the Creator.

In the early 20th century, the same rationale relied upon in *Bradwell* was used to uphold protectionist laws that regulated working conditions for women. In *Muller v. Oregon* (1908), the Supreme Court upheld a state law that restricted working hours for women employed in a laundry, based on their physical characteristics and maternal functions. In *Radice v. New York* (1924), the Court upheld a law barring women from working in restaurants between the hours of 10:00 p.m. and 6:00 a.m. to protect them from exposure to the dangers of night life in the big city.

Sex discrimination cases began to proliferate in the 1940s, largely as a result of the changed experiences of women during World War II. The courts, however, continued to dismiss these challenges. *Goesart v. Cleary* (1948) involved a challenge to a Michigan law that prohibited women from being licensed as barmaids unless they were the wives or daughters of the (male) owner. The Supreme Court upheld the state's statute, arguing in part (p. 465):

> The Fourteenth Amendment did not tear history up by the roots, and the regulation of the liquor traffic is one of the oldest and most untrammeled of legislative powers. Michigan could, beyond question, forbid all women from working behind a bar. . . . The fact that women may now have achieved the virtues that men have long claimed as their prerogatives, and now indulge in vices that men have long practiced, does not preclude the States from drawing a sharp line between the sexes.

In 1961, the Court heard the case of Gweldolyn Hoyt, who killed her husband with a baseball bat because he had been unfaithful (*Hoyt v. Florida*). She argued that the state of Florida had violated her rights under the equal protection clause by trying her in front of an all-male jury. The Court disagreed, concluding that it was permissible for states to preclude women from jury service because of their role in the family. Notice that this is essentially the same issue that was addressed in *Strauder v. West Virginia*, except that case involved the racial composition of juries and was decided (in the plaintiff's favor) 82 years earlier! This underscores the fact that although the pursuits of equal rights for women and racial minorities have in some ways followed a similar path, the timetables have been vastly different.

One reason involves the level of scrutiny used by the courts to analyze these discrimination cases. When it came to race, strict scrutiny was applied. With sex discrimination, however, the courts traditionally applied minimal scrutiny. Minimal scrutiny is the easiest burden for the state to meet, requiring only that the challenged law be rationally related to some legitimate government interest. Laws subjected to minimal scrutiny are nearly always upheld.

The Modern Cases

The landscape for women began to change in the 1970s with a district court case, *Seidenberg v. McSorleys Old Ale House* (1970). In that case, the court struck down a New York statute that excluded women from a pub that had served only men for 115 years. The court applied minimal scrutiny but found no rational basis for the law. A Supreme Court case quickly followed on its heels. *Reed v. Reed* (1971) involved an Idaho statute that delineated who was legally entitled to administer the estate of someone who died *intestate* (without a will). It set forth a hierarchy of categories, starting with the surviving spouse, moving on to the children of the deceased, and so on. The third category read "the father or mother." The law specified that when members of the same category both sought to administer the estate, the male must be preferred. That is what happened here; the mother sued and the case reached the U.S. Supreme Court. In analyzing the case, the Court applied minimal scrutiny but struck down the law as violating the equal protection clause. This was the first time in history that the U.S. Supreme Court struck down a law on the basis of sex discrimination.

The times were ripe for this response. The early 1970s, as previously discussed, was a period of significant growth in the women's movement. In 1972, the U.S. Congress passed the Equal Rights Amendment; although it ultimately failed to attract sufficient popular support for ratification by the states, it was emblematic of the times. In 1973, the Supreme Court heard another important sex discrimination case, *Frontiero v. Richardson*. This case involved a law that treated men and women differently in terms of their eligibility for military spousal allowances. Whereas women could automatically be claimed as dependents by their husbands, the reverse was not true; a woman in the military seeking benefits for her husband was required to prove that he was dependent on her for more than half of his support. The Court struck down the law as violating the equal protection clause. More significantly, it applied strict scrutiny. Similar cases followed, all of which applied strict scrutiny to sex-based classifications, even when men were the aggrieved population. That approach continued until the 1976 case of *Craig v. Boren*.

Craig v. Boren involved an Oklahoma statute that prohibited the sale of 3.2 (low-alcohol) beer to women younger than 18 and men younger than 21. A young man brought a challenge, claiming that it was a violation of equal protection to have one minimum age for women and another for men. The Supreme Court agreed and struck down the law. However in doing so, it applied an entirely new level of scrutiny—neither minimal nor strict. In essence, the Court abandoned its two-tier approach to equal protection analysis and adopted a third level of scrutiny for sex discrimination cases. *Intermediate* (or *heightened*) *scrutiny* requires that a sex-based classification be "substantially related to an important government objective." As Table 17.1 illustrates, this standard falls between the other two. Applying strict scrutiny almost always results in striking down a law, and applying minimal scrutiny almost always results in upholding a law; cases in which intermediate scrutiny is applied can go either way.

A little more explanation might be helpful. We consider it permissible to treat different groups of people differently when there are relevant differences between them. As discussed in Chapter 16, differences based on race or national origin are almost never considered to be relevant; the Court regards these as *suspect classifications* and affords them special protection against discrimination by requiring a compelling justification for treating them differently. Over time, the courts have enunciated the following criteria to define a suspect classification:

- A discrete, identifiable group
- Isolated or segregated from the rest of society
- Has experienced historical discrimination
- Lacks political power
- Is defined by an immutable characteristic not readily amenable to change

To date, only race and national origin have consistently met these criteria. Once a classification is determined to be suspect, it triggers the application of strict scrutiny; in other words, the state's justification is very closely examined and the discriminatory law is generally struck down.

Sex is considered a *semi-suspect* classification because sometimes there are relevant differences between men and women and sometimes there are not. The courts do not subject these classifications to the same exacting scrutiny they apply to race, but they do subject them to greater scrutiny than is applied in most other kinds of cases. Since *Craig v. Boren,* the courts have consistently applied intermediate scrutiny to sex discrimination claims under the equal protection clause.

Rights in Employment

The presence and role of women in the workforce has changed significantly over time. Throughout the 19th and early 20th centuries, women in the United States were primarily engaged in service provision and household-related work (Barney, 2006). Opportunities

TABLE 17.1 **Levels of Scrutiny Under Equal Protection Analysis**

Classification	Level of Scrutiny	Government Purpose	Relationship of Classification to Purpose
Suspect (race)	Strict	Compelling	Necessarily related
Semi-suspect (sex)	Intermediate	Important	Substantially related
Non-suspect	Minimal	Legitimate	Rationally related

for female workers expanded significantly during World War II. During this period, women assumed jobs traditionally held by men, while men served in the armed forces (Groneman & Norman, 1994). Although men returned to their jobs after the war, the presence of women in the workforce remained strong.

Today, women comprise nearly half of all U.S. workers and more than three-quarters of American women ages 25-54 participate in the labor force (Barsh & Yee, 2011). Figure 17.1 illustrates the changes in women's workforce participation over time, including projections for the years to come.

In the event that women experience discrimination on the job, their rights are protected not only by the 14th Amendment's equal protection clause, but by the Civil Rights Act of 1964 and the Equal Pay Act of 1963.

Compensation and Equal Pay

The Equal Pay Act of 1963 prohibits employers from paying workers of one sex less than workers of the other for equal work. Claims under the Equal Pay Act are filed with the Equal Employment Opportunity Commission (EEOC), discussed in Chapter 16. The EEOC has sole responsibility for administering and enforcing the Equal Pay Act.

As is often the case, the seemingly simple notion of "equal pay for equal work" turns out to be quite complex. How does the law view "equality" with respect to both pay and work? The law defines pay as including all forms of compensation including not only salary, but also bonuses, insurance, vacation time, sick leave, clothing allowances, and transportation (Player, 2004). This was demonstrated in *Arizona Governing Committee v. Norris* (1983), in which a state employee in Arizona brought a claim against her employer for discriminating in the provision of retirement benefits. The

FIGURE 17.1   **Civilian Labor Force Participation Rates by Sex (Real and Projected)**

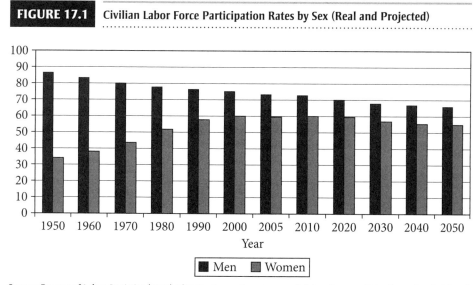

Source: Bureau of Labor Statistics (2007) Changes in men's and women's labor force participation rates. Retrieved from http://www.bls.gov/opub/ted/2007/jan/wk2/art03.htm.

state supreme court ruled in her favor, holding that Title VII (which includes relevant provisions of the Equal Pay Act) prohibits an employer from paying women a lower monthly annuity than men when they have contributed the same amount into the plan over a comparable period of time.

As for the meaning of "equal work," the Fair Pay Act defines it as "jobs that require equal skill, effort, and responsibility, and are performed under similar working conditions" (§206 U.S.C. 29[d][1]). There are exceptions for factors unrelated to sex, including merit and seniority. Not surprisingly, questions remain regarding how to gauge the equality of work since no two situations are completely alike. Courts will typically look at the actual duties performed, although unless a man and a woman are executing the same tasks on the same shift in the same unit of the same company, the analysis must be more complex. In *Hodgson v. Miller Brewing Co.* (1974), female employees filed a discrimination claim based on the company's relegation of female employees to one shift during daytime hours. The company also paid female employees 70 cents less per hour, and those employees working at night received extra pay as a shift differential. The Court found the company in violation of the Equal Pay Act on three counts: relegating all women to the day shift; paying women less overall for work that required equal skill, effort and responsibility; and awarding additional pay for the night shift which was available only to male employees.

Comparable Worth

One of the shortcomings of the notion of equal pay is that it fails to account for the tendency of women to work in lower-paying occupations than men. Ideally, pay should be a function of the value of the labor provided, regardless of its exact contours and who is performing it. We know, however, that job allocation continues to reflect historical norms and social traditions. Although there is a great deal of variation globally across cultures and economies with respect to what jobs are considered men's work and women's work, many jobs in the United States are impacted by preconceived notions of gender. Women tend to dominate in jobs such as teaching, nursing, and social work, which pay "women's wages" (Becker et al., 2001). This segregation of the sexes in regard to employment is striking and has huge implications for the prospect of equal pay. In 2010, the Institute for Women's Policy Research documented a 51% sex segregation index for women with some level of college education in the civilian labor force (Hegewisch, Liepmann, Hayes, & Hartmann, 2010). This means that more than half of women in the workforce would have to change jobs for the sexes to be equally distributed across occupations. In terms of pay, data from the U.S. Bureau of Labor Statistics indicate that although women comprise 48.9% of the full-time year-round workforce, median annual wages are more than $10,000 less for women than for men (DeNavas-Walt, Proctor, & Smith, 2011). Table 17.2 shows the states with the largest and smallest wage gaps between college-educated men and women in full-time, year-round positions.

The reasons behind these discrepancies are many. There is evidence that women are not as proactive as men when it comes to negotiating salaries (Elmasry, 2011). Women and men also have different relationships to the workforce. Whereas most men have a fairly straightforward attachment to the labor force as the "breadwinners," women are more likely to be balancing work and family. In an effort to remediate these issues, several

TABLE 17.2 Best and Worst States for Equal Pay in the United States

Best States			Worst States		
Rank	State	Women's Earnings as a Percentage of Men's	Rank	State	Women's Earnings as a Percentage of Men's
1	West Virginia	89	42	Washington	71
2	District of Columbia	89	43	Massachusetts	70
3	Vermont	83	44	Florida	70
4	Alaska	82	45	Kansas	70
5	New York	82	46	Alabama	69
6	Maine	82	47	South Carolina	68
7	Idaho	82	48	Indiana	67
8	North Dakota	81	49	Virginia	67
9	Nevada	78	50	New Jersey	66
10	California	78	51	Louisiana	64

Source: Adapted from *State Median Annual Earnings and Earnings Ratio for Full-Time, Year-Round Workers Age 16 and Older* by Gender, 2009 fact sheet. Copyright © by the American Association of University Women. Reprinted with permission.

states have adopted comparable worth standards under which men and women filling jobs of similar value receive equal pay. Essentially, this involves evaluating positions, ranking them in terms of importance, and determining pay scales accordingly. In 2001, Maine became the first state to require equal pay for comparable worth not only for public employees but for private sector employees as well. The U.S. government has yet to adopt a comparable worth standard. Evaluation data from implementation of comparable worth in Ontario (Canada) show a reduction in the wage gap of 25% but also reveal difficulty in attracting new employers to the province from outside Canada (Becker et al., 2001; Weaver, 1991).

The struggle for equal pay persists. The National Committee for Pay Equity, an advocacy coalition of which NASW is a member, sponsors a national day of action each year to promote fair pay and economic justice for women and minorities. The date for Equal Pay Day varies each year, falling on the day that symbolizes how far into the current year women must work to earn what men earned in the previous calendar year. In 2012, Equal Pay Day fell on April 17. This means that it took women 107 extra days of work to close the sex-based wage gap with men (National Committee on Pay Equity, 2012).

Hiring, Promotion, and Termination

Hiring, promotion, and termination represent other areas in which workplace discrimination can occur. They are governed by Title VII of the Civil Rights Act of 1964, which addresses not only sex-based discrimination, but also discrimination based on race, color, religion, and national origin. Ironically, sex was added to the bill at the last minute, as an attempt to torpedo its passage. Instead, the bill passed with "sex" firmly embedded among the enumerated protected classes. Employment discrimination against groups identified under Title VII is illegal under both state and federal law, and some states have enacted additional legislation that prohibits employment discrimination. As described in Chapter 16, claims under Title VII are filed with the EEOC. If the case ultimately goes to court, the plaintiff must establish a *prima facie* case of discrimination, at which point the burden of proof shifts to the defendant to produce a legitimate, nondiscriminatory reason for the employment action. Another defense to a charge of sex discrimination is business necessity. Winning a sex discrimination case may result in a monetary award or in *injunctive relief*—for example, prohibiting an employer from engaging in a particular behavior or ordering that a worker be reinstated.

Not unlike cases of race discrimination, proving discrimination is easiest in the presence of policies or practices that explicitly disadvantage one sex or the other. When a policy or practice is neutral on its face, proving sex discrimination can be more difficult. Here, the rules governing disparate treatment and disparate impact come into play. Most difficult of all is proving a case on the basis of a de facto classification that results in disparities in working conditions or wages. All of this is similar to what was discussed in the previous chapter in relation to employment discrimination based on race.

The details of filing an EEOC claim became headline news in 2007 in connection with the U.S. Supreme Court case of *Ledbetter vs. Goodyear Tire Co*. In that case, a woman who had worked for the company for 19 years brought an action under Title VII, claiming that the company had failed to evaluate her fairly and that she had thus been denied equal pay on the basis of sex under the company's merit plan. Although she and her male coworkers started with the same pay, at the time of her retirement she was earning less than the lowest-paid man. Although a jury in the lower court found in her favor, the court of appeals ruled that she had failed to file her claim with the EEOC in a timely manner; claims must be filed within 180 days of the discriminatory action. She argued that her pay during the 180-day window was affected by decisions that had been made by her employer over the course of many years. The U.S. Supreme Court, in a 5–4 decision authored by Justice Alito, agreed with the court of appeals and Ledbetter lost. Justice Ginsburg, writing for the dissent, argued that applying the 180-day limit did not make sense because pay discrimination often occurs in small increments that cannot be readily detected by an employee. In response to the Supreme Court's holding, Congress enacted the Lilly Ledbetter Fair Pay Act of 2009, which clarifies that claims for pay discrimination must be filed with the EEOC within 180 days of the most recent discriminatory act when discrimination has occurred over a period of time. This effectively reverses the Supreme Court's ruling.

Although the *Ledbetter* case ultimately had a happy ending, another recent Supreme Court case once again interpreted the law to make it more difficult for people claiming sex discrimination to prevail. *Wal-Mart Stores, Inc. v. Dukes* (2011) concerned the largest class action job discrimination case in history, potentially affecting 1.5 million women who claimed to have suffered pay and promotion bias at the hands of their employer. At issue was the question of whether the women joining the suit could properly be certified as a class—that is, whether they were similarly situated and could join their individual claims to sue as a single group. Although the lower courts ruled in their favor, the U.S. Supreme Court found in favor of their employer, Wal-Mart. In writing for a five-member majority, Justice Scalia argued that the women had failed to identify any specific company policy that had a common effect on all of the women in the class; he said that the women were trying to sue for millions of different employment decisions at once. The dissenting justices argued that discrimination resulted from widespread bias that suffused the company culture, brought about by stereotypes that demeaned women. They chastised the majority for ignoring what united the women's claims and examining only their differences. In the end, the Court established a new and more rigorous definition of what is required to initiate a class action suit; this is bound to be disadvantageous to those seeking redress from discrimination.

Sexual Harassment

Sexual harassment is another pervasive form of discrimination in the workplace. Unwelcome sexual advances, requests for sexual favors, and other verbal or physical overtures of a sexual nature can constitute sexual harassment when submission to, or rejection of, this behavior explicitly or implicitly affects an individual's employment; unreasonably interferes with an individual's job performance; or creates an intimidating, hostile, or offensive work environment.

As one might expect, sexual harassment is often emotionally volatile and the law has been subject to repeated interpretation and clarification. Claims of sexual harassment are evaluated in terms of three main qualities: circumstance, conduct, and degree of severity or pervasiveness. The *circumstances* under which sexual harassment occurs can be quite varied. According to the EEOC (2002), the scope of harassment includes the following:

- The victim may be a man or a woman, and the harasser may be a man or a woman. Both opposite-sex and same-sex victimization is recognized.
- The harasser may be the victim's supervisor, an agent of the employer, a supervisor in another area, a coworker, or a nonemployee.
- The victim does not have to be the person who is actually harassed but may be anyone affected by the offensive conduct.
- Unlawful sexual harassment may occur even if the victim suffers no economic injury and is not discharged.

The harasser's *conduct* must be unwelcome. Many types of conduct can be interpreted as unwelcome under the right conditions, including the following:

- **Oral or Written Statements.** These include comments about a person's clothing, personal behavior, or body; sexual or sex-based jokes; requests for sexual favors or repeated attempts to ask someone out; sexual innuendoes; rumors about a person's personal or sex life; and threats against a person.
- **Physical Acts.** These include assault; impeding or blocking a person's movement; inappropriate touching of a person or their clothing; and kissing, hugging, patting, or stroking.

- **Nonverbal Behavior.** This includes looking up and down a person's body; derogatory gestures or expressions of a sexual nature; following someone around the office, to their home, and so on.
- **Visual Behaviors.** These include creating, displaying, or sharing posters, drawings, pictures, screensavers, or emails of a sexual nature.
- **Nonsexual Conduct.** This includes harassment that is not sexual in nature but is directed at a person because of his or her sex.

Finally, the degree of *severity or pervasiveness* must be sufficient to "alter the conditions of the [victim's] employment and create an abusive working environment" (Kleinschmidt, 2005, p. 1123). Severity has to do with the egregiousness of the act, and pervasiveness relates to its duration and consistency over time.

In addition to these characteristics, two major types of harassment have developed in the law: quid pro quo and hostile environment:

- **Quid Pro Quo Harassment.** *Quid pro quo* is a Latin term that refers to an exchange of goods or services. In the harassment context, it refers to when a subordinate is promised a job benefit in exchange for submitting to an unwelcome sexual advance, usually from someone in a position of power. For example, a supervisor tells an employee that he will recommend her for a raise if she agrees to go out with him.
- **Hostile Environment Harassment.** This type of harassment exists when an employee is subjected to unwelcome comments, behaviors, or materials of a sexual nature as a repeated part of the workday. In these cases, the courts examine the frequency and severity of the action in question. Unlike *quid pro quo* harassment, hostile environment harassment can be perpetrated not only by supervisors, but also by coworkers or even customers (MacKinnon, 2001, p. 942). Unless an action is exceptionally egregious, isolated incidents are generally not sufficient to warrant a finding of hostile environment sexual harassment.

Not surprisingly, defining a hostile work environment as sexual harassment was initially controversial. What put it on the map was *Meritor Savings Bank v. Vinson* (1986), in which an assistant branch manager sued, claiming that her supervisor had sexually harassed her during her first 4 years on the job. At first she had refused his advances, but she later submitted out of fear that he would fire her if she failed to acquiesce. She argued that his actions created a hostile work environment. The bank pointed out that she had regularly been promoted and was never denied any economic or tangible benefit. Thus, they claimed, no discrimination had taken place. The Supreme Court found in the employee's favor, concluding that Title VII's language regarding the "terms, conditions and privileges of employment" is meant to be broadly interpreted to "strike at the entire spectrum of disparate treatment of men and women."

Although *quid pro quo* and hostile environment harassment can be easily distinguished in theory, in reality they are harder to differentiate since *quid pro quo* harassment invariably creates a hostile work environment. In any event, both types of sexual harassment are legally actionable and both carry the same consequences. Their only difference concerns the conditions under which companies can be held vicariously liable for the behavior of individuals within their employ. With *quid pro quo* harassment, a company is liable for a supervisor's behavior if it culminates in a tangible employment action such as resignation or administrative leave—or, in the case of unfulfilled threats, if the harassment is severe and pervasive. In cases involving a hostile work environment, the company is liable for harassment by its employees unless it can demonstrate that (1) it exercised reasonable care to prevent and promptly correct any harassing behavior, and (2) the employee unreasonably failed to take advantage of any opportunities provided by the employer or to avoid harm.

An important case regarding an employer's vicarious liability for *quid pro quo* harassment by a supervisor is *Burlington Industries v. Ellerth* (1998). In that case, an employee alleged that she was repeatedly subjected to "boorish and offensive remarks and gestures" by her immediate supervisor. Although she rebuffed all of his advances, she placed particular emphasis on several instances when he suggested, after advising her to "loosen up," that he could make her life "very hard or very easy at Burlington." She testified that she did not complain about his harassment while she was still there for fear that doing so would jeopardize her job. She sought to recover from both her supervisor and the company. The employer argued that it should take more than a threat to make companies financially responsible for a supervisor's conduct and that, in the absence of a definitive job action such as termination or demotion, it should not be held liable. Ultimately, the Supreme Court sided with the employee, holding that an employee can sue for sexual harassment even in the absence of any adverse, tangible consequences and can recover against the company without showing that it was in any way at fault for the supervisor's actions. If a threat is made but not carried out, however, it must meet the "severe or pervasive" test in order to constitute sexual harassment.

Imposing liability on an employer for behavior by individuals within the company helps shift the risks and burdens associated with sexual harassment from the employee to the employer. It essentially requires employers to promulgate policies and enforce procedures prohibiting sexual harassment, train and sensitize their staff, and establish a mechanism for grievances to be heard. These policies and procedures have the potential to decrease the incidence of sexual harassment, enabling women to achieve their full potential in the workplace (Equal Rights Advocates, 2011).

Pursuing a Claim with the EEOC

Although the number of sexual harassment complaints filed with the EEOC has declined from approximately 16,000 in 2007 to 12,000 in 2010, they still comprise the largest share (30%) of all complaints filed (EEOC, 2010). Even so, research on sexual harassment suggests significant underreporting. Although one in four women reports having experienced sexual harassment at work, only 41% of them reported it to their employer (MacKinnon, 2001; Langer, 2011).

When an employee believes that she or he has been the victim of sex-based employment discrimination, a claim must be filed with the EEOC before a private lawsuit can be brought. Because bias in compensation, hiring, promotion, termination, and sexual harassment are all considered workplace discrimination, the EEOC's protocol for evaluating their validity is the same. The complainant has the burden of proving that the details of the case are consistent with the law's definition of sex discrimination. Sex discrimination claims follow the same process outlined in Chapter 16 in relation to race discrimination. An investigation is initiated, after which the case may be resolved through settlement, mediation, conciliation, a trial, or dismissal.

Rights in Education

In addition to addressing discrimination in the workplace, the Civil Rights Act addresses discrimination in education. Specifically, Title IX prohibits sex discrimination in federally funded educational institutions:

> No person shall, on the basis of sex, be excluded from participation in, be denied the benefits of, or subjected to discrimination under any program or activity receiving Federal financial assistance. (20 U.S.C §1681[a])

Note that only programs or activities receiving federal funds are covered by the requirements of Title IX. Early cases, most notably *Grove City College v. Bell* (1984), interpreted this provision narrowly. In that case, a small college had consistently declined federal financial assistance; many of its students, however, were recipients of scholarships and other financial aid administered by the U.S. Department of Education. The Supreme Court concluded that this does indeed qualify as federal financial assistance, but it limited the applicability of Title IX to the college's financial aid office. This logic was overturned by the enactment of the Civil Rights Restoration Act of 1987, which specified that Title IX applies to the entire institution if any part of the institution is the recipient of federal funds.

SINGLE-SEX EDUCATION

Single-sex education in private schools has long been commonplace, but it has only recently begun to make a significant showing in the public school arena. In single-sex education, male and female students attend separate schools or classes. Although popular in earlier decades, by 1995 there were only two single-sex public schools in the United States (Weil, 2008). Today, however, the National Association for Single Sex Public Education (NASSPE, 2011a) counts more than 100 single-sex public schools and almost 400 public schools that provide single-sex classes (other than for physical education, health, or sex education).

This resurgence derives from a belief that students—both male and female—achieve greater academic success and have better attitudes toward school when taught in single-sex environments. Opponents, on the other hand, are concerned that single-sex academic settings reinforce negative gender stereotypes, offer no social benefits, and provide little in the way of opposite-sex role models for students (Jost, 2002).

With the 1972 enactment of Title IX, single-sex education became less common. Under Title IX, sex discrimination in federally funded educational institutions is prohibited unless it is part of an affirmative action plan. The law requires that males and females have equal educational experiences in school, which is best accomplished through coeducational instruction (Pollard, 1999).

In 2006, the U.S. Department of Education issued new regulations for the No Child Left Behind Act (NCLB) addressing single-sex education in public schools. *Single-sex classes* may be offered within coed schools as long as the school (1) has an acceptable rationale for offering a single-sex class in that subject, (2) makes a coeducational class in the same subject available at a geographically accessible location, and (3) conducts a biennial review to determine whether single-sex classes are necessary as a remedy for past inequities (NASSPE, 2011b). *Single-sex schools* are permissible as long as substantially equal courses, services, and facilities are provided at other schools in the same school district; these other schools may be single sex or coeducational (NASSPE, 2011b).

The courts have both affirmed and struck down single-sex educational programs. In *Vorchheimer v. School District of Philadelphia* (1976), a female high school student was denied admission to Central High School, an all-male public school. Because there was an equally prestigious all-female magnet program at Girls High, the U.S. Supreme Court ruled that Central High School's admissions requirements did not violate the equal protection clause of the 14th Amendment. Twenty years later, the U.S. Supreme Court struck down the male-only admissions policy at the Virginia Military Institute (VMI), the last all-male public university in the United States.

Pursuant to a lower court decision, VMI attempted to meet the equal protection requirement by establishing a parallel female-only program at Mary Baldwin College, a women's college. However, in *United States v. Virginia* (1996), the Supreme Court found that the parallel program fell short of being comparable to VMI in rigor, reputation, facilities, courses, financial opportunities, faculty, and alumni connections.

On balance, it seems that single-sex education is permissible as long as an alternative of substantially equal quality is readily available. Although some observers see parallels between racially segregated schools and same-sex education, single-sex schools remain legally acceptable.

Sex Discrimination in Athletics

Despite the absence of any explicit mention of sports in the language of the statute, Title IX is best known for its impact on high school and college athletics. Sex discrimination challenges by women in the athletic arena typically have one of two aims: permitting females to play on the same teams with males or requiring the creation of separate programs for females (MacKinnon, 2001). Each is problematic in its own way. When women have argued for inclusion on male teams, courts have concluded that females are fundamentally different from males both physically and psychologically, and thus not "similarly situated" to perform at the same level. This reasoning has been used to justify more restrictive rules for female sports. The alternate approach, separate all-girl teams, requires high schools, colleges, and universities to commit additional funding which, depending on the level of female interest in a particular sport, may not be the best use of resources. Also, the issue of comparable worth is inadequately addressed when girls are given their own team but are prohibited from playing with boys. This impasse has created a serious tension between "the need of individual women to play on men's teams in order to play their best, and the need of most women to play with the best women in order to have a team at all" (MacKinnon, 2001, p. 371).

Cohen v. Brown University (1996) involved a claim that the university had violated Title IX in the operation of its intercollegiate athletics program. In response to a university-wide cost-cutting directive, the university relegated its women's gymnastics and volleyball teams to being donor funded rather than university funded. At the same time, it made the same change in relation to two men's teams, golf and water polo. Although the university's actions appeared to be even-handed, the plaintiffs argued that at the time the changes were made, the university's male athletes already enjoyed a disproportionately large percentage of university funding and had more options available to them for sports participation than women did. As a result, the lack of funding for gymnastics and volleyball represented a discriminatory act on the part of the university, disproportionately affecting female athletes. In deciding the case, the Court applied a three-prong test developed by the Office for Civil Rights (OCR) in the U.S. Department of Education, which has jurisdiction over Title IX claims. Under that test, a federally funded institution is protected from a discrimination claim if it can demonstrate that

1. The intercollegiate participation opportunities for male and female students are substantially proportionate to their respective enrollments.
2. If members of one sex have been and continue to be underrepresented among intercollegiate athletes, the program is being expanded to respond to that group's developing interests and abilities.
3. If the members of one sex are underrepresented among intercollegiate athletes, and the institution cannot show a continuing practice of program expansion as cited above, it can demonstrate that the interests and abilities of that sex have been fully and effectively accommodated by the present program. (44 Fed Reg. at 71,418)

The circuit court found that the university had failed to meet every prong of the three-part test. It rejected the university's argument that it had accommodated the interests of female athletes to the same degree as male athletes—but that there was simply less interest on the part of women. According to the court, "Interest and ability rarely develop in a vacuum: They develop as a function of opportunity and experience" (p. 179). Premising athletic opportunity on a showing of relative interest gives credence to stereotypes and ignores the long tradition of sex discrimination in sports.

Sex Discrimination in Educational Programs

Although the vast majority of cases brought under Title IX are related to athletics, Title IX also addresses issues of exclusion and harassment in education proper. Courts have interpreted Title IX to prohibit institutions from discriminating on the basis of sex by (1) denying any person aid, benefits, or services including course offerings, extracurricular activities, financial aid, facilities, and housing; (2) providing different aid, benefits, or services or providing them in a different manner; (3) subjecting any person to separate or different rules of behavior, sanctions, or treatment, including rules pertaining to appearance; (4) providing significant assistance or acting as a sponsor to any organization that discriminates on the basis of sex; and (5) limiting the enjoyment of any right, privilege, advantage or opportunity.

In *Franklin v. Gwinnett County Public Schools* (1992), a female high school student alleged that a coach at her school (who was also one of her teachers) had persistently sexually harassed her both at school and at her home. She also claimed that he had forced her to have sex with him. The girl reported the incident to the school, but no action was taken; in fact, the school encouraged her not to press charges. The coach agreed to resign on the condition that all charges be dropped, and the school closed its investigation. As a result of the trauma she experienced, the student was forced to switch schools. She also filed a sex discrimination and harassment suit under Title IX because the school qualified as an institution receiving federal financial assistance. The Supreme Court found in the student's favor and ruled, for the first time, that individuals subjected to discrimination in violation of Title IX could seek monetary damages.

Pursuing a Title IX Claim

Title IX claims are overseen by the U.S. Department of Education's Office for Civil Rights (OCR). Anyone who believes he or she has been discriminated against by a publicly funded educational institution on the basis of sex may file a grievance with OCR. It is also permissible for nonvictims to file on a victim's behalf. Claimants are encouraged to first seek resolution of the complaint through the offending institution's grievance process. If a claim is pursued through OCR, it can be initiated by submitting a written statement describing the alleged discriminatory act, when it occurred, to whom it occurred, and the name of the offending institution. The role of OCR is evaluation, assessment, and correction of institutional policy. The claims process and its duration are depicted in Figure 17.2.

A Title IX case may be filed with the courts either in conjunction with an OCR hearing or after the hearing has been completed. Unlike OCR complaints, which may be filed by someone other than the actual victim, law suits may only be filed by the person who has directly experienced the discrimination. A lawsuit may provide more immediate relief because a temporary restraining order can be filed against the offending institution. Finally, unlike OCR, the court can award monetary damages to a successful plaintiff (Women's Sports Foundation, 2009). In sum, Title IX complaints filed with OCR are more likely to stimulate long-term changes with respect to an educational institution's treatment of the sexes, whereas lawsuits filed in court are better suited to resolving individual cases quickly and definitively.

FIGURE 17.2   **OCR Timeline for Title IX Complaint Resolution**

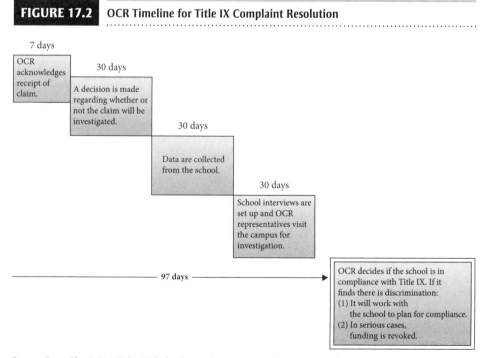

Source: From *Play Fair: A Title IX Playbook For Victory, A Women's Sports Foundation Educational Guide.*
Copyright © 2009 by Women's Sports Foundation. Reprinted with permission. .

In 2012, Title IX marked its 40th anniversary. Research shows that since its inception, Title IX has generated an explosive increase in athletic opportunities for females. In 1971, fewer than 300,000 girls participated in high school sports. By 2003, that number increased to more than 2.7 million, a jump of 900% (Kiefer, 2003). Progress at the university level has been somewhat slower. Many coaches believe that the law unfairly diverts funding away from male athletic programs, which are more cost effective. Whereas men's sports in the United States generate a median of $22.56 million annually, women's sports pull in only about $836,000 per year (Joyner, 2010). Given these numbers, it is no surprise that many coaches and administrators would prefer to see the Title IX criteria relaxed. Men's athletic programs also continue to receive disproportionate funding for scholarships, recruitment, and facilities management (Sullivan, 2010). These subtle and not-so-subtle differences in the treatment of male and female athletes attest to the fact that Title IX still has a long way to go before its promise is fully realized.

Summary and Conclusion

The struggle for women's rights has continued for more than a century. Cases brought under the equal protection clause of the 14th Amendment began to recognize sex discrimination in the early 1970s, with the courts eventually settling on the application of intermediate scrutiny. Cases alleging employment discrimination can also be brought under the Equal Pay Act or Title VII of the Civil Rights Act. Claims related to bias in compensation, hiring, promotion, termination, or sexual harassment must be filed with the Equal Employment Opportunity Commission before a private lawsuit can be initiated. Title IX of the Civil Rights Act prohibits discrimination in publicly funded educational institutions. Most claims that are filed relate to bias in school athletic programs. The U.S. Department of Education's Office for Civil Rights is responsible for processing claims and working with educational institutions to enforce Title IX's requirements. Social workers should be familiar with the processes for combating sex discrimination and must remain active in ensuring the equal treatment of women under the law.

Sample Case

Following is a case concerning the employment rights of pregnant women. Read the majority and dissenting opinions carefully, and consider the questions that follow.

CLEVELAND BOARD OF EDUCATION v. LAFLEUR
414 U.S. 632 (1974)

Mr. Justice Stewart delivered the opinion of the Court.

The respondents . . . and Petitioner . . . are female public school teachers. During the 1970–1971 school year, each informed her local school board that she was pregnant; each was compelled by a mandatory maternity leave rule to quit her job without pay several months before the expected birth of her child. These cases call upon us to decide the constitutionality of the school boards' rules.

Jo Carol LaFleur and Ann Elizabeth Nelsonare are junior high school teachers employed by the Board of Education of Cleveland, Ohio. Pursuant to a rule first adopted in 1952, the school board requires every pregnant school teacher to take maternity leave without pay, beginning five months before the expected birth of her child. Application for such leave must be made no later than two weeks prior to the date of departure. A teacher on maternity leave is not allowed to return to work until the beginning of the next regular school semester which follows the date when her child attains the age of three months. A doctor's certificate attesting to the health of the teacher is a prerequisite to return; an additional physical examination may be required. The teacher on maternity leave is not promised reemployment after the birth of the child; she is merely given priority in reassignment to a position for which she is qualified. Failure to comply with the mandatory maternity leave provisions is ground for dismissal.

Neither Mrs. LaFleur nor Mrs. Nelson wished to take an unpaid maternity leave; each wanted to continue teaching until the end of the school year. Because of the mandatory maternity leave rule, however, each was required to leave her job in March 1971.

. . . Susan Cohen was employed by the School Board of Chesterfield County, Virginia. That school board's maternity leave regulation requires that a pregnant teacher leave work at least four months prior to the expected birth of her child. Notice in writing must be given to the school board at least six months prior to the expected birth date. A teacher on maternity leave is declared re-eligible for employment when she submits written notice from a physician that she is physically fit for re-employment, and when she can give assurance that care of the child will cause only minimal interference with her job responsibilities. The teacher is guaranteed re-employment no later than the first day of the school year following the date upon which she is declared re-eligible.

Mrs. Cohen informed the Chesterfield County School Board in November, 1970, that she was pregnant and expected the birth of her child about April 8, 1971. She initially requested that she be permitted to continue teaching until April 1, 1971. The school board rejected the request, as it did Mrs. Cohen's subsequent suggestion that she be allowed to teach until January 21, 1971, the end of the first school semester. Instead, she was required to leave her teaching job on December 18, 1970.

This Court has long recognized that freedom of personal choice in matters of marriage and family life is one of the liberties protected by the Due Process Clause of the Fourteenth Amendment [e.g.] *Roe v. Wade.*

. . . The question before us in these cases is whether the interests advanced in support of the rules of the Cleveland and Chesterfield County School Boards can justify the particular procedures they have adopted.

The school boards in these cases have offered two essentially overlapping explanations for their mandatory maternity leave rules. First, they contend that the firm cutoff dates are necessary to maintain continuity of classroom instruction, since advance knowledge of when a pregnant teacher must leave facilitates the finding and hiring of a qualified substitute. Secondly, the school boards seek to justify their maternity rules by arguing that at least some teachers become physically incapable of adequately performing certain of their duties during the latter part of pregnancy. By keeping the pregnant teacher out of the classroom during these final months, the maternity leave rules are said to protect the health of the teacher and her unborn child, while at the same time assuring that students have a physically capable instructor in the classroom at all times. ***

We . . . conclude that the arbitrary cutoff dates embodied in the mandatory leave rules before us have no rational relationship to the valid state interest of preserving continuity of instruction. As long as the teachers are required to give substantial advance notice of their condition, the choice of firm dates later in pregnancy would serve the boards' objectives just as well, while imposing a far lesser burden on the women's exercise of constitutionally protected freedom.

The question remains as to whether the cutoff dates at the beginning of the fifth and sixth months can be justified on the other ground advanced by the school boards—the necessity of keeping physically unfit teachers out of the classroom. . . .

The mandatory termination provisions of the Cleveland and Chesterfield County rules surely operate to insulate the classroom from the presence of potentially incapacitated pregnant teachers. But the question is whether the rules sweep too broadly. . . . That question must be answered in the affirmative, for the provisions amount to a conclusive presumption that every pregnant teacher who reaches the fifth or sixth month of pregnancy is physically incapable of continuing. There is no individualized determination by the teacher's doctor . . . as to any particular teacher's ability to continue at her job. . . . ***

We conclude, therefore, that neither the necessity for continuity of instruction nor the state interest in keeping physically unfit teachers out of the classroom can justify the sweeping mandatory leave regulations that the Cleveland and Chesterfield County School Boards have adopted. ***

In addition to the mandatory termination provisions, both the Cleveland and Chesterfield County rules contain limitations upon a teacher's eligibility to return to work after giving birth. Again, the school boards offer two justifications for the return rules— continuity of instruction and the desire to be certain that the teacher is physically competent when she returns to work. As is the case with the leave provisions, the question is not whether the school board's goals are legitimate, but rather whether the particular means chosen to achieve those objectives unduly infringe upon the teacher's constitutional liberty. ***

The respondents . . . do not seriously challenge either the medical requirements of the Cleveland rule or the policy of limiting eligibility to return to the next semester following birth. The provisions concerning a medical certificate or supplemental physical examination are narrowly drawn methods of protecting the school board's interest in teacher fitness; these requirements allow an individualized decision as to the teacher's condition, and thus avoid the pitfalls of the presumptions inherent in the leave rules. Similarly, the provision limiting eligibility to return to the semester following delivery is a precisely drawn means of serving the school board's interest in avoiding unnecessary changes in classroom personnel during any one school term.

The Cleveland rule, however, does not simply contain these reasonable medical and next semester eligibility provisions. In addition, the school board requires the mother to wait until her child reaches the age of three months before the return rules begin to operate. The school board has offered no reasonable justification for this supplemental limitation, and we can perceive none.

Thus, we conclude that the Cleveland return rule, insofar as it embodies the three-month age provision, is wholly arbitrary and irrational, and hence violates the Due Process Clause of the Fourteenth Amendment. The age limitation serves no legitimate state interest and unnecessarily penalizes the female teacher for asserting her right to bear children.

For the reasons stated, we hold that the mandatory termination provisions of the Cleveland and Chesterfield County maternity regulations violate the Due Process Clause of the Fourteenth Amendment, because of their use of unwarranted conclusive presumptions that seriously burden the exercise of protected constitutional liberty. For similar reasons, we hold the three-month provision of the Cleveland return rule unconstitutional.

Mr. Justice Rehnquist, with whom The Chief Justice Joins, Dissenting.

The Court rests its invalidation of the school regulations involved in these cases on the Due Process Clause of the Fourteenth Amendment, rather than on any claim of sexual discrimination under the Equal Protection Clause of that Amendment. My Brother STEWART thereby enlists the Court in another quixotic engagement in his apparently unending war on irrebuttable presumptions. ***

As THE CHIEF JUSTICE pointed out in his dissent last year: Literally thousands of state statutes create classifications permanent in duration, which are less than perfect, as all legislative classifications are, and might be improved on by individualized determinations.. . . Hundreds of years ago in England, before Parliament came to be thought of as a body having general lawmaking power, controversies were determined on an individualized basis without benefit of any general law. Most students of government consider the shift from this sort of determination . . . to have been a significant step forward in the achievement of a civilized political society. It seems to me a little late in the day for this Court to weigh in against such an established consensus. ***

All legislation involves the drawing of lines, and the drawing of lines necessarily results in particular individuals who are disadvantaged by the line drawn being virtually indistinguishable for many purposes from those individuals who benefit from the legislative classification. The Court's disenchantment with "irrebuttable presumptions," and its preference for "individualized determination," is, in the last analysis, nothing less than an attack upon the very notion of lawmaking itself.

The lines drawn by the school boards in the city of Cleveland and Chesterfield County in these cases require pregnant teachers to take forced leave at a stage of their pregnancy when medical evidence seems to suggest that a majority of them might well be able to continue teaching without any significant possibility of physical impairment. But, so far as I am aware, the medical evidence also suggests that, in some cases, there may be physical impairment at the stage of pregnancy fastened on by the regulations in question, and that the probability of physical impairment increases as the pregnancy advances. If legislative bodies are to be permitted to draw a general line anywhere short of the delivery room, I can find no judicial standard of measurement which says the ones drawn here were invalid. I therefore dissent.

Questions

1. What did the maternity leave policies of the Cleveland and Chesterfield County School Boards require? What were the purposes behind each of these requirements? Did the Court find these purposes legitimate? Do you? Why or why not?

2. How did the Court ultimately rule? Why?

3. Notice when this case was decided. How does it reflect the historical context of the times?

4. The court analyzes this case using the due process clause. If the case were decided today using the equal protection clause, what level of scrutiny would be applied? What does that level of scrutiny require? Would the policies survive? Why or why not?

5. The majority of the court objects to the use of an *irrebuttable presumption* and favors an individualized approach. The dissent sees advantages in the use of a presumption. What exactly is a presumption? What presumption is inherent in the school boards' maternity policies? In your view, are presumptions a good way or a bad way to operate? Why?

CHAPTER 17 PRACTICE TEST

The following questions will test your application and analysis of the content found within this chapter. For additional assessment, including licensing exam type questions on applying chapter content to practice behaviors, visit **MySearchLab**.

1. The Equal Pay Act requires that
   a. women and men be paid the same for performing the same duties.
   b. women and men be paid the same for performing work of the equal value.
   c. women be paid at least 80% of what men are paid for the same work.
   d. women be hired into jobs traditionally occupied by men.

2. The U.S. Supreme Court's decision in the Lilly Ledbetter case
   a. allowed women to go directly to court, rather than having to file a complaint with the EEOC.
   b. made it easier for women to file claims of sex discrimination.
   c. made it more difficult for women to file claims of sex discrimination.

   d. was reinforced by federal legislation.

3. Steven brings a sexual harassment suit against his boss, Marvin. He claims that Marvin routinely pats his butt when they pass each other in the hallway. If Steven loses, it will be because
   a. Marvin didn't mean any harm.
   b. Steven was never threatened with losing his job.
   c. the behavior was not unwelcome.
   d. the law does not apply to harassment between persons of the same sex

4. Under the equal protection clause, sex discrimination is analyzed using
   a. minimal scrutiny.
   b. intermediate scrutiny.
   c. strict scrutiny.
   d. the rational basis test.

5. Discuss the legality and desirability of single-sex educational institutions. How do they compare to racially segregated schools? Is the distinction warranted? Why or why not?

6. Has Title IX been successful in rectifying sex discrimination in school sports? What obstacles must be overcome for it to be more successful in the future?

MYSEARCHLAB CONNECTIONS

Reinforce what you learned in this chapter by studying videos, cases, documents, and more available at **www.MySearchLab.com**.

Watch these Videos

⋆ Working Mothers
  • *What additional protections would be important in securing the place of women in the workforce?*

Read these Cases/Documents

Δ National Organization from Women, Statement of Purpose (1966)
  • *What ideals and goals animated the women's movement of the 1960s and 1970s?*

Explore these Assets

• Interactive Case Study: Women's Struggle for Equality
• Website: National Organization for Women

Research these Topics

• women in the military
• women in politics

Assess Your Knowledge

Go to **MySearchLab** to test your knowledge of key topics in this chapter with topic-specific quizzes. Conclude your assessment by completing the chapter exam.

⋆ = CSWE Core Competency Asset   Δ = Case Study

Chapter **18**

....

Legal Rights of Sexual Minorities

Before exploring what social workers need to know about the legal protections afforded lesbian, gay, bisexual, and transgender (LGBT) individuals, it is important that we have a fundamental understanding of the population itself. Because so much confusion surrounds various aspects of sexual identity, we begin by defining the terms typically used to describe them.

Sex is the term used to describe a person's biological identity; people are characterized as *male* or *female*. *Gender* is a set of "socially constructed roles, behaviors, activities, and attributes that a given society considers appropriate" (World Health Organization, 2011). Gender is classified into *feminine* and *masculine*. *Gender identity*, which is defined as "one's internal, personal sense of being a man or a woman," may differ from a person's sex. This is not to be confused with *sexual identity* or *sexual orientation*, which refers to someone's "emotional, romantic, or sexual feelings toward other people" (Glossary, 2011).

This chapter provides background information on the LGBT population, explains how discrimination is treated under the Constitution's due process and equal protection clauses, and examines the rights of sexual minorities in relation to employment, military service, and marriage. The treatment of sexual minorities in other countries is highlighted, and the sample case addresses the exclusion of gays and lesbians from private membership organizations.

Background

In 1948, Alfred Kinsey, after an extensive and controversial study of human sexuality, concluded that 10% of American men were gay. This statistic continues to be widely cited as representing the percentage of gay men and lesbians in society. In a 2002 Gallup poll, respondents estimated the proportion of gay and lesbian Americans at 22% (Robinson, 2002). In reality, there is no definitive and accurate measure of the size of the LGBT population. The U.S. census does not specifically ask respondents to identify their sexual orientation or gender identity, so conclusions must be drawn from the respondent's living situation and marital status. This tends to exclude single or non-cohabiting individuals, bisexual individuals living in heterosexual relationships, and transgender individuals who are asked to select the sex with which they identify (U.S. Census Bureau, 2010).

Demographic Characteristics

The inability to accurately capture the number of LGBT individuals makes it difficult to have a clear understanding of other demographic characteristics as well. Census data and other research findings do provide some insight, despite their limitations. Of the 5.5 million unmarried couples in the United States, 13% are same-sex couples (American Psychological Association [APA], 2011). White people are slightly overrepresented in cohabitating same-sex relationships, whereas every other racial group listed in the census (African Americans, Latinos, Asians/Native Hawaiians, and Other Pacific Islanders) is underrepresented (U.S. Census Bureau, 2010). Estimates further suggest that more than 110,000 same sex couples have children (Gates, 2012). Same-sex couples reside in all but 22 of the nation's 3,140 counties in the 50 states. They are concentrated in certain parts of the country, with 4.8% living in the New York City metropolitan area and 4.2% living in the Los Angeles/Long Beach area of California.

Unfortunately, people who identify as lesbian, gay, bisexual, or transgender are especially susceptible to discrimination and to socioeconomic disadvantage. Although LGBT individuals as a group are better educated than the general public, they have lower earnings. Gay men earn up to 32% less than similarly qualified heterosexual men. The disparity is greater among transgender individuals, up to 64% of whom report incomes of less than $25,000 per year. LGBT individuals are also disproportionately represented in the lowest income brackets. Whereas 5.9% of the general population has an annual salary of less than $10,000, 14% of LGBT individuals fall within that category (APA, 2011).

LGBT youth are at particular disadvantage. Many experience homelessness; an estimated 20% to 40% of all homeless youth identify as LGBT. Approximately 26% report being ejected from their parents' homes after "coming out." Homelessness is associated with increased drug use, risky sexual behaviors, poor mental health, diminished access to education, and reduced social support (APA, 2011).

Summary of Federal Laws

The social, political, and legal environment for LGBT individuals continues to undergo enormous change. Many of these changes occur at the state level, including those addressing marriage equality, nondiscrimination policies, adoption rights, and birth certificate regulations. Nonetheless, some federal laws and policies continue to be important. Among them are the following:

- **Matthew Shepard and James Byrd Jr. Hate Crimes Prevention Act (P.L. 111-84).** This law expanded the federal Hate Crimes Act by including crimes motivated by bias against the victim's actual or perceived gender, sexual orientation, gender identity, or disability. It also requires the FBI to maintain statistics regarding hate crimes involving gender and gender identity. This is the first federal law to extend legal protections to transgender individuals.
- **Don't Ask, Don't Tell Repeal Act (P.L. 111-321).** The original Don't Ask, Don't Tell policy was a compromise allowing lesbians and gay men to serve in the military, provided that they not disclose their sexual orientations. The law, however, did not prevent service members from being dishonorably discharged if their identities came to light. A bill repealing this policy was enacted in 2010 and is currently being implemented.
- **Defense of Marriage Act (P.L. 104-199).** The Defense of Marriage Act (DOMA) allows states to decline to recognize same-sex marriages legally performed in other states. DOMA also defines the terms *spouse* and *marriage* for purposes of federal law, requiring that the partnership be between one man and one woman.

Several additional bills have been introduced in Congress but have not yet succeeded in becoming law. These include the Respect for Marriage Act, which would repeal DOMA; the Employment Non-Discrimination Act (ENDA), which would protect LGBT individuals from workplace discrimination; and the Safe Schools Improvement Act, which would require schools to adopt codes of conduct that prohibit harassment and bullying on the basis of sexual orientation and gender identity.

Sexual Orientation and the Constitution

Just as the courts' treatment of women under the Constitution reflects women's evolving role in society and accompanying changes in public attitudes, the same is true for the courts' treatment of sexual orientation. The women's movement of the 1960s and 1970s formed a backdrop for landmark reproductive rights decisions establishing a constitutional privacy right for women, epitomized by *Griswold v. Connecticut* (contraception) and *Roe v. Wade* (abortion). The women's movement, in turn, provided impetus for the gay rights movement. The brutal 1969 police raid of the Stonewall Inn, a gay bar in New York City, spurred widespread riots and mobilized gay and lesbian activists in their quest for greater self-determination and legal recognition. One of the first agenda items was to seek repeal of state laws criminalzing sodomy. By the mid- to late-1980s, however, the country's growing tolerance of homosexuality was abruptly halted by the paralyzing fear that accompanied the emerging AIDS epidemic. Since AIDS was originally understood to be a "gay disease," the resultant backlash against the gay community played out in the Supreme Court's early cases concerning sexual orientation.

Setting the Standard

It was during this period that the Court issued an extremely important ruling that profoundly affected the course of gay rights for more than two decades. *Bowers v. Hardwick* (1986) involved a challenge to a Georgia law that criminalized sodomy, which it defined as oral or anal sex. The maximum penalty was 20 years in prison. The backstory to this case is recounted by the plaintiff, Michael Hardwick. It started with an encounter with a police officer, Officer Torick, as Hardwick was leaving a gay bar where he worked. The officer picked him up and ticketed him on the pretext of drinking in public. Hardwick failed to appear for his court date because the summons issued by the officer was inaccurately marked. Two hours after the initial hearing time, Officer Torick appeared at Hardwick's home with a warrant for his arrest, which he apparently had processed himself. Upon receiving the warrant, Hardwick went down to the station, explained the situation, and the judge fined him $50 and let him go. Three weeks later, Hardwick was severely beaten by a group of men outside his home who seemed to know his identity. After recovering from his injuries, Hardwick awoke one night to find Officer Torick standing in his bedroom, watching him and a friend in bed. The two men were arrested for violating the anti-sodomy law (Irons, 1990).

Hardwick's case was picked up by the American Civil Liberties Union, which had been looking for test cases to challenge state sodomy laws. When the U.S. Supreme Court granted *certiorari*, it was the first time the Court had ever agreed to hear a gay rights case. At trial, the attorney general who represented the state relied largely on analogies to other "deviate" practices, including sadomasochism, group orgies, and "transvestism"—and drew a connection between gay sodomy and AIDS. He also cautioned that striking down Georgia's law would lead to legitimizing other social ills, including adultery, incest, and bestiality. The attorney for Hardwick argued that the case was about whether the government has a right to dictate how people behave in the bedroom. The American Psychological Association and the American Public Health Association filed a joint *amicus* brief that included 91 citations to the medical and social science literature (Irons, 2006). It showed that 80% of married couples engage in oral or anal sex and that 95% of American men, both gay and straight, had engaged in oral sex—the implication being that all of them could be found in violation of the Georgia law.

The Court in *Bowers* could have analyzed this case according to the equal protection clause but instead chose to analyze it as a due process case in the tradition of the reproductive rights cases. Under a due process analysis, the threshhold question is whether the law in question burdens a *fundamental right*. If so, the state must show that its purpose is so compelling that it warrants superseding the exercise of that right. Contrary to all expectations, a 5–4 majority of the Court declined to recognize engaging in sodomy as a fundamental right and the Court thus upheld the Georgia statute. It distinguished this case from the reproductive rights cases by saying that those were about procreation; this was simply about sex. The Court also noted that this country has a long history of prohibiting homosexual sodomy, that approximately half the states criminalize it, and that the voters of Georgia obviously believe it to be immoral and unacceptable.

The dissent argued that the reproductive rights cases are not about procreation but rather about the ability to define one's identity, which includes one's sexuality. The issue, therefore, is not whether there is a fundamental right to engage in sodomy but whether there is a fundamental right to control the nature of one's intimate associations with others. As for justifying Georgia's law by citing the long history of disapproval toward homosexual conduct, Justice Blackmun (quoting Oliver Wendell Holmes) wrote, "It is revolting to have no better reason for a rule of law than that it was laid down in the time of Henry IV. It is still more revolting if the grounds upon which it was laid down have vanished long since, and the rule simply persists from blind imitation of the past" (p. 199).

One of the great ironies of the 5–4 decision in *Bowers v. Hardwick* is that Justice Powell, upon reflection, concluded that he had "probably made a mistake" in casting his swing vote for the majority (Greenhouse, 1990). Three years after retiring from the bench (and four years after deciding *Bowers*), he conceded that the dissent had the better argument. Had he voted the other way at the time, the history of securing legal rights for sexual minorities would look quite different.

The impact of *Bowers v. Hardwick* can readily be seen in the subsequent cases to come before the courts. An example is the 1987 D.C. Court of Appeals case of *Padula v. Webster*. In that case, an applicant for a position with the FBI was rejected, despite good scores, because the background investigation disclosed that she was gay. The court approached this as an equal protection case but declined to apply either intermediate scrutiny (as applied to sex-based classifications) or strict scrutiny (as applied to race and national origin). Needless to say, the FBI's actions were upheld. In applying minimal scrutiny, the court found that the FBI had a legitimate interest in protecting the agency's credibility and in avoiding the risk of blackmail. The agency's refusal to hire sexual minorities was found to be rationally related to those interests.

Perhaps the most significant part of the court's opinion was its reason for failing to apply a heightened level of scrutiny to the case. The court reasoned that if gay men and lesbians are defined by behavior that can be criminalized—as in *Bowers v. Hardwick*—then they are undeserving of the special legal consideration afforded a suspect or semi-suspect class. This argument continued to dominate the landscape for years to come.

Moving Forward

The first significant sexual orientation case to reach the Supreme Court since *Bowers v. Hardwick* was *Romer v. Evans* (1996). This was an equal protection case concerning a constitutional amendment, approved by 53% of Colorado's voters, that would have prohibited the state and all jurisdictions within the state from including sexual orientation in their antidiscrimination ordinances. Although the lower court found the law unconstitutional using strict scrutiny, the Supreme Court applied minimal scrutiny. Even so, the Court struck the law down. The Court found it too broad a measure to be credible and concluded that its only possible motivation was *animus* (hostility) toward sexual minorities. Unlike *Bowers v. Hardwick*, in which the plaintiffs were expecting a victory but did not get one, no one was willing to bet on the outcome here because three of the five justices in the *Bowers* majority, and three of the four dissenters, were no longer on the Court. The *Romer v. Evans* decision was the first time in history that the U.S. Supreme Court invalidated a measure because it discriminated against lesbians and gay men. Meanwhile, Justice Scalia, who wrote on behalf of the three dissenting justices, called the Court's holding "terminal silliness." Applying minimal scrutiny, he would have upheld the law because of the state's legitimate interest in preserving traditional sexual mores.

The biggest breakthrough on the constitutional front came in 2003 with *Lawrence v. Texas*. In this landmark case, a challenge was brought against a Texas statute that criminalized oral and anal sex between same-sex couples. The facts of the case were reminiscent of those in *Bowers v. Hardwick*, decided nearly two decades earlier. This case, too, involved a man who was arrested in his own home for engaging in sex with another man. Like *Bowers v. Hardwick*, this case was decided on due process grounds. In a 6–3 opinion, however, the Court struck down the Texas antisodomy law as unconstitutional and explicitly overruled the holding in *Bowers v. Hardwick*, saying it "was not correct when it was decided and it is not correct today" (p. 578). In reaching its decision, the Court borrowed liberally from the dissent in *Bowers*. It reframed the issue from the fundamental right to engage in sodomy to the fundamental freedom to control one's intimate associations. The Court took issue with the version of history that had been presented in *Bowers,* noting that antisodomy laws had rarely been enforced against consenting adults. It rejected the notion that the government should be foisting individual moral views on society at large. Finally, it noted a recent trend toward increased recognition of rights for sexual minorities and concluded that no government interest was urgent enough to justify impinging on this fundamental right.

The National Association of Social Workers (NASW) submitted an *amicus* brief in the *Lawrence v. Texas* case. It argued that

- Homosexuality is a normal form of human sexuality, not a mental disorder.
- Suppressing sexual intimacy among same-sex partners would deprive gay men and lesbians of the opportunity to participate in a fundamental aspect of the human experience.
- Antisodomy statutes, such as the one in Texas, reinforce prejudice, discrimination, and violence against gay men and lesbians. (NASW, 2003)

To summarize, discrimination based on sexual orientation has been considered by the courts only relatively recently. It was not until 1986 that the U.S. Supreme Court even agreed to hear such a case, and it was not until 1996 that the Court struck down a law as impermissibly discriminating against gay men and lesbians. The bookend cases of *Bowers v. Hardwick* and *Lawrence v. Texas* are emblematic of the progress that has been achieved over the past two decades of constitutional analsyis.

Rights in Employment

In contrast to racial minorities and women, sexual minorities are entitled to no protection against workplace discrimination under federal law. Title VII of the Civil Rights Act, which prohibits discrimination in regard to the compensation, terms, conditions, or privileges of employment, applies only to race, color, religion, sex, and national origin; it excludes sexual orientation. Despite repeated efforts to recognize LGBT discrimination in federal employment law, no protections currently exist to prevent sexual minorities from being unfairly refused employment, harassed, fired, or subjected to inequitable conditions or benefits. The Employment Non-Discrimination Act (ENDA), which is modeled on Title VII and would remedy this serious omission, has been introduced in every Congress since 1994, with one exception. It was voted on once in the U.S. Senate in 1995 and failed by a single vote, and it was passed by the House of Representatives in 2007 but was never taken up by the Senate. Like Title VII, ENDA would apply to businesses of more than

15 employees and would be enforced by the Equal Employment Opportunity Commission. The most recent version would address intentional discrimination (as opposed to disparate impact) based on real or perceived sexual orientation and gender identity.

Some states and localities have filled the vacuum left by the absence of federal law. Fifteen states have policies that protect against workplace discrimination on the basis of both sexual orientation and gender identity (see Figure 18.1); 21 states have employment laws that protect workers based on sexual orientation only (Human Rights Campaign, 2011b). In addition to these state laws, 240 local jurisdictions have ordinances outlawing sexual orientation discrimination; approximately 60 of these include gender identity. The business sector also has begun to address the problem. Ninety-four percent of Fortune 100 companies and 87% of Fortune 500 companies protect against discrimination on the basis of sexual orientation, with 69% and 46% (respectively) also covering gender identity (Althauser & Greenberg, 2011).

Although this is a start, it is far from adequate. After all, 28 states still permit discrimination on the basis of sexual orientation and 38 have yet to outlaw discrimination based on gender identity or expression—despite the fact that 73% of the public (including majorities from both major political parties) favors employment protections for LGBT individuals (Althauser & Greenberg, 2011; Human Rights Campaign, 2011a).

FIGURE 18.1   **State Nondiscrimination Laws Affecting Sexual Minorities**

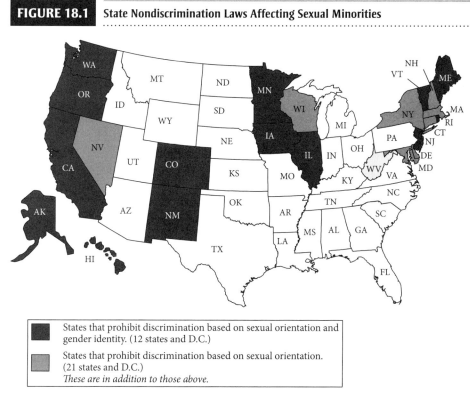

States that prohibit discrimination based on sexual orientation and gender identity. (12 states and D.C.)

States that prohibit discrimination based on sexual orientation. (21 states and D.C.)
These are in addition to those above.

Hiring, Promotion, Harassment, and Termination

The absence of federal protection for sexual minorities has palpable consequences. In a survey of 1,205 LGBT respondents, 39% reported experiencing harassment in the workplace because of their sexual orientation. Frequent or very frequent harassment was most common for lower-income workers and those in the southern and mountain states (Lambda Legal & Deloitte Financial Advisory Services, 2006). According to other research, as many as 28% of LGBT individuals report having been passed over for a promotion, and as many as 17% report not having been hired or having been fired on the basis of their sexual orientation (Althauser & Greenberg, 2011). There is also a wage gap between gay and straight members of both sexes, with gay and bisexual men earning 11% to 27% less than their heterosexual counterparts, and lesbians and bisexual women earning 12% to 30% less than their heterosexual counterparts. Given the combined effects of sex discrimination and sexual orientation discrimination, gay women earned least of all (Burns, 2012; Eskridge & Hunter, 1997). Gender nonconforming and transgender individuals are at particular risk of being subjected to adverse employment conditions: 90% report having been mistreated or harassed on the job, and 47% reported being denied a promotion, denied a position, or fired because of their identity (National Center for Transgender Equality, 2011). They are twice as likely as others to be unemployed, four times as likely to live in poverty, and 20% report currently being or having been homeless (Althauser & Greenberg, 2011).

Because no federal law explicitly prohibits employment discrimination on the basis of sexual orientation or sexual identity, sexual minorities have used Title VII's prohibition against sex discrimination to advance their allegations. One of the earliest and most important of these cases is *Price Waterhouse v. Hopkins* (1989). In this case, the accounting firm's only female candidate for partner had her candidacy put on hold as a result of what she alleged were sexual stereotypes. Although the company agreed that she had many solid qualifications, several of her coworkers had raised concerns about her interpersonal skills, describing her as overly aggressive, unduly harsh, "macho," and impatient. She was also criticized for using profanity and was advised to take a "course at charm school." One coworker indicated that he thought she was overcompensating for being a woman. Finally, she was told that if she wanted to improve her chances, she should "walk more femininely, talk more femininely, dress more femininely, wear make-up, have her hair styled, and wear jewelry" (p. 235). She sued under Title VII, claiming sex discrimination. The Supreme Court agreed that the company's reliance on sex stereotypes constituted impermissible sex discrimination under Title VII. It also concluded that when a mix of permissible and impermissible motives governs an employer's actions, the company must prove by a preponderance of the evidence that it would have made the same decision in the absence of discrimination. This case brought what we now think of as gender identity or sexual expression (being targeted for not conforming to cultural norms of masculinity and femininity) under the umbrella of sex discrimination.

Also brought under Title VII was *Oncale v. Sundowner Offshore Services* (1998). In that case, a male employee quit his job after being repeatedly sexually harassed by his male supervisors. The Supreme Court here broke new ground, concluding that same-sex sexual harassment falls within the protections of Title VII, regardless of whether or not the harasser is gay.

Building on these decisions, the Sixth Circuit Court of Appeals heard *Smith v. City of Salem* in 2004. It involved a firefighter who was undergoing transition from male to female. When his superiors were advised of his status, he was suspended. He brought suit under Title VII. Citing the Supreme Court's earlier holding that Title VII protects against both sex discrimination and gender discrimination (*Price Waterhouse v. Hopkins*), the court of appeals ruled that the plaintiff had an actionable claim. Although not decided by the Supreme Court, this case was important in providing legal recourse for transgender individuals.

More recently, the District of Columbia considered a similar case in *Schroer v. Library of Congress* (2008). In that case, a decorated U.S. Army veteran of 25 years was offered and accepted a job as a terrorism research analyst with the Library of Congress. Before the paperwork had been completed and the arrangements finalized, however, the candidate explained that he was in the planning stages of transitioning from male to female. The offer of hire was rescinded, and the victim brought a sex discrimination suit under Title VII. The employer offered numerous justifications for its decision, all of which were dismissed by the court as being mere pretexts for discrimination. The court concluded that discriminating against someone for transitioning from one sex to the other is a form of sex discrimination and therefore falls within the protections of the Civil Rights Act. Much to the delight of the advocacy community, the Obama administration declined to appeal the ruling.

Employment Benefits for Partners and Families

LGBT individuals, like anyone else, not only work for a source of income but to secure benefits that will help them care for themselves and their loved ones. Too often, these benefits are legally unavailable to sexual minorities and their families. The Family and Medical Leave Act (FMLA), for example, requires employers to grant up to 12 weeks of unpaid sick leave to eligible employees. Guidance from the Department of Justice has clarified that any employee, regardless of identity, can take time off to care for a child for whom he or she has parenting responsibilities, even if there is no legal bond between them. On the other hand, there is no requirement that employers grant leave to care for a same-sex partner or spouse (Human Rights Campaign, 2011c).

A similar deficiency can be found in the Consolidated Omnibus Budget Reconciliation Act (COBRA) of 1986, which many people depend on to extend their health insurance benefits when they might otherwise have ended because of job loss or job transition. Although some employers have chosen to extend this benefit to same-sex partners or spouses and their children, the law does not require that they do so (Human Rights Campaign, 2011c).

In one case that is emblematic of the difficulties faced by LGBT employees, a social worker in Colorado sued after being denied family sick leave benefits to care for her same-sex partner (*Ross v. Denver Department of Health and Hospitals*, 1994). The state court of appeals ruled against her. Although she argued that the state's prohibition against discrimination based on sexual orientation was controlling, the court concluded that it does not change the definition of "immediate family" in the regulations governing sick leave benefits. Because the definition does not include same-sex partners, her employer was under no obligation to provide the benefits.

Fortunately, a number of employers in both the public and private sectors have begun to voluntarily provide partner benefits. As of 2011, this included 83% of Fortune 100 companies and 58% of Fortune 500 companies (Human Rights Campaign, 2011c).

Legal Rights and Military Service

One of the areas in which sexual minorities have made visible strides is in relation to military service. Although there is a long tradition of discrimination on the basis of sexual orientation, growing public objection first gave rise to compromise legislation permitting sexual minorities to serve if they kept their orientation to themselves, then finally to the right to serve their country openly. This evolution has come amid tremendous controversy and acrimony. Other nations including Britain, Australia, and Israel have long permitted LGBT people to serve in the military without incident (MSNBC, 2009).

History and Scope

The first occasion of an American soldier being removed from the military for same-sex intimacy was in 1778. Expulsions, however, were rare until World War I, when the armed forces investigated and removed service members for engaging in sodomy or being "effeminate" in nature. Before World War II, the military began screening male service members for homosexuality, although women were not investigated for lesbianism until the end of the war. Although some individuals were court-marshaled for their homosexuality, others were quietly ushered out of the service. It was not until after the Stonewall Riots in 1969 that service members who had been discharged began suing for the right to serve. Unfortunately, any gains made as a result of these challenges resulted in the adoption of even stricter military policies regarding homosexuality (Eskridge & Hunter, 1997). In 1993, Congress enacted a compromise policy known as Don't Ask, Don't Tell (DADT), which prohibited the military from asking about a service member's sexual orientation and permitted LGBT individuals to serve as long as they did not disclose their status. By the time DADT was repealed in 2010, it is estimated that as many as 14,500 people had lost their positions under the policy (Servicemembers Legal Defense Network, 2011).

Seeking Redress through the Courts

Beginning in the late 1980s, the courts heard a number of challenges to the military's policy on gay service members. Most were heard at the circuit court level, not by the U.S. Supreme Court. Two of these cases were noteworthy in that they applied different levels of scrutiny and reached different results.

In *Watkins v. U.S. Army* (1988), the Ninth Circuit heard the case of a young recruit who, in filling out the army's pre-induction medical form, acknowledged that he had "homosexual tendencies." He was nonetheless inducted and served for 14 years with distinction. In 1981, the army adopted new regulations that mandated the discharge of all gays; Watkins was discharged and denied reenlistment. He challenged the action under the equal protection clause. Unlike in *Padula v. Webster* (the FBI case discussed earlier in this chapter), the court ruled in the plaintiff's favor. Of key importance was the fact that the army regulations at issue here penalized homosexual *status* rather than homosexual *conduct*. The court went further and defined LGBT individuals as a suspect class deserving of strict scrutiny. Under that analysis, it found no compelling interest on the part of the state and concluded that even if the state's interest (maintaining morale and discipline) were compelling, a policy of excluding gays and lesbians from the military was not necessary to achieve it.

In a very similar case, the D.C. Court of Appeals considered an equal protection challenge brought by a student at the Naval Academy who was required to leave after he admitted to being gay (*Steffan v. Perry*, 1994). Although he acknowledged that the regulations permitted termination for both engaging in homosexual conduct and intending to engage in homosexual conduct, he argued that the military could not punish him solely on the basis of his status. The court applied minimal scrutiny and upheld the Naval Academy's actions. It concluded that it was reasonable to presume that someone who is gay is likely to engage in, or intend to engage in, homosexual conduct.

The most recent twist on the question of gay men and lesbians in the military came in the form of a case brought by the Log Cabin Republicans, a nonprofit organization that challenged the federal DADT policy on both free speech and due process grounds (*Log Cabin Republicans v. United States*, 2010). A California District Court found in favor of the plaintiffs, ruling the policy unconstitutional. The court found that DADT violates free speech rights because it prohibits gay service members from speaking freely about their sexual orientation, while permitting straight service members to talk about their sexual orientation, spouses, or significant others. Although the court recognized that the military has a substantial interest in restricting some speech, it found that DADT was far broader than necessary to effectively promote those interests. As for due process, *Lawrence v. Texas* established a fundamental right to control one's intimate associations; DADT burdens that right. Although the military has a substantial interest in maintaining military readiness and unit cohesion, the court found no evidence that these are advanced by DADT; in fact, most testimony suggested that it actually undermines these goals. Subsequent to the decision, enforcement of DADT was halted, Congress repealed the law, and sexual minorities now have the legal right to serve openly in the armed forces.

Marriage Equality

The fight for marriage equality has consumed the attention of legislatures and courts throughout the country. Advocates continue to press for increased recognition of same-sex partnerships, and opponents continue to argue for the retention of traditional values. While these battles rage on, public support for same-sex marriage continues to increase. Four separate polls conducted during an 8-month span in 2010 and 2011 all found that a majority of Americans (51%) favor marriage rights for LGBT couples (Silver, 2011). As Figure 18.2 illustrates, although opinions on the issue vary by generation, political party affiliation, and race, support within all groups has increased dramatically since 1996. Support for same-sex marriage is highest among Millennials (those born after 1980), followed in descending order by members of Generation X (born 1965–1980), Baby Boomers (born 1946–1964), and the Silent Generation (born 1928–1945). In terms of political party affiliation, support is highest among Democrats. Support is also higher among Whites than Blacks. Despite these variations, the trajectory clearly shows increasing support for marriage equality over time.

The struggle to define same-sex relationships in the United States has generated a plethora of terms that can sometimes be confusing. For our purposes, the terms *same-sex marriage* and *marriage equality* will be used to describe a marriage between partners of the same sex, and *partnership recognition* will be used when the partnership is not necessarily a marriage.

FIGURE 18.2	Generational, Partisan, and Racial Differences in Views of Gay Marriage

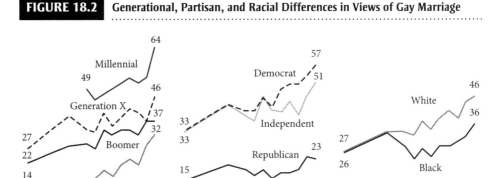

Source: From *Growing Public Support for Same-Sex Marriage* by the Pew Research Center for the People & the Press, a project of the Pew Research Center, February 7, 2012. Copyright © 2012 by the Pew Research Center, http://pewforum.org. Reprinted with permission.

Federal Marriage Rights and Laws

Whatever religious, political, or personal meanings individuals attach to the term *marriage*, one thing remains clear: Those who are granted marriage rights have access to many federal benefits that are unavailable to single people and those in unrecognized partnerships. The Government Accountability Office identified more than 1,000 provisions under federal law in which marriage is a factor in determining eligibility for benefits, rights, or privileges (Partners Task Force for Gay and Lesbian Couples, 2005). A few examples follow:

- Social Security
- Housing
- Food Stamps
- Taxation
- Employment benefits
- Veterans' benefits
- Protection from domestic violence
- Family and Medical Leave
- Immigration and naturalization

The benefits of marriage are unmistakably etched into the social and economic fabric of American society. These continue to be out of reach for the vast majority of LGBT couples.

The only federal law directly targeting same-sex marriage is DOMA. It defines marriage as a union between one man and one woman. It also permits states not to recognize same-sex unions from other states. This law has kept same-sex married partners from receiving a host of federal benefits, including those related to inheritance, survivorship, Social Security, and federal employee benefits (Human Rights Campaign, 2011c). Although DOMA will continue to be enforced, the Obama administration has announced that it will no longer defend the law when its constitutionality is challenged. As of this writing, several legal challenges to DOMA are still pending. A federal district court in Massachusetts decided one important challenge. *Gill v. Office of Personnel Management* (2010) was a case brought by seven same-sex couples married in Massachusetts and three survivors of same-sex spouses, also married in Massachusetts. They challenged their denial of a range of benefits, including federal health benefits, Social Security retirement and survivor benefits, and the right to file a joint federal income tax return. The court found that even applying minimal scrutiny, DOMA violated the equal protection clause. In fact, the court concluded that there was no legitimate purpose served by the law; the only viable explanation was disapproval of same-sex marriage. Another case, heard the same day by the same judge (*Massachusetts v. U.S Department of Health and Human Services*, 2010), challenged DOMA under the 10th Amendment, claiming that it intruded on state authority. A challenge was also brought under the spending clause, claiming that it required the state to engage in discrimination in order to be eligible for federal funds. The court agreed, ruling in favor of the plaintiffs and finding DOMA unconstitutional. Congressional Republicans appealed these decisions to the U.S. Supreme Court, which is expected to hear the combined cases during its 2012 term.

State Recognition of Partnership Rights

A state can grant partnership recognition in a number of ways. The terms used to describe these arrangements vary from state to state and may have different meanings from one state to another. Most common are *domestic partnerships* and *civil unions*. Both are intended to provide some or all of the legal benefits of marriage.

Advocates for marriage argue that it has the advantage of being a universally recognized and instantly understood institution, unlike domestic partnerships and civil unions. Creating these other categories of partnership recognition inevitably relegates them to a status inferior to marriage. Some believe that even if the same benefits are bestowed, these differences in terminology reinforce the notion that LGBT couples are different from, and less deserving than, their straight counterparts (National Organization for Women, 2009). Opponents of same-sex marriage argue that marriage is a sacred institution that has always been understood to involve one man and one woman; they fear that granting marriage rights to same-sex couples will open the door to recognizing homosexuality as a legitimate "lifestyle."

The landscape regarding partnership rights for LGBT couples continues to evolve. Social workers have a responsibility to stay informed of these developments so we can help our clients pursue their legal rights. As of 2011, six states and the District of Columbia permit same-sex marriage; the states are Connecticut, Iowa, Massachusetts, New Hampshire, New York, and Vermont. Meanwhile, nine states allow domestic partnerships or civil unions: California, Delaware, Hawaii, Illinois, Nevada, New Jersey, Oregon, Rhode Island, and Washington. In addition, Maryland is the only state to recognize same-sex marriages originating in other jurisdictions (Human Right Campaign, 2011d).

The issue of same-sex marriage provides an excellent example of the interaction between legislatures and courts. In the 1993 case of *Baehr v. Lewin*, the Supreme Court of Hawaii found that the denial of marriage licenses to same-sex couples violated the state constitution. As a result of the court's decision, the state constitution was quickly amended to vest decision making in the legislature rather than the courts. Needless to say, the legislature subsequently voted to prohibit same-sex marriage. The backlash following the *Baehr* decision had even greater repercussions; it gave rise to passage of DOMA. Between 1973 and 2005, a total of 42 states enacted laws similar to DOMA, and many approved amendments to their state constitutions reaffirming a limited definition of marriage (Vestal, 2007).

One of the most interesting sagas concerns same-sex marriage rights in California. In 2000, California began recognizing domestic partnerships. In 2004, San Francisco began issuing marriage licenses to same-sex couples on its own authority, in contravention of state law. The state decided that the mayor had overstepped his bounds and the marriages were nullified. In 2007, after multiple attempts, a bill was passed to legalize same-sex marriage. Governor Schwarzenegger vetoed it. The following year, the California Supreme Court heard the cases of four same-sex couples who sought to have their marriages from San Francisco recognized. The court ruled that the state constitution recognizes a fundamental right to marry that applies equally to same-sex couples.

It was in response to this ruling that a referendum was held, calling for an amendment to the state constitution that would define marriage as a union between a man and a woman. The measure, known as Proposition 8, passed in 2008 with 52% of the vote. In 2010, *Perry v. Schwarzenegger* was brought in U.S. District Court for the Northern District of California, challenging the constitutionality of Proposition 8. After an exhaustive consideration of the arguments on both sides, the court ruled that Proposition 8 violates both the due process and equal protection clauses of the 14th Amendment. The court was unable to find any legitimate justification for the law, let alone a compelling one; it thus concluded that Proposition 8 fails even under minimal scrutiny. Twelve days after the ruling, the Ninth Circuit Court of Appeals issued a *stay* (delaying enforcement of the judgment) pending appeal.

LGBT RIGHTS IN A GLOBAL CONTEXT

Internationally, the rights afforded sexual minorities vary greatly by region and by culture. Many cultures retain social taboos against homosexuality that have led to its criminalization. In total, homosexual acts are illegal in 76 countries (Bruce-Jones & Itaborahy, 2011).

Depending on the country, laws criminalizing homosexuality may include (Amnesty International, 2008; Bruce-Jones & Itaborahy, 2011; Human Rights Watch, 2008):

- Punishing people solely on the basis of their sexual orientation. This includes laws prohibiting sodomy or other sexual activity between same-sex couples.

- Punishing gender identity. This includes punishing people for imitating the appearance of the opposite sex.

- Outlawing the "promotion" of homosexuality, or inciting others to engage in sexual activity with a person of the same sex.

- Requiring different ages of consent for homosexual intercourse than for homosexual intercourse. Fourteen countries currently have such laws.

- Executing people based on their sexual orientation or gender identity. Currently, gay men can receive the death penalty for sexual relations with another man in five countries: Iran, Saudi Arabia,

Yemen, Mauritania, and Sudan, as well as some parts of Nigeria and Somalia. Lesbians may be executed for sexual relations with another woman in four countries.

- Punishing same-sex relations with long prison sentences. In Sri Lanka, a gay man can receive up to 12 years in prison, in Malaysia up to 20, and in Uganda same-sex sexual relations may be punished with life imprisonment. In addition to the obvious consequences of these laws, there are additional insidious ones. Policies that criminalize homosexuality may result in arbitrary arrests based on allegations about sexual orientation and may serve as a state-sanctioned justification for violence against LGBT individuals in the community.

Despite the prevalence of anti-LGBT legislation and attitudes worldwide, some regions have made great strides in safeguarding the rights of sexual minorities. England and Scotland repealed their laws criminalizing homosexuality in 1967 and 1980, respectively. More recently, Kyrgyzstan decriminalized homosexuality in 2004, Nicaragua in 2007, and Nepal in 2008 (Amnesty International, 2008). Meanwhile, same-sex marriage is legal in 10 countries: the Netherlands, Belgium, Spain, Canada, South Africa, Norway, Sweden, Portugal, Iceland, and Argentina, as well as in Mexico City and several U.S. states (Associated Press, 2010, 2011). This is consistent with the position of NASW, which is "committed to advancing policies and practices that will improve the status and equality of all lesbian, gay, bisexual and transgender people" (NASW, n.d.). NASW continues to be involved in international advocacy efforts to combat laws that discriminate against people on the basis of their sexual orientation or gender identity.

The Future

In 2004, NASW adopted a strongly worded position statement in support of marriage equality, reaffirming our ethical obligation to promote social justice and prevent discrimination on the basis of sexual orientation (NASW, 2004). In addition to engaging in advocacy and assisting LGBT clients in understanding their legal rights, social workers can help correct misinformation and combat stereotypes concerning LGBT individuals, couples, and families.

Given the increased public acceptance of both partnership recognition and same-sex marriage, more and more states are expected to extend legal recognition to LGBT couples. Meanwhile, the Respect for Marriage Act—a bill that would repeal the federal Defense of Marriage Act—has been introduced in both the Senate (S. 598) and the House of Representatives (H.R. 1116). The Senate bill, sponsored by Sen. Dianne Feinstein (D-CA) has 32 cosponsors as of this writing; the House bill, sponsored by Rep. Jerrold Nadler (D-NY), has 154 cosponsors. President Obama has announced his support for the bill.

Summary and Conclusion

Despite a growing trend toward their recognition and acceptance, sexual minorities continue to experience discrimination and socioeconomic disadvantage. LGBT youth and transgender individuals are at particular risk. The first case in which the U.S. Supreme Court considered a case involving the constitutional rights of sexual minorities came in 1986, in the midst of public panic regarding the AIDS epidemic. That case, which upheld state criminal sodomy statutes, set the tone for many years to come. It was not until a decade later that the Court first struck down a law that discriminated on the basis of sexual orientation. In 2003, the Court finally recognized the right of LGBT individuals to enjoy the same privacy rights heterosexuals enjoy under the Constitution.

Equal rights in employment settings are hampered by the exclusion of sexual orientation and gender identity from Title VII of the Civil Rights Act. A number of states and localities have responded by enacting their own nondiscrimination laws. A number of legal challenges involving discrimination based on gender identity, gender expression, and sex stereotyping have successfully been brought under the guise of sex discrimination. The landscape in terms of military service has changed dramatically as the result of the repeal of Don't Ask, Don't Tell. The fight for marriage equality has also resulted in some victories, including several successful challenges to the Defense of Marriage Act in federal district court; the issue may well reach the U.S. Supreme Court in the near future. Social workers should monitor developments related to the legal rights of sexual minorities and continue to advocate for change.

Sample Case

This case concerns a First Amendment challenge to discrimination based on sexual orientation. Read the opinion and consider the questions that follow.

BOY SCOUTS OF AMERICA v. DALE
530 U.S. 640 (2000)

Chief Justice Rehnquist delivered the opinion of the Court.

Petitioners are the Boy Scouts of America and the Monmouth Council, a division of the Boy Scouts of America (collectively, Boy Scouts). The Boy Scouts is a private, not-for-profit organization engaged in instilling its system of values in young people. The Boy Scouts asserts that homosexual conduct is inconsistent with the values it seeks to instill. Respondent is James Dale, a former Eagle Scout whose adult membership in the Boy Scouts was revoked when the Boy Scouts learned that he is an avowed homosexual and gay rights activist. The New Jersey Supreme Court held that New Jersey's public accommodations law requires that the Boy Scouts admit Dale. This case presents the question whether applying New Jersey's public accommodations law in this way violates the Boy Scouts' First Amendment right of expressive association. We hold that it does.

James Dale entered scouting in 1978 at the age of eight. . . . Dale became a Boy Scout in 1981 and remained a Scout until he turned 18. By all accounts, Dale was an exemplary Scout. In 1988, he achieved the rank of Eagle Scout, one of Scouting's highest honors.

Dale applied for adult membership in the Boy Scouts in 1989. The Boy Scouts approved his application for the position of assistant scoutmaster of Troop 73. Around the same time, Dale left home to attend Rutgers University. After arriving at Rutgers, Dale first acknowledged to himself and others that he is gay. He quickly became involved with, and eventually became the co-president of, the Rutgers University Lesbian/Gay Alliance. In 1990, Dale attended a seminar addressing the psychological and health needs of lesbian and gay teenagers. A newspaper covering the event interviewed Dale about his advocacy of homosexual teenagers' need for gay role models. In early July 1990, the newspaper published the interview and Dale's photograph. . . . Later that month, Dale received a letter from Monmouth Council Executive James Kay revoking his adult membership. Dale wrote to Kay requesting the reason for Monmouth Council's decision. Kay responded by letter that the Boy Scouts "specifically forbid membership to homosexuals." ***

In Roberts v. United States Jaycees, 468 U. S. 609, 622 (1984), we observed that "implicit in the right to engage in activities protected by the First Amendment" is "a corresponding right to associate with others in pursuit of a wide variety of political, social, economic, educational, religious, and cultural ends." This right is crucial in preventing the majority from imposing its views on groups that would rather express other, perhaps unpopular, ideas. Government actions that may unconstitutionally burden this freedom may take many forms, one of which is "intrusion into the internal structure or affairs of an association" like a "regulation that forces the group to accept members it does not desire."

The forced inclusion of an unwanted person in a group infringes the group's freedom of expressive association if the presence of that person affects in a significant way the group's ability to advocate public or private viewpoints. ***

The record reveals the following. The Boy Scouts is a private, nonprofit organization. According to its mission statement: "It is the mission of the Boy Scouts of America to serve others by helping to instill values in young people and, in other ways, to prepare them to make ethical choices over their lifetime in achieving their full potential. The values we strive to instill are based on those found in the Scout Oath and Law:

On my honor I will do my best
To do my duty to God and my country
And to obey the Scout Law;
To help other people at all times;
To keep myself physically strong,
Mentally awake, and morally straight.
A Scout is:
Trustworthy, Obedient
Loyal, Cheerful
Helpful, Thrifty
Friendly, Brave
Courteous, Clean
Kind, Reverent"

Thus, the general mission of the Boy Scouts is clear: "[T]o instill values in young people." The Boy Scouts seeks to instill these values by having its adult leaders spend time with the youth members, instructing and engaging them in activities like camping, archery, and fishing. During the time spent with the youth members, the scoutmasters and assistant scoutmasters inculcate them with the Boy Scouts' values—both expressly and by example. It seems indisputable that an association that seeks to transmit such a system of values engages in expressive activity.

Given that the Boy Scouts engages in expressive activity, we must determine whether the forced inclusion of Dale as an assistant scoutmaster would significantly affect the Boy Scouts' ability to advocate public or private viewpoints. This inquiry necessarily requires us first to explore, to a limited extent, the nature of the Boy Scouts' view of homosexuality.

The values the Boy Scouts seeks to instill are "based on" those listed in the Scout Oath and Law. The Boy Scouts explains that the Scout Oath and Law provide "a positive moral code for living; they are a list of 'do's' rather than 'don'ts.'" The Boy Scouts asserts that homosexual conduct is inconsistent with the values embodied in the Scout Oath and Law, particularly with the values represented by the terms "morally straight" and "clean." ***

We must then determine whether Dale's presence as an assistant scoutmaster would significantly burden the Boy Scouts' desire to not "promote homosexual conduct as a legitimate form of behavior." As we give deference to an association's assertions regarding the nature of its expression, we must also give deference to an association's view of what would impair its expression. That is not to say that an expressive association can erect a shield against antidiscrimination laws simply by asserting that mere acceptance of a member from a particular group would impair its message. But here Dale, by his own admission, is one of a group of gay Scouts who have become leaders in their community and are open and honest about their sexual orientation. . . . Dale's presence in the Boy Scouts would, at the very least, force the organization to send a message, both to the youth members and the world, that the Boy Scouts accepts homosexual conduct as a legitimate form of behavior.

Having determined that the Boy Scouts is an expressive association and that the forced inclusion of Dale would significantly affect its expression, we inquire whether the application of New Jersey's public accommodations law to require that the Boy Scouts accept Dale as an assistant scoutmaster runs afoul of the Scouts' freedom of expressive association. We conclude that it does. ***

We are not, as we must not be, guided by our views of whether the Boy Scouts' teachings with respect to homosexual conduct are right or wrong; public or judicial disapproval of a tenet of an organization's expression does not justify the State's effort to compel the organization to accept members where such acceptance would derogate from the organization's expressive message. "While the law is free to promote all sorts of conduct in place of harmful behavior, it is not free to interfere with speech for no better reason than promoting an approved message or discouraging a disfavored one, however enlightened either purpose may strike the government."

The judgment of the New Jersey Supreme Court is reversed, and the cause remanded for further proceedings not inconsistent with this opinion.

It is so ordered.

Justice Stevens, with whom Justice Souter, Justice Ginsburg and Justice Breyer join, dissenting.

New Jersey "prides itself on judging each individual by his or her merits" and on being "in the vanguard in the fight to eradicate the cancer of unlawful discrimination of all types from our society." Since 1945, it has had a law against discrimination. The law broadly protects the opportunity of all persons to obtain the advantages and privileges "of any place of public accommodation." The New Jersey Supreme Court's construction of the statutory definition of a "place of public accommodation" has given its statute a more expansive coverage than most similar state statutes. And as amended in 1991, the law prohibits discrimination on the basis of nine different traits including an individual's "sexual orientation." The question in this case is whether that expansive construction trenches on the federal constitutional rights of the Boy Scouts of America (BSA). ***

In this case, Boy Scouts of America contends that it teaches the young boys who are Scouts that homosexuality is immoral. Consequently, it argues, it would violate its right to associate to force it to admit homosexuals as members, as doing so would be at odds with its own shared goals and values. ***

To bolster its claim that its shared goals include teaching that homosexuality is wrong, BSA directs our attention to two terms appearing in the Scout Oath and Law. The first is the phrase "morally straight," which appears in the Oath; the second term is the word "clean," which appears in a list of 12 characteristics together comprising the Scout Law. ***

It is plain as the light of day that neither one of these principles . . . says the slightest thing about homosexuality. Indeed, neither term in the Boy Scouts' Law and Oath expresses any position whatsoever on sexual matters. ***

In light of BSA's self-proclaimed ecumenism, furthermore, it is even more difficult to discern any shared goals or common moral stance on homosexuality. . . . BSA surely is aware that some religions do not teach that homosexuality is wrong. ***

The evidence before this Court makes it exceptionally clear that BSA has, at most, simply adopted an exclusionary membership policy and has no shared goal of disapproving of homosexuality. . . . A State's antidiscrimination law does not impose a "serious burden" or a "substantial restraint" upon the group's "shared goals" if the group itself is unable to identify its own stance with any clarity. ***

To prevail in asserting a right of expressive association as a defense to a charge of violating an antidiscrimination law, the organization must at least show it has adopted and advocated an unequivocal position inconsistent with a position advocated or epitomized by the person whom the organization seeks to exclude. ***

In its briefs, BSA implies, even if it does not directly argue, that Dale would use his Scoutmaster position as a "bully pulpit" to convey immoral messages to his troop, and therefore his inclusion in the group would compel BSA to include a message it does not want to impart. . . .

BSA has not contended, nor does the record support, that Dale had ever advocated a view on homosexuality to his troop before his membership was revoked. Accordingly, BSA's revocation could only have been based on an assumption that he would do so in the future. But the only information BSA had at the time it revoked Dale's membership was a newspaper article describing a seminar at Rutgers University on the topic of homosexual teenagers that Dale attended. . . . From all accounts Dale was a model Boy Scout and Assistant Scoutmaster up until the day his membership was revoked, and there is no reason to believe that he would suddenly disobey the directives of BSA because of anything he said in the newspaper article. ***

The majority, though, does not rest its conclusion on the claim that Dale will use his position as a bully pulpit. Rather, it contends that Dale's mere presence among the Boy Scouts will itself force the group to convey a message about homosexuality. ***

It is not likely that BSA would be understood to send any message, either to Scouts or to the world, simply by admitting someone as a member. Over the years, BSA has generously welcomed over 87 million young Americans into its ranks. . . . The notion that an organization of that size and enormous prestige implicitly endorses the views that each of those adults may express in a non-Scouting context is simply mind boggling. Indeed, in this case there is no evidence that the young Scouts in Dale's troop, or members of their families, were even aware of his sexual orientation, either before or after his public statements at Rutgers University. ***

Unfavorable opinions about homosexuals "have ancient roots." *Bowers* v. *Hardwick*, 478 U. S. 186, 192 (1986). . . . Over the years, however, interaction with real people, rather than mere adherence to traditional ways of thinking about members of unfamiliar classes, have modified those opinions. . . . That such prejudices are still prevalent and that they have caused serious and tangible harm to countless members of the class New Jersey seeks to protect are established matters of fact that neither the Boy Scouts nor the Court disputes. . . .

I respectfully dissent.

Questions

1. This case represents a conflict between two important rights. What are they?

2. Given the information presented, do you agree with the majority that disapproval of homosexuality is an integral part of the Boy Scouts' message? Or do you agree with the dissent that it is not? Why?

3. If the Boy Scouts had excluded an African American (rather than a gay man) from membership claiming that including him would run counter to its emphasis on being "clean," do you think the Court would have reached the same conclusion? Why or why not?

4. Where do you believe the line should be drawn between the obligation not to discriminate and the right of a private organization to choose its members? Which is more important? Why?

CHAPTER 18 PRACTICE TEST

The following questions will test your application and analysis of the content found within this chapter. For additional assessment, including licensing-exam type questions on applying chapter content to practice behaviors, visit **MySearchLab**.

1. The U.S. Supreme Court
   a. consistently applies strict scrutiny in LGBT discrimination cases.
   b. first invalidated a law that discriminated against gay men and lesbians in 1996.
   c. continues to uphold laws that criminalize sodomy.
   d. struck down the Defense of Marriage Act.

2. Sexual minorities
   a. are easily identified in census data.
   b. are explicitly protected from workplace discrimination by federal law.
   c. are less well educated than the population at large.
   d. earn less than their heterosexual counterparts.

3. Which of the following is TRUE?
   a. The United States is the first country in the world to allow gays and lesbians to openly serve in the military.

   b. Don't Ask, Don't Tell was repealed by Congress in 2010.
   c. The issue of LGBT service in the military has never come before the courts.
   d. Don't Ask, Don't Tell has never been ruled unconstitutional.

4. Nelson applies for a job at a local bank in his small, southern town. He contacts the branch manager the following week and is told that another candidate was selected instead—one who they believe "would be more acceptable to the customers." Nelson interprets this to mean that he was passed over because he is gay. Nelson has a viable claim of sexual orientation discrimination
   a. under Title VII of the Civil Rights Act.
   b. under Title IX of the Civil Rights Act.
   c. under the recently enacted Employment Non-Discrimination Act.
   d. if his state or county prohibits LGBT discrimination in employment.

5. Discuss how the legislative and judicial branches of government have each contributed to the current legal status of marriage equality in the United States. In your view, when and how will the issue ultimately be resolved? Explain.

6. Given your understanding of the law in relation to sexual minorities, identify and discuss three specific things that social workers can and should do to secure social justice for members of the LGBT community.

MYSEARCHLAB CONNECTIONS

Reinforce what you learned in this chapter by studying videos, cases, documents, and more available at **www.MySearchLab.com.**

Watch these Videos

* Gay Marriage
  * *What has been accomplished, to date, in the pursuit of marrige equality? What steps remain?*

Read these Cases/Documents

Δ Transgender People
* *What are some of the barriers to employment encountered by those who are transgender? How can they be addressed by legal reforms? By agency policies? By individual employers and coworkers?*

Explore these Assets

* Website: Gay and Lesbian Alliance Against Defamation (GLAAD), The

Research these Topics

* the politics of same-sex marriage
* discrmination and gender identity

Assess Your Knowledge

Go to **MySearchLab** to test your knowledge of key topics in this chapter with topic-specific quizzes. Conclude your assessment by completing the chapter exam.

---

* = CSWE Core Competency Asset   Δ = Case Study

Chapter **19**

Legal Rights of Immigrants

Immigration law is exceedingly complex. While many other special populations have realized substantial gains in terms of equal treatment, a hostile public climate has driven the adoption of laws that increasingly curtail immigrant rights. Some of these laws address immigrants broadly, but most target those who are undocumented. For social workers, this represents a critical social justice issue. The National Association of Social Workers "has a special interest in the impact of refugee and immigration policies on families and children" (NASW, 2006). NASW supports legislation that promotes social justice for all immigrants, regardless of their immigration status.

Given that the issue of immigrant rights continues to be a social and political flash-point in many areas of the country, it is important for social workers to be knowledgeable about the rights that are both afforded and denied them. This chapter presents background information about America's immigrant population, explains some of the basic terminology related to immigration law, and explores the rights of immigrants in relation to public benefits, employment, and detention and removal. A special section highlights the controversy surrounding birthright citizenship and the sample case addresses the right to a public school education.

Background

According to the 2009 American Community Survey, a total of 38.5 million people, or 12.5% of the U.S. population, are foreign born (Grieco & Trevelyan, 2010). The foreign-born population is composed of naturalized U.S. citizens, legal permanent residents, temporary residents, and immigrants without authorization. For purposes of our discussion, the terms *unauthorized immigrant* and *undocumented immigrant* will be used interchangeably to describe those individuals sometimes referred to as *illegal immigrants*, an unnecessarily derogatory term. We also use the term *immigrant* in place of the term *alien* to describe those present in the United States who were not born U.S. citizens.

Brief History and Rationale

Prior to the Revolutionary War and for the hundred years that followed, immigration to the United States was unrestricted because immigrants were needed to supplement the existing labor supply. This period of free immigration ended with passage of the Immigration Act of 1882, which excluded undesirables, including convicts, paupers, and the "mentally defective." That same year, the Chinese Exclusion Act sought to exclude Chinese nationals who were no longer needed to supply cheap labor for the railroad industry. The Chinese Exclusion Act was eventually repealed in 1943, when the Chinese became important allies during World War II (Chang-Muy & Congress, 2009). Immigration was further limited by the Immigration Act of 1917, the Quota Law of 1921, and the Immigration Law of 1924 which excluded many noncitizens from Southern and Eastern Europe, required literacy tests, and capped the number of immigrants permitted from countries outside the Western Hemisphere (Legomsky & Rodriguez, 2009). In 1952, Congress passed the Immigration and Nationality Act (INA), which has remained the cornerstone of U.S. immigration policy. The INA continued to permit immigration based on a quota system until it was amended in 1965 to prohibit restrictions premised on race, sex, and nationality (Legomsky & Rodriguez, 2009).

The reasons for migration are many. Lee (1966) coined the *push-pull theory* of immigration, which states that immigrants are pushed from their home countries by economic hardship and political, religious, or social oppression—and pulled to another country by the prospects of a better economy and political freedom. People immigrate to the United States in order to escape environmental disasters, poverty, political instability, and violence. Many seek better wages or working conditions, social and religious freedom, or the opportunity to reunite with family (Chang-Muy & Congress, 2009).

For social workers, working with immigrant clients can be challenging. It is important to understand the entirety of their experience including what life was like in their country of origin; their reasons for immigrating; any difficulties they faced in the course of their journey; and the impact of separation from their home communities, cultures, and supports (Drachman, 1992). It is also extremely helpful to understand how they are regarded under American law; in this way, we can assist them in exercising the rights they have and advocate for the rights denied them.

Immigration Status

Residents of the United States fall under various classifications that determine the terms under which they may remain in the country. These statuses are summarized here:

- **Citizens.** Anyone born in the United States is automatically a citizen under the terms of the U.S. Constitution. Immigrants to the United States can become *naturalized citizens.* In most instances, this requires being a legal permanent resident for at least 5 years; residing continuously in the United States; being of good moral character; being able to read, write, and speak basic English; and passing a civics exam (U.S. Citizenship and Immigration Services [USCIS], 2011).

- **Temporary residents.** Noncitizens who enter the United States under temporary visas are classified as nonimmigrants under the Immigration and Nationality Act. Nonimmigrants may enter as tourists, students, or workers—most often to assume positions in the health care industry, as agricultural workers, or at jobs requiring skilled and unskilled labor. *Temporary protected status* (TPS) may be granted to nationals who cannot return safely to their home countries because of armed conflict or natural disaster (USCIS, 2011).

- **Legal Permanent Residents (LPRs).** These are noncitizens who have been admitted to the United States with the intention of remaining indefinitely. Legal permanent residents are able to get a "green card" and work in the United States. Most people gain LPS status by being sponsored by a family member or employer.

- **Refugees**. These are people who leave their home countries and are unable or unwilling to return because of a well-founded fear of persecution based on race, religion, nationality, political opinion, or membership in a particular social group. Refugees must be sponsored by an individual or organization and can apply for LPR status after 1 year in the United States.

- **Asylees.** These are noncitizens who meet the definition of refugee but enter the United States without first securing refugee status. They can apply for asylum upon entry, within 1 year of entry, or when threatened with deportation (Weissbrodt & Danielson, 2005).

- **Undocumented Immigrants.** These are people who are present in the United States without authorization after having overstayed a legal visa or having entered the country absent official permission.

In addition, several conditions warrant *special status*. Victims of human trafficking may be eligible for a *T-Visa*, which allows for temporary residency in the United States followed by eligibility to apply for legal permanent status. The *U-Visa* is available to victims of serious crime who cooperate with police; like the T-Visa, it can lead to LPR status and a path to citizenship. Under the *Violence Against Women Act* (VAWA), undocumented immigrants who have been abused by their U.S. citizen or LPR spouses may be eligible for relief from deportation. Finally, undocumented youth in state custody for whom reunification is not an option may be eligible for *Special Immigrant Juvenile Status* (SIJS), allowing them to attain LPR status when they transition to adulthood.

Knowing within which category an immigrant falls can be extremely helpful because many rights are specifically premised on immigration status. Making this determination, however, can be difficult; some immigrants are unclear about their legal status, whereas others are reluctant to disclose their status for fear of being detected and deported. Social workers should always be sensitive to the risks that are potentially involved in an immigrant disclosing his or her status and should take the obligation to maintain confidentiality seriously (Rome, 2010).

Demographic Profile

The current attention to immigration issues, much of it punitive, results from rapid growth among mostly Latino immigrants that has changed the composition of numerous American cities and states. This trend is expected to continue. By 2050, an estimated one in five Americans will be an immigrant, with Latino immigrants comprising nearly 30% of the total U.S. population (Passel & Cohn, 2008a).

Of the approximately 38.5 million immigrants currently living in the United States, 43.7% are naturalized citizens. Of those remaining, an estimated 12.5% are LPRs. The vast majority of new LPRs were born in Mexico, followed in descending order by China, the Philippines, India, and the Dominican Republic (Batalova & Terrazas, 2010; Monger, 2010; Rytina, 2010). A total of 74,602 refugees were admitted into the United States in 2009; this is the largest number admitted in a decade. Nearly 68% were from Iraq, Burma, and Bhutan (Batalova & Terrazas, 2010). California and Texas are home to the largest number of new refugees. In addition to those granted refugee status, more than 21,000 people were granted asylum in 2010; most were from China, Ethiopia, and Haiti (Li & Batalova, 2011).

The size of the undocumented immigrant population is notoriously difficult to track. Estimates by the Pew Hispanic Center suggest that there are 11.1 million undocumented immigrants currently living in the United States, 47% of whom have arrived since 2000. Those who are undocumented represent 28% of the foreign-born population, nearly 4% of the total U.S. population, and more than 5% of the U.S. workforce (Batalova & Terrazas, 2010; Passel & Cohn, 2009). Approximately 80% of the undocumented population is from Latin America, primarily from Mexico. According to the Department of Homeland Security, 24% of undocumented immigrants reside in California, down from 30% in 2000. This decrease reflects the fact that settlement patterns have become more dispersed. As Figure 19.1 illustrates, immigrants are finding their way to a larger number of destination states. Even so, immigrants continue to be disproportionately represented in California, Texas, Florida, New York, and Illinois (Hoefer, Rytina, & Baker, 2010).

Of special interest to many social workers is the fact that 23.8% of U.S. children younger than age 17 have at least one immigrant parent (Batalova & Terrazas, 2010). Meeting their needs poses particular challenges for policy makers, the legal system, and service providers alike.

Summary of Federal Laws

Unlike many of the legal issues discussed elsewhere in this book, immigration has traditionally been regarded as lying largely within the domain of the federal government. Among the important federal laws most relevant to immigrant rights are the following:

- **Immigration Reform and Control Act of 1986 (IRCA, P.L. 99-603).** This law granted legal status to immigrants who had resided continuously within the United States without authorization since 1982, legalized the status of certain agricultural workers, increased penalties for employers who knowingly hire undocumented workers, and increased border enforcement.
- **Illegal Immigration Reform and Immigrant Responsibility Act of 1996 (IIRIRA, P.L. 104-208).** This law took a "get tough" approach to undocumented

FIGURE 19.1 States with the Largest and Fastest Growing Immigrant Populations

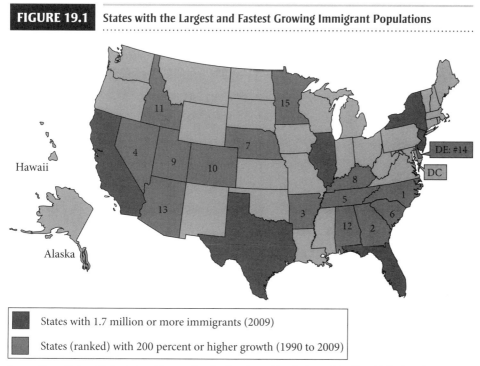

Legend:
- States with 1.7 million or more immigrants (2009)
- States (ranked) with 200 percent or higher growth (1990 to 2009)

Source: From *States with Largest and Fastest Growing Immigrant Populations originally* published on the Migration Policy Institute Data Hub, www.migrationpolicy.org/datahub. Reprinted with permission.

immigration by making it more difficult to sponsor noncitizens for immigration, expanding the definition of deportable offenses, restricting judicial review of removal orders and opportunities for relief, and allowing deportation of noncitizens who become public charges within 5 years of entering the United States.

- **Homeland Security Act of 2002 (P.L. 107-296).** This law, enacted in the aftermath of the September 11, 2001 attacks, reorganized the federal government's administrative structure by creating a new Department of Homeland Security. The new department includes U.S. Customs and Border Protection, Immigration and Customs Enforcement (ICE), and U.S. Citizenship and Immigration Services (USCIS), all of which are involved in the enforcement of federal immigration law.

In recent years, states have begun to assert themselves more boldly, sometimes in ways that seek to expand the rights of immigrants and sometimes in ways that further restrict them. The question of what rightly falls within the federal government's purview and what falls to the states continues to dominate much of the immigration debate. In 2012, the U.S. Supreme Court considered this issue in *Arizona v. United States.* A 5-3 majority (Justice Kagan recused herself) invalidated 3 of the 4 contested provisions of Arizona's law, including making it a state crime for unauthorized immigrants to reside in Arizona or apply for a job, and allowing police to arrest anyone they believe has committed a deportable offense. The majority, however, upheld the state's right to require police to arrest those whom they have probable cause to believe are in the country illegally and to hold them until their status is checked with federal officials. Arizona's law is one of several state laws being challenged in court; others include those in Alabama, Georgia, Indiana, Utah, and South Carolina (Richey, 2011). Although the Supreme Court has ruled on so-called *federal preemption* (whether state immigration enforcement runs afoul of federal prerogatives), it has yet to hear a challenge based on the link between such enforcement and racial profiling or other civil rights violations.

BIRTHRIGHT CITIZENSHIP

The 14th Amendment to the U.S. Constitution states that "all persons born or naturalized in the United States and subject to the jurisdiction thereof are citizens of the United States and of the State in which they reside." Initially adopted to ensure that African Americans could become citizens, the *citizenship clause* has been interpreted to afford U.S. citizenship to anyone born on U.S. soil, including children of undocumented immigrants. According to the U.S. Census Bureau's March 2009 Current Population Survey, 8% of U.S. births in 2008 were to undocumented immigrants, totaling an estimated 340,000 children (Passel & Cohn, 2009). Approximately 37% of undocumented immigrants have U.S.-born children, and an estimated 5.1 million citizen children have parents who are undocumented (Passel & Taylor, 2010). In 2008, 8.8 million people, including 4 million children, lived in mixed-status families (Passel & Cohn, 2009).

Opponents of undocumented immigration often refer to U.S. citizen children of undocumented immigrants as *anchor babies*, the idea being that undocumented parents give birth to children on U.S. soil in order to further their own quest for legal residency. In actuality, research suggests that most undocumented immigrants come to the United States for better paying jobs, not so they can give birth on American soil; the small fraction who do come while pregnant are likely seeking higher quality medical care (Lacey, 2011; Passel & Taylor, 2010). Furthermore, in order to sponsor an undocumented parent, a child must be at least age 21 and have sufficient earnings to qualify, and the parent must spend at least 10 years outside the United States before applying for a green card. Nevertheless,

numerous bills have been introduced in Congress over the past decade seeking to exclude U.S.-born children of undocumented immigrants from citizenship based on a reinterpretation of the citizenship clause. These bills, including the LEAVE Act, the ENFORCE Act, the Citizenship Reform Act, the RIGHT Act, and the No Sanctuary for Illegals Act, have been uniformly unsuccessful, although many have been introduced multiple times. Currently pending is the Birthright Citizenship Act of 2011, introduced by Rep. Steve King (R-IA) and Senator David Vitter (R-LA); as of this writing, the House bill (H.R. 140) has 90 cosponsors and the Senate bill (S. 723) has 4. Like many of the other bills introduced to date, it would limit U.S. citizenship to children who have at least one citizen or LPR parent.

Meanwhile, state governments continue their efforts to force federal action on immigration by introducing their own draconian reforms. Arizona, Indiana, Mississippi, Texas, Oklahoma, and South Dakota have introduced birthright citizenship bills at the state level. A group calling itself State Lawmakers for Legal Immigration has forged an interstate compact under which at least 14 states are seeking to create a new kind of birth certificate that would identify children of undocumented immigrants. The Arizona state Senate Appropriations Committee has already given its blessing to both the birthright citizenship and birth certificate bills (SB 1309 and SB 1308, respectively). There are serious questions about the constitutionality of both proposals.

Revoking birthright citizenship for children of undocumented immigrants would have far-reaching consequences. Because a number of significant rights and benefits are premised on citizenship status, many children would be added to the rolls of those deprived of important assistance. Furthermore, children who now have the option of remaining in the United States in the event that their parents are deported would face their own inevitable deportation as well. Social workers should be actively engaged in opposing these inequitable proposals. We are in an excellent position to add to the body of literature on why people choose to immigrate and to educate the public about the myths that underlie the *anchor baby* idea. We must also help defeat both federal and state attempts to redefine citizenship rights under the 14th Amendment and to brand children of undocumented immigrants with separate birth certificates. These policies disrespect diversity and will likely engender increased divisiveness and discrimination.

Immigration and the Equal Protection Clause

A number of equal protection cases have been brought alleging discrimination based on *alienage* (country of origin) under a variety of federal and state laws. The majority involve differential treatment of citizens and LPRs, the two categories that are most alike. When federal immigration laws have been challenged, the courts have been reluctant to intervene because it is clear that the federal government has sole responsibility for deciding who may immigrate and under what circumstances. In fact, no challenge to a federal immigration law has ever been successful on equal protection grounds. Not only have the courts applied minimal scrutiny, the easiest threshold to meet, but in some cases they have based their decisions on an even less stringent finding that the classification was not *wholly irrational*. A good example is *Matthews v. Diaz* (1976), where the Supreme Court upheld a law under which federal Medicare benefits were provided only to citizens and to LPRs who had been in the country for at least 5 years. This tendency to treat federal immigration laws with deference has extended to the most recently enacted welfare law, the 1996 Personal Responsibility Act. In *City of Chicago v. Shalala* (1999), the Seventh Circuit applied minimal scrutiny and upheld the denial of Supplemental Security Income and food stamps to noncitizens.

When it comes to state laws, the situation is quite different. Initially, back in 1886, the U.S. Supreme Court ruled that the 14th Amendment applies to citizens and noncitizens alike. In deciding the case of *Yick Wo v. Hopkins*, the Court struck down a San Francisco ordinance that applied different requirements to laundries owned by Chinese residents and White residents, effectively barring the former from earning a living. For many years that followed, however, discriminatory laws enforced by the states were routinely upheld. Throughout the late 19th and early 20th centuries, when immigration to the United States was especially heavy, the courts found a variety of ways to allow states to maintain laws that disadvantaged immigrants (Weissbrodt & Danielson, 2005).

This began to turn around with the 1915 case of *Traux v. Raich*. This case concerned an Arizona law that required private employers to ensure that at least 80% of their workforce was comprised of U.S.-born citizens. The Supreme Court struck down the law, arguing that regulating the employment of LPRs impinged on the federal government's role in relation to immigration; it further concluded that the law's sole purpose was to discriminate. The next time the Court struck down an immigration law was more than 30 years later, in

Takahashi v. Fish and Game Commission (1948). This case involved a California law that discriminated against Japanese residents by restricting fishing licenses to those eligible for citizenship (which, at the time, Japanese nationals were not).

In the 1970s, this tougher approach to state laws that discriminate against immigrants culminated in *Graham v. Richardson* (1971). In that case, the U.S. Supreme Court concluded that noncitizens constitute a suspect classification and that alienage, like race, was deserving of strict scrutiny. The Court consequently struck down an Arizona law under which a disabled 64-year-old LPR from Mexico was denied state-administered Medicaid benefits because of her immigration status. This case was heard together with another case involving an LPR from Scotland who was denied benefits under Pennsylvania's state public assistance program. The Court soundly rejected the states' rationale that they were conserving limited benefits for their own citizens. Throughout the 1970s, lower courts struck down a whole host of state laws using strict scrutiny. These included, for example, a New York law barring noncitizens from working in civil service positions, a Connecticut law allowing only U.S. citizens to practice law, a Puerto Rican law limiting engineering licenses to citizens, and a New York law that denied college financial assistance to LPRs and other noncitizens unless they applied for citizenship status (Weissbrodt & Danielson, 2005).

By the end of the 1970s, the tide had again turned, this time away from the use of strict scrutiny. State statutes that drew distinctions between citizens and noncitizens in relation to "political" functions were upheld by state courts; for example, noncitizens in New York were barred from serving as state troopers and being certified as public school teachers, while California permitted only citizens to be employed as probation officers. Courts also upheld discriminatory state laws found to be consistent with federal policy (including restrictions on the receipt of Temporary Assistance for Needy Families [TANF] benefits). Some states, meanwhile, have continued to apply strict scrutiny. Given these inconsistencies, the only conclusion that can be drawn is that challenges to discriminatory state policies are more likely to be successful than challenges to federal law—although even with state laws, the Court has yet to settle on a consistent approach.

Access to Public Benefits

The rights of immigrants in relation to public benefits changed dramatically with the enactment of two laws in 1996: the Personal Responsibility and Work Opportunity Reconciliation Act (PRWORA, commonly referred to as *welfare reform*) and the IIRIRA. Contrary to what many believe, these laws had a significant impact not only on unauthorized immigrants but also on those legally in the country. The original definition of "federal public benefits" was extremely broad. It restricted immigrants' access to grants, contracts, loans, professional licenses, and commercial licenses, along with retirement, welfare, health, disability, public or assisted housing, postsecondary education, food assistance, unemployment compensation, and any other benefit for which payments or assistance is provided to an individual, household, or family by an agency of the United States or by public funds. The Department of Health and Human Services later narrowed the list, but it remains the case that new and stringent eligibility requirements apply to benefits under the Low-Income Home Energy Assistance Program (LIHEAP), the Children's Health Insurance Program (CHIP), TANF, Foster Care and Adoption Assistance, the Child Care and Development Fund (CCDF), Medicare, and nonemergency Medicaid, among others (Broder & Blazer, 2011).

Benefit Eligibility

The Personal Responsibility Act created two categories of immigrants for purposes of determining access to federal benefit programs: qualified immigrants and not qualified immigrants. *Qualified immigrants* include the following:

- LPRs (people with green cards)
- Refugees and asylees
- Certain battered spouses and children
- Certain victims of trafficking

All other immigrants, including undocumented immigrants and many people lawfully present in the United States, are considered *not qualified* (Broder & Blazer, 2011). Eligibility rules for both categories are summarized in Table 19.1. Because of the complexity of the governing laws and regulations, this information is designed to provide an overview only.

TABLE 19.1   **Eligibility of Qualified and Non-Qualified Immigrants for Federal Public Benefits**

Program	Qualified Immigrants Eligible Only If	Not Qualified Immigrants Eligible Only If
Supplemental Security Income (SSI)	• LPR with 40 quarters of work	• Receiving SSI on August 22, 1996
	• At least 5 years in qualified immigrant status	• Victims of trafficking and their derivative beneficiaries, but only for first 7 years after status granted
	• Granted refugee status or asylum	
	• Veteran or active duty military; spouse, un-remarried surviving spouse or child	
Food Stamps	• Under age 18	• Victims of trafficking and their derivative beneficiaries
	• Granted refugee status or asylum	
	• At least 5 years in qualified immigrant status	

(continued)

TABLE 19.1 **Eligibility of Qualified and Non-Qualified Immigrants for Federal Public Benefits (continued)**

Program	Qualified Immigrants Eligible Only If	Not Qualified Immigrants Eligible Only If
	• Receiving disability-related assistance	
	• LPR with 40 quarters of work	
	• Age 65 or older and lawfully residing in the U.S. on August 22, 1996	
	• Veteran or active duty military; spouse, un-remarried surviving spouse or child	
Temporary Assistance to Needy Families (TANF)	• Granted refugee status or asylum	• Victims of trafficking and their derivative beneficiaries
	• At least 5 years in qualified immigrant status	
	• Veteran or active duty military; spouse, un-remarried surviving spouse or child	
Medicaid	• Granted refugee status or asylum	• Receiving SSI on August 22, 1996
	• Receiving federal foster care funds	• Victims of trafficking and their derivative beneficiaries
	• At least 5 years in qualified immigration status	
	• Veteran or active duty military; spouse, un-remarried surviving spouse or child	
Children's Health Insurance Program (CHIP)	• Granted refugee status or asylum	• Victims of trafficking and their derivative beneficiaries
	• At least 5 years in qualified immigrant status	
	• Veteran or active duty military; spouse, un-remarried surviving spouse or child	

(continued)

Program	Qualified Immigrants Eligible Only If	Not Qualified Immigrants Eligible Only If
Medicare, Part A (Hospitalization)	• Eligible	• Lawfully present and eligible for assistance based on employment record
Public Housing and Section 8 Housing	• Certain abused spouses and children (If one member of the household is eligible on the basis of immigration status, the family may reside in the housing but the subsidy will be pro-rated.)	• Victims of trafficking and their derivative beneficiaries
Social Security	Eligible	• Lawfully present in the U.S.
		• Receiving assistance based on an application filed before December 1,1996

Source: From Guide to Immigrant *Eligibility for Federal Programs*. Copyright © 2002 by the National Immigration Law Center. Reprinted with permission.

Contrary to what the term would suggest, "qualified" immigrants face significant restrictions in accessing benefits. LPRs are eligible to apply for most benefits only after they have been in the United States for at least 5 years; in many cases, they must also have at least 40 quarters of work history. In certain cases, humanitarian immigrants such as refugees, asylees, and victims of human trafficking are eligible to receive benefits for a period of only 7 years after their status is granted, although some may be eligible for a 2-year extension (Broder & Blazer, 2011; Zimmerman & Tumlin, 1999).

Most immigrants petitioning for residency in the United States are required to have a sponsor submit an affidavit of support. The sponsor promises to financially support the immigrant if necessary and must demonstrate the financial ability to do so (Legomsky & Rodriguez, 2009). If the immigrant attempts to apply for public assistance, the sponsor's income is added to the immigrant's income, which invariably puts the immigrant over the maximum amount permitted for benefit eligibility (Chang-Muy & Congress, 2009).

Immigrants who are "not qualified" are excluded from all major federal benefit programs with the exception of emergency services under Medicaid, immunizations, short-term emergency disaster relief, and treatment for communicable diseases (Zimmerman & Tumlin, 1999). Despite the fact that many undocumented immigrants pay taxes and contribute to Social Security, the IIRIRA prohibits these immigrants from ever receiving Social Security benefits (Legomsky & Rodriguez, 2009). A number of states have passed legislation allowing otherwise not qualified immigrants to receive state-funded services. For example, all states provide access to the Supplemental Nutrition Program for Women, Infants, and Children (WIC), and many provide health care coverage to children and pregnant women (Chang-Muy & Congress, 2009).

Barriers to Access

Even immigrants who are eligible may face barriers in actually obtaining public benefits. The confusing mix of state and federal laws can leave many clients, eligibility workers, and service providers uncertain about who is eligible for what, resulting in immigrants mistakenly being deemed ineligible when they actually are qualified for benefits. Eligibility workers should be trained in the laws of their state in order to ensure that they are providing competent advice and assistance. Social workers must be knowledgeable in order to serve as effective advocates for immigrant clients, ensuring that they are able to access the benefits they need.

Lack of language-appropriate services can impede immigrants' access to public benefits as well, even though Title VI of the Civil Rights Act of 1964 prohibits agencies from discriminating against recipients of federal funding on the basis of national origin and requires that they implement measures to provide language assistance (Chang-Muy & Congress, 2009).

Widespread confusion has also arisen over a provision allowing immigration officials to deny entry into the country or applications for LPR status if they determine that the immigrant is likely to become *public charge* (Broder & Blazer, 2011). Despite clarification that receipt of noncash benefits will not jeopardize an immigrant's status, some agencies continue to provide inaccurate information and many immigrants refrain from taking advantage of available benefits for fear of being deemed a public charge.

Imposition of complex and confusing rules, restricted eligibility, and a hostile public climate have had a chilling effect that has kept some qualified immigrants from seeking the benefits to which they are entitled. Following passage of the Personal Responsibility Act, for example, there was a huge drop in food stamp use even by eligible noncitizens. In mixed–status families, noncitizen parents may fail to access benefits to which their U.S.-born children are fully entitled because of their own fears of being detected and deported (Van Hook & Balisreri, 2006). Similarly, although children in undocumented immigrant families are eligible for discounted immunizations and emergency medical care, lack of certainty about eligibility rules and fear of deportation prevent many parents from seeking these critical health care services for their children (Kullgren, 2003).

Partly as a result of their limited access to the nation's safety net, immigrants are disproportionately represented among U.S. residents living in poverty (Zimmerman & Tumlin, 1999). Undocumented immigrants in particular are more likely than American citizens to be poor, lack health insurance, and experience food insecurity. They have higher rates of unemployment and lower educational attainment and are more likely to face significant language barriers (Passel & Cohn, 2009). Restricted access to food stamps and Medicaid may place children at increased risk of long-term physical, cognitive, and developmental deficits (Van Hook & Balisreri, 2006). Meanwhile, immigrant adults who fail to access emergency health care services for communicable diseases may endanger not only their own health but the public health as well (Kullgren, 2003).

Ethical Issues for Social Workers

Given the current public climate favoring anti-immigrant policies and practices, social workers may be confronted by troubling ethical dilemmas. This often occurs when the law requires one course of action and our Code of Ethics requires another (Reamer, 2008). The first step in reconciling these discrepant expectations is to become familiar with the relevant laws in the jurisdictions where we practice. Unfortunately, some of us fail to do so; instead, we behave based on faulty assumptions or our own personal biases. In one alarming case, a social worker under contract with the Florida Department of Children and Families arranged a visit between two children and their undocumented mother and grandparents, specifically for the purpose of allowing local authorities to apprehend them and turn them over to ICE for deportation (Florida Immigrant Coalition, 2009). Although the vast majority of social workers would recognize this example as a flagrant violation of social work ethics, not every case is so clear. The reality, as discussed earlier, is that there are limits on the federal benefits to which noncitizens are entitled, and a number of states and localities have passed laws making social workers complicit in their efforts to further marginalize the immigrant population. In 2004, Arizona voters approved a ballot initiative (Proposition 200) requiring all public employees to verify a prospective recipient's immigration status before providing any public benefit, and to report to authorities those who are unable to produce documentation of their legal status. Anyone providing services to someone not legally present in the United States is subject to a fine and/or jail time (Furman, Langer, Sanchez, & Negi, 2007). A number of localities have similarly attempted to enlist service providers in their quest to discourage immigrants from settling within their borders. In 2005, the town of Herndon, Virginia, opened a day labor center that drew the ire of some local residents. The town council insisted that the center's operators check immigration status and serve only those who could document that they were in the country legally; the operators of the center refused. The town council tried to find another group to operate the center, but none would agree to comply with its terms. Meanwhile, a circuit court judge ruled that the town's policy of serving only "legal" immigrants was a violation of both the First Amendment and the equal protection clause (*Town of Herndon v. Thomas*, 2007). Rather than serve all immigrants regardless of status, however, the town council voted to shut the site down (Turque, 2007).

These examples illustrate how easily immigration policies can create serious ethical dilemmas for social workers when we have to decide between embracing our professional ethics and adhering to the law (Furman et al., 2007; Padilla, Shapiro, Fernández-Castro, & Faulkner, 2008). Fortunately, efforts to enact similar laws on the federal level have thus far been unsuccessful. For example, the Border Protection, Terrorism, and Illegal Immigration Control Act of 2005 (H.R. 4437) would have criminalized assisting, transporting, or harboring undocumented immigrants, potentially jeopardizing the provision of health care and social services. The bill passed in the House of Representatives but died in the U.S. Senate (Dolgoff, Loewenberg, & Harrington, 2009; Padilla et al., 2008).

Reporting an immigrant's status to authorities or denying immigrants services flies in the face of our professional commitment to maintaining client confidentiality and ensuring that all people have equal access to resources, employment, services, and opportunities. How, then, should we respond when the law conflicts with our ethical obligations? The NASW Code of Ethics directs us to make a responsible effort to resolve the conflict in a manner that is consistent with our professional values and principles, and to seek consultation before acting (NASW, 2008). Meanwhile, if social workers believe that a legal mandate is ethically questionable, we should use our experience in working with immigrants to effectively advocate for policy change (Padilla, 1997). According to former

NASW president Elvira Craig de Silva, "As social workers, we must present a politically active, united front to stem the disappearance of services and resources and ensure equal protection from discrimination for all immigrants, refugees and undocumented individuals who come to live in the U.S. To do nothing is to ignore the core of who we are and what our profession stands for*" (De Silva, 2006).

Access to Public Education

Surprisingly, as Chapter 20 explains, the U.S. Constitution embodies no explicit right to an education. Yet we consider an education an indispensible asset in this country, fundamental to achieving self-sufficiency, success, and the ability to compete in the global economy. In a landmark 1982 case, the U.S. Supreme Court ruled that although no one is guaranteed a public education, the equal protection clause prohibits states from financing the education of some children while declining to finance the education of undocumented immigrant children. That case, *Plyler v. Doe,* appears as the sample case at the end of the chapter.

For border states in particular, the costs of educating immigrant children are substantial. Thus the Supreme Court's decision has not deterred states from seeking to avoid providing undocumented immigrant children with a public education. In 1994, California voters approved Proposition 187, which, among other provisions, barred the state's school districts from enrolling undocumented children. The law was subsequently overturned in *League of United Latin American Citizens v. Wilson* (1995), relying on the Supreme Court's decision in *Plyler v. Doe.* More than 15 years later, in 2011, Arizona introduced a bill that contemplates similar action. SB 1611 would make proof of citizenship a requirement for admission to taxpayer-supported schools, depriving immigrant children from kindergarten through college of a public education (Sayani, 2011). That same year, Alabama enacted legislation requiring public schools to determine each student's immigration status and submit annual reports to the State Board of Education. Fortunately, unless and until the courts rule otherwise, immigrants retain a constitutional right to public education, regardless of their status.

Of course, merely permitting enrollment is not enough. Immigrants face additional barriers to educational success, including limited English proficiency, work and family responsibilities, and financial insecurity. Only two-thirds of immigrants older than age 25 who are not naturalized have a high school education (Erisman & Looney, 2007). Fry (2010) reports that only 48% of foreign-born Latino adults graduated from high school and of those who drop out, only 5% obtain a GED.

Language barriers are a significant obstacle for many immigrant students. The number of students with limited English proficiency (LEP) in public schools increased by 56% between 1995 and 2005, while the entire student population increased by only 2.6%. As discussed in Chapter 16, research shows a wide achievement gap between LEP and non-LEP students on standardized tests that continues throughout childhood and adolescence (Batalova, Fix, & Murray, 2007; Fry, 2007). Title VI of the Civil Rights Act of 1964 and the Equal Educational Opportunities Act (EEOA) of 1974 require school districts to take action to ensure that students' language barriers do not impede equal participation in educational programs. Schools are required to assess students' English proficiency and provide

---

*Excerpt from *A United Front on Immigration* by Elvira Craig de Silva, from NASW News, February 2006, Volume 51(2). Copyright © 2006 by the National Association of Social Workers, Inc. Reprinted with permission.

English as a Second Language (ESL) instruction when necessary. The U.S. Department of Justice is responsible for monitoring and enforcing the implementation of these programs.

The controversy regarding immigrants and education applies to higher education as well; immigrants comprise just 12% of undergraduate college students (Erisman & Looney, 2007). Latino immigrants are underrepresented in this group, accounting for only 30% of those immigrants attending college. Immigrant students are less likely to earn a bachelor's degree than their citizen counterparts, instead earning certificates or associates degrees. Although undocumented immigrants are permitted to attend public universities, they face numerous challenges as a result of their immigration status. Undocumented students are ineligible for governmental grants, loans, or work-study programs, leaving many unable to afford a college education. In addition, the IIRIRA bars undocumented immigrants from paying in-state tuition rates unless the state specifically passes legislation to authorize it. To date, 12 states have done so. California, Connecticut, Illinois, Kansas, Nebraska, New Mexico, New York, Oklahoma, Texas, Utah, and Washington allow undocumented immigrants to enroll as in-state students in their public universities. Although Maryland enacted such a law in 2011, a successful petition drive among opponents resulted in the law being shelved pending the results of a ballot referendum in 2012. Most of the state laws require that the student has lived in the state for a certain number of years, graduated from high school there, and plans to apply for legalized status (National Immigration Law Center, 2012). A number of states have also made undocumented students eligible for scholarships derived from non-state sources.

The federal DREAM Act was first introduced in the U.S. Senate in 2001 and has been reintroduced in every Congress since. Under the DREAM Act, undocumented youth who arrived in the United States before age 16, have lived in the United States for 5 years, graduated from a U.S. high school, and were of "good moral character" would be granted conditional permanent residency status for 6 years. If within those 6 years, the individual completes at least 2 years of college or serves for 2 years in the military, he or she would be eligible to apply for U.S. citizenship (Lee, 2006). The most recent version of the legislation was defeated in the 111th Congress in December 2010 by a Senate filibuster. In 2012, President Obama circumvented Congress and initiated a "deferred action" policy that allows undocumented youth who came to the United States as children to avoid deportation for two years while they work or attend college. Although as many as 1.7 million people are expected to qualify, the costs of a college education may prove to be prohibitive for many; the policy also falls short of creating a path to citizenship. Many consider it an important step forward, but a temporary solution at best.

Rights in Employment

Under U.S. law, noncitizens are permitted to work in the United States only if they are LPRs, refugees, or asylees, or they have a nonimmigrant status that allows them to be employed. The United States permits 140,000 noncitizens per year to immigrate for employment purposes; priority is given to those with extraordinary potential or advanced degrees. Noncitizen workers may also enter the United States on temporary work visas in order to help employers meet an immediate need for extra labor (Weissbrodt & Danielson, 2005). Until the passage of the Immigration Reform and Control Act in 1986, there were no restrictions on immigrants seeking work or employers hiring them, regardless of their status. Today, noncitizens who work without authorization and employers who knowingly hire unauthorized workers are subject to penalties under the law. Nonetheless, many undocumented immigrants find work in the U.S. economy, often in low-paying or high-risk jobs, including agriculture, construction, manufacturing, and food services (Chang-Muy & Congress, 2009).

Decent jobs are one of the primary motivations that drive immigrants to come to the United States. Even though some of their earnings go back to family members in their countries of origin, they also contribute to the U.S. economy by renting apartments, establishing small businesses, and purchasing goods. Between 1990 and 2001, half of all new workers in the United States were recent immigrants; between 2000 and 2004, they accounted for approximately 60% of workforce growth (Chang-Muy & Congress, 2009). Not surprisingly, immigrant workers earn less on average than their citizen counterparts, with undocumented families earning approximately 40% less than documented immigrants or U.S.-born families (Passel, 2005). Undocumented workers are overrepresented in low-wage jobs; although they comprise approximately 5% of the total workforce, they make up a full 20% of those doing low-wage work.

Rights in the Workplace

Immigrants, both documented and undocumented, have rights in employment. They are covered by Title VII of the Civil Rights Act, which protects against workplace discrimination based on race, color, national origin, religion, and sex. Immigrant workers are also protected by federal wage and hour laws and are entitled to a minimum wage and overtime payments under the Fair Labor Standards Act (FLSA). All workers also have the right to be paid for work performed. In *Patel v. Quality Inn South* (1988), the 11th Circuit Court of Appeals considered the case of a man from India who remained in the United States after the expiration of his tourist visa, performing maintenance work at a hotel in Alabama. After more than 2 years there, he sued the hotel for wage and overtime violations. The court found in his favor, concluding that all workers are entitled to the protections of the FLSA. They reasoned that even if their employment is not legal, denying undocumented immigrants these protections might incentivize employers to hire them at less than the minimum wage.

Immigrants also have the right to unionize in the workplace, regardless of their status. In the 1984 Supreme Court case of *Sure-Tan, Inc. v. NLRB*, the Court held that undocumented workers who were reported to immigration authorities in retaliation for union organizing could sue under the National Labor Relations Act (NLRA). Although the Court reached a similar conclusion in the 2002 case of *Hoffman Plastic Compounds, Inc. v. NLRB*, it nonetheless found that an undocumented worker who was fired because of his union affiliation was not entitled to reinstatement or back pay. The Court seems to be saying that undocumented immigrants have a right to union participation and must be compensated for work actually performed, but those who are illegally employed are not entitled to back pay for work that was not performed.

Under the Occupational Safety and Health Act (OSHA) of 1970, workers also have the right to a safe and healthy workplace. Despite being covered by OSHA, foreign-born workers comprised 69% of workplace fatalities in 2002, although they accounted for only 15% of the U.S. workforce (Chang-Muy & Congress, 2009). They also experience significantly higher rates of occupational injury than their native counterparts (Orrenius & Zavodny, 2009). This raises the question of whether immigrants are eligible to receive workers' compensation payments to subsidize the costs of medical care and lost earnings.

Although the terms of these laws vary by state, at least two cases (one in Michigan and one in Pennsylvania) have permitted employers to avoid providing workers' compensation to injured workers who are on the job illegally (Weissbrodt & Danielson, 2005).

Verifying Immigration Status

The Immigration Reform and Control Act (IRCA) of 1986 amended the INA to make it illegal for an employer to knowingly recruit, hire, or continue to employ anyone who is not authorized to work in the United States. As a result, many otherwise law-abiding individuals have been forced to acquire false documentation in order to secure employment. The practice of purchasing false documents has led to the creation of E-Verify, an Internet-based program that allows employers to verify a worker's employment eligibility. For the most part, participation in E-Verify is voluntary, although some states (including Arizona and Mississippi) mandate its use. If a worker's name and Social Security number do not match the entry in E-Verify, ICE issues a *no-match letter* to the employer, who must then either investigate the worker's documentation further or terminate the employee. Since its inception, the program has been plagued by widespread problems, including erroneous no-match letters resulting from misspellings, inconsistent representations of surnames originally in other languages, name changes through marriage or divorce, and long delays in updating information. These errors disproportionately affect foreign-born U.S. citizens, with almost 10% mistakenly being told they are not eligible for employment; this is 30 times the rate for native-born U.S. citizens. The program's opponents argue that use of the program discriminates against workers perceived to be foreign, and that its effectiveness in preventing the employment of undocumented immigrants is questionable.

In 2011, the U.S. Supreme Court upheld an Arizona law mandating the use of E-Verify and permitting the revocation of business licenses held by companies that knowingly hire undocumented workers (*Chamber of Commerce v. Whiting*). The primary question was whether the state is preempting federal law. Opponents argued that the Arizona law conflicts with provisions of IRCA, but the majority of the Court found the law permissible because the issuing of business licenses was the province of the state.

Exploitation in the Workplace

IRCA's prohibition against hiring undocumented immigrants has resulted in a dramatic increase in exploitation (Legomsky & Rodriguez, 2009). Documented and undocumented immigrants are overrepresented in low-wage industries and are frequently paid at or below the minimum wage. Many immigrants in the service and construction sectors, for example, receive no overtime pay and no benefits and are frequently exploited through nonpayment of wages. Some employers charge immigrants for transportation or levy fees for services such as cashing payroll checks. Immigrants also experience mandatory extra hours, few regular breaks, poor or dangerous working conditions, and a high incidence of workplace injuries (Bloomekatz, 2007; Valenzuela, 2003).

Poor command of the English language and low levels of education make immigrants susceptible to exploitation. Many are ignorant of their employment rights or are unaware of how to pursue them. In addition, their marginalized status contributes to their vulnerability (Heyman, 1998; Valenzuela, 2003). Immigrants employed under temporary work visas are often powerless; when their visas expire, employers know that they will either leave the country or become undocumented, making them less likely to report workplace abuses. Immigrants have little leverage against their employers; they often fear demotion, harassment, termination, or exposure to federal authorities if they fail to acquiesce to adverse conditions or treatment (Bloomekatz, 2007). Finally, immigrants may not report exploitation because they are accustomed to the standards of employment in their home countries, which are often worse than those in the United States.

Workplace Raids

One enforcement mechanism used by ICE to identify and detain unauthorized workers is workplace raids. The number and frequency of these raids increased dramatically during the George W. Bush administration, going from a total of 500 in 2005 to 1,000 in 2006 (Dettlaff & Phillips, 2007). Relatively few of the arrests made as a result of these raids were for criminal conduct. Between 2002 and 2007, only 863 workplace arrests were for actual crimes, compared to 4,077 for unauthorized presence in the United States (U.S. Immigration and Customs Enforcement, 2007). The constitutionality of these enforcement actions was upheld in *INS v. Delgado* (1984). In that case, the Supreme Court ruled that questioning factory workers about their immigration status during a factory raid did not constitute a "seizure" under the Fourth Amendment because the workers were permitted to continue with their work and to move about the workplace during the investigation.

Contrary to the picture painted in the *Delgado* case, however, those who have been subjected to raids describe having been kept in their place of business for hours on end, deprived of the opportunity to eat, drink, or use the bathroom. Witnesses to raids contend that Latino workers are singled out for greater scrutiny than White workers, leading to accusations of racial profiling (Hing, 2009). In addition, few immigrants arrested during raids are provided with interpreters who speak their native language (Ackermann, 2010). Finally, although most undocumented immigrants caught in raids are charged, there is little prosecution of the employers who are also breaking the law. In Postville, Iowa, a 2008 raid on an Agriprocessors plant disrupted a union organizing campaign and interfered with an investigation into alleged child labor law violations (Chang-Muy & Congress, 2009). Although nearly 400 workers were arrested, not a single company official was prosecuted. This reflects national trends. While the number of workers arrested in workplace raids rose from just over 500 in 2002 to nearly 5,000 in 2008, only 90 arrests involved officials of the employing companies (Hsu, 2008).

The negative impact of raids on families and communities is also well documented. When parents are picked up in workplace raids, children may be stranded at school or day care, or left entirely without supervision. Parents sometimes end up signing voluntary departure papers and leaving the country before they can contact their families (Capps, Castaneda, Chaudry, & Santos, 2007). The long-term effects of raids on children include anxiety, depression, feelings of abandonment, emotional trauma, eating and sleeping disorders, posttraumatic stress disorder, and behavioral changes (Capps et al., 2007; Kremer, Moccio, & Hammell, 2009). After raids, immigrant communities suffer increased social isolation because many people fear arrest if they venture outside. They also suffer economic hardship when, in the absence of the breadwinner, extended family members must assume responsibility for the children whose parents were detained or removed.

The Obama administration has distanced itself from the large-scale raids that characterized the Bush administration, focusing instead on charging employers who illegally hire immigrant workers (Slevin, 2010). Between 2008 and 2010, the administration quadrupled the number of employer audits; it fined businesses a total of $6.9 million in 2010, compared with $675,000 just two years earlier (Bennett, 2011; Preston, 2010).

Detection, Detention, and Removal

As a result of changes to federal, state, and local immigration laws, *detection, detention, and deportation* (also known as *removal*) have become more common in recent years, affecting all noncitizens regardless of their immigration status. Enforcement of immigration laws has become more zealous, with record high numbers of immigrants detained until deportation. In addition, partnerships between local law enforcement and ICE have increased the ability of local police forces to apprehend those suspected of immigration violations.

Detection

The IIRIRA altered the long-standing policy that the federal government has sole authority over immigration concerns. As a result of these changes, state and local authorities are now empowered to enter into agreements with ICE that allow local law enforcement officials to enforce immigration laws. These agreements, known as *287(g) agreements*, are presently operating in 72 jurisdictions in 24 states. Specifically, they delegate authority to local law enforcement to screen people for immigration status, identify violators, and detain them until federal authorities take custody. These charges initiate the deportation process (Capps, Rosenblum, Rodriguez, & Chishti, 2011). Between 2006 and 2009, 287(g) agreements led to the identification of 120,000 undocumented immigrants (Feere, 2009).

The Obama administration has announced its intention to prioritize identifying and removing those undocumented immigrants who represent security threats, have committed serious crimes, or have multiple immigration violations. Although the overall number of deportations increased by 6% between 2008 and 2010, the number of criminals deported increased by 70% (Bennett, 2011). There is little evidence that these new priorities have had an appreciable impact on local enforcement activities, however. Nationally, only about half of those picked up through 287(g) agreements have committed serious crimes; the other half are guilty of misdemeanors, primarily traffic offenses. A recent study found that policies among jurisdictions vary; some are implementing targeted programs that focus on the Obama priorities, whereas others continue to implement universal programs aimed at identifying as many undocumented immigrants as possible (Capps et al., 2011).

Critics have voiced concern that permitting local law enforcement officers to check immigration status will lead to racial profiling and contrived arrests. There are reports that Hispanic-looking drivers have been pulled over for alleged traffic infractions, presumably as a pretext for verifying their immigration status (Mauldin, 2010). Another criticism of the program is that it negatively affects communities by leading immigrants to avoid public places, undermining their trust in law enforcement and making them less likely to report crimes and cooperate in investigations (Capps et al., 2011; Rome, 2010). On another front, the Secure Communities program, initiated by ICE in 2007, requires local law enforcement to send the fingerprints of everyone arrested—for everything from traffic violations to homicides—to be checked against U.S. immigration records (U.S. Immigration and Customs Enforcement, n.d.). If a fingerprint is matched to Department of Homeland Security immigration databases, ICE is notified—even if the noncitizen has not been convicted of a crime. As of October 2010, Secure Communities has been implemented in 33 states and has been responsible for the removal of tens of thousands of undocumented immigrants (Immigration Policy Center, 2010; Vedantam, 2010).

One of the criticisms of Secure Communities is that no training is provided to the local law enforcement officers who participate (National Immigration Forum, n.d.). As with the 287(g) programs, there are also concerns about racial profiling, contrived stops and arrests, and the fact that the vast majority of those identified have committed only minor offenses. Several localities have attempted to opt out of the Secure Communities program, including Arlington County (VA), the District of Columbia, San Francisco, and Santa Clara County (CA). Contrary to what was widely believed to be true, ICE has indicated that, for all intents and purposes, participation is required (Vedantam, 2010).

Detention

ICE holds immigrant detainees in a network of 400 jails and detention facilities, where more than 30,000 detainees can be found on any given day. The Department of Homeland Security reported detaining a total of 383,524 immigrants in 2009 (Department of Homeland Security, 2010); approximately 70% of these detainees are held in county jails under contract with the federal government (Kalhan, 2010). Detention is mandatory for all noncitizens in deportation proceedings for aggravated felony convictions (discussed later), as well as for those with pending asylum cases (Rotolo, 2008; Legomsky & Rodriguez, 2009). Approximately two-thirds of detainees are subject to mandatory detention, and almost half of all removal proceedings involve a person who is detained (Kalhan, 2010).

The conditions faced by immigrants in detention suggest violations of both human rights and legal due process. There is little oversight by ICE of local county jails where the majority of detained immigrants are held. Although immigration proceedings are considered civil, immigration detainees are held in the same units as violent criminals. The American Civil Liberties Union and Amnesty International have documented substandard conditions in these facilities including overcrowding, poor ventilation, unacceptable food quality, unsanitary living quarters, and nonfunctioning showers and toilets. In addition, detainees complain about lack of access to telephones, limited visitation hours, physical and verbal abuse, and inadequate access to health care. Since 2003, more than 100 detainees have died while in ICE custody, often because their health needs have gone untreated during detention (Kalhan, 2010).

Because immigration violations are classified as noncriminal offenses under the law, the legal safeguards and protections that attach in criminal proceedings are unavailable; in essence, although detainees are incarcerated, they enjoy few legal rights. Detainees have no right to receive *Miranda* warnings; no right to a jury trial; and in cases of mandatory detention, they have no right to bail. Immigrant detainees do not have the right to a speedy trial; this can result in detention lasting months or years if the person contests his or her deportation. Finally, the one legal right that is arguably most critical, the right to counsel, is often beyond a detainee's reach. The government is under no obligation to provide a lawyer free of charge as it does in criminal cases; as a result, approximately 84% of detainees lack access to counsel (American Civil Liberties Union, n.d.). Without the assistance of a lawyer, detainees have difficulty contacting witnesses and gathering evidence to defend themselves against the charges.

The challenges of detention are particularly acute for unaccompanied, undocumented minors. Like adult detainees, they have no right to free legal representation and must hire their own attorneys or navigate the complexities of the immigration process on their own. Youth with legal representation are four times more likely to win their cases, thereby avoiding long-term detention and deportation; however, only about 50% of unaccompanied youth have access to attorneys and only about 10% appear with immigration lawyers in court. As a result, these youth must often make tremendously difficult decisions—including whether to opt for voluntary departure or for a hearing with an immigration judge—without the benefit of legal counsel.

The Supreme Court case of *Flores v. Reno* (1993) resulted in a negotiated settlement between the Immigration and Naturalization Service (INS) and the plaintiffs, a group of unaccompanied, undocumented children. Under the agreement, the INS must recognize the special vulnerability of minors, hold them in the least restrictive setting possible, and permit them to be released to someone who will keep them safe and ensure their appearance in immigration court even if that person is not a parent or legal guardian. Although some concerns remain about the implementation of the *Flores* agreement, many improvements have been documented. In 2002, responsibility for unaccompanied immigrant children was transferred from the INS to the Division of Unaccompanied Children's Services (DUCS) within the Office of Refugee Resettlement in the U.S. Department of Health and Human Services. While 34% of unaccompanied, undocumented children were placed in jail-like settings under the INS, less than 2% are now placed in secure facilities (Bump & Gozdziak, 2007). According to observers, however, more progress needs to be made. The majority of youth are still held in large, institution-style settings rather than in noninstitutional settings such as shelter facilities, group homes, or short-term foster care (Barth, 2002). DHS also continues to operate family detention centers where entire undocumented families are held together. These too have been subject to criticism with reports indicating that children are sometimes separated from their parents as punishment, receive little education, and are subjected to crowded and unsanitary living conditions (Women's Commission for Refugee Women and Children, 2007).

Removal

Laws enacted in the late 1990s significantly expanded the circumstances under which noncitizens can be deported (now called *removed*). In 2009, an estimated 393,000 noncitizens were removed from the United States with the majority (72%) being deported to Mexico (Department of Homeland Security, 2010). Under current law, those who enter the country without authorization are subject to deportation, as are those who overstay or violate the terms of their visas. Documented immigrants can be deported if they commit an aggravated felony.

The term *aggravated felony* has a different meaning under immigration law than we might suppose. The offenses covered by the term are not necessarily the most egregious crimes, nor are they necessarily even felonies. Aggravated felonies include drug offenses, traffic offenses, assault, larceny, weapons violations, forgery, invasion of privacy, liquor violations, tax evasion, obstruction of justice, gambling, threats, obscenity, and others, many of which qualify as misdemeanors under state law. The proportion of immigrants who are deported for serious, violent crimes is small. Between 1997 and 2007, 72% of all deportations were for nonviolent offenses. In 2009, aggravated assault accounted for only 1% of removals and homicide accounted for only 0.3% (Human Rights Watch, 2009). The minor crimes that most often lead to deportation of noncitizens are marijuana possession, traffic offenses, and disorderly conduct.

Conviction of an aggravated felony carries serious consequences. Regardless of immigration status, time spent in the United States, or the severity of the offense, there is no eligibility for relief from deportation. Noncitizens removed because of an aggravated felony conviction are permanently barred from reentering the United States (Human Rights Watch, 2007; Legomsky & Rodriguez, 2009, 575; Rome, 2010). Furthermore, the expanded definition of aggravated felony applies retroactively. Noncitizens with convictions for offenses that did not trigger deportation when committed are now deportable, even if they served their sentences and have since been law-abiding in every way (Human Rights Watch, 2007; Rome, 2010). These individuals are often unaware that they are deportable until they attempt to naturalize, reenter the United States from abroad, attempt to renew their LPR status, or have an encounter with law enforcement officials (Chang-Muy & Congress, 2009).

As discussed in Chapter 12, the U.S. Supreme Court decided an important case concerning the right to effective assistance of counsel under the Sixth Amendment. *Padilla v. Kentucky* (2010) concerned an LPR from Honduras who had resided in the United States for 40 years and had served in the military during the Vietnam War. While working as a truck driver, he was convicted of transporting marijuana. After consulting with his attorney, he decided to plead guilty in exchange for a reduced charge. In making that decision, he relied on his attorney's assurance that he had nothing to worry about in terms of his immigration status because he had been in the country so long. In fact, the attorney was wrong. As an aggravated felony, his drug conviction was a deportable offense. Padilla argued that his right to effective assistance of counsel had been violated. The Court agreed, ruling that an attorney representing a noncitizen has an obligation to advise him or her of the possible immigration consequences of a guilty plea. As a result of this decision, noncitizens in criminal proceedings have the right to be correctly informed about how a conviction could affect their immigration status.

Generally speaking, noncitizens are entitled to a *removal hearing* before being deported, regardless of whether they are in the country with or without authorization. An exception is that those denied admission at the border can be removed without the benefit of a hearing unless they request asylum. The first step in the hearing process is the issuance of a Notice to Appear, which advises the court and the noncitizen of the grounds for removal. It must also advise the noncitizen of his or her rights, including the right to hire counsel, offer evidence, examine the evidence against him or her, and cross-examine witnesses. Failure to appear for scheduled proceedings may result in an order for removal *in absentia*. Assuming the noncitizen appears for the hearing, others present will include the immigration judge, ICE's counsel (who acts as prosecutor), the noncitizen's counsel (if any), and witnesses. Although there is no requirement that an interpreter be provided, the courts have found that failure to do so may violate due process. ICE has the burden of proving, by clear and convincing evidence, that the person is removable under the law.

In addition to making more immigrants deportable, current law restricts the opportunities for relief from deportation. To be eligible for *cancellation of removal,* noncitizens must have spent 10 years living in the United States and be law-abiding citizens of good moral character. They must also demonstrate that removal would cause *exceptional and extremely unusual hardship*. This standard is so difficult to meet that approvals have averaged only 1,268 annually despite the fact that the government is permitted to grant up to 4,000 petitions each year (Feinstein, 2004).

Many advocates take issue with U.S. deportation policies, citing violations of civil and human rights. Although noncitizens in deportation proceedings are entitled to hire legal counsel, none is provided to them by the government because deportation is classified as a civil, not a criminal, proceeding (Schoenholz & Bernstein, 2008). Immigrants without legal counsel are far less successful at winning their cases and avoiding deportation than immigrants who are represented by an attorney. Removal policies also adversely affect family unity, a core value of the Universal Declaration of Human Rights and the International Covenant on Civil and Political Rights (Human Rights Watch, 2007). This is especially true when undocumented parents have U.S.-born children, as is often the case. Parents who are deported face an untenable choice: They can allow their citizen children to remain in the United States and endure the family separation, or they can deprive their children of their citizenship rights in order to keep the family intact. The failure of the system to consider the best interests of the child runs contrary to the U.N. Convention on the Rights of the Child and to social work values (Rome, 2010). Finally, U.S. immigration law also permits the deportation of refugees who have been convicted of an aggravated felony. As a result, many refugees who commit relatively minor crimes are forced to return to a country where they could face persecution; this violates the Refugee Convention, which has been ratified by the United States (Human Rights Watch, 2009).

Summary and Conclusion

Immigrants comprise a growing sector of the U.S. population. Because of the likelihood that we will encounter immigrants in our social work practices and communities, it is important that we be familiar with their needs, their contributions, and the ways in which immigration laws affect their lives. Although both citizens and noncitizens are protected by the equal protection clause of the Constitution, no federal immigration law has ever been struck down as unconstitutional. Meanwhile, the courts have variously applied both strict scrutiny and minimal scrutiny to state laws with unpredictable results. Since 1996, immigrants have had limited access to public benefit programs, many of which exclude undocumented immigrants entirely and subject those with authorized status to strict eligibility criteria. All immigrants are entitled by law to a public education, although ineligibility for financial assistance makes college impossible for many. Immigrants enjoy workplace protections, including the right to join a union, be paid a minimum wage, and receive workers' compensation, but they continue to be vulnerable to exploitation by employers who are rarely penalized for labor violations. Finally, the delegation of immigration enforcement powers to the states has resulted in many immigrants being detained and deported, raising concerns about civil and human rights violations. Social workers must help ensure that the needs of immigrants are met, regardless of their status, and that they are afforded the rights due them under law. We must also advocate for policies—both nationally and locally—that treat immigrants with dignity and respect.

Sample Case

What follows is an excerpt from the majority opinion in *Plyer v. Doe,* a case concerning the right of undocumented immigrant children to a public education. Although this case was decided more than 25 years ago, its central issue remains controversial. Read the case and consider the questions that follow.

PLYER v. DOE
457 U.S. 202 (1982)

Justice Brennan delivered the opinion of the Court.

The question presented by these cases is whether, consistent with the Equal Protection Clause of the Fourteenth Amendment, Texas may deny to undocumented school-age children the free public education that it provides to children who are citizens of the United States or legally admitted aliens. ***

In May, 1975, the Texas Legislature revised its education laws to withhold from local school districts any state funds for the education of children who were not "legally admitted" into the United States. The 1975 revision also authorized local school districts to deny enrollment in their public schools to children not "legally admitted" to the country. These cases involve constitutional challenges to those provisions.

The Fourteenth Amendment provides that

[n]o State shall . . . deprive any person of life, liberty, or property, without due process of law; nor deny to *any person within its jurisdiction* the equal protection of the laws (Emphasis added).

Appellants argue at the outset that undocumented aliens, because of their immigration status, are not "persons within the jurisdiction" of the State of Texas, and that they therefore have no right to the equal protection of Texas law. We reject this argument. Whatever his status under the immigration laws, an alien is surely a "person" in any ordinary sense of that term. Aliens, even aliens whose presence in this country is unlawful, have long been recognized as "persons" guaranteed due process of law by the Fifth and Fourteenth Amendments. Indeed, we have clearly held that the Fifth Amendment protects aliens whose presence in this country is unlawful from invidious discrimination by the Federal Government. . . .

In appellants' view, persons who have entered the United States illegally are not "within the jurisdiction" of a State even if they are present within a State's boundaries and subject to its laws. Neither our cases nor the logic of the Fourteenth Amendment support that constricting construction of the phrase "within its jurisdiction." ***The Fourteenth Amendment to the Constitution is not confined to the protection of citizens. It says:

> Nor shall any state deprive any person of life, liberty, or property without due process of law; nor deny to any person within its jurisdiction the equal protection of the laws.

These provisions are universal in their application, to all persons within the territorial jurisdiction, without regard to any differences of race, of color, or of nationality, and the protection of the laws is a pledge of the protection of equal laws. *Yick Wo v. Hopkins,* 118 U.S. 356 at 369 (emphasis added). ***

Our conclusion that the illegal aliens who are plaintiffs in these cases may claim the benefit of the Fourteenth Amendment's guarantee of equal protection only begins the inquiry. The more difficult question is whether the Equal Protection Clause has been violated by the refusal of the State of Texas to reimburse local school boards for the education of children who cannot demonstrate that their presence within the United States is lawful, or by the imposition by those school boards of the burden of tuition on those children. It is to this question that we now turn.

The Equal Protection Clause directs that "all persons similarly circumstanced shall be treated alike." But so too, "[t]he Constitution does not require things which are different in fact or opinion to be treated in law as though they were the same." The initial discretion to determine what is "different" and what is "the same" resides in the legislatures of the States. A legislature must have substantial latitude to establish classifications that roughly approximate the nature of the problem perceived, that accommodate competing concerns both public and private, and that account for limitations on the practical ability of the State to remedy every ill. In applying the Equal Protection Clause to most forms of state action, we thus seek only the assurance that the classification at issue bears some fair relationship to a legitimate public purpose.

But we would not be faithful to our obligations under the Fourteenth Amendment if we applied so deferential a standard to every classification. The Equal Protection Clause was intended as a restriction on state legislative action inconsistent with elemental constitutional premises. Thus, we have treated as presumptively invidious those classifications that disadvantage a "suspect class," or that impinge upon the exercise of a "fundamental right."***

Sheer incapability or lax enforcement of the laws barring entry into this country, coupled with the failure to establish an effective bar to the employment of undocumented aliens, has resulted in the creation of a substantial "shadow population" of illegal migrants—numbering in the millions—within our borders. This situation raises the specter of a permanent caste of undocumented resident aliens, encouraged by some to remain here as a source of cheap labor, but nevertheless denied the benefits that our society makes available to citizens and lawful residents. The existence of such an underclass presents most difficult problems for a Nation that prides itself on adherence to principles of equality under law.

The children who are plaintiffs in these cases are special members of this underclass. Persuasive arguments support the view that a State may withhold its beneficence from those whose very presence within the United States is the product of their own unlawful conduct. These arguments do not apply with the same force to classifications imposing disabilities on the minor children of such illegal entrants. ***

[V]isiting . . . condemnation on the head of an infant is illogical and unjust. More-over, imposing disabilities on the . . . child is contrary to the basic concept of our system that legal burdens should bear some relationship to individual responsibil-ity or wrongdoing. Obviously, no child is responsible for his birth, and penalizing the . . . child is an ineffectual—as well as unjust—way of deterring the parent. *Weber v. Aetna Casualty & Surety Co.*, 406 U.S. 164, 175 (1972).

Of course, undocumented status is not irrelevant to any proper legislative goal. Nor is undocumented status an absolutely immutable characteristic, since it is the product of conscious, indeed unlawful, action. But § 21.031 is directed against children, and imposes its discriminatory burden on the basis of a legal characteristic over which children can have little control. It is thus difficult to conceive of a rational justification for penalizing these children for their presence within the United States. Yet that appears to be precisely the effect of § 21.031.

Public education is not a "right" granted to individuals by the Constitution. *San Antonio Independent School Dist. v. Rodriguez*, 411 U.S. 1, 35 (1973). But neither is it merely some governmental "benefit" indistinguishable from other forms of social welfare legisla-tion. Both the importance of education in maintaining our basic institutions and the last-ing impact of its deprivation on the life of the child mark the distinction. The "American people have always regarded education and [the] acquisition of knowledge as matters of supreme importance." 411 U.S. 1, 35 (1973). ***

. . . We cannot ignore the significant social costs borne by our Nation when select groups are denied the means to absorb the values and skills upon which our social order rests. In addition to the pivotal role of education in sustaining our political and cultural heritage, denial of education to some isolated group of children poses an affront to one of the goals of the Equal Protection Clause: the abolition of governmental barriers presenting unreasonable obstacles to advancement on the basis of individual merit. ***

. . . What we said 28 years ago in *Brown v. Board of Education* still holds true:

> Today, education is perhaps the most important function of state and local govern-ments. Compulsory school attendance laws and the great expenditures for education both demonstrate our recognition of the importance of education to our democratic society. It is required in the performance of our most basic public responsibilities, even service in the armed forces. It is the very foundation of good citizenship. Today it is a principal instrument in awakening the child to cultural values, in preparing him for later professional training, and in helping him to adjust normally to his envi-ronment. In these days, it is doubtful that any child may reasonably be expected to succeed in life if he is denied the opportunity of an education. Such an opportunity, where the state has undertaken to provide it, is a right which must be made available to all on equal terms.

These well-settled principles allow us to determine the proper level of deference to be afforded § 21.031. Undocumented aliens cannot be treated as a suspect class, because their presence in this country in violation of federal law is not a "constitutional irrele-vancy." Nor is education a fundamental right; a State need not justify by compelling neces-sity every variation in the manner in which education is provided to its population. *See San Antonio Independent School Dist. v. Rodriguez, supra*, at 28–39. But more is involved in these cases than the abstract question whether § 21.031 discriminates against a suspect class, or whether education is a fundamental right. Section 21.031 imposes a lifetime hardship on a discrete class of children not accountable for their disabling status. The stigma of illiteracy will mark them for the rest of their lives. By denying these children a basic education, we deny them the ability to live within the structure of our civic institutions, and foreclose any realistic possibility that they will contribute in even the smallest way to the progress of our Nation. In determining the rationality of § 21.031, we may appropriately take into account its costs to the Nation and to the innocent children who are its victims. In light of these countervailing costs, the discrimination contained in § 21.031 can hardly be considered rational unless it furthers some substantial goal of the State. ***

. . . [W]e discern three colorable state interests that might support § 21.031. First, appellants appear to suggest that the State may seek to protect itself from an influx of illegal immigrants. While a State might have an interest in mitigating the potentially harsh economic effects of sudden shifts in population, § 21.031 hardly offers an effective method of dealing with an urgent demographic or economic problem. There is no evidence in the record suggesting that illegal entrants impose any significant burden on the State's economy. To the contrary, the available evidence suggests that illegal aliens underutilize public services, while contributing their labor to the local economy and tax money to the state fisc. The dominant incentive for illegal entry into the State of Texas is the availability of employment; few if any illegal immigrants come to this country, or presumably to the State of Texas, in order to avail themselves of a free education. Thus, even making the doubtful assumption that the net impact of illegal aliens on the economy of the State is negative, we think it clear that "[c]harging tuition to undocumented children constitutes a ludicrously ineffectual attempt to stem the tide of illegal immigration," at least when compared with the alternative of prohibiting the employment of illegal aliens.

Second, while it is apparent that a State may "not . . . reduce expenditures for education by barring [some arbitrarily chosen class of] children from its schools," *Shapiro v. Thompson,* 394 U.S. 618, 633 (1969), appellants suggest that undocumented children are appropriately singled out for exclusion because of the special burdens they impose on the State's ability to provide high-quality public education. But the record in no way supports the claim that exclusion of undocumented children is likely to improve the overall quality of education in the State. As the District Court . . . noted, the State failed to offer any credible supporting evidence that a proportionately small diminution of the funds spent on each child [which might result from devoting some state funds to the education of the excluded group] will have a grave impact on the quality of education.

And, after reviewing the State's school financing mechanism, the District Court . . . concluded that barring undocumented children from local schools would not necessarily improve the quality of education provided in those schools. Of course, even if improvement in the quality of education were a likely result of barring some *number* of children from the schools of the State, the State must support its selection of *this* group as the appropriate target for exclusion. In terms of educational cost and need, however, undocumented children are "basically indistinguishable" from legally resident alien children.

Finally, appellants suggest that undocumented children are appropriately singled out because their unlawful presence within the United States renders them less likely than other children to remain within the boundaries of the State, and to put their education to productive social or political use within the State. Even assuming that such an interest is legitimate, it is an interest that is most difficult to quantify. The State has no assurance that any child, citizen or not, will employ the education provided by the State within the confines of the State's borders. In any event, the record is clear that many of the undocumented children disabled by this classification will remain in this country indefinitely, and that some will become lawful residents or citizens of the United States. It is difficult to understand precisely what the State hopes to achieve by promoting the creation and perpetuation of a subclass of illiterates within our boundaries, surely adding to the problems and costs of unemployment, welfare, and crime. It is thus clear that whatever savings might be achieved by denying these children an education, they are wholly insubstantial in light of the costs involved to these children, the State, and the Nation.

If the State is to deny a discrete group of innocent children the free public education that it offers to other children residing within its borders, that denial must be justified by a showing that it furthers some substantial state interest. No such showing was made here. Accordingly, the judgment of the Court of Appeals in each of these cases is *Affirmed.*

Questions

1. How would you summarize the arguments in favor of providing undocumented children with a public education? Which social work values support this position?

2. Although not reprinted here, four justices on the Court joined a dissenting opinion. What would you suppose their arguments were? Do you think any of these arguments have merit? Explain.

3. This case was brought under the equal protection clause. What level of scrutiny does the Court appear to be applying? How can you tell?

4. Do you think that undocumented immigrants should be considered a suspect class, like racial and ethnic minorities? How are these groups the same? How are they different?

5. In the past few years, a number of states have proposed or adopted laws requiring that schools ascertain the immigration status of all students who enroll. Would you support such legislation? Why or why not?

6. If *Plyer v. Doe* were reconsidered today, what do you think the outcome would be? Why?

CHAPTER 19 PRACTICE TEST

The following questions will test your application and analysis of the content found within this chapter. For additional assessment, including licensing-exam type questions on applying chapter content to practice behaviors, visit **MySearchLab**.

1. Laura is a 17-year-old who was smuggled out of her native Honduras as part of a human-trafficking ring. Once in the United States, she was forced into prostitution. When the police picked her up, she was threatened with deportation because of her undocumented status. Because of her circumstances, Laura could be eligible for immigration relief under

   a. Special Immigrant Juvenile Status.

   b. T-Visa.

   c. U-Visa.

   d. Violence Against Women Act.

2. Undocumented immigrants are eligible for

   a. emergency Medicaid.

   b. food stamps.

   c. Social Security.

   d. TANF.

3. Juan came to the United States with his mother when he was an infant. Both are undocumented.

His mother is desperate for Juan to have a good education. Which of the following is true regarding his legal rights?

   a. The right to an education is a fundamental right, explicitly guaranteed by the Constitution.

   b. He can attend a public elementary or secondary school regardless of his immigration status.

   c. When he applies to college, he can receive student financial aid.

   d. He is prohibited by law from attending a public university.

4. Immigrant workers

   a. are entitled to earn the minimum wage.

   b. are excluded from employment discrimination protections under Title VII.

   c. are not permitted to unionize.

   d. have experienced less exploitation since federal law made it illegal to hire unauthorized immigrants.

5. A number of policies adopted since the 1990s have resulted in increased detection, detention, and deportation of immigrants. These include E-Verify, workplace raids, 287(g) agreements, Secure Communities, the expanded definition of aggravated felonies, and limitations on "cancellation of removal." Discuss one of these policies, including what it is, how it works, and its impact on immigrants and immigrant families.

6. What is birthright citizenship? Explore the likely consequences of revoking birthright citizenship for children of undocumented parents. Finally, frame an argument against such proposals, drawing on social work values and ethics.

MYSEARCHLAB CONNECTIONS

Reinforce what you learned in this chapter by studying videos, cases, documents,
and more available at **www.MySearchLab.com.**

Watch these Videos

* English: Who Needs It?
  - *If the United States were to adopt an "English as the official language" or "English only" policy, what would the impact be on immigrants? On American communities? Should social workers support such a policy? Why or why not?*
* Court Rules on Hazelton's Immigration Laws (2010)
  - *How should courts go about balancing the civil liberties of unauthroized immigrants against the concerns of the communities in which they settle? Which, if any, restrictions on employment, housing, and government benefits should be upheld?*

Read these Cases/Documents

Δ Undocumented Mexicans
  - *How do current immigration laws affect the well-being of undocumented children and families in the child welfare system?*

Research these Topics

- Real ID
- the politics of immigration reform
- training for immigration judges

Assess Your Knowledge

Go to **MySearchLab** to test your knowledge of key topics in this chapter with topic-specific quizzes. Conclude your assessment by completing the chapter exam.

⋆ = CSWE Core Competency Asset   Δ = Case Study

Chapter **20**

Legal Rights of Students

In our society, as in many others, the childhood years are closely associated with school attendance. Here in the United States, education through high school and beyond is recognized as an indispensible asset. The government has acknowledged its importance through the passage of compulsory school attendance laws, and research increasingly demonstrates that graduates enjoy increased productivity and earnings (Bureau of Labor Statistics, 2012). Despite its importance, the right to an education is not explicitly guaranteed by the Constitution. Ironically, however, it is enshrined in international human rights treaties, including the Convention on the Rights of the Child and the Universal Declaration on Human Rights.

Although there is no constitutional right to an education per se, the law has frequently examined the applicability of both constitutional and statutory rights to students in the school setting. Previous chapters have explored the educational rights of racial minorities, women, and immigrants. This chapter examines the rights of all students under the First, Fourth, Eighth, and Fourteenth Amendments to the Constitution, as well as the rights of students with disabilities under the Individuals with Disabilities Education Act (IDEA). A special section highlights the issue of disciplining students with special needs, and the sample case examines the right to special education. All social workers should be aware of the legal rights of students because so many of us work with young people and their families; school social workers in particular should be conversant with how legal rights are shaped by the school setting.

Background

The United States has a highly developed educational infrastructure. There are 98,000 public elementary and secondary schools in the United States (including approximately 5,000 charter schools) serving more than 49.4 million students, and approximately 33,300 private schools serving approximately 6 million students (National Center for Education Statistics [NCES], 2010). An additional 1.5 million children are home schooled (NCES, 2009). The student/teacher ratio is 15.3 to 1 in public schools and 12.9 to 1 in private schools. Public elementary and secondary schools are expected to spend approximately $525 billion during the 2011–2012 school year and graduate a total of 3.2 million young people (NCES, 2010).

Of course, these national data mask the significant discrepancies in opportunity and achievement that continue to plague our educational system. As of 2009, approximately 3 million youth between ages 16 and 24 were neither enrolled in school nor had earned a high school diploma or equivalent. This dropout rate was highest for Hispanics (17.6%), followed in descending order by African Americans (9.3%), Whites (5.2%), and Asian/Pacific Islanders (3.4%). Dropout rates for youth with disabilities were approximately twice as high as for their nondisabled peers. Finally, dropout rates for immigrant youth and for youth living in poverty were especially pronounced (Chapman, Laird, Ifill, & KewalRamani, 2011). Geography also plays a role in educational opportunity. Although expenditures per pupil averaged $10,297 nationally in 2008, New York spent an average of $11,572 per student, while Utah spent only $3,886 (Zhou & Johnson, 2010). On-time high school completion rates also vary considerably from state to state, ranging from a high of 90.7% in Wisconsin to a low of 56.3% in Nevada. Overall, those states with the highest completion rates are congregated in the Midwest; those with the lowest rates are located in the South (Chapman et al., 2011). Despite its comparative wealth, the United States is struggling to compete with many other nations when it comes to student knowledge, skills, school enrollment, and graduation rates (Organisation for Economic Co-Operation and Development, 2010).

Many of these inequities are perpetuated by our reliance on local property taxes to finance education. This method of financing was challenged in the 1973 U.S. Supreme Court case of *San Antonio Independent School District v. Rodriguez*, in which plaintiffs argued—unsuccessfully—that children in poverty constitute a suspect class deserving of strict scrutiny, and that public education is a fundamental right. Rejecting both contentions, the Court found that Texas's use of property taxes to finance its public schools was rationally related to the goal of local control; therefore, despite the drastic inequities it produced, the financing scheme was considered constitutional. Since that time, the battle for school finance reform has shifted to the state level, with states including Alabama, Ohio, and Massachusetts enjoying some success in shifting educational resources to those most in need; school finance equalization on a larger scale, however, remains an elusive ideal (Heise, 2008).

Education has traditionally been a state and local concern, with the federal government playing only a minor role. This is reflected in the fact that federal funding accounts for only 10.8% of all education expenditures (U.S. Department of Education, 2011). State laws, for example, define the expectations for school attendance. Since the mid-19th century, these compulsory education laws have required children to attend school or receive education through other means, until a specified age (National Conference of State

Legislatures [NCSL], 2012). States including Delaware and Maryland require children to attend school from the ages of 5 to 16. Other states, such as California, Texas, and Virginia, require that children attend until they reach the age of 18 (National Center for School Engagement, 2003). Failing to comply with compulsory education laws can have legal repercussions, resulting in charges of truancy or fines. State laws also define school enrollment criteria, grade-level curricula, and graduation requirements. Local school district policies typically govern school behavioral expectations and disciplinary actions. The federal role in education, which has grown in recent years, is focused on ensuring educational opportunity for minorities, women, disadvantaged students, and students with disabilities; providing student financial aid; and holding states accountable for student achievement. The right to special education is outlined in the Individuals with Disabilities Education Act (20 U.S.C.A. §§1400-1485), and the No Child Left Behind Act of 1991 (P.L. 107-110) addresses student achievement. Various provisions of the U.S. Constitution also safeguard the rights of students. Following is a discussion of student rights in relation to freedom of expression, search and seizure, school discipline, and special education.

Freedom of Expression

An important right afforded all Americans is the right to freedom of expression. The First Amendment states, "Congress shall make no law respecting an establishment of religion, or prohibiting the free exercise thereof; or abridging the freedom of speech, or of the press; or the right of the people peaceably to assemble, and to petition the Government for a redress of grievances." Although explicitly granted in the Constitution, there has been considerable debate about whether, and how, these rights apply to students in a school setting. At one time, attending school was regarded as a privilege and schools were given wide latitude to regulate student behavior. Today, courts recognize that students indeed have rights deserving of protection; these rights, however, are balanced against the need to maintain order and safety in schools, and to promote the educational mission (Alexander & Alexander, 2009).

Freedom of Speech

As a general matter, because of their immaturity, the rights of children and youth can legally be curtailed to a greater degree than can those of adults. Several Supreme Court cases provide guidance as to when, and under what circumstances a school can limit a student's freedom of speech. Perhaps the most famous case on this topic is *Tinker v. Des Moines Independent School District* (1969), which involved three students in Iowa who planned to publicize their opposition to the war in Vietnam by wearing black armbands to school. In anticipation of the protest, school officials established a policy prohibiting the wearing of armbands and threatening suspension for those who failed to remove them. The students proceeded to wear the armbands as planned and were subsequently suspended. They and their parents filed suit, claiming that the school's actions violated their First Amendment right to free speech. Although the lower courts ruled in favor of school authorities, a seven-justice majority of the Supreme Court reversed, ruling in favor of the students. Asserting that the wearing of black armbands is a form of free speech guaranteed by the

Constitution, Justas Fortas wrote, "It can hardly be argued that either students or teachers shed their constitutional rights to freedom of speech or expression at the schoolhouse gate" (p. 506). That being said, the Court proceeded to acknowledge that although schools possess the authority to establish rules and maintain order, this particular student action was "a silent, passive expression of opinion" that neither disrupted the school's work nor interfered with the rights of other students (p. 508). The takeaway message from *Tinker* is that student speech cannot be abridged simply because it is controversial; there must be evidence that it will substantially interfere with school operations or discipline.

Subsequent decisions suggest that *Tinker* was the high-water mark in terms of student free speech rights. Two Supreme Court rulings in the 1980s affirmed the right of schools to curtail student expression. *Bethel School District v. Fraser* (1986) involved a high school student who gave a speech at an assembly attended by more than 600 classmates. The speech, nominating a fellow student for student government office, was riddled with sexual innuendo; the student was subsequently suspended. He later filed suit, claiming that his First Amendment right to free speech had been violated. Distinguishing the speech in this case from the political message associated with the armbands worn by the students in *Tinker*, the Court found in favor of the school district by a 7–2 vote. The Court held that schools have a legitimate and appropriate interest in prohibiting "vulgar and offensive" language that is inconsistent with the fundamental values of public education.

Just two years later, in *Hazelwood School District v. Kuhlmeier* (1988), students enrolled in a journalism class filed suit after two articles they had written were removed from the student newspaper before publication because the instructor considered them inappropriate. One concerned the students' experiences with pregnancy and the other concerned the impact of divorce on students at the school. The Supreme Court ruled in favor of the school district, finding no violation of the students' First Amendment rights. According to Justice White, unlike *Tinker*, which involved student expression that happened to occur on school property, the newspaper's production was a school-sponsored activity over which the faculty had final authority. Under these circumstances, the school was within its rights to delete material it considered to be in conflict with "legitimate pedagogical concerns" (p. 273). Justices Brennan and Marshall dissented, arguing that the school newspaper was designed to serve as a forum for the expression of diverse viewpoints. Because the articles neither disrupted class work nor impinged on the rights of others, their removal constituted impermissible censorship under the First Amendment.

More recently, in the case of *Morse v. Frederick* (2007), a student was suspended for displaying a 14-foot banner that read "BONG HITS 4 JESUS" during a class trip to the Olympic Torch Relay in Juneau, Alaska. The student sued the school, claiming that the suspension violated his First Amendment right to free speech. The U.S. Supreme Court disagreed. The Court noted that the display occurred in the midst of other students, during school hours, at a school-sanctioned activity. Because the banner was "reasonably viewed as promoting illegal drug use" in contravention of school district policy, it was constitutionally permissible for the school to restrict the speech. Deterring drug use by students was recognized as an important interest on the part of the school. The three dissenting justices took issue with the majority's conclusion that the banner's message was meant to promote drug use, deferring to Frederick's own admission that it was simply nonsense designed to attract the television cameras. According to the dissent, an ambiguous message like the one in *Frederick* should hardly be sufficient to justify the stifling of student speech.

What can we conclude from this? First, it is clear that political speech, as in *Tinker*, is regarded by the Court as deserving of special protection. Second, when the expression occurs as part of a school-sanctioned event, school authorities appear to have greater latitude in sanctioning it—especially if they believe it interferes with the school's educational mission or threatens the safety of the student body.

Freedom of Dress and Appearance

In addition to oral and written communication, how one chooses to dress may be regarded as a form of expression. Although the U.S. Supreme Court has yet to hear a case involving school uniforms, several lower courts have considered the constitutionality of school dress codes. In 2001, the Fifth Circuit Court of Appeals upheld a policy requiring students to wear uniforms in the case of *Canady v. Bossier Parish School Board*. In reaching its decision, the Court applied a four-prong test. Under that test, a dress code policy will be upheld if (1) the school board has the power to make such a policy, (2) the policy promotes a substantial interest of the school board, (3) the adoption of the policy is not an attempt to censor student expression, and (4) the policy restricts student expression only to the degree necessary to promote the school board's interests. In the *Canady* case, the court found that the policy was permissible because it enhanced the educational process by reducing the occurrence of disciplinary problems, it was value neutral, and students had opportunities to express themselves through avenues other than clothing.

A number of cases have addressed attempts to restrict the wearing of alcohol-, drug-, or gang-related apparel in schools. In *Jenglin v. San Jacinto Unified School District* (1993), a California district court considered a policy prohibiting students from wearing clothing bearing the names of professional sports teams or colleges. The court found the policy constitutionally permissible as applied at the high school level, where evidence suggested a gang presence in the school and a connection between gangs and the attire in question. However, it struck down the policy as applied at the elementary and junior high school levels, where the gang presence was negligible, and there was nothing to suggest that the attire was likely to create a substantial disruption. Similarly, in *McIntyre v. Bethel School Independent District No. 3* (1992), an Oklahoma district court considered the constitutionality of a dress code that prohibited the wearing of a shirt parodying a liquor advertisement. It found in favor of the students, noting that the school failed to demonstrate that wearing the shirt would interfere with schoolwork or pose a disciplinary problem. In *Chalifoux v. New Caney Independent School District* (1997), students in a Texas school were prohibited from wearing rosary beads on the theory that they constituted a gang symbol. The district court found in favor of the students, reasoning that surely the school could find alternative means of controlling gang activity and ensuring school safety without categorically trampling on students' First Amendment rights.

Other cases have addressed the wearing of earrings and other accessories, hair length, and tattoos. Particularly at the elementary school level, school policies prohibiting the wearing of earrings by male students have been upheld under the theory that they undermine school discipline and are contrary to the fostering of a positive educational environment (*Hines v. Caston School Corp.*, 1995; *Jones v. W.T. Henning Elementary School*, 1998). At the high school level, prohibiting male students from wearing earrings has received mixed reviews from the courts. In some jurisdictions, courts have found personal appearance to rise to the level of a fundamental right; when that is the case, the students generally prevail, because it is difficult for the state to meet its burden of showing that wearing an earring creates substantial and material disruption, jeopardizes student safety, undermines the educational program, or interferes with the rights of other students. When personal appearance is *not* considered to be a fundamental right, school systems are more likely to prevail because they need only demonstrate that there is a rational basis for the policy. With hair length in particular, the courts have increasingly deferred to the judgment of school authorities, except when hair length was determined to be related to the students' heritage, religion, race, or nationality (*Alabama & Coushatta Tribes of Texas v. Big Sandy School District*, 1993).

Freedom of Religion

Other issues related to freedom of expression that may arise in the school environment revolve around religion. This continues to be a highly controversial area in which the courts' interpretation of the First Amendment continues to evolve. Two constitutional provisions are at issue: the *establishment clause*, which is designed to create a wall of separation between church and state, and the *free exercise clause*, which guarantees each individual the right to believe as he or she chooses. Among the specific issues the courts have considered are prayer in schools and the use of school facilities for religious purposes.

Three cases heard by the U.S. Supreme Court in close succession, *Engel v. Vitale* (1962), *School District of Abington Township v. Schempp* (1963), and *Murray v. Curlett* (1963), laid the groundwork for limiting the practice of beginning each school day with prayers and Bible verses. The Court struck down these practices as First Amendment violations of the establishment clause, clarifying that although it is permissible to study the Bible or religion as part of a secular academic program, it is impermissible to use the classroom to promote religion. In the years since, states have attempted to circumvent this prohibition by setting aside class time for meditation, silence, quiet reflection, or voluntary prayer. The results have been mixed. An Alabama statute calling for a period of silence for "meditation or voluntary prayer" in public schools was struck down because it was apparent from the legislative history that the law's purpose was religious rather than secular (*Wallace v. Jaffree,* 1985). On the other hand, "moment of silence" policies in Georgia (*Brown v. Gwinnett County School District,* 1997) and Virginia (*Brown v. Gilmore,* 2001) were upheld by the circuit courts because they permitted students to use the time as they saw fit, without expressly encouraging religious activity.

Organized prayer at high school graduation ceremonies has been invalidated (*Lee v. Weisman,* 1992), as have student-initiated graduation prayers (*Gearon v. Loudoun County School Board,* 1993), prayers before and after athletic games (*Santa Fe Independent School District v. Doe,* 2000), and prayer at school board meetings (*Coles v. Cleveland Board of Education,* 1999). On the other hand, the performance of religious music by public school choirs has repeatedly been upheld. The bottom line seems to be that mandatory prayer, as well as prayer conducted as part of a school-sponsored activity, is impermissible unless its purpose can be shown to be secular. Despite the wealth of legal authority, however, this issue continues to be litigated.

A challenge to the words "under God" in the Pledge of Allegiance was heard by the U.S. Supreme Court in 2004 (*Elk Grove Unified School District v.Newdow*). In that case, a student who considered himself an atheist claimed that inclusion of those words consti-tuted a violation of the establishment clause. The Court declined to decide the merits of the case because the boy's father, who had brought the case, lacked standing as a noncus-todial parent. The Ninth Circuit Court of Appeals, however, later considered the issue in *Newdow v. Rio Linda Union School District* (2010). That court upheld as constitutional the teacher-led recitation of the Pledge of Allegiance, despite its inclusion of the words "under God." According to the court's majority, the historical context of the pledge makes clear that the phrase's purpose was to inspire patriotism, not to endorse religion. Meanwhile, more blatant religious activity continues in many public schools across the country. As recently as 2011, for example, the American Civil Liberties Union (ACLU) filed a law suit against a South Carolina public school system where students were required to attend a worship rally, encouraged to pray, and directed to sign a pledge dedicating themselves to Jesus (ACLU, 2011).

Another issue that has received considerable attention is the use of public school facili-ties by religious groups. Since passage of the Equal Access Act of 1984 (20 U.S.C. §§4071-4074), federal law has dictated that any school district permitting student organizations to use its facilities after hours must make those facilities equally available to student religious groups. This signaled an important shift in our understanding of the First Amendment: Student religious activity on public school grounds was now regarded as protected by the free exercise clause, rather than prohibited by the establishment clause. This trend of valu-ing religious expression over the maintenance of separation between church and state con-tinues to the present day.

Freedom of Assembly

The Equal Access Act specifies that if a public secondary school receiving federal funds allows even a single non-curricular student group to use its facilities outside regular in-structional hours, it must allow meetings of all other non-curricular groups regardless of their religious, political, philosophical, or other content. Ironically, the same conservative Christian groups that spearheaded the law's initial passage have since sought to exclude lesbian, gay, bisexual, and transgender (LGBT) support groups from meeting on school property. In one case, a Kentucky high school had gone so far as to shut down all student clubs, rather than allow meetings of the Gay Straight Alliance (GSA). Several lower court cases have been brought challenging these exclusionary policies, and in each case the stu-dents have prevailed (*Boyd County High School Gay Straight Alliance v. Board of Educ. of Boyd County*, 2003; *Colin v. Orange Unified School District*, 2000). In a 2006 case involv-ing students at a Minnesota high school, the Eighth Circuit even ruled that the GSA was entitled to have access to the school's public address system, yearbook, and all other forms of communication used by other student groups (*Straights and Gays for Equality v. Osseo Area Schools*). In 2000, the National Association of Social Workers (NASW) joined an *amicus* brief supporting the GSA in a case before the 10th Circuit Court of Appeals (*East High Gay/Straight Alliance v. Board of Education of Salt Lake City School District*). The suit was later withdrawn when the school district voluntarily reinstated non-curricular clubs, allowing the GSA to meet,

In sum, the courts have concluded that although students retain their constitutional First Amendment rights to freedom of speech, religion, and assembly, those rights are not identical to those enjoyed by adults. When a student's speech, dress, or religious expression can reasonably be expected to trigger a significant disruption to school order or is contrary to the school's educational mission, those rights may be curtailed. In most instances, the school must demonstrate that policies limiting student rights are rationally related to a legitimate purpose. The courts approach these "freedom of expression" cases by balancing the civil liberties of students against the school's broader mission to provide a safe environment for learning.

Search and Seizure

Many American students today engage in behaviors that place them at risk, including carrying a weapon or using illegal drugs. According to a 2010 report by the Centers for Disease Control (CDC), 17.5% of students in the United States had carried a weapon to school in the previous 30 days, nearly 50% had smoked cigarettes at least once in their lifetime, more than 70% had ever consumed alcohol, and approximately 40% had used marijuana at least once. In addition, 2.5% reported having used heroin, 4.1% had used methamphetamines, 6.4% had used cocaine, 6.7% had used Ecstasy, 11.7% had used inhalants, and 20.2% took prescription drugs without a doctor's prescription. Many of these students had used alcohol, tobacco, or other drugs while at school, and 22.7% reported having been offered, sold, or given an illegal drug on school property.

In response to concerns arising from the risks associated with these unhealthy behaviors, government authorities, school districts, and schools have implemented policies designed to locate and confiscate contraband on school premises. The Fourth Amendment protects citizens from "unreasonable searches and seizures." This section explores how the courts have applied this right to students in the school setting.

Searches of Student Property

In 1985, the U.S. Supreme Court heard a landmark case involving a school's search of a student's belongings (*New Jersey v. T.L.O*). In this case, two 14-year-old students were caught smoking in a school bathroom. In a follow-up conversation with the assistant vice principal, one of the girls admitted to the offense, but the other did not. The assistant vice principal subsequently searched the purse belonging to the latter girl (T.L.O.) and found not only cigarettes, but also marijuana, paraphernalia, and other items suggesting she was engaged in dealing drugs. After being confronted with this evidence, T.L.O. admitted to selling marijuana to other students. The confiscated items were turned over to the police, T.L.O. was suspended from school, and charges were brought against her in juvenile court. In the course of the proceedings, T.L.O. filed a motion to suppress the items found in her purse, arguing that the vice principal had violated her Fourth Amendment right to be free from unreasonable search and seizure. The lower court held that students in school maintain their rights under the Fourth Amendment but concluded that the search was reasonable. The New Jersey Supreme Court reversed, finding the search unreasonable. The Supreme Court again reversed, concluding that there was no violation of T.L.O.'s Fourth Amendment rights. The Court addressed two important questions in its ruling: first, whether Fourth Amendment rights apply in the school setting, and second, whether the search conducted by the school officials in *T.L.O.* met the required standard of reasonableness.

In response to the first question, the Court affirmed that searches conducted by public school officials must indeed comply with the Fourth Amendment because school officials are acting as representatives of the state, rather than as surrogate parents. In response to the second question, the Court noted that although students maintain an expectation of privacy on school grounds, school officials must be afforded some flexibility to discipline students in the interests of maintaining order and ensuring safety. To this end, unlike law enforcement, school officials need not obtain a warrant, nor do they need probable cause before searching a student's belongings. The only requirement is that the search be reasonable, given the totality of the circumstances. Determining the *reasonableness* of a search involves answering two questions: (1) whether the search was justified at the time of initial suspicion, and (2) whether the ensuing search was "reasonably related in scope to the circumstances which justified the interference in the first place" (p. 341). According to the Court, the first criterion is met when there are "reasonable grounds for suspecting that the search will turn up evidence that the student has violated or is violating either the law or the rules of the school" (p. 342). The second criterion is met when the search is performed in accordance with its stated objective and is "not excessively intrusive in light of the age and sex of the student and the nature of the infraction" (p. 342). In the case of *New Jersey v. T.L.O.*, the Court found the school's search of the student's purse to be reasonable and therefore constitutional.

In the years since, the lower courts have decided numerous cases applying the holding and rationale of *T.L.O.* to other search situations. For example, the New Jersey Supreme Court in 2010 concluded that a search of students' cars on school property is constitutional as long as it is conducted pursuant to reasonable suspicion (*State v. Best*). Also in 2010, a Mississippi federal district court upheld the seizure of a student's cell phone and the search of its contents in light of the school's policy banning cell phones from school property (*J.W. v. DeSoto County Sch. Dist.*). The general test applied in each case was that of "reasonableness" as defined in *New Jersey v. T.L.O.*

Locker searches seem to present more of a challenge. Most states, including for example Georgia, Maryland, and Wisconsin have concluded that students have no expectation of privacy in their lockers because the lockers are considered to be the property of the school rather than the student. Consequently, students have no protection against locker searches and seizures. At the other end of the spectrum is Massachusetts, which maintains that students retain a substantial expectation of privacy in their lockers. Virginia has staked out a middle ground; it recognizes a student expectation of privacy, but one that is significantly limited. Those of us who are school social workers need to be familiar with the search and seizure policy in our states and local school districts so we can advise students of their rights and be sure that our own behavior is consistent with prevailing legal standards.

Strip Searches

Not surprisingly, searches of a person's body are held to a higher legal standard than are searches of a person's possessions; they involve a greater expectation of privacy and are inherently more invasive. Nonetheless, their constitutionality is determined using the same *T.L.O.* standards that govern searches of property. The search must be reasonable; this means that the school official has a reasonable suspicion that a law or school rule has been violated, and the search is conducted in the least intrusive manner possible.

The object of the search seems to weigh heavily in determining its reasonableness. Strip searches for drugs, for example, are often permitted because of the threat drugs pose to student health and safety (*Williams by Williams v. Ellington*, 1991; *Cornfield by Lewis v. Consolidated High School*, 1993), whereas searches for stolen money are not (*Bellnier v. Lund*, 1977; *Konop v. Northwestern School District*, 1998). The source of the tip on which the school official's suspicion is based may also enter into the equation. When another student is the informant and that student's trustworthiness is suspect, the reasonableness requirement is unlikely to be met; when multiple sources provide the information generating the suspicion, however, the search is more likely to be considered reasonable (*Cornfield by Lewis v. Consolidate High School*, 1993).

In 2009, the U.S. Supreme Court decided *Safford Unified School District v. Redding*, a case in which a 13-year-old student was strip searched by school personnel. Another student had reported that Redding had pain relief pills in her possession, which she was distributing to other students in violation of school policy. After an initial interview with the principal and a search of her backpack produced no evidence of the pills, Redding was taken to the school nurse's office where, in the presence of the school nurse and an administrative assistant, she was required to remove her clothing and pull out her bra and underpants for further inspection. No pills were found. Redding filed suit claiming that her Fourth Amendment rights had been violated. The district court found no Fourth Amendment violation, but the circuit court reversed. The U.S. Supreme Court affirmed the constitutionality of searching Redding's outer clothing and backpack but concluded that the search of Redding's underwear was unreasonable according to the standard enunciated by the Court in *New Jersey v. T.L.O.* Here, the Court explained, the "content of the suspicion failed to match the degree of intrusion" (p. 2642). Given the limited threat of the specific drugs in question (the equivalent of two Advil® or one Aleve®), the absence of any indication that Redding was distributing them to other students in large enough quantities to imperil their safety, and the absence of any suggestion that she was hiding the pills in her underwear, the search was considered excessively intrusive. The Court cited NASW's *amicus* brief to support its contention that, given Redding's sex and age, such a search is likely to be experienced as embarrassing, frightening, humiliating, and traumatic.

Drug Testing

Drug testing in schools also raises Fourth Amendment issues, because the collection and testing of a blood or urine specimen is legally considered to be a search. Although *T.L.O.* provides some guidance on the permissibility of searching an individual student's person or belongings when there is a reasonable suspicion of drug use, the courts have since addressed the more difficult question of whether and under what circumstances a school can require random drug tests when there is no reason to suspect wrongdoing on the part of any individual student. The first major case on this issue was *Vernonia School District v. Acton* (1995), in which the U.S. Supreme Court upheld an Oregon school district policy requiring random drug testing as a condition of participating in school sports. The policy was instituted with considerable parent support after less intrusive strategies (including offering classes aimed at preventing drug use and utilizing drug-sniffing dogs) had been attempted. Specifically, the program required students to sign a consent form and obtain the written consent of their parents in order to participate in their desired sport. All students would be tested at the beginning of the season and then would be tested randomly throughout the season. The testing involved entering a restroom facility with a same-sex adult and producing a urine sample to be given to the adult whose presence served to ensure that the sample had not been altered. The samples were then sent to an independent laboratory to be tested for illicit drugs. Students with positive results could be mandated to participate in a treatment program or be suspended from their team for two or more seasons.

A seventh-grade student, James Acton, and his parents refused to consent to mandatory drug testing, and James was consequently denied participation in the school's football program. The parents filed suit, claiming that the drug-testing policy violated the Fourth Amendment, but the U.S. Supreme Court upheld the policy as constitutional. First, the Court reasoned that although students have a reduced expectation of privacy in school, student athletes have an even lesser expectation of privacy because they regularly perform private activities, such as dressing or showering, in common areas. Second, the Court found that the means of obtaining the urine samples was relatively unobtrusive and therefore acceptable. Third, the Court affirmed the importance of preventing drug use in schools, given its adverse consequences for the individuals involved as well as its impact on the learning environment. Finally, the Court acknowledged that drug use poses a particular hazard for student athletes because of their increased risk of injury. The school district's policy was upheld as reasonable and therefore constitutional.

The question raised in *Vernonia* has since been considered in relation to a more sweeping drug-testing policy. In 2002, the U.S. Supreme Court considered an Oklahoma school district policy requiring all middle and high school students to consent to random drug tests as a condition of participating in any extracurricular activity (*Board of Education v. Earls*). Unlike the policy in *Vernonia*, which pertained only to athletics, the policy in *Earls* applied equally to those in marching band, show choir, Future Farmers of America, Future Homemakers of America, cheerleading, the Academic Team, and the National Honor Society. Relying on the reasoning in *Vernonia*, the Supreme Court upheld the policy against a Fourth Amendment challenge by two students. In a 5–4 decision, the Court reasoned that students in extracurricular activities have a reduced expectation of privacy compared to the student body at large, the method of drug testing was minimally invasive, and the school district has a legitimate interest in preventing drug use by students. In defense of the last assertion, the Court noted both the presence of drugs at the school in question and the nationwide drug epidemic, which "makes the war against drugs a pressing concern in every school" (p. 834). These two cases, taken together, suggest that a school's interest in preventing drug use supersedes the rights of students to be free from drug tests administered in the absence of specific suspicion of wrongdoing.

School Discipline

The 14th Amendment to the Constitution guarantees that no individual be deprived of "life, liberty, or property without due process of law." So how does this apply within the school setting? Traditionally, schools freely imposed suspensions or expulsions based on the assertion that attending school was a privilege; under this framework, school personnel had complete authority to withhold education when a student behaved in a manner that was contrary to school rules. More recently, however, the courts have acknowledged that young people cannot be deprived of an education without being afforded due process of law (Alexander & Alexander, 2009).

In this context, *due process* refers to the procedures that are required before one can be deprived of life, liberty, or property. These procedural requirements typically include notice of the intended deprivation, a fair hearing, and the opportunity to present one's case. The seminal decision on this topic is *Goss v. Lopez* (1975). In that case, nine high school students in Ohio received 10-day suspensions without the benefit of a hearing; they consequently filed suit, claiming a violation of their 14th Amendment due process rights. In a 5–4 decision, the U.S. Supreme Court first concluded that the due process clause applies to suspensions and expulsions from the educational system because liberty and property rights are implicated. The Court then went on to specify that due process requires notice of the charges and the intended disciplinary consequences, along with an opportunity for the student to present his or her side of the story.

Although there are some similarities between school disciplinary hearings and civil or criminal legal proceedings, there are also important differences. The Court in *Goss v. Lopez* deliberately stopped short of requiring that students facing brief suspensions have the full panoply of rights afforded at trial. For example, there is no guaranteed right to legal representation, to confront or call witnesses, or to freedom from self-incrimination. In addition, although hearsay is inadmissible in the courtroom, it has been deemed admissible in the context of formal school disciplinary hearings. Of course, school authorities are always free to provide students with additional legal safeguards if they so choose, and lengthier suspensions or expulsions may require additional procedures to meet the demands of the due process clause.

Disciplinary hearings should be conducted prior to the implementation of the punishment if at all possible. In some cases, however, an immediate temporary suspension may be required. The Court in *Goss v. Lopez* specified that "students whose presence poses a continuing danger to persons or property or an ongoing threat of disrupting the academic process may be immediately removed from school" (p. 582). In these cases, formal proceedings are still expected to take place as soon as possible.

Zero-Tolerance Policies

One of the most potent factors affecting school disciplinary actions and the rights of students is the notion of *zero tolerance*. Zero tolerance refers to policies under which harsh penalties are triggered by even a single infraction of the rules. Under many zero-tolerance policies, mandatory suspension and expulsion have become the primary means of achieving school discipline. Although zero-tolerance policies do not deny due process of law, they do prescribe nonnegotiable penalties (Alexander & Alexander, 2009).

Prompted by concerns about rising youth crime in the late 1980s and early 1990s, Congress passed the Gun-Free Schools Act of 1994 (McAndrews, 2001), which was later reauthorized as part of the No Child Left Behind Act of 2001. The act requires that every school district receiving federal funding implement a one-year mandatory expulsion for students who possess a firearm on school grounds. It also requires that students be referred to juvenile or criminal justice authorities if the behavior constitutes a criminal offense. Although the law does provide an opportunity for school officials to mitigate the harshness of the punishment on a case-by-case basis, it nonetheless became a catalyst for the widespread adoption of mandatory exclusionary discipline policies. Within a few short years, all 50 states had adopted some variation of the policy (Collins, Goodman, & Moulton, 1990). These policies vary across states and within states by school district. Nationally, 94% of schools report having zero-tolerance policies for firearms, 91% for other weapons, 87% for alcohol, 88% for drugs, 79% for violence, and 79% for tobacco (NCES, 1998). Other behaviors governed by these policies include profanity, immoral conduct, sexual harassment, gang membership, disruptive behavior, disobedience, excessive tardiness and absenteeism, unauthorized possession of a cell phone, destruction or stealing of school property, and unauthorized occupancy of school grounds (Rutherford Institute, 2001). These policies have served to "crack down" on undesirable behaviors. However, they have also been widely criticized as ineffective and unfair. Countless examples exist of zero-tolerance policies being applied to seemingly minor infractions that pose little actual danger to the student community. In middle schools, for example, disrespect and disobedience are the most common reasons for suspension, with tardiness and truancy not far behind. Many behaviors that were previously handled within the school have now become the province of the juvenile and criminal justice systems, resulting in a "school-to-prison pipeline" (American Psychological Association, 2008).

Students have been removed for bringing Midol®, Tylenol®, and other over-the-counter medications to school in violation of antidrug policies. In Colorado, a 10-year-old girl was suspended after giving her teacher the small knife her mother put in her lunchbox, along with an apple (Cauchon, 1999). Other examples include a 5-year-old student in California who was expelled after finding a razor blade at his bus stop and bringing it to school to show the teacher; a 17-year-old junior in Chicago who was arrested and expelled for shooting a paper clip with a rubber band; and a 9-year-old boy in Virginia who was suspended for a day and interviewed by police for distributing Certs Concentrated Mints that were considered to be look-alike drugs (Skiba & Peterson, 1999).

Supporters of zero-tolerance policies believe they send a quick and clear message that certain behaviors are simply unacceptable in the school setting, allowing all students to feel safer while at school. Critics, however, question the effectiveness of these policies and note that separation from school through suspension or expulsion may lead to worse educational outcomes for the student, including loss of educational opportunities, poor school performance, and even dropout (National Association of School Psychologists, 2001). The consequences for students of color and students with disabilities—both overrepresented among those suspended or expelled—are especially striking (Civil Rights Project, 2000; Skiba, Michael, Nardo, & Peterson, 2002). A concern voiced by professionals and parents alike relates to the absence of "common sense" when meting out punishment; many of these policies fail to distinguish between serious and lesser offenses and leave no discretion to school authorities to consider the individual circumstances involved. Both the American Bar Association and the American Academy of Pediatrics have issued policy statements citing the potential for suspension and expulsion to negatively impact both adolescent development and community health.

Opposition to zero tolerance intensified following the 2009 suicide of an 11th-grade student in Virginia who was facing an expulsion hearing after being found with marijuana on school grounds. Virginia law mandates expulsion under these circumstances and leaves no discretion to school authorities (Fisher, 2009). In January 2011, a football player in the same school district was removed from school and recommended for expulsion, despite never having violated school rules in the past; he had been caught with a capsule of synthetic marijuana (a legal substance). He committed suicide while awaiting transfer to another high school in the area (Reitzes, 2011). Outrage over the harsh zero-tolerance policies that precipitated these young men's tragic deaths has resulted in the formation of grassroots anti-zero-tolerance policy organizations, such as FairfaxZeroToleranceReform .org. These groups join other, well-established advocacy organizations in voicing opposition to these policies.

The courts, meanwhile, have widely upheld zero-tolerance policies even when the offense is committed unknowingly or there is no intent to harm. In *Ratner v. Loudoun County Public Schools* (2001), for example, a middle school student confiscated a knife from a classmate who was suicidal and put it in his own locker. The knife was discovered by school officials, who praised him for acting in the suicidal student's best interest. Nonetheless, he was given a long-term suspension under the district's zero-tolerance policy. The Fourth Circuit upheld the suspension. As long as a zero-tolerance policy is clearly stated, has been adopted by the school district, specifies the covered offenses, and has been disseminated to students, it is likely to be upheld. When harsh punishments are instituted in schools, as they are under zero-tolerance policies, it is especially important that the procedural guarantees of the due process clause be adhered to; social workers should be vigilant in ensuring that students' legal rights are realized.

Corporal Punishment

Corporal punishment, defined as causing a person physical discomfort or pain as a means of discipline for misbehavior, has been widely debated and researched over the years. This issue was previously discussed in the context of child abuse and neglect. Here we explore the issue of physical punishment in the context of the school environment.

Like other forms of school discipline, corporal punishment has historically been widely accepted. School authorities were considered to be acting *in loco parentis* (in place of the parent) and therefore were at liberty to punish children as they saw fit. Corporal punishment has typically involved striking a student with a wooden paddle, ruler, belt, or other object on various parts of the body for behaving in a manner contrary to school rules. Its use is intended to stop the student's behavior, prevent it from recurring, and serve as a cautionary example to other students (American Academy of Child and Adolescent Psychiatry, 1988).

The U.S. Supreme Court heard two corporal punishment cases in the mid-1970s. In *Baker v. Owen* (1975), the Court affirmed a North Carolina district court decision permitting the punishment of children in schools over their parents' objections. The Court reasoned that although parents generally have the right to control the disciplining of their children, the school "has a countervailing interest in maintenance of order in the school . . . sufficient to sustain the right of teachers and school officials to administer reasonable corporal punishment for disciplinary purposes" (p. 296). The Court's opinion also articulated guidelines for corporal punishment, specifying that (1) children must be notified in advance of which behaviors are subject to punishment, (2) less drastic disciplinary measures must be attempted first, (3) only reasonable force can be used, (4) a second staff person must be present as a witness, and (5) parents can request a written explanation of the reason for the punishment and the names of those who observed it.

Two years later, the Court heard the landmark case of *Ingraham v. Wright* (1977). Two middle school students in Florida, James Ingraham and Roosevelt Andrews, brought the case. The operative school board policy in that district authorized teachers to physically discipline students who disobeyed the rules by striking them up to five times on the buttocks with a wooden paddle of prescribed measurements. The policy also prohibited punishment that was degrading or unduly severe, and required teachers to consult with the principal before administering the punishment. In both students' cases, however, the principal was not consulted and the students sustained significant injuries as a result of the paddling. Ingraham was struck 20 times on the buttocks while being held over a table after he failed to respond promptly to his teacher's directions. He required medical attention and missed 11 days of school. Andrews testified that on two occasions he was struck on the arm and lost full use of the limb for a week. The students filed suit, claiming that the school had violated their Eighth Amendment right to be free from cruel and unusual punishment, and their 14th Amendment right to procedural due process. The district court found in favor of the school and the court of appeals reversed, finding in favor of the students.

In a 5–4 decision, the Supreme Court rejected both constitutional claims and upheld the use of corporal punishment as constitutional. It held that the Eighth Amendment, originally intended to apply to prisoners in the criminal justice system, is inapplicable to children in schools. It further held that it would be impractical to require 14th Amendment due process protections (notice and a hearing) every time a teacher sought to administer corporal punishment. On the other hand, the Court clarified that corporal punishment is permissible only when it is reasonably necessary for the proper education and discipline of the child, and warned that excessive corporal punishment could subject teachers to civil or criminal liability.

When *Ingraham v. Wright* was decided in 1977, the use of corporal punishment in schools was widespread. Today, although less common, it remains legal in 21 states (Human Rights Watch, 2008). Research has highlighted the practice's ineffectiveness and negative consequences (Center for Effective Discipline, 2008; Human Rights Watch, 2008; NASW, 2009). Many professional groups have called for the practice to be discontinued, including NASW, the American Academy of Pediatrics, the National Education Association, the American Bar Association, the National Association of School Psychologists, the National Mental Health Association, the National PTA, and the American Academy of Child and Adolescent Psychiatry. NASW's policy statement on Physical Punishment of Children is unequivocal in noting that "the use of physical force against people, especially children, is antithetical to the best values of a democratic society and of the social work profession" (p. 254).

Since the Supreme Court handed down its ruling in *Ingraham*, several lower courts have heard cases regarding the use of corporal punishment in schools. Generally speaking, the outcomes appear to turn on whether the court regards the administration of the punishment as reasonable under the circumstances. An Eleventh Circuit case, *Neal v. Fulton County Board of Education* (2000), is illustrative. In that case, a high school freshman, Durante Neal, was slapped in the face by a fellow member of the varsity football team during practice. When he reported the incident, the coach suggested he learn to handle his own affairs. Neal took a metal weight lock from the coaches' office, put it in his gym bag, and hit the teammate with it when he again approached Neal after practice. A fight ensued and the coach intervened—but, rather than break up the fight, he hit Neal with the weight lock, knocking his eye out of its socket and leaving him permanently blind in one eye. Neal filed suit, claiming his constitutional rights had been violated. Although the district court dismissed the case, finding that no constitutional rights were implicated, the court of appeals reversed. The court noted that the punishment here was not carried out pursuant to an established school board policy and that the Constitution does protect a student against corporal punishment that is "intentional, obviously excessive, and creates a foreseeable risk of serious injury" (p. 1069).

Social workers can play an important role in contributing to the literature on corporal punishment, promoting alternative disciplinary measures, working with students facing disciplinary action, and advocating for the elimination of physical punishment in schools. Given the profession's commitment to safeguarding the rights and well-being of those most vulnerable, the continuing use of corporal punishment is unacceptable. Beyond its negative effects generally, research shows that it disproportionately impacts children of color and those with disabilities. While Black children comprise 17% of the school-age population in the United States, they comprise nearly 36% of children receiving corporal punishment (Children's Defense Fund, 2011). As highlighted elsewhere in this chapter, students with disabilities are also disproportionately punished. A bill to ban corporal punishment in public and private schools receiving federal funds was introduced in Congress by Rep. Carolyn McCarthy (D-NY). The Ending Corporal Punishment in Schools Act of 2011 (H.R. 3027) would also provide grants for schools to implement positive behavioral supports, a strengths-based, evidence-supported intervention aimed at improving school climate and reducing disciplinary referrals. Social workers should actively promote this proposal and others like it.

Special Education

Law and social work also converge when it comes to special education. This is an area of particular relevance for social workers in schools. The number of children receiving special education services has increased dramatically in recent years, from 8.4% in 1976–1977 to 13.4% in 2007–2008. While the total number of elementary and secondary school students increased by 10% between 1976 and 2007, the number of children receiving special education services increased by 81%. Of those receiving special education services, 90% are categorized as having "mild disabilities" and 10% have severe disabilities, including autism, severe intellectual deficits, blindness, and deafness (Snyder & Dillow, 2010). This rapid growth in the special education population is in part a function of teachers' improved ability to recognize students with special needs.

Rights Under Federal Law

The Individuals with Disabilities Education Act (IDEA, 20 U.S.C. §§1400-1487) is the primary federal law addressing special education. Two other laws complement it: Section 504 of the Rehabilitation Act of 1973 and the Americans with Disabilities Act (ADA). Originally enacted in 1990 and amended several times since, IDEA grew out of the Education for All Handicapped Children Act of 1975 (EHA, P.L. 94-142). IDEA guarantees every child "a free and appropriate public education" in the least restrictive environment appropriate to his or her needs. Part B of the act addresses special education and related services for children ages 3–21, and Part C addresses early intervention services from birth through age 2.

IDEA, like its predecessor, was enacted to correct long-standing injustices faced by children with disabilities who were often excluded from the educational system. As recently as 1970 (when women and African Americans were making significant civil rights gains), only one in five children with disabilities was being educated in U.S. schools. Many states excluded certain children by law, including those who were deaf, blind, emotionally disturbed, or intellectually disabled. Local school districts excluded more than a million children each year, and another 3.5 million received little or no meaningful instruction. As a result, parents in 26 states brought challenges in court, using the same equal protection arguments that had successfully been made in *Brown v. Board of Education* relative to African American children. Two cases, *Pennsylvania Association for Retarded Citizens (PARC) v. Commonwealth of Pennsylvania* (1971) and *Mills v. Board of Education of the District of Columbia* (1972), were particularly significant; they articulated the basic rights that formed the foundation for the EHA and later for IDEA (National Council on Disability, 2000; Palmaffy, 2001).

Under IDEA, states must provide a *free and appropriate public education* to all children with disabilities. The law sets out an elaborate set of processes by which this is accomplished. Those processes are depicted in Illustration 20.1. Under a provision called *child find*, schools are mandated to seek out and identify students needing special education and refer them for evaluation. Parents can also request an evaluation. A multidisciplinary team of school personnel determines whether or not the child meets the eligibility criteria for special educational services under IDEA, based on multiple sources of information including input from the parents (Atkins-Burnett, 2007). If the child is determined to be eligible, an *individualized education program* (IEP) is developed to guide the delivery of services. The IEP must

- Describe the child's current levels of academic achievement and functional performance
- Specify measurable annual goals
- Explain how the child's progress toward the goals will be measured
- Identify the special education and related services that will be provided
- Indicate the anticipated frequency of services and when they will begin
- Specify any accommodations necessary to measure the child's achievement on state or local standardized tests
- Describe the extent to which the child will be able to participate alongside nondisabled children in regular classes

DISCIPLINING STUDENTS WITH DISABILITIES

As educational rights for children with special needs expanded under the Education for All Handicapped Children Act and later IDEA, schools were faced with the mounting dilemma of whether and how to discipline children with disabilities. While school officials retained an important interest in securing the safety and order of the educational environment, parents reacted strongly to the disciplining of their disabled children who, in many cases, were incapable of conforming their behavior to standard classroom expectations. A series of court decisions informed the development of a complex set of rules governing the disciplining of students with special needs.

Generally speaking, the courts have been consistent in holding that IDEA prohibits school districts from punishing students for behavior that is related to their disabilities (O'Neil, 2005). This has generated a backlash, with some perceiving a double standard under which special needs students are treated differently from their nondisabled peers, often in response to the same unacceptable behaviors (Proffitt-Dupre, 2000).

One of the first issues to be considered by the courts was expulsion. Before a student with a disability can be expelled, a multidisciplinary team must make a *manifestation determination* as to whether or not the child's inappropriate behavior is a result of his or her disability (*Doe v. Koger*, 1979). Parents have the right to challenge the determination in court. If the determination reveals that the behavior *is* the result of a disability, the child cannot be expelled. However, the school must develop an appropriate intervention plan for the child based on a functional behavioral assessment, or review and modify the existing plan to address the behavior at issue. If, on the other hand, the behavior is *unrelated* to the disability, the child can be disciplined like any other child but must continue to receive services (*S-1 v. Turlington*, 1981). Early versions of IDEA contained a legal presumption that inappropriate behavior by special needs children is a manifestation of their disability. That presumption was removed from the law in 2004.

The most important U.S. Supreme Court case on the topic of disciplining children with special needs is *Honig v. Doe* (1988). That case involved two children with emotional disabilities in California whom the school district had suspended and sought to expel because of violent and disruptive behavior resulting from their disabilities. A seven-member majority of the court ruled that school authorities may remove a child (or place the child in an interim alternative educational setting) for up to 10 days under these circumstances, but a longer exclusion from school (absent consent of the parents) is considered an impermissible change in placement. Under what is referred to as the *stay-put* provision of IDEA, students have the right to remain in their school while any proceedings are pending.

An exception was introduced following the enactment of the Gun Free Schools Act of 1994. Today, students with disabilities can be suspended for up to 45 days, without a manifestation determination, for weapons and drug violations or for inflicting "serious bodily injury" on another person (20 U.S.C. § 1415[d][1][G]). It is also possible for a hearing officer to keep a child in an interim alternative educational placement for up to 45 days based on substantial evidence that the "current placement will likely result in harm to the child or others" and that the school has "made reasonable efforts to minimize the risk of harm in the current placement" (Atkins-Burnett, 2007, p. 204).

Even though the law has provided safeguards to prevent students with disabilities from being inappropriately disciplined—and has recognized their right to receive ongoing services as part of a free and appropriate public education—research shows that students with disabilities are more often subject to school discipline than their nondisabled peers (e.g., Losen & Gillespie, 2012). School social workers have an important role to play in helping to ensure that disciplinary measures are equitably applied to all students within the school setting.

ILLUSTRATION 20.1

IEP Flowchart

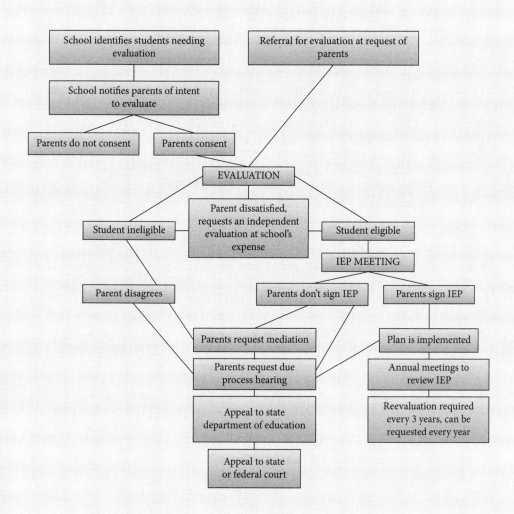

School identifies students needing evaluation

Referral for evaluation at request of parents

School notifies parents of intent to evaluate

Parents do not consent

Parents consent

EVALUATION

Parent dissatisfied, requests an independent evaluation at school's expense

Student ineligible

Student eligible

IEP MEETING

Parent disagrees

Parents don't sign IEP

Parents sign IEP

Parents request mediation

Plan is implemented

Parents request due process hearing

Annual meetings to review IEP

Appeal to state department of education

Reevaluation required every 3 years, can be requested every year

Appeal to state or federal court

Development of the IEP is a collaborative effort on the part of a team that includes the parent(s), at least one regular education teacher, at least one special education teacher, a representative of the local educational agency, someone able to interpret the assessment results, other individuals with relevant expertise, and (when appropriate) the student. Social workers often serve as members of the IEP team or are consulted by team members prior to the meeting.

Under IDEA, if a school district is unwilling or unable to provide a disabled child with a free and appropriate public education, parents have the right to withdraw the child from public school and place him or her in a private school. Under these circumstances, parents are entitled to have the school district reimburse the cost of a private school education. If the district declines to do so, the parents can request an administrative hearing and eventually take their case to court. It is important to understand, however, that parents and schools often have different interpretations of what constitutes a free and appropriate public education. According to the U.S. Supreme Court in *Board of Education v. Rowley* (1982), a free and appropriate public education requires only that level of service reasonably calculated to provide the child with an educational benefit. In other words, the quality and quantity of services must enable the student to proceed to the next grade level and achieve average grades, but no more. Schools need not maximize the child's potential nor provide extraordinary educational interventions. The child in *Rowley*, a deaf first-grader in New York, was able to perform adequately in school by reading her teachers' lips. Her parents argued, however, that she could excel if she were given access to a sign language interpreter. When the school refused to include interpreting services in the IEP, Rowley's parents sought a hearing. The hearing examiner found for the school and Rowley's parents appealed. The district court ruled that because of the disparity between the child's potential and her performance, she was not being provided a free and appropriate public education as contemplated by IDEA. The court of appeals affirmed, but a six-person majority of the Supreme Court reversed—concluding that the school's obligation under IDEA had been met.

One of the hallmarks of IDEA is its insistence that children with disabilities be educated in the *least restrictive environment* (LRE). For many children, this means being educated in a regular classroom. From 1998 to 2007, the percentage of children with disabilities spending more than 80% of their time in general education classrooms jumped from 32% to 57% (National Center for Education Statistics, 2010). This is an aspect of IDEA that remains controversial and is often litigated. The Ninth Circuit Court of Appeals, in *Sacramento City Unified School District v. Rachel H.* (1994), provided a four-point test for determining a child's proper placement. It required that the following factors be balanced: (1) the educational benefits of full-time placement in a regular class, (2) the nonacademic benefits of such a placement, (3) the effect the special needs child has on the teacher and children in the regular class, and (4) the costs of mainstreaming the child. Although support for the general notion of educating children in the least restrictive environment remains widespread, some critics question the wisdom of the law's presumption in favor of educating all disabled children in regular classrooms. Instead, they favor a continuum of settings that includes (from least to most restrictive) instruction in regular classes, special classes in a regular school, instruction in a special school, home instruction, and if necessary, instruction in a hospital or other institutional settings. They argue that *full inclusion* (educating in a regular classroom) should never occur at the expense of an appropriate education. Rather, the first step should be determining what services are necessary for a particular child and then providing those services in as integrated a setting as possible (Blanck, Hill, Siegal, & Weatherstone, 2009; Colker, 2006).

In addition to special educational services, IDEA requires that schools provide *related services* that are necessary to help students benefit from their education. IDEA identifies a wide range of such services, including (but not limited to) transportation, speech pathology and audiology, occupational therapy, therapeutic recreation, school nurse services, psychological services, counseling, and *social work services.* Needless to say, there is an important role here for social workers who may be called upon to conduct biopsychosocial assessments, provide individual or group counseling, address issues in a child's living environment that impact his or her performance, and mobilize resources to support the child's learning.

Under IDEA, parents retain the right to challenge an IEP—either through mediation or by requesting a *due process hearing* in front of an administrative law judge. The school district can also seek a hearing if, for example, it wishes to change an IEP and the parents withhold their consent. All parties to the hearing are entitled to be represented by counsel, to present evidence, and to cross-examine witnesses. If either party is dissatisfied with the results of the hearing, the decision can be appealed to state or federal court (Alexander & Alexander, 2009). The U.S. Supreme Court ruled in 2005 that the burden of proof rests with whichever party brings the action; in other words, parents challenging an IEP bear the burden of proving the case (*Schaffer v. Weast*). Given the complexity of the process, some fear that this may discourage parents from pursuing their cases or may disadvantage those who choose to do so.

Parents may also challenge an IEP's implementation. Courts generally defer to the school district in these cases, unless the parent can show that there has been a *material failure* to implement the IEP's terms. In other words, the services actually provided must fall "significantly short" of the services agreed upon (Alexander & Alexander, 2009). Minor deviations from the plan are unlikely to result in a victory for the parents.

Disproportionality

Children of color are overrepresented in special education programs, although there are enormous geographic variations. Nationally, minority children comprise the majority of students receiving special education in the United States (U.S. Commission on Civil Rights, 2009), with African American and American Indian/Alaska Native children being 1.5 times as likely as students from all other racial/ethnic groups to be classified as having disabilities. African American children are more than twice as likely to be labeled emotionally disturbed and three times as likely to be labeled intellectually disabled as students from all other racial and ethnic groups combined. American Indian/Alaska Native children are 3.6 times more likely to be labeled developmentally delayed (Gould, 2009). Particularly troublesome are research findings confirming that minority children in predominantly White school districts are more likely to be placed in special education programs than minority children in more integrated school districts (Ladner, 2009). Once referred for special education, minority students are also more likely than their White counterparts to be placed in self-contained classrooms rather than in regular education classes. Whereas 54.7% of White students in 2003 were placed in regular classrooms for most of the day, only 38.6% of African American students were afforded the same opportunity (Gould, 2009).

Students with limited English proficiency (LEP) are also disproportionately represented in special education programs. Research suggests that as many as three-fourths of LEP students enrolled in special education programs are improperly placed (Zamora, 2009). While the overall number of students with limited English proficiency increased by 61% between 1997 and 2007, the number receiving special education more than doubled (Monroe, 2009). Contrary to what might be expected, the majority of LEP students (76% in elementary schools and 56% in secondary schools) are U.S.-born citizens. More than half of the LEP students in public secondary schools are second- or third-generation Americans (Capps et al., 2005). Because English language learners tend to perform poorly on standardized achievement tests, they are often misclassified as disabled (Zamora, 2009). Research suggests that those who receive all their instruction in English are nearly three times as likely to be referred for special education as those who receive some support in their native language (Artiles & Ortiz, 2002).

A California district court addressed the issue of misclassification in *Diana v. State Board of Education* (1970). In that case, Mexican American schoolchildren whose first language was Spanish had been placed in classes for children with mental retardation after taking an intelligence test in English. More extensive testing, however, revealed that seven of the nine children were not intellectually disabled. The court mandated that all Mexican American and Chinese American children be reevaluated in their native language and that intelligence tests used for assessment reflect the children's native culture. More generally, the court held that (1) if a student's primary language is not English, tests must be administered both in English and the student's first language, and (2) tests used for assessment purposes must be free of cultural bias. The efficacy of intelligence tests was also challenged in the 1984 case of *Larry P. v. Riles*. This class action resulted from San Francisco's disproportionate placement of African American children in classes for students with intellectual disabilities. Although only 28.5% of the district's students were Black, Black students comprised 66% of the students in these special education classes. The Ninth Circuit Court of Appeals banned the use of culturally biased I.Q. tests and mandated that the state instead adopt a multifaceted approach to student evaluation. It also required that the state monitor the representation of African American students in special education classes, and implement corrective action when disproportionality is observed.

Numerous theories have been offered to explain the overrepresentation of minorities and English language learners in special education programs. Historically, special education classes were used as "dumping grounds" for disruptive students; some believe that this still accounts for the disproportionate placement of African American boys in special classes. As one source says, " I believe the staff and faculty are afraid of boys of color. . . . The simplest way to deal with it is to teach the kids who are easy to teach and warehouse the most difficult ones" (Salzman, 2005). Some observers point to the subjectivity of decisions made by school officials, whereas others believe that educators misinterpret culturally normative behaviors as evidence of disability. Students of color may experience difficulty connecting with curricula that are designed for dominant student groups, and teachers may incorrectly interpret disinterest as an inability to learn. As noted earlier, the use of culturally biased intelligence tests can also result in students being inappropriately labeled as disabled (National Education Association, 2007). Some attribute the overuse of special education to perverse financial incentives that favorably compensate school districts for special education placements (Ladner, 2009). Others note the interrelationship among minority status, limited English proficiency, special education placements, and poverty, suggesting that more is at play than simple misdiagnosis (Felton, 2009; Reschly, 2009). Whatever the cause, there is widespread agreement that teachers must be better trained in distinguishing linguistic barriers from cognitive deficits, and culturally normative behaviors from disability. In addition, there is an urgent need to maximize federal financial support for special education. Far from realizing the 40% contribution originally projected, federal funding continues to hover around 16.5%.

Senator Tom Harkin's (D-IA) IDEA Full Funding Act (S. 1403), introduced in 2011, would gradually increase the federal share of special education funding to 40% by 2021. Social workers can support needed special education services by advocating for passage of this and other bills that would strengthen our commitment to serving children in need. We can also use our cultural competence and understanding of person-in-environment to ensure that children are properly identified and served when it comes to special education.

Summary and Conclusion

The right to an education, although not guaranteed by the U.S. Constitution, is afforded through compulsory school attendance laws. States shoulder the bulk of responsibility for financing and implementing public education, with the federal government assuming a more modest role. Although the United States boasts a quality educational system overall, significant disparities in access and opportunity continue to disadvantage low-income children and children of color. Although students are afforded a number of constitutional rights in the school setting, these rights are sometimes subjugated to the exigencies of maintaining order and protecting the educational mission. This balancing approach to civil liberties in schools has been applied by the Supreme Court in cases addressing the First Amendment's freedom of speech and press, freedom of religion, and freedom of assembly. When it comes to search and seizure, the scope of student rights depends on the likely expectation of privacy, the invasiveness of the search, and the importance of the search's objective. The courts have increasingly recognized student rights in relation to school discipline, especially when it comes to due process. The continued use of corporal punishment and the implementation of zero-tolerance policies are inconsistent with social work values.

The scope of student rights should be of great interest to social workers. Schools are an important system in any family's environment. School social workers in particular have an obligation to ensure the realization of student rights and help students and their parents navigate the legal terrain when necessary. As advocates for students, social workers can help educate the school community about student needs and evidence-based interventions. The expertise of social workers is particularly valuable in assessing and planning for students with special needs, and in working with school personnel and families around disciplinary actions. Finally, social workers should promote school policies and programs that increase equity across the student population.

Sample Case

The First Circuit Court of Appeals decided the following case. Although it was brought under the Education for All Handicapped Children Act, it applies equally to the Individuals with Disabilities Education Act. Read the case, think about the material in the chapter concerning the right to special education, and answer the questions that follow.

TIMOTHY W. v. ROCHESTER SCHOOL DISTRICT
875 F.2d 954 (1989)

Bownes, Circuit Judge.

Plaintiff-appellant Timothy W. appeals an order of the district court which held that under the Education for All Handicapped Children Act, a handicapped child is not eligible for special education if he cannot benefit from that education. . . . We reverse.

Background

Timothy W. was born two months prematurely on December 8, 1975 with severe respiratory problems, and shortly thereafter experienced an intracranial hemorrhage, subdural effusions, seizures, hydrocephalus, and meningitis. As a result, Timothy is multiply handicapped and profoundly mentally retarded. He suffers from complex developmental disabilities, spastic quadriplegia, cerebral palsy, seizure disorder and cortical blindness. His mother attempted to obtain appropriate services for him, and while he did receive some services from the Rochester Child Development Center, he did not receive any educational program from the Rochester School District when he became of school age.

On February 19, 1980, the Rochester School District convened a meeting to decide if Timothy was considered educationally handicapped under the state and federal statutes, thereby entitling him to special education and related services. The school district heard testimony from Dr. Robert Mackey, Timothy's pediatrician and Medical Consultant for SSI (Supplemental Security Income Program), to the effect that Timothy was severely handicapped. Dr. Mackey recommended the establishment of an educational program for Timothy, which emphasized physical therapy and stimulation. Reports by Susan Curtis, M.S., and Mary Bamford, O.T.R., an occupational therapist, also recommended an educational program consisting of occupational therapy and increasing Timothy's responses to his environment. Testimony of Timothy's mother indicated that he responded to sounds. Carrie Foss, director of the Rochester Child Development Center, testified that Timothy localized sound, responded to his name, and responded to his mother. On the other hand, Dr. Alan Rozycki, a pediatrician at the Hitchcock Medical Center, reported that Timothy had no educational potential, and Dr. Patricia Andrews, a developmental pediatrician, stated that hydrocephalus had destroyed part of Timothy's brain. The school district adjourned without making a finding. In a meeting on March 7, 1980, the school district decided that Timothy was not educationally handicapped—that since his handicap was so severe he was not "capable of benefitting" from an education, and therefore was not entitled to one.***

On July 5, 1988, the district court rendered its opinion. . . . It first ruled that "under EAHCA [the Education for All Handicapped Children Act], an initial determination as to the child's ability to benefit from special education, must be made in order for a handicapped child to qualify for education under the Act. The court then reviewed the materials, reports and testimony and found that "Timothy W. is not capable of benefitting from special education.... As a result, the defendant [school district] is not obligated to provide special education under EAHCA." Timothy W. has appealed this order.

The primary issue is whether the district court erred in its rulings of law. Since we find that it did, we do not review its findings of fact.***

The language of the Act could not be more unequivocal. The statute is permeated with the words "*all* handicapped children" whenever it refers to the target population. It never speaks of any exceptions for severely handicapped children. Indeed . . .the Act gives priority to the most severely handicapped. Nor is there any language whatsoever which requires as a prerequisite to being covered by the Act, that a handicapped child must demonstrate that he or she will "benefit" from the educational program. Rather, the Act speaks of the *state's* responsibility to design a special education and related services program that will meet the unique "needs" of all handicapped children. The language of the Act in its entirety makes clear that a "zero-reject" policy is at the core of the Act, and that no child, regardless of the severity of his or her handicap, is to ever again be subjected to the deplorable state of affairs which existed at the time of the Act's passage, in which millions of handicapped children received inadequate education or none at all. In summary, the Act mandates an appropriate public education for all handicapped children, regardless of the level of achievement that such children might attain.***

The Act was a response to tomes of testimony and evidence that handicapped children were being systematically excluded from education outright, or were receiving grossly inadequate education. The Office of Education provided Congress with a report documenting that there were eight million handicapped children, and that more than four million of them were not receiving an appropriate education, including almost two million who were receiving no education at all.

In mandating a public education for all handicapped children, Congress explicitly faced the issue of the possibility of the non-educability of the most severely handicapped. The Senate Report stated, "The Committee recognizes that in many instances the process of providing special education and related services to handicapped children is *not guaranteed to produce any particular outcome*."***

Thus, the district court's major holding, that proof of an educational benefit is a prerequisite before a handicapped child is entitled to a public education, is specifically belied, not only by the statutory language, but by the legislative history as well. We have not found in the Act's voluminous legislative history, nor has the school district directed our attention to, a single affirmative averment to support a benefit/eligibility requirement. But there is explicit evidence of a contrary congressional intent, that no guarantee of any particular educational outcome is required for a child to be eligible for public education.***

The district court relied heavily on *Board of Education v. Rowley* in concluding that as a matter of law a child is not entitled to a public education unless he or she can benefit from it. The district court, however, has misconstrued *Rowley*. In that case, the Supreme Court held that a deaf child, who was an above average student and was advancing from grade to grade in a regular public school classroom, and who was already receiving substantial specialized instruction and related services, was not entitled, in addition, to a full time sign-language interpreter, because she was already benefitting from the special education and services she was receiving. The Court held that the school district was not required to maximize her educational achievement. It stated, "if personalized instruction is being provided with sufficient supportive services to permit the child to benefit from the instruction . . . the child is receiving a 'free appropriate public education' as defined by the Act,"*** and that "certainly the language of the statute contains no requirement . . . that States maximize the potential of handicapped children."***

Rowley focused on the level of services and the quality of programs that a state must provide, not the criteria for *access* to those programs.*** The Court's use of "benefit" in *Rowley* was a substantive limitation placed on the state's choice of an educational program; it was not a license for the state to exclude certain handicapped children. In ruling that a state was not required to provide the maximum benefit possible, the Court was not saying that there must be proof that a child will benefit before the state is obligated to provide any education at all. Indeed, the Court in *Rowley* explicitly acknowledged Congress' intent to ensure public education to all handicapped children without regard to the level of achievement that they might attain. . . . Thus, the intent of the Act was more to open the door of public education to handicapped children on appropriate terms than to guarantee any particular level of education once inside.***

Rowley simply does not lend support to the district court's finding of a benefit/eligibility standard in the Act. As the Court explained, while the Act does not require a school to maximize a child's potential for learning, it does provide a "basic floor of opportunity" for the handicapped. . . . Nowhere does the Court imply that such a "floor "contains a trap door for the severely handicapped.***

Conclusion

The statutory language of the Act, its legislative history, and the case law construing it, mandate that all handicapped children, regardless of the severity of their handicap, are entitled to a public education. The district court erred in requiring a benefit/eligibility test as a prerequisite to implicating the Act. School districts cannot avoid the provisions of the Act by returning to the practices that were widespread prior to the Act's passage, and which indeed were the impetus for the Act's passage, of unilaterally excluding certain handicapped children from a public education on the ground that they are uneducable. The law explicitly recognizes that education for the severely handicapped is to be broadly defined, to include not only traditional academic skills, but also basic functional life skills, and that educational methodologies in these areas are not static, but are constantly evolving and improving. It is the school district's responsibility to avail itself of these new approaches in providing an education program geared to each child's individual needs. The only question for the school district to determine, in conjunction with the child's parents, is what constitutes an appropriate individualized education program (IEP) for the handicapped child. We emphasize that the phrase "appropriate individualized education program" cannot be interpreted, as the school district has done, to mean "no educational program."***

The judgment of the district court is reversed, judgment shall issue for Timothy W. The case is remanded to the district court which shall retain jurisdiction until a suitable individualized education program (IEP) for Timothy W. is effectuated by the school district. Timothy W. is entitled to an interim special educational placement until a final IEP is developed and agreed upon by the parties. The district court shall also determine the question of damages. Costs are assessed against the school district.

QUESTIONS

1. Stated briefly, what was the court's holding in this case? How did it reach its conclusion?

2. According to the court, IDEA presumes that there are no uneducable children. Do you agree? What sort of "education" should Timothy receive?

3. How would you counter the argument that, given finite financial resources, students who can benefit from an education should get priority over children like Timothy?

4. Timothy's parents fought for services for their child for 9 years, bringing their case before the school, a hearing examiner, and the courts. Few parents have the time, the resources, or the know-how to be so persistent. The IEP process alone is enough to overwhelm many parents who feel out of their depth in the company of school officials and other experts. If you were a school social worker, what knowledge and skills could you bring to a case like Timothy's? What roles could you play in the special education process? How could you be helpful?

CHAPTER 20 PRACTICE TEST

The following questions will test your application and analysis of the content found within this chapter. For additional assessment, including licensing-exam type questions on applying chapter content to practice behaviors, visit **MySearchLab**.

1. When Bernadette moved to a new school, she was horrified to discover that the school had a dress code prohibiting, among other things, the wearing of bandanas. In fact, Bernadette prided herself on her amazing collection of bandanas, which spanned the entire color spectrum. She tried wearing one to school the first week, but she was caught by the assistant principal and disciplined. If Bernadette were to challenge the dress code, claiming that it violated her First Amendment rights, what would be the likely result?

   a. She would win because how one dresses is considered a form of free speech.

   b. She would win because she had her parents' permission.

   c. She would lose because bandanas are associated with gang activity in that neighborhood.

   d. She would lose because free speech rights do not apply to students.

2. Performing religious songs as part of a school chorus concert is permissible because

   a. audience members are free to leave if they object.

   b. the concert's purpose is secular.

   c. more than one religion is being represented.

   d. the establishment clause does not apply to schools.

3. Corporal punishment in schools

   a. has consistently been upheld by the U.S. Supreme Court.

   b. no longer takes place.

   c. has a proven deterrent effect on misbehavior.

   d. is supported by NASW, except when applied to students with disabilities.

4. According to the courts, IDEA requires that students with disabilities

   a. be educated in separate, special education classes.

   b. be provided with sufficient services to allow them to achieve average grades.

   c. be provided with sufficient services to maximize their potential.

   d. defer to the school's judgment regarding the appropriateness of the IEP.

5. Are locker searches in schools constitutional? Explain how the courts have ruled on this issue and why.

6. Discuss the arguments for and against zero-tolerance policies in schools. Which arguments do you personally find most compelling? Which arguments do you think policy makers would find most persuasive? Why?

MYSEARCHLAB CONNECTIONS

Reinforce what you learned in this chapter by studying videos, cases, documents, and more available at **www.MySearchLab.com**.

Read these Cases/Documents

Δ Dylan James: A Case in School Social Work Practice

- *What alternatives to "zero tolerance" could be used with disruptive students?*

Explore these Assets

- Website: Center for the Study and Prevention of Violence
- Website: School Social Work Association of America

Research these Topics

- confidentialty in school settings
- mainstreaming children on the autism spectrum
- cross-dressing in schools

Assess Your Knowledge

Go to **MySearchLab** to test your knowledge of key topics in this chapter with topic-specific quizzes. Conclude your assessment by completing the chapter exam.

⋆ = CSWE Core Competency Asset   Δ = Case Study

Appendix I

SELECTED AMENDMENTS TO THE
U.S. CONSTITUTION (ABRIDGED)

Amendment I

Congress shall make no law respecting an establishment of religion, or prohibiting the free exercise thereof; or abridging the freedom of speech, or of the press; or the right of the people peaceably to assemble, and to petition the Government for a redress of grievances.

Amendment II

A well regulated Militia, being necessary to the security of a free State, the right of the people to keep and bear Arms, shall not be infringed.

Amendment IV

The right of the people to be secure in their persons, houses, papers, and effects, against unreasonable searches and seizures, shall not be violated, and no Warrants shall issue, but upon probable cause, supported by Oath or affirmation, and particularly describing the place to be searched, and the persons or things to be seized.

Amendment V

No person shall be held to answer for a capital, or otherwise infamous crime, unless on a presentment or indictment of a Grand Jury, except in cases arising in the land or naval forces, or in the Militia, when in actual service in time of War or public danger; nor shall any person be subject for the same offence to be twice put in jeopardy of life or limb; nor shall be compelled in any criminal case to be a witness against himself, nor be deprived of life, liberty, or property, without due process of law; nor shall private property be taken for public use, without just compensation.

Amendment VI

In all criminal prosecutions, the accused shall enjoy the right to a speedy and public trial, by an impartial jury of the State and district wherein the crime shall have been committed, which district shall have been previously ascertained by law, and to be informed of the nature and cause of the accusation; to be confronted with the witnesses against him; to have compulsory process for obtaining witnesses in his favor, and to have the Assistance of Counsel for his defense.

Amendment VIII

Excessive bail shall not be required, nor excessive fines imposed, nor cruel and unusual punishments inflicted.

Amendment IX

The enumeration in the Constitution, of certain rights, shall not be construed to deny or disparage others retained by the people.

Amendment X

The powers not delegated to the United States by the Constitution, nor prohibited by it to the States, are reserved to the States respectively, or to the people.

Amendment XIII

Section 1. Neither slavery nor involuntary servitude, except as a punishment for crime whereof the party shall have been duly convicted, shall exist within the United States, or any place subject to their jurisdiction.

Amendment XIV

Section 1. All persons born or naturalized in the United States and subject to the jurisdiction thereof, are citizens of the United States and of the State wherein they reside. No State shall make or enforce any law which shall abridge the privileges or immunities of citizens of the United States; nor shall any State deprive any person of life, liberty, or property, without due process of law; nor deny to any person within its jurisdiction the equal protection of the laws.

Amendment XV

Section 1. The right of citizens of the United States to vote shall not be denied or abridged by the United States or by any State on account of race, color, or previous condition of servitude.

Amendment XIX

The right of citizens of the United States to vote shall not be denied or abridged by the United States or by any State on account of sex. Congress shall have power to enforce this article by appropriate legislation.

Amendment XXIV

Section 1. The right of citizens of the United States to vote in any primary or other election for President or Vice President, for electors for President or Vice President, or for Senator or Representative in Congress, shall not be denied or abridged by the United States or any State by reason of failure to pay any poll tax or other tax.

Amendment XXVI

Section 1. The right of citizens of the United States, who are eighteen years of age or older, to vote shall not be denied or abridged by the United States or by any State on account of age.

Appendix II

GLOSSARY

Adjudication. The determination of a judgment; decision at the conclusion of a trial

Administrative law. Laws made by the executive branch of government

Affirm. Uphold a decision previously made by a lower court

Affirmative action. Policies or practices designed to compensate for a history of discrimination against women and racial minorities

Aggravated felony. In immigration law, a category of offenses for which an immigrant can be deported

Aggravating factors. Circumstances that weigh in favor of a harsher sentence in criminal proceedings

Alienage. A person's noncitizen status

Amicus curiae. Non-parties who submit briefs to the court in order to inform decision making; literally, a friend of the court

Arraignment. The first step in a criminal proceeding whereby the defendant is formally charged and enters a plea

Assisted outpatient treatment. Alternative sentence permitted by some states when civil commitment is unnecessary but voluntary compliance with outpatient treatment is unlikely

Asylee. A noncitizen who meets the definition of refugee but enters the country without first securing refugee status

Bona fide occupational qualification (BFOQ). A type of discrimination in employment that is legally acceptable because it is necessary to the normal functioning of a business

Burden of proof. The obligation of one party, typically the plaintiff, to convince the court of the truth of an allegation

Case law. Law made by the judicial branch of government

Circuit court of appeals. Part of a system of federal courts that hears appeals from U.S. district courts

Civil commitment. The involuntary hospitalization of a person with mental illness who is a danger to self or others

Civil proceedings. Cases designed to resolve disputes between two parties; not criminal

Civil union. Also called *domestic partnership*; a type of partnership recognized in some states that affords the members of a same-sex couple some or all of the legal rights afforded to married couples

Class action. A suit brought by members of a group on behalf of all those who are similarly situated

Concurring opinion. An opinion written by a judge who agrees with the outcome of the majority's opinion but offers different reasons

Courts of limited jurisdiction. Courts that hear only certain types of cases, such as traffic courts, immigration courts, or bankruptcy courts

Criminal proceedings. Cases brought by the government against someone who has allegedly violated a criminal law

Damages. Monetary compensation awarded to the party who prevails

De facto. As a matter of practice, not as a matter of law

Defendant. The party defending against a lawsuit

De jure. As a matter of law

Delinquency. Acts committed by juveniles that are unlawful for both juveniles and adults

Discovery. A pretrial procedure in which one party gains information about the case held by the other

Disparate impact. When a law that appears to be neutral has a disproportionate effect on one group compared to another

Disparate treatment. When a law deliberately treats one group differently from another

District court. A court that has jurisdiction over a distinct geographical area that includes a state or part of a state

Diversity jurisdiction. The right of federal courts to hear cases involving disputes between citizens of different states

Due process. The constitutional guarantee enshrined in the 5th and 14th Amendments to the U.S. Constitution stipulating that the government may not deprive an individual of life, liberty, or property in the absence of certain procedures

Equal protection. The constitutional guarantee enshrined in the 14th Amendment to the U.S. Constitution that protects against discrimination

Executive branch. The branch of the government that is responsible for enforcement of laws

Ex parte order. An order requested by one party in the absence of another; an exception to the basic rule that both parties must be present at any argument before a judge

Expert witness. A witness whose purpose is to help educate the court about issues that require special knowledge

Fact witness. A direct observer of events that are relevant to the case being presented in court

Forensic interview. A highly structured interview designed to gather factual information for use as evidence in court

Grand jury. A jury convened to determine whether the facts presented by the prosecution are sufficient proof of guilt to warrant a trial

Guardian at litem. An individual assigned by the court to represent the interests of a child or incapacitated adult in a legal proceeding

Hearsay. Information that the witness knows only secondhand, usually inadmissible as evidence in court

Hostile environment. A type of sexual harassment whereby an employee is subjected to repeated unwelcome comments, behaviors, or materials of a sexual nature

Indictment. A formal accusation submitted to the grand jury by the prosecutor, charging someone with a crime

Informed consent. The right of an individual to make a voluntary, well-informed decision

Intermediate scrutiny. Also called *heightened scrutiny*; under equal protection analysis, requires that a statute that treats different groups differently be substantially related to an important government purpose

Judicial review. The court's power to rule on a law's validity

Judiciary. The branch of government charged with interpreting the nation's laws

Juvenile court. Tribunal designed to hear cases involving youthful offenders

Legal custody. Authority to make major, long-term decisions about a child's health, education, and welfare

Legal permanent resident. A person residing in the United States with authorization who has not yet been granted citizenship; a "green card" holder

Legislation. Bills passed by the legislative branch and signed by the chief executive; also called *statutes* or *ordinances*

Legislature. The branch of the government responsible for passing laws

Magistrate. A public official with limited judicial powers

Malpractice. A professional breach of conduct prohibited by law

Minimal scrutiny. Also called *rational basis test*; under equal protection analysis, requires that a statute that treats different groups differently be rationally related to a legitimate government purpose

Miranda **warnings.** The requirement that law enforcement inform people in custody of their legal rights

Mitigating factors. Circumstances that weigh in favor of a lighter sentence in criminal proceedings

Naturalized citizen. A person born in another country who has been granted the rights of citizenship in the United States

Nolo contendere. A plea by which the defendant does not admit guilt but accepts punishment for the charges

Ordinances. Laws passed by local governments

Parens patriae. A legal doctrine that allows government to intervene to protect people who are vulnerable

Peremptory challenges. The procedure by which attorneys are permitted to dismiss members of a jury pool without providing a reason

Plaintiff. Also known as the petitioner; the party bringing a lawsuit

Plea agreement. A negotiated agreement between a prosecutor and a defendant in which a defendant pleads guilty in exchange for a lesser charge

Power of attorney. The legal authorization for one person to act on another's behalf

Precedent. Also known as *stare decisis*, the practice of relying on prior court rulings in deciding a case

Pretrial conference. A meeting of both parties designed to clarify the issues for trial

Prima facie. A case supported by at least the minimum amount of evidence required; in some instances, once a *prima facie* case is made, the burden of proof shifts to the opposing party

Privilege. The right to keep confidential information from being divulged in a court proceeding

Probable cause. Facts sufficient to warrant a belief that a crime has been committed

Probation. An alternative to incarceration that allows a convicted defendant to be released into the community with supervision

Prosecutorial discretion. The right of a prosecutor to decide whether or not to pursue a case

Protective order. A type of restraining order issued to protect an individual from harmful contact or threatening behavior by another

Quid pro quo harassment. A type of sexual harassment whereby a subordinate is promised a job benefit in exchange for submitting to an unwelcome sexual advance

Recidivism. The act of engaging in repeat offending

Refugee. A person outside his or her home country who is unable or unwilling to return because of well-founded fear of persecution; basis for a special immigration status

Remand. Returning a case to the lower court so that it can determine the outcome consistent with the higher court's ruling

Removal. In immigration law, the current term to describe deportation

Reverse. Vacate and change the ruling of a lower court

Rules of evidence. The body of law governing the admissibility of evidence in court

Special immigrant juvenile status (SIJS). A status afforded undocumented youth in state custody for whom family reunification is not an option, and who cannot return to their country of origin; permits adjustment of status to legal permanent resident

Standard of proof. The level of certainty and degree of evidence needed to establish a case

Status offense. An act that is unlawful for juveniles but not adults

Statute of limitations. The period within which a lawsuit may be filed

Statutes. Laws passed by the legislature

Statutory law. Laws enacted through the legislative process

Strict scrutiny. Under equal protection analysis, the most searching level of inquiry; requires that a statute that treats different groups differently be necessary to achieve a compelling government purpose

Subpoena. A legally enforceable demand to testify in court or submit documents or other evidence

Suspect classification. In equal protection analysis, a discrete group that has been historically disadvantaged and warrants special protection from discrimination

T-Visa. A special visa afforded certain victims of trafficking

Unauthorized immigrant. A person residing in the United States without proper documentation; also called *undocumented* or *illegal immigrant*

U-Visa. A special visa afforded victims of serious crimes who agree to cooperate with police

Voir dire. The process by which attorneys select or reject jurors; also the questioning of an expert witness's qualifications to testify

Writ of certiorari. Notification by the U.S. Supreme Court that it will agree to hear an appeal from a lower court.

References

Chapter 1

Albert, R. (2000). *Law and social work practice.* New York: Springer Publishing Co.

Arnason, S., Fish, D. G., & Rosenzweig, E. P. (2001). Elder law and elder care: A team response to the needs of elderly clients. *Journal of Gerontological Social Work, 34*(3), 3–11.

Barsky, A. E., & Gould, J. W. (2002). *Clinicians in court: A guide to subpoenas, testifying, and everything else you need to know.* New York: The Guilford Press.

Batson v. Kentucky, 476 U.S. 79 (1986).

Berman, G., & Feinblatt, J. (2005). *Good courts: The case for problem-solving justice.* New York: The New Press.

Berman, G., Rempel, M., & Wolf, R.V. (Eds.) (2007). *Documenting results: Research on problem-solving justice.* New York: Center for Court Innovation.

Brennan, W. C., & Khinduka, S. K. (1971). Role expectations of social workers and lawyers in the juvenile court. *Crime and Delinquency Quarterly, 17,* 191–201.

Burgess, A. W. (2002). Domestic violence: How many steps forward? How many steps back? *Online Journal of Issues in Nursing,* 7 (1). Retrieved from http://www.nursingworld.org//MainMenuCategories/ANAMarketplace/ANAPeriodicals/OJIN/TableofContents/Volume72002/No1Jan2002/DomesticViolenceOverview.aspx

Casey, P. M., & Rottman, D. B. (2003). *Problem-solving courts: Models and trends.* Williamsburg, VA: National Center for State Courts.

Center for Social Services Research. (2002). *Child welfare and the courts: An exploratory study of the relationship between two complex systems.* Berkeley: University of California. Retrieved from http://cssr.berkeley.edu/pdfs/CWCandCourtsEntire.pdf

Coleman, B. (2001). Lawyers who are also social workers: How to effectively combine two different disciplines to better serve clients. *Journal of Law and Policy, 7,* 131–158.

Coleman, S. (1999). *Students' and professionals' attitudes, knowledge, perceptions and beliefs about forensic social work practice* (Unpublished master's thesis). University of Redlands, Redlands, CA.

Day, P. J. (2009). *A new history of social welfare.* Boston: Pearson/Allyn & Bacon.

Diamond, S. S., Rose, M. R., & Murphy, B. (2006). Revisiting the unanimity requirement: The behavior of the non-unanimous civil jury. *Northwestern University Law Review, 100*(1), 201–230.

Fogelson, F. B. (1970). How social workers perceive lawyers. *Social Casework, 51*(2), 95–101.

Freedberg, S. (1993). The feminine ethic of care and the professionalization of social work. *Social Work, 38*(5), 535–540.

Galowitz, P. (1999). Collaboration between lawyers and social workers: Re-examining the nature and potential of the relationship. *Fordham Law Review, 67*(5), 2123–2154.

Glover, T., & Burke, T. (2007). Jury-rigging: Computer program vs. jury consultant. *Campbell Law Observer.* Retrieved from http://www.radford.edu/~tburke/Burke/jury.pdf

Golick, T., & Lessem, J. (2004). A law and social work clinical program for the elderly and disabled: Past and future challenges. *Journal of Law and Policy, 14,* 183–208.

Hijiya, J. A. (1980). Four ways of looking at a philanthropist: A study of Robert Weeks deForest. *Proceedings of the American Philosophical Society, 124*(6), 404–418.

J.E.B. v. Alabama, 511 U.S. 127 (1994).

Kearney, R. C., & Sellers, H. T. (1997). Gender bias in court personnel administration. *Judicature 81*(1), 8–14.

Kelly, L., Smith, N., & Gibson, S. (2009). From intervention roles to multidisciplinary practice. In T. Maschi, C. Bradley, & K. Ward (Eds.), *Forensic social work: Psychosocial and legal issues in diverse practice settings.* New York: Springer Publishing Company.

Kelso, R. W. (1929). The historical steps by which law and social work are coming together. *Annals of the American Academy of Political and Social Science, 145*(Part I), 17–22.

Khadaroo, S. T. (2011, Sept. 2). Feds warn colleges: Handle sexual assault reports properly. *Christian Science Monitor.* Retrieved from http://www.msnbc.msn.com/id/44376767/ns/us_news-christian_science_monitor/t/feds-warn-colleges-handle-sexual-assault-reports-properly/#.Tv8u5Vbdk3E

Lau, J. A. (1983). Lawyers vs. social workers: Is cerebral hemisphericity the culprit? *Child Welfare, 62,* 21–29.

Madden, R. G., & Wayne, R. H. (2003). Social work and law: A therapeutic jurisprudence perspective. *Social Work, 48*(3), 338–347.

Mirchandani, R. (2008). Beyond therapy: Problem-solving courts and the deliberative democratic state. *Law and Social Inquiry, 33,* 853–893.

Mitchell, O., Wilson, D.B., Eggers, A., & MacKenzie, D.L. (2012). Drug courts' effects on criminal offending for juveniles and adults. *Campbell Systematic Reviews,* DOI 10.4073/CST.2012.4

National Association of Social Workers. (2011a). *Social workers in Congress (112th Congress).* Washington, DC: Author.

National Association of Social Workers. (2011b). *Social workers in state and local office.* Retrieved from http://www.socialworkers.org/pace/state.asp

Pierce, C. T., Gleason-Wynn, P., & Miller, M. G. (2001). Social work and law: A model for implementing social services in a law office. *Journal of Gerontological Social Work, 34*(3), 61–71.

Ritter, J. A. (2007). Evaluating the political participation of licensed social workers in the new millennium. *Journal of Policy Practice, 6*(4), 61–78.

Ritter, J. A., Vakalahi, H. G. O., & Kiernan-Stern, M. (2009). *101 careers in social work*. New York: Springer Publishing Co.

Roberts, A. R., & Brownell, P. (1999). A century of forensic social work: Bridging the past to the present. *Social Work, 44*(4), 359–369.

Rome, S. H. (2008). Forensic social work. In T. Mizrahi & L.E. Davis (Eds.), *Encyclopedia of social work* (20th ed., pp. 221–223). Washington, DC and New York: NASW Press and Oxford University Press.

Rome, S. H., & Hoechsttetter, S. (2010). Social work and civic engagement: The political participation of professional social workers. *Journal of Sociology and Social Welfare, 37*(3), 107–129.

Rome, S. H., Hoechstetter, S., & Wolf-Branigin, M. (2010). Pushing the envelope: Empowering clients through political action. *Journal of Policy Practice, 9*(3–4), 201–219.

Russel, R. (1988). Role perceptions of attorneys and caseworkers in child abuse cases in juvenile court. *Child Welfare, 67*, 205–216.

Saltzman, A., & Furman, D. (1999). *Law in social work practice*. Chicago, IL: Nelson-Hall.

Sloane, H. (1967). Relationship of law and social work. *Social Work, 12*(1), 86–92.

Smith, A. D. (1970). The social worker in the legal setting: A study of interprofessional relationships. *Social Service Review, 44*(2), 155–168.

Solomon, P., & Draine, J. (1995). Issues in serving the forensic client. *Social Work, 40*(1), 25–33.

St. Joan, J. (2001). Building bridges, building walls: Collaboration between lawyers and social workers in a domestic violence clinic and issues of client confidentiality. *Clinical Law Review, 7*(2), 403–468.

Staller, K. M., & Kirk, S. A. (1998). Knowledge utilization in social work and legal practice. *Journal of Sociology & Social Welfare, 25*(3), 91–113.

Stein, T. J. (2004). *The role of law in social work practice and administration*. New York: Columbia University Press.

Taylor, S. (2005). Educating future practitioners of social work and law: Exploring the origins of inter-professional misunderstanding. *Children and Youth Services Review, 28*(6), 638–653.

Tyuse, S. W., & Linhorst, D. M. (2005). Drug courts and mental health courts: Implications for social work. *Health and Social Work, 30*(3), 233–240.

Vandervort, F. (2008). Legal ethics and high child welfare turnover: An unexplored connection. *Children and Youth Services Review, 30*(5), 546–563.

Weil, M. (1982). Research on issues in collaboration between social workers and lawyers. *Social Service Review, 56*(3), 393–405.

Weinstein, J. (1997). And never the twain shall meet: The best interests of children and the adversary system. *University of Miami Law Review, 52*, 79–175.

Weinstein, J. B. (1999). When is a social worker as well as a lawyer needed? *Journal of the Institute for the Study of Legal Ethics, 2*, 391–399.

Wiggins, R. (2009). *Collaboration of social work students and public defenders: A how-to manual* (Unpublished thesis project). George Mason University, Fairfax, VA.

Wiglesworth, A., Mosqueda, L, Burnight, K., Younglove, T., & Jeske, D. (2006). Findings from an elder abuse forensic center. *The Gerontologist, 46*(2), 277–283.

Winegar, T. (2006). *Voir dire*. Retrieved from http://www.toddw.com/3A_Voir_Dire.pdf

Young, P. (2009, Jan.). Social work students provide needed services for prisoners through Michigan Prison Reentry Initiative. News Release. Retrieved from http://www.emich.edu/univcomm/releases/release.php?id=1242305208

Chapter 2

ABC News (2009, March 16). How do celebrity salaries compare with ours? Retrieved from http://abcnews.go.com/GMA/WaterCooler/story?id=124545&page=1

Atkins v. Virginia, 536 U.S.304 (2002).

Baker, P. (2005, Sept. 6). Bush nominates Roberts as chief justice: President seeks quick approval with another seat left to fill. *Washington Post*, p. A1.

Baum, L. (2007). *The Supreme Court* (9th ed.). Washington, DC: CQ Press.

Betts v. Brady, 316 U.S. 455 (1942).

Board of Education v. Earls, 536 U.S. 822 (2002).

Bowers v. Hardwick, 478 U.S. 186 (1986).

Brown v. Board of Education, 347 U.S. 483 (1954).

Bush v. Gore, 531 U.S. 98 (2000).

Citizens United v. Federal Election Commission, 130 S.Ct. 876 (2010).

Danielson v. Dennis, Case No. 06SA174, Colorado Supreme Court (July 31, 2006).

DeShaney v. Winnebago Co. Department of Social Services, 489 U.S. 189 (1989).

District of Columbia v. Heller, 128 S.Ct. 2783 (2008).

Elk Grove Unified School District v. Newdow, 542 U.S. 1 (2004).

Forest Grove School District v. T.A., 129 S.Ct. 987 (2009).

Gideon v. Wainwright, 518 U.S. 515 (1996).

Graham v. Florida, 130 S.Ct. 2011 (2010).

Greenhouse, L. (1987, Oct. 24). Bork's nomination is rejected 58-42; Reagan "saddened." *New York Times*. Retrieved from http://www.nytimes.com/1987/10/24/politics/24REAG.html?pagewanted=1

Gonzales v. Carhart, 550 U.S. 124 (2007).

Grunwald, M., Becker, J., & Russakoff, D. (2005, Nov. 1). Comparisons to Scalia, but also to Roberts. *Washington Post*, p. A1.

Irons, P. (2006). *A people's history of the Supreme Court: The men and women whose cases and decisions have shaped our Constitution*. New York: Penguin Books.

Johnson v. State, 602 So.2d. 1288 (1992).

Kennedy v. Louisiana, 554 U.S. 407 (2008).

Korematsu v. United States, 323 U.S. 214 (1944).

Landes, W. M., & Posner, R. A. (2009). Rational judicial behavior: A statistical study. *The Journal of Legal Analysis, 1*(2), 775–831.

Lane, C. (2005, Sept. 4). Chief Justice William H. Rehnquist dies. *Washington Post,* p. A1.

Lawrence v. Texas, 539 U.S. 558 (2003).

Ledbetter v. Goodyear Tire and Rubber Co., 550 U.S. 618 (2007).

Monahan, J., & Walker, L. (1998). *Social science in law: Cases and materials* (4th ed.). Westbury, NY: The Foundation Press.

Montebello Rose Co. v. Agricultural Labor Relations Bd., 173 Cal. Rptr. 856 (1981).

Muller v. Oregon, 208 U.S. 412 (1908).

National Association of Social Workers. (2005). NASW opposes Roberts court nomination. *NASW News, 50*(9).

National Association of Social Workers (2006). NASW opposes court nominee Samuel Alito. *NASW News, 51*(1).

National Federation of Independent Business v. Sebelius, No. 11–393 (June 28, 2012).

National Taxpayers Union. (2010). *Salaries for members of Congress, Supreme Court justices, and the president.* Retrieved from http://www.ntu.org/on-capitol-hill/pay-and-perks/salaries-for-members-of.html

O'Brien, D. (2005). *Storm center: The Supreme Court in American politics* (7th ed.). New York: W. W. Norton & Company.

People v. Cabral, 15 Cal. Rptr.2d 866 (1993).

Perry v. Schwarzenegger, U.S. District Court for the Northern District of California, No C 09-2292 VRW (2010).

Roe v. Wade, 410 U.S. 113 (1973).

Roper v. Simmons, 543 U.S. 551 (2005).

Silverstein, M. (2007). *Judicious choices: The new politics of Supreme Court confirmations* (2nd ed.). New York: W. W. Norton & Company.

Stanford v. Kentucky, 392 U.S. 361 (1989).

Stenberg v. Carhart, 530 U.S. 914 (2000).

Trinidad School District No. 1 v. Lopez, No. 97SC124, Colorado Supreme Court (1998).

United States v. Virginia, 518 U.S. 515 (1996*).*

Varnum v. Brien, 763 N.W.2d 862 (2009).

Vernonia School District v. Acton, 515 U.S. 646 (1995).

Chapter 3

American Academy of Child and Adolescent Psychiatry (1997). Summary of the practice parameters for child custody evaluation. *Journal of American Academy of Child and Adolescent Psychiatry, 36*(12), 1784–1787.

American Academy of Psychiatry and the Law. (2005). American Academy of Psychiatry and the Law: Ethics guidelines for the practice of forensic psychiatry. Retrieved from http://www.aapl.org/ethics.htm

Ashford, J. B. (2009). Overview of forensic social work. In A. R. Roberts (Ed.), *Social workers' desk reference* (pp. 1055–1060). New York: Oxford University Press.

Barker, R. L. (2003). *The social work dictionary* (5th ed.). Washington, DC: NASW Press.

Barker, R. L., & Branson, D. M. (2000). Forensic Social Work: Legal Aspects of Professional Practice (2nd ed.). Binghamton, NY: Haworth Press.

Barsky, A. E., & Gould, J. W. (2002). *Clinicians in court: A guide to subpoenas, depositions, testifying, and everything else you need to know.* New York: Guilford Press.

Bow, J. N., & Quinnell, F. A. (2002). A critical review of child custody evaluation reports. *Family Court Review, 40*(2), 164–176.

Collins, R., Lincoln, R., & Frank, M. G. (2002). Effect of rapport in forensic interviewing. *Psychiatry, Psychology, and Law, 9*(1), 69–78.

Cross, T. P., Jones, L. M., Walsh, W. A., Simone, M., Kolko, D. J., Szczepanski, J., & Magnuson, S. (2008). Evaluating children's advocacy centers' response to child sexual abuse. Retrieved from http://www.ncjrs.gov/pdffiles1/ojjdp/218530.pdf

Dix, G. E., & Poythress Jr., N. G. (1981). Propriety of medical dominance of forensic mental health practice: The empirical evidence. *Arizona Law Journal, 23*(3), 961–989.

Faller, K. C. (2007). *Interviewing children about sexual abuse: Controversies and best practice.* New York: Oxford University Press.

Gifis, S. (2008). Direct examination. *Dictionary of Legal Terms* (4th ed.), Hauppauge, NY: Barron's.

Guidelines for forensic evaluation. (2004). Federal Bureau of Prisons—Clinical Practice Guidelines. Retrieved from http://www.federaldefender.net/Documents/Scrolling%20Banner/BOP%20Guidelines.pdf

Hornor, G. (2008). Child advocacy centers: Providing support to primary care providers. *Journal of Pediatric Health Care, 22*(1), 35–39.

Hughes, D., & O'Neal, B. (1983). A survey of current forensic social work. *Social Work, 28,* 393–394.

Knoll, J. L., & Resnick, P. J. (2007). Insanity defense evaluations: Toward a model for evidence- based practice. *Brief Treatment and Crisis Intervention Advance Access, 8,* 92–110.

Kuehnle, K. (1998). Ethics and the forensic expert: A case study of child custody involving allegations of child sexual abuse. *Ethics and Behavior, 8*(1), 1–18.

Massachusetts Department of Mental Health, Forensic Services (2008). *Report writing guidelines.* Retrieved from http://www.mass.gov/eohhs/docs/dmh/publications/mgl-guidelines.pdf

McNamee, C., & Mulford, C. (2007). *Innovations assessment of the elder abuse forensic center of Orange County, California.* Washington, DC: National Institute of Justice. Retrieved from http://www.ncjrs.gov/pdffiles1/nij/grants/220331.pdf

Merriam-Webster (1997). Cross-examination. *Dictionary of Law.* Springfield, MA: Author.

National Association of Social Workers. (2008). Code of Ethics. Retrieved from http://www.naswdc.org/pubs/code/code.asp

North Carolina Division of Social Services & the Family and Children's Resource Program (2000, Aug.). Preparing for your day in court. *Children's Services Practice Notes, 5*(3), 1–8.

Rich, J. (2010). Psychological testing. Retrieved from http://www.psychologicaltesting.com/forensic.htm

Rome, S. H. (2008). Forensic social work. In T. Mizrahi & L. E. Davis (Eds.), *Encyclopedia of social work* (20th ed., pp. 221–223). Washington, DC, and New York: NASW Press and Oxford University Press.

San Francisco Elder Abuse Forensic Center. (2011). What is an elder abuse forensic center? Retrieved from http://www.sfeafc.org/about/whatisaneafc.html

Schneider, D. C., Mosqueda, L., Falk, E., & Huba, G. J. (2010). Elder abuse forensic centers. *Journal of Elder Abuse & Neglect, 22*(3–4), 255–274.

Simone, M., Cross, T.P., Jones, L.M., & Walsh, W.A. (2005). Children's advocacy centers: Understanding the impact of a phenomenon. In K.A. Kendall-Tacket & S.M. Giacomoni (Eds.), *Child victimization : Maltreatment, bullying and dating violence, prevention and intervention* (pp. 22:1–22:24). Kinsgston, NJ: Civil Research Institute.

Swenson, L. C. (1997). *Psychology and law* (2nd ed.). Pacific Grove, CA: Brooks/Cole.

Tuberous Sclerosis Alliance (TSA). (2010). Guardianship. Retrieved from http://www.tsalliance.org/pages.aspx?content=62

Voskanian, P. H. (2011). General and forensic psychiatry. Retrieved from http://www.forensic-psychiatrist.com/Competency.html

Wakefield, H. (2006). Guidelines on investigatory interviewing of children: What is the consensus in the scientific community? *American Journal of Forensic Psychology, 24*(3), 57–74.

Yuille, J. C., Hunter, R., Joffe, R., & Zaparniuk, J. (1993). Interviewing children in sexual abuse cases. In G. S. Goodman & B. L. Bottoms (Eds.), *Child victims, child witnesses: Understanding and improving children's testimony* (pp. 95–115). New York: Guilford Press.

Chapter 4

American Bar Association (ABA). (2001). *Standards on state judicial selection: Report of the Commission on State Judicial Selection Standards.* Chicago, IL: Author.

American Judicature Society (AJS). (2008). *Judicial selection in the states: How it works, why it matters.* Retrieved from http://www.judicialselection.us/uploads/documents/JudicialSelectionBrochureemail_A2E54457CD359.pdf

American Judicature Society. (2010). *Judicial selection in the states: Appellate and general jurisdiction courts.* Retrieved from http://www.judicialselection.us/uploads/documents/Judicial_Selection_Charts_1196376173077.pdf

American Judicature Society. (2011). *Federal judicial selection: Federal judicial nominating commissions.* Retrieved from http://www.judicialselection.us/federal_judicial_selection/federal_judicial_nominating_commissions.cfm?state=FD

Barker, R. L., & Branson, D. M. (2000). *Forensic social work: Legal aspects of professional practice* (2nd ed.). New York: Haworth Press.

Barksy, A. E., & Gould, J. W. (2002). *Clinicians in court: A guide to subpoenas, depositions, testifying, and everything else you need to know.* New York: Guilford Press.

Berkson, L.C., Caufield, R., & Reddick, M. (2010). *Judicial selection in the United States: A special report.* Chicago, IL: American Judicature Society.

Bostic v. State, 772 P.2d 1089.

Brand, R. (2010). A look at federal judicial selection. *The Advocate, 53*, 82–84.

Chemerinsky, E. (2003). Ideology and the selection of federal judges. *U.C. Davis Law Review, 36*, 619–631.

Collins, P. M. (2004). Friends of the court: Examining the influence of amicus curiae participation in U.S. Supreme Court litigation. *Law & Society Review, 38*(4), 807–832.

Collins, P. M. (2007). Lobbyists before the U.S. Supreme Court: Investigating the influence of amicus curiae briefs. *Political Research Quarterly, 60*(1), 55–70.

Committee for Economic Development (CED). (2002). *Justice for hire: A statement on national policy.* New York: Author.

Corbally, S. F., & Bross, D. C. (2001). A practical guide for filing *amicus briefs* in state appellate courts. Retrieved from http://www.naccchildlaw.org/resource/resmgr/amicus_curiae/amicuspracticalguide.pdf

Corbally, S. F., Bross, D. C., & Flango, V. E. (2004). Filing of amicus curiae briefs in state courts of last resort: 1960–2000. *The Justice System Journal, 25*, 39–56.

Epstein, L., & Knight, J. (1998). *The choices justices make.* Washington, DC: CQ Press.

Flango, V. E., Bross, D. C., & Corbally, S. F. (2006). Amicus curiae briefs: The court's perspective. *Justice System Journal, 27*(2), 180–190.

Foggan, L. A., & Dancey, Z. D. (2004, April). Writing persuasive briefs and recruiting amicus support. *For The Defense,* 35–38.

Giles, M. W., Hettinger, V. A., & Peppers, T. (2001). Picking federal judges: A note on policy and partisan selection agendas. *Political Research Quarterly, 54*(3), 623–641.

Gothard, S. (1989). Power in the court: The social worker as an expert witness. *Social Work, 34*(1), 65–67.

Jaffee v. Redmond, 518 U.S. 1 (1996).

Jost, K. (2009). Judicial elections. *CQ Researcher, 19*(16), 373–396.

Justice at Stake. (2011). Campaign money data. Retrieved from http://www.justiceatstake.org/state/campaign_money_data.cfm

Kearney, J. D., & Merrill, T. W. (2000). The influence of amicus curiae briefs on the Supreme Court. *University of Pennsylvania Law Review, 148*, 743–855.

Kennedy v. Louisiana, 554 U.S. 407 (2008).

L.G. v. State of Alaska, 14 P.3d 946 (2000).

Mallory v. Ohio, 38 F. Supp.2d 525 (1997).

National Association of Social Workers. (2011). About the amicus brief database. Retrieved from http://www.socialworkers.org/ldf/brief_bank/about.asp

North Carolina Division of Social Services (2000). Preparing for your day in court. Children's Services Practice Notes. Retrieved from http://www.practicenotes.org/vol5_no3/preparing_for_day_court.htm

Pollack, D. (2004). Being deposed—literally. *Policy & Practice, 62*(3), 26.

Polowy, C. I., & Gilbertson, J. (2004). *Social workers as expert witnesses.* Washington, DC: National Association of Social Workers Legal Defense Fund.

Sarnoff, S. (2004). Social workers and the witness role: Ethics, laws, and roles. *Journal of Social Work Values & Ethics, 1*(1). Retrieved from http://www.socialworker.com/jswve/content/view/10/30/

Schouten, F. (2010, March 3). States act to revise judicial selection. *USA Today.* Retrieved from http://www.usatoday.com/news/politics/2010-03-30-judges_N.htm

Schultz, L. (1989). The social worker as an expert witness in suspected child abuse cases: A primer for beginners. *Issues in Child Abuse Accusations, 1*(2). Retrieved from http://www.ipt-forensics.com/journal/volume1/j1_2_4.htm

Simpson, R. W., & Vasaly, M. R. (2004). *The amicus brief: How to be a good friend of the court* (2nd ed.). Chicago, IL: American Bar Association.

Wheeler, R. (2009). The changing face of the federal judiciary. Governance Studies at Brookings. Retrieved from http://www.brookings.edu/~/media/Files/rc/papers/2009/08_federal_judiciary_wheeler/08_federal_judiciary_wheeler.pdf

Chapter 5

Abille v. United States, 482 F. Supp. 703 (N.D. Cal. 1980).

Albert, R. (2000). *Law and social work practice* (2nd ed.). New York: Springer.

Barsky, A. E., & Gould, J. W. (2002). *Clinicians in court: A guide to subpoenas, depositions, testifying, and everything else you need to know.* New York: Guilford Press.

Code of Virginia § 54.1-2969 (E).

Cool v. Olson, Circuit Ct., Outagamie Co., Wisconsin, Case No. 94 CV 707 (1997).

Cournoyer, B. (2008). *The social work skills workbook.* Belmont, CA: Brooks/Cole.

Court of Appeal affirms Orange County jury finding CPS liable to mother for $4.9 million in damages (2010, June 17). Retrieved from http://www.scribd.com/doc/33308170/Court-of-Appeal-Affirms-Orange-County-Jury-Finding-Cps-Liable-to-Mother-for-4-9-Million-in-Damages

Cruzan v. Missouri Department of Health, 497 U.S. 261 (1990).

Davis, N., Pohlman, A., Gehlbach, B., Kress, J. P., McAtee, J., Herlitz, J., & Hall, J. (2003). Improving the process of informed consent in the critically ill. *Journal of the American Medical Association, 289*(15), 1963–1968. doi:10.1001/jama.289.15.1963

Deardorff, W. W. (2010). Internet based treatment: A comprehensive review and ethical issues. Retrieved from http://www.behavioralhealthce.com/index.php/component/courses/?task=view&cid=69

Dickson, D. T. (1995). *Law in the health and human services: A guide for social workers, psychologists, psychiatrists, and related professionals.* New York, NY: Free Press.

Dolgoff, R., Loewenberg, F.M., & Harrington, D. (2009). *Ethical decisions for social work practice.* Belmont, CA: Thompson Brooks/Cole.

EMDR Institute (2011). Eye movement desensitization and reprocessing. Retrieved from http://www.emdr.com

Fox, S. (2005). Health information online. Pew Internet and American Life Project, November 2004 Survey. Retrieved from http://www.pewinternet.org/Reports/2005/Health-Information-Online

Hamman v. County of Maricopa, 775 P.2d 1122 (1989).

Houston-Vega, M., Nuehring, E. M., & Daguio, E. R. (1997). *Prudent practice: A guide for managing malpractice risk.* Washington, DC: NASW Press

In re A.C., 573 A.2d 1235 (1990).

Israel, A. B. (2011). *Using the law: Practical decision making in mental health.* Chicago, IL: Lyceum.

Jacobs, D. (2003). Suicide assessment. University of Michigan Depression Center Colloquium Series. Retrieved from http://www.stopasuicide.org

Jacobs, D., & Brewer, M. (2004). APA practice guideline provides recommendations for assessing and treating patients with suicidal behaviors. *Psychiatric Annals, 34*(5), 373–380.

Jaffee v. Redmond, 518 U.S. 1 (1996).

Macarov, D. (1990). Confidentiality in the human services. *International Journal of Sociology and Social Policy, 10*(4/5/6), 65–81. doi:10.1108/eb013102

Minnesota Coalition Against Sexual Assault. (2010). Minor consent for medical and mental health treatment. Retrieved from http://www.mncasa.org/Documents/svji_facts_2_2801476753.pdf

National Association of Social Workers. (2004). *Client confidentiality & privileged communications.* Washington, DC: Author.

National Association of Social Workers. (2005a). *NASW procedures for professional review: Revised* (4th ed). Retrieved from http://www.naswdc.org/nasw/ethics/procedures.asp

National Association of Social Workers. (2005b). Social workers and record retention requirements. In *Legal issue of the month.* Retrieved from http://www.socialworkers.org/ldf/legal_issue/200510.asp?back=yes&print=1

National Association of Social Workers. (2007). *Social workers and the legal rights of children.* Washington, DC: Author.

National Association of Social Workers (2008a). Code of Ethics. Retrieved from http://www.naswdc.org/pubs/code/code.asp

National Association of Social Workers. (2008b). Social workers and "duty to warn" state laws. In *Legal issue of the month.* Retrieved from http://www.naswdc.org/ldf/legal_issue/2008/200802.asp?back=yes

National HIV/AIDS Clinicians' Consultation Center. (2011). Compendium of state HIV testing laws. Retrieved from http://www.nccc.ucsf.edu/consultation_library/state_hiv_testing_laws/

Oregon Health Authority. (2011). Minor rights: Access and consent to health care. Retrieved from http://public.health.oregon.gov/HealthyPeopleFamilies/Youth/Documents/MinorConsent.pdf

Patterson, W. M., Dohn, H. H., Bird, J., & Patterson, G. A. (1983). Evaluation of suicidal patients: The SAD PERSONS scale. *Psychosomatics, 24*(4), 343–349.

Postel, M.G., deHaan, H.A., & DeJong, C.A.J. (2008). E-therapy for mental health problems: A systematic review. *Telemedicine and E-Health, 14*(7), 7-7-714.

Reamer, F. G. (1991). AIDS, social work, and the "duty to protect." *Social Work, 36*(1), 56–60.

Reamer, F. G. (2003). *Social work malpractice and liability: Strategies for prevention* (2nd ed.). New York: Columbia University Press.

Recupero, P. R., & Rainey, S. E. (2005). Informed consent to e-therapy. *American Journal of Psychotherapy, 59*(4), 319–331.

Relf v. Weinberger, 372 F. Supp. 1196 (1974).

Roberts, A. R., Monferrari, I., & Yeager, K. R. (2008). Avoiding malpractice lawsuits by following risk assessment and suicide prevention guidelines. *Brief Treatment and Crisis Intervention, 8*(1), 5–14.

Saltzman, A., & Furman, D. M. (1999). *Law in social work practice* (2nd ed.). Chicago, IL: Nelson-Hall.

Santhiveeran, J. (2009). Compliance of social work e-therapy websites to the NASW Code of Ethics. *Social Work in Health Care, 48*(1), 1–13. doi:10.1080/00981380802231216

Sard v. Hardy, 379 A.2d 1014 (1977).

Sarnoff, S. (2004). Social workers and the witness role: Ethics, laws, and roles. *Journal of Social Work Values and Ethics, 1*(1). Retrieved from http://www.socialworker.com/jswve/content/view/10/30/

Shapiro, D. L., & Smith, S. R. (2011). *Malpractice in psychology: A practical resource for clinicians.* Washington, DC: American Psychological Association.

Strom-Gottfried, K. (2000). Ensuring ethical practice: An examination of NASW Code violations, 1986–1997. *Social Work, 45*(3), 251–261.

Strong, P. (2010). Online counseling therapy service via Skype. *Psychology Today.* Retrieved from http://www.psychologytoday.com/blog/the-mindfulness-approach/201007/online-counseling-therapy-service-skype

Swenson, L. C. (1997). *Psychology and law for the helping professions* (2nd ed.). Pacific Grove, CA: Brooks/Cole.

Tarasoff v. Regents of the University of California, 551 P.2d 334 (1976).

Zinermon v. Burch, 494 U.S. 113 (1990).

Chapter 6

American Humane. (2008). What should I know about reporting child abuse or neglect? Retrieved from http://www.americanhumane.org/about-us/newsroom/fact-sheets/reporting-child-abuse-neglect.html

Anonymous v. Vella, U.S. Dist. LEXIS 30880; 64 Fed. R. Serv. 3d 585 (2006).

Bennett, S. (2005). Review of current global trends in child protection policy and legislation. *The Link, 13*(3)/*14*(1). Chicago: International Society for Protection of Children.

Bonner, B. (2005). Deinstitutionalization program observed in Belarus. *The Link, 13*(3)/*14*(1). Chicago: International Society for Protection of Children.

Bourg Carter, S. (2009). *Children in the courtroom: Challenges for lawyers and judges* (2nd ed.). Louisville, CO: National Institute for Trial Advocacy (NITA).

Camreta v. Greene, 131 S.Ct. 2020 (2011).

Chalk, R., Gibbons, A., & Scarupa, H. J. (2002). *The multiple dimensions of child abuse and neglect: New insights into an old problem.* Washington, DC: Child Trends. Retrieved from http://www.childtrends.org/Files/ChildAbuseRB.pdf

Child Welfare Information Gateway (2006a). Long-term consequences of child abuse and neglect. Retrieved from http://www.childwelfare.gov/pubs/factsheets/long_term_consequences.cfm

Child Welfare Information Gateway. (2006b). Working with the courts in child protection. Retrieved from http://www.childwelfare.gov/pubs/usermanuals/courts/chaptertwo.cfm

Child Welfare Information Gateway. (2007a). Definitions of child abuse and neglect: Summary of state laws. Retrieved from http://www.childwelfare.gov/systemwide/laws_policies/statutes/defineall.pdf.

Child Welfare Information Gateway. (2007b). Penalties for failure to report and false reporting of child abuse and neglect: Summary of state laws. Retrieved from http://www.childwelfare.gov/systemwide/laws_policies/statutes/report.cfm

Child Welfare Information Gateway. (2008). Mandatory reporters of child abuse and neglect. Retrieved from http://www.childwelfare.gov/systemwide/laws_policies/statutes/manda.pdf

Child Welfare League of America. (2009). Learning about out-of-home placement services. *A family's guide to the child welfare system.* Retrieved from http://www.cwla.org/childwelfare/fg05.pdf

City of Charleston v. Ferguson, 532 U.S. 67 (2001).

Clark, H. H., Jr., & Estin, A. R. (2000). *Cases and problems on domestic relations* (6th ed.). St. Paul, MN: West Group.

Clement, M. (1997). *The juvenile justice system: Law and process.* Boston: Butterworth-Heinemann.

Council on Virginia's Future. (2010). Virginia performs: Child abuse and neglect. Retrieved from http://vaperforms.virginia.gov/indicators/healthFamily/childAbuse.php

Coy v. Iowa, 487 U.S. 1012 (1988).

Crosson-Tower, C. (2008). *Understanding child abuse and neglect* (7th ed.). Boston: Pearson Education.

Crosson-Tower, C. (2009) *Exploring child welfare: A practice perspective* (5th ed.). Boston: Pearson Education.

De Bellis, M., & Thomas, L. (2003). Biologic findings of post-traumatic stress disorder and child maltreatment. *Current Psychiatry Reports*, 5, 108–117.

DeShaney v. Winnebago County Department of Social Services, 109 S.Ct. 108 (1989).

Downs, S. W., Moore, E., & McFadden, J. (2009) *Child welfare and family services: Policies and practice* (8th ed.). Boston: Pearson Education.

Dube, S. R., Anda, R. F., Felitti, V. J., Chapman, D., Williamson, D. F., & Giles, W. H. (2001). Childhood abuse, household dysfunction and the risk of attempted suicide throughout the life span: Findings from the Adverse Childhood Experiences Study. *Journal of the American Medical Association, 286,* 3089–3096.

Dumaret, A., & Rosset, D. (2005) Adoption and child welfare protection in France. *Early Child Development and Care, 175*(7/8), 661–670.

English, D. J., Widom, C. S., & Brandford, C. (2004). Another look at the effects of child abuse. *NIJ Journal, 251,* 23–24.

Essali, A. (2005). Symposium on child protection held in Syria. *The Link, 13*(3)/*14*(1). Chicago: International Society for Protection of Children.

Faller, K. C. (2007). *Interviewing children about sexual abuse.* New York: Oxford University Press.

Gardner, D. (2008). *Youth aging out of foster care: Identifying strategies and best practices.* Washington, DC: National Association of Counties.

Goldstein, R. D. (1999). *Child abuse and neglect: Cases and materials.* St. Paul, MN: West Group.

Hagele, D. M. (2005). The impact of maltreatment on the developing child. *North Carolina Medical Journal, 66(5),* 356–359.

Idaho v. Wright, 497 U.S. 805 (1990).

Katz, I., & Hetherington, R. (2006). Co-operating and communicating: A European perspective on integrating services for children. *Child Abuse Review, 15(6),* 429–439.

Kelley, B. T., Thornberry, T. P., & Smith, C. A. (1997). *In the wake of childhood maltreatment.* Washington, DC: National Institute of Justice. Retrieved from http://www.ncjrs.gov/pdffiles1/165257.pdf

Madden, R. G., & Parody, M. (1997). Between a legal rock and a practice hard place: Legal issues in "recovered memory" cases. *Clinical Social Work Journal, 25*(2), 223–247.

Maryland v. Craig, 497 U.S. 836 (1990).

McCarthy, J., Marshall, A., Collins, J., Arganza, G., Deserly, K., & Milon, J. (2003). *A family's guide to the child welfare system.* Washington, DC: The Child Welfare League of America.

Meyer v. Nebraska, 262 U.S. 390 (1923).

Missouri Department of Social Services. (2008). Investigation response. *Child Welfare Manual,* Sec. 2, Chapter 4, Attachment L. Retrieved from http://www.dss.mo.gov/cd/info/cwmanual/section2/ch4/sec2ch4attachl.htm

Missouri Department of Social Services. (2009). Older youth program. Retrieved from http://www.dss.mo.gov/cd/chafee/index.htm

Morgan, S., & Khan, A. (2011). Social workers and child protection investigations. Retrieved from https://www.socialworkers.org/ldf/legal_issue/2011/201101.asp?back=yes

Myers, B. (2008, June 3). After 4 girls' slayings, welfare agency floods family court with abuse cases. *The Examiner.* Retrieved from http://washingtonexaminer.com/article/80775

Myers, J. E. B. (1998). *Legal issues in child abuse and neglect practice.* Thousand Oaks, CA: Sage Publications.

National Association of Social Workers. (2011). *Camreta Amicus Brief* (No. 09-1454). Retrieved from http://www.socialworkers.org/assets/secured/documents/ldf/briefDocuments/Camreta%20v.%20Greene.pdf

National Clearinghouse on Child Abuse & Neglect Information. (2001). *Prevention pays: The costs of not preventing child abuse and neglect.* Washington, DC: U.S. Department of Health and Human Services.

National CASA Association. (2012). About us. Retrieved from http://www.casaforchildren.org/site/c.mtJSJ7MPIsE/b.5301303/k.6FB1/About_Us__CASA_for_Children.htm

New Jersey Division of Youth and Family Services v. S.S., 855 A.2d 8 (2004).

North Carolina Administrative Office of the Courts. (n.d.). Juvenile court proceeding chart. Retrieved from http://www.nccourts.org/Citizens/CPrograms/Improvement/Documents/Juvenilecourtprocess-rev3.pdf

Parham v. J.R., 442 U.S. 584 (1979).

Pecora, P. J., Williams, J., Kessler, R. C., Downs, A. C., O'Brien, K., Hiripi, E., & Morello, S. (2003). Assessing the effects of foster care: Early results from the Casey national alumni study. Retrieved from http://www.casey.org/Resources/Publications/pdf/CaseyNationalAlumniStudy_FullReport.pdf

Persky, A.S. (2012). Beyond the Penn State scandal: Child abuse reporting laws. *D.C. Bar.* Retrieved from http://www.dcbar.org/for_lawyers/resources/publications/washington_lawyer/june_2012/childabuse.cfm

Pierce v. Society of Sisters, 268 U.S. 510 (1925).

Prevent Child Abuse New York. (2003). The costs of child abuse and the urgent need for prevention. Retrieved from http://www.preventchildabuseny.org/files/6213/0392/2130/costs.pdf

Qiao, D. P., & Chane, Y. C. (2005) Child abuse in China: A yet-to-be acknowledged "social problem" in the Chinese mainland. *Child and Family Social Work, 10(1),* 21–27.

Ramona v. Isabella, No. 61898 (Cal., Napa County Super. Ct.) (1994).

Ramsey, S. H., & Abrams, D. E. (2003). *Children and the law in a nutshell* (2nd ed.). St. Paul, MN: West.

Santosky v. Kramer, 455 U.S. 745 (1982).

Schneider, C. E., & Brinig, M. R. (2000). *An invitation to family law: Principles, process and perspectives* (2nd ed.). St. Paul, MN: West Group.

Schuyler Center for Analysis and Advocacy (2008). *Teenage births: Outcomes for young parents and their children.* Albany, NY: Author.

Silverman, A. B., Reinherz, H. Z., & Giaconia, R. M. (1996). The long-term sequelae of child and adolescent abuse: A longitudinal community study. *Child Abuse and Neglect, 20*(8), 709–723.

State Court Administrative Office, Child Welfare Services Division. (2008). *Conducting effective post-termination review hearings.* Lansing, MI: Author.

Suter v. Artist M., 503 U.S. 347 (1992).

Tang, C. M. (2006). Developmentally sensitive forensic interviewing of preschool children: Some guidelines drawn from basic psychological research. *Criminal Justice Review, 31(2),* 132–145.

Troxel v. Granville, 530 U.S. 57 (2000).

U.S. Department of Health and Human Services, Office on Child Abuse and Neglect. (2003). Child protective services: A guide for caseworkers. Retrieved from http://www.childwelfare.gov/pubs/usermanuals/cps/cpsf.cfm

U.S. Department of Health and Human Services, Administration for Children and Families. (2009). Child Abuse Prevention and Treatment Act as amended by Keeping Children and Families Safe Act of 2003. Retrieved from http://www.acf.hhs.gov/programs/cb/laws_policies/cblaws/capta03/capta_manual.pdf

U.S. Department of Health and Human Services, Administration on Children, Youth, and Families. (2011a). Child maltreatment 2009. Retrieved from http://www.acf.hhs.gov/programs/cb/pubs/cm10/cm10.pdf

U.S. Department of Health and Human Services, Administration on Children and Families. (2011b). The AFCARS report.

Retrieved from http://www.acf.hhs.gov/programs/cb/stats_research/afcars/tar/report18.htm

Vandervort, F. (2008). Legal ethics and high child welfare turnover: An unexplored connection. *Children and Youth Services Review, 30*(5), 546–563.

Wakefield, H. (2006). Guidelines on investigatory interviewing of children: What is the consensus in the scientific community? *American Journal of Forensic Psychology, 24*(3), 57–74.

Wald, M., & Martinez, T. (2003). Connected by 25: Improving the life chances of the country's most vulnerable 14–24 year olds. Retrieved from http://www.hewlett.org/uploads/files/ConnectedBy25.pdf

Watts-English, T., Fortson, B. L., Gibler, N., Hooper, S. R., & De Bellis, M. (2006). The psychobiology of maltreatment in childhood. *Journal of Social Sciences, 62*(4), 717–736.

Wheeler v. United States, 159 U.S. 523 (1895).

Chapter 7

Abrams, D. E., & Ramscy, S. H. (Eds.). (2000). *Children and the law*. Saint Paul, MN: West Group.

Abrams, D. E., Cahn, N. R., Ross, C. J., & Meyer, D. D. (2009). *Contemporary family law*. St. Paul, MN: Thomson Reuters.

Administration for Children and Families. (2011a). Children in public foster care on September 30th of each year who are waiting to be adopted, FY 2002–FY 2010. Retrieved from http://www.acf.hhs.gov/programs/cb/stats_research/afcars/waiting2010.pdf

Administration for Children and Families. (2011b). The AFCARS report: Preliminary FY 2010 estimates as of June 2011. Retrieved from http://www.acf.hhs.gov/programs/cb/stats_research/afcars/tar/report18.pdf

Adoption Advisor. (n.d.). Overview of Virginia laws. Retrieved from http://theadoptionadvisor.com/information/virginia/va-overview/

American Psychiatric Association. (2002). Adoption and Co-parenting of Children by Same-sex Couples. Retrieved from http://gbge.aclu.org/sites/default/files/images/stories/oppo12.pdf

Atwood, T. C. (2007a). Consent or coercion: How mandatory open records harm adoption. In T. C. Atwood, L. A. Allen, V. C. Ravenel, & N. F. Callahan (Eds.), *Adoption factbook IV* (pp. 461–468). National Council for Adoption. Retrieved from https://www.adoptioncouncil.org/images/stories/documents/adoptionfactbookiv1.pdf.

Atwood, T. C. (2007b). The jury is in regarding adoption openness. In T. C. Atwood, L. A. Allen, V. C. Ravenel, & N. F. Callahan (Eds.), *Adoption factbook IV* (pp. 453–454). National Council on Adoption. Retrieved from https://www.adoptioncouncil.org/images/stories/documents/adoptionfactbookiv1.pdf

Averett, P., Nalavany, B., & Ryan, S. (2009). An evaluation of gay/lesbian and heterosexual adoption. *Adoption Quarterly, 12*(3–4), 129–151.

Bartholet, E. (2007a). International adoption: The child's story. *Georgia State Law Review, 24*, 333–379.

Bartholet, E. (2007b). International adoption: Thoughts on the human rights issues. *Buffalo Human Rights Law Review, 13*, 151–203.

Burr v. Board of County Commissioners of Stark County, 23 Ohio St. 3d 69 (1986).

Child Welfare Information Gateway. (2006). *The basics of adoption practice: A bulletin for professionals*. Washington, DC: U.S. Department of Health and Human Services.

Child Welfare Information Gateway (2008). Stepparent adoption. Washington, DC: Author.

Child Welfare Information Gateway. (2010a). Adoption options. Retrieved from http://www.childwelfare.gov/pubs/f_adoptoption.cfm#pubadopt

Child Welfare Information Gateway. (2010b). The adoption home study process. Retrieved from http://www.childwelfare.gov/pubs/f_homstu.cfm

Child Welfare Information Gateway. (n.d.). Adopting children through a public agency (foster care). Retrieved from http://www.childwelfare.gov/adoption/adoptive/foster_care.cfm

Craft, C. (2011). Why choose an open adoption? Retrieved from http://adoption.about.com/od/adopting/a/whyopenadoption.htm

Crosson-Tower, C. (2001). *Exploring child welfare: A practice perspective*. Boston: Allyn & Bacon.

Daly, K. J., & Sobol, M. P. (1994). Public and private adoption: A comparison of service and accessibility. *Family Relations, 43*(1), 86–93.

Doe v. Sundquist, 2 S.W.3d 919 (1999).

Emmanel, J. (2010). Beyond wrongful adoption: Expanding adoption agency liability to include a duty to investigate and a duty to warn. *Golden Gate Law Review, 29*(2), 181–233.

Fair, L. M. (2008). Shame on U.S.: The need for uniform open adoption records legislation in the United States. *Santa Clara Law Review, 48*, 1039–1067.

Fields, T. A. (1996). Declaring a policy of truth: Recognizing the wrongful adoption claim. *Boston College Law Review, 37*(5), 975–1018.

Freundlich, M. (1999). Reforming the Interstate Compact on the Placement of Children. The Evan B. Donaldson Adoption Institute. Retrieved from http://www.adoptioninstitute.org/policy/inters2.html

Gates, G. J., Badgett, M. V. L., Macomber, J. E., & Chambers, K. (2007). *Adoption and foster care by gay and lesbian parents in the United States*. Washington, DC: The Urban Institute. Retrieved from http://www.urban.org/UploadedPDF/411437_Adoption_Foster_Care.pdf

Grotevant, H. D., Perry, Y. V., & McRoy, R. G. (2007). Openness in adoption: Outcomes for adolescents within their adoptive kinship networks. In T. C. Atwood, L. A. Allen, V. C. Ravenel, & N. F. Callahan (Eds.), *Adoption factbook IV* (pp. 439–452). Sterling, VA: PMR Printing Company.

Hansen, M. E. & Pollack, D. (2007). Transracial adoption of black children: An economic analysis. Retrieved from http://law.bepress.com/cgi/viewcontent.cgi?article=9198&context=expresso

Hollinger, J. H. (1993). Adoption law. *The Future of Children, 3*(1), 43–61.

Human Rights Campaign. (2010). State laws and legislation: Adoption. Retrieved from http://www.hrc.org/laws-and-legislation/state/c/adoption

Infant Adoption Training Initiative. (n.d). Frequently asked questions about adoption in Alabama. Retrieved from http://iaatp .com/docs/Alabama-frequentlyAskedQuestionsOct08.pdf

Krause, H. D., & Meyer, D. D. (2007). *Family law* (5th ed). St. Paul, MN: Thomson/West.

LeCheminant, J. D. (2007). How court-enforceable contact agreements undermine the adoptive family. *Adoption factbook IV*. National Council for Adoption. Retrieved from https://www .adoptioncouncil.org/images/stories/documents/adoptionfact bookiv1.pdfMatter of Adoption of Evan, 583 N.Y.S.2d 997 (1992).

Meracle v. Children's Service Society, 437 N.W.2d 532 (1989).

McDermott, M. T. (1993). Agency versus independent adoption: The case for independent adoption. *The Future of Children, 3*(1), 146–152.

M.H. & J.L.H. v. Caritas Family Services, 488 N.W.2d 282 (1992).

Michael J. v. County of Los Angeles Department of Adoptions, 201 Cal. App. 3d 859 (1988).

Mississippi Choctaw Indians v. Holyfield, 490 U.S. 30 (1989).

Price, S. (2004) Adoption: Birth mothers' rights to revoke consent. Retrieved from http://www.cga.ct.gov/2004/rpt/2004-R-0661.htm

Roe v. Catholic Charities, 588 N.E.2d 354 (1992).

Sakai, C., Lin, H., & Flores, G. (2011). Health outcomes and family services in kinship care. *Archives of Pediatrics and Adolescent Medicine, 165*(2), 150–165.

Stein, T. J. (2004). *The role of law in social work practice and administration*. New York: Columbia University Press.

U.S. Department of State. (n.d.). Child citizenship Act of 2000. Retrieved from http://travel.state.gov/visa/immigrants/types/ types_1312.html

U.S. Department of State. (2010a). Intercountry adoption. Retrieved from http://www.adoption.state.gov

U.S. Department of State. (2010b). FY 2010 annual report on intercountry adoptions. Retrieved from http://adoption.state.gov/ content/pdf/fy2010_annual_report.pdf

U.S. Department of State. (2011). Intercountry adoption. Retrieved from http://adoption.state.gov/country_information/alerts_ notices.php

Wadlington, W., & O'Brien, R. C. (1998). *Domestic relations*. Westbury, NY: The Foundation Press.

Zinn, A. (2009). Foster family characteristics, kinship, and permanence. *Social Service Review, 83*(2), 185–219.

Chapter 8

Aaby, B. J. (2009). Understanding the Uniform Child Custody Jurisdiction Enforcement Act. *American Journal of Family Law, 22(1)*, 11–19.

Abrams, D. E., Cahn, N. R., Ross, C. J., & Meyer, D. D. (2009). *Contemporary family law* (2nd ed). St. Paul, MN: Thomson/West.

American Bar Association (n.d.). Deciding factors in awarding child custody. Retrieved from http://www.americanbar.org/ groups/public_education/resources/law_issues_for_consumers/ custody_options.html

Baerber, D. R., Galatzer-Levy, R., Gould, J. W., & Nye S. G. (2002). A methodology for reviewing the reliability and relevance of child custody evaluations. *Journal of the American Academy of Matrimonial Lawyers, 18*, 35–73.

Bolotin, L. (2008). When parents fight: Alaska's presumption against awarding custody to perpetrators of domestic violence. *Alaska Law Review, 25*, 263–301.

Carter, K. J. (2006). The best interest test and child custody: Why transgender should not be a factor in custody determinations. *Health Matrix, 16, 209–256*.

Child Welfare Information Gateway. (2008). Determining the best interests of the child: Summary of state laws. Retrieved from http://www.childwelfare.gov/systemwide/laws_policies/statutes/ best_interest.cfm

Clement, M. (1997). *The juvenile justice system: Law and process*. Boston: Butterworth-Heinemann.

Cohen, O., & Shnit, D. (2001). Social workers' recommendations on the non-custodial father's visitation rights with his preschool children. *International Social Work, 44*(3), 311–328.

Downs, S. W., Moore, E., & McFadden, J. (2009) *Child welfare and family services: Policies and practice* (8th ed.). Boston: Pearson Education.

Ex Parte Devine, 398 So. 2d 686 (1981).

Feldman v. Feldman, 358 N.Y.S.2d 507 (1974).

Foster v. Alston, 7 Miss. 406 (1842).

Goldstein, J., Freud, A., & Solnit, A. (1973). *Beyond the best interests of the child*. New York: The Free Press.

Hans, J. D. (2002). Stepparenting after divorce: Stepparents' legal position regarding custody, access, and support. *Family Relations, 51*(4), 301–307.

Hoff, P. (2001, Dec.). The Uniform Child-Custody Jurisdiction and Enforcement Act. *Juvenile Justice Bulletin*. Washington, DC: U.S. Department of Justice, Office of Juvenile Justice and Delinquency Prevention.

Keith, P. M. (2002). Grandparent visitation rights: An inappropriate intrusion or appropriate protection? *International Journal on Aging and Human Development, 54*(3), 191–204.

Kelly, J. B. (1994). The determination of child custody. *The Future of Children: Children and Divorce, 4(1)*, 121–142.

Ken R. v. Arthur Z., 682 A.2d 1267 (1996).

Kennedy v. Kennedy, 376 N.W. 2d 702 (1985).

Krause, H. D., & Meyer, D. D. (2007). *Family law in a nutshell* (5th ed.). St Paul, MN: Thomson/West.

LawFirms.com (2012). Joint legal custody. Retrieved from http:// www.lawfirms.com/resources/family/child-custody/joint-legal- custody.htm

Lewis, K. (2009). *Child custody evaluations by social workers: Understanding the five stages of custody*. Washington, DC: NASW Press.

M.A.B. v. R.B., 510 N.Y.S.2d 960 (1986).

M.B.B. v. E.R.W., 100 P.3d 415 (2004).

Morgan v. Foretich, 546 A. 2d 407(1988).

Palmore v. Sidoti, 466 U.S. 429 (1984).

Pikula v. Pikula, 374 N.W.2d at 712 (1985).

Ricks, S. (1984). Determining child custody: Trends, factors, and alternatives. *Family Court Review, 22(1)*, 65–70.

Usack v. Usack, 793 N.Y.S.2d 223 (2005).

Chapter 9

Advocates for Human Rights. (2010). Effects of domestic violence on children. Retrieved from http://www.stopvaw.org/Effects_ of_Domestic_Violence_on_Children.html

American Bar Association. (2010). Commission on domestic violence. Retrieved from http://www.americanbar.org/groups/domestic_violence/resources/statistics.html

American Law and Legal Information. (2010). Domestic violence—arrest policies. Retrieved from http://law.jrank.org/pages/1004/Domestic-Violence-Arrest-policies.html#ixzz0zPz1jsMq

Bureau of Justice Statistics (2012). Homicide trends in the U.S.: Intimate homicide. Retrieved from http://bjs.ojp.usdoj.gov/content/homicide/tables/intimatestab.cfm

Campbell, J. C., Webster, D., Koziol-McLain, J., Block, C., Campbell, D., Curry, M. A. … Laughon, K. (2003). Risk factors for femicide in abusive relationships: Results from a multisite case control study. *American Journal of Public Health. 93*(7), 1089–1097.

Dalton, C., & Schneider, E. M. (2001). *Battered women and the law.* New York: Foundation Press.

Dixon v. United States, 548 U.S. 1 (2006).

Domestic Violence and Sexual Assault Data Resource Center. (2011). Domestic violence legislation. Retrieved from http://www.jrsa.org/dvsa-drc/national-summary.shtml

Domestic Violence Resource Center. (2011). Domestic violence statistics. Retrieved from http://www.dvrc-or.org/domestic/violence/resources/C61/

Dugan, M. K., & Hock, R. R. (2006). *It's my life now: Starting over after an abusive relationship or domestic violence* (2nd ed.). New York: Routledge.

Felson, R.B., Ackerman, J.M., & Gallagher, C. (2005). Police intervention and the repeat of domestic assault. U.S. Department of Justice. Retrieved from https://www.ncjrs.gov/pdffiles1/nij/grants/210301.pdf

Finn, J. (2004). A survey of online harassment at a university campus. *Journal of Interpersonal Violence, 19*(4), 468–483.

Fritzler, R. B., & Simon, L. M. J. (2000). Creating a domestic violence court: Combat in the trenches. *Court Review, 28.*

Goodno, N. H. (2007). Cyberstalking, a new crime: Evaluating the effectiveness of current state and federal laws. Retrieved from http://www.law.missouri.edu/lawreview/docs/72-1/Goodno.pdf

Herrell, S. B. & Hofford, M. (1990). Family violence: Improving court practice. *Juvenile and Family Court Journal, 41*(5), 1–59.

Hines, D. A., & Malley-Morrison, K. (2005). *Family violence in the United States: Defining, understanding, and combating abuse.* Thousand Oaks, CA: Sage Publications.

Hirschel, D. (2008). Domestic violence cases: What research shows about arrest and dual arrest rates. Washington, DC: National Institute of Justice. Retrieved from http://www.nij.gov/publications/dv-dual-arrest-222679/dv-dual-arrest.pdf

Klein, A. R. (2008). Practical implications of current domestic violence research. Part II: Prosecution. Washington, DC: U.S. Department of Justice. Retrieved from https://www.ncjrs.gov/pdffiles1/nij/grants/222320.pdf

Lapidus, L. M., Martin, E. J., & Luthra, N. (2009). *The rights of women: The authoritative ACLU guide to women's rights.* New York: New York University Press.

Lemon, N. K. D. (2009). *Domestic violence law* (3rd ed.). Berkeley, CA: West/Thomson Reuters.

Liz Claiborne Inc. (2009). Teen dating abuse report 2009. Teenage Research Unlimited. Retrieved from http://loveisnotabuse.com/c/document_library/get_file?p_l_id=45693&folderId=72612&name=DLFE-202.pdf

McVeigh, K. (2011, April 8). Cyberstalking now more common than face-to-face stalking. Retrieved from http://www.guardian.co.uk/uk/2011/apr/08/cyberstalking-study-victims-men

Mills, L. G. (2008). *Violent partners: A breakthrough plan for ending the cycle of abuse.* New York: Basic Books.

National Center for Victims of Crime. (2012). Domestic/partner intimate violence. Retrieved from: http://victimsofcrime.org/library/crime-information-and-statistics/domestic-partner-intimate-violence

National Conference of State Legislatures. (2011). State cyberstalking and cyberharassment laws. Retrieved from http://www.ncsl.org/default.aspx?tabid=13495

National Institute of Justice. (2009). Practical implications of current domestic violence research: For law enforcement, prosecutors and judges. Retrieved from https://www.ncjrs.gov/pdffiles1/nij/225722.pdf

National Network to End Domestic Violence (2012). Domestic violence counts 2011: A 24-hour census of domestic violence shelters and services. Retrieved from http://nnedv.org/docs/Census/DVCounts2011/DVCounts11_NatlReport_BW.pdf

People v. Romero, 10 Cal. App. 4th 1150 (1992).

Ptacek, J. (2001). Battered women in the courtroom: The power of judicial response. *Crime, Law & Societal Change, 35,* 363.

Rennison, C. M. (2003). Bureau of Justice Statistics crime data brief: Intimate partner violence, 1993–2001. Retrieved from http://bjs.ojp.usdoj.gov/content/pub/pdf/ipv01.pdf

Silverman, J. G., Raj, A., Mucci, L. A., & Hathaway, J. E. (2001). Dating violence against adolescent girls and associated substance use, unhealthy weight control, sexual at risk behavior, pregnancy, and suicidality. *Journal of the American Medical Association, 286*(5), 572–579.

Stalking Resource Center. (2012). The national center for victims of crime: Stalking fact sheet. Retrieved from http://www.victimsofcrime.org/our-programs/stalking-resource-center/stalking-information#vic

State v. Kelly, 478 A.2d 364 (1984).

State v. Wanrow, 559 P.2d 548 (1977).

Stiles, M.M. (2002). Witnessing domestic violence: The effect in children. *American Family Physician, 66*(11), 2052–2067.

Tayak, R. (2010). Punishment for domestic violence. Retrieved from http://www.domesticviolencedefense.com/criminal_case/punishment.html

Thurman v. City of Torrington, 595 F.Supp.1521 (1984).

Tjaden, P., & Theonnes, N. (2000). Extent, nature, and consequences of intimate partner violence. Retrieved from http://www.ojp.usdoj.gov/nij/pubs-sum/181867.htm

UNICEF (2006). Behind closed doors: The impact of domestic violence on children. Retrieved from http://www.unicef.org/protection/files/BehindClosedDoors.pdf

United States Department of Justice. (2005). Family violence statistics. Retrieved from http://bjs.ojp.usdoj.gov/content/pub/pdf/fvs02.pdf

United States Department of Justice. (2010a). Domestic violence. Retrieved from http://www.ovw.usdoj.gov/domviolence.htm

United States Department of Justice. (2010b). Stalking victimization in the United States special report. Retrieved from http://www.ovw.usdoj.gov/aboutstalking.htm

United States Department of Justice. (2010c). The facts about the Violence Against Women Act. Retrieved from http://www.ovw.usdoj.gov/docs/vawa.pdf

Weber, J. (2000). Domestic violence courts: Components and considerations. *Journal of the Center for Families, Children, and the Courts, 2,* 23–29.

Whitfield, C. L., Anda, R. F., Dube, S. R., & Felitle, V. J. (2003). Violent childhood experiences and the risk of intimate partner violence in adults: Assessment in a large health maintenance organization. *Journal of Interpersonal Violence, 18,* 166–185.

Chapter 10

Acierno, R., Hernandez-Tejada, M., Muzzy, W., & Steve, K. (2009). *National elder mistreatment study.* Washington, DC: National Institute of Justice.

Administration on Aging. (2010a). Projected future growth of the older population by age: 1900 to 2050 with chart of the 65+ population (Excel Chart). Retrieved from http://www.aoa.gov/AoARoot/Aging_Statistics/future_growth/future_growth.aspx

Administration on Aging. (2010b). Older Americans Act. Retrieved from http://www.aoa.gov/AoA_programs/OAA/index.aspx

Administration on Aging (2012). Profile of older Americans. Retrieved from http://www.aoa.gov/AoARoot/Aging_Statistics/Profile/index.aspx

American Academy of Family Physicians. (2009). Advance directives and do not resuscitate orders. Retrieved from http://familydoctor.org/online/famdocen/home/pat-advocacy/endoflife/003.html

American Bar Association, Commission on Law and Aging. (2006). Judicial determination of capacity of older adults in guardianship proceedings. Retrieved from http://www.abanet.org/aging/docs/judges_book_5–24.pdf

American Bar Association, Commission on Law and Aging (2009). Report to House of Delegates. Retrieved from http://www.abanet.org/aging/guardianship/lawandpractice/pdfs/111A_February_2009.pdf

Baxter v. Montana, 2009 MT 449 (2009).

Bonnie, R. J., & Wallace, R. B. (Eds.). (2003). *Elder mistreatment: Abuse, neglect, and exploitation in an aging America.* Washington, DC: National Academies Press.

Bovbjerg, B. D. (2006). *Guardianships: Little progress in ensuring protection for incapacitated elderly people.* Testimony before the Special Committee on Aging, U.S. Senate. Washington, DC: U.S. Government Accountability Office.

Centers for Disease Control. (2006). Public health and aging: Trends in aging—United States and worldwide. Retrieved from http://www.cdc.gov/mmwr/preview/mmwrhtml/mm5206a2.htm

Crampton, A. (2004). The importance of adult guardianship for social work practice. *Journal of Gerontological Social Work, 43*(2), 117–129.

Dickson, D. T. (1995). *Law in the health and human services: A guide for social workers, psychologists, psychiatrists, and related professionals.* New York: The Free Press.

Elder Justice Coalition. (2010, March 22). Elder justice bills clear Congress, Obama to sign into law. Press Release. Retrieved from http://www.elderjusticecoalition.com/docs/Elder-Justice-Coalition-March_22_2010.pdf

Equal Employment Opportunity Commission. (2008). Facts about age discrimination. Retrieved from http://www.eeoc.gov/facts/age.html

Frolik, L. A., & Kaplan, R. L. (2006). *Elder law: In a nutshell* (4th ed.). St. Paul, MN: Thomson/West.

Generations United. (2009). Public policy agenda for the 111th Congress. Washington, DC: Author. Retrieved from http://www.gu.org/LinkClick.aspx?fileticket=AjtJgDnlsSU%3D&tabid=157&mid=606

Ginsberg, L., & Miller-Cribbs, J. (2005). *Understanding social problems, policies, and programs* (4th ed.). Columbia: University of South Carolina Press.

Gonzales v. Oregon, 546 U.S. 243 (2006).

Gross v. FBL Financial Services, Inc., 129 S.Ct. 2343 (2009).

Letiecq, B. L., Bailey, S. J., & Porterfield, F. (2008). "We have no rights, we get no help": The legal and policy dilemmas facing grandparent caregivers. *Journal of Family Issues, 29*(8), 995–1012.

McClennen, J. (2010). *Social work and family violence: Theories, assessment, and intervention.* New York: Springer Publishing.

Metzger, M., & Kaplan, K. O. (2001). *Transforming death in America: A state of the nation report.* Washington, DC: Last Acts, Partnership for Caring.

Miller v. Youakim, 44 U.S. 125 (1979).

Mor-Barak, M. E., & Tynan, M. (1993). Older workers and the workplace: A new challenge for occupational social work. *Social Work, 38*(1), 45–55.

National Alliance for Caregiving. (2009). Caregiving in the U.S. 2009. Retrieved from http://assets.aarp.org/rgcenter/il/caregiving_09_fr.pdf

National Association of Adult Protective Services Administrators. (2001). Elder abuse awareness kit: A resource kit for protecting older people and people with disabilities (Resource Kit). Retrieved from www.ncea.aoa.gov/NCEAroot/Main_Site/pdf/basics/speakers.pdf

National Association of Social Workers. (2009). Policy statement: End of life care. *Social Work Speaks.* Washington, DC: Author.

National Association of Social Workers. (2010). *NASW Standards for social work practice with family caregivers of older adults.* Washington, DC: NASW Press.

National Center on Elder Abuse. (2007). Elder abuse/mistreatment defined. Retrieved from http://www.ncea.aoa.gov/NCEAroot/Main_Site/FAQ/Basics/Definition.aspx

National Committee for the Prevention of Elder Abuse (2008). What is elder abuse? Retrieved from http://www.preventelderabuse.org/elderabuse/

National Council on Aging. (n.d.). Aging fact sheet. Retrieved from http://www.ncoa.org/public-policy-action/health-care-reform/elder-justice/elder-abuse-fact-sheet.html

National Hospice and Palliative Care Organization. (n.d.). What are advance directives? Retrieved from http://www.caringinfo.org/i4a/pages/index.cfm?pageid=3285

Nerenberg, L. (2008). *Elder abuse prevention: Emerging trends and promising strategies*. New York: Springer Publishing.

O'Connor v. Consolidated Coin Caterers Corp., 517 U.S. 308 (1996).

Pillemer, K., & Finkelhor, D. (1988). The prevalence of elder abuse: A random sample survey. *The Gerontologist, 28*, 51–57.

Price Waterhouse v. Hopkins, 490 U.S. 228 (1989).

Richardson, V. E., & Barusch, A. S. (2006). *Gerontological practice for the twenty-first century: A social work perspective*. New York: Columbia University Press.

Roby, J. L., & Sullivan, R. (2000). Adult protection service laws: A comparison of state statutes from definition to case closure. *Journal of Elder Abuse and Neglect, 12*(3/4), 17–51.

Roy, K. K. (2003). Sleeping watchdogs of personal liberty: State laws disenfranchising the elderly. *Elder Law Journal, 11*(1), 109–140.

Simmons, T., & Lawler Dye, J. (2003). Grandparents living with grandchildren: 2000 Census Brief. Retrieved from http://www.census.gov/prod/2003pubs/c2kbr-31.pdf

Smith v. City of Jackson, 544 U.S. 228 (2005).

Straka, S. M., & Montminy, L. (2006). Responding to the needs of older women experiencing domestic violence. *Violence Against Women, 12*(3), 251–267.

Teaster, P. B., Dugar, T. A., Mendiono, M. S., Abner, E. L., Cecil, K. A., & Otto, J. M. (2006). *The 2004 survey of state adult protective services: Abuse of adults 60 years of age and older*. National Center on Elder Abuse. Retrieved from http://www.ncea.aoa.gov/ncearoot/main_site/pdf/2-14-06%20final%2060+report.pdf

Tennessee Employment Law Center. (2010). Age Discrimination in Employment Act (ADEA). Retrieved from http://www.tennesseeemploymentlawcenter.com/adea.html

Tremblay, K. R., Jr., Barber, C. E., & Kubin, L. (2006). Grandparents: As parents. Colorado State University Extension. Retrieved from http://www.ext.colostate.edu/pubs/consumer/10241.html

United Nations, Department of Social and Economic Affairs. (2009). *World population ageing*. New York: Author.

University of Miami. (2009). Decision-making: Autonomy, valid consent, and guardianship. Retrieved from http://www.miami.edu/index.php/ethics/projects/geriatrics_and_ethics/decision-making_autonomy_valid_consent_and_guardianship/

U.S. Census Bureau. (2009). Grandparents as caregivers. Retrieved from http://www.census.gov/newsroom/releases/archives/facts_for_features_special_editions/cb09-ff16.html

U.S. Department of Housing and Urban Development (2009). Intergenerational housing needs and HUD program options. Retrieved from http://www.huduser.org/Publications/pdf/intergenerational.pdf

U.S. Department of Labor, Bureau of Labor Statistics. (2009). Occupational outlook handbook, 2010–2011 edition. Retrieved from www.bls.gov/oco/ocos060.htm#outlook

U.S. General Accounting Office. (2001). *Demographic trends pose challenges for employers and workers*. GAO-02085. Washington, DC: Author.

Vacco v. Quill, 521 U.S. 793 (1997).

Van Loon, R. A. (1999). Desire to die in terminally ill people: A framework for assessment and intervention. *Health and Social Work, 24*(4), 260–268.

Virginia Department of Social Services. (2008). Adult protective services in the Commonwealth. Retrieved from http://www.dss.virginia.gov/files/division/dfs/as/aps/intro_page/learn_more/aps_power_point_11_2_11.pdf

von Wachter, T. (2009). The end of mandatory retirement in the US: Effects on retirement and implicit contracts. Retrieved from http://www.columbia.edu/~vw2112/papers/vonwa_mr_2009.pdf

Wallace, G. (2001). Grandparent caregivers: Emerging issues in elder law and social work practice. *Journal of Gerontological Social Work, 34*(3) 127–130.

Warren, M. K. (2001) *Grandparent visitation rights: A legal research guide*. Buffalo, NY: William S. Hein & Co.

Washington v. Glucksberg, 521 U.S. 702 (1997).

Wasik, J. F. (2000, March/April). The fleecing of America's elderly. *Consumers Digest*.

Zachary, M. K. (2000). Age discrimination—Part II: The private employee. *Supervision, 61*(9), 22–27.

Chapter 11

American Bar Association. (2004). Adolescence, brain development, and legal culpability. Retrieved from http://www.americanbar.org/content/dam/aba/publishing/criminal_justice_newsletter/crimjust_juvjus_Adolescence.authcheckdam.pdf

Aronson, J. D. (2009). Neuroscience and juvenile justice. *Akron Law Review, 42*, 917–930.

Bilchik, S. (1999). Juvenile justice: A century of change. *1999 National Report Series*. Washington, DC: Office of Juvenile Justice and Delinquency Prevention. Retrieved from http://www.ncjrs.gov/pdffiles1/ojjdp/178995.pdf

Bostwick, L. (2010). *Policies and procedures of the Illinois juvenile justice system*. Chicago: Illinois Criminal Justice Information Authority.

Breed v. Jones, 421 U.S. 519 (1975).

Bureau of Labor Statistics. (2009). Probation officers and correctional treatment specialists. *Occupational Outlook Handbook, 2010–11 Edition*. Retrieved from http://www.bls.gov/oco/ocos265.htm

Campaign for Youth Justice. (2011). State trends: Victories from 2005–2010. Washington, DC: Author. Retrieved from http://www.campaignforyouthjustice.org/documents/CFYJ_State_Trends_Report.pdf

Center for Children's Law and Policy. (2010). JJDPA reauthorization. Retrieved from http://www.cclp.org/JJDPA_reauthorization.php

Centers for Disease Control and Prevention. (2007). Effects on violence of laws and policies facilitating the transfer of youth from the juvenile to the adult justice system. Retrieved from http://www.cdc.gov/MMWR/PDF/rr/rr5609.pdf

Coalition for Juvenile Justice. (2006). What are the implications of adolescent brain development for juvenile justice? Retrieved from http://www.juvjustice.org/media/resources/public/resource_138.pdf

Cocozza, J. J., & Skowyra, K. R. (2000). Youth with mental health disorders: Issues and emerging responses. *Office of Juvenile Justice and Delinquency Prevention Journal, 7*(1), 3–13.

Feld, B. C. (2003). *Juvenile justice administration: In a nutshell.* St. Paul, MN: Thompson/West.

Feld, B.C. (2006). Juveniles' competence to exercise Miranda rights: An empirical study of policy and practice. *Minnesota Law Review, 91,* 26–100.

Ferguson, A. B., & Douglas, A. C. (1970). A study of juvenile waiver. *San Diego Law Review, 7*(1), 39–54.

Goldstein, N.E.S., Condie, L.O., Kalbeitzer, R., Osman, D., & Geier, J.L. (2003). Juvenile offender Miranda rights comprehension and self-reported likelihood of offering false confessions. *Assessment, 10*(4), 359–369.

Graham v. Florida, 130 S.Ct. 2011 (2010).

Griffin, P. (2008a). Purpose clause. National Center for Juvenile Justice. Retrieved from http://www.ncjj.org/Topic/Purpose-Clause.aspx/

Griffin, P. (2008b). Different from adults: An updated analysis of juvenile transfer and blended sentencing laws, with recommendations for reform. National Center for Juvenile Justice. Retrieved from http://www.ncjj.org/PDF/MFC/MFC_Transfer_2008.pdf

Griffin, P., Addie, S., Adams, B., & Firestine, K. (2011). Trying juveniles as adults: An analysis of state transfer laws and reporting. Office of Juvenile Justice and Delinquency Prevention. Retrieved from http://www.ncjj.org/pdf/Transfer_232434.pdf

Griffin, P., Szymanski, L., & King, M. (2006). National overviews. *State Juvenile Justice Profiles.* Pittsburgh, PA: National Center for Juvenile Justice. Retrieved from http://www.ncjj.org/Research_Resources/State_Profiles.aspx

Griffin, P., Torbet, P., & Szymanski, L. (1998). Trying juveniles as adults in criminal court: An analysis of state transfer provisions. Retrieved from http://www.ojjdp.gov/pubs/tryingjuvasadult/toc.html

Grisso, T. (1980). Juveniles' capacities to waive *Miranda* rights: An empirical analysis. *California Law Review, 68,* 1134–1166.

In re Gault, 397 U.S. 1 (1967).

In re J.M., 519 A.2d 497 (1992).

In re Winship, 397 U.S. 358 (1970).

Institute for Youth Development (1998). Youth facts: Violence and Youth. Retrieved from http://www.youthdevelopment.org/download/violence.pdf

J.D.B. v. North Carolina, No. 09-11121 (June 16, 2011).

Kurlycheck, M. C., & Johnson, B. D. (2004). The juvenile penalty: A comparison of juvenile and young adult sentencing outcomes in criminal court. *Criminology, 42*(2), 485–517.

Mack, J. (1909). The juvenile court. *Harvard Law Review, 23*(104), 449–476.

National Association of Social Workers. (2009). *Social work speaks: 2009–2012.* Washington, DC: NASW Press.

National Association of Social Workers. (2010). *The juvenile justice system.* Washington, DC: NASW Press.

Oklahoma Publishing Company v. Oklahoma City, 430 U.S. 308 (1977).

Puzzanchera, C. (2009). Juvenile arrests 2008. *Juvenile Justice Bulletin.* Retrieved from www.ncjrs.gov/pdffiles1/ojjdp/228479.pdf

Puzzanchera, C., & Adams, B. (2011). Juvenile arrests 2009. Retrieved from http://www.ojjdp.gov/pubs/236477.pdf

Puzzanchera, C., Adams, B., & Sickmund, M. (2010). *Juvenile court statistics 2006–2007.* Pittsburgh, PA: National Center for Juvenile Justice.

Redding, R. E. (2003). The effects of adjudicating and sentencing juveniles as adults: Research and policy implications. *Youth Violence and Juvenile Justice, 1*(2), 128–155.

Rightmer, T. (2005). Arrested development: Juveniles' immature brains make them less culpable than adults. *Quinnipiac Health Law Journal, 9*(1), 1–32.

Roper v. Simmons, 543 U.S. 551 (2005).

Schall v. Martin, 467 U.S. 2553 (1984).

Scott, E.S., & Steinberg, L. (2008). *Rethinking juvenile justice.* Cambridge, MA: Harvard University Press.

Sickmund, M. (2003). OJJDP national report series: Juveniles in court. Retrieved from https://www.ncjrs.gov/html/ojjdp/195420/contents.html

Smith v. Daily Mail Publishing Company, 443 U.S. 97 (1979).

Snyder, H. N., & Sickmund, M. (2006). *Juvenile offenders and victims: 2006 national report.* Pittsburgh, PA: National Center for Juvenile Justice.

Witt, P. H. (2003). Transfer of juveniles to adult court: The case of H.H. *Psychology, Public Policy, and Law, 9*(4), 361–380.

Yarborough v. Alvarado, 541 U.S. 652 (2004).

Chapter 12

American Civil Liberties Union. (2002). Know your rights: The Prison Litigation Reform Act. Retrieved from http://www.aclu.org/images/asset_upload_file79_25805.pdf

American Civil Liberties Union. (2010). ACLU-PA and civil rights firm file class action lawsuit against Philadelphia police department for racial profiling. Retrieved from http://www.aclupa.org/pressroom/aclupaandcivilrightsfirmfi.htm

American Civil Liberties Union. (2011a). ACLU-PA reaches agreement with City of Philadelphia in stop-and-frisk challenge. Retrieved from http://www.aclupa.org/pressroom/aclupareachesagreementwith.htm

Amnesty International USA. (2004). *Threat and humiliation: Racial profiling, domestic security, and human rights in the United States.* New York: Author.

Argersinger v. Hamlin, 407 U.S. 25 (1972).

Bell v. Wolfish, 441 U.S. 520 (1979).

Bounds v. Smith, 430 U.S. 817 (1977).

Branham, L. S. (2005). *The law and policy of sentencing and corrections: In a nutshell.* St. Paul, MN: West Publishing Co.

Brown v. Plata, 131 S.Ct. 1910 (2011).

Dickerson v. U.S., 530 U.S. 428 (2000).

Dolgoff, R., & Feldstein, D. (2009). Social welfare programs: Sustaining the quality of life. In R. Dolgoff & D. Feldstein (Eds.), *Understanding social welfare: A search for social justice.* (8th ed., pp. 271–272). Boston, MA: Pearson Education.

Estelle v. Gamble, 378 U.S. 546 (1964).

Federal Bureau of Investigation. (2010a). Arrests. *Crime in the United States.* Retrieved from http://www2.fbi.gov/ucr/cius2009/arrests/index.html

Federal Bureau of Investigation. (2010b). *Regional crime rates.* Retrieved from http://www.fbi.gov/about-us/cjis/ucr/crime-in-the-u.s/2010/crime-in-the-u.s.-2010/offenses-known-to-law-enforcement/standard-links/region

Federal Bureau of Investigation. (2010c). *Crime in the United States by community type, 2009*. Retrieved from http://www2.fbi.gov/ucr/cius2009/data/table_02.html

Ferguson v. City of Charleston, 532 U.S. 67 (2001).

Fields v. Smith, Nos. 10-2339, 10-2466 (Aug. 5, 2011).

Fleisher, M. S., & Decker, S. H. (2001). An overview of the challenge of prison gangs. *Corrections Management Quarterly, 5*(1), 1–9.

Fox, J. A., & Zawitz, M. W. (2010). *Homicide trends in the U.S.* Bureau of Labor Statistics. Retrieved from http://bjs.ojp.usdoj.gov/content/homicide/race.cfm

Frescoln, K. (2009). Drug treatment courts. *North Carolina Medical Journal, 70*(1), 66–69.

Gelman, A., Fagan, J., & Kiss, A. (2007). An analysis of the New York City Police Department's "stop-and-frisk" policy in the context of claims of racial bias. *Journal of the American Statistical Association, 102*(479), 813–823.

Georgia v. Randolph, 547 U.S. 103 (2006).

Gideon v. Wainwright, 72 U.S. 335 (1963).

Gould, J., & Mastrofski, S. (2004). Suspect searches: Assessing police behavior under the U.S. Constitution. *Criminology and Public Policy, 3,* 315–362.

Hunter v. Underwood, 471 U.S. 222 (1985).

Inciardi, J. A., Martin, S. S., & Butzin, C. A. (2004). Five-year outcomes of therapeutic community treatment of drug-involved offenders after release from prison. *Crime & Delinquency, 50*(1), 88–107.

Jacobs v. West Feliciana Sheriff's Department, 378 U.S. 546 (1964).

James, D. J., & Glaze, L. E. (2006). *Mental health problems of prison and jail inmates*. Bureau of Justice Statistics. Retrieved from http://bjs.ojp.usdoj.gov/index.cfm?ty=pbdetail&iid=789

Johnson v. California, 543 U.S. 499 (2005).

Katz v. United States, 389 U.S. 347 (1967).

Kyllo v. United States, 533 U.S. 27 (2001).

Lavender, G. (2011, Oct. 17). Why California prisoners press on with hunger strike. *The Guardian*. Retrieved from http://www.guardian.co.uk/commentisfree/cifamerica/2011/oct/17/california-prisoners-hunger-strike

Mapp v. Ohio, 367 U.S. 643 (1961).

Maschi, T., Bradley, C., & Ward, K. (Eds.). (2009). *Forensic social work: Psychosocial and legal issues in diverse practice settings*. New York: Springer Publishing Company.

Mauer, M., & Kansal, T. (2005). *Barred for life: Voting rights restoration in permanent disenfranchisement states*. Washington, DC: The Sentencing Project.

Miranda v. Arizona, 384 U.S. 436 (1966).

National Association of Social Workers. (2009). *Social work speaks, 2009-2012*. Washington, DC: NASW Press.

National Center on Addiction and Substance Abuse. (2010). *Behind bars II: Substance abuse and America's prison population*. New York: Columbia University.

National Institute on Drug Abuse. (2008). Research report series: Therapeutic community. Retrieved from http://www.drugabuse.gov/publications/research-reports/therapeutic-community

National Reentry Resource Center. (n.d.). Second Chance Act. Retrieved from http://www.nationalreentryresourcecenter.org/about/second-chance-act

National Women's Law Center (2010). *Mothers behind bars: A state-by-state report card and analysis of confinement of pregnant and parenting women and the effect on their children*. Washington, DC: Author.

Neubauer, D. W., & Fradella, H. F. (2011). *America's courts and the criminal justice system* (10th ed.). Belmont, CA: Wadsworth.

New York Civil Liberties Union. (n.d.). Stop and frisk practices. Retrieved from http://www.nyclu.org/issues/racial-justice/stop-and-frisk-practices

Padilla v. Kentucky, 200 U. S. 321 (2010).

Perlin, M. L., & Dlugacz, H. A. (2009). It's doom alone that counts: Can international human rights law be an effective source of rights in correctional conditions litigation? *Behavioral Sciences & the Law, 27*(5), 675–694.

Pew Center on the States. (2009). One in 31 U.S. adults are behind bars, on parole, or probation. Retrieved from http://www.pewtrusts.org/news_room_detail.aspx?id=49696

Pew Center on the States (2011). *State of recidivism: The revolving door of America's prisons*. Washington, DC: The Pew Charitable Trusts.

Popple, P. R., & Leighninger, L. (2005). *Social work, social welfare, and American society* (6th ed.). Boston, MA: Pearson.

Powell v. Alabama, 287 U.S. 45 (1932).

Project Vote. (2010). Restoring voting rights to former felons. Retrieved from http://projectvote.org/felon-voting/340-restoring-voting-rights-to-former-felons.html

Quigley, B. (2010). Fourteen examples of racism in the criminal justice system. Retrieved from http://www.huffingtonpost.com/bill-quigley/fourteen-examples-of-raci_b_658947.html

Rachlin, A. (2007). Rights of defense. *Governing Magazine*. Retrieved from http://meetings.abanet.org/webupload/commupload/CR209700/sitesofinterest_files/RIGHTSOFDEFENSEGoverningMagazineJanuary2007.pdf

Rand, M. R. (2009). *Criminal victimization, 2008*. Bureau of Justice Statistics. Retrieved from http://bjs.ojp.usdoj.gov/content/pub/pdf/cv08.pdf

Richardson v. Ramirez, 418 U.S. 24 (1974).

Ridgeway, G. (2007). *Analysis of racial disparities in the New York Police Department's stop, question, and frisk practices*. Rand Corporation. Retrieved from http://www.rand.org/content/dam/rand/pubs/technical_reports/2007/RAND_TR534.pdf

Robinson v. California, 70 U.S. 660 (1962).

Rudolf, J. (2012, May 16). Stop and frisk lawsuit gains class action status, judge slams NYPD over policy. Huffington Post. Retrieved from http://www.huffingtonpost.com/2012/05/16/stop-and-frisk-nypd_n_1522733.html

Schneckloth v. Bustamonte, 412 U.S. 218 (1973).

Siegel, L. J. (2010). *Introduction to criminal justice* (12th ed.). Belmont, CA: Wadsworth.

Stevens, M. (2003). Stop and frisk law: A guide to doctrines, tests, and special circumstances. Retrieved from http://faculty.ncwc.edu/mstevens/410/410lect12.htm

Tapia v. United States, 70 U.S. 660 (1962).

Terry v. Ohio, 392 U.S. 1 (1968).

Truman, J.L. (2011). Crime victimization, 2010. Bureau of Justice Statistics. Retrieved from http://www.bjs.gov/index.cfm?ty=pbdetail&iid=2224

Turner v. Safley, 482 U.S. 78 (1987).

U.S. Department of Justice (2012). Justice Department settles lawsuit against the Berkeley, S.C., sheriff's office for violating detainees' first amendment religious and speech rights. [Press Release]. Retrieved from http://www.justice.gov/opa/pr/2012/January/12-crt-040.html

Viglione, J., Hannon, L., & DeFina, R. (2011). The impact of light skin on prison time for Black female offenders. *The Social Science Journal, 48*(1), 250–258.

Vitek v. Jones, 445 U.S. 480 (1980).

Weeks v. United States, 232 U.S. 383 (1914).

Wheeler, D. P., & Patterson, G. (2008). Prisoner reentry. *Health and Social Work, 33*(2), 145–147.

Wolff v. McDonnell, 418 U.S. 539 (1974).

Chapter 13

American Association of Intellectual and Developmental Disabilities. (2010). Definition of intellectual disability. Retrieved from http://www.aaidd.org/content_100.cfm?navID=21

American Civil Liberties Union. (2003a). Race and the death penalty. Retrieved from http://www.aclu.org/capital-punishment/race-and-death-penalty

American Civil Liberties Union. (2003b). Mental retardation and the death penalty. Retrieved from http://www.aclu.org/capital-punishment/mental-retardation-and-death-penalty

American Civil Liberties Union. (2009). Mental illness and the death penalty. Retrieved from http://www.aclu.org/capital-punishment/report-mental-illness-and-death-penalty

American Civil Liberties Union of Virginia. (2003). *Broken justice: The death penalty in Virginia.* Richmond, VA: Author. Retrieved from http://www.aclu.org/files/FilesPDFs/broken_justice.pdf

Amnesty International. (2010a). Executions by state. Retrieved from http://www.amnestyusa.org/our-work/issues/death-penalty/us-scheduled-executions/executions-by-state

Amnesty International (2010b). Death penalty and race. Retrieved from http://www.amnestyusa.org/our-work/issues/death-penalty/us-death-penalty-facts/death-penalty-and-race

Amnesty International (2011). *Death sentences and executions 2010.* London: Author.

Amnesty International. (2012). Abolitionist and retentionist countries. Retrieved from http://www.amnesty.org/en/death-penalty/abolitionist-and-retentionist-countries

Atkins v. Virginia, 536 U.S. 304 (2002).

Baze v. Rees, 553 U.S. 35 (2008).

Blackstone, W. (1979). *Commentaries on the laws of England (1765–1769), Volume 4.* Chicago: University of Chicago Press.

Branch v. Texas, 408 U.S. 238 (1972).

Centers for Disease Control and Prevention. (n.d.). Intellectual disability. Retrieved from http://www.cdc.gov/ncbddd/actearly/pdf/parents_pdfs/IntellectualDisability.pdf

Clark County Prosecutors Office. (2008). Methods of execution. Retrieved from http://www.clarkprosecutor.org/html/death/methods.htm

Cochran, J. K., & Chamlin, M. B. (2000). Deterrence and brutalization: The dual effects of executions. *Justice Quarterly, 17*(4), 685–706.

Coker v. Georgia, 433 U.S. 584 (1977).

Death Penalty Information Center. (2012a). States with and without the death penalty. Retrieved from http://www.deathpenaltyinfo.org/states-and-without-death-penalty

Death Penalty Information Center. (2012b). History of the death penalty. Retrieved from http://www.deathpenaltyinfo.org/history-death-penalty

Death Penalty Information Center. (2012c). State by state database. Retrieved from http://www.deathpenaltyinfo.org/state_by_state

Death Penalty Information Center. (2012d). Facts about the death penalty. Retrieved from http://www.deathpenaltyinfo.org/documents/FactSheet.pdf

Death Penalty Information Center (2012e). Execution list 2012. Retrieved from http://www.deathpenaltyinfo.org/execution-list-2012

Death Penalty Information Center (2012f). Women and the death penalty. Retrieved from http://www.deathpenaltyinfo.org/women-and-death-penalty

Death Penalty Information Center (2012g). Methods of execution. Retrieved from http://www.deathpenaltyinfo.org/methods-execution

Dieter, R. C. (n.d.). The death penalty and human rights: U.S. death penalty and international law. Retrieved from www.deathpenaltyinfo.org/Oxfordpaper.pdf

Dieter, R. C. (1998). The death penalty in black and white: Who lives, who dies, who decides. Retrieved from http://www.deathpenaltyinfo.org/death-penalty-black-and-white-who-lives-who-dies-who-decides

Ehrlich, I. (1975). The deterrent effect of capital punishment. *The American Economic Review, 65*(3), 397–417.

Ford v. Wainwright 477 U.S. 399 (1986).

Furman v. Georgia, 408 U.S. 238 (1972).

Gallup. (2010). Death penalty. Retrieved from http://www.gallup.com/poll/1606/death-penalty.aspx

General Accounting Office (1996). Death penalty sentencing: Research indicates pattern of racial disparities. In H.A. Bedau (Ed.), *The death penalty in america: current controversies* (pp. 268–274). New York: Oxford University Press.

General Assembly of the United Nations. (1948). Universal Declaration of Human Rights. Retrieved from http://www.un.org/en/documents/udhr/

Gregg v. Georgia, 428 U.S. 153 (1976).

Innocence Project. (n.d.) About the Innocence Project. Retrieved from http://www.innocenceproject.org

Jacobs, D., & Kent, S. L. (2007). The determinants of executions since 1951: How politics, protests, public opinion, and social divisions shape capital punishment. *Social Problems, 54*(3), 297–318.

Kennedy v. Louisiana, 128 S.Ct. 2641 (2008).

McCleskey v. Kemp, 481 U.S. 279 (1987).

Messerli, J. (2009). Should the death penalty be banned as a form of punishment? Retrieved from http://www.balancedpolitics.org/death_penalty.htm

National Association of Social Workers. (2009). Capital punishment and the death penalty. *Social Work Speaks*. Washington, DC: NASW Press.

Panetti v. Quarterman, 551 U.S. 930 (2007).

Pataki, G.E. (1997, March). Death penalty is a deterrent. *USA Today*. Retrieved from http://www.prodeathpenalty.com/articles/pataki.htm

Penry v. Lynaugh, 492 U.S. 302 (1989).

Prison Policy Initiative. (2003). Crime & punishment in the U.S.: Death row demographics. Retrieved from http://www.prisonpolicy.org/prisonindex/deathpenalty.html

Radelet, M. L., & Akers, R. L. (1996). Policy and perspectives: Deterrence and the death penalty. The view of experts. *The Journal of Criminal Law and Criminology, 87*(1), 1–16.

Roper v. Simmons, 543 U.S. 551 (2005).

Schroeder, J. (2003). Forging a new practice area: Social work's role in the death penalty mitigation investigations. *Families in Society, 84*(3), 423–432.

Schroeder, J., Guin, C. C., Pogue, R., & Bordelon, D. (2006). Mitigating circumstances in death penalty decisions: Using evidence-based research to inform social work practice in capital trials. *Social Work, 51*(4), 355–364.

Stanford v. Kentucky, 492 U.S. 361 (1989).

Stolzenberg, L., & D'Alessio, S. J. (2004). Capital punishment, execution publicity and murder in Houston, Texas. *The Journal of Criminal Law and Criminology, 94*(2), 351–380.

Thompson v. Oklahoma, 487 U.S. 815 (1988).

Trop v. Dulles, 356 U.S. 86 (1958).

Unah, I., & J. Boger, J. (2001). *Race and the death penalty in North Carolina, An empirical analysis: 1993–1997*. The Common Sense Foundation, North Carolina Council of Churches. Retrieved from http://www.unc.edu/~jcboger/NCDeathPenaltyReport2001.pdf

Chapter 14

Annas, G. (2010). Resurrection of a stem-cell funding barrier: Dickey-Wicker in court. *The New England Journal of Medicine 363*(18), 1687–1689.

Application of Milton S. Hershey Medical Center, 595 A.2d 1290 (1990).

Arias, E. (2010). United States life tables, 2006. *National Vital Statistics Reports, 58*(21), 1–40.

AVERT. (n.d). South East Asia HIV & AIDS statistics. Retrieved from http://www.avert.org/aids-hiv-south-east-asia.htm

Blas, E., Sommerfeld, J., & Kurup, A.S. (Eds.). (2011). Social determinants approaches to public health: From concept to practice. World Health Organization. Retrieved from http://whqlibdoc.who.int/publications/2011/9789241564137_eng.pdf

Bongso, A., & Richards, M. (2004). History and perspective of stem cell research. *Best Practice and Research Clinical Obstetrics and Gynecology 18*(6), 827–842.

Bragdon v. Abbott, 524 U.S. 624 (1998).

Buck v. Bell, 274 U.S. 200 (1927).

Bullard, R. D. (2002). Poverty, pollution, and environmental racism: Strategies for building healthy and sustainable communities. Atlanta, GA: Environmental Justice

Resource Center. Retrieved from http://www.ejrc.cau.edu/PovpolEj.html

Carey v. Population Services International, 431 U.S. 678 (1977).

Center for HIV Law and Policy. (2011). Prosecutions for HIV exposure in the United States, 2008–2011. Retrieved from http://www.hivlawandpolicy.org/resources/view/456

Center for Reproductive Rights. (2011). Contraceptive access in the United States. Retrieved from http://reproductiverights.org/en/project/contraceptive-access-in-the-united-states

Centers for Disease Control and Prevention. (2006). Cases of HIV infection and AIDS in the United States and dependent areas, 2006. Retrieved from http://www.cdc.gov/hiv/surveillance/resources/reports/2006report/index.htm

Centers for Disease Control and Prevention. (2010a). 1 in 5 men who have sex with men in 21 cities in U.S. have HIV; nearly half unaware. Retrieved from http://www.cdc.gov/nchhstp/newsroom/ngmHAAD2010PressRelease.html

Centers for Disease Control and Prevention. (2010b). New CDC analysis reveals strong link between poverty and HIV infection. Retrieved from http://www.cdc.gov/nchhstp/Newsroom/povertyandhivpressrelease.html

Centers for Disease Control and Prevention. (2011a). Diagnoses of HIV infection and AIDS in the United States and dependent areas, 2009. Retrieved from http://www.cdc.gov/hiv/surveillance/resources/reports/2009report/index.htm

Centers for Disease Control and Prevention. (2011b). Health disparities and inequalities report—United States, 2011. Retrieved from http://www.cdc.gov/mmwr/pdf/other/su6001.pdf

Chalk v. United States, 840 F.2d 701 (1988).

Davis v. Davis, 842 S.W.2d 588 (1992).

Doe v. Borough of Barrington, 729 F. Supp. 376 (1990).

Doe v. City of New York, 15 F.3d 264 (1994).

Dolgoff, R., & Feldstein, D. (2007). *Understanding social welfare: A search for social justice*. Boston: Pearson Education.

Duncan, C. (2008). The future of DNA evidence. *Journal of Forensic Identification 58*(3), 283–295.

Eisenstadt v. Baird, 405 U.S. 438 (1972).

Furrow, B. R., Greaney, T. L., Johnson, S. H., Jost, T. S., & Schwartz, R. L. (2008). *Health law: Cases, materials and problems* (6th ed.). St. Paul, MN: Thomson/West.

Gonzales v. Carhart, 550 U.S. 124 (2007).

Goodman, E. (1989, March 10). Ethics and the petri dish. *San Francisco Chronicle*, p. A-33, col. 4.

Griswold v. Connecticut, 381 U.S. 479 (1965).

Guttmacher Institute. (2011). State policies in brief: Minors' access to contraceptive services. Retrieved from http://www.guttmacher.org/statecenter/spibs/spib_MACS.pdf

Guyer, M., & Collins, F. (1995). How is the Human Genome Project doing, and what have we learned so far? *Proceedings of the National Academy of Sciences of the United States of America, 92*(24), 10841–10848.

Harris, G. (2011, Dec. 11). Plan to widen availability of morning-after pill is rejected. *The New York Times*. Retrieved from http://www.nytimes.com/2011/12/08/health/policy/sebelius-overrules-fda-on-freer-sale-of-emergency-contraceptives.html

Hofrichter, R., & Bhatia, R. (Eds.). (2010). *Tackling health inequities through public health practice.* New York: Oxford University Press.

In re Baby M., 537 F.2d 1227 (1988).

Irons, P. (2006). *A people's history of the Supreme Court.* New York: Penguin Books.

Irvine, L., Elliott, L., Wallace, H., & Crombie, I. K. (2006). A review of major influences on current public health policy in developed countries in the second half of the 20th century. *The Journal of the Royal Society for the Promotion of Health, 126*: 73–78. doi: 10.1177/1466424006063182

Jacoby, M.B., Sullivan, T.A., & Warren, E. (2001). Rethinking the debates over health care financing: Evidence from the bankruptcy courts. *New York University Law Review, 76*(2), 375–418.

James, S. D., & Hutchison, C. (2012, Jan. 10). NC to compensate victims of sterilization in 20th century eugenics program. ABC News. Retrieved from http://abcnews.go.com/Health/Womens Health/north-carolina-compensate-victims-eugenics-program-sterilized/story?id=15328707#.UCEYHaAw_jA

John B. v. The Superior Court of Los Angeles County, S128248 (2006).

Jordan, M. (2011, July 26). White-minority wealth gap widens. *The Wall Street Journal.* Retrieved from http://online.wsj.com/article/SB10001424053111904772304576468333980952942.html

Karger, H., & Stoesz, D. (2008). *American social welfare policy: A pluralist approach.* Boston: Pearson Education.

Klitzman, R. (2010). Views of discrimination among individuals confronting genetic disease. *Journal of Genetic Counseling 19*(1), 68–83.

Koehler, J. (2001). When are people persuaded by DNA match statistics? *Law and Human Behavior 25*(5), 493–513.

Lapham, E.V., Kozma, C., & Weiss, J.O. (1996). Genetic discrimination: Perspectives of Consumers. *Science, 274*, 621–624.

Lawrence, J. (2000). The Indian Health Service and the sterilization of Native American women. *The American Indian Quarterly, 24*(3), 400–419.

Malamud, M. (2010). As Idaho law takes effect, measures are "area of continuing legal controversy." *NASW News 55*(7).

Miller, J. (2006). The unconscionability of conscience clauses: Pharmacists' consciences and women's access to contraception. *Health Matrix, 16*(237), 289–330.

Montalvo v. Radcliffe, 67 F.3d 873 (1999).

National Association of Social Workers. (2003). *NASW standards for integrating genetics into social work practice.* Washington, DC: Author. Retrieved from http://www.naswdc.org/practice/standards/geneticsstdfinal4112003.pdf

National Association of Social Workers. (2005). Standards for social work practice in health care settings. Retrieved from http://www.socialworkers.org/practice/standards/NASWHealthCareStandards.pdf

National Association of Social Workers. (2009a). Family planning and reproductive choice. *Social Work Speaks: 2009–2012.* Washington, DC: NASW Press.

National Association of Social Workers. (2009b). Health care policy. *Social Work Speaks, 2009–2012.* Washington, DC: NASW Press.

National Association of Social Workers. (2011). Social workers and health care reform. Retrieved from http://www.socialworkers.org/ldf/legal_issue/2011/042011.asp

National Association of Social Workers. Retrieved from http://www.socialworkers.org/ldf/legal_issue/2010/201005.asp

National Conference of State Legislatures. (2011). Abortion laws. Retrieved from http://www.ncsl.org/default.aspx?tabid=14401

National Federation of Independent Business v. Sebelius, 567 U.S. _ (2012).

Open Society Institute. (2008). 10 reasons to oppose the criminalization of HIV exposure or transmission. Retrieved from http://www.soros.org/sites/default/files/10reasons_20081201.pdf

Planned Parenthood v. Casey, 505 U.S. 833 (1992).

Planned Parenthood v. Danforth, 428 U.S. 52 (1976).

Provider refusal and conscience clause controversies. (May 2011). National Association of Social Workers. Retrieved from: https://www.socialworkers.org/ldf/legal_issue/2011/052011.asp?back=yes

Ricks v. Budge, 64 P.2d 208 (1937).

Roe v. Wade, 410 U.S. 113 (1973).

School Board of Nassau County v. Arline, 480 U.S. 273 (1987).

Skinner v. Oklahoma, 316 U.S. 535 (1942).

Social workers and conscience clauses. (2010, May).

Stein, T. J. (1998). *The social welfare of women and children with HIV and AIDS.* New York: Oxford University Press.

Strug, D. L., Grube, B. A., & Beckerman, N, L. (2002). Challenges and changing roles in HIV/AIDS social work, *Social Work in Health Care, 35*(4), 1–19.

Sutton v. United Air Lines, 527 U.S. 471 (1999).

United Nations Programme on HIV/AIDS (UNAIDS). (n.d). Regions. Retrieved from http://www.unaids.org/en/regionscountries/regions/

U.S. Census Bureau. (2009). Health insurance highlights: 2009. Retrieved from http://www.census.gov/hhes/www/hlthins/data/incpovhlth/2009/highlights.html

Vozzella, L. (2012, Aug. 6). Arlington delegate seeks reparations for sterilization victims. *The Washington Post.* Retrieved from http://www.washingtonpost.com/blogs/virginia-politics/post/arlington-delegate-seeks-reparations-for-sterilization-victims/2012/08/06/96cf3aa8-dfee-11e1-a19c-fcfa365396c8_blog.html

Walker v. Pierce, 560 F.2d 609 (1977).

Ward, E., Halperin, M., Schrag, N., Cokknides, V., DeSantis,, C., Brandi, P, Siegel, R., Stewart, A., & Jemal, A. (2008). Association of insurance with cancer care utilization and outcomes. *CA: A Cancer Journal for Clinicians, 58*(1), 9–31.

Webster v. Reproductive Health Services, 492 U.S. 490 (1989).

Whalen v. Roe, 97 S.Ct. 869 (1977).

Williams, R. A. (Ed.). (2007). *Eliminating health disparities in America.* Totowa, NJ: Humana Press.

Williams v. United States, 242 F.3d 169 (2001).

Wilper, A. P., Woolhandler, S., Lasser K. E., McCormick, D., Bor, D. H., & Himmelstein, D. U. (2009). Health insurance and mortality in U.S. adults. *American Journal of Public Health, 99*(12), 1–7.

Wolf, L. E., & Lo, B. (2001). Ethical dimensions of HIV/AIDS. University of California, San Francisco. Retrieved from http://hivinsite.ucsf.edu/InSite?page=kb-08-01-05#S3.1X

World Health Organization. (2010). Definition of health. Retrieved from https://apps.who.int/aboutwho/en/definition.html

World Health Organization. (2012). HIV/AIDS. Retrieved from http://www.who.int/immunization/topics/hiv/en/index1.html

Chapter 15

Addington v. Texas, 441 U.S. 418 (1979).

Advocacy Treatment Center. (2011). Assisted outpatient treatment laws. Retrieved from http://www.treatmentadvocacycenter.org/solution/assisted-outpatient-treatment-laws

Ake v. Oklahoma, 470 U.S. 68 (1985).

American Academy of Child and Adolescent Psychiatry. (2010). ADHD: A guide for families. Retrieved from http://www.aacap.org/cs/adhd_a_guide_for_families/how_common_is_adhd

American Law Institute. (1962). *Model penal code.* Philadelphia, PA: Author.

Arnold, R.P. (2012). The insanity defense among the states. Retrieved from http://criminal.findlaw.com/criminal-procedure/the-insanity-defense-among-the-states.html

Backlar, P., McFarland, B. H., Swanson, J. W., & Mahler, J. (2001). Consumer, provider, and informal caregiver opinions on psychiatric advance directives. *Administration and Policy in Mental Health, 28*(6), 427–441.

Carr, L. W. (2004, July). *Wyatt v. Stickney: A landmark decision.* Alabama Disabilities Advocacy Program. Retrieved from http://www.adap.net/Wyatt/landmark.pdf

Centers for Disease Control and Prevention. (2009). 2004 National Nursing Home Survey. Retrieved from http://www.cdc.gov/nchs/nnhs.htm

Dusky v. United States, 362 U.S. 402 (1960).

Epright, C. E. (2010). Coercing future freedom: Consent and capacities for autonomous choice. *Journal of Law, Medicine, & Ethics, 38*, 799–806.

In re K.L., 774 N.Y.S.2d 472 (2004).

Insel, T. R. (2008). Assessing the economic costs of serious mental illness. *American Journal of Psychiatry, 165*(6), 663–665.

Israel, A. B. (2011). *Using the law: Practical decision making in mental health.* Chicago: Lyceum Books.

Jackson v. Indiana, 406 U.S. 715 (1972).

James, D. J., & Glaze, L. E. (2006, September 6). Mental health problems of prison and jail inmates. Bureau of Justice Statistics. Retrieved from http://bjs.ojp.usdoj.gov/index.cfm?ty=pbdetail&iid=789

Jones v. United States, 48 U.S. 681 (1983).

Kansas v. Crane, 534 U.S. 407 (2002).

Kansas v. Hendricks, 521 U.S. 346 (1997).

Kessler, R. C., Berglund, P. A., Demler, O., Jin, R., & Walters, E. E. (2005). Lifetime prevalence and age-of-onset distributions of DSM-IV disorders in the National Comorbidity Survey Replication (NCS-R). *Archives of General Psychiatry*, *62*(6), 593–602.

Kumar, A. (2011, February 21). Cost to keep sexual offenders in check is escalating for Virginia. *The Washington Post.* Retrieved from http://www.washingtonpost.com/wp-dyn/content/article/2011/02/21/AR2011022105330.html

Levin, A. (2012, March 16). Long, winding road ends in settlement of D.C. MH care suit. *Psychiatric News, 47*(6), 6b–7.

Mechanic, D. (2008). *Mental health and social policy: Beyond managed care.* Boston: Pearson/Allyn and Bacon.

Melville, J. D., & Naimark, D. (2003). Punishing the insane: The verdict of guilty but mentally ill. *Journal of the American Academy of Psychiatry and the Law, 30*(4), 353–355.

Mental Health America. (2011). Confining sexual predators in the mental health system. Retrieved from http://www.mentalhealthamerica.net/go/position-statements/55

Moscicki, E. K. (2001). Epidemiology of completed and attempted suicide: Toward a framework for prevention. *Clinical Neuroscience Research, 1*(5), 310–323.

National Association of Anorexia Nervosa and Associated Disorders. (2011). Eating disorders statistics. Retrieved from http://www.anad.org/get information/about-eating-disorders/eating-disorders-statistics/

National Center on Addiction and Substance Abuse. (2010). *Behind bars II: Substance abuse and America's prison population.* New York: Columbia University.

National Coalition for the Homeless. (2009). Mental illness and homelessness. Retrieved from http://www.nationalhomeless.org/factsheets/Mental_Illness.pdf

National Institute of Mental Health. (2010). Statistics. Retrieved from http://www.nimh.nih.gov/statistics/index.shtml

National Institute of Mental Health (2012). The numbers count: Mental disorders in America. Retrieved from http://www.nimh.nih.gov/health/publications/the-numbers-count-mental-disorders-in-america/index.shtml

National Institute on Alcohol Abuse and Alcoholism. (2011). Substance abuse among the military, veterans, and their families. Retrieved from http://drugabuse.gov/tib/vet.html

National Resource Center on Psychiatric Advance Directives. (2011). Glossary. Retrieved from http://www.nrc-pad.org/content/blogsection/20/69/

Nemade, R., & Dombeck, M. (2009). Schizophrenia symptoms, patterns and statistics and patterns. Retrieved from http://www.mentalhelp.net/poc/view_doc.php?type=doc&id=8805

O'Connor v. Donaldson, 422 U.S. 563 (1975).

Popple, P.R., & Leighninger, L. (2005). *Social work, social welfare, and American society.* Boston, MA: Pearson Education.

President's New Freedom Commission on Mental Health. (2003). Achieving the promise: Transforming mental health care in America. Retrieved from http://store.samhsa.gov/shin/content//SMA03-3831/SMA03-3831.pdf

Protection and Advocacy System v. City of Albuquerque, 195 P.3d 1 (2008).

Public Broadcasting System. (2011). Insanity defense FAQs. Retrieved from http://www.pbs.org/wgbh/pages/frontline/shows/crime/trial/faqs.html

Rennie v. Klein, 653 F.2d 836 (1978).

Seling v. Young, 531 U.S. 250 (2001).

Sell v. United States, 539 U.S. 166 (2003).

Sheetz, B. M. (2007). The choice to limit choice: Using psychiatric advance directives to manage the effects of mental illness and support self-responsibility. *University of Michigan Journal of Law Reform, 40*(2), 401–434.

Simpson, G. A., Cohen, R. A., Pastor, P.N., & Reuben, C. A. (2008). Use of mental health services in the past 12 months by children aged 4–17 years: United States, 2005–2006. Centers for Disease Control and Prevention. Retrieved from http://www.cdc.gov/nchs/data/databriefs/db08.htm

Substance Abuse and Mental Health Services Administration. (2004). 2003 national survey on drug use and health. Retrieved from http://oas.samhsa.gov/nhsda/2k3nsduh/2k3Results.htm

Substance Abuse and Mental Health Services Administration. (2005). Quick guide for mental health professionals based on tip 42: Substance abuse treatment for persons with co-occurring disorders. Retrieved from http://kap.samhsa.gov/products/tools/cl-guides/pdfs/QGMHP_TIP42.pdf

Substance Abuse and Mental Health Services Administration. (2010). *Mental health, United States, 2008*. Rockville, MD: Center for Mental Health Services, Substance Abuse and Mental Health Services Administration.

Swanson, J. W., Van McCrary, S., Swartz, M. S., Van Dorn, R. A., & Elbogen, E. B. (2007). Overriding psychiatric advance directives: Factors associated with psychiatrists' decision to preempt patients' advance refusal of hospitalization and medication. *Law and Human Behavior, 31*(1), 77–90.

Swartz, M. (2008). Psychiatric advance directives: A tool for patients and clinicians. Retrieved from http://www.miwatch.org/2008/04/psychiatric_advance_directives.html

Swerdlow-Freed, D. H. (2003). Assessment of competency to stand trial and criminal responsibility. *Michigan Criminal Law Annual Journal, 1*(1), 24–28.

Treatment Advocacy Center. (2011). Consequences of non-treatment: Fact sheet. Retrieved from http://www.treatmentadvocacycenter.org/resources/consequences-of-lack-of-treatment/violence/1384

United States v. Comstock, 200 U. S. 321 (2010).

Wang, S. S. (2007, November 27). Helping mental patients gain some control over treatment. *The Wall Street Journal: Health Journal*, p. D1. Retrieved from http://online.wsj.com/public/article/SB119612505203604609.html?mod=blog

World Health Organization. (2008). The global burden of disease: 2004 update. Retrieved from http://www.who.int/healthinfo/global_burden_disease/GBD_report_2004update_AnnexA.pdf

Wu, E. Q., Birnbaum, H. G., Ball, D. E., Kessler, R. C., Moulis, M., & Aggerwal, J. (2005). The economic burden of schizophrenia in the United States in 2002. *Journal of Clinical Psychiatry, 66*(9), 1122–1129.

Wyatt v. Stickney, 325 F.Supp. 781 (1971).

Wyatt v. Stickney, 344 F.Supp. 373 (1972).

Chapter 16

Board of Education of Oklahoma City v. Dowell, 498 U.S. 237 (1991).

Brown v. Board of Education, 347 U.S. 483 (1954).

Brown v. Board of Education, 348 U.S. 294 (1955).

Calderón, M., Slavin, R., & Sánchez, M. (2011). Effective instruction for English learners. *The Future of Children, 21*(1), 103–127.

Callahan, R. M. (2005). Tracking and high school English learners: Limiting opportunity to learn. *American Educational Research Journal, 42*(2), 305–328.

Callahan, R., Wilkinson, L., & Muller, C. (2008). School context and the effect of ESL placement on Mexican-origin adolescents' achievement. *Social Science Quarterly, 89*(1), 177–200.

Callahan, R., Wilkinson, L., Muller, C., & Frisco, M. (2009). ESL placement and schools: Effects on immigrant achievement. *Educational Policy, 23*(2), 355–384.

Castañeda v. Pickard, 648 F.2d 989 (1981).

City of Richmond v. Croson, 488 U.S. 469 (1989).

Clark, C. S. (1995). Housing discrimination. *CQ Researcher, 5*(8), 169–192.

DeNavas-Walt, C., Proctor, B. D., & Smith, J. C. (2010). *Income, poverty, and health insurance coverage in the United States: 2009*. Washington, DC: U.S. Government Printing Office. Retrieved from http://www.census.gov/prod/2010pubs/p60-238.pdf

Equal Employment Opportunity Commission. (2010). Employment tests and selection procedures. Retrieved from http://www.eeoc.gov/policy/docs/factemployment_procedures.html

Federal Bureau of Investigation. (n.d). Hate crime—Overview. Retrieved from http://www.fbi.gov/about-us/investigate/civilrights/hate_crimes/overview

Federal Bureau of Investigation. (2008). Hate Crimes Statistics Act. Retrieved from http://www2.fbi.gov/ucr/hc2008/hatecrimestatistics.html

Federal Bureau of Investigation. (2011). Hate crime statistics, 2010. Retrieved from http://www.fbi.gov/about-us/cjis/ucr/hate-crime/2010/narratives/hate-crime-2010-incidents-and-offenses

Gratz v. Bollinger, 539 U.S. 244 (2003).

Griggs v. Duke Power Co., 401 U.S. 424 (1971).

Grutter v. Bollinger, 539 U.S. 306 (2003).

Hirbayashi v. United States, 320 U.S. 81 (1943).

Hobbs, F., & Stoops, N. (2002). *Demographic trends in the 20th century*. Washington, DC: U.S. Government Printing Office.

Irons, P. (2006). *A people's history of the Supreme Court: The men and women whose cases and decisions have shaped our constitution*. New York: Penguin Books.

Johnson, L. B. (1965). To fulfill these rights. Commencement address at Howard University. Retrieved from http://www.lbjlib.utexas.edu/johnson/archives.hom/speeches.hom/650604.asp

Jones v. Mayer, 392 U.S. 409 (1968).

Katel, P. (2008). Affirmative action. *CQ Researcher, 18*(36), 841–864.

Kochlar, R., Fry, R., Taylor, P., Velasco, G., & Motel, S. (2011). *Wealth gaps rise to record highs between Whites, Blacks and Hispanics*. Washington, DC: Pew Research Center.

Korematsu v. United States, 323 U.S. 214 (1944).

Lau v. Nichols, 414 U.S. 563 (1974).

Levinson, R. B. (2011). Gender-based affirmative action and reverse gender bias: Beyond Gratz, Parents Involved, and Ricci. *Harvard Journal of Law & Gender, 34*(1), 1–36.

Li, B. (2007). From bilingual education to OELALEAALEPS: How the No Child Left Behind Act has undermined English language learners' access to a meaningful education. *Georgetown Journal on Poverty Law & Policy, 14*(3), 539–572.

Lindsey v. Normet, 405 U. S. 56 (1972).

Logan, J. R., & Stults, B. J. (2011). The persistence of segregation in the metropolis: New findings from the 2010 census. Retrieved from http://www.s4.brown.edu/us2010/Data/Report/report2.pdf

Loving v. Virginia, 388 U.S. 1 (1967).

McDonald, L., & Powell, J. A. (1998). *The rights of racial minorities.* New York: Puffin Books.

McDonnell Douglas Corp. v. Green, 411 U.S. 792 (1973).

Mitchell, C. (2005). English only: The creation and maintenance of an academic underclass. *Journal of Latinos and Education, 4*(4), 253–270.

National Association of Social Workers. (2009). Language and cultural diversity in the United States. *Social Work Speaks* (8th ed.). Washington, DC: NASW Press.

National Fair Housing Alliance (2011). *The big picture: How fair housing organizations challenge systemic and institutionalized discrimination.* Washington, DC: Author.

Onwuachi-Willig, A., Houh, E., & Campbell, M. (2008). Cracking the egg: Which came first—stigma or affirmative action? *California Law Review, 96*, 1299–1352.

Pellegrinelli, L. (2010, December 2). *All things considered* [Audio podcast]. National Public Radio. Retrieved from http://www.npr.org/2010/12/02/131761843/Hate-Crime-Statistics-Lack-Key-Facts

Plessy v. Ferguson, 163 U.S. 537 (1896).

Regents of the University of California v. Bakke, 438 U.S. 265 (1978).

Ricci v. DeStefano, 129 S.Ct. 2658 (2009).

Shelley v. Kraemer, 334 U.S. 1 (1948).

Society for Human Resource Management. (2011). Uniform guidelines on employee selection procedures of 1978. Retrieved from http://www.shrm.org/LegalIssues/FederalResources/FederalStatutesRegulationsandGuidanc/Pages/Uniformguidelinesonselectionprocedures.aspx

Spencer v. Kugler, 404 U.S. 1027 (1972).

Stein, S. (2008, August 14). Census projections; U.S. will be half minority by 2042. *The Huffington Post.* Retrieved from http://www.huffingtonpost.com/2008/08/14/census-projections-us-wil_n_118878.html

Strauder v. West Virginia, 100 U.S. 303 (1879).

Swann v. Charlotte-Mecklenberg Board of Education, 402 U.S. 1 (1971).

Turner, M. A., Ross, S. L., Galster, G. C., Yinger, J., Godrey, E. B., Bednarz, B. A., & Zhao, B. (2002). *Discrimination in metropolitan housing markets: National results from phase I of HDS2000.* Washington, DC: The Urban Institute.

U.S. Census Bureau. (2008). Percent of the projected population by race and Hispanic origin for the United States: 2010 to 2050. Retrieved from http://www.census.gov/population/www/projections/summarytables.html

U.S. Census Bureau. (2011). Overview of race and Hispanic origin 2010. Retrieved from http://www.census.gov/prod/cen2010/briefs/c2010br-02.pdf

U.S. Department of Housing and Urban Development. (2002). Fair housing: Equal opportunity for all [Brochure]. Washington, DC: Author.

U.S. Department of Housing and Urban Development. (2008). *The state of fair housing: FY 2008 annual report on fair housing.* Washington, DC: Author.

Vieira, N. (1990). *Constitutional civil rights.* St. Paul, MN: West Publishing Company.

Village of Arlington Heights v. Metropolitan Housing Development Corporation, 429 U.S. 252 (1977).

Washington v. Davis, 426 U.S. 229 (1976).

Willborn, S. L., Schwab, S. J., Burton, J. F., & Lester, G. L.L. (2007). *Employment law: Cases and materials.* Newark, NJ: LexisNexis Group.

Yasui v. United States, 320 U.S. 115 (1943).

Chapter 17

American Association of University Women. (n.d.). State median annual earnings and earnings ratio for full-time, year-round workers age 16 and older by gender, 2009. Retrieved from http://www.aauw.org/learn/research/statedata/upload/gendergap2009_data.pdf

Arizona Governing Committee v. Norris, 43 U.S. 1073 (1983).

Barney, W. L. (2006). *A companion to 19th century America.* Hoboken, NJ: Wiley-Blackwell.

Barsh, J., & Yee, L. (2011). *Unlocking the full potential of women in the U.S. economy.* Retrieved from http://online.wsj.com/public/resources/documents/WSJExecutiveSummary.pdf

Becker, M., Bowman, C. G., & Torrey, M. (2001). *Feminist jurisprudence: Taking women seriously* (2nd ed.). St. Paul, MN: West Publishing Co.

Bradwell v. Illinois, 83 U.S. 130 (1873).

Bureau of Labor Statistics. (2007). Changes in men's and women's labor force participation rates. Retrieved from http://www.bls.gov/opub/ted/2007/jan/wk2/art03.htm

Burlington Industries v. Ellerth, 524 U.S. 742 (1998).

Cohen v. Brown University, 101 F.3d 155 (1996).

Craig v. Boren, 429 U.S. 190 (1976).

DeNavas-Walt, C., Proctor, B.D., & Smith, J.C. (2011). *Income, poverty, and health insurance coverage in the United States: 2010.* Washington, DC: U.S. Census Bureau.

Elmasry, F. (2011, March 7). U.S. women can't close the pay gap. *Voice of America.* Retrieved from http://www.voanews.com/english/news/usa/US-Women-Cant-Close-the-Pay-Gap-117530324.html

Equal Rights Advocates. (2011). Sexual harassment in the workplace. Retrieved from http://www.equalrights.org/professional/sexhar/work/workplac.asp

Franklin v. Gwinnett County Public Schools, 503 U.S. 60 (1992).

Frontiero v. Richardson, 411 U.S. 677 (1973).

Goesart v. Cleary, 335 U. S. 464 (1949).

Groneman, C., & Norton, M. B. (1994). *"To toil the livelong day": America's women at work, 1780–1980.* Ithaca, NY: Cornell University Press.

Grove City College v. Bell, 465 U.S. 555 (1984).

Hegewisch, A., Liepmann, H., Hayes, J., & Hartmann, H. (2010). *Separate and not equal? Gender segregation in the labor market and the gender wage gap.* Washington, DC: Institute for Women's Policy Research.

Hodgson v. Miller Brewing Co., 457 F.2d 221 (1974).

Hoyt v. Florida, 368 U.S. 57 (1961).

Jost, K. (2002). Single-sex education. *CQ Researcher, 12*(25), 569–592.

Joyner, J. (2010, August 27). College athletics losing money. Outside the Beltway. Retrieved from http://www.outsidethebeltway.com/college-athletics-losing-money/

Kiefer, H. M. (2003, January 28). What do Americans see in Title IX's future? Gallup, Inc. Retrieved from: http://www.gallup.com/poll/7663/what-americans-see-title-ixs-future.aspx

Kleinschmidt, H. L. (2005). Reconsidering severe or pervasive: Aligning the standard in sexual harassment and racial harassment causes of action. *Indiana Law Journal*, 1119, 1123–1129.

Langer, G. (2011, Nov. 16). One in four U.S. women reports workplace harassment. *ABC News.* Retrieved from http://abcnews.go.com/blogs/politics/2011/11/one-in-four-u-s-women-reports-workplace-harassment/

Ledbetter v. Goodyear Tire Co., 550 U.S. 618 (2007).

MacKinnon, C. A. (2001). *Sex equality.* New York: Foundation Press.

Meritor Savings Bank v. Vinson, 447 U.S. 57 (1986).

Muller v. Oregon, 208 U.S. 412 (1908).

National Association for Single Sex Public Education. (2011a). Single-sex schools/schools with single-sex class/what's the difference? Retrieved from http://www.singlesexschools.org/schools-schools.htm#22

National Association for Single Sex Public Education. (2011b). The legal status of single-sex public education. Retrieved from http://www.singlesexschools.org/legal.html

National Committee for Pay Equity (2012). Equal pay day. Retrieved from http://www.pay-equity.org/day.html

Player, M. A. (2004). *Federal law of employment discrimination in a nutshell* (5th ed.). St. Paul, MN: West Publishing Co.

Pollard, D. S. (1999). *Single-sex education.* Newton, MA: WEEA Equity Resource Center.

Radice v. New York, 264 U. S. 292 (1924).

Reed v. Reed, 404 U.S. 71 (1971).

Seidenberg v. McSorley's Old Ale House, 317 F. Supp. 593 (1970).

Sexual Harassment Support. (2011). Sexual harassment in the workplace. Retrieved from http://sexualharassmentsupport.org/SHworkplace.html

Sullivan, J. (2010, October 19). False start. *CommonWealth Magazine.* Retrieved from http://www.commonwealthmagazine.org/News-and-Features/Features/2010/Fall/False-start.aspx

Thomas, C. S. (2001). *Sex discrimination in a nutshell* (2nd ed.). St. Paul, MN: West Publishing Co.

United States v. Virginia, 518 U.S. 515 (1996).

U.S. Equal Employment Opportunity Commission. (2002). Facts about sexual harassment. Retrieved from http://www.eeoc.gov/facts/fs-sex.html

U.S. Equal Employment Opportunity Commission. (2010). Sexual harassment charges EEOC and FEPAs combined FY 1997–FY 2010. Retrieved from http://www.eeoc.gov/eeoc/statistics/enforcement/sexual_harassment.cfm

Vorchheimer v. School District of Philadelphia, 430 U.S. 703.

Wal-Mart Stores, Inc. v. Dukes, 131 S.Ct. 2541 (2011).

Weaver, K. (1991). Comparable worth in the United States and the Canadian province of Ontario. *British Columbia International and Comparative Law Review, 14*(1), 137–158.

Weil, E. (2008, March 2). Teaching boys and girls separately. *The New York Times Magazine.* Retrieved from http://www.nytimes.com/2008/03/02/magazine/02sex3-t.html?pagewanted=all

Women's Sports Foundation. (2009). Play fair: A title IX playbook for victory. Retrieved from http://www.avca.org/includes/media/docs/Play-Fair-Final.pdf

Chapter 18

Althauser, S., & Greenberg, S. (2011). FAQ: The Employment Non-Discrimination Act. Center for American Progress. Retrieved from http://www.americanprogress.org/issues/2011/07/enda_faq.html/

American Psychological Association. (2011). Lesbian, gay, bisexual, and transender persons and socioeconomic status. Retrieved from http://www.apa.org/pi/ses/resources/publications/factsheet-lgbt.aspx

Amnesty International. (2008). *Love, hate and the law: Decriminalizing homosexuality.* London: Author.

Associated Press. (2010, March 4). Mexico City's gay marriage law takes effect. MSNBC. Retrieved from http://www.msnbc.msn.com/id/35714490/ns/world_news-americas/#storyContinued

Associated Press. (2011, March 14). 10 countries now allow same-sex marriage. *The Washington Post.* Retrieved from http://www.washingtonpost.com/wp-dyn/content/article/2011/03/14/AR2011031402821.html

Baehr v. Lewin, 852 P.2d 44 (1993).

Bowers v. Hardwick, 478 U.S. 186 (1986).

Bruce-Jones, E., & Itaborahy, L. P. (2011). State-sponsored homophobia: A world survey of laws criminalizing same-sex sexual acts between consenting adults. The International Lesbian, Gay, Bisexual, Trans and Intersex Association. Retrieved from http://www.europarl.europa.eu/meetdocs/2009_2014/documents/droi/dv/4_04ilgareport_/4_04ilgareport_en.pdf

Burns, C. (2012). The gay and transgender wage gap. Center for American Progress. Retrieved from http://www.americanprogress.org/issues/2012/04/lgbt_wage_gap.html

Eskridge, W. N., & Hunter, N. D. (1997). *Sexuality, gender, and the law.* Westbury, NY: The Foundation Press.

Gates, G.J. (2012). Family formation and raising children among same-sex couples. National Council on Family Relations. Retrieved from http://williamsinstitute.law.ucla.edu/wp-content/uploads/Gates-Badgett-NCFR-LGBT-Families-December-2011.pdf

Gill v. Office of Personnel Management, 699 F.Supp.2d 374 (2010).

Glossary. (2011). Straight for equality. Retrieved from http://community.pflag.org/page.aspx?pid=619

Greenhouse, L. (1990, Nov. 5). Washington talk; When second thoughts in case come too late. *The New York Times.* Retrieved from http://www.nytimes.com/1990/11/05/us/washington-talk-when-second-thoughts-in-case-come-too-late.html

Human Rights Campaign. (2011a). Employment Non-Discrimination Act. Retrieved from http://www.hrc.org/laws-and-legislation/federal-legislation/employment-non-discrimination-act

Human Rights Campaign. (2011b). Statewide employment laws and policies. Retrieved from http://www.hrc.org/files/assets/resources/Employment_Laws_and_Policies.pdf

Human Rights Campaign. (2011c). Benefits. Retrieved from http://www.hrc.org/issues/pages/benefits

Human Rights Campaign. (2011d). Marriage Equality and other relationship recognition laws. Retrieved from http://www.hrc.org/files/assets/resources/Relationship_Recognition_Laws_Map%281%29.pdf

Human Rights Watch. (2008). Kuwait: Repressive dress-code law encourages police abuse. Retrieved from http://www.hrw.org/news/2008/01/16/kuwait-repressive-dress-code-law-encourages-police-abuse

Irons, P. (1990). *The courage of their convictions: Sixteen Americans who fought their way to the Supreme Court.* New York: Penguin Books.

Irons, P. (2006). *A people's history of the Supreme Court.* New York: Penguin Books.

Lambda Legal & Deloitte Financial Advisory Services. (2006). 2005 workplace fairness survey. Retrieved from http://data.lambdalegal.org/pdf/641.pdf

Lawrence v. Texas, 539 U.S. 558 (2003).

Log Cabin Republicans v. United States, 716 F.Supp.2d 884 (2010).

Massachusetts v. U.S. Department of Health and Human Services, 698 F.Supp.2d 234 (2010).

MSNBC. (2009, July 12). Gays in military not an issue for many nations. Retrieved from http://www.msnbc.msn.com/id/31878625/ns/us_news-military/t/gays-military-not-issue-many-nations/#.TnZoiOzIiSo

National Association of Social Workers. (n.d.). Gender equity. Retrieved from http://www.naswdc.org/practice/intl/issues/gender.asp

National Association of Social Workers. (2003). Social workers and legal developments in gay rights. Retrieved from https://www.socialworkers.org/ldf/legal_issue/200311.asp

National Association of Social Workers. (2004). Same-sex marriage position statement. Retrieved from http://www.naswdc.org/diversity/lgb/062804.asp?print=1

National Center for Transgender Equality. (2011). Injustice at every turn: Executive summary. Retrieved from http://transequality.org/PDFs/Executive_Summary.pdf

National Organization for Women. (2009). Equal marriage NOW: Civil marriage v. civil unions. Retrieved from http://www.now.org/issues/marriage/marriage_unions.html

Oncale v. Sundowner Offshore Services, 523 U.S. 75 (1998).

Padula v. Webster, 822 F.2d 97 (1987).

Partners Task Force for Gay and Lesbian Couples. (2005). List of federal marriage laws—2003. Retrieved from http://www.buddybuddy.com/mar-g03.html

Perry v. Schwarzenegger, 704 F. Supp. 2d 921 (2010).

Price Waterhouse v. Hopkins, 490 U.S. 228 (1989).

Robinson, J. (2002, October 8). What percentage of the population is gay? Gallup.com. Retrieved from http://www.gallup.com/poll/6961/what-percentage-population-gay.aspx

Ross v. Denver Department of Health and Hospitals, 883 P.2d 516 (1994).

Romer v. Evans, 517 U.S. 620 (1996).

Schroer v. Library of Congress, Case 1:05-cv-01090-JR (September 19, 2008).

Servicemembers Legal Defense Network. (2011). About "Don't Ask, Don't Tell." Retrieved from http://www.sldn.org/pages/about-dadt

Silver, N. (2011, April 20). Gay marriage opponents now in minority. *The New York Times.* Retrieved from http://fivethirtyeight.blogs.nytimes.com/2011/04/20/gay-marriage-opponents-now-in-minority/

Smith v. City of Salem, 378 F.3d 566 (2004).

Steffan v. Perry, 41 F.3d 677 (1994).

U.S. Census Bureau. (2010). The census: A snapshot. Retrieved from 2010.census.gov/partners/pdf/factSheet_General_LGBT.pdf

Vestal, C. (2007). Gay marriage ripe for court decisions in three states. Pew Research Center. Retrieved from http://pewresearch.org/pubs/418/gay-marriage-ripe-for-court-decisions-in-three-states

Watkins v. United States Army, 875 F.2d 699 (1989).

World Health Organization. (2011). Gender, woman and health: What do we mean by "sex" and "gender"? Retrieved from www.who.int/gender/whatisgender/en/

Chapter 19

Ackermann, D. (2010). A matter of interpretation: How the language barrier and the trend of criminalizing illegal immigration caused a deprivation of due process following the Agriprocessors, Inc. raids. *Columbia Journal of Law and Social Problems, 43*(3), 363.

American Civil Liberties Union (n.d.). Immigration detention. Retrieved from http://www.aclu.org/immigrants-rights/detention

Arizona v. United States, 567 U.S. _ (2012).

Barth, R. P. (2002). *Institutions vs. foster homes: The empirical base for the second century of debate.* Chapel Hill: University of North Carolina, Chapel Hill, School of Social Work, Jordan Institute for Families.

Batalova, J., Fix, M., & Murray, J. (2007). *Measures of change: The demography and literacy of adolescent English learners—A report to the Carnegie Corporation of New York.* Washington, DC: Migration Policy Institute.

Batalova, J., & Terrazas, A. (2010). Frequently requested statistics on immigrants and immigration in the United States. Migration Policy Institute. Retrieved from http://migrationinformation.com/USFocus/display.cfm?ID=818#9

Bennett, B. (2011, Jan. 27). Republicans want a return to workplace immigration raids. *Los Angeles Times.* Retrieved from http://articles.latimes.com/2011/jan/27/nation/la-na-immigration-raids-20110127

Bloomekatz, R. (2007). Rethinking immigration status discrimination and exploitation in the low-wage workplace. *UCLA Law Review, 54*(6), 1963–2010.

Broder, T., & Blazer, J. (2011). Overview of immigrant eligibility for federal programs. National Immigration Law Center. Retrieved from https://nilc.org/access-to-bens.html

Bump, M., & Gozdziak, E. (2007). The care of unaccompanied undocumented children in federal custody: Issues and options. *Protecting Children: A Professional Publication of American Humane, 23*(1), 67–83.

Capps, R., Castaneda, R. M., Chaudry, A., & Santos, R. (2007). *Paying the price: The impact of immigration raids on America's children.* Washington, DC: National Council of La Raza.

Capps, R., Rosenblum, M. R., Rodriguez, C., & Chishti, M. (2011). *Delegation and divergence: A study of 287(g) state and local immigration enforcement.* Washington, DC: Migration Policy Institute.

Chamber of Commerce v. Whiting, No. 09-115 (May 26, 2011).

Chang-Muy, F., & Congress, E. P. (2009). *Social work with immigrants and refugees: Legal issues, clinical skills, and advocacy.* New York: Springer Publishing.

City of Chicago v. Shalala, 189 F.3d 598 (1999).

De Silva, E. (2006). A united front on immigration. *NASW News, 54*(2). Retrieved from http://www.naswdc.org/pubs/news/2006/02/desilva.asp

Department of Homeland Security, Office of Immigration Statistics. (2010). Immigration enforcement actions: 2009. Retrieved from http://www.dhs.gov/xlibrary/assets/statistics/publications/enforcement_ar_2009.pdf

Dettlaff, A., & Phillips, S. D. (2007). *Immigration enforcement considerations for child welfare systems.* Chicago, IL: Jane Addams College of Social Work.

Dolgoff, R., Loewenberg, F. M., & Harrington, D. (2009). *Ethical decisions for social work practice.* Belmont, CA: Thomson Brooks/Cole.

Drachman, D. (1992). A stage-of-migration framework for service to immigrant populations. *Social Work, 37*(1), 68–72.

Erisman, W., & Looney, S. (2007). *Opening the door to the American dream: Increasing higher education access and success for immigrants.* Washington, DC: Institute for Higher Education Policy.

Feere, J. D. (2009). Memorandum: The Obama administration's 287(g): An analysis of the new MOA. Center for Immigration Studies. Retrieved from http://www.cis.org/articles/2009/undermining287g.pdf

Feinstein, D. (2004, June 4). Senator Feinstein questions deportation of long-term, law-abiding undocumented immigrants. Retrieved from http://votesmart.org/public-statement/40813/senator-feinstein-questions-deportation-of-long-term-law-abiding-undocumented-immigrants

Flores v. Reno, 507 U.S. 292 (1993).

Florida Immigrant Coalition. (2009). Overzealous immigration enforcement hurts and angers community members. Media Alert. Retrieved http://floridaimmigrant.org/default.asp?PageNum=555

Fry, R. (2007). *How far behind in math and reading are English language learners?* Washington, DC: Pew Hispanic Center.

Fry, R. (2010). *Hispanics, high school dropouts and the GED.* Washington, DC: Pew Hispanic Center.

Furman, R., Langer, C. L., Sanchez, T. W., & Negi, N. L. (2007). A qualitative study of immigration policy and practice dilemmas for social work students. *Journal of Social Work Education, 43*(1), 133–146.

Graham v. Richardson, 403 U.S. 365 (1971).

Grieco, C. M., & Trevelyan, E. N. (2010). Place of birth of the foreign-born population: 2009. American Community Survey Briefs, U.S. Census Bureau. Retrieved from http://www.census.gov/prod/2010pubs/acsbr09-15.pdf

Heyman, J. (1998). State effects on labor exploitation: The INS and undocumented immigrants at the Mexico–United States border. *Critique of Anthropology, 18*(2), 157–180.

Hing, B. O. (2009). Institutional racism, ICE raids, and immigration reform. *University of San Francisco Law Review, 44(2)*, 307–352.

Hoefer, M., Rytina, N., & Baker, B. C. (2010). Population estimates: Estimates of the unauthorized immigrant population residing in the United States: January 2009. Department of Homeland Security, Office of Immigration Statistics. Retrieved from http://www.dhs.gov/xlibrary/assets/statistics/publications/ois_ill_pe_2009.pdf

Hoffman Plastic Compounds, Inc. v. NLRB, 535 U.S. 137 (2002).

Hsu, S.S. (2008, May 18). Immigration raid jars a small town. *The Washington Post.* Retrieved from http://www.washingtonpost.com/wp-dyn/content/article/2008/05/17/AR2008051702474.html

Human Rights Watch. (2007). *Forced apart: Families separated and immigrants harmed by U.S. deportation policy.* New York: Author.

Human Rights Watch. (2009). *Forced apart (by the numbers): Noncitizens deported for mostly nonviolent offenses.* New York: Author.

Immigration Policy Center. (2010, November 4). Secure communities: A fact sheet. Retrieved from http://www.immigrationpolicy.org/just-facts/secure-communities-fact-sheet

INS v. Delgado, 466 U.S. 210 (1984).

Kalhan, A. (2010). Rethinking immigration detention. *Columbia Law Review Sidebar, 110*, 42–58.

Kremer, J. D., Moccio, K. A., & Hammell, J. W. (2009). *Severing a lifeline: The neglect of citizen children in America's immigration enforcement policy.* Minneapolis, MN: Dorsey & Whitney LLP.

Kullgren, J. T. (2003). Restrictions on undocumented immigrants' access to health services: The public health implications of welfare reform. *American Journal of Public Health, 93*(10), 1630–1633.

Lacey, M. (2011, Jan. 4). Birthright citizenship looms as next immigration battle. *The New York Times.* Retrieved from http://www.nytimes.com/2011/01/05/us/politics/05babies.html?pagewanted=all

League of United Latin American Citizens v. Wilson, 908 F. Supp. 755 (1995).

Lee, E. S. (1966). A theory of migration. *Demography, 3*(1), 47–57.

Lee, Y. (2006). To dream or not to dream: A cost-benefit analysis of the Development, Relief, and Education for Alien Minors (DREAM) Act. *Cornell Journal of Law and Public Policy, 16*(1), 231–258.

Legomsky, S. H., & Rodriguez, C. M. (2009). *Immigration and refugee law and policy* (5th ed.). St. Paul, MN: West Group.

Li, M., & Batalova, J. (2011). Refugees and asylees in the United States. Migration Policy Institute. Retrieved from http://www.migrationinformation.org/USFocus/display.cfm?ID=851

Matthews v. Diaz, 426 U.S. 67 (1976).

Mauldin, E. (2010). DHS Office of Inspector General Report: ICE reforms fail to solve fundamental 287(g) problems. National Immigration Law Center. Retrieved from http://www.nilc.org/287g-OIG-report-2010-04-29.html

Migration Policy Institute. (2011). *States with largest and fastest growing immigrant populations.* Retrieved from http://www.migrationinformation.org/datahub/maps.cfm

Monger, R. (2010). Annual flow report: U.S. legal permanent residents: 2009. Department of Homeland Security, Office of Immigration Statistics. Retrieved from http://www.dhs.gov/xlibrary/assets/statistics/publications/lpr_fr_2009.pdf

National Association of Social Workers. (2006). *Social work speaks: NASW policy statements, 2006–2009.* Washington, DC: NASW Press.

National Association of Social Workers. (2008). *Code of ethics.* Retrieved from http://www.socialworkers.org/pubs/code/code.asp

National Immigration Forum. (n.d.). Secure communities. Retrieved from http://www.immigrationforum.org/images/uploads/Secure_Communities.pdf

National Immigration Law Center. (2012). Basic facts about in-state tuition for undocumented immigrant students. Retrieved from http://www.nilc.org/basic-facts-instate.html

Orrenius, P.M., & Zavodny, M. (2009). Do immigrants work in riskier jobs? *Demography, 46*(3), 535–551.

Padilla, Y. C. (1997). Immigrant policy: Issues for social work practice. *Social Work, 42*(6), 595–608.

Padilla, Y. C., Shapiro, E. R., Fernández-Castro, M. D., & Faulkner, M. (2008). Our nation's immigrants in peril: An urgent call to social workers. *Social Work, 53*(1), 5–8.

Padilla v. Kentucky, 466 U. S. 668 (2010).

Passel, J. S. (2005). *Unauthorized migrants: Numbers and characteristics.* Washington, DC: Pew Hispanic Center.

Passel, J. S., & Cohn, D. (2008a). *U.S. population projections 2005–2050.* Washington, DC: Pew Hispanic Center.

Passel, J. S., & Cohn, D. (2008b). *Trends in unauthorized immigration: Undocumented inflow now trails legal inflow.* Washington, DC: Pew Hispanic Center.

Passel, J. S., & Cohn, D. (2009) A portrait of unauthorized immigrants in the United States (Research Report). The Pew Hispanic Center. Retrieved from http://pewhispanic.org/files/reports/107.pdf

Passel, J. S., & Taylor, P. (2010). Unauthorized immigrants and their U.S.-born children. (Research Report). The Pew Hispanic Center. Retrieved from http://pewhispanic.org/files/reports/125.pdf

Patel v. Quality Inn South, 846 F.2d 700 (1988).

Plyer v. Doe, 457 U.S. 202 (1982).

Preston, J. (2010, July 9). Illegal workers swept from jobs in "silent raids." *New York Times.* Retrieved from http://www.nytimes.com/2010/07/10/us/10enforce.html

Reamer, F. G. (2008). When ethics and law collide. *Social Work Today, 8*(5). Retrieved from http://www.socialworktoday.com/archive/EoESepOct08.shtml

Richey, W. (2011, Dec. 12). Supreme Court takes Arizona immigration law case in key test of federal power. *The Christian Science Monitor.* Retrieved from http://www.csmonitor.com/USA/Justice/2011/1212/Supreme-Court-takes-Arizona-immigration-law-case-in-key-test-of-federal-power

Rome, S. H. (2010). Promoting family integrity: The Child Citizen Protection Act and its implications for public child welfare. *Journal of Public Child Welfare, 4*(3), 245–262.

Rotolo, L. (2008). *Detention and deportation in the age of ICE: Immigrant and human rights in Massachusetts.* Boston, MA: American Civil Liberties Union.

Rytina, N. (2010). Population estimates: Estimates of the legal resident population in 2009. Department of Homeland Security, Office of Immigration Statistics. Retrieved from http://www.dhs.gov/xlibrary/assets/statistics/publications/lpr_pe_2009.pdf

Sayani, D. (2011, Feb. 24). New Arizona immigration bill dubbed "SB 1070 on steroids." The New American. Retrieved from http://www.thenewamerican.com/usnews/immigration/item/2069-new-arizona-immigration-bill-dubbed-sb-1070-on-steroids

Schoenholtz, A. I., & Bernstein, M. (2008). Improving immigration adjudications through competent counsel. *Georgetown Journal of Legal Ethics, 21*(1), 55–60.

Slevin, P. (2010, July 26). Deportation of illegal immigrants increases under Obama administration. *The Washington Post.* Retrieved from http://www.washingtonpost.com/wp-dyn/content/article/2010/07/25/AR2010072501790.html?hpid=topnews

Sure-Tan Inc., v. NLRB, 67 U.S. 883 (1984).

Takahashi v. Fish and Game Commission, 334 U.S. 410 (1948).

Town of Herndon v. Thomas, MI-2007-644 (Cir. Ct. Fairfax County, 2007).

Traux v. Raich, 239 U. S. 33 (1915).

Turque, B. (2007, Sept. 6). Herndon to shut down center for day laborers. *The Washington Post.* Retrieved from http://www.washingtonpost.com/wp-dyn/content/article/2007/09/05/AR2007090502600.html

U.S. Citizenship and Immigration Services. (2011). Citizenship through naturalization. Retrieved from http://www.uscis.gov/portal/site/uscis/menuitem.eb1d4c2a3e5b9ac89243c6a7543f6d1a/?vgnextoid=d84d6811264a3210VgnVCM100000b92ca60aRCRD&vgnextchannel=d84d6811264a3210VgnVCM100000b92ca60aRCRD

U.S. Immigration and Customs Enforcement. (n.d.). Secure communities. Retrieved from http://www.ice.gov/secure_communities/

U.S. Immigration and Customs Enforcement. (2007). ICE fiscal year 2007 annual report: Protecting national security and upholding public safety. Retrieved from http://www.ailadownloads.org/advo/ICEFY2007AnnualReport.pdf

Valenzuela, A. (2003). Day labor work. *Annual Review of Sociology, 29,* 307–333.

Van Hook, J., & Balisreri, K. S. (2006). Ineligible parents, eligible children: Food stamps receipt, allotments, and food insecurity among children of immigrants. *Social Science Research, 35*(1), 228–251.

Vedantam, S. (2010, Oct. 1). No opt-out for immigration enforcement. *The Washington Post.* Retrieved from http://www.washingtonpost.com/wp-dyn/content/article/2010/09/30/AR2010093007268.html

Weissbrodt, D., & Danielson, L. (2005). *Immigration law and procedure.* Minneapolis: Thomson/West.

Women's Commission for Refugee Women and Children & Lutheran Immigration and Refugee Service. (2007). *Locking up family values: The detention of immigrant families.* New York: Author.

Yick Wo v. Hopkins, 118 U.S. 356 (1886).

Zimmerman, W., & Tumlin, K. C. (1999). *Patchwork policies: State assistance for immigrants under welfare reform* (Occasional Paper Number 24). Washington, DC: The Urban Institute.

Chapter 20

Alabama v. Coushatta Tribes of Texas v. Big Sandy School District, 817 F. Supp. 1319 (1993).

Alexander, K., & Alexander, M. D. (2009). *The law of schools, students and teachers* (4th ed.). St. Paul, MN: West Publishing Co.

American Academy of Child and Adolescent Psychiatry. (1988). *Policy statements: Corporal punishment in schools.* Retrieved from http://www.aacap.org/cs/root/policy_statements/corporal_punishment_in_schools

American Civil Liberties Union. (2011). *Anderson v. Chesterfield County School District.* Retrieved from http://www.aclu.org/religion-belief/anderson-v-chesterfield-county-school-district

American Psychological Association. (2008). Are zero tolerance policies effective in the schools? *American Psychologist, 63*(9), 852–862.

Artiles, A. J., & Ortiz, A. A. (2002). *English language learners with special education needs: Identification, assessment, and instruction.* Washington, DC: Center for Applied Linguistics.

Atkins-Burnett, S. (2007). Children with disabilities. In P. Allen-Meares (Ed.), *Social work services in schools* (pp. 182–221). Boston, MA: Pearson Education.

Baker v. Owen, 423 U.S. 907 (1975).

Bethel School District v. Fraser, 478 U.S. 675 (1986).

Blanck, P., Hill, E., Siegal, C. D., & Waterstone, M. (2009). *Disability civil rights law and policy.* St. Paul, MN: Thomson Reuters.

Board of Education v. Earls, 536 U.S. 822 (2002).

Boyd County High School Gay Straight Alliance v. Board of Educ. of Boyd County, 258 F.Supp.2d 667 (2003).

Bureau of Labor Statistics (2012). Education pays. Retrieved from http://www.bls.gov/emp/ep_chart_001.htm

Canady v. Bossier Parish School Board, 240 F.3d 437 (2001).

Capps, R., Fix, M., Murray, J., Ost, J., Passel, J., & Herwantoro, S. (2005). *The new demography of America's schools: Immigration and the No Child Left Behind Act.* Washington, DC: The Urban Institute.

Cauchon, D. (1999, April 13). Zero-tolerance policies lack flexibility. Retrieved from http://www.usatoday.com/educate/ednews3.htm

Center for Effective Discipline. (2008). Facts vs. opinion: School corporal punishment. Retrieved from http://www.stophitting.com/index.php?page=factsvsopinions

Centers for Disease Control and Prevention. (2010). Youth risk behavior surveillance—United States, 2009. Retrieved from http://www.cdc.gov/mmwr/pdf/ss/ss5905.pdf

Chalifoux v. New Caney Independent School District, 976 F. Supp. 659 (1997).

Chapman, C., Laird, J., Ifill, N., & KewalRamani, A. (2011). Trends in high school dropout and completion rates in the United States: 1972–2009. National Center for Education Statistics. Retrieved from http://nces.ed.gov/pubs2012/2012006.pdf

Children's Defense Fund. (2011*). Portrait of inequality 2011: Black children in America.* Retrieved from http://www.childrensdefense.org/programs-campaigns/black-community-crusade-for-children-II/bccc-assets/portrait-of-inequality.pdf

Civil Rights Project of Harvard University and the Advancement Project. (2000). *Opportunities suspended: The devastating consequences of zero-tolerance and school discipline policies.* Washington, DC: Authors.

Colin v. Orange Unified School District, 83 F. Supp. 2d 1135 (2000).

Colker, R. (2006). The disability presumption: Thirty years later. *University of Pennsylvania Law Review, 154*(4), 789–862.

Collins, J. L., Goodman, R. A., & Moulton, A. D. (1990). Healthy and safe school environment: A CDC review of school laws and policies concerning child and adolescent health. *Journal of School Health, 78*(2), 101–111.

Diana v. State Board of Education, CA 70 RFT (N.D. Cal. 1970).

Doe v. Koger, 480 F. Supp. 225 (1979).

Elk Grove Unified School District v. Newdow, 542 U.S. 1 (2004).

Engel v. Vitale, 370 U.S. 421 (1962).

Felton, R. M. (2009). Minorities and limited English proficient students in special education. In *Minorities in Special Education.* Washington, DC: U.S. Commission on Civil Rights. Retrieved from http://www.usccr.gov/pubs/MinoritiesinSpecialEducation.pdf

Fisher, M. (2009, April 5). Unbending rules on drugs in schools drive one teen to the breaking point. Retrieved from http://www.washingtonpost.com/wp-dyn/content/article/2009/04/04/AR2009040402596.html

Gearon v. Loudoun County School Board, 844 F. Supp. 1097 (1993).

Goss v. Lopez, 419 U.S. 565 (1975).

Gould, M. (2009). National Council on Disability written remarks. In *Minorities in Special Education.* Washington, DC: U.S. Commission on Civil Rights. Retrieved from http://www.usccr.gov/pubs/MinoritiesinSpecialEducation.pdf

Hazelwood School District v. Kuhlmeier, 484 U.S. 260 (1988).

Heise, M. (2008). The story of *San Antonio Independent School Dist. v. Rodriguez:* School finance, local control, and constitutional limits. In M. A. Olivas & R. G. Schneider (Eds.), *Education law stories* (pp. 51-82). New York: Foundation Press.

Hines v. Caston School Corp., 651 N.E. 2d 330 (1995).

Honig v. Doe, 484 U.S. 305 (1988).

Human Rights Watch. (2008). *A violent education: Corporal punishment of children in U.S. public schools.* New York: Author.

Ingraham v. Wright, 430 U.S. 651 (1977).

J.W. v. DeSoto County School. District (N.D. Miss. Nov. 11, 2010).

Jenglin v. San Jacinto Unified School District, 872 F. Supp. 1459 (1993).

Jones v. W.T. Henning Elementary School, 721 So.2d 530 (1998).

Konop v. Northwestern School District, 26 F. Supp. 2d 1189 (1998).

Ladner, M. (2009). Minority children and special education: Evidence of racial bias and strategies to avoid misdiagnosis. In *Minorities in Special Education.* Washington, DC: U.S. Commission on Civil Rights. Retrieved from http://www.usccr.gov/pubs/MinoritiesinSpecialEducation.pdf

Larry P. v. Riles, 93 F. 2d 969 (1984).

Lee v. Weisman, 505 U.S. 577 (1992).

Losen, D.J., & Gillespie, J. (2012). Opportunities suspended: The disparate impact of disciplinary exclusion from school. The Center for Civil Rights Remedies. Retrieved from http://civilrightsproject.ucla.edu/resources/projects/center-for-civil-rights-remedies/school-to-prison-folder/federal-reports/upcoming-ccrr-research/losen-gillespie-opportunity-suspended-ccrr-2012.pdf

McAndrews, T. (2001, March). *Zero-tolerance policies.* Retrieved from https://scholarsbank.uoregon.edu/xmlui/bitstream/handle/1794/3369/digest146.pdf?sequence=1

McInyre v. Bethel School Independent District No. 3, 804 F. Supp 1415 (1992).

Mills v. Board of Education of the District of Columbia, 348 F. Supp. 866 (1972).

Monroe, S. (2009). Minorities and limited English proficient students in special education. In *Minorities in Special Education.* Washington, DC: U.S. Commission on Civil Rights. Retrieved from http://www.usccr.gov/pubs/MinoritiesinSpecialEducation.pdf

Morse v. Frederick, 551 U.S. 393 (2007).

Murray v. Curlett, 83 S.Ct. 869 (1963).

National Association of School Psychologists. (2001). Zero tolerance and alternative strategies: A fact sheet for educators and policymakers. Retrieved from http://www.nasponline.org/resources/factsheets/zt_fs.aspx

National Association of Social Workers. (2009). Physical punishment of children. *Social Work Speaks.* Washington, DC: NASW Press.

National Center for Education Statistics. (1998). Violence and discipline problems in U.S. public schools: 1996–97. Retrieved from http://nces.ed.gov/surveys/frss/publications/98030/index.asp?sectionid=5

National Center for Education Statistics (2009). Fast facts: Home-schooling. Retrieved from http://nces.ed.gov/fastfacts/display.asp?id=91

National Center for Education Statistics. (2010). Fast facts: Back to school statistics. Retrieved from http://nces.ed.gov/fastfacts/display.asp?id=372

National Center for School Engagement. (2003). Compulsory attendance laws listed by state. Retrieved from http://www.schoolengagement.org/TruancypreventionRegistry/Admin/Resources/Resources/15.pdf

National Conference of State Legislatures. (2012). Compulsory education. Retrieved from http://www.ncsl.org/default.aspx?tabid=12943

National Council on Disability. (2000). Back to school on civil rights. Retrieved from http://www.ncd.gov/publications/2000/Jan252000#3

National Education Association (2007). Truth in labeling: Disproportionality in special education. Retrieved from http://www.nccrest.org/Exemplars/Disporportionality_Truth_In_Labeling.pdf

Neal v. Fulton County Board of Education, 229 F.3d 1069 (2000).

New Jersey v. T.L.O., 469 U.S. 325 (1985).

Newdow v. Rio Linda Union School District, 597 F.3d 1007 (2010).

O'Neil, G. (2005). School discipline and educationally disabled students. Retrieved from http://www.educationlawconsortium.org/forum/2005/papers/oneil.pdf

Organisation for Economic Co-Operation and Development. (2010). PISA 2009 key findings: Vol. 1, What students know and can do. Retrieved from www.oecd.org/edu/pisa/2009

Palmaffy, T. (2001). The evolution of the federal role. In C. E. Finn Jr., A. J. Rotherham, & C. R. Hokanson Jr. (Eds.), *Rethinking special education for a new century.* Thomas B. Fordham Foundation and Progressive Policy Institute. Retrieved from http://www.edexcellencemedia.net/publications/2001/200105_rethinkingspecialed/special_ed_final.pdf

Proffitt-Dupre, A. (2000). A study in double standards, discipline and the disabled student. *Washington Law Review, 75*(1), 1–96.

Ratner v. Loudoun County Public Schools, 16 Fed. Appx. 140 (2001).

Reitzes, S. (2011, March 22). Fairfax suicide leads to criticism of zero tolerance policies. Retrieved from http://www.thechurchillobserver.com/news/2011/03/22/fairfax-suicide-leads-to-criticism-of-zero-tolerance-policies/

Reschly, D. J. (2009). Minority special education disproportionality: Findings and misconceptions. In *Minorities in Special Education.* Washington, DC: U.S. Commission on Civil Rights. Retrieved from http://www.usccr.gov/pubs/MinoritiesinSpecialEducation.pdf

Rutherford Institute. (2001). *Zero-tolerance and school discipline policies.* Charlottesville, VA: Author.

S-1 v. Turlington, 635 F.2d 342 (1981).

Sacramento City Unified School District v. Rachel H., 14 F.3d 1398 (1994).

Safford Unified School District v. Redding, 129 S.Ct. 2633 (2009).

Salzman, A. (2005, Nov. 20). Special education and minorities. *The New York Times.* Retrieved from http://www.nytimes.com/2005/11/20/nyregion/nyregionspecial2/20ctspecial.html?pagewanted=all

San Antonio Independent School District v. Rodriguez, 411 U.S. 1 (1973).

Santa Fe Independent School District v. Doe, 530 U.S. 290 (2000).

Schaffer v. Weast, 546 U.S. 49 (2005).

School District of Abington Township v. Schempp, 374 U.S. 203 (1963).

Skiba, R., & Peterson, R. (1999). The dark side of zero tolerance—Can punishment lead to safe schools? *The Phi Delta Kappan, 80*(5), 372–376, 381–382.

Skiba, R., Michael, R. S., Nardo, A. C., & Peterson, R. (2002). The color of discipline: Sources of racial and gender disproportionality in school punishment. *The Urban Review, 34*(4), 317–342.

Snyder, T. D., & Dillow, S. A. (2010). *Digest of education statistics 2009.* Washington, DC: National Center for Education Statistics, U.S. Department of Education.

State v. Best, 987 A.2d 605 (2010).

Straights and Gays for Equality v. Osseo Area Schools, 471 F.3d 908 (2006).

Tinker v. Des Moines Independent School District, 393 U.S. 503 (1969).

U.S. Commission on Civil Rights (2009). *Minorities in special education.* Washington, DC: Author.

U.S. Department of Education. (2011). The federal role in education. Retrieved from http://www2.ed.gov/about/overview/fed/role.html

Vernonia School District v. Acton, 515 U.S. 646 (1995).

Wallace v. Jaffree, 472 U.S. 38 (1985).

Williams by Williams v. Ellington 936 F.2d 881 (1991).

Zamora, P. (2009). Minorities in special education. In *Minorities in Special Education.* Washington, DC: U.S. Commission on Civil Rights. Retrieved from http://www.usccr.gov/pubs/MinoritiesinSpecialEducation.pdf

Zhou, L., & Johnson. F. (2010). Revenues and expenditures for public elementary and secondary education: School year 2007–08. National Center for Education Statistics. Retrieved from http://nces.ed.gov/pubs2010/2010326.pdf

Index